# U.S. ARMY SPECIAL OPERATIONS TARGET INTERDICTION COURSE

## SNIPER TRAINING AND EMPLOYMENT

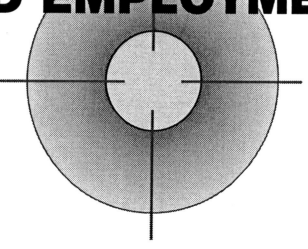

PALADIN PRESS · BOULDER, COLORADO

*U.S. Army Special Operations Target Interdiction Course: Sniper Training and Employment*

Reprint edition published 1999 by Paladin Press

ISBN 10: 1-58160-043-7
ISBN 13: 978-1-58160-043-8

Printed in the United States of America

Published by Paladin Press, a division of
Paladin Enterprises, Inc.,
Gunbarrel Tech Center
7077 Winchester Circle
Boulder, Colorado 80301 USA
+1.303.443.7250

Direct inquiries and/or orders to the above address.

PALADIN, PALADIN PRESS, and the "horse head"
design are trademarks belonging to Paladin Enterprises and
registered in United States Patent and Trademark Office.

Visit our Web site at www.paladin-press.com

# SPECIAL OPERATIONS SNIPER TRAINING AND EMPLOYMENT

## Table of Contents

3

## Chapter 1

## THE SPECIAL OPERATIONS SNIPER

### 1-1. PURPOSE

The purpose of this manual is to provide doctrinal guidance on the mission, selection of personnel, organization, equipment, training, skills, and employment of the Special Operations Sniper.

### 1-2. SCOPE

This manual addresses three distinct audiences:

o    The commander. This manual provides specific guidance on the nature, role, candidate selection, organization, and employment of sniper personnel.

o    The trainer. This manual provides a reference for the development of training programs.

o    The sniper. This manual contains detailed information on the fundamental knowledge, skills, and employment methods of snipers throughout the entire Operational Continuum.

This manual describes those segments of sniping that are unique to Special Operations Forces (SOF). It also describes those portions of conventional sniping that are necessary to train indigenous forces.

### 1-3. GENERAL

The Special Operations (SO) sniper is a selected volunteer specially trained in advanced marksmanship and fieldcraft skills who can engage selected targets from concealed positions at ranges and under conditions that are not possible for the normal rifleman, in support of Special Operations Forces (SOF) missions.

### 1-4. MISSION

Nature of Special Operations.
SO are actions conducted by specially organized, trained, and equipped military and paramilitary forces to achieve military, political, economic, or psychological objectives by nonconventional means in hostile, denied, or politically sensitive areas. They are conducted in peace, conflict, and war, independently or in coordination with operations of conventional forces. Politico-military considerations frequently shape SO, requiring clandestine,

1

covert or low-visibility techniques, and oversight at the national level. SO usually differ from conventional operations in their degree of risk, operational techniques, mode of employment, independence from friendly support, and dependence upon operational intelligence and indigenous assets.

Public law (10 USC 167) states that SO activities include the following as far as they relate to SO:

o       Direct action (DA).

o       Strategic reconnaissance, which the US Special Operations Command (USSOCOM) has incorporated into a broader activity called special reconnaissance (SR).

o       Unconventional warfare (UW).

o       Foreign internal defense (FID).

o       Civil affairs (CA).

o       Psychological operations (PSYOP).

o       Counterterrorism (CT).

o       Humanitarian assistance (HA).

o       Theater search and rescue (SAR).

o       Such other activities as may be specified by the National Command Authorities (NCA).

SOF are those forces specifically organized, trained, and equipped to conduct SO activities or provide direct support (DS) to other SOF. They provide a versatile military capability to defend US national interests. They are an integral part of the total defense posture of the United States and a strategic instrument of national policy. These forces serve as force multipliers. They can function in an economy of force role to provide substantial leverage at a reasonable cost and effort. SOF thus provide military options for national response that can stabilize an international situation with minimum risk to US interests.

The SO sniper will normally be employed to conduct:

Unconventional Warfare (UW).

Foreign Internal Defense (FID).

Direct Action (DA).

Special Reconnaissance (SR).

2

Counter Terrorism (CT).

During peacetime, SO snipers may also be used to:

Assist foreign governments.

Train foreign military snipers.

Conduct counterterrorism operations.

Safeguard US citizens and property abroad.

Conduct recovery operations.

Conduct deception operations.

Conduct show of force operations.

Conduct rescue operations.

Conduct operations that support the National Command Authority's (NCA) strategic goals.

The SO sniper supports these missions with the following:

Engaging long-range targets with precision fire.

Obtaining and reporting enemy intelligence information.

## 1-5. SELECTION OF PERSONNEL

The purpose of this section is to establish doctrinal guidelines for the selection and assessment of SOF sniper candidates. It is critically important for the commander to monitor evaluation and selection procedures, since each unit may have a different mission. There are no absolutes for the selection of SOF snipers; however, there are diagnostic tests, organizational indicators, and trends that will serve to assist the commander in identifying potential snipers.

Candidates for sniper training must be carefully screened. The rigorous training program and the great personal risk in combat require high motivation and the ability to learn a variety of skills. The proper mental conditioning cannot always be taught or instilled by training.

Many well-disciplined individuals can rapidly compose themselves after a fleeting surrender to excitement, fear, or indecisiveness. In the sniper's profession an instant of uncontrolled emotion can be fatal. The sniper must possess true

3

emotional balance, a perpetual self-possession, and serenity developed from maturity and patience. The hunter who experiences "buck-fever" may lose the deer; the sniper who cannot control his emotions may lose his life.

The sniper must be capable of calmly and deliberately killing targets that may not pose an immediate threat to him. It is much easier to kill in self-defense or in the defense of others than it is to kill without apparent provocation. The sniper must not be susceptible to emotions such as anxiety or remorse. Candidates whose motivation toward sniper training rests mainly in the desire for the prestige from serving in a unique role may not be capable of the cold rationality that the sniper's job requires. To kill in this fashion requires mental discipline and the belief in the rightness and moral correctness of the mission. The sniper must be able to live with himself afterward, sorting out his feelings of right and wrong, without carrying disabling emotional baggage.

Diagnostic and aptitude testing may be implemented at the discretion of the commander. Certain testing procedures may be quite lengthy and tedious and are therefore subject to limitations of time, equipment, and facilities. It is recommended, however, that psychological evaluation of a candidate be at least partially determined through the use of the Minnesota Multi-Phasic Personality Inventory (MMPI). This test, if properly administered, gives the commander a personality profile of the individual. It can assist the commander in evaluating whether the candidate can function in confined spaces, can work independently, and has the potential to function as a sniper.

The tests are more than simple mental analyses. Psychological screening establishes a profile of characteristics that indicate if an individual would be a successful sniper. Testing eliminates candidates who would not perform well in combat. In the past, some trained snipers have refused to shoot targets that were not a direct threat to them, or, after shooting an enemy, refused to shoot again. Psychological screening is intended to identify individuals who would have these problems.

Other tests that may be used by the commander are:

    o    The California Psychological Inventory. This test measures normality traits that can enhance or inhibit the ability to accomplish a given mission. Specifically, it measures self-confidence, achievement potential, motivation levels, and trainability.

    o    The Meyer Briggs Test. This test indicates the method by which an individual analyzes data, feelings, senses, perceptions, or judgment.

4

o     The Otis Intelligence Test.   This correlates an
individual's IQ with his adaptability; the higher the IQ, the
easier it is to train an individual.

o     The Group-Embedded Figures Test.   This test
determines perceptual and cognitive thinking ability.

The commander, in order to achieve the best candidate, should
talk to a qualified psychologist, and explain what he is looking
for in a candidate.   That way, when a candidate is tested, the
psychologist can then sit down with the commander and give him the
best recommendation on the candidate's psychological profile.

The current method for the selection of snipers within a unit
has been for each unit to establish its own selection criteria.
This method, while addressing the current needs of the unit, may
lead to inconsistency in future sniper selection.

To aid the commander in his selection of sniper candidates,
there are several concrete prerequisites that should be met by the
candidates prior to acceptance into the sniper program.

To meet the administrative prerequisites, the sniper candidate
should:

o     Be a member of the SOF (Active and Reserve
Components), or be a selected DOD personnel.

o     Have a passing score on the Army Physical Fitness
Test (APFT) within one (1) month of the beginning of the sniper
training program.

o     Have scored expert with the M16A1/A2 rifle IAW
Chapter 3, Section III, FM 23-9 (M16A1 and M16A2 Rifle
Marksmanship) within one (1) month of training.   Preferably, the
candidate repeatedly scores expert during his biannual
qualification.

o     Have no record of drug or alcohol abuse.

o     Have no record of punishment under the Uniform Code
of Military Justice during his current enlistment.

o     Have a GT score of 110 or above, an SC score of 110
or above, or a CO score of 110 or above.

o     Be in the pay grade of E4 or above.

o     Have 20/20 vision, correctable IAW Chapter 32, paragraph 7-3g, AR 40-501 (Standards of Medical Fitness).   Glasses are
a liability unless the individual is otherwise highly qualified.

o    Have had a psychological evaluation conducted under the direction of, and approved by a qualified medical expert. This examination will include, as a minimum, the MMPI and a psychiatric history mental status examination.

o    Have at least 12 months of service remaining on active duty after completion of the sniper course.

o    Have a SECRET clearance.

Note:    All of the above are prerequisites to enter the Special Operations Target Interdiction Course at Fort Bragg, North Carolina.

Personal prerequisites may be determined by the commander through background checks, interviews, records review, and counseling sessions. Recommended personal prerequisites should include, but are not limited to, the following:

o    Experience as a hunter or woodsman.

o    Experience as a competitive marksman.

o    Interest in weapons.

These first three personal prerequisites are particularly important when it comes to sustaining sniper skills, because the sniper with these characteristics will have a greater desire to practice these tasks as they are part of his avocation.

o    Ability to make rapid, accurate assessments and mental calculations.

o    Ability to maintain an emotionally stable personal life.

o    Ability to function effectively under stress.

o    Possession of character traits of patience, attention to detail, perseverance, and physical endurance.

o    Ability to focus completely.

o    Ability to endure solitude.

o    Objectivity to the extent that one can stand outside oneself to evaluate a situation.

o    Ability to work closely with another individual in confined spaces and under stress.

o    Freedom from certain detrimental personal habits such as the use of tobacco products and alcohol. The use of these are a liability unless the candidate is otherwise highly qualified. (These traits, however, should not be the sole disqualifier.)

o    First class APFT scores with a high degree of stamina, and preferably solid athletic skills and abilities.

o    An attitude of determination is the most important.

After the commander has selected the sniper candidate, he must assess the individual's potential as a sniper. This assessment may be made by a thorough review of the candidate's records, objective tests, and subjective evaluations. The length of time a commander may devote to a candidate's assessment will vary with his resources and the mission. Normally, two or three days will suffice to complete an accurate assessment.

Assessment testing should include both written and practical tests. Practical examinations will actively measure the candidate's physical ability to perform the necessary tasks and subtasks involved in sniping. Written examinations will evaluate the candidate's comprehension of specific details.

Assessment testing must objectively and subjectively determine an individual's potential as a sniper. Objectivity measures the capacity to learn and perform in a sterile environment. Subjectivity assesses actual individual performance.

Objective assessment tests are presented as a battery grouped by subject matter and may be presented either as practical or written examinations. The following are some examples of objective testing:

o    The shooting battery consists of a number of tests designed to evaluate the theoretical and practical applications of rifle marksmanship.

o    The observation and memory battery consists of a number of tests designed to evaluate the candidate's potential for observation and recall of specific facts.

o    The intelligence battery consists of standard military tests and previously mentioned specialized tests.

o    The critical decision test consists of a number of tests designed to evaluate the candidate's ability to think quickly and use sound judgment.

o    The motor skills battery will test hand-eye coordination.

Subjective assessment tests are designed to gain insight into the candidate's personality. Although the candidate is constantly observed in the selection and assessment process, specific tests may be designed to identify desirable and undesirable character traits. All subjective testing should be conducted or monitored by a trained psychologist (well versed in sniper selection). Examples of possible subjective test batteries include, but not limited to, the following:

o    The interview. This should identify the candidate's motivation for becoming a sniper and examine his expectations concerning the training.

o    The suitability inventory. This test basically compares the sniper candidate to a "predetermined profile" containing the characteristics, skills, motivations, and experience a sniper should possess.

Selection is conducted at the conclusion of the assessment program by a committee of assessors. While the commander should monitor all candidate selections, it is important for the committee to make the decision to preserve consistency and to rule out individual bias. The procedure for selection should be accomplished by a quorum during which the candidates are rated on a progressive scale. Candidates should be chosen based on their standing, in conjunction with the needs of the unit. At this time the best qualified soldiers should be selected; alternate and future candidates may also be identified. Additionally, the following guidelines should be adhered to:

o    Candidates should not be apprised of their status during selection.

o    Non-volunteers should not be considered.

o    The best qualified candidates should be selected first.

o    Soldiers not meeting set prerequisites should not be entered into the program.

## 1-6.  QUALIFICATIONS OF SOTIC GRADUATES

Upon completion of the Special Operations Target Interdiction Course (SOTIC), the sniper is capable of shooting groups within two minutes of angle (MOA). This is grouping within 12 inches at 600 meters. He is able to: hit moving targets at 400 meters; hit head-sized targets at 200 meters with a three-second exposure; and move within 200 meters of an observer undetected. He understands camouflage and concealment, observation techniques, reporting techniques, hide site selection, and hide construction. He is capable of first-round hits on man-sized targets out to 600 meters 100 percent of the time, and out to 900 meters 70 percent of the time. While this may sound impressive, it is not the desired final product. In order for the sniper to be "fully" qualified, he must be able to group within 6-7 inches at 600 meters. In other words, he must continually strive to improve in the art of sniping.

The only way the sniper can improve is through a comprehensive sniper sustainment training program. This program must not just sustain the sniper at his present level, it must challenge him to improve and better his skills. The program is mandatory in accordance with USASFC(A) Reg 350-1 (Component Training), and should be used as frequently as possible, with two weeks every six months as a minimum. Sniping skills are extremely perishable, and without this program the sniper will rapidly lose his skills and become ineffective.

## 1-7. THE SNIPER TEAM

In special operations, snipers are assigned in pairs. The sniper pair consists of two equally trained snipers who provide mutual security and support for each other. Snipers are employed in pairs for the purpose of enhancing the team's effectiveness and diminishing the stress that a single sniper would be more apt to encounter. Sniper pairs may also engage targets more rapidly and may stay in the field for longer periods of time than a single sniper.

When employed, the more experienced of the pair will act as the observer during the shot. This is especially important on a high priority target. The more experienced sniper is better able to read winds and give the shooter a compensated aim point which takes into account the effects of the environment, and consequently, better ensures a first-round hit. Additionally, a high priority target may warrant that both snipers engage the target to ensure a hit. The two man concept permits this flexibility.

Experience in World War I, World War II, etc., has shown that deploying snipers in pairs as a sniper/observer team significantly increases the success rate of the missions. With few exceptions, snipers who are deployed singularly have shown a marked decrease in their effectiveness and performance almost immediately after the start of the mission. This is due to the individual becoming overwhelmed with concern for his security, the tasks to be accomplished, and his own emotions, i.e., fear, loneliness, etc.

## 1-8. SNIPER TEAM ORGANIZATION

9

Sniper teams are organized into two-man pairs. The sniper team is the basic operational organization for the employment of snipers, and is the cornerstone of viable sniper employment and effectiveness. Snipers are trained to operate in two-man sniper teams. Either member of the pair can perform the function of the sniper (with the M24 or a specially selected weapon); the other member is armed with the standard service rifle or the M21/LSR and performs the function of the observer. The two-man team is the smallest organization recommended. It offers mobility, concealment, and flexibility. The sniper pair can maintain continuous observation of an area while alternating security, sleeping, eating, etc., and relieving the stress inherent in a single-man operation. The coach-shooter relationship of the sniper pair is invaluable in target acquisition, estimation of range to targets, observation of bullet trace and impact, and offering corrections to targets engaged. Additionally, the mutual support of two snipers working together is a significant morale factor during employment in combat environments or extended missions.

Under certain circumstances the team may be augmented with a squad to platoon-sized element. This element could be used for security, hide construction, or as a cover for a stay-behind operation. If the augmentation is for security purposes, the security element must be located far enough away from the team to prevent its compromise. Eight hundred to 1,000 meters is a starting guideline that must be modified according to the situation and the terrain. It is critical to mission success that the sniper team and the augmentation unit be thoroughly familiar with each other and have well developed SOPs.

Organizational grouping of snipers above the sniper team level is normally accomplished through the expedient pooling of sniper teams into larger organizations. Such centralized grouping of sniper assets can prove beneficial to their employment for specific missions as opposed to sniper teams working independently. Centralized control should be managed by the sniper specialist within the unit. Regardless of any provisional or temporary sniper grouping, sniper teams should not be split; they are most effectively employed in the pairs in which they have trained.

# Chapter 2

## SPECIAL OPERATIONS SNIPER EQUIPMENT

Snipers, by the nature of their mission, must learn to exploit the maximum potential from all of their equipment. The organizational level of employment, and the mission will determine the type and amount of equipment needed. Snipers will carry only that equipment necessary for the successful accomplishment of their mission.

## 2-1.  SNIPER WEAPON SYSTEMS (SWS)

### M24 SWS

The current SWS is the M24 sniper rifle with the Leupold & Stevens Ultra 10X M3A rifle scope. The M24 is based on the Remington Model 700 long action with an adjustable trigger. The barrel is a heavy, 5 groove, 11.2 inch twist, stainless steel target barrel. The stock is constructed of fiberglass, graphite, and kevlar with an adjustable butt plate. The weapon is constructed to be accurate within 1/2 minute of angle (MOA) or 1/2 inch groups at 100 yards. The M24 is currently chambered for the 7.62 mm NATO cartridge. When it is chambered for the .300 Winchester Magnum cartridge, the M24 will be known as the Medium Sniper Rifle (MSR). The M24 is issued two per Operational Detachment.

The components of the M24 SWS (Figure 2-1-1) are as follows:

o    Bolt action rifle

o    Fixed 10x telescope, L&S M3A

o    System case

o    Scope case

o    Detachable iron sights (front and rear)

o    Deployment case and kit (Figure 2-1-1A)

o    Optional bipod

o    Cleaning kit

o    Soft rifle case

o    Operator's manual

1

The safety. The safety is located on the right rear side of the receiver and provides protection against accidental discharge under normal usage when properly engaged. The sniper should follow the rules below.

To engage the safety, place it in the "S" position (Figure 2-1-2).

Always place the safety in the "S" position before handling, loading, or unloading the weapon.

When the weapon is ready to be fired, place the safety in the "F" position (Figure 2-1-3).

Bolt assembly. The bolt assembly locks the round into the chamber and extracts the round from the chamber. The sniper should follow the rules below:

To remove the bolt from the receiver, place the safety in the "S" position, raise the bolt handle, and pull it back until it stops. Push the bolt stop release up (Figure 2-1-4) and pull the bolt from the receiver.

To replace the bolt, ensure the safety is in the "S" position, align the lugs on the bolt assembly with the receiver (Figure 2-1-5), slide the bolt all the way into the receiver, and then push the bolt handle down.

Trigger assembly. Pulling the trigger fires the rifle when the safety is in the "F" position. The operator may adjust the trigger pull force from a minimum of 2 pounds to a maximum of 8 pounds. This is done using the 1/16-inch allen wrench provided in the deployment kit. Turning the trigger adjustment screw (Figure 2-1-6) clockwise will increase the force needed to pull the trigger. Turning it counterclockwise will decrease the force needed. This is the only trigger adjustment the sniper should make. (CAUTION! Too light of an adjustment will cause the weapon to discharge when disengaging the safety, loading, or if the weapon is dropped while the safety is in the "F" position.)

Stock adjustment. The M24 has a mechanism for adjusting the length of pull of the stock. The thick wheel provides this adjustment. The thin wheel is for locking this adjustment (Figure 2-1-6A). Turn the thick wheel clockwise to lengthen the stock, or counterclockwise to shorten the stock. To lock the position of the shoulder stock, turn the thin wheel clockwise against the thick wheel. To unlock the position of the shoulder stock, turn the thin wheel counterclockwise away from the thick wheel. The length of pull is adjusted so that when the butt of the rifle is placed alongside the shooting forearm against the base of the bicep, the trigger finger's first joint is in line with the trigger.

Inspection. The M24 is designed to be repaired by the operator. Deficiencies that cannot be repaired by the sniper will require manufacturer warranty work. Refer to TM 9-1005-306-10 that is furnished with each weapon system. The sniper should check the following areas when inspecting the M24:

o    The appearance and completeness of all parts.

o    The bolt to ensure it has the same serial number as the receiver, and that it locks, unlocks, and moves smoothly.

o    The safety to ensure it can be positively placed into the "S" and "F" positions easily without being too difficult or moving too freely.

o    The trigger to ensure the weapon will not fire when the safety is in the "S" position, and that it has a smooth, crisp trigger pull when the safety is in the "F" position.

o    The action screws (front of the internal magazine and rear of the trigger guard) for proper torque (65 inch-pounds).

o    The telescope mounting ring nuts for proper torque (65 inch-pounds).

o    The stock for any cracks, splits, or any contact it may have with the barrel.

o    The telescope for obstructions such as dirt, dust, and moisture, and loose or damaged lenses.

Iron sights. The M24 has a backup sighting system consisting of detachable front and rear iron sights. To install the iron sights, the sniper must first remove the telescope. The sniper should follow the rules below.

To attach the front sight to the barrel, align the front sight and the front sight base dovetails and slide the sight over the base. Next, tighten the screw slowly, ensuring that the screw seats into the recess in the sight base (Figure 2-1-7).

To attach the rear sight to the receiver, remove one of the three set screws, and align the rear sight with the rear sight base located on the left rear of the receiver (Figure 2-1-8). Tighten the screw to secure the sight to the base.

Loading. The M24 has an internal, five-round capacity magazine. To load the rifle, th sniper should:

o    Point the weapon in a safe direction.

o    Ensure the safety is in the "S" position.

3

o       Raise the bolt handle and pull it back until it stops.

o       Push five rounds of 7.62 mm ammunition one at a time through the ejection port into the magazine. Ensure that the bullet end of the rounds is aligned toward the chamber.

o       Push the rounds fully rearward in the magazine.

o       Once the five rounds are in the magazine, push the rounds downward while slowly pushing the bolt forward over the top of the first round.

o       Push the bolt handle down. The magazine is now loaded.

o       To chamber a round, raise the bolt and pull it back until it stops.

o       Push the bolt forward. The bolt strips a round from the magazine and pushes it into the chamber.

o       Push the bolt handle down.

o       To fire, place the safety in the "F" position and pull the trigger.

Shipment for Uncorrectable Maintenance. See TM 9-1005-306-10.

## M21 SWS

The National Match M14 rifle and its telescope make up the M21 SWS (Figure 2-1-9). The M21 is a match-grade M14 rifle equipped with a 3-9x adjustable ranging telescope (ART I/II). The M21 is accurized IAW United States Army Marksmanship Training Unit specifications and has the same basic design and operation as the standard M14 rifle (FM 23-8), except for specially selected and hand-fitted parts. The M21 has been replaced by the M24; however, the M21 is still in use throughout the US Army. Once the M24 is fully fielded, the M21 can be used as the sniper team defensive-/back-up SWS. The future SOF Light Sniper Rifle (LSR) is be based on the M14 action, and will be issued two per Operational Detachment.

### Description:

o       The barrel is match-grade, gauged and selected to ensure correct specification tolerances. The bore is not chrome-lined.

o       The stock is walnut and impregnated with an epoxy.

o       The receiver is individually custom-fitted to the stock with a metal-filled epoxy compound.

4

o     The firing mechanism is reworked and polished to provide for a crisp hammer release. Trigger weight is between 4.5 and 4.75 pounds.

o     The flash suppressor is fitted and reamed to improve accuracy and eliminate any misalignment.

o     The gas cylinder and piston are reworked and polished to improve operation and reduce carbon buildup.

o     The gas cylinder and lower band are permanently attached to each other.

o     The entire rifle is composed of parts that are carefully selected, fitted, and assembled.

Inspection. Deficiencies discovered during inspection will be reported to the unit armorer. The sniper should inspect the following areas:

o     The appearance and completeness of all parts. Shiny surfaces should be treated.
o     The flash suppressor for misalignment, burrs, or evidence of bullet tipping. The suppressor should be tight on the barrel.

o     The front sight to ensure that it is tight, that the blade is square, and that all edges and corners are sharp.

o     The gas cylinder to ensure that it fits tightly on the barrel. The gas plug should be firmly tightened.

o     The forward band on the stock to ensure that it does not bind against the gas cylinder front band.

o     The handguard to ensure that it is not binding against the receiver, the top of the stock, or the operating rod.

o     The firing mechanism to ensure the weapon will not fire with the safety "on," and that it has a smooth, crisp trigger pull when the safety is "off."

o     The rear sight tension by turning the aperture up to the "10" position. Press down on the top of the aperture with the thumb. If the aperture can be pushed down, the tension must be readjusted.

o     The stock for splits or cracks.

Iron Sights. The M21 SWS is equipped with National Match front and rear sights (Figure 2-1-10). The front sight is used to obtain a battle zero for windage, so that the rear sight can be centered on its markings.  The front sight is moved in the opposite direction that the sniper wants the shot group to move.

The rear sight has a pinion assembly that adjusts the elevation of the aperture.  When the sniper turns the elevation knob clockwise, it raises the point of impact.  Turning it counterclockwise lowers the point of impact.  Each click of the knob is worth 1 MOA.  The hooded aperture is also adjustable and provides .5 MOA changes in elevation.  Rotating the aperture so that the indication notch is at the top raises the point of impact .5 MOA.  Rotating the indication notch to the bottom lowers the point of impact.  The windage knob adjusts the lateral movement of the rear sight.  Turning the knob clockwise moves the point to impact to the right and turning it counterclockwise moves the point of impact to the left.  Each click of the windage knob is .5 MOA.

Loading and Unloading.  When the sniper loads the M21, he locks the bolt to the rear and place the weapon in the safe position.  Insert the magazine into the magazine well by pushing up, then pulling the bottom of the magazine to the rear until the magazine catch gives an audible click.  To chamber a round, pull the bolt slightly to the rear to release the bolt catch, then release the bolt.  (CAUTION!  Do not "ride" the bolt forward.  Allow the mainspring to close the bolt.)  To unload the M21, first place the weapon on "safe."  Depress the magazine release latch, and move the magazine in a forward and downward motion at the same time.  Lock the bolt to the rear and remove the chambered round.


## 2-2.  TELESCOPIC SIGHTS

A telescopic sight mounted on the rifle allows the sniper to detect and engage targets more effectively than he could by using the iron sights.  Unlike sighting with iron sights, the target's image in the telescope is on the same focal plane as the aiming point (reticle).  This allows for a clearer picture of the target and reticle because the eye can focus on both simultaneously.

Another advantage of the telescope is its ability to magnify the target.  This increases the resolution of the target's image, making it clearer and more defined.    The average unaided human eye can distinguish detail of about 1 inch at 100 meters (1 MOA).  Magnification, combined with well-designed optics, permit resolution of this 1 inch divided by the magnification.  Thus, a 1/4 MOA of detail can be seen with a 4-power scope at 100 meters, or 1 inch of detail can be seen at 600 meters with a 6-power scope.

Additionally, telescopic sights magnify the ambient light, making shots possible earlier and later during the day.  Although a telescope helps the sniper to see better, it does not help him to shoot better.

## Leupold & Stevens M3A Telescope

**Description.** The M3A is a fixed 10x telescope with a ballistic drop compensator dial for bullet trajectory from 100 to 1,000 meters. The elevation knob is marked in 50-meter increments, and has one MOA elevation adjustments. The windage knob is in 1/2 MOA increments, and a third knob provides for focus/parallax adjustment. The reticle is a duplex cross hair with 3/4 MOA mil dots (Figure 2-2-1). The mil dots are 1 mil apart, center to center, with a possible 10 mils vertical and 10 mils horizontal. The mil dots are used for range estimation, holdover, windage holds, and mover leads.

The design and operating principle of the M3A scope is different from the ART series of telescopes. The major difference in the M3A is the adjustment method used to compensate for the trajectory of the bullet at varying distances.

The M3A consists of: the telescope, a fixed mount, a detachable sun shade for the objective lens, and dust covers for the objective and ocular (eyepiece) lens.

The telescope has a fixed 10x magnification, which gives the sniper better resolution than with the ART series.

There are three knobs located midway on the tube: the focus/parallax, elevation, and windage knobs (Figure 2-2-2).

**Adjustments.** The focus/parallax knob is located on the left side of the tube. It is used to focus the target's image onto the same focal plane as the reticle, thereby reducing parallax to a minimum. Parallax is the apparent movement of the sight picture on the reticle when the eye is moved from side to side or up and down. The focus knob has two extreme positions indicated by the infinity mark and the largest of four dots. Adjustments between these positions focus images from less than 50 meters to infinity.

The elevation knob is located on top of the tube. This knob has calibrated index markings from 1 to 10. These marking represent the elevation setting adjustments needed at varying distances: 1 = 100 meters, 10 = 1,000 meters. Each click of the elevation knob equals 1 MOA.

The windage knob is located on the right side of the tube. This knob is used for lateral adjustments. Turning the knob in the direction indicated moves the point of impact in that direction. Each click on the windage knob equals 1/2 MOA.

The eyepiece is adjusted by turning it in or out of the tube until the reticle appears crisp and clear to the assigned operator. Focusing the eyepiece should be done after mounting the telescope on the rifle. Grasp the eyepiece and back it away from the lock ring. Do not attempt to loosen the lock ring first; it will automatically loosen when the eyepiece is backed away (no tools are needed). The eyepiece is rotated several turns to move it at least 1/8 inch. This much change is needed to achieve any measurable effect on the reticle clarity. Look through the scope at the sky or a blank wall, and check to see if the reticle appears sharp and crisp.

Scope Mount. The scope mount consists of a base plate with four screws and a pair of scope rings (each with an upper and lower ring half) with eight ring screws (Figure 2-2-3). The base plate is mounted to the rifle by screwing the four base plate screws through the plate and into the top of the receiver. The screws must not protrude into the receiver and interrupt the functioning of the bolt. It is advisable to use medium strength "Loctite" on these four baseplate screws for a more permanent attachment. After the base plate is mounted, the scope rings are mounted.

When the sniper mounts the scope rings, he should select one of slots on the mounting base and engage the ring bolt spline with the selected slot. Push the ring forward to get spline-to-base contact as the mount ring nut is tightened. Check the eye relief. If the telescope needs to be adjusted, the ring nuts are loosened and the ring bolts are aligned with the other set of slots on the base; and the process is repeated. Ensure that the cross hairs are perfectly aligned (vertically and horizontally) with the rifle. Any cant will cause misses at longer ranges. Once satisfied with the eye relief obtained (approximately 3 to 3 1/2 inches), tighten the ring nuts to 65 inch-pounds using the T-handle torque wrench (found in the deployment case).

Operation. When using the telescope, the sniper should simply look at the target, focus the telescope, determine the distance to the target by using the mil dots on the reticle, and then adjust the elevation knob for the estimated range. Place the cross hair on the desired point of impact.

## Adjustable Ranging Telescopes

The adjustable ranging telescope (ART) is a component of the M21 SWS. The two types of ARTs found on the M21 are the ART I and ART II. Both telescopes share the same basic design and operating principle. Therefore, they will be described together, with their differences highlighted.

Description. The ART is a 3- 9x variable telescopic sight modified for use with the sniper rifle. This telescope has a ballistic cam mounted to the power adjustment ring on the ART I (Figure 2-2-4). The ART II has a separate ballistic cam and power ring (Figure 2-2-5). The ART is mounted on a spring-loaded base that is adapted to fit the M14. The lens surfaces are coated with a hard film of magnesium fluoride for maximum light transmission. It is transported in a hard carrying case when not mounted to the rifle.

These telescopes have modified reticles. The ART I has the basic cross hair design with two horizontal stadia lines that appear at the target's distance, 15 inches above and 15 inches below the cross hair intersection. It also has two vertical stadia lines that appear at the target's distance, 30 inches to the left and 30 inches to the right of the cross hair intersection (Figure 2-2-6). The ART II reticle consists of three posts: two horizontal and one bottom vertical post (Figure 2-2-7). The thickness of these posts represents 1 meter at the target's distance. The reticle has a basic cross hair with two dots on the horizontal line that appear at the target's distance, 30 inches to the left and 30 inches to the right of the cross hair intersection.

A ballistic cam is attached to the power adjustment ring on the ART I, and the ART II has a separate power adjustment ring and ballistic cam.

The power ring on both telescopes increases and decreases the magnification, while the ballistic cam raises and lowers the telescope to compensate for elevation.

Adjustments. The sniper should make focus adjustments by screwing the eyepiece into or away from the telescope tube until the reticle appears crisp and black. (Procedure detailed in Appendix I).

Located midway on the scope tube are the elevation and windage turrets with dials that are used for zeroing adjustments. These dials are graduated in 1/2 MOA increments. Turning the dial will move the point of impact as indicated on the dial.

Scope Mount. The ART mount is made of light-weight aluminum and consists of a side-mounting plate and a spring-loaded base with attached telescope mounting rings. The mount is designed for low-profile mounting of the telescope to the rifle, using the mounting guide grooves and threaded hole(s) on the left side of the M14 receiver. The ART I has one thumbscrew that screws into the left side of the receiver (Figure 2-2-8). The ART II mount has two thumbscrews; one is screwed into the left side of the receiver, and the other is screwed into the modified cartridge clip guide in front of the rear sight (Figure 2-2-9).

Operation. The ART telescopes are designed to automatically adjust for the needed elevation at ranges from 300 to 900 meters. This is done by increasing or decreasing the magnification of the telescope until a portion of the target's image matches the represented measurement of the telescope's reticle.
ART I: The power ring on the ART I is adjusted until 30 inches of an object or a person's image (beltline to the top of the head) fits exactly in between the horizontal stadia lines (Figure 2-2-10).

ART II: The power ring on the ART II is adjusted until 1 meter (about 40 inches) of an object or person's image (crotch to the top of the head) appears equal to one of the posts in the reticle (Figure 2-2-11).

When the power ring is turned to adjust the target's image to fit the reticle, the ballistic cam is also turned. This raises or lowers the telescope itself to compensate for elevation. Once the telescope's magnification is properly adjusted to bracket the target, the ballistic cam has adjusted the telescope for the proper elevation needed to engage the target at that distance.

The ART II has a locking thumbscrew located on the power ring to connect and disconnect the power ring from the ballistic cam. This allows the sniper to adjust the telescope onto the target (auto-ranging mode) and then disengage the locking thumbscrew to increase magnification (manual mode) without affecting the elevation adjustment.

## 2-3. AMMUNITION

7.62x51mm NATO M118 Special Ball or M852 National Match ammunition is used with the SWSs. The SWS must be re-zeroed every time the type or lot of ammunition is changed. The ammunition lot number is printed on the cardboard box, metal can, and wooden crate the ammunition is packaged in. The sniper should maintain this information in the weapon's data book.

Snipers should always attempt to use match-grade ammunition when available because of its greater accuracy and lower sensitivity to environmental effects. However, if match-grade ammunition is not available, or if the situation requires, a different grade of ammunition may be used. Standard-grade ammunition may not provide the same level of accuracy or point of impact as match-grade ammunition. In the absence of match-grade ammunition, firing tests should be conducted to determine the most accurate lot of ammunition available. Once a lot of ammunition is identified as meeting the requirements, this lot should be used as long as it is available.

<u>**Types and Characteristics**</u>
<u>M118 Special Ball</u>. The M118 Special Ball bullet consists of a gilding metal jacket and a lead antimony slug. It is a boat-tailed bullet (the rear of the bullet is tapered to reduce drag) and has a nominal weight of 173 grains (most are closer to 175 grains). The tip of the bullet is not colored. The base of the cartridge is stamped with the NATO standardization mark (circle and cross hair), manufacturer's code, and year of manufacture. Its primary use is against personnel. Its accuracy standard requires a 10-shot group to have an extreme spread of not more than 12 inches at 550 meters (2 MOA) when fired from an accuracy barrel in

a test cradle.  The stated velocity of 2550 feet per second (fps) is measured at 78 feet from the muzzle.  The actual <u>muzzle</u> velocity of this ammunition is 2610 fps.  M118 is the primary choice for both the M24 and M21 SWSs because the telescopic sights are ballistically matched to this ammunition out to 1,000 and 900 meters, respectively.

<u>M852 National Match (open-tip)</u>.  As of October 1990 the Department of State, Army General Counsel, and the Offices of the Judge Advocate General concluded that the use of open-tip ammunition does not violate the laws-of-war obligation of the United States.  This ammunition may be employed in peacetime or in wartime missions of the Army, Navy, and Marine Corps.

Description.  The M852 bullet is boat-tailed, 168 grains in weight, and has an open tip.  The open tip is a shallow aperture (about the diameter of the wire in a standard-size straight pin or paper clip) in the nose of the bullet.  Describing this bullet as a hollow point is misleading in law-of-war terms.  A hollow-point bullet is typically thought of in terms of its ability to expand upon impact with soft tissue.  Physical examination of the M852 open-tip bullet reveals that its opening is small in comparison to the aperture of hollow-point hunting bullets.  For example, the 165 grain hunting bullet is a true hollow-point, boat-tailed bullet with an aperture much larger in size than that of the M852's bullet.  It also contains serrations cut into the jacket to ensure expansion.  In the M852, the open tip is closed as much as possible to provide better aerodynamics and contains no serrations.  The lead core of the M852 bullet is entirely covered by the bullet jacket.

Purpose.  The small, shallow aperture in the M852 provides a bullet design that offers maximum accuracy at long ranges.  The jacket is rolled around its core from base to tip; standard military bullets and other match bullets have their jacket rolled around its core from tip to base, leaving an exposed lead core at the base.  The design of the M852 was to produce a bullet that would not expand or flatten easily upon impact with the human body or otherwise cause wounds greater than those caused by standard military small-arms ammunition.

Performance.  Other than its superior long-range accuracy capabilities, the M852 was examined with regard to its performance upon impact with the human body or in artificial material that approximates soft human tissue.  In some cases, the bullet will break up or fragment after entry into soft tissue.  Fragmentation depends on many factors, including the range to the target, velocity at the time of impact, degree of yaw of the bullet at the point of impact, or the distance traveled point-first within the body before yaw is induced.  The M852 was not designed to yaw intentionally or break up upon impact.  These characteristics are common to all military rifle bullets.  There was little discernible difference in bullet

11

fragmentation between the M852 and other military small-arms bullets. Some military ball ammunition of foreign manufacture tends to fragment sooner in human tissue or to greater degree, resulting in wounds that would be more severe than those caused by the M852 bullet.

> NOTE:     M852 is the best substitute for M118 taking the following limitations into consideration:

o     The M852's trajectory is not identical to the M118's trajectory, therefore, it is not matched ballistically with the M3A or ART I/II telescopes.

o     M852 is not suited for target engagement beyond 600 to 700 meters because the 168 grain bullet is not ballistically suitable. This bullet will drop below the sound barrier just beyond this distance. The severe turbulence that it encounters as it becomes sub-sonic affects its accuracy at distances beyond 600 to 700 meters.

M82 Blank. The M82 blank ammunition is used during sniper field training. It provides the muzzle blast and flash that can be detected by trainers during the exercises that evaluate the sniper's ability to conceal himself while firing his weapon.

## Alternative Ammunition

If match-grade ammunition is not available, standard 7.62x51mm NATO ball ammunition can be used. However, the M3A and ART I/II telescopes' bullet drop compensators are designed for M118 Special Ball, and there would be a significant change in zero. Standard ammunition should be test-fired and the ballistic data recorded in the data book. Standard ball ammunition should be used in an emergency situation only.

M80/M80E1 Ball. The M80 and M80E1 ball cartridge bullet consists of a gilding metal jacket with a lead antimony slug. It is boat-tailed and weighs 147 grains. The tip of the bullet is not colored. It is primarily used against personnel. Its accuracy standard requires a 10-shot group to have an extreme spread of not more than 24 inches at 550 meters (4 MOA) when fired from an accuracy barrel in a test cradle. The muzzle velocity of this ammunition is 2800 fps. The base of the cartridge is stamped with the NATO standardization mark, manufacturer's initials, and the date of manufacture. Several lots should be test-fired prior to use due to the reduced accuracy and fluctuation in lots. The most accurate lot that is available in the largest quantity (to minimize test repetition) should be selected for use.

M62 Tracer. The M62 tracer bullet consists of a gilding metal-clad steel jacket, a lead antimony slug, a tracer subigniter, and igniter composition. It has a closure cap and weighs 141 grains. The bullet tip is painted orange (NATO identification for tracer ammunition). It is used for observation of fire, incendiary, and signaling purposes. Tracer ammunition is manufactured to have an accuracy standard that requires 10-shot groups to have an extreme spread of not more than 36 inches at 550 meters (6 MOA). The base of the cartridge is stamped with the NATO standardization mark, manufacturer's initials, and date of manufacture. The amount of tracer ammunition fired through SWSs should be minimized because of its harmful effect on the precision-made barrel.

## Round Count Book

The sniper maintains a running count of the number and type of rounds fired through the SWS. It is imperative to accurately maintain the round count book as the SWS should be re-barreled after 10,000 rounds of firing or after a noticeable loss of accuracy.

## 2-4. OBSERVATION DEVICES

Aside from the rifle and telescopic sight, the sniper's most important tools are optical devices. The categories of optical equipment normally employed by snipers are: binoculars, telescopes, range finders, and night vision devices. Selected optical equipment for special purposes will be discussed.

## Binoculars

Every sniper should be issued binoculars; they are the snipers' primary tool for observation. Binoculars provide an optical advantage not found with telescopes or other monocular optical devices. The binoculars' typically larger objective lens, lower magnification, and binocular characteristics add depth and field of view to an observed area. Many types of binoculars are available. Binocular selection should take the following into account:

o    Durability. The binoculars must be able to withstand rough use under field conditions. They must be weatherproof--sealed against moisture that would render them useless due to internal fogging. Binoculars with individually-focussed eyepieces can more easily be made waterproof than centrally-focussed binoculars. Most waterproof binoculars offered have individually-focussed eyepieces.

o    Size. Snipers' binoculars should be relatively compact for ease of handling and concealment.

o    Moderate magnification. Binoculars of 6 to 8 power are best suited for sniper work. Higher magnifications tend to limit the field of view for any given size of objective lens. Additionally, higher magnifications tend to intensify hand movements during observation, and compresses depth perception.

13

o     Lens   diameter.      Binoculars   with   an   objective   lens
diameter  of  35  to  50  mm  should  be  considered  the  best  choice.
Larger lenses permit more light to enter; therefore, the 50 mm lens
would be more effective in low-light conditions.

o     Mil   scale.     The   binoculars   should   have   a   mil   scale
incorporated into the field of view for range estimation.

<u>Method of holding binoculars</u>.     Binoculars should be held
lightly, resting on, and supported by the heels of the hands.   The
thumbs are positioned to block out light that would enter between
the eyes and the eyepieces.   The eyepieces are held lightly to the
eyes  to  avoid  transmitting  body  movement.     Whenever  possible,  a
stationary rest should support the elbows.  An alternate method for
holding  the  binoculars  is  to  move  the  hands  forward,  cupping  them
around the sides of the objective lenses.   This keeps light from
reflecting   off   the   lenses,   which   would   reveal   the   sniper's
position.   The sniper should <u>always</u> be aware of reflecting light.
The  sniper  should  operate  from  within  shadows  or  cover  the  lens
with an extension or thin veil (example: nylon stocking).
<u>Adjustments</u>.   Interpupillary adjustment is the movement of the
monocles to fit an individual's eyes.   Interpupillary distance is
the distance between the eyes.   The monocles are hinged together
for ease of adjustment.   The hinge is adjusted until the field of
vision  ceases  to  be  two  overlapping  circles  and  appears  as  a
single,  sharply  defined  circle.     The  setting  on  the  hinge  scale
should be recorded for future use.

Every  individual  and  each  eye  of  that  individual  requires
different focus settings.   The sniper should adjust the focus for
each  eye  in  the  following  manner:   with  <u>both</u>  eyes  open,  look  at  a
distant object, then through the binoculars at this same object.
Place  one  hand  over  the  objective  lens  of  the  right  monocle  and
turn  the  focussing  ring  of  the  left  monocle  until  the  object  is
sharply defined.   Uncover the right monocle and cover the left one.
Rotate  the  focussing  ring  of  the  right  monocle  until  the  object  is
sharply  defined.    Uncover  the  left  monocle.    The  object  should  be
clear  to  both  eyes.    The  sniper  should  glance  frequently  at  the
distant  object  with  his  eyes  during  this  procedure  to  ensure  that
his  eyes  are  not  compensating  for  an  out-of-focus  condition.    Read
the  diopter  scale  on  each  focussing  ring  and  record  for  future
reference.   Correctly focussed binoculars will prevent eye strain
when observing for extended periods.

<u>Eye fatigue</u>.   Prolonged use of the binoculars or telescope
will cause eye fatigue, reducing the effectiveness of observation.
Periods of observation with optical devices should be limited to 30
minutes, followed by a minimum of 15 minutes rest.   Eye strain can
be minimized during observation by glancing away at green grass or
any other natural, subdued color.

<u>M22 Binoculars</u>

14

The M22 binoculars (Figure 2-4-1) are the newest in the inventory, and are general issue. These binoculars have the same features as the M19, plus fold-down eyepiece cups for personnel who wear glasses, to reduce the distance between the eyes and the eyepieces. It also has protective covers for the objective and eyepiece lenses. The binoculars have laser protection filters on the insides of the objective lenses (<u>DIRECT SUNLIGHT REFLECTS OFF OF THESE LENSES!</u>). The reticle pattern (Figure 2-4-2) is different from the M19's reticle.

## <u>Observation Telescope M49 and Tripod</u>

<u>Description</u>. The M49 observation telescope is a prismatic optical instrument of 20 power magnification (Figure 2-4-3). The lenses are coated with magnesium fluoride for improved light-transmitting capability. It is carried by the sniper team whenever needed for the mission. The telescope is used by the designated observer to assist in observation and selection of targets while the sniper is in the position to fire. Properly used, the M49 telescope can significantly enhance the success of the snipers' mission by allowing them to conduct a superior target analysis, reading of the current environmental conditions, and make spotting corrections by observing bullet trace and impact. The high magnification of the telescope makes observation, target detection, and target identification possible where conditions such as range would otherwise prevent identification. Camouflaged targets and those in deep shadows are more readily detected.

<u>Operation of the M49</u>. An eyepiece cover cap and objective lens cover are used to protect the optics when the telescope is not in use. Care must be taken to prevent cross-threading of the fine threads. The eyepiece focusing sleeve is turned clockwise or counterclockwise until the image can be clearly seen by the operator.

<u>Operation of the M15 Tripod</u>. The height adjusting collar is used to maintain a desired height for the telescope. The collar is held in position by tightening the clamping screw. The shaft rotation locking thumb screw clamps the tripod shaft at any desired azimuth. The elevating thumbscrew is used to adjust the cradle of the tripod, and to increase or decrease the angle of elevation of the telescope. The tripod legs can be held in an adjusted position by tightening the screw nut at the upper end of each leg.

<u>Setting up the M49 and Tripod</u>. Spread the legs and place the tripod on a level position on the ground so that the cradle is level with the target area. Place the telescope through the strip loop of the tripod and tighten the strap to keep the telescope in place and steady. If the tripod is not carried, an expedient rest should be used for the scope. The scope needs a steady position to maximize its capabilities and minimize eye strain.

## 2-5. NIGHT VISION DEVICES

Snipers use night vision devices (NVDs) to accomplish their mission during limited visibility operations. NVDs can be employed as observation aids, weapons sights, or both.

**Employment factors.** First- and second-generation NVDs amplify the ambient light to provide an image of the observed area or target. These NVDs will not function in total darkness because they do not project their own light source, and therefore, require target illumination. NVDSs work best on bright, moonlit nights. When there is no light or the ambient light level is low (such as in heavy vegetation), the use of artificial or infrared light improves the NVD's performance.

Fog, smoke, dust, hail, or rain limit the range and decrease the resolution of NVDs.

NVDs do not allow the operator to see through objects in the field of view. The operator will experience the same range restrictions when viewing dense wood lines as he would when using other optical sights.

Initially, an operator may experience eye fatigue when viewing for prolonged periods. Initial exposure should be limited to 10 minutes, followed by a 15 minute rest period. After several periods of viewing, the observation time limit can be safely extended. To aid in maintaining continuous observation and to reduce eye fatigue, the operator should alternate his viewing eyes often.

## Night Vision Sight, AN/PVS-2

The AN/PVS-2 is a first-generation NVD (Figure 2-5-1). It can resolve images in low ambient light conditions better than second-generation NVDs can. However, first-generation NVDs are larger and heavier. Characteristics of the AN/PVS-2 are as follows:

| | |
|---|---|
| Length | 18.5 inches |
| Width | 3.34 inches |
| Weight | 5 pounds |
| Magnification | 4 power |
| Range | dependent on ambient light conditions |
| Field of view | 171 mils |
| Focus range | 4 meters to infinity |

## Night Vision Sight, AN/PVS-4

The AN/PVS-4 is a portable, battery-operated, electro-optical instrument that can be hand-held for visual observation or weapon-mounted for precision fire at night (Figure 2-5-2). The observer can detect and resolve distant targets through the unique capability of the sight to amplify reflected ambient light (moon, stars, or skyglow). The sight is passive; thus, it is free from enemy detection by visual or electronic means. This sight, with the appropriate adapter bracket, can be mounted on the M16, M21, or M24.

Second-generation NVDs, characterized by the AN/PVS-4, possess the advantage of smaller size and weight over first-generation NVDs. However, they do not possess the extreme low-light capability of the first-generation devices. The AN/PVS-4 also offers advantages of internal adjustments, changeable reticles, and protection from blooming (the effect of a single light source, such as a flare or streetlight, which would overwhelm the entire image). Characteristics of the AN/PVS-4 are as follows:

| | |
|---|---|
| Length | 12 inches |
| Width | 3.75 inches |
| Weight | 3.5 pounds |
| Magnification | 3.6 power |
| Range | 400 meters/starlight, 600 meters/moon- light for a man-sized target |
| Field of view | 258 mils |
| Focus range | 20 feet to infinity |

Uses. When mounted on the M16 rifle, the AN/PVS-2/4 is effective in achieving a first-round hit out to and beyond 300 meters, depending upon the light conditions. The AN/PVS-2/4 is mounted on the M16 since the NVD's limited range does not make its use practical for the 7.62 mm sniper weapon systems. This avoids problems that may occur when removing and replacing the NVD. The NVD provides an effective observation capability during limited visibility operations. The NVD does not give the width, depth, or clarity of daytime optics. However, a well-trained operator can see enough to: analyze the tactical situation, detect enemy targets, and engage targets effectively. The sniper team uses the AN/PVS-2/4 to:

o    Enhance their night observation capability.

o    Locate and suppress hostile fire at night.

o    Deny enemy movement at night.

17

o    Demoralize the enemy with effective first-round hits
     at night.

     Snipers should weigh the advantages and disadvantages between
the AN/PVS-2 and the AN/PVS-4 when the choice is available.  The
proper training and knowledge with NVDs cannot be overemphasized.
The results obtained with NVDs will be directly attributable to the
sniper's skill and experience in their employment.

## KN200/KN250 Image Intensifier (SIMRAD)

     The KN200/250 image intensifier (Figure 2-5-3) increases the
use of the existing M3A telescope.  It is mounted as an add-on unit
and enables the sniper to aim through the eyepiece of the day sight
both during day and night--an advantage not achieved with
traditional types of NVDs.  Sudden illumination of the scene does
not affect sighting abilities.  These image intensifiers can be
used with both second- and third-generation image intensifier tubes
and do not require modification.  The exact position of the image
intensifier relative to the day sight is not critical due to the
unique design.  As boresighting is not required, the mounting
procedures take only a few seconds.  The KN200/250 technical
specifications:

|  | KN200 | KN250 |
|---|---|---|
| Magnification | 1 X   +/- 1% | |
| Field of View | 10 degrees | 12 degrees |
| Mounting Tolerance | +/- 1 degree | |
| Objective Lens | 100 mm | 80 mm |
| Focusing Range | Fixed | |
| Battery Life | 40 hours at 25 degrees C with two alkaline AA cells | |
| Operating Temperature | -30 to +50 degrees C | |
| Weight (excluding bracket) | 1.4 kg | 0.7 kg |

## Night Vision Goggles, AN/PVS-5

     The AN/PVS-5 is a lightweight, passive night vision system
that gives the sniper team another means of observing an area
during limited visibility (Figure 2-5-4).  The sniper normally
carries the goggles, because the observer has the M16 mounted with
the NVD.  The goggles' design make them easier to view with.
However, the same limitations that apply to the nightsight also
apply to the goggles.

## Night Vision Goggles, AN/PVS-7 Series

18

The night vision goggles, AN/PVS-7 (Figure 2-5-5) can be used instead of the AN/PVS-5 goggles. These goggles provide better resolution and viewing ability than the AN/PVS-5 goggles. The AN/PVS-7 series goggles come with a head-mount assembly that allows them to be mounted in front of the face to free both hands. The goggles can be used without the mount assembly for hand-held viewing. (See TM 11-5855-262-10-1).

## Laser Observation Set, AN/GVS-5

Depending on the mission, snipers can use the AN/GVS-5 to determine increased distances more accurately. The AN/GVS-5 (Figure 2-5-6) is an individually operated, hand-held, distance-measuring device designed for distances from 200 to 9,990 meters (with an error of plus or minus 10 meters). It measures distances by firing an infrared beam at a target and measuring the time the reflected beam takes to return to the operator. It then displays the target distance, in meters, inside the viewer. The reticle pattern in the viewer is graduated in 10-mil increments and has display lights to indicate low battery and multiple target hits. If the beam hits more than one target, the display gives a reading of the closest target hit. The beam that is fired from the set poses a safety hazard; therefore, snipers planning to use this equipment should be thoroughly trained in its safe operation. (See TM 11-5860-201-10).

## Mini-Eyesafe Laser Infrared Observation Set, AN/PVS-6

The AN/PVS-6 (Figure 2-5-7) contains the following components: mini-eyesafe laser range finder; batteries, BA-6516/U, non-rechargeable, lithium thionyl chloride; carrying case; shipping case; tripod; lens cleaning compound and lens cleaning tissue; and operator's manual. The laser range finder is the major component of the AN/PVS-6. It is lightweight, individually operated, and hand-held or tripod-mounted; it can accurately determine ranges from 50 to 9,995 meters in 5-meter increments and displays the range in the eyepiece. It can also be mounted with and boresighted to the night observation device, AN/TAS-6, Long-range.

## 2-6. STANDARD MISSION EQUIPMENT

The sniper team determines the type and quantity of equipment to be carried by a METT-T analysis. A sniper team, due to unique mission requirements, only carries mission-essential equipment. This is only a partial listing. See Appendix M for a detailed listing.

Each sniper team should be equipped with the following:

o    M24 SWS (with 100 rounds ammunition M118 or M852).

o    Sniper's data book, mission logbook, range cards, wind tables, and slope dope.

o    M21 SWS/LSR/service rifle (w/NVD as appropriate) (with 200-210 rounds ammunition).

o    M49 20x spotting scope with M15 tripod (or equivalent 15-20x fixed power scope, or 15-45x zoom spotting scope).

o    Binoculars (preferably 7 x 50 power with mil scale).

o    M9/Service pistols (with 45 rounds 9mm ball ammunition).

o    Night vision devices (as needed).

o    Radio(s).

o    Camouflaged clothing (constructed by the sniper).

o    Compass (the M2 is preferable).

o    Watches (sweep second hand with luminous dial and water-proof).

o    Maps/sector sketch material.

o    M18A1/M67/CS grenades (as needed).

o    Special mission equipment.

## Additional Equipment

There is no limit to the diversity of equipment that the sniper may use for normal or special missions. The key to proper selection of equipment is a careful mission analysis, and to take only what is necessary for the mission. Too much equipment can seriously hamper the sniper's mobility, endurance, and stealth. Recommended additional equipment:

o    Sling. The standard issue web sling or leather sling is used by the sniper to aid in firing the rifle if a solid rest is not available. However, the leather sling should be the primary sling used. The web sling is not suitable for sling-supported positions.

o    Uniform. In most cases, snipers will use more sophisticated camouflage than most soldiers. Due to their methods of employment, snipers rely heavily on camouflage for protection.

o    Ghillie suit. The ghillie suit is a camouflage uniform that is covered with irregular strips of colored burlap or similar material. These strips are folded in half and sewn mainly to the back, legs, arms, and shoulders of the suit. The strips are then frayed or cut to give the suit the appearance of vegetation. A close-net veil can be sewn to the back of the neck and shoulders of the suit and draped over the head when needed. The veil will help

20

break the outline of the head and conceal the lens of the telescope, ejecting brass cases, etc..

When deploying with regular troops, snipers should wear the uniform of those personnel. Wearing an item such as the ghillie suit will spotlight the snipers in contrast with the regular troops and make them a prime target to the enemy, especially enemy snipers.

o  Watch.  There are several types of military wristwatches that have a "luminous dial" or face.  The precise time is important to the sniper for intelligence reporting and mission planning. Watches can be used for orientation and direction finding if the compass should become inoperative.  Watches can help to judge distance by sound using the "crack-thump" or "flash-bang" methods.

o  Compass. Snipers will employ the compass in conjunction with the map to aid in orientation.  They may use the M2 compass rather than the standard lensatic compass.  The M2's ability to measure angles is useful, particularly in urban terrain. Additionally, the mirror can be used as an improvised periscope for looking around or over obstacles or for signaling.

o  Maintenance equipment.  During missions of short duration, snipers may opt to leave maintenance equipment in the rear.  However, for missions of long duration or distance this equipment must be taken.  Maintenance equipment can include items such as weapon and optical cleaning equipment for short missions, or it can include tools and replacement parts for missions in protracted environments such as FID or UW operations.  The amount and type of maintenance equipment that is needed will also be governed by support maintenance available in any given operation area.  Due to the match quality of the M21 sniper weapon, any maintenance beyond the organizational level should be performed by a qualified national match armorer.

o  Communications.  The diversity of communications equipment available to snipers is extensive.  Selection considerations include: transmission range, multiple frequencies, secure operations, and portability.

o  Measuring Ruler.  A standard 10 to 25 foot metal carpenter's tape ruler allows the sniper to measure items in his operational area.  This information may be incorporated into his "cheat book."

o  Calculator.  The sniper team needs a pocket-size calculator to calculate distances when using the mil-relation formula.  Solar-powered calculators usually work fine, but under limited visibility conditions, battery power may be preferred.  If a battery-powered calculator is to be used in low-light conditions, it should have a lighted display.

21

o    Other items.  Knives, bayonets, entrenching tools, wire cutters, pruning shears, and rucksacks, will be employed as the mission and common sense dictate.  The sniper team is best quali- fied to determine which particular items will be carried for each given mission.


## 2-7.  SPECIAL MISSION EQUIPMENT

### Special Weapons

Special weapons include any weapons that are designed for a specific purpose or employed to meet specific mission requirements. Because of the sniper's mission, special weapons should possess three basic characteristics: durability, simplicity, and accuracy. The weapons must be durable enough to withstand the conditions en- countered in combat, simple enough to minimize failure, yet accurate enough for sniping.  The weapons should be capable of grouping consistently into two MOA out to 600 meters (approximately a 12-inch group).  The accuracy of special weapons may be improved by various modifications to the weapons themselves and/or selection of certain types of ammunition.  Examples of special weapons:

o    Bolt-action target rifles.

o    Foreign sniper weapons (procured out of need, compatibil- ity, or to provide a foreign "signature").

o    Large-bore, long-range sniper rifles.

o    Telescope-mounted handguns  (e.g., XP100 or the Thompson Center Contender), for easy concealment or use as light multi- mission SWSs.

o    Suppressed weapons.

### Suppressed Weapons

The suppressor is a device designed to deceive observers forward of the sniper as to the exact location of the weapon and the sniper.  It accomplishes this by disguising the signature in two ways.  First, it reduces the muzzle blast to such an extent that it becomes inaudible a short distance from the weapon.  This makes the exact sound location extremely difficult, if not impossible to locate.  Secondly, it suppresses the muzzle flash at night making visual location equally difficult.  This is critical during night operations.

Noise Sources.  When a rifle, or any high muzzle velocity weapon is fired, the resulting noise is produced by two separate sources.  Depending on distance and direction from the weapon, the two noises may sound as one or as two closely spaced different sounds.  These sounds are the muzzle blast and the ballistic crack, or sonic boom, produced by the bullet.

The muzzle blast is generated by the blast wave created by the high velocity gases escaping into the atmosphere behind the bullet. This noise is relatively easy to locate as it emanates from a single, fixed point.

Ballistic crack results from the supersonic speed of the bullet which compresses the air ahead of it exactly in the same fashion as a supersonic jet creates a sonic boom. The only difference is that the smaller bullet produces a sharp crack rather than a large overpressure wave with its resulting louder shock wave.

Unlike the muzzle noise which emanates from a fixed point, the ballistic crack radiates backwards in a conical shape similar to a bow wave from a boat, from a point slightly ahead of the moving bullet. Thus, the sonic boon created by the supersonic bullet moves at the velocity of the bullet away from the muzzle noise and in the direction of the target. Location and identification of the initial source of the shock wave is extremely difficult because the moving wave strikes the ear at nearly 90 degrees to the point of origin. Attention is thus drawn to the direction from which the wave is coming rather than towards the initial source, the firing position (Figure 2-7-1).

## Special Surveillance Devices

In some circumstances, snipers may employ special surveillance devices in their mission. Employment of this special equipment will normally involve added weight and bulk that will limit the sniper's mobility. Examples of such devices include, but are not limited to, the following:

o    Unertl 100 mm team spotting scope. This spotting scope is a standard team scope for most marksmanship units and should be used for sniper training purposes. The scope's increased field of view will greatly enhance the team's observation capability in static positions.

o    Crew-served NVDs. These devices are commonly employed in conjunction with crew-served weapons (as typified by the AN/TVS-5) or night observation (typified by the AN/TVS-4). They offer a significant advantage over their smaller counterparts in surveillance, target acquisition, and night observation (STANO). However, their weight and bulk normally limit their use to static operations.

o    Thermal imagery. Thermal imagery is a relatively new tool available to the sniper team. Equipment such as the AN/PAS-7 offers a thermal imagery device in a portable package. Thermal imagery can enhance STANO operations when employed with more conventional equipment, or it can provide continuous surveillance when ambient light conditions (such as starlight and moonlight) do not exist for light-intensification devices.

23

o    Radars and sensors.  Just as the sniper's surveillance operations should be integrated into the overall surveillance plan, the sniper should strive to make maximum use of any surveillance radars and sensors in the area of operation.  Snipers will not normally employ these items themselves, but through coordination with using or supporting units.  The snipers may be able to use the target data that the radars and sensors can acquire.  However, it must be kept in mind that these devices are subject to human error, interpretation, and enemy countermeasures.  Total reliance on their intelligence could prove detrimental or misleading.

## 2-8.  CARE AND CLEANING OF THE SNIPER WEAPON SYSTEMS

Maintenance is any measure taken to keep the system in top operating condition.  It includes: inspection, repair, cleaning, and lubrication.  Inspection reveals the need for repair, cleaning, or lubrication.  A weapon, sheltered in garrison and infrequently used, must be inspected often to detect dirt, moisture, and signs of corrosion, and it must be cleaned accordingly.  A weapon in use and subject to the elements, however, requires no inspection for cleanliness, since the fact of its use and exposure is sufficient evidence that it requires repeated cleaning and lubrication.  The sniper couples his cleaning with a program of detailed inspection for damage or defect.

## Rifle maintenance tools and supplies:

o    One-piece plastic-coated .30 cal cleaning rod with jag (36").

o    Bronze bristle bore brushes (.30 and .45 calibers).

o    Cleaning patches (small and large sizes).

o    Shooter's Choice Bore Solvent (Carbon cleaner), ("SCBS").

o    Sweets 7.62 Copper Remover (Copper cleaner), ("SWEETS") (Shooter's Choice Copper Remover is the second choice).

o    Shooter's Choice "Rust Prevent".

o    Cleaner, Lubricant, Preservative ("CLP").

o    Rifle grease.

o    Bore guide (long action).

o    Q-tips.

o    Pipe cleaners.

o    Medicine dropper.

o    Shaving brush.

o    Tooth brush.

o    Pistol cleaning rod.

o    Rags.

o    Camel hair brush.

o    Lens paper.

o    Lens cleaning fluid (denatured or isopropyl alcohol).

**When to clean the rifle:**
    <u>Before firing</u>.  The rifle must always be cleaned prior to firing.  Firing a weapon with a dirty bore or chamber will multiply and speed up any corrosive action.  Oil in the bore and chamber of even a clean rifle will cause pressures to vary and first-round accuracy will suffer.  Clean and dry the bore and chamber prior to departure on a mission and use extreme care to keep the rifle clean and dry en route to the objective area.  Firing a rifle with oil or moisture in the bore will cause a puff of smoke that can disclose the firing position.

    <u>After firing</u>.  The rifle must be cleaned after is has been fired, because firing produces deposits of primer fouling, powder ashes, carbon, and metal fouling.  Although modern ammunition has a non-corrosive primer which makes cleaning easier, the primer residue can still cause rust if not removed.  Firing leaves two major types of fouling that requires different solvents to remove: <u>carbon</u> fouling and <u>copper</u> jacket fouling.  The rifle must be cleaned within a reasonable interval--a matter of hours--after cessation of firing.  Common sense should preclude the question as to the need for cleaning between rounds.  Repeated firing will not injure the weapon if it was properly cleaned before the first round.

    The M24 SWS will be disassembled only when absolutely necessary, not for daily cleaning.  An example of this would be to remove an obstruction that is stuck between the stock and the barrel.  When disassembly is required, the recommended procedure is:

o    Place the weapon so that it is pointing in a safe direction.

o    Ensure the safety is in the "S" position.

o    Remove the bolt assembly.

o    Loosen the mounting ring nuts (2) (Figure 2-8-1) on the telescope and remove the telescope.

o    Remove the action screws (2) (Figure 2-8-2).

o    Lift the stock from the barrel assembly (Figure 2-8-3).

o    For further disassembly, refer to TM 9-1005-306-10.

## Cleaning procedure

o    Lay the rifle on a cleaning table or other flat surface with the muzzle away from the body and the sling down. Make sure not to strike the muzzle or telescopic sight on the table. The "MTM" cleaning cradle is ideal for holding the rifle.

o    Always clean the bore from the chamber toward the muzzle, attempting to keep the muzzle lower than the chamber to prevent bore cleaner from running into the receiver or firing mechanism. Be careful not to get any type of fluid between the receiver and the stock. If fluid does get between the stock and receiver, the receiver will actually "slide" on the bedding every time the rifle recoils, thereby decreasing accuracy and increasing wear and tear on the receiver and bedding material.

o    Always use a bore guide to keep the cleaning rod centered in the bore during the cleaning process.

o    First, push several patches saturated with SCBS through the barrel to loosen the powder fouling and begin the solvent action on the copper jacket fouling.

o    Saturate the bronze bristle brush (NEVER USE STAINLESS STEEL BORE BRUSHES--THEY WILL SCRATCH THE BARREL!) with SCBS (shake bottle regularly to keep the ingredients mixed) using the medicine dropper to prevent contamination of the SCBS. Run the bore brush through a MINIMUM of 20 times. Ensure that the bore brush passes completely through the barrel before reversing its direction, otherwise the bristles will break off.

o    Using a pistol cleaning rod and a .45 caliber bore brush, clean the chamber by rotating the patch-wrapped brush 8 to 10 times. DO NOT scrub the brush in and out of the chamber.

o    Push several patches saturated with SCBS through the bore to push out the loosened powder fouling.

o    Continue using the bore brush and patches with SCBS until the patches come out without traces of the black/gray powder fouling and are becoming increasingly green/blue. This indicates that the powder fouling has been removed, and that only the copper fouling remains. Remove the SCBS from the barrel with several clean patches. This is important because the different solvents should never be mixed in the barrel.

o    Push several patches saturated with SWEETS through the bore, using a scrubbing motion to work the solvent into the copper. Let the solvent work for 10-15 minutes (NEVER LEAVE SWEETS IN THE BARREL FOR MORE THAN 30 MINUTES!)

o    While waiting, scrub the bolt with the toothbrush moistened with SCBS and wipe down the remainder of the weapon with a cloth.

o    Push several patches saturated with SWEETS through the barrel. They will appear dark blue at first, indicating the amount of copper fouling removed. Continue this process until the saturated patches come out without the trace of blue/green. If the patches continue to come out dark blue after several treatments with SWEETS, use the bronze brush saturated with SWEETS to increase the scrubbing action. Be sure to clean the bronze brush thoroughly afterwards with hot running water ("Quick Scrub Cleaner/Degreaser" is preferred) as the SWEETS acts upon its bristles as well.

o    When the barrel is completely clean, dry it with several tight fitting patches. Also, dry out the chamber using the .45 brush with a patch wrapped around it.

o    Run a patch saturated with Shooter's Choice Rust Prevent (not CLP) down the barrel and chamber if the weapon is to be stored for any length of time. Stainless steel barrels are not immune from corrosion. Be sure to remove the preservative by running dry patches through the bore and chamber prior to firing.

o    Place a small amount of rifle grease on the rear surfaces of the bolt lugs. This will prevent galling of the metal surfaces.

o    Wipe down the complete weapon exterior (if it is not covered with camouflage paint) with a CLP-saturated cloth to protect it during storage.

## M21 Care and Maintenance
Extreme care has been used in building this sniper rifle. A similar degree of attention must be devoted to its daily care and maintenance.

The rifle should not be disassembled by the sniper for normal cleaning and lubrication. Disassembly should be performed only by the armorer during scheduled inspections or repair, and it will be thoroughly cleaned and lubricated at that time.

The recommended procedure for cleaning and lubricating the rifle is similar to the M24 with the following additions:

o    The bore is cleaned from the muzzle end of the barrel, so extra care must be taken during cleaning.  A satisfactory muzzle guide can be made from an expended 12 gauge shotgun shell, with the primer pocket drilled out and polished to fit the one-piece, <u>plastic-coated</u> cleaning rod.

o    Clean the receiver, other interior areas, and the flash suppressor with a tooth brush, rag, and patches.

o    Do not put bore cleaner in the gas port!  It will increase carbon buildup and restrict free movement of the gas piston.

o    Before firing, lubricate the rifle by placing a light coat of grease on the operating rod handle track, camming surfaces in the hump of the operating rod, the bolt's locking lug track, and in between the front band lip of the gas system and the metal band on the lower front of the stock.

## Barrel Break-in Procedure

To maximize barrel life, accuracy, and minimize the cleaning requirement, the following barrel break-in procedure must be used. This procedure is best done when the SWS is new or newly rebarreled.  The break-in period "laps in" the barrel by polishing the barrel surface under heat and pressure.  The barrel must first be cleaned completely of all fouling, both powder and copper.  The barrel is dried, and one round is fired.  The barrel is then completely cleaned using Shooter's Choice Solvent and then Sweet's 7.62 copper remover.  Again, the barrel must be completely cleaned. Another round is fired.  This procedure of firing one shot, then cleaning, etc. must be done for a total of 10 rounds.  After the 10th round, the SWS is then tested for groups by firing three (3) round shot groups, with a complete barrel cleaning between shot groups for a total of five shot groups (15 rounds total).  The barrel is now broken in, and will provide superior accuracy and a longer usable barrel life.  Additionally, the barrel will be easier to clean because the surface is smoother.  Again, the barrel should be cleaned at least every 50 rounds to maximize barrel life.

## Storage

The M24 and M21 SWSs should be stored as follows:

o    Clear the SWS, close the bolt, and squeeze the trigger.

o    Open the lens caps to prevent gathering of moisture.

o    Hang the weapon upside down by the rear sling swivel.

o    Place all other items in the system case (M24).

o    Transport the weapon in the system case during non-tactical  situations.

28

o     Protect the weapon at all times during tactical movement.

## Optical Equipment Maintenance
Dirt, rough handling, or abuse of optical equipment will result in inaccuracy and malfunction. When not in use, the rifle and scope should be cased, and the lenses should be capped.


## Cleaning the Lenses
Lenses are coated with a special magnesium fluoride reflection-reducing material. The coat is very thin and great care is required to prevent damage to it.

To remove dust, lint, or other foreign matter from the lens, brush it lightly with a clean camel hair brush.

To remove oil or grease from the optical surfaces, apply a lens tissue with a drop of lens cleaning fluid or rubbing alcohol. Carefully wipe off the lens surface in circular motions, from the center to the outside edge. Dry off the lens with a clean lens tissue. In the field, if the proper supplies are not available, breath heavily on the glass and wipe with a soft, clean cloth.

## Handling Telescopes
Telescopes are delicate instruments and must be handled with care. The following precautions will prevent damage:

o     Check and tighten all mounting screws periodically and always prior to an operation. Be careful not to change coarse windage adjustment.

o     Keep lenses free from oil and grease and never touch them with the fingers. Body grease and perspiration injure them. Keep lenses capped.

o     Do not force elevation and windage screws or knobs.

o     Do not allow the telescope to remain in direct sunlight, and avoid letting the sun's rays shine through the lens. Lenses magnify and concentrate sunlight into a pinpoint of intense heat which is focused on the mil scale reticle. This may melt the mil dots and damage the telescope internally. Keep the lenses covered and the entire telescope covered when not firing or observing.

o     Avoid dropping the telescope or striking it with another object. This could damage it severely and permanently, as well as change the zero.

o     To avoid damage to the telescope or any other sniper equipment, the snipers or armorers should be the only personnel handling the equipment. Anyone who does not know how to use this equipment properly could cause damage.

29

## Maintenance and Care in Cold Climates

<u>Rifle</u>. In temperatures below freezing, the rifle must be kept free of moisture and heavy oil, both of which will freeze, causing working parts to freeze or operate sluggishly. The rifle should be stored in a room with the temperature equal to the outside temperature. If the rifle is taken into a warm area, condensation will occur, thus requiring a thorough cleaning and drying before being taken into the cold. Otherwise, the condensation will cause icing on exposed metal parts and optics.

The firing pin should be disassembled and cleaned thoroughly with a degreasing agent. It should then be lubricated with CLP. Rifle grease will harden and cause the firing pin to fall sluggishly.

On weapons with wood stocks such as the M21, the stock must be sealed with danish oil or the equivalent. If moisture gets into the wood, then freezes, the stock will crack.

<u>Optical Equipment</u>. In extreme cold, care must be taken to avoid condensation and the congealing of oil on the glass.

If not excessive, condensation can be removed by placing the instrument in a warm place. Concentrated heat must not be applied, because it will cause expansion and damage. Moisture may also be blotted from the optics with lens tissue or a soft, dry cloth.

In cold temperatures, oil will thicken and cause sluggish operation or failure. Focusing parts are particularly sensitive to freezing oils. Breathing will form frost, so the optical surfaces must be cleaned with lens tissue, preferably dampened lightly with alcohol. Do not, however, apply the alcohol directly to the glass.

## Maintenance and Care after Salt Water Exposure

<u>Rifle</u>. Salt water and salt water atmosphere have extreme and very rapid corrosive effects on metal. During periods of this exposure, the rifle must be checked frequently and cleaned as often as possible, even if it means only lubricating the weapon. The weapon should always be well lubricated, including the bore, except when actually firing. Before firing, always run a dry patch through the bore, if possible.

## Maintenance and Care during Jungle Operations (High Humidity)

<u>Rifle</u>.
Use more lubricant.
Keep the rifle cased when not in use.
Protect from rain and moisture whenever possible.
Keep ammunition clean and dry.
Clean rifle, bore, and chamber daily.
Keep the telescope caps on when not in use. If moisture or fungus develops inside the telescope, get a replacement.

Clean and dry the stock daily.
Dry the carrying case and rifle in the sun whenever possible.

## Maintenance and Care during Desert Operations
Rifle.
Keep the weapon completely dry and free of CLP and grease except on the rear of the bolt lugs.
Keep the rifle free of sand by use of a carrying sleeve or the case when not in use.
Protect the weapon by using a wrap. Slide the wrap between the stock and barrel then cross over on top of the scope, cross under the weapon (over magazine) and secure. The weapon can still be placed into immediate operation but all critical parts are covered. The sealed hard case is preferred in the desert if the situation permits.
Keep the telescope protected from the direct rays of the sun.
Keep ammunition clean and protected from the direct rays of the sun.
Use a toothbrush to remove sand from the bolt and receiver.
Clean the bore and chamber daily.
Protect the muzzle and receiver from blowing sand by covering with a clean cloth.
To protect the free-floating barrel of the weapon, take an 8- or 9-inch strip of cloth and tie a knot in each end. Before going on a mission, slide the cloth between the barrel and stock all the way to the receiver and leave it there. When in position, slide the cloth out, taking all restrictive debris and sand with it.

## Maintenance and Care, Hot Climate and Salt Water Exposure
Optical Equipment.
Optics are especially vulnerable to hot, humid climates and salt water atmosphere.
Sun rays. Optical equipment must NOT be exposed to direct sunlight in a hot climate.
Humidity and salt air. In these environments, the optical instruments must be inspected and cleaned frequently to avoid rust and corrosion. A light film of oil is beneficial.
Perspiration. Perspiration from the hands is a contributing factor to rusting. After being handled, instruments must be thoroughly dried and lightly oiled.


## 2-9. TROUBLESHOOTING THE SNIPER WEAPON SYSTEMS

If a weapon malfunction occurs, the following lists indicate the possible malfunctions and corrective actions.

## M24 Malfunctions and Corrections
The following list does not reflect all malfunctions that may occur, or all causes and corrective actions. If a malfunction is not correctable, the complete weapon system must be turned in to

the proper maintenance/supply channel for return to the contractor (see shipment, TM 9-1005-306-10).

| Malfunction | Cause | Correction |
|---|---|---|
| Fail to fire | Safety in "S" position | Move safety to "F" position |
| | Defective ammunition | Eject round |
| | Firing pin damaged | Change firing pin assembly |
| | Firing pin binds | Change firing pin assembly |
| | Firing pin protrudes | Change firing pin assembly |
| | Firing control out of adjustment | Turn complete system in to the maintenance/supply channel for return to contractor |
| | Trigger out of adjustment | Turn in as above |
| | Trigger does not retract | Turn in as above |
| | Trigger binds on trigger guard | Turn in as above |
| | Firing pin does not remain in cocked position with bolt closed | Turn in as above |
| Bolt binds | Action screw protrudes into bolt track | Turn in as above |
| | Scope base protrudes into bolt track | Turn in as above |
| Fail to feed | Bolt override of cartridge | Seat cartridge fully rearward in magazine |
| | Cartridge stems chamber | Pull bolt fully rearward; remove stemmed cartridge from ejection port area; reposition cartridge fully in the magazine |
| | Magazine in backward | Remove magazine spring, and reinstall with long leg follower |
| | Weak or broken magazine spring | Replace spring |

32

| | | |
|---|---|---|
| Fail to eject | Broken ejector | Turn the complete weapon system in to the maintenance/ supply channel for return to contractor |
| | Fouled ejector plunger | Inspect and clean bolt face; if mal- function continues, turn in as above |
| Fail to extract | Broken extractor | Turn in as above |

## M21 Malfunctions and Corrections

The following, lists pertinent information for the operator. If the weapon becomes unserviceable, it must be turned in for service by a school-trained National Match armorer.

| Malfunction | Cause | Correction |
|---|---|---|
| Failure to load | Dirty or deformed magazine | Clean or replace |
| | Damaged magazine tube | Replace magazine |
| | Dirty magazine | Clean |
| | Damaged or broken magazine spring | Replace magazine |
| | Damaged or broken follower | Replace magazine |
| | Loose or damaged floor plate | Replace magazine |
| Magazine inserts with difficulty | Bent or damaged magazine | Replace magazine |
| | Excessive dirt in receiver | Clean |
| | Round not completely seated in magazine | Remove round; insert properly |
| | Deformed or operating rod spring guide | Evacuate to authorized armorer |
| | Damaged magazine latch | Evacuate to authorized armorer |
| | Magazine latch movement restricted | Check movement; if necessary; if bent or distorted, evacuate to authorized armorer |
| Magazine not retained in weapon | Magazine latch damaged | Evacuate to authorized armorer |
| | Magazine latch spring damaged | Evacuate to authorized armorer |

33

| | | |
|---|---|---|
| | Magazine latch plate damaged or missing | Replace magazine |
| | Deformed or damaged operating rod spring guide | Evacuate to authorized armorer |
| | Locking recess at top front of magazine deformed | Replace magazine |
| | Magazine not fully installed | Remove; install correctly (make sure latch clicks) |
| Fail to feed | Weak or broken spring | Replace magazine |
| | Damaged magazine | Replace magazine |
| | Damaged or deformed stripping lug on bolt | Evacuate to authorized armorer |
| | Short recoil | See short recoil |
| | Dirty ammunition and/or magazine | Clean ammunition and/or magazine |
| | Weak or broken operating rod spring | Evacuate to authorized armorer |
| | Restricted movement of, or damaged operating rod | Evacuate to authorized armorer |
| Bolt fails to close tightly | Cartridge case holding bolt out of battery | Pull bolt assembly to rear and remove deformed cartridge; clean ammunition and/or barrel and chamber |
| | Dirty chamber | Clean chamber |
| | Extractor does not snap over rim of cartridge case | Evacuate to authorized armorer |
| | Frozen or blocked ejector spring and plunger | Evacuate to authorized armorer |
| | Restricted movement of, or damaged operating rod spring | Evacuate to authorized armorer |
| | Bolt not fully rotated and locked in receiver | Evacuate to authorized armorer |
| | Weak or broken operating rod spring | Evacuate to authorized armorer |
| | Damaged receiver | Evacuate to authorized armorer |

34

| | | |
|---|---|---|
| Fail to fire | Bolt not fully locked | (See bolt fails to move forward and close tightly) |
| | Defective ammunition | Replace ammunition |
| | Firing pin worn, damaged, or movement restricted | Evacuate to authorized armorer |
| | Broken hammer | Evacuate to authorized armorer |
| | Weak or broken hammer spring | Evacuate to authorized armorer |
| | Hammer and trigger lugs or sear worn or broken, causing hammer to ride the bolt assembly forward | Evacuate to authorized armorer |
| Short recoil | Gas plug loose or missing | Tighten plug if loose; evacuate to authorized armorer if missing |
| | Restricted movement of operating rod assembly | Evacuate to authorized armorer |
| | Bolt binding | Clean |
| | Gas cylinder lock not fully installed | Evacuate to authorized armorer |
| | Gas piston restricted | Evacuate to authorized armorer |
| | Damaged connector assembly | Evacuate to authorized armorer |
| | Partially closed spindle valve | Evacuate to authorized armorer |
| | Defective ammunition | Replace ammunition |
| Fail to extract | Spindle valve closed | Evacuate to authorized armorer |
| | Cartridge seized in chamber | Remove |
| | Short recoil | (See short recoil) |
| | Damaged or deformed extractor | Evacuate to authorized armorer |
| | Weak, deformed or or frozen extractor plunger assembly | Evacuate to authorized armorer |
| | Ruptured or separated cartridge | Evacuate to authorized armorer |

35

| | | |
|---|---|---|
| Fail to eject | Short recoil | (See short recoil) |
| | Weak, deformed or frozen extractor plunger assembly | Evacuate to authorized armorer |
| Fail to hold bolt rearward | Damaged or deformed magazine follower | Replace magazine |
| | Damaged bolt lock | Evacuate to authorized armorer |
| | Bolt lock movement restricted | Evacuate to authorized armorer |
| | Weak or broken magazine spring | Replace magazine |

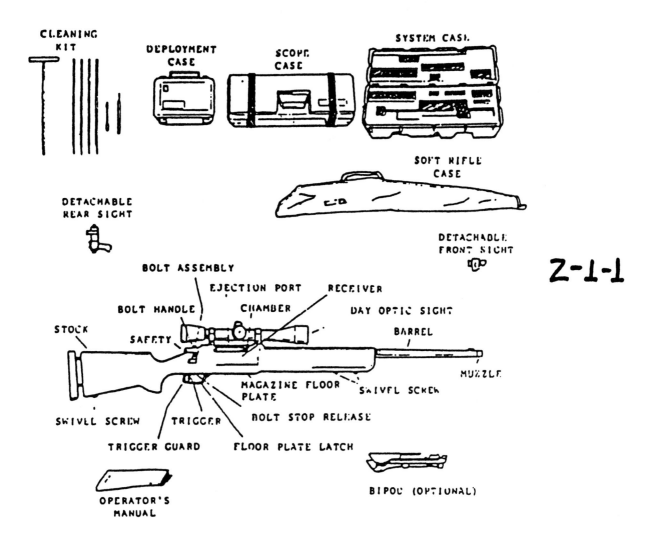

CLEANING KIT

DEPLOYMENT CASE

SCOPE CASE

SYSTEM CASE

SOFT RIFLE CASE

DETACHABLE REAR SIGHT

DETACHABLE FRONT SIGHT

2-1-1

BOLT ASSEMBLY
EJECTION PORT
RECEIVER
BOLT HANDLE
CHAMBER
DAY OPTIC SIGHT
STOCK
SAFETY
BARREL
MUZZLE
MAGAZINE FLOOR PLATE
SWIVEL SCREW
SWIVEL SCREW
TRIGGER
BOLT STOP RELEASE
TRIGGER GUARD
FLOOR PLATE LATCH

BIPOD (OPTIONAL)

OPERATOR'S MANUAL

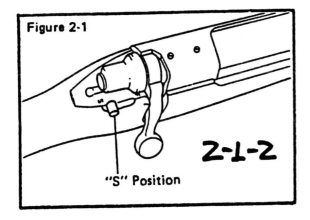

Figure 2-1

2-1-2

"S" Position

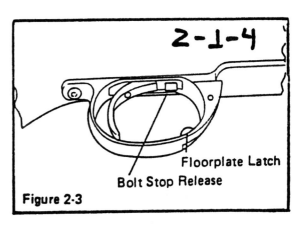

2-1-4

Floorplate Latch
Bolt Stop Release

Figure 2-3

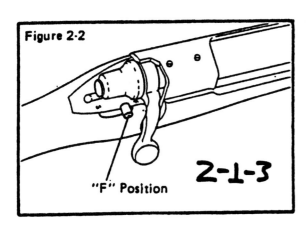

Figure 2-2

2-1-3

"F" Position

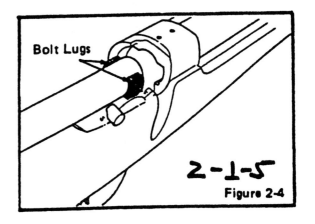

Bolt Lugs

2-1-5

Figure 2-4

# DEPLOYMENT KIT

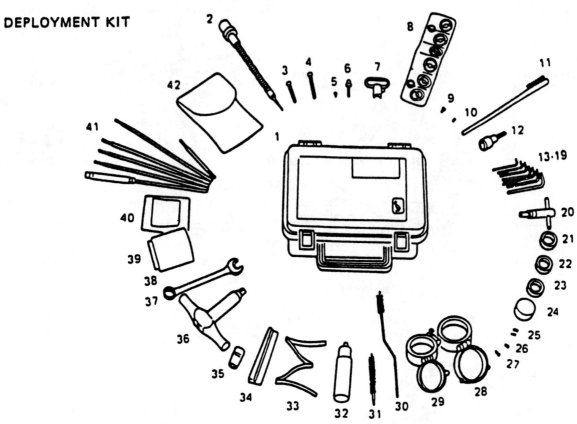

## DEPLOYMENT KIT

| | | | | |
|---|---|---|---|---|
| 1 | Deployment Case | 24 | Day Optic Sight Adj. Dial Dust Cover |
| 2 | Firing Pin Assembly | 25 | Day Optic Sight Ring Screws |
| 3 | Front Guard Screw | 26 | Day Optic Sight Base Screw Front |
| 4 | Rear Guard Screw | 27 | Day Optic Sight Base Screw Rear |
| 5 | Front Sight Base Screw | 28 | Day Optic Sight Dust Cover, Front |
| 6 | Swivel Screw | 29 | Day Optic Sight Dust Cover Rear |
| 7 | Swivel, Sling | 30 | Brush, Chamber |
| 8 | Front Sight Insert Kit | 31 | Brush, Bore |
| 9 | Rear Sight Base Screw | 32 | Oil Bottle |
| 10 | Trigger Pull Adj. Screw | 33 | Magazine Spring |
| 11 | Brush, Cleaning Small | 34 | Magazine Follower |
| 12 | Socket Wrench Attachment 3/8" Drive Hex Bit 5/32" | 35 | Socket, Socket Wrench 1/2" |
| 13 | .050" Key, Socket Head Screw | 36 | T-Handle Torque Wrench |
| 14 | 1/16" Key, Socket Head Screw | 37 | Wrench, Box and Open 1/2" |
| 15 | 5/64" Key, Socket Head Screw | 38 | Rear Sight Base Plug Screw |
| 16 | 3/32" Key, Socket Head Screw | 39 | Day Optic Sight Sunshade |
| 17 | 7/64" Key, Socket Head Screw | 40 | Swabs, Cleaning, Small Arms |
| 18 | 1/8" Key, Socket Head Screw | 41 | Cleaning Rod Kit |
| 19 | 5/32" Key, Socket Head Screw | 42 | Lens Cleaning Kit |
| 20 | T-handle Combo Wrench | | |
| 21 | Day Optic Sight Windage Dial w/ Screws | | |
| 22 | Day Optic Sight Elevation Dial w/Screws | | |
| 23 | Day Optic Sight Focus Dial w/ Screws | | |

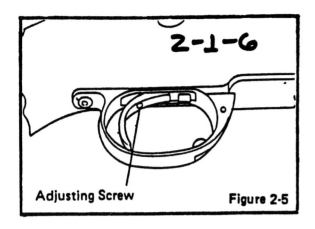

**2-1-6**

Adjusting Screw

Figure 2-5

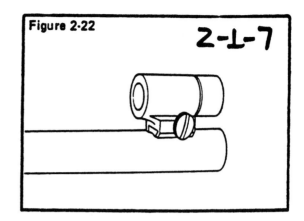

Figure 2-22

**2-1-7**

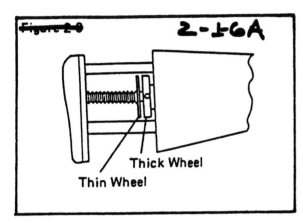

Figure 2-6

**2-1-6A**

Thick Wheel

Thin Wheel

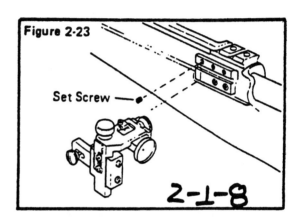

Figure 2-23

Set Screw

**2-1-8**

**2-1-9**

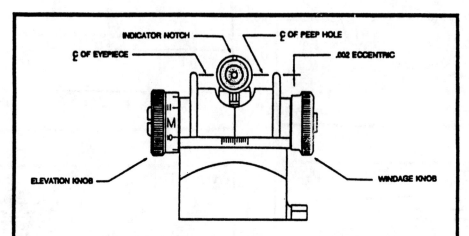

INDICATOR NOTCH

℄ OF PEEP HOLE

℄ OF EYEPIECE

.002 ECCENTRIC

M

ELEVATION KNOB

WINDAGE KNOB

## 1. NATIONAL MATCH REAR SIGHT ASSEMBLY WITH 1/2 MINUTE WINDAGE AND 1/2 MINUTE ELEVATION

a.   The two aperture assemblies are identical except for the eyepieces which have different peep hole diameters. The aperture with .0595 peep hole will be installed as standard with the .0520 diameter aperture available as an alternate.

The hooded eyepiece is designed to eliminate glare and reflections on the sight aperture, and to provide 1/2 minute changes in elevation. Each eyepiece is selectively fitted and matched with its individual aperture. It should not be attempted to disassemble the aperture assembly or to change eyepieces on an aperture.

The peep hole is .002 vertically eccentric with other diameters of the eyepiece. Rotating the eyepiece 180° clockwise or counter-clockwise raises and lowers the line of sight. Two spring loaded balls in the eyepiece engage a vertical "V" notch in the face of the aperture to retain the eyepiece in each position. The position of the eyepiece is indicated by a notch at the rear face of the eyepiece.

Each click of the elevation knob gives a change of 1 minute. Rotating the eyepiece so that the indicator notch is at the top, moves the point of impact of the bullet up 1/2 minute. With the indicator notch at the bottom, point of impact of the bullet will be moved down 1/2 minute.

b.   The National Match sight base marked "NM/2A" is undercut to accept the hooded eyepiece. The 64 pitch thread of this sight base and of the National Match windage knob produce a 1/2 minute change in windage for each click of the knob. Thus the National Match Rear Sight is capable of 1/2 minute sight changes for both windage and elevation.

c.   The National Match front sight has a blade width of .065 minus .005, and is identified by the letters "NM" and the numbers "062" on its right side. The width of the sight blade of the standard M1 or M14 rifle is .084 minus .010.

## 2. FITTING THE NM REAR SIGHT APERTURE

a.   Using a fine file, modify the underside and end of the aperture as shown, so that the aperture will not bottom out in the rear sight receiver well.

b.   To fit the aperture to the NM/2A base, the outside edges have to be brought in by stoning or with a fine file. Remove the same amount of metal from both sides slowly, checking the fit often. you want this to be a tight fit with no play from left to right.

METAL REMOVED AS SHOWN

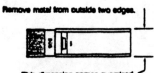

Remove metal from outside two edges.

This dimension comes oversized.

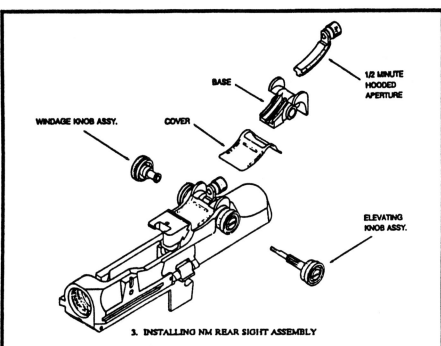

**3. INSTALLING NM REAR SIGHT ASSEMBLY**

Extreme care should be used in handling the parts. Both the windage knob and rear sight base have a fine pitch thread. Because of the precision made threads, particular attention should be given to the following, prior to, and during assembly:

a. Insert rear sight base through the opening of the cover.

b. Place the front lip of cover into the recess at the forward portion of rear sight receiver well. Raise the base slightly, exposing the rear portion of the cover. With a screwdriver, apply pressure to rear of cover in a horizontal direction until the cover snaps into place and is firmly retained by the receiver.

c. Insert the aperture assembly, into the aperture groove in the base and lower until it bottoms against the receiver.

d. Caution should be exercised in starting windage knob threads into rear sight base to preclude danger of cross threading. Mating threads must be free of all foreign matter.

With the left hand, apply pressure to the base forward and to the right of the receiver. Insert and turn windage knob carefully to engage the mating threads. Continue to turn windage knob until the base is tightly seated against the right receiver ear.

e. Insert pinion of elevating knob assembly through the hole on left side of receiver ear, meshing the pinion teeth with mating teeth of the aperture. Simultaneously align by feel, the flat at the end of pinion shaft with mating contour of the lock, housed in the windage knob. Thread the rear sight nut (in the windage knob) onto the pinion shaft. (Some manipulation of parts may be necessary to permit assembly). Tighten rear sight nut until both elevating and windage knobs become inoperative. By backing off the rear sight nut one or more clicks (one-half turn per click) both knobs will then be operative. The graduation mark on rear sight base can be aligned with graduation mark on the receiver.

f. Tighten the rear sight screw securely. Settings of various ranges are obtained in terms of the number of clicks from the lowest position of the aperture once the sight has been "zeroed" in at the respective ranges. Once sight settings have been established, the rear sight mechanism should be left intact to preserve sight zero.

―――――――――――――――AVAILABLE FROM―――――――――――――――

PHONE
(301) 490-9485

# FULTON ARMORY
8725 Bollman Place #1
Savage, Maryland
20763

FAX
(301) 490-9547

# M24 DAY OPTIC SIGHT

2-2-1 ™

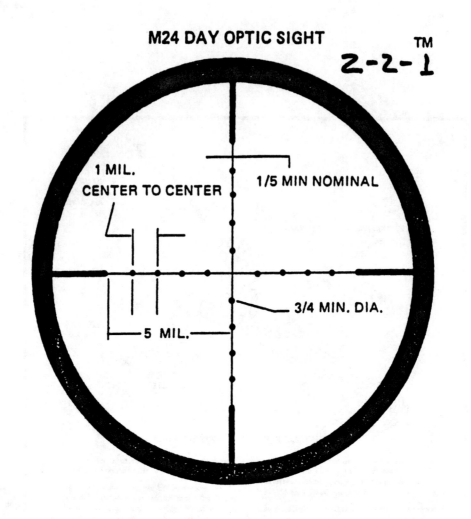

1 MIL.
CENTER TO CENTER

1/5 MIN NOMINAL

3/4 MIN. DIA.

5 MIL.

2-2-2

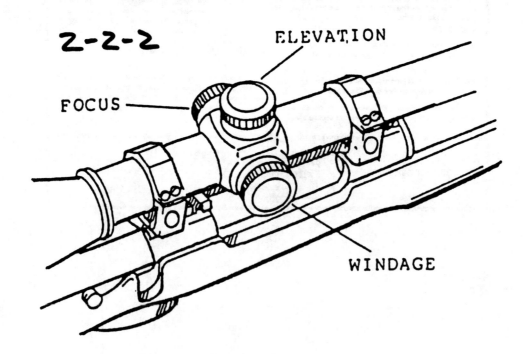

ELEVATION

FOCUS

WINDAGE

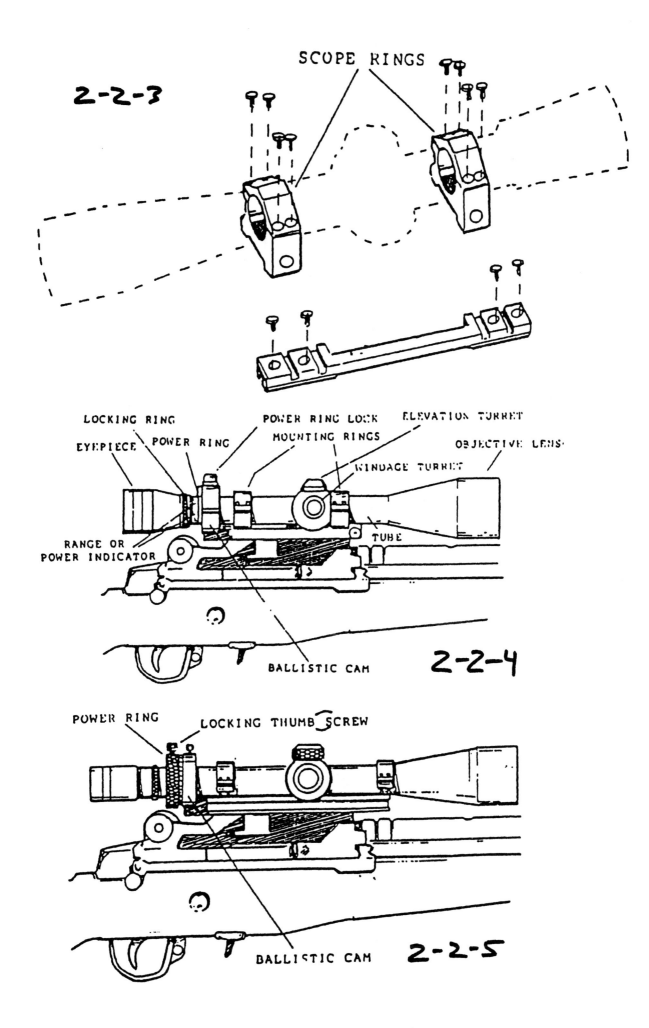

2-2-3

SCOPE RINGS

LOCKING RING · POWER RING LOCK · ELEVATION TURRET
EYEPIECE · POWER RING · MOUNTING RINGS · OBJECTIVE LENS
WINDAGE TURRET
RANGE OR POWER INDICATOR
TUBE
BALLISTIC CAM · 2-2-4

POWER RING · LOCKING THUMB SCREW
BALLISTIC CAM · 2-2-5

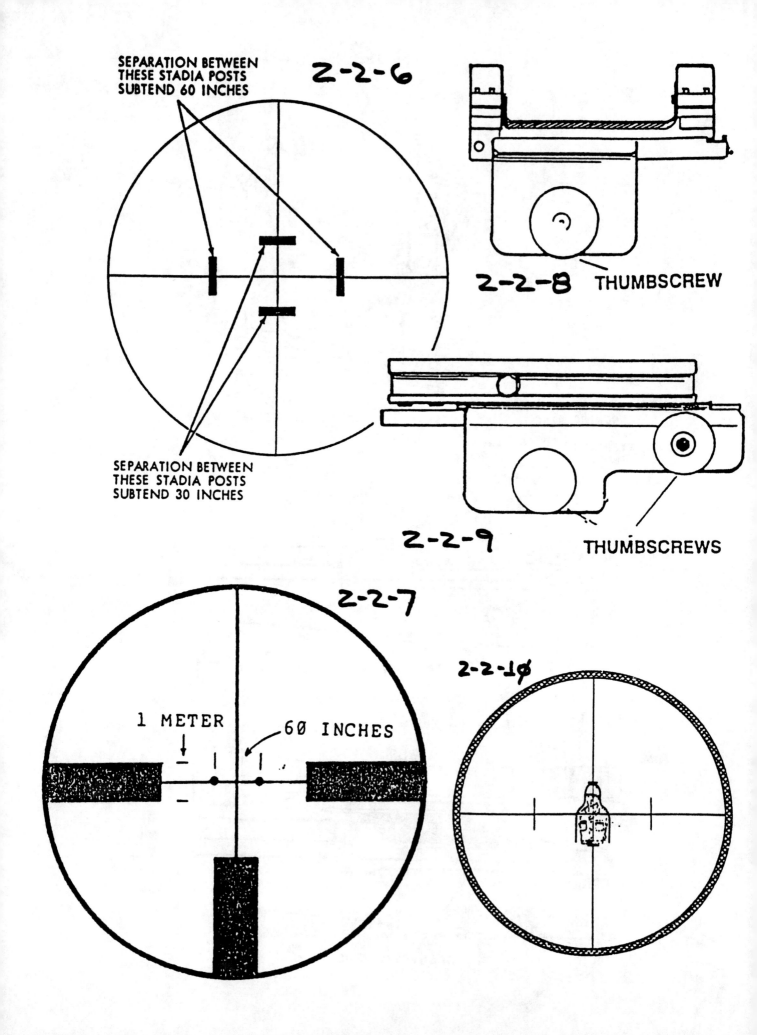

SEPARATION BETWEEN
THESE STADIA POSTS
SUBTEND 60 INCHES

2-2-6

2-2-8  THUMBSCREW

SEPARATION BETWEEN
THESE STADIA POSTS
SUBTEND 30 INCHES

2-2-9  THUMBSCREWS

2-2-7

1 METER     60 INCHES

2-2-10

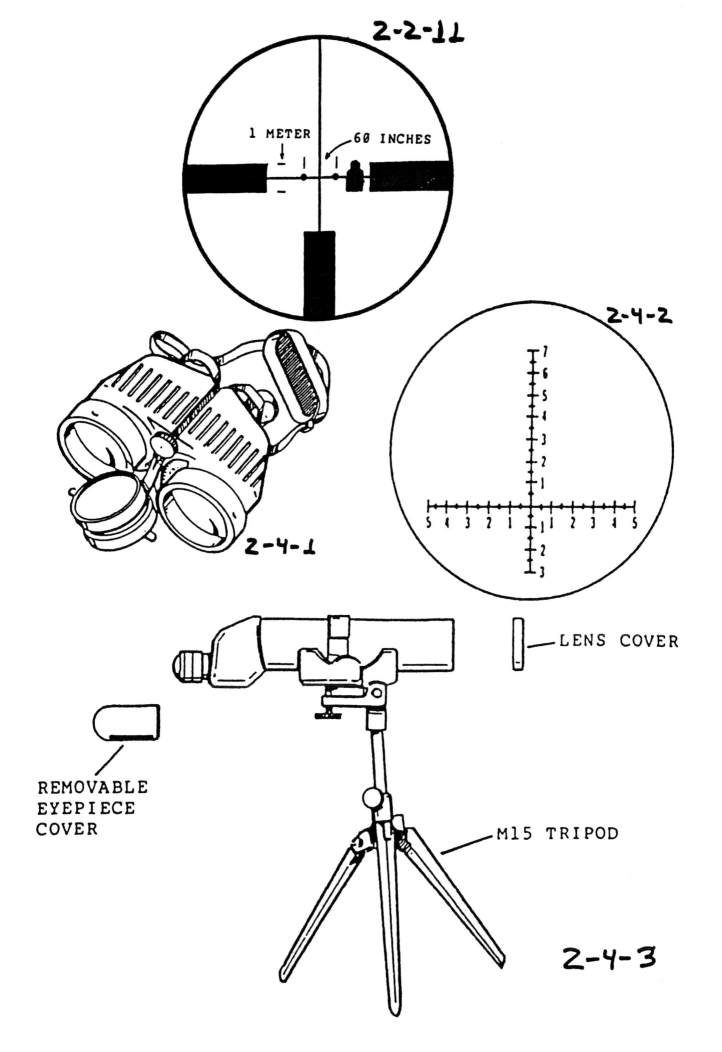

2-2-11

1 METER

60 INCHES

2-4-2

2-4-1

LENS COVER

REMOVABLE
EYEPIECE
COVER

M15 TRIPOD

2-4-3

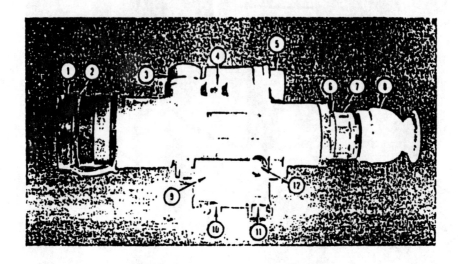

1   Lens cap.
2   Range focusing ring.
3   Oscillator cap.
4   Power switch.
5   Battery cap.
6   Diopter scale.

7   Eyepiece focusing ring.
8   Rubber eyeshield.
9   Boresight mount assembly.
10  Mount lock knobs (2).
11  Elevation adjustment knob.
12  Azimuth adjustment knob.

*Figure 21. Night vision sight, individual served weapon, AN/PVS-2.*

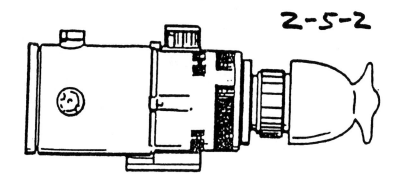

**2-5-2**

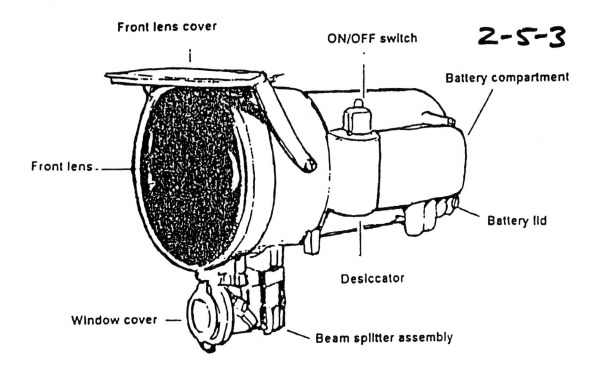

**2-5-3**

Front lens cover

ON/OFF switch

Battery compartment

Front lens

Battery lid

Window cover

Desiccator

Beam splitter assembly

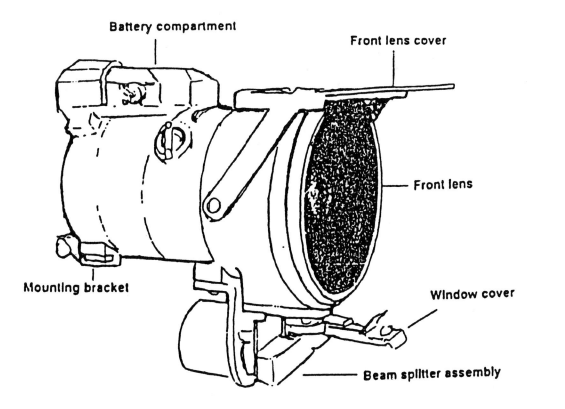

Battery compartment

Front lens cover

Front lens

Mounting bracket

Window cover

Beam splitter assembly

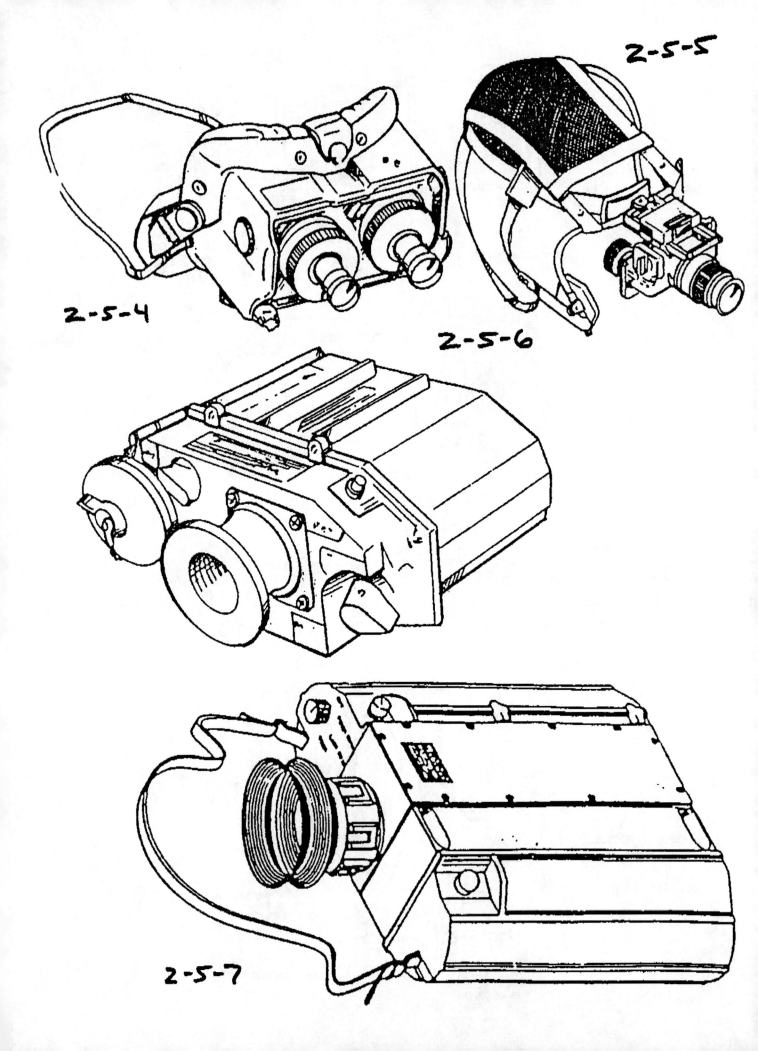

2-5-5

2-5-4

2-5-6

2-5-7

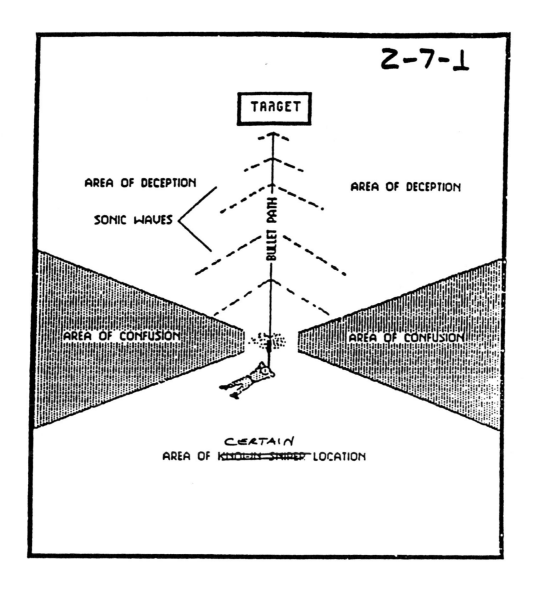

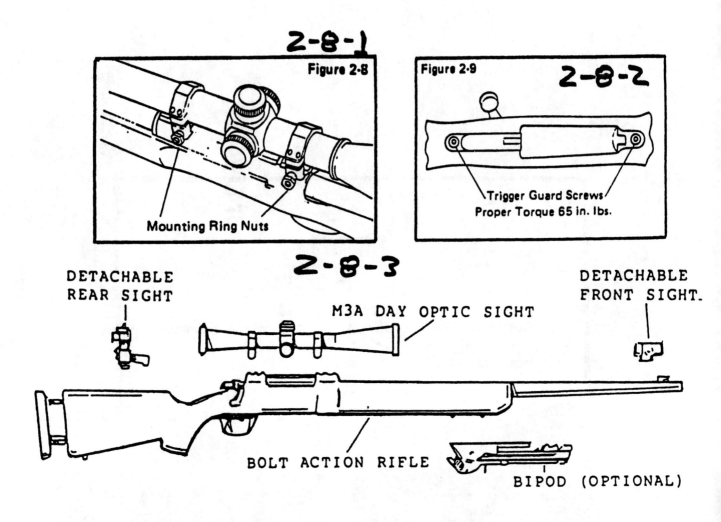

2-8-1

Figure 2·8

Mounting Ring Nuts

2-8-2

Figure 2·9

Trigger Guard Screws
Proper Torque 65 in. lbs.

2-8-3

DETACHABLE
REAR SIGHT

M3A DAY OPTIC SIGHT

DETACHABLE
FRONT SIGHT.

BOLT ACTION RIFLE

BIPOD (OPTIONAL)

(a)   MAJOR ASSEMBLIES

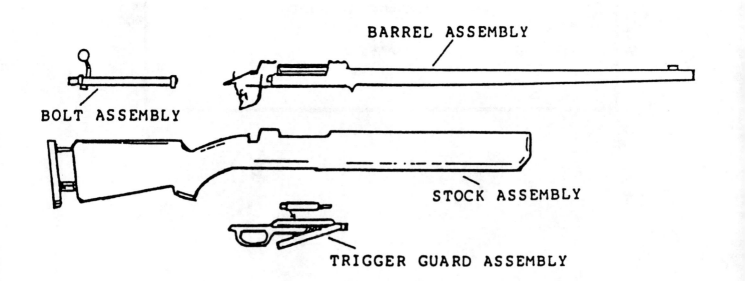

BARREL ASSEMBLY

BOLT ASSEMBLY

STOCK ASSEMBLY

TRIGGER GUARD ASSEMBLY

# Chapter 3

## MARKSMANSHIP TRAINING

### 3-1. OVERVIEW

The role of the Special Operations sniper is to engage targets with precision rifle fire. The sniper's skill with a rifle is the most vital skill in the art of sniping. This skill is extremely perishable. Sniper marksmanship differs from basic rifle marksmanship only in the degree of expertise. The sniper, using basic and advanced marksmanship as building blocks, must adapt the conventional methods of shooting to meet sniping's unique requirements. The sniper is required to make first-round hits in a field environment under less than ideal conditions. Sniper techniques may seem to contradict commonly accepted marksmanship techniques, but the sniper must adapt if he is to be successful. Snipers must become experts in marksmanship. The fundamentals are developed into fixed and correct shooting habits that become instinctive. This is the: "Conditioning of the nervous system."

**Standards of Performance**

Snipers should maintain their proficiency at the following **minimum** standards:

    o   100 % hits on stationary targets at ranges of less than 600 meters.

    o   70 % hits on stationary targets at ranges from 600 to 900 meters.

    o   70 % hits on moving targets at ranges of less than 500 meters.

### 3-2. SHOOTING POSITIONS

Sniper shooting positions are characterized by one word: STABILITY. Unlike the target shooter who must shoot from different positions of varying stability to satisfy marksmanship rules, the sniper searches for the most stable position possible. He is not trying to see if he can hit the target--he must know he can hit the target! A miss could mean a failed mission or his life. A good position enables the sniper to relax and concentrate when preparing to fire. Sniper shooting positions must be solid, stable, and durable.

The sniper seeks the most stable position possible. Whether prone, kneeling, or standing, the sniper's position should be supported. To achieve this, he should seek shooting rests or supports. Shooting from a rest helps to eliminate human factors such as heartbeat, muscular tension, and fatigue. A rest can

1

support both the front and the rear of the rifle, as in the case of benchrest shooting.

Regardless of the rest selected (tree, dirt, sandbag, etc.), the sniper should prevent any objects from contacting the barrel. During the firing process, the barrel vibrates like a tuning fork, and any disturbance to this harmonic motion will result in an erratic shot. Additionally, a hard support will normally cause the rifle to change its point of impact. The sniper can help to eliminate this problem by shooting from objects of similar hardness. The sniper's hat, glove, or sock filled with sand or dirt can be placed between the rifle forestock and shooting support to add consistency from range to combat. A support or rest offers a tremendous advantage to the sniper and must be used whenever possible. Accuracy with a rifle is a product of consistency, and a rest offers consistency to shooting positions.

On the battlefield, the sniper must assume a steady firing position with maximum use of cover and concealment. Considering the variables of terrain, vegetation, and the tactical situation, the sniper can use many variations of the basic positions. When assuming a firing position, he must adhere to the following basic rules:

o    The sniper's most frequently used and most stable position should be the prone position or its variations.

o    Use any support available.

o    Avoid touching the support with the barrel of the weapon since it interferes with the barrel harmonics and creates shot displacement.

o    Use a cushion between the weapon and the support.

o    Do not allow the side of the weapon to rest against the support. This will have an effect on the weapon during recoil, and may affect the point of impact.

o    Never cant the weapon while firing or aiming. The sniper should tilt his head to the weapon, not the weapon to his head.

## The Three Elements of a Good Position
The three elements of a good position are: bone support, muscular relaxation, and a natural point of aim on the aiming point.

o    <u>Bone support</u>. Positions are designed as foundations for the rifle, and good foundations for the rifle are important to the sniper. When a sniper establishes a weak foundation (position) for the rifle, the position will not withstand the repeated recoil of the rifle in a string of rapid fire shots or deliver the support

2

necessary for precise shooting. Therefore, the shooter will not be able to apply the marksmanship fundamentals properly. Proper bone support is a learned process; only through practice (dry fire, live fire) will the sniper gain proficiency in this skill.

o    <u>Muscular relaxation</u>. The sniper must learn to relax as much as possible in the various firing positions. Undue muscle strain or tension causes trembling, which is transmitted to the rifle. However, in all positions, a certain amount of controlled muscular tension is needed. For example, in a rapid-fire position there should be pressure on the spot weld. Only through practice and achieving a natural point of aim will the sniper learn muscular relaxation.

o    <u>Natural point of aim on the aiming point</u>. In aiming, the rifle becomes an extension of the body, so it is necessary to adjust the body position until the rifle points naturally at the target. To avoid the use of muscles to aim at a target, the sniper must shift his entire firing position to move his natural point of aim to the desired point of impact. This is achieved by the following process:

o    Assume a good steady position.

o    Close both eyes and relax as if preparing to fire.

o    Open both eyes to see where the weapon is pointing.

o    Leave the non-firing elbow in place, and shift the legs, torso, and firing elbow left or right.

o    Repeat the process until the weapon points naturally at the desired point of impact.

The sniper can change the elevation of a natural point of aim by leaving the elbows in place and sliding the body forward or rearward. This causes the muzzle of the weapon to drop or rise, respectively. Minor adjustments to the natural point of aim can be made by the right leg (right-handed shooter). The sniper moves the lower leg in the opposite direction that he wants the sight to go. Another consideration is to maintain a natural point of aim after the weapon has been fired; therefore, proper bolt operation becomes critical. The sniper must practice reloading while in the prone position without removing the butt of the weapon from the firing shoulder.

The two techniques for accomplishing this task are as follows:

o    After firing, move the bolt slowly while canting the weapon to the right. Execution of this task causes the spent cartridge to fall next to the weapon rather than flying through the air.

3

o    After firing, move the bolt to the rear with the thumb of the firing hand. Using the index and middle fingers, reach into the receiver and catch the spent cartridge case as it is being ejected. This technique does not require canting the weapon.

NOTE:    The sniper conducts bolt operation under a veil or equivalent camouflage to improve concealment.

## Factors Common to All Positions

Establishing a mental checklist of steady position elements greatly enhances the sniper's ability to achieve a first-shot hit. This checklist includes the five factors inherent to a good firing position:

o    Non-firing hand.

o    Placement of the rifle butt.

o    Firing hand.

o    Elbows.

o    Stock weld.

o    <u>Non-firing hand</u>. Use the non-firing hand as a support. The non-firing hand should either support the forestock or the butt of the weapon. Never grasp the forestock with the non-firing hand. Let the weapon rest in the non-firing hand. If the sniper grasps the weapon, the recoil and muscle tremor will cause erratic shots. If the non-firing hand is used to support the butt, place the hand next to the chest and rest the tip of the butt on it. Ball the hand into a fist to raise or loosen the fist to lower the weapon's butt. A preferred method to do this is to hold a sock full of sand in the non-firing hand and place the weapon butt on the sock. This reduces body contact with the weapon. To raise the butt, squeeze the sock. To lower it, loosen the grip on the sock.

o    <u>Placement of the rifle butt</u>. Place the rifle butt firmly in the pocket of the shoulder. Proper placement of the butt helps to steady the rifle and lessen recoil. The key to the correct rifle butt method is consistent rearward pressure by the shooting hand and correct placement in the shoulder. A hard hold versus a very light hold may change bullet impact. Again, consistency is important. Insert a pad on the ghillie suit where contact with the butt is made to reduce the pulse beat and breathing effects, which can be transmitted to the weapon.

o    <u>Firing hand</u>. Grasp the small of the stock firmly but not rigidly with the shooting hand. Exert pressure rearward, mainly with the middle and ring fingers of the firing hand. Do not "choke" the small of the stock. A choking-type grip can cause a twisting action during recoil. In addition, do not steer the rifle

with the hand or shoulder.  Make large windage adjustments by al-
tering the natural point of aim, not by leaning or steering the
rifle, as this will cause the rifle to steer in that direction
during recoil.  The thumb can be wrapped over the top of the small
of the stock and used to grasp, or it can be laid alongside or on
top of the stock in a relaxed manner.  Place the index finger on
the trigger, ensuring that it does not touch the stock of the
weapon and will not disturb the lay of the rifle when the trigger
is pulled.  Maintain a steady rearward pressure on the weapon when
shooting.  This will help steady the weapon.

    o    Elbows.  Find a comfortable position that provides the
greatest support.

    o    Stock weld.  The stock weld is the point of firm contact
between the sniper's cheek and the stock.  The cheek is placed on
the stock in a position that gives proper eye relief.  The stock
weld will differ from position to position.  However, due to the
position of the telescope on the sniper rifle and the necessity to
have eye relief, the sniper may not get a normal spot weld.  The
important consideration is to get firm contact so that the head and
weapon recoil as one unit, thereby facilitating rapid recovery.
The point on the weapon should be a natural point where eye relief
can be maintained.  Place the cheek in the same place on the stock
with each shot.  A change in stock weld tends to cause misalignment
with the sights, thus creating misplaced shots.  This is more of a
problem when using iron sights, than with the telescopic sight that
is properly adjusted to eliminate parallax.

    Once a spot or stock weld is obtained, the same positioning
should be used for each shot.  Stay with the weapon, do not lift
the head from the stock during recoil, and maintain the spot weld
or cheek weld.  During the initial period of firing, the cheek may
become tender and sore.  To prevent this and to prevent flinching,
press the face firmly against the stock.

**Sniper Shooting Positions**

    o    Prone Supported Position
    The sniper first selects his firing position.  He picks
a position that gives the best observation, fields of fire, and
concealment.  He then assumes a comfortable prone position and
prepares a firing platform for his rifle (Figure 3-2-1).  The rifle
platform should be as low to the ground as possible.  The rifle
should rest on the platform in a balanced position to the rear of
the upper sling swivel and forward of the magazine.  Care must be
taken to ensure that the operating parts, the magazine, and the
barrel do not touch the support, as contact will cause erratic
shots.  The sniper then forms a wide, low bipod with his elbows.
He grips the small of the stock with his firing hand, thumb over or
alongside the small of the stock and the forefinger (just in front
of the first joint) on the trigger, and pulls the butt of the rifle

5

into his firing shoulder. He then places the non-firing hand under the toe of the stock, palm down, and places the lower sling swivel into the web of the thumb and forefinger. The fingers and thumb of the non-firing hand can be adjusted by curling the fingers and thumb into a fist or relaxing the fingers and thumb and laying them flat. In this manner the sniper can raise or lower the barrel onto the target. As an alternative, a sock filled with sand or dirt can be placed under the toe of the stock. The sniper then grips the sock with the non-firing hand and by squeezing the sock or relaxing pressure on it, he can lower or raise the barrel onto the target. This method is extremely stable and accurate. However, the sniper must ensure that the sock is filled only to the size of a softball as a minimum or a large grapefruit as a maximum. He then relaxes into a comfortable supported position, removing his non-firing hand from the stock when necessary to manipulate the scope. He can change magazines with either hand, or he can reload single rounds into the M24 with the firing hand while supporting the rifle at the toe of the stock with the non-firing hand. When firing from this position, the sniper must have a clear field of fire. This is extremely important because the shot may become erratic if the bullet strikes a leaf, grass, or twig.

o    Hawkins Position
        The Hawkins position is used when a low silhouette is desired. This position is very useful when firing from a small depression, a slight rise in the ground, or from a roof (Figure 3-2-2). This is the steadiest of all shooting positions. Concealment is also greatly aided by the Hawkins position because the firer is lying flat on the ground. This position cannot be used on level ground since the muzzle cannot be raised high enough to aim at the target.

        The Hawkins position is similar to the prone supported position, except that the support of the weapon is provided by the non-firing hand. Grasp the front sling swivel with the non-firing hand, forming a fist to support the front of the weapon. Make sure that the wrist and elbow are locked straight; the recoil is taken up entirely by the non-shooting arm. Otherwise, the face will absorb the weapon's recoil. Lie flat on the ground, either directly behind the rifle (Canadian version) or angled off to one side (British version). Place the rear or toe of the stock under the armpit, resting the stock on the ground if possible. It will appear as though the sniper is lying on the rifle. Make minor adjustments in muzzle elevation by tightening or relaxing the fist of the non-firing hand. If more elevation is required, place a support under the non-firing fist.

        If using the Canadian version, place the butt of the rifle in the shoulder. If using the British version, tuck the butt under the armpit. The sniper should always use what is the most comfortable.

6

o   <u>Prone Unsupported Position</u>
The prone unsupported position is only used when a suitable support is not available, but the prone position is required for stability and concealment (Figure 3-2-3). The sniper faces the target squarely with the sling attached to the non-shooting arm above the bicep and lies down facing the target, legs straight to the rear. The non-shooting elbow is extended so that it is in line with body and the target and as far under the rifle as comfortable. With the shooting hand, push forward on the butt of the stock and fit it into the pocket of the shoulder. Place the shooting side elbow down wherever it feels natural and grasp the grip of the stock, pulling it firmly into the shoulder. The sniper lets his cheek rest naturally on the stock where he can see through the sights and acquire the target. He draws his shooting side knee up to a comfortable position so as to take the weight off of the diaphragm. A natural point of aim is obtained by adjusting the elevation by sliding the body forward or rearward and adjusting the breathing.

o   <u>Prone Backward Shooting Position</u>
The prone backward shooting position is used when the terrain or situation dictates (Figure 3-2-4). This position provides a higher angle of fire as required when shooting uphill and other positions are inadequate. Also, the sniper would use this position when he must engage a target to his rear but cannot turn around because of the enemy situation or hide constrictions. The sniper assumes a comfortable position on his side with both legs bent for support and stability. The sniper places the butt of the SWS into the pocket of his shoulder where it meets the armpit. He attempts to support his head for better stability and comfort. The small exit pupil of the telescope requires the sniper to maintain a solid hold and center the exit pupil in the field of the telescope to minimize the errors in sight alignment.

o   <u>Sitting Supported Position</u>
To assume this position, prepare a firing platform for the rifle or rest the rifle on the raised portion of the position (Figure 3-2-5). Ensure that the barrel or operating parts do not touch the support. Assume a comfortable sitting position to the rear of the rifle, grasp the small of the stock with the firing hand, and place the butt of the rifle into the shoulder pocket. Place the non-firing hand on the small of the stock to assist in getting a stock weld and the proper eye relief.
Rest the elbows on the inside of the knees in a manner similar to the standard crossed-leg position. Adjust the position by varying the position of the elbows on the inside of the knees or by varying the body position. This position may be tiring; therefore, the firing mission should be alternated frequently between the sniper team members.

o   <u>Sitting Unsupported Position</u>

7

The sniper faces his body 30 degrees away from the target in the direction of the shooting hand. He sits down and crosses his ankles so that the non-shooting side ankle is across the shooting side ankle (Figure 3-2-6). The sling is properly adjusted for the sitting position. The shooting hand palm places the butt of the stock into the shoulder while allowing the weapon to rest on the non-shooting hand. The shooting hand pulls the stock firmly into the shoulder. The elbows rest inside the knees and the body is leaned forward. Direct contact between the points of the elbows and the points of the knees is not permitted, so that the bones and not the muscles support the weapon. The stock is held high enough in the shoulder to require only a slight tilt of the head to acquire the sights, without canting the weapon. The muzzle is lowered and raised by moving the non-shooting hand forward and backward on the forestock. The breath is held when the sights are on the target.

The cross-leg position is assumed in the same way as the sitting position, but the sniper faces 45 to 60 degrees away from the target and crosses his legs instead of his ankles.

    o    <u>Kneeling Supported Position</u>
The supported kneeling position is used when it is necessary to quickly assume a position and there is insufficient time to assume the prone position (Figure 3-2-7). It can also be used on level ground or on ground that slopes upward where fields of fire or observation preclude using the prone position.

This position is assumed in much the same manner as the standard kneeling position, except that a tree or some other immovable object is used for support, cover, or concealment. Support is acquired by contact with the calf and knee of the leading leg, the upper forearm, or the shoulder or possibly by resting the rifle on the hand lightly against the support. As with other supported positions, the sniper ensures that the operating parts and the barrel do not touch the support. Since the area of support provided is greatly reduced, bone support is maximized.
The position is assumed in the following manner (right-handed firers use these techniques; left-handed firers do the opposite). The sniper faces the direction of the target, 45 degrees to the right. He kneels down and places the right knee on the ground. Keeping the left leg as vertical as possible, he sits back on the right heel, placing it as directly under the spinal column as possible. A variation is to turn the toe inward and sit squarely on the right foot. The small of the stock is grasped with firing hand, and the fore-end of the weapon is cradled in a crook formed with the left arm. The butt of the weapon is placed in the pocket of the shoulder, then the meaty underside of the left elbow is placed on top of the left knee. Reaching under the weapon with the left hand the sniper lightly grasps the firing arm. He relaxes forward and into the support, using the left shoulder as a contact

8

point.  This reduces transmission of the pulse beat into the sight picture.  A tree, building, or vehicle can be used for support.

o    <u>Sling Supported Kneeling Position</u>
        If vegetation height presents a problem, the kneeling position can be raised by using the rifle sling (Figure 3-2-8). This position is assumed executing the first three steps for assuming a kneeling supported position.  With the leather sling mounted to the weapon, the sling is turned one-quarter turn to the left. The lower part of the sling will then form a loop.  The left arm is placed through the loop; the sling is pulled up the arm and placed on the upper arm above the bicep.  The sling is tightened on the arm by manipulating the upper and lower parts of the sling, if time permits.  The arm is rotated in a clockwise motion around the sling and under the rifle with the sling secured to the upper arm.  The fore-end of the stock is placed in the "V" formed by the thumb and forefinger of the left hand.  Relax the left arm, and let the sling support the weight of the weapon.  The flat part of the rifle is placed behind the point of the left elbow on top of the left knee. The left hand pulls back along the fore-end of the rifle toward the trigger guard to add to stability.

o    <u>Squatting Position</u>
        The squatting position is used during hasty engagements or when other more stable positions would be unacceptable due to inadequate height or concealment (Figure 3-2-9).  The sniper assumes this position by facing 45 degrees away from his direction of fire, feet shoulder-width apart, and simply squats.  The sniper can either rest his elbows on his knees or wrap them over his knees.  Body configuration will determine the most comfortable and stable technique to use.  Solid supports can also be used for the sniper to lean up against, or to lean back into.

o    <u>Standing Supported Position</u>
        The supported standing position is used under the same circumstances as the supported kneeling position, where time, field of fire, or observation preclude the use of other, more stable positions.  It is the least steady of the supported positions and should be used only as a last resort (Figure 3-2-10).

    This position is assumed in much the same manner as the standard standing position, except that a tree or some other immovable object is used for support.  Support is acquired by contact with the leg, body, or arm or by resting the rifle lightly against the support.  The sniper ensures that the support makes no contact with operating parts or the barrel of the rifle.

    To assume this position with horizontal support, such as a wall or ledge, proceed as follows.  The sniper locates a solid object for support. Branches are avoided as they tend to sway when the wind is present.  The fore-end of the weapon is placed on top of the support; the butt of the weapon is then placed into the

9

pocket of the shoulder. A "V" is formed with the thumb and forefinger of the non-firing hand. Place the nonfiring hand, palm facing away, against the support with the fore-end of the weapon resting in the V of the hand. This steadies the weapon and allows quick recovery from recoil.

A vertical support such as a tree, telephone pole, corner of building, or vehicle, may be used (Figure 3-2-10A). Locate the stable support. Then face 45 degrees to right of target, and place the palm of the non-firing hand at arm's length against the support. Lock the arm straight, let the lead leg buckle, and place body weight against the non-firing hand. Keep the trail leg straight. Place the fore-end of the weapon in the V formed by extending the thumb of the non-firing hand. Exert more pressure to the rear with the firing hand.

o    <u>Standing Unsupported or Off-hand Position</u>
This position is the least desirable because it is the least stable and most exposed of all the positions (Figure 3-2-11). The situation may dictate that this position must be used. The sniper faces perpendicular to the target, facing in the direction of his shooting hand, with his legs spread about shoulder width apart. He grasps the pistol grip of the stock with his shooting hand and supports the fore-end with the non-shooting hand. He raises the stock of the weapon so that the toe of the stock fits into the pocket of the shoulder and the weapon is lying on its side away from the body. The weapon is rotated until the weapon is vertical and the shooting elbow is parallel with the ground. The non-shooting elbow is pulled into the side to support the weapon with the arm and rib cage. The sniper tilts his head slightly toward the weapon to obtain a natural spot or cheek weld and to align his eye with the sights. If his eye is not aligned with the sights, he adjusts his head position until the front sight and the target can be seen through the rear sight. Once in position he looks through his sights and moves his entire body to get the sights on target. He does not muscle the weapon onto the target. The sniper rests the rifle on a support to relax his arm muscles after firing the shot and following through.

o    <u>Other Supported Positions</u>
During training in fundamentals, positions are taught in a step-by-step process. The sniper is guided through a series of precise movements until he obtains the correct position. The purpose of this is to ensure that he knows and correctly applies all of the factors that can assist him in holding the rifle steady. As the sniper perfects the standard and supported positions, he can then use his ingenuity to devise other supported positions. Through practice he will gradually become accustomed to the feel of these positions and will know instinctively when his position is correct. This is particularly important in combat, as the sniper must be able to assume positions rapidly and be prepared to enhance the stability of the position by adapting it to any available

10

artificial support.  Significant nonstandard supported positions
are as follows:

* **Foxhole Supported Position**
This position is used primarily in prepared
defensive areas where there is time for preparation.  In this type
of position, the sling may be used for added support or sandbags or
other material to provide a stable firing platform.

* **Tree Supported Position**
This position is used when observation and firing
into an area cannot be accomplished from the ground.  The important
consideration when using this position is to select a tree that is
inconspicuous, one that is strong enough to support the sniper's
weight, and one that affords concealment.  The sniper must remember
that he limits his avenues of escape when in a tree.

* **Bench Rest Position**
This position can be used when firing from a
building, a cave, or a deeply shaded area.  The sniper can use a
built-up platform or table, with a sitting aid, and a rifle
platform for stability.  This is a stable position and one that
will not tire the sniper.  When using this position, the sniper
should stay deep in the shadows to prevent detection by the enemy.

## Field-Expedient Weapon Support
Support of the weapon is critical to the sniper's success in
engaging targets.  Unlike a well-equipped firing range with
sandbags for weapon support, the sniper will encounter situations
where weapon support relies on common sense and imagination.  The
following items are commonly used as field-expedient weapon
supports:

o  **Sand Sock**.  The sniper needs the sand sock when
delivering precision fire at long ranges.  He uses a standard-
issued, olive-drab wool sock filled one-half to three-quarters full
of sand and knotted off (Figure 3-2-12).  He places it under the
rear sling swivel when in the prone supported position for added
stability.  By limiting minor movements and reducing pulse beat,
the sniper can concentrate on trigger control and aiming.  He uses
the non-firing hand to grip the sand sock, rather than the rear
sling swivel.  The sniper makes minor changes in muzzle elevation
by squeezing or relaxing his grip on the sock.  He also uses the
sand sock as padding between the weapon and a rigid support.

o  **Rucksack**.  If the sniper is in terrain bare of any
natural support, he may use his rucksack (Figure 3-2-13).  He must
consider the height and presence of rigid objects within the
rucksack.  The rucksack must conform to weapon contours to add
stability.

11

o      Sandbag.  The sniper can fill and empty a sandbag on site (Figure 3-2-14).

o      Tripod.  The sniper can build a field-expedient tripod by tying together three 12-inch long sticks (one thicker than the others) with 550 cord or the equivalent (Figure 3-2-15).  When tying the sticks, he wraps the cord at the center point and leaves enough slack to fold the legs out into a triangular base.  Then, he places the fore-end of the weapon between the three uprights.  A small camera table tripod padded with a sock full of sand or dirt can also be used.

o      Bipod.  The sniper can build a field-expedient bipod by tying together two 12-inch sticks, thick enough to support the weight of the weapon (Figure 3-2-16).  Using 550 cord or the equivalent, he ties the sticks at the center point, leaving enough slack to fold them out in a scissor-like manner.  He then places the weapon between the two uprights.  The bipod is not as stable as other field-expedient items, and it should be used only in the absence of other techniques.

o      Forked Stake.  The tactical situation determines the use of the forked stake (Figure 3-2-17).  Unless the sniper can drive a forked stake into the ground, this is the least desirable of the techniques; that is, he must use his non-firing hand to hold the stake in an upright position.  Delivering long-range precision fire is a near-impossibility due to the unsteadiness of the position.  The sniper should practice using these supports at every opportunity and select the one that best suits his needs.  He must train as if in combat to avoid confusion and self-doubt.

## Slings
The M1907 National Match leather sling is superior to the standard web sling when used as a shooting aid.  Snipers who use a sling when shooting should be aware of the possibility of a zero change.  If the weapon is zeroed using a sling support, the point of impact may change when/if the sling is removed.  This is most noticeable in rifles with stocks that contact the barrel, such as the M21.  The sling must be adjusted for each position.  Each position will have a different point in which the sling is at the correct tightness.  The sniper counts the number of holes in the sling and writes these down so that he can properly adjust the sling from position to position.

## 3-3.  TEAM FIRING TECHNIQUES

A successful sniper team consists of two intelligent and highly versatile members:  the sniper and the observer.  Each must be able to move and survive in a combat environment.  The sniper's special mission is to deliver precision fire on targets that may rule out the use of conventional-size fighting forces. They must also:

o       Calculate the range to the target

o       Determine the effects of weather on ballistics

o       Make necessary sight changes

o       Observe bullet impact

o       Quickly critique performance before any subsequent shots

This calls for a coordinated, efficient team effort.

## Sniper and Observer Responsibilities

Each member of the sniper team has specific responsibilities when engaged in eliminating a target. Only through repeated practice can the team begin to function properly. Responsibilities of team members are as follows:

The sniper:

o       Builds a steady, comfortable position

o       Locates and identifies the designated target

o       Estimates the range to the target

o       Correctly dials in proper elevation and windage to engage the target

o       Notifies observer of readiness to fire

o       Takes aim at the designated target

o       Controls breathing at natural respiratory pause
o       Executes proper trigger control

o       Follows through

o       Makes an accurate and timely shot call

o       Prepares to fire subsequent shots, if necessary

The observer:

o       Properly positions himself.

o       Selects an appropriate target. The target closest to the team presents the greatest threat. If multiple targets are visible

13

at various ranges, the engagement of closer targets allows the sniper to confirm his zero and ensure his equipment is functioning properly. The observer must consider existing weather conditions before trying a shot at a distant target (effects of weather increase with range).

o    Assists in range estimation.

o    Calculates the effect of existing weather conditions on ballistics. Weather conditions include detecting elements of weather (wind, light, temperature, humidity) that will affect bullet impact, and calcualting the sight adjustments to ensure a first-round hit.

o    Reports sight adjustment data to sniper.

o    Uses the M49 spotting telescope for shot observation. He aims and adjusts the telescope so that both the downrange indicators and the target are visible.

o    Critiques performance. He asks the sniper for a shot call and compares sight adjustment data with bullet impact if the target is hit. He gives the sniper an adjustment and selects a new target if changes are needed. If the target is missed, the observer follows the above procedure and questions the sniper about his performance and shot call so that subsequent sight adjustments ensure a target hit.

## Sniper and Observer Positioning

The sniper should find a place on the ground that allows him to build a steady, comfortable position with the best cover, concealment, and visibility of the target area. Once established, the observer should position himself out of the sniper's field of view on his firing side.

The closer the observer gets his spotting telescope to the sniper's line of bore, the easier it is to follow the trace (path) of the bullet and observe impact. A position at 4 to 5 o'clock (7 to 8 o'clock for left-handed firers) off the firing shoulder and close to (but not touching) the sniper is best (Figure 3-3-1).

If the sniper is without weapon support in his position, he must use the observer's body as a support. This support is not recommended since the sniper must contend with his own movement and the observer's body movement. The sniper should practice and prepare to use an observer-supported position, if needed. A variety of positions can be used; however, the two most stable are when the observer is in a prone or sitting position.

o    _Prone_. To assume the prone position, the observer lies at a 45- to 75-degree angle to the target and observes the area through his spotting telescope. The sniper assumes a prone -

supported position, using the back of the observer's thigh for support (Figure 3-3-2). Due to the offset angle, the observer may only see the bullet impact.

        o     <u>Sitting</u>. If vegetation height prevents the sniper from assuming a prone position, the sniper has the observer face the target area and assume a cross-legged sitting position. The observer places his elbows on his knees to stabilize his position. For observation, the observer uses binoculars held in his hands. The spotting telescope is not recommended due to its higher magnification and the unsteadiness of this position. The sniper places the fore-end of the weapon across the observer's trapezius muscle on his non-firing side (Figure 3-3-3), stabilizing the weapon with the forefinger of the non-firing hand (Figure 3-3-4). The sniper is behind the observer in an open-legged, cross-legged, or kneeling position, depending on the target's elevation (Figure 3-3-5). When using these positions, the sniper's effective engagement of targets at extended ranges is difficult and used only as a last resort. When practicing these positions, the sniper and observer must enter respiratory pause together to eliminate breathing movement.

## 3-4.  SIGHTING AND AIMING

    The sniper's use of iron sights serves mainly as a back-up system to his optical sight. However, iron sights are an excellent means of training for the sniper. The sniper is expected to be proficient in the use of iron sights before he obtains formal sniper training, and he must remain proficient. By utilizing iron sights during training, the sniper is forced to maintain his concentration on the fundamentals of shooting. For a review of basic rifle marksmanship, reference should be made to FM 23-8 (<u>M14 and M14A1 Rifle and Rifle Marksmanship</u>), FM 23-9 (<u>M16A1 and M16A2 Rifle Marksmanship</u>). While these manuals are good for a basic review, some modifications in shooting techniques may be made.

    The sniper begins the aiming process by aligning the rifle with the target when assuming a firing position. He should point the rifle naturally at the desired point of aim. If his muscles are used to adjust the weapon onto the point of aim, they will automatically relax as the rifle fires, and the rifle will begin to move towards its natural point of aim. Because this movement begins just before the weapon discharges, the rifle is moving as the bullet leaves the muzzle. This causes displaced shots with no apparent cause (recoil disguises the movement). By adjusting the weapon and body as a single unit, rechecking, and readjusting as needed, the sniper achieves a true natural point of aim. Once the position is established, the sniper then aims the weapon at the exact point on the target. Aiming involves three factors: eye relief, sight alignment, and sight picture.

## Eye Relief

This is the distance from the sniper's firing eye to the rear sight or the rear of the telescope tube. When using iron sights, the sniper ensures that this distance remains constant from shot to shot to preclude changing what he views through the rear sight. However, relief will vary from firing position to firing position and from sniper to sniper, according to the sniper's neck length, his angle of head approach to the stock, the depth of his shoulder pocket, and his firing position. This distance (Figure 3-4-1) is more rigidly controlled with telescopic sights than with iron sights. The sniper must take care to prevent eye injury caused by the telescope tube striking his eyebrow during recoil. Regardless of the sighting system he uses, he must place his head as upright as possible with his firing eye located directly behind the rear portion of the sighting system. This head placement also allows the muscles surrounding his eye to relax. Incorrect head placement causes the sniper to look out of the top or corner of his eye, resulting in muscular strain. Such strain leads to blurred vision and can also cause eye strain. The sniper can avoid eye strain by not staring through the iron or telescopic sights for extended periods. The best aid to consistent eye relief is maintaining the same stock weld from shot to shot. The reason for this is that as the eye relief changes, a change in sight alignment will occur. Normal eye relief for the rear aperture size on the M21 and M24 is 2 3/4 to 3 1/2 inches. Maintaining eye relief is a function of the position and uses either spot weld or stock weld. Once the shooter is ready to fire, it is imperative that he concentrate on the front sight and not the target.

## Sight Alignment

With iron sights, sight alignment is the relationship between the front and rear sights as seen by the sniper (Figure 3-4-2). The sniper centers the top edge of the front sight blade horizontally and vertically within the rear aperture. (The center of aperture is easiest for the eye to locate and allows the sniper to be consistent in blade location.) With telescopic sights, sight alignment is the relationship between the cross hairs (reticle) and a full field of view as seen by the sniper. The sniper must place his head so that a full field of view fills the tube, with no dark shadows or crescents to cause misplaced shots. He centers the reticle in a full field of view, ensuring the vertical cross hair is straight up and down so that the rifle is not canted. Again, the center is easiest for the sniper to locate, and allows for consistent reticle placement. Sight alignment is the most critical factor in aiming. An error in sight alignment increases proportionately with range and will result in increased misses.

While centering the front sight works well, other techniques also work well and the sniper should try each to find which works best for him. The front sight of the M21 has a sight block and a hex-head screw. By using the hex-head screw as a reference point, the shooter can place the screw at the bottom of the rear aperture.

By having two round reference points, the eye and the mind work together automatically to center the hex at the same point. Another technique the shooter may use is to divide the hex-head screw in half and center it on the bottom of the rear aperture. Still another technique is to center the sight block on the bottom of the rear aperture. Any of these techniques work well. It matters only that the shooter is comfortable with the technique. The M24 has a hooded front sight, which simplifies sight alignment. The front sight hood is centered in the rear sight aperture.

## Sight Picture

With iron sights, the sight picture is the relationship between the front sight blade, the rear aperture, and the target as seen by the sniper (Figure 3-4-3). The sniper centers the top edge of the blade in the rear aperture. He then places the top edge of the blade in the center of the largest visible mass of the target (disregard the head and use the center of the torso). With telescopic sights, sight picture is the relationship between the reticle and full field of view and the target as seen by the sniper (Figure 3-4-4). The sniper centers the reticle in a full field of view. He then places the reticle center on the largest visible mass of the target (as in iron sights). The center of mass of the target is easiest for the sniper to locate, and it surrounds the intended point of impact with a maximum amount of target area. When aiming, the sniper concentrates on the front sight, not the target. This is critical to detect any errors in sight alignment, which is more important than the sight picture.

When aiming, the sniper has several choices of where to hold the front sight:

o       The center hold. The center hold places the front sight on the desired point of impact. The problem with this is that the front sight blocks part of the target. This is probably the best sight picture for combat use because it is the most "natural" for US Army-trained soldiers.

o       The six o'clock hold. This hold places the target on top of the front sight. The main problem is that it is easy for the front sight to "push up" into the target, causing the round to go high.

o       The line of white hold. The line of white allows a strip of contrasting color to show between the target and the front sight. This permits the shooter to see the entire target and prevents the front sight from going high or low without the shooter noticing it.

## Sight Alignment Error

When sight alignment and sight picture are perfect (regardless of sighting system) and all else is done correctly, the shot will hit center of mass on the target. However, with an error in sight alignment, the bullet is displaced in the direction of the error. Such an error creates an angular displacement between the line of sight and the line of bore. This displacement increases as range increases; the amount of bullet displacement depends on the size of alignment error. Close targets show little or no visible error. Distant targets can show great displacement or can be missed altogether due to severe sight misalignment. An inexperienced marksman is prone to this kind of error, since he is unsure of what correctly aligned sights look like (especially telescopic sights). When a sniper varies his head position (and eye relief) from shot to shot, he is apt to make sight alignment errors while firing (Figure 3-4-5).

## Sight Picture Error

An error in sight picture is an error in the placement of the aiming point. This causes no displacement between the line of sight and the line of bore. The weapon is simply pointed at the wrong spot on the target. Because no displacement exists as range increases, close and far targets are hit or missed depending on where the front sight or the reticle is when the rifle fires (Figure 3-4-6). All snipers face this kind of error every time they shoot. Regardless of firing position stability, the weapon will always be moving. A supported rifle moves much less than an unsupported one, but both still move in what is known as a wobble area. The sniper must adjust his firing position so that his wobble area is as small as possible and centered on the target. With proper adjustments, the sniper should be able to fire the shot while the front sight blade or reticle is on the target at, or very near, the desired aiming point. How far the blade or reticle is from this point when the weapon fires is the amount of sight picture error all snipers face. Also, the sniper should not attempt to aim for more than five or six seconds without blinking. This will be an additional strain on the eye and will "burn" the sight alignment and sight picture into the retina. This will cause minor changes in sight alignment and sight picture to go unnoticed.

## Dominant Eye

Some individuals may have difficulty aiming because of interferences from their dominant eye, if this is not the eye used in the aiming process. This may require the sniper to fire from the other side of the weapon (right-handed firer will fire left-handed). To determine which eye is dominant, hold an index finger 6 to 8 inches in front of your eyes. Close one eye at a time while looking at the finger; one eye will make the finger appear to move and the other will not. The eye that does not make the finger appear to move is the dominant eye. If the sniper does not have a cross-dominant problem, it is best to aim with both eyes open. This allows him to see naturally and helps him relax. Also, with both eyes open, the sniper can find targets more quickly in his telescopic sight. Closing one eye puts an unnatural strain on the aiming eye and limits the sniper's protective peripheral vision.

## Advantages of Telescopic Sights

Telescopic sights offer many advantages.  They are:

    o    Extremely accurate aiming, which enables the sniper to
fire at distant, barely perceptible, and camouflaged targets that
are not visible to the naked eye.

    o    Rapid aiming, because the sniper's eye sees the cross
hairs and the target with equal clarity in the same focal plane.

    o    Accurate fire under conditions of unfavorable illumina-
tion (such as at dawn and dusk) and during periods of limited
visibility (moonlight and fog).

    With all of its advantages, there are a few considerations
that the sniper must keep in mind when using telescopes.  The
telescopic sight will never make a poor shooter any better.  The
only advantage to the telescopic sight is that the target and the
reticle are on the same focal plane, and the magnficiation provides
a more distinct aiming point.  The magnification is also a
disadvantage, as it also magnifies aiming and holding errors.
Although technically there is no sight alignment with the
telescopic sight, if the eye is not centered on the scope,
shadowing will occur.  This error will have the same effect as
improper sight alignment.  The bullet will strike at a point
opposite the shadow and will increase in error as the distance
increases.

    Improper head placement on the stock is the main cause of
shadowing.  Due to the scope being higher than the iron sights, it
is difficult to obtain a good solid stock weld.  If this is a
problem,  temporary cheek rests can be constructed using Kotex, T-
shirts, or any material that can be removed and replaced.  This
will assist the sniper in obtaining a good stock weld and will help
to keep his head held straight for sighting.


## Aiming With Telescopic Sights

    A telescopic sight allows aiming without using the organic
rifle sights.  The line of sight is the optical axis that runs
through the center of the lens and the intersection of the cross
hairs.  The cross hairs and the image of the target are in the
focal plane of the lens (that plane which passes through the lens
focus, perpendicular to the optical axis).  The sniper's eye sees
the cross hairs and the image of the target with identical
sharpness and clarity.  To aim with a telescope, the sniper must
position his head at the exit pupil of the telescope eyepiece so
that the line of sight of his eye coincides with the optical axis
of the telescope.  He then centers the cross hairs on the target.


## Eye Relief

    In aiming, the eye must be located 3 to 3 3/4 inches from the
exit pupil of the eyepiece.  This distance, the eye relief, is

fairly large, but it is necessary to ensure safety from recoil and to obtain a full field of vision.

## Shadow Effects

During aiming, the sniper must ensure that there are no shadows in the field of vision of the telescope. If the sniper's eye does not have proper eye relief, a circular shadow will occur in the field of vision, reducing the field-of-vision size, hindering observation, and in general, making aiming difficult. If the eye is positioned incorrectly in relation to the main optical axis of the telescope (shifted to the side), crescent-shaped shadows will occur on the edges of the eyepiece. They can occur on either side, depending upon the position of the axis of the eye with respect to the optical axis of the telescope. If these crescent-shaped shadows are present, the bullets will strike to the side away from them. This error is the same as a sight alignment error with iron sights.

## Head Adjustments

If the sniper notices shadows on the edges of the field of vision during aiming, he must find a head position in which the eye will see clearly the entire field of vision of the telescope. Consequently, in order to ensure accurate aiming with a telescope, the sniper must direct his entire attention to keeping his eye on the optical axis of the telescope, and he must have the intersection of the cross hairs coincide exactly with the aiming point. However, his concentration must be on the cross hairs and not the target. It is important not to stare at the cross hairs while aiming.

## Canting

Canting is the act of tipping the rifle to either side of the vertical, causing misplaced and erratic shot grouping.

## Point of Aim

The point of aim should not be the center of mass, unless required by the situation. The best point of aim is anywhere within the triangle formed by the the base of the neck and the two nipples (Figure 3-4-7). This will maximize the probability of hitting major organs and vessels, and rendering a clean one-shot kill. The optional point of aim if the upper chest hold is not available is the centerline below the belt. The pelvic girdle is rich in major blood vessels and nerves. A hit here will cause a mechanical collapse or mechanical dysfunction. This is also an advantage if the target is wearing body armor, which usually only covers the upper chest. The final point of aim is the head hold (Figures 3-4-8,9,10). This is very difficult to achieve because of its size and constant motion. The advantage of the head hold is incapacitation well under 1 second if the correct placement is achieved. This hold is well suited for hostage situations where closer ranges are the norm, and instant incapacitation is required. The exact hold is along the plane formed by the nose and the two ear canals. The target is the brain stem, to severe the spinal cord from the medulla oblongata. Note that the point of aim is not the forehead nor between the eyes. This would result in a hit that is too high.

What the sniper is trying to severe or pulverize is the target's brain stem, the location where the spinal cord connects to the brain. Nerves that control motor function are channeled through here, and the lower third of the stem (the medulla) controls breathing and heartbeat. Hit here, the target will not experience even reflexive motor action. His entire body will instantly experience what is called "flaccid paralysis"; all of his muscles will suddenly relax, incapable of any motion of any kind thereafter. The sniper can tell how successful his head shot was by watching how his target falls. If the target goes straight down, limp, or pitches forward, there is a high assurance of fatality. If the target falls to the side, the target has only been partially incapacitated.

For a chest shot that is ideally placed mid-sternum, the bullet will strike the largest and hardest of the bones overlying the vital organs. When the bullet strikes and severs the target's spine, his legs will buckle under flaccid paralysis. His arms, however, may not be incapacitated instantly. With a chest shot, even though the suspect may technically be "dead" from the devastation of the round, there may be a brief and dangerous delay before he acts dead. His brain may not die for one to two minutes after his heart has ceased to function. During this time, his brain may command his arms to commit a simple, final act. The sniper anticipates these possibilities and delivers an immediate second round if the suspect is not fully down and out and/or anyone is within his sphere of danger.

## 3-5. BREATH CONTROL

Breath control is important to the aiming process. If the shooter breathes while trying to aim, the rise and fall of his chest will cause the rifle to move vertically. Sight alignment is accomplished while the shooter is breathing, but he must be able to hold his breath to complete the process of aiming. To properly hold his breath, the shooter inhales, exhales normally, and stops at the moment of natural respiratory pause. If the shooter does not have the correct sight picture, then he must change his position.
A respiratory cycle lasts four to five seconds. Inhalation and exhalation require only about two seconds. Thus, between each respiratory cycle, there is a pause of two to three seconds. This pause can be expanded to 12 to 15 seconds without any special effort or unpleasant sensation; however, the maximum safe pause is 8 to 10 seconds. The shooter must fire the shot during an extended pause between breaths or start the process over again. During the

respiratory pause, the breathing muscles are relaxed, and the shooter thus avoids straining the diaphragm (Figure 3-5-1).

A shooter should assume his position and breathe naturally until his hold begins to settle. Many shooters then take a slightly deeper breath, exhale and pause, expecting to fire the shot during the pause. If the hold does not settle sufficiently to allow the shot to be fired, the shooter resumes normal breathing and repeats the process.

The respiratory pause should never feel unnatural. If the pause is extended for too long, the body suffers from oxygen deficiency and sends out signals to resume breathing. These signals produce slight involuntary movements in the diaphragm and interfere with the shooter's ability to concentrate. The heart rate also increases and there is a decrease of oxygen to the eyes. This causes the eyes to have difficulty focusing and this results in eye strain. During multiple, rapid-fire engagements, the breathing cycle should be forced through a rapid, shallow cycle between shots instead of trying to hold the breath or breathing. Firing should be accomplished at the forced respiratory pause.

The natural tendency of the weapon to rise and fall during breathing allows the sniper to fine tune his aim by holding his breath at the point in which the sights rest on aiming point.

## 3-6. TRIGGER CONTROL

Trigger control is the most important component of the sniper marksmanship fundamentals. It is defined as causing the rifle to fire when the sight picture is at its best, without causing the rifle to move. Trigger squeeze, on the other hand, is defined as the independent action of the forefinger on the trigger, with a uniformly increasing pressure straight to the rear until the rifle fires. Trigger control is the last task to be accomplished before the weapon fires. It is more difficult to apply when using a telescope or when a firing position becomes less stable. Misses are usually caused by the aim being disturbed as the bullet leaves the barrel, or just before it leaves the barrel, and is the result of a shooter jerking the trigger or flinching. The trigger need not be jerked violently to spoil the aim; even a slight, sudden pressure of the trigger finger is enough to cause the barrel to waver and spoil the sight alignment. Flinching is an involuntary movement of the body--tensing of the muscles of the arm, the neck, or the shoulder in anticipation of the shock of recoil or the sound of the rifle firing. A shooter can correct these errors by understanding and applying proper trigger control.

Proper trigger control occurs when the sniper places his firing finger as low on the trigger as possible and still clears the trigger guard, thereby achieving maximum mechanical advantage.

22

The sniper engages the trigger with that part of his firing finger that allows him to pull the trigger straight to the rear. A firm grip on the rifle stock is essential for trigger control. If the sniper begins his trigger pull from a loose grip, he tends to squeeze the stock as well as the trigger and thus loses trigger control. To avoid transferring movement of the finger to the entire rifle, the sniper should see daylight between the trigger finger and the stock as he squeezes the trigger, straight to the rear. To ensure a well-placed shot, he fires the weapon when the front blade or reticle is on the desired point of aim.

The sniper maintains trigger control best by assuming a stable position, adjusting on the target, and beginning a breathing cycle. As the sniper exhales the final breath toward a natural respiratory pause, he secures his finger on the trigger. On the M21, he will take up the slack in the trigger until resistance is felt. As the front blade or reticle settles on the desired point of aim, and the natural respiratory pause is entered, the sniper applies initial pressure. He increases the tension on the trigger during the respiratory pause as long as the front blade or reticle remains in the area of the target that ensures a well-placed shot. If the front blade or reticle moves away from the desired point of aim on the target, and the pause is free of strain or tension, the sniper stops increasing the tension on the trigger, waits for the front blade or reticle to return to the desired point, and then continues to squeeze the trigger. The shooter perfects his aim while continuing the steadily increasing pressure until the hammer falls. This is trigger control. If movement is too large for recovery or if the pause has become uncomfortable (extended too long), the sniper should carefully release the pressure on the trigger and begin the respiratory cycle again.

Most successful snipers agree that the trigger slack should be taken up with a heavy initial pressure. Concentration should be focused on the perfection of the sight picture as trigger control is automatically applied. Concentration, especially on the front sight or reticle is the greatest aid to prevent flinching and jerking.

The methods of trigger control involve a mental process, while pulling the trigger is a mechanical process. Two methods of trigger control are used to pull the trigger: the smooth motion or constant pressure trigger pull and the interrupted trigger pull.

o    Smooth Motion/Constant Pressure Trigger Pull. In the smooth motion trigger pull the shooter takes up the slack with a heavy initial pressure and, when the sight picture settles, pulls the trigger with a single, smooth action. This method is used when there is a stationary target and the position is steady. This type of trigger control will help prevent flinching, jerking, and bucking the weapon.

o    Interrupted Trigger Pull.   In the interrupted trigger
pull the shooter applies pressure to the trigger when the sight
picture begins to settle, and as long as the sight picture looks
good or continues to improve.   If the sight picture deteriorates
briefly, the shooter maintains the pressure at a constant level and
increases it when the picture again begins to improve.   This
technique is used in the standing position due to the lack of
stability of the position, and the sniper may apply smooth motion
trigger pull or pressure.   This is necessary because of the wobble
area or wavering of the sights around, through, or in the target or
aiming point due to the instability of the position.   If, while
controlling the pressure, an error occurs in the sight alignment or
sight picture that is great enough to cause the shot to miss the
target, the sniper holds the pressure that he has on the trigger
until   the   correct   sight   alignment   or   sight   picture   is
reestablished.   He then continues the pressure or repeats this
technique until he fires the rifle.   The sniper does not jerk the
trigger when the sights are aligned and the "perfect" sight picture
occurs.

Another type of trigger control that is not really separate
from the previous two is called the "Infantry Trophy trigger pull."
This is only applicable to semiautomatic weapons.   It is extremely
effective during multiple engagements, or when time is critical.
After engaging the first target, the sniper maintains the pressure
on the trigger with his trigger finger.   During the forced
inhalation of the breathing cycle, the sniper gently releases the
pressure slightly on the trigger until he feels the sear engage.
This is usually indicated by a tactile and audible click.   He then
enters the normal cycle of the trigger control, perfecting the
sight picture until the next shot is released.   This is continued
until the sniper is out of targets or ammunition.   This technique
minimizes the distance that the trigger and trigger finger must
travel between shots.

Trigger control is not only the most important fundamental of
marksmanship but also the most difficult to master.   The majority
of shooting errors stems directly or indirectly from the improper
application of trigger control.   Failure to hit the target
frequently results from the sniper jerking the trigger or applying
pressure on both the trigger and the side of the rifle.   Either of
these actions can produce a miss.   Therefore, instructors should
always check for indications of improper trigger control, since an
error in this technique can start a chain reaction of other errors.
Some of the indications of improper trigger control are:

o    Flinching.   Flinching is an involuntary muscular
reaction or tension in anticipation of recoil or muzzle blast.   It
is indicated by moving the head, closing the eyes, tensing the non-
firing arm, moving the shoulders to the rear, or a combination of
these.

24

o    Bucking.  Bucking is an attempt to anticipate and take up the recoil before it occurs by tensing the shoulder muscles and moving the shoulder forward.

o    Jerking.  Jerking is an attempt to make the rifle fire at a certain instant by rapidly applying pressure on the trigger.

Trigger control can be developed into a reflex action.  The sniper can develop his trigger control to the point that pulling the trigger requires no conscious effort.  The sniper will be aware of the pull, but he will not be consciously directing it.  Everyone exhibits this type of reflex action in daily living.  The individual who walks or drives a car while carrying on a conversation is an example.  He is aware of his muscular activity, but is not planning it.  He is thinking about the conversation.

Trigger control is taught in conjunction with positions.  When positions and trigger control are being taught, an effective training aid for demonstrating the technique of trigger control with reference to the interrupted or controlled pressure, is the wobble sight and target simulator.  The wobble sight may be used with a fixed target simulator to demonstrate wobble area, adjustment of natural point of aim, breathing, and trigger control.

In all positions, dry firing is one of the best methods of developing proper trigger control.  In dry firing, not only is the coach able to detect errors, but the individual shooter is able to detect his own errors, since there is no recoil to conceal the rifle's undesirable movements.  Where possible, trigger control practice should be integrated into all phases of marksmanship training.  The mastery of trigger control takes patience, hard work, concentration, and a great deal of self-discipline.


3-7.  THE INTEGRATED ACT OF FIRING ONE ROUND

Once the sniper has been taught the fundamentals of marksmanship, his primary concern is to apply this knowledge in the performance of his mission.  An effective method of applying fundamentals is through the use of the integrated act of firing one round.  The integrated act is a logical, step-by-step development of the fundamentals, whereby the sniper develops habits to fire each shot exactly the same.  Thus he achieves the marksmanship goal that a sniper must strive for:  "one shot--one kill."

The integrated act of firing can be divided into four distinct phases:

Preparation Phase.  Before departing the preparation area, the sniper ensures that:

o    The team is mentally conditioned and knows what mission they are to accomplish.

o    A systematic check is made of equipment for completeness and serviceability including, but not limited to:

*    Properly cleaned and lubricated rifles.

*    Properly mounted and torqued scopes.

*    Zero-sighted systems and recorded data in the sniper data book.

*    The study of weather conditions to determine their possible effects on the team's performance of the mission.

Before-Firing Phase.  On arrival at the mission site, the team exercises care in selecting positions.  The sniper ensures that the selected positions complement the mission's goal.  During this phase, the sniper:

o    Maintains strict adherence to the fundamentals of position.  He ensures that the firing position is as relaxed as possible, making the most of available external support.  He also makes sure the support is stable, confirms to the position, and allows a correct, natural point of aim for each designated area or target.

o    Once in position, he remove the scope covers and checks the field(s) of fire, making any needed corrections to ensure clear, unobstructed firing lanes.

o    Makes dry-firing and natural point of aim checks.

o    Double-checks ammunition for serviceability and completes final magazine loading.

o    Notifies the observer he is ready to engage targets.  The observer must be constantly aware of weather conditions that may affect the accuracy of the shots.  He must also stay ahead of the tactical situation.

Firing Phase.  Upon detection, or if directed to a suitable target, the sniper makes appropriate sight changes, aims, and tells the observer he is ready to fire.  The observer then gives the needed windage and observes the target.  To fire the rifle, the sniper should remember the key word, "BRASS".  Each letter is explained as follows:

o    Breathe.  The sniper inhales and exhales to the natural respiratory pause.  He checks for consistent head placement and stock/spot weld.  He ensures eye relief is correct (full field of view through the scope; no shadows present.)  At the same time, he begins aligning the cross hairs or front blade with the target at the desired point of aim.

o    Relax. As the sniper exhales, he relaxes as many muscles as possible, while maintaining control of the weapon and position.

o    Aim. If the sniper has a good, natural point of aim, the rifle points at the desired target during the respiratory pause. If the aim is off, the sniper should make a slight adjustment to acquire the desired point of aim. He avoids "muscling" the weapon toward the aiming point.

o    Slack. The first stage of the two-stage trigger (the slack, M21 only) must be taken up with heavy initial pressure. Most experienced snipers actually take up the slack and get initial pressure as they reach the respiratory pause. In this way, the limited duration of the pause is not used up by manipulating the slack in the trigger.

o    Squeeze. As long as the sight picture is satisfactory, the sniper should squeeze the trigger. The pressure applied to the trigger must be straight to the rear without disturbing the lay of the rifle or the desired point of aim.

After-Firing Phase. The sniper's after-firing actions include observing the target area to certify the hit, observing the enemy reaction, acquiring another target, and avoiding compromise of his position. The sniper must analyze his performance. If the shot impacted at the desired spot (a target hit), it may be assumed the integrated act of firing one round was correctly followed. If, however, the shot was off call, the sniper and observer must check for possible errors.

o    Failure to follow the key word, BRASS (partial field of view, breath held incorrectly, trigger jerked, rifle muscled into position, and so on).

o    Target improperly ranged with scope (causing high or low shots).

o    Incorrectly compensated for wind (causing right or left shots).

o    Possible weapon/ammunition malfunction (used only as a last resort when no other errors are detected).

Once the probable reasons for an off-call shot is determined, the sniper must make note of the errors. He pays close attention to the problem areas to increase the accuracy of future shots.

27

## Follow-through

Applying the fundamentals increases the odds of a well-aimed shot being fired. When mastered, additional skills can make that first-round kill even more of a certainty. One of these skills is the follow-through.

Follow-through is a continued mental and physical application of the fundamentals after each round is fired. It is the act of continuing to apply all of the sniper marksmanship fundamentals as the weapon fires as well as immediately after it fires. It consists of:

o    Keeping the head in firm contact with the stock (stock weld).

o    Keeping the finger on the trigger all the way to the rear.

o    Continuing to look through the rear aperture or scope tube.

o    Keeping muscles relaxed.

o    Avoiding reaction to recoil and/or noise.

o    Releasing the trigger only after the recoil has stopped.

Good follow-through ensures that the weapon is allowed to fire and recoil naturally. The sniper/rifle combination reacts as a single unit to such actions. From a training viewpoint, follow-through may allow the sniper to observe the strike of his bullet in relation to his aiming point and help him rapidly correct and adjust his sights for a second shot. Also, a good follow-through will indicate to the sniper the quality of his natural point of aim. The weapon should settle back on target. If it does not, then muscles were used to get the weapon on target.

## Calling the Shot

Calling the shot is being able to tell where the round should impact on the target. Because live targets invariably move when hit, the sniper will find it almost impossible to use his telescope to locate the target after the round is fired. Using iron sights, the sniper will find that searching for a downrange hit is beyond his abilities. He must be able to accurately call his shots. Proper follow-through will aid in calling the shot. The dominant factor in shot calling is, however, where the reticle or post is located when the weapon discharges. This location is called his final focus point.

With iron sights, the final focus point should be on the top edge of the front sight blade. The blade is the only part of the sight picture that is moving (in the wobble area). Focusing on it aids in calling the shot and detecting any errors in sight alignment or sight picture. Of course, lining up the sights and the target initially requires the sniper to shift his focus from the target to the blade and back until he is satisfied that he is properly aligned with the target. This shifting exposes two more facts about eye focus. The eye can instantly shift focus from near objects (the blade) to far objects (the target). The eye cannot, however, be focused so that two objects at greatly different ranges (again the blade and target) are both in sharp focus. After years of experience, many snipers find that they no longer hold final focus on the front sight blade. Their focus is somewhere between the blade and the target. This act has been related to many things, from personal preference to failing eyesight. Regardless, inexperienced snipers are still advised to use the blade as a final focus point.

The final focus is easily placed with telescopic sights because of the sight's optical qualities. Properly focused, a scope should present both the field of view and the reticle in sharp detail. Final focus should then be on the target. While focusing on the target, the sniper moves his head slighty from side to side. The reticle may seem to move across the target face, even though the rifle and scope are motionless. This movement is parallax. Parallax is present when the target image is not correctly focused onto the reticle's focal plane. Therefore, the target image and the reticle appear to be in two separate positions inside the scope, causing the effect of reticle movement across the target. A small amount of parallax is unavoidable throughout the range of the ART series of scopes. The M3A on the M24 has a focus/parallax adjustment that eliminates parallax. The sniper should adjust this knob until the target's image is on the same focal plane as the reticle. To determine if the target's image appears at the ideal location, the sniper should move his head slightly left and right to see if the reticle appears to move. If it does not move, the focus is properly adjusted and no parallax is present.

In calling the shot, the sniper predicts where the shot will hit the target. The sniper calls the shot while dry firing and actual firing by noting the position of the sights in relation to the aiming point the instant the round is fired. If his shot is not on call, the sniper must review the fundamentals to isolate his problem or make a sight change as indicated to move his shot to his point of aim. Unless he can accurately call his shots, the sniper will not be able to effectively zero his rifle.

## 3-8. DETECTION AND CORRECTION OF ERRORS

During the process of teaching or using the fundamentals of marksmanship, it will become evident that errors may plague any shooter. When an error is detected, it must be corrected.

Sometimes errors are not obvious, and this is when a coach or instructor will be invaluable. The procedure for correcting errors is to pinpoint or isolate the error, prove to the sniper that he is making this error, and convince him that through his own efforts and concentration he can correct his error. Knowing what to look for through analysis of the shot groups, observation of the sniper, questioning of the sniper, and review of the fundamentals of training exercises will assist the coach in this process.

## Target Analysis
Target or shot group analysis is an important step in the process of detection and correction of errors (Figure 3-8-1). When analyzing a target, errors in performance should be correlated to loose groups, the shape of groups, and the size of groups. With some snipers, especially the experienced, this cannot be done readily. However, the coach must be able to discuss the probable error. A bad shot group is seldom caused by only one error. It should also be remembered that in the initial analysis of groups, the coach must take into consideration the capabilities of the sniper as well as those of the weapon and the ammunition.

## Observation of the Sniper
When the coach or instructor has an indication that the sniper is committing one or more errors, it will usually be necessary for the coach or instructor to observe this sniper while he is in the act of shooting to pinpoint his errors. If the coach or instructor has no indication of the sniper's probable errors, the initial emphasis should be on firing position and breath control. Next, the coach or instructor should look for the most common errors-- anticipation of the shot and improper trigger control. If observing the sniper fails to pinpoint his errors, the coach or instructor must then question him.

## Questioning the Sniper
The coach or instructor should ask the sniper if he can detect his errors. He should have the sniper explain the firing procedure, to include position, aiming, breath control, trigger control, and follow-through. If questioning does not reveal all of the errors, the coach or instructor should talk the sniper through the correct procedure for firing one round.

## Review the Fundamentals
The coach or instructor should talk the sniper through the following procedures: setting the sights, building the position, aligning the sights, checking the natural point of aim, adjusting the natural point of aim, controlling the breath, obtaining a sight picture, focussing on the front sight, controlling the trigger, follow through, and calling the shot. If errors still exist, there are several training exercises that can help to pinpoint them.
## Training Exercises

These training exercises or devices can be used at any time to supplement the detection procedure. (See FM 23-8, <u>M14 and M14A1 Rifles and Rifle Marksmanship</u>).

o     Trigger exercise.

o     Metal disk exercise.

o     Ball and dummy exercise.

o     Blank target firing exercise.

o     M2 aiming device.

o     Air rifles.

When the sniper leaves the firing line, he compares weather conditions to the information needed to hit the point of aim/point of impact. Since he fires in all types of weather conditions, he must be aware of temperature, light, mirage, and wind. The sniper must consider other major points or tasks:

o  Compare sight settings with previous firing sessions. If the sniper always has to fine-tune for windage or elevation, there is a chance he needs a sight change (slip a scale).

o  Compare ammunition by lot number for the best rifle and ammunition combination.

o  Compare all groups fired under each condition. Check the low and high shots as well as those to the left and the right of the main group--the less dispersion, the better. If groups are tight, they are easily moved to the center of the target; if loose, there is a problem. Check the telescope focus and make sure the rifle is cleaned correctly. Remarks in the data book will also help.

o  Make corrections. Record corrections in the data book, such as position and sight adjustment information to ensure retention.

o  Analyze a group on a target. This is important for marksmanship training. The firer may not notice errors during firing, but errors become apparent when analyzing a group. This can only be done if the data book has been used correctly.

A checklist that will aid in shot group/performance analysis follows:

*  Group tends to be low and right.

31

o   Left hand not positioned properly.

o   Right elbow slipping.

o   Improper trigger control.

* Group scattered about the target.

o   Improper trigger control.

o   Incorrect eye relief, sight picture/alignment.

o   Failure to focus on the front sight (iron sights).

o   Stock weld changed.

o   Unstable firing position.

* Good group with several erratic shots.

o   Flinching.  Shots may be anywhere.

o   Bucking.  Shots from 7 to 10 o'clock.

o   Jerking.  Shots may be anywhere.

* Group strung up and down through the target.

o   Breathing while firing.

o   Improper vertical alignment of sights.

o   Stock weld changed.

o   Bad lot of ammunition.

* Compact group out of the target.

o   Incorrect zero.

o   Failure to compensate for wind.
o   Bad natural point of aim.

o   Scope shadow.

* Group center of the target out the bottom.

o   Scope shadow.

o   Position of the rifle changed in the shoulder.

  o Sling sliding down the arm.

  o Position too low.

 * Horizontal group across the target.

  o Scope shadow.

  o Canted weapon.

  o Bad natural point of aim.

  o Incorrect sight alignment.

  o Failure to compensate for changing winds.

  o Loose position.

  o Muscling the rifle.

As the stability of a firing position decreases, the wobble area increases. The larger the wobble area, the harder it is to fire the shot without reacting to it. This reaction occurs when the sniper:

 o Anticipates recoil. The firing shoulder begins to move forward just before the round fires.

 o Jerks the trigger. The trigger finger moves the trigger in a quick, chopping, spasmodic attempt to fire the shot before the front blade or reticle can move away from the desired point of aim.

 o Flinches. The sniper's entire upper body (or parts thereof) overreacts to anticipated noise or recoil. This is usually due to being unfamiliar with the weapon.

 o Avoids recoil. The sniper tries to avoid recoil or noise by moving away from the weapon or closing the firing eye just before the round fires. This, again, is caused by a lack of knowledge of the weapon's actions upon firing.


## 3-9. APPLICATION OF FIRE

Following the Austrian-Prussian War of 1866, the Prussian Army began a systematic study of the effectiveness and control of small arms fire. The result of this study, conducted over a six-year period, was the introduction of the science of musketry, a misnomer as all major armies were by then equipped with rifles. Musketry is the science of small arms fire under field conditions, as opposed to range conditions, and is concerned entirely with firing at unknown distances; thus, the importance of the study of musketry to

33

the sniper. The material presented is merely an overview of the fundamentals of musketry. At the peak of the study of musketry as a martial science, schools of musketry often extended their courses to six weeks duration. Only the introduction of machine guns and automatic small arms precipatated the doctrine of its study, although various aspects of musketry were retained as separate subjects, such as judging distances and issuing fire control orders. This ties together the scattered remnants of the study of musketry as it pertains to sniping.

All weapon sights are constructed with a means of adjustment. Although the technicalities of adjustment may vary with weapon type, or means of sighting, generally the weapon sight will be correctable for windage and elevation. The specific method by which adjustment is accomplished is angular displacement of the sight in relation to the bore of the rifle. This angular displacement is measured in minutes of angle (MOA).

## Minute of Angle

A minute of angle is the unit of angular measure which subtends 1/60 of 1 degree of arc. With few exceptions the universal method of weapon sight adjustment is in fractions, or multiples, of minutes of angle. A minute of angle subtends a distance of 1.0472 inches at 100 yards and 2.8 centimeters at 100 meters. Since a minute of angle is an angular unit of measure, the arc subtended by a minute of angle increases proportionately with distance (Figure 3-9-1).

It is recognized that fractions are difficult to work with when making mental calculations. For this reason the conventional dictum of shooters that assumes one minute of angle is the equivalent of 1 inch at 100 yards will be followed. It will also be assumed that one minute of angle is the equivalent of 3 centimeters at 100 meters. By rounding off the angular displacement of the minute of angle in this manner, only one-half inch of accuracy at 1,000 yards and 2 centimeters at 1,000 meters is lost. Data will be presented in both the English and the Metric system. This will permit the sniper to use whichever system he is most comfortable with.

## Sight Corrections

With the knowledge of how much the displacement of one minute of angle at a given distance is, it is now possible to calculate sight corrections. All that the sniper needs to know is how many minutes of angle, or fractions of a minute of angle, each sight graduation (known as "clicks") equals. This is dependent on the type of sight used.

To determine the amount of correction required in minutes of angle for the English system, the error in inches is divided by the range expressed in whole numbers. The correction formula is:

$$\text{MINUTES} = \frac{(\text{ERROR}) \ (\text{inches})}{\text{RANGE (expressed in whole numbers)}}$$

To determine the amount of correction required in minutes of angle using the metric system, the error in centimeters is divided by the range expressed in whole numbers, then the resultant is divided by 3. The correction formula is:

$$\text{MINUTES} = \frac{\text{ERROR (centimeters)}}{\text{RANGE (expressed in whole numbers)} \times 3}$$

There will arise occasions when the impact of a shot is observed, but there is no accurate indication of how much the error is in inches or centimeters. Such occasions may occur when there is a great distance between the aiming point and the impact point or when there is a lack of an accurate reference. It is possible to determine the distance of the impact point from the point of aim in mils, then to convert the mils to minutes of angle. The conversion factor is:

1 MIL = 3.375 MINUTES OF ANGLE

EXAMPLE: When a round is fired the impact of the round is observed to be several feet to the right of the target. The observer notes the impact point and determines it to be 2 mils to the right of the aiming point.

3.375 x 2 = 6.75 MINUTES

The table below gives the inch equivalents of mils at the given ranges of 91 meters to 1,000 meters and 100 yards to 1,000 yards. This will aid the sniper in computing his sight change in mils for a given distance to the target with a given miss in estimated inches. For example, a miss of 28 inches left at 400 yards would be a 2 mil hold to the right.

## MIL VALUE

| RANGE | INCHES | RANGE | INCHES |
|---|---|---|---|
| 91 meters (100 yds) | 3.6 | 549 meters (600 yds) | 22.0 |
| 100 meters | 4.0 | 600 meters | 24.0 |
| 183 meters (200 yds) | 7.0 | 640 meters (740 yds) | 25.0 |
| 200 meters | 8.0 | 700 meters | 27.5 |
| 274 meters (300 yds) | 11.0 | 731 meters (800 yds) | 29.0 |
| 300 meters | 12.0 | 800 meters | 31.5 |
| 365 meters (400 yds) | 14.0 | 823 meters (900 yds) | 32.5 |
| 400 meters | 15.75 | 900 meters | 35.5 |
| 457 meters (500 yds) | 18.0 | 914 meters (1,000 yds) | 36.0 |
| 500 meters | 20.0 | 1,000 meters | 39.0 |

## METRIC/ENGLISH EQUIVALENTS

| METRIC 1 MOA (CM) | YARDS | METERS/YARDS | METERS | ENGLISH 1 MOA (IN) |
|---|---|---|---|---|
| 3 | 109 | 100 | 91 | 1 |
| 4.5 | 164 | 150 | 137 | 1.5 |
| 6 | 219 | 200 | 183 | 2 |
| 7.5 | 273 | 250 | 228 | 2.5 |
| 9 | 328 | 300 | 274 | 3 |
| 10.5 | 383 | 350 | 320 | 3.5 |
| 12 | 437 | 400 | 365 | 4 |
| 13.5 | 492 | 450 | 411 | 4.5 |
| 15 | 546 | 500 | 457 | 5 |
| 16.5 | 602 | 550 | 503 | 5.5 |
| 18 | 656 | 600 | 549 | 6 |
| 19.5 | 711 | 650 | 594 | 6.5 |
| 21 | 766 | 700 | 640 | 7 |
| 22.5 | 820 | 750 | 686 | 7.5 |
| 24 | 875 | 800 | 731 | 8 |
| 25.5 | 929 | 850 | 777 | 8.5 |
| 27 | 984 | 900 | 823 | 9 |
| 28.5 | 1039 | 950 | 869 | 9.5 |
| 30 | 1094 | 1000 | 914 | 10 |
| 31.5 | 1148 | 1050 | 960 | 10.5 |
| 33 | 1203 | 1100 | 1005 | 11 |

## Applied Ballistics

Ballistics, the study of projectiles in motion, can be broken down into three major areas. Interior or internal ballistic deals with the bullet in the rifle from primer detonation until it leaves the muzzle of the weapon. Exterior (also external) ballistics picks up after the bullet leaves the muzzle of the weapon and extends through the trajectory until the bullet impacts on the target or point of aim. Terminal ballistics is the study of what the bullet does upon impact with the target. Terminal velocity, location of the hit, and the bullet's design and construction will determine the effectiveness of the terminal ballistics.

When it is fired, a bullet travels a straight path in the bore of the rifle as long as it is confined in the barrel. As soon as the bullet is free of this constraint (exits the barrel), it immediately begins to fall, due to the effects of gravity, and its motion is retarded, due to air resistance. The path of the bullet through the air, as a result of these two influences, is called the bullet's trajectory.

If the barrel is horizontal, the forward motion imparted to the bullet by the detonation of the cartridge will cause it to travel in the direction of point A, but air resistance and the pull of gravity will cause it to strike point B (Figure 3-9-2). So as soon as the bullet is free from the constraint of the barrel, it begins to pull from the horizontal.

In order for point A to be struck, the barrel of the rifle must be elevated to some predetermined angle (Figure 3-9-3). The bullet's initial impulse will be in the direction of point C. However, because of initial angle, the bullet will fall, due again to air resistance and gravity, to point A. This initial angle is known as the angle of departure.

The size of the angle of departure depends on the shape of the trajectory and varies with the range or distance from the muzzle to the target, and for any given range, the angle of departure varies with the determining factors of the trajectory. The form of the trajectory is influenced by:

      o    The initial velocity (muzzle velocity).

      o    The angle of departure.

      o    Gravity.

      o    Air resistance.

      o    The rotation of the projectile (bullet) about its axis.

The relationship between initial velocity and air resistance is that the greater the amount of air resistance the bullet must overcome, the faster the bullet slows down as it travels through the air. A bullet with a lower initial velocity will be retarded less by air resistance and will retain a greater proportion of its initial velocity over a given distance. This relationship is important in that a light projectile with a higher initial (or short range) velocity will have a "flatter" initial trajectory but will have less initial and retained energy with which to incorporate the target, will be deflected more by wind, and will have a steeper trajectory at longer ranges. A comparatively heavy projectile will have a lower initial velocity and a steeper initial trajectory, will not retain its energy over a great distance (retained energy is proportional to the mass of the projectile), will be deflected less by wind, and will have a "flatter" long-range trajectory.

Angle of departure is the angle to which the muzzle of the rifle must be elevated above the horizontal in order for the bullet to strike a distant point. When the bullet departs the muzzle of the rifle, it immediately begins to fall to earth due to the constant pull of gravity. The angle of departure increases the height the bullet must fall before it reaches the ground. If a rifle barrel were set horizontally in a vacuum, a bullet fired from the barrel would reach the ground at a distant point at the same moment that a bullet merely dropped from the same height as the barrel would reach the ground. Despite the horizontal motion of the bullet, its velocity in the vertical plane is constant (due to the constant effect of gravity). Angle of departure in the air, however, is directly related to the time of flight of the projectile in that medium. The greater the angle at which the projectile departs the muzzle, the more time in the air it will retain and, therefore, the further it will travel before it strikes the ground. However, at the 45 degree point, the effect of gravity causes the bullet to begin to lose distance.

The angle of departure is not constant. Although the angle of departure may remain fixed, a number of variables will influence the angle of departure in a series of shots fixed at the same given distance. The differences in the internal ballistics of a given lot of ammunition will have an effect. A muzzle velocity, within a proven lot, will often vary as much as 60 feet per second between shots. Imperfections in the human eye will cause the angles of departure of successive shots to be inconsistent. Imperfections in the weapon, such as a faulty bedding, a worn bore, or worn sight adjustments are variables. Errors in the way the rifle is held or canted will affect the angle of departure. These are just a few of the factors that cause differences in the angle of departure, and these are the main reasons why successive shots under seemingly identical conditions do not hit at the same point on the target.

Gravity as an influence on the shape of a bullet's trajectory is a constant force. It neither increases nor decreases over time or distance. It is present, but given the variable dynamics

39

influencing the flight of a bullet, it is unimportant. Given that both air resistance and gravity influence the motion of a projectile, the initial velocity of the projectile and the air resistance are interdependent and indirectly influence the shape of the trajectory.

The single most important variable affecting the flight of a bullet is air resistance. It is air resistance, not gravity, that determine the shape of a bullet's trajectory. If gravity alone were the determining factor, the trajectory would have the shape of a parabola, where the angle of fall would be the same (or very nearly so) as the angle of departure. The result of air resistance, however, is that the shape of the trajectory is an elipse, where the angle of fall is steeper than the angle of departure.

The lands and grooves in the bore of the rifle impart a rotational motion to the bullet about its own axis. This rotational motion causes the projectile, as it travels through the air, to shift in the direction of rotation (in almost all cases to the right). This results in a drift that is caused by air resistance. A spinning projectile behaves precisely like a gyroscope. Pressure applied to the front of the projectile (air resistance) retards its forward motion but does not significantly upset its stability. However, upward pressure applied to the underside of the projectile, due to its downward travel caused by gravity, causes it to drift in the direction of spin. Fortunately, this drift is relatively insignificant at all but the greatest ranges (more than 1,000 yards).

Due to the combined influences just discussed, the trajectory of the bullet first crosses the line of sight (LOS) with a scarcely perceptible curve. The trajectory continues to rise to a point a little more than halfway to the target, called the maximum ordinate, beyond which it curves downward with a constantly increasing curve (possibly recrossing the LOS) until it hits the target (or ground). The point where the LOS meets the target is the point of aim (POA). The point where the bullet (trajectory) strikes the target is the point of impact (POI). Theoretically, the POA and the POI should coincide. In practical terms, because of one or more of the influences discussed, they rarely do. The greater the skill of the shooter and the more perfect the rifle and ammunition, the more often these two points will coincide.

The part of the trajectory between the muzzle and the maximum ordinate is called the rising branch of the trajectory, while the part beyond the maximum ordinate is called the falling branch of the trajectory. It is with the falling branch that we are most concerned, for this part of the trajectory contains the target and the ground in its vicinity. In computing the height of the trajectory, assuming the LOS is horizontal, and at regular intervals (usually 100 yards) the height of trajectory is measured and recorded as the ordinate. The distance from the muzzle to the ordinate known as the abscissa. The distance in front of the muzzle, within which the bullet does not rise higher than the object fired at, is called the danger space of the rising branch of the trajectory. The falling branch of the trajectory also contains a danger space. The point where the bullet falls into the height of the target and continues to the ground is known as the danger space of the falling branch of the trajectory.

Assuming that the point of aim is taken at the center of the target, the extent of the danger space is dependent upon (Figure ?):

    o    The height of the firer, whether he is standing, kneeling, or prone.

    o    The height of the target, whether he is standing, kneeling, or prone.

    o    The "flatness" of the trajectory--the ballistic properties of the cartridge used.

    o    The angle of the line-of-sight--above or below the horizontal.

    o    The slope of the ground where the target resides.

The point of aim also has a significant influence on the extent of the danger space. If the point of aim is taken at the top of the target, the total danger space will lie entirely behind the target. If the point of aim is taken at the foot of the target, the total danger space will lie entirely in front of the target. Thus, the extent of the total danger space, including the target, will be determined by where the point of aim is taken on the target. Only when the point of aim is at the center of the target will the total danger space (in relative terms) extend an equal distance in front of and behind the target.

## Shot Groups
If a rifle is fired a great number of times under conditions as nearly uniform as possible, the bullets striking the target will group themselves about a central point called the center of impact and will form a circular or eliptical group. The dimensions and shape of this shot group will vary, depending on the distance of the target from the firer. The circle, or elipse, formed by these shots constantly increases in size with the range. The line connecting the centers of impact of all shots at all ranges measured is called the mean trajectory, and the core containing the circumferences of all the circles would mark the limits of the sheaf. The mean trajectory is the average trajectory; all ordinates are compared to it, and angles of departure and fall refer only to it.

41

The pattern on the target made by all of the bullets is called the shot group. If the shot group is received on a vertical target, it is called a vertical shot group. If the group is received on a horizontal target, it is called a horizontal shot group. A large number of shots will form a shot group having the general shape of an elipse, with its major axis vertical. The shots will be symmetrically grouped about the center of impact, not necessarily about the point of aim. They will be grouped more densely near the center of impact than at the edges, and half of all the shots will be found in a strip approximately one-fourth the size of the whole group. The width of this strip is called the mean (or the 50 percent dispersion) vertical if measured vertically, or the mean lateral if measured laterally.

When considering the horizontal shot group, the mean lateral dispersion retains its same significance, but what is called the mean vertical dispersion on a vertical target is known as the mean longitudinal dispersion on a horizontal target. There is a significant relationship between the size, or dimensions, of a shot group and the size, or dimensions, of the target fired at. With a shot group of fixed dimensions, when the target is made sufficiently large, all shots fired will strike the target. Conversely, with a very small target, only a portion of the shots fired will strike the target; the rest of the shots will pass over, under, or to the sides of the target.

It is evident that the entire study of the practical application of exterior ballistics--hitting a target of variable dimensions at unknown distances--is one of the probability of a shot group of fixed dimensions (the firer's grouping ability) conforming to the dimensions of a given target. Added to this probability is the ability of the firer to compensate for environmental conditions and maintain an accurate zero.

One of the greatest paradoxes of sniping is that an average marksman has a greater probability of hitting targets at unknown distances than a good marksman if their respective abilities to judge distances and environmental conditions and maintain an accurate zero are equal. (The classification of "good marksman" and an "average marksman" refers only to the shooter's grouping ability.) A good marksman who has miscalculated wind or who is not accurately zeroed would expect to miss the target entirely. An average marksman, under identical conditions, would expect to obtain at least a few hits on the target; or if only one shot were fired, would have a high probability of obtaining a first-round hit. The above statement does not mean that average marksmen make better snipers. It does mean that the better the individual shoots (the better his grouping ability is), the more precise his ability to judge distance, calculate wind, and maintain his zero must be.

The entire study of practical exterior ballistics is the state of applying a shot group or a sheaf of shots over an estimated distance against a target of unknown or estimated dimensions and estimating the probability of obtaining a hit with a single shot contained within the sheaf of shots previously determined through shot group practices.

## Influence of Ground on the Shot Group (Sheaf of Shots)

When firing at targets at unknown distances under field conditions, the sniper must taken into consideration the lay of the ground and how it will affect his probable chances of hitting the target aimed at. Generally, the ground a sniper fires over will:

o    Be level.

o    Slope upward.

o    Slope downward.

As discussed previously, danger space is the distance measured above the line of sight within which the trajectory does not rise above the highest point of the target nor fall below its lowest point. The extent of the danger space depends on:

o    The relationship between the trajectory and the line of sight, or angle of fall, and therefore on the range curvature of the trajectory.

o    The height of the target.

o    The point of aim--the point where the line of sight meets the target.

o    The point of impact.

NOTE:    The longer the range, the shorter the danger space, due to the increasing curvature of the trajectory.

The displacing of the center of impact from the center of the target is a factor that must also be considered; it will often be the controlling factor. The danger space at ranges under 700 yards is affected by the position of the firer (height of the muzzle above the ground). The danger space increases as the height of the muzzle decreases. At longer ranges, no material effect is felt from different positions of the firer.

The influence of the ground on computing hit probability on a target at unknown distances results in the necessity of distinguishing between danger space and swept space (which are functions of the mean trajectory) and between these (danger space and swept space) and the dangerous zone (which is a function of the whole or a part of the cone of fire). For a given height of target and point of aim, the danger space is of fixed dimensions, while the swept space varies in relation with the slope of the ground.

43

Swept space is shorter on rising ground and longer on falling ground than the danger space. All the functions of the dangerous zone, such as the density of the group at a given distance from the center of impact, are correspondingly modified.


## 3-10. BALLISTICS

As applied to sniper marksmanship, ballistics may be defined as the study of the firing, flight, and effect of ammunition. Proper execution of marksmanship fundamentals and a thorough knowledge of ballistics ensure the successful completion of the mission. Tables and formulas in this section should be used only as guidelines since every rifle performs differently. Maximum ballistics data eventually result in a well-kept data book and knowledge gained through experience.

### Types of Ballistics
Ballistics may be divided into three distinct types: internal, external, and terminal.

o    Internal. The interior workings of a weapon and the functioning of its ammunition (what happens in the barrel).

o    External. The flight of the bullet from the muzzle to the target.

o    Terminal. What happens to the bullet after it hits the target.

### Terminology
To fully understand ballistics, the sniper should be familiar with the following terms:

Muzzle velocity--The speed of a bullet as it leaves the rifle barrel, measured in feet per second (fps). It varies according to various factors, such as ammunition type and lot number, temperature and humidity.

Line of Sight--A straight line from the eye through the aiming device to the point of aim.

Line of Departure--The line defined by the bore of the rifle or the path the bullet would take without gravity.

Trajectory--The path of the bullet as it flies to the target.

Midrange Trajectory/Maximum Ordinate--The highest point the bullet reaches on its way to the target. This point must be known to engage a target that requires firing underneath an overhead obstacle, such as a bridge or a tree. Inattention to midrange

44

trajectory may cause the sniper to hit the obstacle instead of the target.

Bullet Drop--How far the bullet drops from the line of departure to the point of impact.

Time of Flight--The amount of time it takes for the bullet to reach the target from the time it exits the rifle.

Retained Velocity--The speed of the bullet when it reaches the target. Due to drag, the velocity will be reduced.


## Effects on Trajectory

Mastery of marksmanship fundamentals and field skills is not the only requirements for being a sniper. Some of the factors that have an influence on the trajectory are:

o   Gravity. The sniper would not have a maximum range without gravity. A fired bullet would continue to move much the same as items floating in space. As soon as the bullet exits the muzzle of the weapon, gravity begins to pull it down, requiring the sniper to use his elevation adjustment. At extended ranges, the sniper actually aims the muzzle of his rifle above his line of sight and lets gravity pull the bullet down into the target. Gravity is always present, and the sniper must compensate for this through elevation adjustments or holdover techniques.

o   Drag. Drag is the slowing effect the atmosphere has on the bullet. This effect either increases or decreases, according to the air--that is, the less dense the air, the less drag and vice versa. Factors affecting drag and air density are: temperature, altitude/ barometric pressure, humidity, bullet efficiency, and the wind.

o   Temperature. The higher the temperature, the less dense the air. If the sniper zeroes at 60 degrees F and he fires at 80 degrees F, the air is less dense, thereby causing an increase in muzzle velocity and higher impact. A 20-degree change equals a one-minute elevation change on the rifle.

o   Altitude/barometric pressure. Since the air pressure is less at higher altitutdes, the air is less dense. Thus, the bullet is more efficient and impacts higher due to less drag. Table 3-1 shows the appropriate effect of change of impact from sea level to 10,000 feet if the rifle is zeroed at sea level. Impact will be the point of aim at sea level. For example, a rifle zeroed at sea level and fired at 700 meters at 5,000 feet will hit 1.6 minutes high.

o   Humidity. Humidity varies along with the altitude and temperature. Table 3-1 considers the changes in altitudes.

Problems can occur if extreme humidity changes exist in the area of operations. That is, when humidity goes up, impact goes down; when humidity goes down, impact goes up. Since impact is affected by humidity, a 20 percent change in humidity equals about one minute as a rule of thumb. Keeping a good data book during training and acquiring experience are the best teachers.

     o     Bullet efficiency. This is called a bullet's ballistic coefficient. The imaginary perfect bullet is rated as being 1.00. Match bullets range from .500 to about .600. The M118 173-grain match bullet is rated at .515.

     o     Wind. Wind is discussed in Chapter 3-13.

| RANGE (METERS) | 2,500 FEET *(ASL) | 5,000 FEET (ASL) | 10,000 FEET (ASL) |
|---|---|---|---|
| 100 | .05 | .08 | .13 |
| 200 | .1 | .2 | .34 |
| 300 | .2 | .4 | .6 |
| 400 | .4 | .5 | .9 |
| 500 | .5 | .9 | 1.4 |
| 600 | .6 | 1.0 | 1.8 |
| 700 | 1.0 | 1.6 | 2.4 |
| 800 | 1.3 | 1.9 | 3.3 |
| 900 | 1.6 | 2.8 | 4.8 |
| 1,000 | 1.8 | 3.7 | 6.0 |

*Above sea level

Table 3-1. Point of impact rise at new elevation (minutes)

## Selected Ballistic Information

| Ammunition | Bullet Type | Ballistic Coefficient | Muzzle Velocity |
|---|---|---|---|
| M193 | 55 FMJBT | .260 | 3200 FPS |
| M80 | 147 FMJBT | .400 | 2808 FPS |
| M118 | 173 FMJBT | .515 | 2610 FPS |
| M852 | 168 HPBT | .475 | 2675 FPS |
| M72 | 173 FMJBT | .515 | 2640 FPS |

3-11.  SNIPER DATA BOOK

The sniper data book contains a collection of data cards. The sniper uses the data cards to record firing results and all elements that had an effect on firing the weapon. This can vary from information about weather conditions to the attitude of the firer on that particular day. The sniper can refer to this information later to understand his weapon, the weather effects, and his shooting ability on a given day. One of the most important items of information he will record is the cold barrel zero of his weapon. A cold barrel zero refers to the first round fired from the weapon at a given range. It is critical that the sniper know this by shooting the first round at different ranges. For example, Monday, 400 meters; Tuesday, 500 meters; Wednesday, 600 meters. When the barrel warms up, later shots begin to group one or two minutes higher or lower, depending on specific rifle characteristics. Information is recorded on DA Form 5785-R (Sniper's Data Card) (Figure 3-11-1). A blank copy of this form is located in appendix N for local reproduction.

When used properly, the data sheet will provide the necessary information for initial sight settings at each distance or range. It also provides a basis for analyzing the performance of the sniper and his rifle and is a valuable aid in making bold and accurate sight changes. The most competent sniper would not be able to consistently hit the center of the target if he were unable to analyze his performance or if he had no record of his performance or conditions affecting his shooting.

**Entries**
The three phases in writing information on the data card are: before firing, during firing, and after firing.

**Before Firing.** Information that is written before firing is:

o      Range. The distance to the target.

o      Rifle and telescope number. The serial numbers of the rifle and telescope.

o      Date. Date of firing.

o      Ammunition. Type and lot number of ammunition.

o      Light. Amount of light (overcast, clear, and so forth).

o      Mirage. Whether a mirage can be seen or not (good, bad, fair, and so forth).

o      Temperature. Temperature on the range.

o      Hour. Time of firing

o    Light (diagram).  Draw an arrow in the direction the light is shining.

o    Wind.  Draw an arrow in the direction that the wind is blowing, and record its average velocity and cardinal direction (N, NE, S, SW, and so forth).

During Firing.  Information that is written while firing is:

o    Elevation.  Elevation setting used and any correction needed.  For example:  The target distance is 600 meters; the sniper sets the elevation dial to 6.  The sniper fires and the round hits the target 6 inches low of center.  He then adds one minute (one click) of elevation (+1).

o    Windage. Windage setting used and any correction needed. For example:  The sniper fires at a 600 meter target with a windage setting on 0; the round impacts 15 inches right of center.  He will then add 2 1/2 minutes left to the windage dial (L/2 1/2).  When firing the M21, the sniper draws the windage holdoff on the silhouette in the "HOLD" box.

o    Shot.  The column of information about a particular shot. For example:  Column 1 is for the first round; column 10 is for the tenth round.

o    Elevation.  Elevation used (ex. 6+1, 6-1).

o    Wind.  Windage used (ex. L/2, 1/2, O, R/1/2).

o    Call.  Where the aiming point was when the weapon fired.

o    Large silhouette.  Used to record the exact impact of the round on the target.  This is recorded by writing the shot's number on the large silhouette in the same place it hit the target.

After Firing.  After firing, the sniper writes any comments about the  firing in the remarks section:

o    Comments about the weapon, firing conditions (time allowed for fire), or his condition (nervous, felt bad, felt good, and so forth).

o    Corrected no-wind zero:  Show the elevation and windage in minutes and clicks that was correct for this position and distance under no-wind conditions.

o    Remarks:  Note any equipment, performance, weather conditions, or range conditions that had a good or bad effect on the firing results.

Analysis

When the sniper leaves the firing line, he compares weather conditions to the information needed to hit the point of aim/point of impact. Since he fires in all types of weather conditions, he must be aware of temperature, light, mirage, and wind. The sniper must consider other possibilities:

o     Compare sight settings with previous firing sessions. If the sniper always has to fine-tune for windage or elevation, there is a chance he needs a sight change (slip a scale).

o     Compare the ammunition by lot number for the best rifle and ammunition combination.

Compare all groups fired under each condition. Check the low and high shots as well as those to the left and the right of the main group. Of course, less dispersion is desired. If groups are tight, they are easily moved to the center of the target; if scattered, there is a problem. Check the telescope focus and ensure that the rifle is cleaned correctly. Remarks in the data book will also help.

Make corrections. Record corrections in the data book, such as position and sight adjustment information to ensure retention. The sniper should compare hits to calls. If they agree, this is an indication that the zero is correct and that any compensation for the effects of the weather is correct. If the calls and hits are consistently out of the target, sight adjustment or more position and trigger control work is necessary.

He should compare the weather conditions and location of the groups on the latest data sheet to previous data sheets to determine how much and in which direction the sights should be moved to compensate for the weather conditions. If better results are obtained with a different sight picture under an unusual light condition, the firer should use this sight picture whenever firing under that particular light condition. A different sight picture may necessitate adjusting the sights. After establishing how much to compensate for the effects of weather or which sight picture works best under various light conditions, the firer should commit this information to memory.

The firing data sheets used for training or zeroing should be kept for future reference. Rather than carrying the firing data sheets during sniper training exercises or combat, the firer can carry or tape on his weapon stock a list of the elevation and windage zeros at various ranges.

## 3-12. ZEROING THE RIFLE

Depending upon the situation, a sniper may be called upon to deliver an effective shot at ranges up to 1,000 meters or more.

This requires the sniper to zero his rifle (with telescopic and iron sights) at most of the ranges that he may be expected to fire. When using telescopic sights, he need only zero for elevation at 300 meters (100 meters for windage) and confirm at the more distance ranges. His success depends on a "one round, one hit" philosophy. He may not get a second shot. Therefore, he must accurately zero his rifle so that when applying the fundamentals he can be assured of an accurate hit.

A zero is the alignment of the sights with the bore of the rifle so that the bullet will impact on the target at the desired point of aim. However, the aiming point, the sight, and the bore will coincide at two points. These points are called the zero.

## Characteristics of the Sniper Rifle Iron Sights

The iron sights of the M24 and the M21 are adjustable for both windage and elevation. While these iron sights are a backup to the telescope, and are used operationally only under extraordinary circumstances, it is in the sniper's best interest to be fully capable with them. Iron sights are excellent for developing marksmanship skills. They force the sniper to concentrate on sight alignment, sight picture, and follow-through. The sights on the M24 and the M21 differ in details, but share many similar operating precedures.

## M24

The M24 has a hooded front sight that has interchangeable inserts. These inserts range from circular discs to posts, each in varying sizes. It is recommended that the sniper use the post front sight to develop the sight picture that is consistent with the majority of US systems. The rear sight is the Palma match sight and has elevation and windage adjustments in 1/4 MOA. The elevation knob is on the top of the sight, and the windage knob is on the right side of the sight. Turning the elevation knob in the dirction marked "UP" raises the point of impact (POI) and turning the windage knob in the direction marked "R" moves the POI to the right.

## M21

The rear sight of the M21 rifle is correctable for both windage and elevation. The windage knob is located on the right of the rear sight mechanism; the elevation knob is on the left. The rear sight also consists of a National Match sight base and a National Match hooded aperture. Each click of the elevation knob on the M21 is worth one MOA and moves the strike of the bullet approximately 1 inch on the target for every 100 meters of range. As the M21 is equipped with a hooded rear-sight aperture, it has a one-half minute elevation change capability. To move the strike of the bullet up one-half minute, the hood must be rotated so that the notch in the hood is up. If the notch in the hood is already up and a one-half minute increase in elevation is desired, the elevation knob must be moved up one click and the hood rotated so that the notch is down. For moving the sights downward, the same procedure is used, but in reverse. The windage knob produces one-half minute change in windage for each click. Thus, the M21 sniper rifle is capable of one-half minute changes in both elevation and windage. The rear sight can be adjusted from 0 to 72 clicks in elevation and 32 clicks to the right and 32 clicks to the left of the center line of the windage gauge.

## Adjustment of the Rear Sight
Mechanical windage zero is determined by aligning the sight base index line with the center line of the windage gauge. The location of the movable index line indicates the windage used or the windage zero of the rifle; for example, if the index line is to the left of the center line of the gauge, this is a left reading; windage zero can be determined by simply counting the number of clicks back to the mechanical zero.

The elevation of any range is determined by counting the number of clicks down to mechanical elevation zero (hooded aperture down for the M21).

Sight adjustment or manipulation is a very important aspect of training that must be thoroughly learned by the sniper. This can best be accomplished through explanation and practical work in the manipulation of the sights.

The rear sight must be moved in the direction that the shot or shot group is to be moved. To move the rear sight or a shot group to the right, the windage knob is turned clockwise. The rule to remember is: "Push right--pull left." To raise the elevation or a shot group, the elevation knob is turned clockwise. To lower the elevation or a shot, the elevation knob is turned counterclockwise.

## Zeroing the Sniper Rifle Using the Iron Sights
The most precise method of zeroing a sniper rifle with the iron sights is to fire the rifle and adjust the sights to hit a given point at a specific range. The rifle is zeroed in 100-meter increments from 100 to 900 meters. The targets are placed at each range; then the sniper fires one or more three-round shot groups at each aiming point, adjusting the rear sight until the center of the shot group and the aiming point coincide at each range. The initial zeroing for each range should be accomplished from the prone supported position. The sniper can then zero from those positions and ranges that are most practical. There is no need to zero from the least steady positions at longer ranges.


Zeroing procedure for iron sights:

    o    Center the front sight on the sight block (M21 only). There is an allen screw at the rear of the front sight. Loosen it and slide the front sight on the block until it is centered. Retighten the allen screw. For the M24, ensure that the front and rear sights are snugly attached to the correct dovetails on the SWS.

    o    Center the rear sight by aligning the sight base index line and the center line for windage guage.  For the M21: rotate the windage knob in one direction until it stops, then backing off 32 clicks.  The index line and windage guage should be aligned. This indicates the mechanical windage zero.

    o    Fire a three-round shot group.   Use a solid prone supported position.  Note the position of the shot group on the target, but do not make any corrections.   Stand up and wait 1 minute, then assume the same position and fire another shot group. By firing two separate groups, the sniper gets a much more accurate indication of errors due to the sight being out of alignment and can prevent errors due to a poor shooting position.

    o    Note the position of the two shot groups in relation to the point of aim.  Determine the amount of error and adjust the rear sight for windage and elevation until the center of the shot group and aiming point coincide at each range.

    o    Determine the elevation zero for each range by counting the number of clicks down to the mechanical elevation zero (hooded aperture index notch down).

    o    The location of the movable index line indicates the windage used or the windage zero of the rifle.   Determine the windage zero by counting the number of clicks back to the mechanical zero.

## M24 Iron Sight Details
    Elevation knob adjustments: By turning the elevation knob located on the top of the rear sight in the "UP" direction raises the point of impact; turning the knob in the opposite direction lowers the point of impact.  Each click of adjustment equals .25 MOA.

    Windage knob adjustments: By turning the windage knob located on the right side of the rear sight in the "R" direction to moves the impact of the round to the right; turning the knob in the opposite direction moves the point of impact to the left.   Each click of adjustment equals .25 MOA.

    Calibrating rear sight: After zeroing the sights to the rifle, loosen the elevation and windage indicator plate screws with the wrench provided.  Align the "0" on the plate with the "0" on the sight body, then retighten the plate screws. Next, loosen the set screws in each knob and align the "0" of the knob with the reference line on the sight.  Press the sight and tighten the set screws.  Sharpen or soften the click to preference by loosening or tightening the spring screws equally on the knob.  Now, windage and elevation corrections can be made and the sniper can return quickly to the "zero" standard.

Graduations: There are 12 divisions or 3 MOA adjustments in each knob revolution. Total elevation adjustment is 60 MOA and total windage adjustment is 36 MOA. Adjustment scales are of the "vernier" type. Each graduation on the scale plate equals 3 MOA. Each graduation on the sight base scale equals 1 MOA.

To use the scales, the sniper:

o    Notes the point at which graduations on both scales are aligned (Figure 3-12-1).

o    Counts the number of full 3 MOA graduations from "0" on the scale plate to "0" on the sight base scale.

o    Adds this figure to the number of MOAs from "0" on the bottom scale to the point where the two graduations are aligned.

## Calibrating the M21 Iron Sight
The index lines on the elevation knob designate hundreds of meters or yards to the target. The elevation knob that is calibrated for meters (most common) has a "M" stamped into its body. The elevation knob that is calibrated in yards does not have the "M" stamped on its body. Every other line is numbered with an even number, lines in between are the odd hundreds of meters. For example, the line marked with a number "2" is the 200m index line. The index line between the numbers 2 and 4 is the 300m index line. If the distance to the target is not in exact hundreds of meters, the elevation knob should be clicked between the index lines to approximate the distance. If the target distance is less than 100m, the 100m setting should be used; the difference in impact is minimal.

To calibrate the elevation knob, the sniper must first zero the rifle at a known distance that correlates to one of the index lines on the elevation knob. (The recommended distance is 300m).

Once zeroing is completed, calibration involves the following steps:

Step 1: Turn the elevation knob forward (down, away from the sniper), and move the rear sight aperture assembly to its lowest setting (mechanical zero), counting the number of clicks. This number of clicks is elevation zero and must be remembered for use in the calibration process. For example, the number will be 10 clicks.

Step 2: Loosen the screw in the center of the elevation knob using a dime or screwdriver (about one turn) until the knob can be rotated forward. Be careful not to loosen the screw too much or it may fall and become lost.  It is critical that once the screw is loosened to never rotate the elevation knob clockwise (up or toward the sniper) during calibration.  This could result in improper calibration.

Step 3:  Turn the elevation knob forward (down, away from the sniper) until the index line on the receiver lines up with the index line on the knob that correlates to the distance at which the rifle was zeroed--for example, 300 yards.  This is the index line between 2 and 4.  If the setting is passed (even by one click), rotate the elevation knob counterclockwise (down, away from the sniper) until the index lines match up.  <u>Never</u> rotate the knob in the UP direction (clockwise, toward the sniper) with the screw in the elevation knob loose.

Step 4:  Remember the number of clicks (for example, 10) when zeroing the rifle and begin rotating the elevation knob counterclockwise (down, away from the sniper).  Count the clicks until the elevation knob has been rotated the same number of clicks that were on the rifle when zeroed.  If too many clicks are used, start over at Step 3.

Step 5:  Now, hold the elevation knob, being careful not to allow it to rotate, then tighten the screw in the center of the elevation knob as tight as possible.  Hold the elevation knob carefully with a pair of pliers to ensure the screw is tight.

Step 6:  To check the calibration, rotate the elevation knob to mechanical zero (all the way down), then count the number of clicks to zero.  This should result in the index line on the receiver being lined up with the correct index line on the elevation knob (between 2 and 4).  If this happens, the rear sight is now calibrated for elevation.  If not, repeat Steps 1 through 5.

## Characteristics of the Sniper Rifle Telescopic Sight

Sniper telescopic sights have turret assemblies for the adjustment of elevation and windage.  The upper assembly is the elevation, and the assembly on the right is for windage.  These assemblies have knobs that are marked for corrections of a given value in the direction indicated by the arrow.  The M3A and the ART series use a similar system for zeroing.  The sniper moves the knobs in the direction that he wants the shot group to move on the target.  See Appendix I for details on the telescopic sights.


## M3A

The M3A is graduated to provide 1 MOA of adjustment for each click of its elevation knob, and 1/2 MOA of adjustment for each click of its windage knob.  This sight is designed to provide audible and tactile clicks.  The elevation turret knob is marked in meters, in 50-meter increments from 100-1000m.

<u>ART I/II</u>

The ART series is graduated to provide 1/2 MOA adjustments for both elevation and windage adjusting screws. These adjustment screws are marked with painted index lines, and are friction only. The sniper must observe the screws while he is making adjustments. The scale on each turret of the ART I and ART II has 48 index lines, each representing a half-minute of movement. At 100 meters, one revolution of the adjusting screw equals 48 half-minutes (48 half-inches) or 24 full minutes (24 inches).

## <u>Zeroing the Sniper Weapon System With the Telescopic Sight</u>

The most precise method of zeroing the sniper rifle for elevation using the scope sight is to fire and adjust the sight to hit a given point at 300 meters. For windage, the scope should be zeroed at 100 meters. This rules out as much wind effect as possible. After zeroing at 100 meters, the sniper should confirm his zero out to 900 meters in 100-meter increments. The bullseye-type target (200 yard targets, NSN SR1-6920-00-900-8204) should be used for zeroing.

The sniper should use the following zeroing procedure:

o    Properly mount the scope to the rifle.

o    Select or prepare a distinct target (aiming cross) at 300 meters for elevation or 100 meters for windage.

o    Assume the supported prone position.

o    Loosen the power ring lock on the ART scopes by turning the knurled nut counterclockwise.

o    Turn the power adjustment ring to the low power/range setting (3 index) on the ART scopes. The M3A is a fixed 10 power scope. Set elevation to the range at which you are presently zeroing.

o    While aiming, superimpose the cross hair over the aiming cross and position the 30-inch target between the vertical stadia marks on the ART I. These are not present on the ART II or the M3A.

o    Fire a three-round shot group and determine its location and distance from the aiming cross.

o    Using the elevation and windage rule, determine the number of clicks (half-minutes of elevation and windage for the ART I and ART II, full minute of elevation for the M3A1) necessary to move the center of the group to the center of the aiming cross.

o    Remove the elevation and windage turret caps and make the necessary sight adjustments. Then replace the turret caps. In making sight adjustments, remember to turn the adjusting screws in the direction that you wish to move the strike of the bullet or group. With the ART I and ART II always go past the intended setting, then return to the setting. Finally, tap the turret to get it to settle.

o    Fire additional groups as necessary to ensure that the center of the shot group coincides with the point of aim at 300 meters.

o    Zero the elevation and windage scales and replace the turret caps.

o    The rifle is now zeroed for 300 meters.

o    To engage targets at other ranges, you need only set the desired range (300 to 900 meters, inscribed on the focusing ring for the ART I or ART II) opposite the reference dot on the top of the scope. For the M3A set the range on the elevation turret. To engage targets at undetermined ranges, range on the target, and in conjunction with ranging, for the ART I and ART II, the ballistic cam will elevate the scope to compensate for trajectory. The M3A must be manually set on the elevation turret after ranging using the mil dots in the scope.

NOTE:    The elevation and windage adjusting screws should not be moved beyond the point where reticle movement stops. The mechanism may become disengaged and require factory repair.

## Adjustable Ranging Telescope (ART I and ART II)

All rifle telescopic sights, regardless of stated instructions, should be placed on 3 power (for ART scopes) and zeroed for windage at 100 meters. This will negate a majority of wind errors and will produce, as closely as possible, a no-wind zero. Once the windage is set on the windage adjustment, it must be zeroed and marked. Elevation for all scopes should be zeroed at 300 meters. Even though the ART II states that the weapon can be zeroed at 100 meters, this is inadvisable due to elevation cam wear, elevation cam post wear, and/or improper height adjustment. Even though the ART scopes should "automatically" adjust for ranges once they have been zeroed, the shooter must shoot each 100-meter increment to confirm auto ranging. If a discrepancy exists, the shooter must record this discrepancy in his shooter's log. This is imperative due to cam wear variances that cause the scope to improperly elevate as the shooter turns the cam. Some ART IIs possess a 100-1000m cam. After zeroing at 300 meters, the shooter must check his zero at 100 and 200 meters as marked on the cam. This is important, as the cam post height adjustment may very well be too low to permit this adjustment. The key to the ART scope system is to remember scope age and wear on the cams. This almost always produces a discrepancy in the auto range system for elevation zero at all the ranges. This does not affect the ability of the scope to range on a target. The 150-450m cam for the ART II suffers the same problems.

Due to the ART scope mounting system and the ART scope ranging cam several items must be checked to maintain consistent grouping. First, the shooter must hand tighten the mounting screws for the ART I and ART II as tight as possible. He should then fire five rounds and retighten the scope. At this time he should mark the knurled knobs and mount to give visual reference to the tightening point. Then after every 5 to 10 rounds of firing, he should visually and manually check for mount tightness. Both scope mounts have a tendency to work loose during firing.

The ART II power ring and range cam can be separated so that the firer can utilize 9x at 300 meters or any other power and range combination. However, this procedure should be used with extreme caution and only in circumstances when only one shot is to be fired. When the power ring and the range cam on the ART II are separated, the power ring remains tight and will hold its position, but the range cam will not. The range cam will float after each shot, changing the elevation. If more than one shot is necessary, the range cam must be checked after each shot. If the power ring and range cam are separated and are not fired for a period of time, the range cam must be checked before the weapon is fired.

AN/PVS-2 Night Vision Device
The AN/PVS-2 may be zeroed during daylight hours or during hours of darkness. However, the operator may experience some difficulty in attempting to zero just before darkness (dusk). The light level is too low at dusk to permit the operator to resolve his zero target with the lens cap cover in place, but the light level at dusk is still intense enough to cause the sight to automatically cut off unless the lens cap cover is in position over the objective lens. The sniper will normally zero the sight for the maximum practical range that he can be expected to observe and fire, depending on the level of illumination.

The sight is zeroed in the following manner:

o       Place or select a distinct target at the desired zeroing range. A steel target provides the easiest target to spot because bullet splash is indicated by a spark as the bullet strikes the steel. Assume the prone supported position, supporting the weapon and night vision sight combination with sandbags or other available equipment that will afford maximum stability.

o       Bore sight the sight to the rifle. To do this, place the iron sight windage and elevation zero on the rifle for the zeroing range and adjust the weapon position until the correct sight picture is obtained on the aiming point at the zeroing range. Move

57

the eye to the night vision sight and observe the location of the reticle pattern in relation to the reference aiming point. If the reference aiming point on the target and the reference point of aim of the reticle pattern do not coincide, move the elevation and azimuth adjustment knobs until these aiming points coincide.

o    Place the reference point of aim of the reticle pattern (Figure 3-12-2) on the center of mass of the target, or on a distinct aiming point on the target, and fire enough rounds to obtain a good shot group. Check the target to determine the center of the shot group in relation to the reticle point of aim.

o    Adjust the night vision sight to move the reticle aiming reference point to the center of the shot group. When making adjustments for errors in elevation or azimuth, move the sight in the direction of the error. For example, if the shot group is high and to the left of the reticle point of aim, compensate for the error by moving the sight to the left and up.

NOTE:    Each click of the azimuth or elevation knob will move the strike of the round 2 inches for each 100 meters of range.

To engage targets at ranges other than the zero range, apply hold-off to compensate for the rise and fall in the trajectory of the round.

## AN/PVS-4 Night Vision Device
Zeroing the AN/PVS-4 is similar to zeroing with standard optical sights because (unlike the AN/PVS-2) the AN/PVS-4 mounts over the bore of the weapons system and has internal windage and elevation adjustments (Figure 3-12-3).

## Factors Affecting or Influencing the SWS Zero
The effects of the weather are the primary causes of error in the strike of the bullet and factors affecting zero. The wind, mirage, light, temperature, and humidity all have an effect on the bullet, the sniper, or both. Sniping is often accomplished under extremes of weather, therefore, all effects must be considered. Wind conditions constantly present the greatest problem to the sniper. The wind has considerable effect on the bullet that increases with the range. Winds also have considerable effect on the shooter. The stronger the wind, the more difficulty the shooter has in holding the rifle steady. Light affects the shooter in different ways. This subject is very controversial as light may or may not have an effect.

## Periodic Checking
A sniper cannot expect his zero to remain absolutely constant. Periodic checking of the zero is required after disassembly of the sniper rifle for maintenance and cleaning, for changes in ammunition lots, as a result of severe weather changes, and to

ensure accuracy of fire to obtain first-shot hits. The rifle must be zeroed by the individual who will use it. Individual differences in stock or spot weld, eye relief, position, and trigger control usually result in each sniper having a different zero with the same rifle or a change in zero after moving from one position to another.

## Confirming Zero

After a rifle has been zeroed and it becomes necessary to confirm this zero for any reason, the rifle can be zeroed again by firing at a known distance with the sight set on the old zero. If a sight adjustment is necessary to hit the aiming point, this zero change will remain constant at all ranges. For example, if firing at a distance of 500 meters with the old zero and it becomes necessary to raise the elevation three clicks to hit the aiming point, the elevation zero should be raised three clicks at all ranges.

## Changing Zero

Before changing the zero, windage, or elevation, the sniper must consider the effects of weather. A sniper rifle can change the zero because of wear, abuse, or repairs, Extreme changes of humidity or temperature can warp the stock or affect the ammunition.

## Field Expedient Zeroing

The sniper may need to confirm his zero in a field environment. A weapon that has been dropped or taken through excessive climatic changes as may be experienced by deploying world-wide are good reasons for confirming the SWS's zero. This method may also be used when the time or the situation does not permit the use of a known distance range. This technique is best used for confirming old zeros.

The sniper will need an observer equipped with binoculars or a spotting telescope to assist him. The sniper and observer pick out an aiming point in the center of an area--hillside, brick house, or any surface where the strike of the bullet can be observed. The range to this point can be determined by the ranging device on the telescope, map survey, by the range card of another weapon, or by ground measurement.

Once the firer has assumed a stable position, the observer must position himself to the rear of the firer and close to him. The observer's binoculars or telescope should be positioned approximately 18 to 24 inches above the weapon and directly in line with the axis of the bore. With his optics in this position, the observer can see the trace of the bullet as it moves downrange. The trace or shock wave of the bullet sets up an air turbulence sufficient enough to be observed in the form of a vapor trail. The trace of the bullet enables the observer to follow the path of the bullet in its trajectory towards its impact area. The trace will

59

disappear prior to impact, making it appear to the inexperienced observer that the bullet struck above or beyond its actual impact point. For example, at 300 meters the trace will disappear approximately 5 inches above the impact point. At 500 meters the trace will disappear approximately 25 inches above the impact point.

Wind causes lateral movement of the bullet. This lateral movement will appear as a drifting of the trace in the direction that the wind is blowing. This movement must be considered when determining windage zero. The observer must be careful to observe the trace at its head and not be misled by the bending tail of the trace in a stout crosswind. Before firing the first round, the sniper must set his sights so that he will hit on or near his aiming point. This sight setting is based on the old zero or an estimate. The sniper fires a shot and gives a call to the observer. If the strike of the bullet could not be observed, the observer gives a sight adjustment based on the trace of the bullet.

If the first shots do not hit the target, the shooter may fire at the four corners of the target. One of the rounds will hit the target, and the shooter can use this hit to make an adjustment to start the zeroing process. Once the strike of the bullet can be observed in the desired impact area, the observer compares the strike with the call and gives sight adjustments until the bullet impact coincides with the aiming point.

## Firing at Targets for which No Definite Zero has been Established

When firing on targets at a range of 100 meters or less, the 100-meter zero should be used. The difference between the impact of the bullet and the aiming point increases as the range increases if the sights are not moved. If the sniper's zero is 46 clicks at 900 meters and 40 clicks at 800 meters and if he establishes the range of the target at 850 meters, he should use a sight setting of 43 clicks rather than using his 800- or 900-meter zero or the hold-off method. At any range, moving the sights is preferred over the hold-off method.

## Firing the 25-Meter Range

Dial the telescope to 300 meters for elevation and to zero for windage. Aim and fire at a target that is at a 25-yard distance. Adjust the telescope until rounds are impacting one (1.0) inch above the point of aim. To confirm, fire the SWS on a KD range out to its maximum effective range.

For iron sights, the sniper may fire on a 25-meter range to obtain a battle-sight zero. The sniper then subtracts one minute (one click) of elevation from the battle-sight zero to get a 200-meter zero. The sniper may then use the following table to determine the necessary increases in elevation to engage targets out to 600 meters:

200 to 300 meters--two minutes.

300 to 400 meters--three minutes.

400 to 500 meters--four minutes.

500 to 600 meters--five minutes.

NOTE:     This table is based on the average change of several sniper rifles, and while the changes may not result in an "exact" point of aim, or point of impact zero, the sniper should not miss his target.

## 3-13.  ENVIRONMENTAL EFFECTS

For the highly trained sniper, the effects of weather are the main cause of error in the strike of the bullet. Wind, mirage, light, temperature, and humidity all have some effect on the bullet, the sniper, or both. Some effects are insignificant, depending on average conditions of sniper employment. However, sniping is often accomplished under extremes of weather; therefore, all effects must be considered.

### Wind Classification

The condition that constantly presents the greatest problem to the sniper is the wind. The wind has a considerable effect on the bullet, and the effect increases with the range. This is due mainly to the slowing of the bullet's velocity combined with a longer flight time. This allows the wind to have a greater effect on the bullet as distances increase. The result is a loss of stability. Wind also has a considerable effect on the sniper. The stronger the wind, the more difficulty the sniper has in holding the rifle steady. The effect on the sniper can be partially offset with good training, conditioning, and the use of supported positions.

Since the sniper must know how much effect the wind will have on the bullet, he must be able to classify the wind. The best method is to use the clock system (Figure 3-13-1). With the sniper at the center of the clock and the target at 12 o'clock, the wind is assigned three values: full, half, and no value. Full value means that the force of the wind will have a full effect on the flight of the bullet. These winds come from 3 and 9 o'clock. Half value means that a wind at the same speed, but from 1,2,4,5,7,8,10, and 11 o'clock, will move the bullet only half as much as a full-value wind. No valued means that a wind from 6 or 12 o'clock will have little or no effect on the flight of the bullet at close ranges. The no-value wind has a definite effect on the bullet at long ranges (beyond 600 meters) if it is not blowing directly from 6 or 12 o'clock. This is the most difficult wind to fire in due to its switching or fishtail effect, which requires frequent sight changes. Depending on the velocity of this type of wind, it may have a slight effect on the vertical displacement of the bullet.

## Wind Velocity

Before adjusting the sight to compensate for wind, the sniper must determine wind direction and velocity. He may use certain indicators to accomplish this. These are range flags, smoke, trees, grass, rain, and the sense of feel. However, the preferred method of determining wind direction and velocity is reading mirage. In most cases, wind direction can be determined simply by observing the indicators.

A common method of estimating the velocity of the wind during training is to watch the range flag (Figure 3-13-2). The sniper determines the angle between the flag and pole, in degrees, then divides by the constant number 4. The result gives the approximate velocity in miles per hour. This is based on the use of the heavier cotton range flags, not nylon flags, which are now used on most ranges.

If no flag is visible, the sniper holds a piece of paper, grass, cotton, or some other light material at shoulder level, then drops it. He then points directly at the spot where it lands and divides the angle between his body and arm by the constant number 4. This gives him the approximate wind velocity in miles per hour (Figure 3-13-3).

If these methods cannot be used, the following information is helpful in determining velocity:

| Wind Velocity (mph) | Effect |
|---|---|
| 0 - 3 | The wind can barely be felt, but may be detected by mirage or smoke drifts. |
| 3 - 5 | The wind can be felt on the face. |
| 5 - 9 | The leaves in the trees and long grass are in constant motion. |
| 9 - 14 | The wind raises dust, loose paper and moves small branches in trees. |
| 14 - 20 | The wind causes small trees to sway. |
| 20 - 26 | There is a strong breeze and the large branches in the trees are in motion. |

## Mirage

A mirage is a reflection of the heat through layers of air at different temperatures and densities as seen on a warm, bright day. With the telescope, the sniper can see a mirage as long as there is a difference in ground and air temperatures. Proper reading of the mirage enables the sniper to estimate wind speed and direction with a high degree of accuracy. The sniper uses the M49 spotting scope to read the mirage. Since the wind nearest to mid-range has the greatest effect on the bullet, he tries to determine velocity at that point. He can do this in one of two ways:

o He focuses on an object at midrange, then places the telescope back on to the target without readjusting the focus.

o He can also focus on the target, then back off the focus one-quarter turn counterclockwise. This makes the target appear fuzzy, but the mirage will be clear.

As observed through the telescope, the mirage appears to move with the same velocity as the wind, except when blowing straight into or away from the telescope. Then, the mirage gives the appearance of moving straight upward with no lateral movement. This is called a boiling mirage. A boiling mirage may also be seen when the wind is constantly changing direction. For example, a full-value wind blowing from 9 o'clock to 3 o'clock suddenly changes direction. The mirage will appear to stop moving from left to right and will present a boiling appearance. When this occurs, the inexperienced observer may direct the sniper to fire with the "0" wind. As the sniper fires, the wind begins blowing from 3 o'clock to 9 o'clock, causing the bullet to miss the target; therefore, firing in a "boil" can hamper shot placement. Unless there is a no-value wind, the sniper must wait until the boil disappears. In general, changes in the velocity of the wind, up to about 12 miles per hour, can be readily determined by observing the mirage (Figure 3-13-4). Beyond that speed, the movement of the mirage is too fast for detection of minor changes. In general, when the waves of the mirage are shallow, its velocity and resultant wind speed are fast.

The true direction of the wind may be determined by traversing the telescope until the heat waves appear to move straight up with no lateral motion (a boiling mirage).

A mirage is particularly valuable in reading no-value winds. If the mirage is boiling, the effective wind velocity is zero. If there is any lateral movement of the mirage at ranges of 300 to 900 meters, it is usually necessary to make windage adjustments.

Another important effect of mirage is the light diffraction caused by the uneven air densities, which are characteristic of heat waves. Depending on atmospheric conditions, this diffraction will cause a displacement of the target image in the direction of the movement of the mirage. Thus if a mirage is moving from left to right, the target will appear to be slightly to the right of its actual location. Since the sniper can only aim at the image received by his eye, he will actually aim at a point which is offset slightly from the center of the target. This error will be in addition to the displacement of the bullet caused by the wind. Since the total effect of the visible mirage (effective wind plus target displacement) will vary considerably with atmospheric conditions and light intensity, it is impossible to predict the amount of error produced at any given place and time. It is only through considerable experience in reading images that the sniper will develop proficiency as a "wind doper."

Before firing, the sniper should check the mirage and make the necessary sight adjustments or holdoff to compensate for any wind. Immediately after firing and before plotting the call in the scorebook, he again checks the mirage. If any changes are noted, they must be considered in relating the strike of the bullet to the call. The above procedure should be used for each shot.

## Conversion of Wind Velocity to Minutes of Angle

All telescopic sights have windage adjustments that are graduated in minutes of angle or fractions thereof. A minute of angle is 1/60th of a degree. This equals about 1 inch (1.0472 inches) for every 100 meters.

        Example:   1 MOA = 2 inches at 200 meters
                   1 MOA = 5 inches at 500 meters

Snipers use minutes of angle to determine and adjust the elevation and windage needed on the telescope. After finding the wind direction and velocity in miles per hour, the sniper must then convert it into minutes of angle, using the wind formula as a rule of thumb only. The wind formula is:

$$\frac{\text{RANGE (hundreds) X VELOCITY (mph)}}{\text{CONSTANT}} = \text{Minutes full-value wind}$$

The constant depends on the target's range, and is due to bullet velocity loss:

        100 to 500   "C" = 15
        600          "C" = 14
        700 to 800   "C" = 13
        900          "C" = 12
       1000          "C" = 11

If the target is 700 meters away and the wind velocity is 10 mph, the formula is:

$$\frac{7 \ X \ 10}{13} = 5.38 \text{ minutes or } 5 \ 1/2 \text{ minutes}$$

This determines the number of minutes for a full-value wind. For a half-value wind, the 5.38 would be divided in half.

The observer makes his own adjustment estimations, then compares them to the wind conversion table, which can be a valuable training tool. He must not rely on this table; if it is lost, his ability to perform the mission could be severely hampered. Until the observer gains skill in estimating wind speed and computing sight changes, he may refer to the wind conversion table (Table 3-1).

## Effects of Light

Light does not affect the trajectory of the bullet; however, it may affect the way the sniper sees the target through the telescope. Light affects different people in different ways. The general tendency, however, is for the sniper to shoot high on a dull, cloudy day and low on a bright, clear day. Extreme light conditions from the left or the right may have an effect on the horizontal impact of a shot group.

This effect can be compared to the refraction (bending) of light through a medium, such as a prism or a fish bowl. The same effect, although not as drastic, can be observed on a day with high humidity and with sunlight from high angles. To solve the problem of light and its effects, the sniper must accurately record the light conditions under which he is shooting. Through experience and study, he will eventually determine the effect of light on his zero. Light may also affect firing of unknown distance ranges since it affects range determination capabilities.

## Effects of Temperature

Temperature has a definite effect on the elevation setting required to hit the center of the target. This is caused by the fact that an increase in temperature of 20 degrees F will increase the muzzle velocity by approximately 50 feet per second. When ammunition sits in direct sunlight, the burn rate of powder is increased. The greatest effect of temperature is on the density of the air. As the temperature rises, the air density is lowered. Since there is less resistance, velocity increases and once again the impact rises. This is in relation to the temperature in which the rifle was zeroed. If the sniper zeroes at 50 degrees and he is now firing at 90 degrees, the impact rises considerably. How high it rises is best determined once again by past firing recorded in the data book. The general rule, however, is that a 20-degree increase from zero temperature will raise the impact by one minute; conversely, a 20-degree decrease will drop impact by one minute.

Elevation above sea level can have an important effect on bullet trajectory. At higher elevations air density, temperature, and air drag on the bullet decrease.

## Effects of Humidity

Humidity varies along with the altitude and temperature. The sniper can encounter problems if drastic humidity changes occur in his area of operation. Remember, if humidity goes up, impact goes down; if humidity goes down, impact goes up. As a rule of thumb, a 20-percent change will equal about one minute, affecting the impact. The sniper should keep a good data book during training and refer to his own record.

To understand the effects of humidity on the strike of the bullet, the sniper must realize that the higher the humidity, the denser the air; thus there is more resistance to the flight of the bullet. This resistance will tend to slow the bullet, and, as a result, the sniper must raise his elevation to compensate for it. The effect of humidity at short ranges is not as noticeable as at longer ranges. The experience of the sniper and his study of hits and groups under varied conditions of humidity will determine the effect of humidity on his zero.

Some snipers fail to note all of the factors of weather. Certain combinations of weather will have different effects on the bullet. For this reason, a sniper may fire two successive days in the same location and under what appears to be the same conditions and yet use two different sight settings. For example, a 30 percent rise in humidity cannot always be determined readily. This rise in humidity makes the air denser. If this heavier air is present with a 10 miles per hour wind, more elevation and more windage will be required to hit the same location than on a day when the humidity is 30 percent lower.

By not considering all the effects of weather, some snipers may tend to overemphasize certain effects, and this will produce bad shots from time to time. Snipers normally fire for a certain period of time under average conditions. As a result they zero their rifles, and (with the exception of minor displacements of shots and groups) they have little difficulty except for the wind. However, a sniper can travel to a different location and fire again and find a change in his zero. Proper recording and study of the weather effects would indicate why the zero changed. Proper recording and study based on experience are all-important with respect to determining the effects of weather. Probably one of the most difficult things to impress upon a sniper is the evidence of a probable change in his zero. If a change is indicated, it should be applied to all ranges.

## 3-14. SLOPE SHOOTING

Most firing practice conducted by the sniper team involves the use of military range facilities, which are relatively flat. However, as a sniper being deployed to other regions of the world, the chance exists of operating in a mountainous or urban environment. This requires target engagements at higher and lower elevations. Unless the sniper takes corrective action, bullet impact will be above the point of aim. How high the bullet hits is determined by the range and angle to the target (Table 3-3). The amount of elevation changed applied to the telescope of the rifle for angle firing is known as slope dope.

| ANGLE: | 5 | 10 | 15 | 20 | 25 | 30 | 35 | 40 | 45 | 50 | 55 | 60 |
|---|---|---|---|---|---|---|---|---|---|---|---|---|
| RANGE (m) | | | | | | | | | | | | |
| 100 | .01 | .04 | .09 | .16 | .25 | .36 | .49 | .63 | .79 | .97 | 1.2 | 1. |
| 200 | .03 | .09 | .2 | .34 | .53 | .76 | 1. | 1.3 | 1.7 | 2. | 2.4 | 2. |
| 300 | .03 | .1 | .3 | .5 | .9 | 1.2 | 1.6 | 2.1 | 2.7 | 3.2 | 3.9 | 4. |
| 400 | .05 | .19 | .43 | .76 | 1.2 | 1.7 | 2.3 | 2.9 | 3.7 | 4.5 | 5.4 | 6. |
| 500 | .06 | .26 | .57 | 1. | 1.6 | 2.3 | 3. | 3.9 | 4.9 | 6. | 7.2 | 8. |
| 600 | .08 | .31 | .73 | 1.3 | 2. | 2.9 | 3.9 | 5. | 6.3 | 7.7 | 9.2 | 10. |
| 700 | .1 | .4 | .9 | 1.6 | 2.5 | 3.6 | 4.9 | 6.3 | 7.9 | 9.6 | 11.5 | 13. |
| 800 | .13 | .5 | 1. | 2. | 3. | 4.4 | 5.9 | 7.7 | 9.6 | 11.7 | 14. | 16. |
| 900 | .15 | .6 | 1.3 | 2.4 | 3.7 | 5.3 | 7.2 | 9.3 | 11.6 | 14.1 | 16.9 | 19. |
| 1000 | .2 | .7 | 1.6 | 2.8 | 4.5 | 6.4 | 8.6 | 11. | 13.9 | 16.9 | 20.2 | 23. |

NOTE: Range given is slant range (meters), not map distance.

Table 3-3. Bullet rise at given angle and range in minutes

The following is a list of compensation factors to use in setting the sights of the sniper weapon system when firing from any of the following angles. To use this table, find the angle at which you must fire and then multiply the estimated range by the decimal figure shown to the right. For example, if the estimated range is 500 meters and the angle of fire is 35 degrees, set the zero of the weapon for:

500 x .82 = 410 meters.

| PERCENT OF SLOPE ANGLE UP OR DOWN | MULTIPLY RANGE BY |
|---|---|
| 05 degrees | .99 |
| 10 degrees | .98 |
| 15 degrees | .96 |
| 20 degrees | .94 |
| 25 degrees | .91 |
| 30 degrees | .87 |
| 35 degrees | .82 |
| 40 degrees | .77 |
| 45 degrees | .70 |
| 50 degrees | .64 |
| 55 degrees | .57 |
| 60 degrees | .50 |
| 65 degrees | .42 |
| 70 degrees | .34 |
| 75 degrees | .26 |
| 80 degrees | .17 |
| 85 degrees | .09 |
| 90 degrees | .00 |

As can be seen, the steeper the angle, the shorter the range will be set on the scope or sights for a first-round hit. Also, the steeper the angle, the more precise you must be in estimating or measuring the angle. Interpolation is necessary for angles between tens and fives.

Example: Find the compensation factor for 72 degrees.

70 degrees = .34; 75 degrees = .26

72 is 40 percent between 70 and 75 degrees

.34 - .26 = .08

.08 X 40 % (.40) = .03

.34 - .03 = .31

## 3-15. HOLDOFF

Holdoff is shifting the point of aim to achieve a desired point of impact. Certain situations, such as multiple targets at varying ranges and rapidly changing winds, do not allow proper windage and elevation adjustments. Therefore, famliarization and practice of elevation and windage holdoff techniques prepare the sniper to meet these situations.

## Elevation

This technique is used only when the sniper does not have time to change his sight setting. The sniper rarely achieves pinpoint accuracy when holding off, since a minor error in range determination or a lack of a precise aiming point might cause the bullet to miss the desired point. He uses holdoff with the telescope only if several targets appear at various ranges, and time does not permit adjusting the scope for each target.

The sniper uses holdoff to hit a target at ranges other than the range for which the rifle is presently adjusted. When the sniper aims directly at a target at ranges greater than the set range, his bullet will hit below the point of aim. At closer distances, his bullet will hit higher than the point of aim. If the sniper understands this and the effect of trajectory and bullet drop, he will be able to hit the target at ranges other than that for which the rifle was adjusted. For example, the sniper adjusts the rifle for a target located 500 meters downrange, but another target appears at a range of 600 meters. The holdoff would be 25 inches; that is, the sniper should hold off 25 inches above the center of visible mass in order to hit the center of mass of that particular target (Figure 3-15-1). If another target were to appear at 400 meters, the sniper would aim 15 inches below the center of visible mass in order to hit the center of mass.

The vertical mil dots on the M3A's reticle can be used as aiming points when using elevation holdoffs (Figure 3-15-2). For example, if the sniper has to engage a target at 500 meters and the scope is set at 400 meters, he would place the first mil dot 5 inches below the vertical line on the target's center mass. This gives the sniper a 15-inch holdoff at 500 meters.

For a 500-meter zero:

o    100 and 400 meters, the waist/beltline.

o    200 and 300 meters, the groin.

o    500 meters, the chest.

o    600 meters, the top of the head.

## Windage

The sniper can use a holdoff to compensate for the effects of wind. When using the M3A scope, the sniper uses the horizontal mil dots on the reticle to hold off for wind. The space between each mil dot equals 3.375 MOA, and a very accurate hold can be determined with the mil dots. For example, if the sniper has a target at 500 meters that requires a 10-inch holdoff, he would place the target's center mass halfway between the cross hair and the first mil dot (1/2 mil) (Figure 3-15-3). When using the horizontal stadia marks on the ART-type scope reticle to measure the required holdoff distance, the sniper must remember to first range-in on the target. He then subdivides the horizontal reticle line within the stadia marks (60 inches) to determine the correct distance for holdoff (Figure 3-15-4). He can also use that reference point as an aiming point or point of aim.

When holding off, the sniper aims into the wind. If the wind is moving from the right to left, his point of aim is to the right. If the wind is moving from left to right, his point of aim is to the left. Constant practice in wind estimation can bring about proficiency in making sight adjustments or learning to apply holdoff correctly. If the sniper misses the target and the impact of the round is observed, he notes the lateral distance of his error and refires, holding off that distance in the opposite direction.

The formula used to find the holdoff distance is:

$$\frac{\text{Clicks (from wind formula) x Range (nearest hundred)}}{2} = \frac{\text{Holdoff}}{\text{(inches)}}$$

Note:    The wind formula must be computed first to find the clicks.

Example:    Range to a target is 400 yards; wind is from 3 o'clock at 8 mph. Find the holdoff required to hit the target (M118).

$$\frac{R \times V}{15} = \text{Clicks} \qquad \frac{4 \times 8}{15} = \frac{32}{15} = 2 \text{ clicks}$$

$$\frac{C \times R}{2} = \frac{\text{Holdoff}}{\text{(inches)}} \qquad \frac{2 \times 4}{2} = \frac{8}{2} = 4 \text{ inches right}$$

Or, these two formulas can be combined into a single equation:

$$\text{Holdoff (inches)} = \frac{(R)(R)(V)}{30}$$

Remember, for a half-value wind, divide clicks by 2, not the holdoff.

## 3-16. ENGAGEMENT OF MOVING TARGETS

The best example of a lead can be demonstrated by a quarterback throwing a pass to his receiver. He has to throw the ball at some point downfield in front of the receiver; the receiver will then run to that point. The same principle applies to shooting at moving targets. Moving targets are the most difficult to hit. When engaging a target that is moving laterally across the line of sight, the sniper must concentrate on moving his weapon

70

with the target while aiming at a point some distance ahead. He must hold this lead, fire, and follow through after the shot. To engage moving targets, the sniper employs the following techniques:

o     Leading

o     Tracking

o     Trapping or ambushing

o     Tracking and holding

o     Firing a snap shot

## Leading
     Engaging moving targets requires the sniper to place the cross hairs ahead of the target's movement. The distance the cross hairs are placed in front of the target's movement is called a lead.

     There are four factors in determining leads:

     o     Speed of the target. As a target moves faster, it will move a greater distance during the bullet's flight. Therefore, the lead increases as the target's speed increases.

     o     Angle of movement. A target moving perpendicular to the bullet's flight path moves a greater lateral distance during its flight time than a target moving at an angle away from or toward the bullet's path. Therefore, a target moving at a 45-degree angle has less lateral movement than a target moving at a 90-degree angle. As the lateral movement increases, the lead must be increased.

     o     Range to the target. The farther away a target is, the longer it takes for the bullet to reach it. Therefore, the lead must be increased as the distance to the target increases.

     o     Wind effects. The sniper must consider how the wind will affect the trajectory of the round. A wind blowing opposite to the target's direction requires more of a lead than a wind blowing in the same direction as the target's movement.

## Tracking
     Tracking requires the sniper to establish an aiming point ahead of the target's movement and to maintain it as the weapon is fired. This requires the weapon and body position to be moved while following the target and firing.

## Trapping or Ambushing
     Trapping or ambushing is the sniper's preferred method of engaging moving targets. The sniper must establish an aiming point

71

ahead of the target that is the correct lead for speed and distance. As the target reaches this point, the sniper fires his weapon. This method allows the sniper's weapon and body position to remain motionless. With practice, a sniper can determine exact leads and aiming points using the horizontal stadia lines in the ART scopes or the mil dots in the M3A. However, the sniper must remember to concentrate on the cross hairs and not on the target, and to not jerk the trigger.

## Tracking and Holding
The sniper uses this technique to engage an erratically moving target. That is, while the target is moving, the sniper keeps his cross hairs centered as much as possible and adjusts his position with the target. When the target stops, the sniper quickly perfects his hold and fires. This technique requires concentration and discipline to keep from firing before the target comes to a complete halt.

## Firing a Snap Shot
A sniper may often attempt to engage a target that only presents itself briefly, then resumes cover. Once he establishes a pattern, he can aim in the vicinity of the target's expected appearance and fire a snap shot at the moment of exposure.

## Lead Description
The sniper not only must determine his target's range but also its angle and speed of travel relative to his line of sight in order to determine the correct lead.

Angle of target movement. A method of estimating the angle of movement of a target moving across the sniper's front is as follows (Figure 3-16-1):

o    Full-value lead target. When only one arm and one side of the target are visible, the target is moving at or near an angle of 90 degrees, and a full-value lead is necessary.

o    Half-value lead target. When one arm and two-thirds of the front or back of the target are visible, the target is moving at approximately a 45 degree angle, and a one-half value lead is necessary.

o    No-lead target. When both arms and the entire front or back are visible, the target is moving directly toward or away from the sniper and will require no lead.

Target speed. Target speed will be a significant factor in determining the lead of the target. Moving targets are generally classified as walking or running. Running targets will require a greater lead than walking targets. Once target speed is determined, the sniper estimates the proper lead for the target at that specific range. Simultaneously, he applies the angle value to his lead estimation for the target (full-lead, half-lead).

For example, a target walking at a 45 degree angle toward the sniper at an average of 300 meters would require a 6-inch lead. This is determined by using the full-value lead of a walking target 300 meters away (a 12-inch lead) and dividing it in half, for a half-value lead (as the target is moving at a 45 degree angle toward the sniper). Wind, once again, must be considered, as this will affect the lead used. For a target moving with the wind, the sniper must subtract the wind value from the lead. Conversely, for a target moving against the wind, the sniper must add the wind value to his lead.

Double leads are sometimes necessary for snipers who use the swing-through method on a target that is moving toward their shooting side. The double lead is necessary because of the difficulty some people have in swinging their weapon smoothly toward their shooting side. Practice on a known-distance range and meticulous record keeping are required to hone a sniper's moving target engagement skill.

## Lead Calculation

The following formulas are used to determine moving target leads:

TIME OF FLIGHT X TARGET SPEED = LEAD

Time of flight: Flight time of the bullet in seconds.

Target speed: Speed of the target in feet per second.

Lead: Distance that the aiming point must be placed ahead of the moving target in feet.

Average speed of a man during:
Slow patrol  = 1 fps/0.8 mph
Fast patrol  = 2 fps/1.3 mph
Slow walk    = 4 fps/2.5 mph
Fast walk    = 6 fps/3.7 mph

To convert leads in feet to meters:

LEAD IN FEET X 0.348 = METERS

To convert leads in meters to mils:

$$\frac{\text{LEAD IN METERS X 1,000}}{\text{RANGE TO TARGET}} = \text{MIL LEAD}$$

73

Once the required lead has been determined, the sniper should use the mil scale in the telescope for precise holdoff. The mil scale can be mentally sectioned into 1/4-mil increments for leads. The chosen point on the mil scale becomes the sniper's point of concentration just as the cross hairs are for stationary targets. The sniper concentrates on the lead point and fires the weapon when the target is at this point.

## Lead Values

Below are the recommended leads for movers at various ranges and speeds:

### LEADS IN MILS

| RANGE | WALKERS | FAST WALKERS | RUNNERS |
|-------|---------|--------------|---------|
| 100 yds | LEADING EDGE | 7 /8 | 1 3/4 |
| 200 yds | 7/8 | 1 1/4 | 1 3/4 |
| 300 yds | 1 1/8 | 1 3/4 | 2 1/4 |
| 400 yds | 1 1/4 | 1 3/4 | 2 1/2 |
| 500 yds | 1 1/4 | 1 3/4 | 2 1/2 |
| 600 yds | 1 1/2 | 2 1/4 | 3 |
| 700 yds | 1 1/2 | 2 1/4 | 3 |
| 800 yds | 1 1/2 | 2 1/2 | 3 |
| 900 yds | 1 3/4 | 2 1/2 | 3 1/2 |
| 1,000 yds | 1 3/4 | 2 1/2 | 3 1/2 |

### LEADS IN MOA

| RANGE | WALKERS | FAST WALKERS | RUNNERS |
|-------|---------|--------------|---------|
| 100 yds | LEADING EDGE | 3 | 6 |
| 200 yds | 3 | 4.5 | 6 |

| 300 yds | 4 | 6 | 8 |
| 400 yds | 4.5 | 6 | 9 |
| 500 yds | 4.5 | 6 | 9 |
| 600 yds | 5 | 7.5 | 10 |
| 700 yds | 5 | 7.5 | 10 |
| 800 yds | 5.5 | 8 | 11 |
| 900 yds | 5.5 | 8 | 11 |
| 1,000 yds | 5.5 | 8 | 11 |

## LEADS IN FEET AND INCHES

| RANGE | WALKERS | FAST WALKERS | RUNNERS |
|---|---|---|---|
| 100 yds | LEADING EDGE | 3" | 6" |
| 200 yds | 6" | 9" | 1' |
| 300 yds | 1' | 1.5' | 2' |
| 400 yds | 1.5' | 2.25' | 3' |
| 500 yds | 2' | 3' | 4' |
| 600 yds | 2.5' | 3.75' | 5' |
| 700 yds | 3' | 4.5' | 6' |
| 800 yds | 3.5' | 5.25' | 7' |
| 900 yds | 4' | 6' | 8' |
| 1,000 yds | 4.5' | 7.25' | 9' |

It is not recommended for snipers to engage runners beyond 500 yards due to the excessive lead required. If a runner is engaged at distances beyond 500 yards, an immediate follow-up shot must be ready.

The classification of a walker, fast walker, and a runner is based on a walker moving at 2 miles per hour, a fast walker at 3 1/2 miles per hour, and a runner at 5 miles per hour.

It must be remembered that the above leads are guides only and starting point leads. Each individual will have his own leads based on how he perceives movement and his reaction time to it.

## Common Errors

When engaging moving targets, the sniper makes common errors because the sniper is under greater stress than with a stationary target. There are more considerations, such as retaining a steady position and the correct aiming point, how fast the target is moving, and how far away it is. The more practice a sniper has shooting moving targets, the better he will become.

Some common mistakes are as follows:

o     The sniper has a tendency to watch his target instead of his aiming point. He must force himself to watch his lead point.

o     The sniper may jerk or flinch at the moment his weapon fires because he thinks he must fire NOW. This can be overcome through practice on a live-fire range.

o     The sniper may hurry and thus forget to apply wind as needed. Windage must be calculated for moving targets just as for stationary targets. Failure to do this when acquiring a lead will result in a miss.

Engaging moving targets not only requires the sniper to determine the target distance and wind effects on the round, but he must also consider the lateral speed of the target, the round's time of flight, and the placement of a proper lead to compensate for both. These added variables increase the chance of a miss. Therefore, the sniper should engage moving targets when it is the only option.

## 3-17. ENGAGEMENT OF SNAP TARGETS

In many instances the sniper will be presented with a target that will show itself for only a brief moment. Under these circumstances it is very important to concentrate on trigger control. Trigger control is modified to a very rapid pull of the finger directly to the rear without disturbing the lay of the weapon.

Another valuable skill for the sniper to learn is the quick-kill shooting technique. The sniper is most vulnerable during movement. Not only will he be compromised because of his heavier equipment requirement, but he will be at a disadvantage because of his large, optically-sighted sniper rifle. Using the quick-kill technique, the sniper or observer can engage a target very rapidly at close range. This is very useful for chance encounters with the enemy and when security is threatened. The rifle is carried pointing to the sniper's front. The muzzle of the weapon will always point where the sniper is looking, not at port arms. When the rifle is raised to shoot, the eye is looking at the target. As the sniper looks at his target, the weapon lines on the target, and at the same movement, the sniper fires. This technique must be practiced to obtain proficiency. It is not "wild shooting", but a learned technique. A close analogy could be made to a skeet shooter who points his shotgun as opposed to sighting it.


## 3-18. SHOOTING THROUGH OBSTACLES AND BARRIERS

### Glass Penetration

Another variable the sniper may encounter is the effect that glass penetration has on exterior and terminal ballistics. The USMC conducted a test by firing at an 8 by 9 inch pane of safety glass at 90 degree and 45 degree angles with the following results:

o Regardless of the angle, the path of the test bullet core was not affected up to 5 feet beyond the point of initial impact.

o At an angle, glass fragments were always blown perpendicular to the glass plate.

o The M118 173 grain bullet's copper jacket fragments upon impact. All of the bullet fragments followed an erratic path both in height and width. Each of the main cores (lead) began to tumble about 2 feet from the initial impact point.

o Due to the lamination of safety glass with a sheet plastic, large fragments of plastic were embedded in the target one foot from the point of impact. Theses fragments were large enough to cause severe wounds.

o Glass fragments did not penetrate targets farther than one foot from the point of impact.

o It can be concluded that anyone near the glass would be injured.

The US Army conducted a penetration test by firing 1 yard from a glass plate and through the glass plate at a silhouette target 100 yards away. Of the 14 test shots through various types of glass, only 2 shots hit the target. Therefore, as indicated by both the USMC and US Army tests, snipers should try to avoid engaging targets requiring glass penetration.

### Penetration Performance of M118 Special Ball

To support the M24 SWS program, two tests were conducted with the M118 Special Ball ammunition at a range of 800 meters. The first test used a test sample of ballistic kevlar, and the second test used a 10-gauge, mild steel plate. Testing personnel positioned a witness plate behind each of these targets. Witness plates consist of a 0.5 mm sheet of 2024T3 aluminum to measure residual velocity/energy. To pass the test, the bullet had to penetrate both the target and witness plate. Results of these tests follow:

    o M118 versus Ballistic Kevlar. When 10 rounds were fired at 13 layers of ballistic kevlar (equivalent to the US personal armor system ground troop vest), full penetration was achieved of both the test sample and the aluminum witness plate.

    o M118 versus Mild Steel Plate. When 20 rounds were fired at a 3.42 mm thick (10-gauge) SAE 1010 or 1020 steel plate (Rockwell hardness of B55 to B70), 16 achieved full penetration of both the test sample and aluminum witness plate. The 4 failing rounds penetrated the steel plate but only dented the witness plate. These 4 rounds were considered to have insufficient terminal energy to be effective.


3-19.  COLD BORE FIRST SHOT HIT

    On a mission, a sniper will rarely get a second shot at the intended target. The sniper must hit his target with the first shot with a high degree of probability. This requirement places a great deal of importance on the maintenance of a solid sniper's log book. Whenever the sniper conducts a live-fire, he should develop a data base on his SWS and its cold bore zero. The sniper uses the integrated act of firing one round to hone his sniping skills. By maintaining a detailed log book, the sniper develops confidence in his system's ability to provide the "one shot--one kill" that is the goal of every sniper. The sniper must pay close attention to the maintenance and cleanliness of his rifle, and his proficiency in the marksmanship fundamentals. This exercise also develops the team work within the sniper pair required to accomplish the mission. The sniper should attempt to obtain his cold bore data at all ranges and climatic conditions. The bore and chamber must be completely dry and free of all lubricants. The exact point of impact of the bullet should be annotated in the log book. Keeping a file of the actual paper targets used in addition to the log book is even better. This data will help to detect trends that can be used to improve the sniper's performance.


3-20.  LIMITED VISIBILITY FIRING

    The US Army currently does not field a completely satisfactory night vision sight for its SWS. The best compromise using issue equipment is to mount a PVS-4 onto a M16A2. This NVD should be kept permanently mounted to avoid zeroing problems. This system is adequate because the rifle's effective range matches that of the

NVD's ability to distinguish target details. The M24 and M21 can be used during limited visibility operations if the conditions are favorable. Moonlight, artificial illumination, and terrain will determine the potential effectiveness. The sniper will find that the reticle will fade out during limited visibility. Rather than trying to strain his eyes to make out the reticle, the sniper should instead use the entire field of view of the telescope as the aiming device. Live fire exercises will help the sniper to determine his own maximum effective range.

Another consideration during limited visibility firing is that of muzzle flash. The M16 and the M21 are both equipped with excellent flash suppressors. The enemy would have to be very close or using NVDs to pinpoint a couple of muzzle flashes. The M24, on the other hand, does not have a flash suppressor at all. The sniper will have to compensate for this deficiency by hide selection, location, and even ammunition lot. A loophole will go a long ways toward minimizing the muzzle flash. The M24's problem will be exacerbated when it is converted to the .300 Win Mag, with its correspondingly larger muzzle flash.

## 3-21. NBC FIRING

Performance of long-range precision fire is difficult at best during NBC conditions. Enemy NBC warfare creates new problems for the sniper. Not only must the sniper properly execute the fundamentals of marksmanship and contend with the forces of nature, he must overcome obstacles presented by protective equipment.

### Protective Mask
The greatest problem while firing the M24 with the M17-series protective mask was that of recoil breaking the seal of the mask. Also, due to filter elements and hard eye lenses, the sniper could not gain and maintain proper stock weld and eye relief. Additionally, the observer could not gain the required eye relief for observation through his M49 spotting telescope. However, testing of the M25-series protective mask provided the following results:

o    Because of its separate filtering canister, the stock weld was gained and maintained with minimal effort.

o    Its flexible face shield allowed for excellent observation. This also allowed the sniper and observer to achieve proper eye relief, which was needed for observation with their respective telescopes.

### Mission Oriented Protection Posture
Firing in MOPP has a significant effect on the ability to deliver precision fire. The following problems and solutions have been identified:

o    Eye relief.  Special emphasis must be made in maintaining proper eye relief and the absence of scope shadow.  Maintaining consistent stock weld is a must.

o    Trigger control.  Problems encountered with trigger control consist of the sense of touch and stock drag.

*    Sense of touch.  When gloves are worn, the sniper cannot determine the amount of pressure he is applying to the trigger.  This is of particular importance if the sniper has his trigger adjusted for a light pull.  Training with a glove will be beneficial; however, the trigger should be adjusted to allow the sniper to feel the trigger without accidental discharge.

*    Stock drag.  While training, the sniper should have his observer watch his trigger finger to ensure that the finger and glove are not touching any part of the rifle but the trigger.  The glove or finger resting on the trigger guard moves the rifle as the trigger is pulled to the rear.  The sniper must wear a well-fitted glove.

o    Vertical Sight Picture.  The sniper naturally cants the rifle into the cheek of the face while firing with a protective mask.  Using the vertical cross hair of the reticle as a reference mark, he keeps the weapon in a vertical position.  Failure to do this will cause shots to hit low and in the direction of the cant.  Also, windage and elevation corrections will not be true.

o    Sniper/Observer Communications.  The absence of a voice-mitter on the M25-series protective mask creates an obstacle in relaying information.  The team either speaks louder or uses written messages.  A system of foot taps, finger taps, or hand signals may be devised.  Communication is a must; training should include the development and practice of communications at different MOPP levels.

The easiest solution to NBC firing with the M24 SWS is to use the Harris bipod.  The bipod helps to stabilize the rifle, and allows the sniper to maintain a solid position behind the rifle as he cants his head to achieve a proper sight picture.  The sniper can also try tilting his head down so that he is looking up through the telescope.  NBC firing must be incorporated into live fire ranges so that the most comfortable and effective position can be developed.  Also, a detailed log book should be developed that addresses the effects of NBC firing.

# TABLE 3-2

WINDAGE HOLD-OFFS IN MILS FOR 7.62mm NM, M118

| Range Meters | Wind Value | 3 MPH Mils | 5 MPH Mils | 7 MPH Mils | 10 MPH Mils | 12 MPH Mils | 15 MPH Mils | 18 MPH Mils | 20 MPH Mils |
|---|---|---|---|---|---|---|---|---|---|
| 200 | 1/2 | 0.0 | 0.0 | 0.0 | 0.0 | 0.0 | 0.25 | 0.25 | 0.25 |
| | FULL | 0.0 | 0.0 | 0.25 | 0.25 | 0.5 | 0.5 | 0.5 | 0.5 |
| 300 | 1/2 | 0.0 | 0.0 | 0.25 | 0.25 | 0.25 | 0.25 | 0.5 | 0.5 |
| | FULL | 0.0 | 0.25 | 0.25 | 0.5 | 0.75 | 0.75 | 1.0 | 1.0 |
| 400 | 1/2 | 0.0 | 0.25 | 0.25 | 0.25 | 0.5 | 0.5 | 0.75 | 0.75 |
| | FULL | 0.25 | 0.25 | 0.5 | 0.75 | 0.75 | 1.0 | 1.25 | 1.5 |
| 500 | 1/2 | 0.0 | 0.25 | 0.25 | 0.5 | 0.5 | 0.75 | 0.75 | 1.0 |
| | FULL | 0.25 | 0.5 | 0.5 | 0.75 | 1.0 | 1.25 | 1.5 | 1.75 |
| 600 | 1/2 | 0.0 | 0.25 | 0.5 | 0.5 | 0.75 | 0.75 | 1.0 | 1.0 |
| | FULL | 0.25 | 0.5 | 0.75 | 1.0 | 1.25 | 1.5 | 2.0 | 2.0 |
| 700 | 1/2 | 0.25 | 0.25 | 0.5 | 0.75 | 0.75 | 1.0 | 1.0 | 1.5 |
| | FULL | 0.5 | 0.75 | 1.0 | 1.25 | 1.5 | 1.75 | 2.25 | 2.5 |
| 800 | 1/2 | 0.25 | 0.5 | 0.5 | 0.75 | 0.75 | 1.0 | 1.25 | 1.5 |
| | FULL | 0.5 | 0.75 | 1.0 | 1.5 | 1.75 | 2.0 | 2.5 | 2.75 |
| 900 | 1/2 | 0.25 | 0.5 | 0.5 | 0.75 | 1.0 | 1.25 | 1.5 | 1.5 |
| | FULL | 0.5 | 0.75 | 1.0 | 1.5 | 1.75 | 2.25 | 2.75 | 3.0 |
| 1000 | 1/2 | 0.25 | 0.5 | 0.75 | 1.0 | 1.0 | 1.25 | 1.5 | 1.75 |
| | FULL | 0.5 | 1.0 | 1.25 | 1.75 | 2.0 | 2.25 | 3.0 | 3.25 |

If engaging a moving target that is moving with the wind then subtract the above values, when moving against the wind then add the above values.

WINDAGE HOLDOFFS IN MINUTES OF ANGLE (MOA) FOR 7.62mm NM, M118

| Range Meters | Wind Value | 3 MPH Min. | 5 MPH Min. | 7 MPH Min. | 10 MPH Min. | 12 MPH Min. | 15 MPH Min. | 18 MPH Min. | 20 MPH Min. |
|---|---|---|---|---|---|---|---|---|---|
| 200 | 1/2 | 0 | 0.5 | 0.5 | 0.5 | 0.5 | 1.0 | 1.0 | 1.0 |
| | FULL | 0.5 | 0.5 | 1.0 | 1.0 | 1.5 | 1.5 | 2.0 | 2.0 |
| 300 | 1/2 | 0.5 | 0.5 | 0.5 | 1.0 | 1.0 | 1.0 | 1.5 | 1.5 |
| | FULL | 0.5 | 1.0 | 1.0 | 1.5 | 2.0 | 2.5 | 3.0 | 3.5 |
| 400 | 1/2 | 0.5 | 0.5 | 1.0 | 1.0 | 1.5 | 1.5 | 2.0 | 2.0 |
| | FULL | 0.5 | 1.0 | 1.5 | 2.0 | 2.5 | 3.5 | 4.0 | 4.5 |
| 500 | 1/2 | 0.5 | 0.5 | 1.0 | 1.5 | 1.5 | 2.0 | 2.5 | 2.5 |
| | FULL | 1.0 | 1.5 | 2.0 | 2.5 | 3.5 | 4.0 | 5.0 | 5.5 |
| 600 | 1/2 | 0.5 | 1.0 | 1.0 | 1.5 | 1.5 | 2.5 | 3.0 | 3.5 |
| | FULL | 1.0 | 1.5 | 2.5 | 3.5 | 4.0 | 5.0 | 6.0 | 6.5 |
| 700 | 1/2 | 0.5 | 1.0 | 1.5 | 2.0 | 2.5 | 2.5 | 3.5 | 4.0 |
| | FULL | 1.0 | 2.0 | 2.5 | 4.0 | 4.5 | 5.0 | 7.0 | 7.5 |
| 800 | 1/2 | 0.5 | 1.0 | 1.5 | 2.0 | 2.5 | 3.5 | 4.0 | 4.5 |
| | FULL | 1.5 | 2.0 | 3.0 | 4.5 | 5.5 | 6.5 | 8.0 | 9.0 |
| 900 | 1/2 | 0.5 | 1.0 | 1.5 | 2.5 | 3.0 | 3.5 | 4.5 | 5.0 |
| | FULL | 1.5 | 2.5 | 3.5 | 5.0 | 6.0 | 7.5 | 9.0 | 10.0 |
| 1000 | 1/2 | 1.0 | 1.5 | 2.0 | 3.0 | 3.5 | 4.5 | 5.5 | 6.0 |
| | FULL | 1.5 | 3.0 | 4.0 | 5.5 | 6.5 | 8.0 | 10.0 | 11.0 |

If engaging a moving target that is moving with the wind then subtract the above values, when moving against the wind then add the above values.

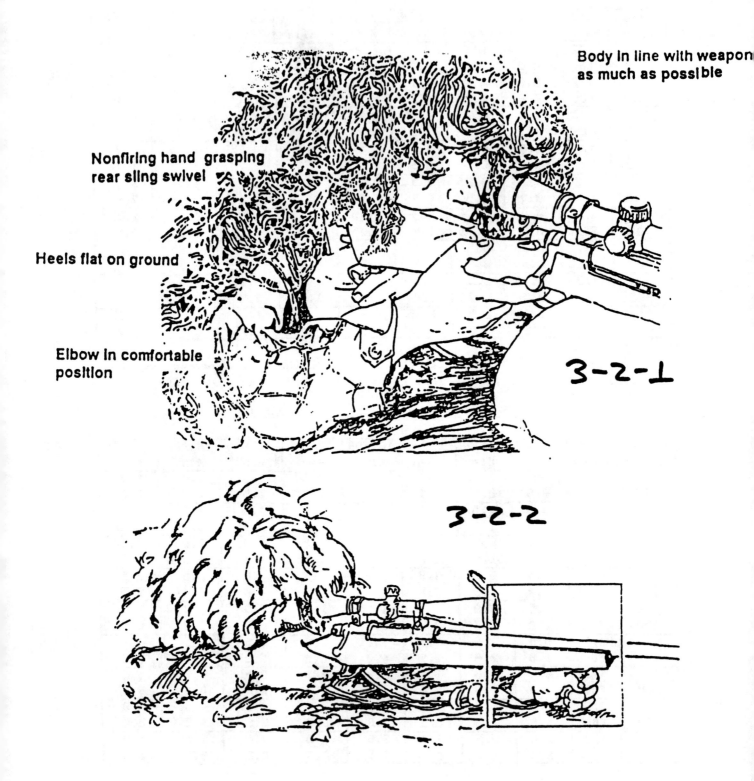

Body in line with weapon
as much as possible

Nonfiring hand grasping
rear sling swivel

Heels flat on ground

Elbow in comfortable
position

3-2-1

3-2-2

The prone position used by David I. Boyd. Note the straight line alignment from the right hand to the right heel shown in the center photo. Proper spot weld is shown in the lower right photo.

teloscope case

3-2-5    N/A

3-2-6

These photos illustrate the sitting
position used by David I. Boyd, 1981
National Highpower Rifle and Service
Rifle Champion.  Boyd is a left-handed
shooter, but the position techniques
shown in these photos can easily be
reversed for right-handed shooters.
The right center photo shows the cant
Boyd must use to shoot sitting.  He
does not recommend canting a highpower
rifle unless it is absolutely necessary
to assume a good position.

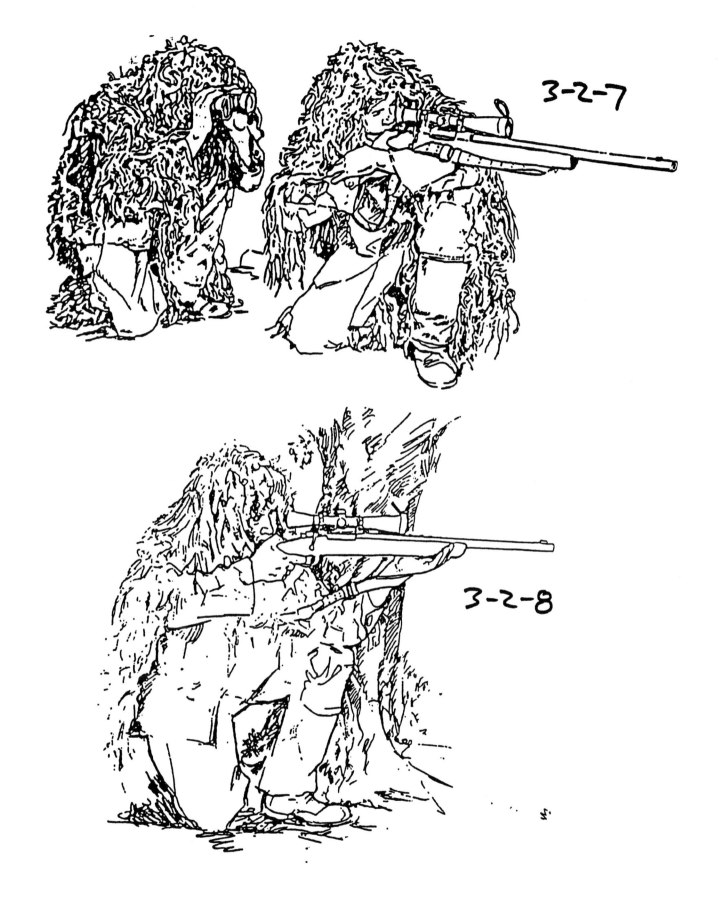

3-2-7

3-2-8

3-2-9 N/A

3-2-1∅

3-2-1∅A

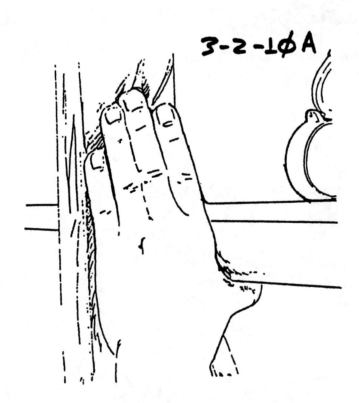

PHOTO D

PHOTO C

Boyd's system of holding his right hand in front of the magazine is shown in Photos C & D. An alternate hand position, not used by Boyd, is shown in Photo E.

PHOTO E

PHOTO A

PHOTO B

The standing position used by David I. Boyd. Note the high left elbow in Photos A & B.

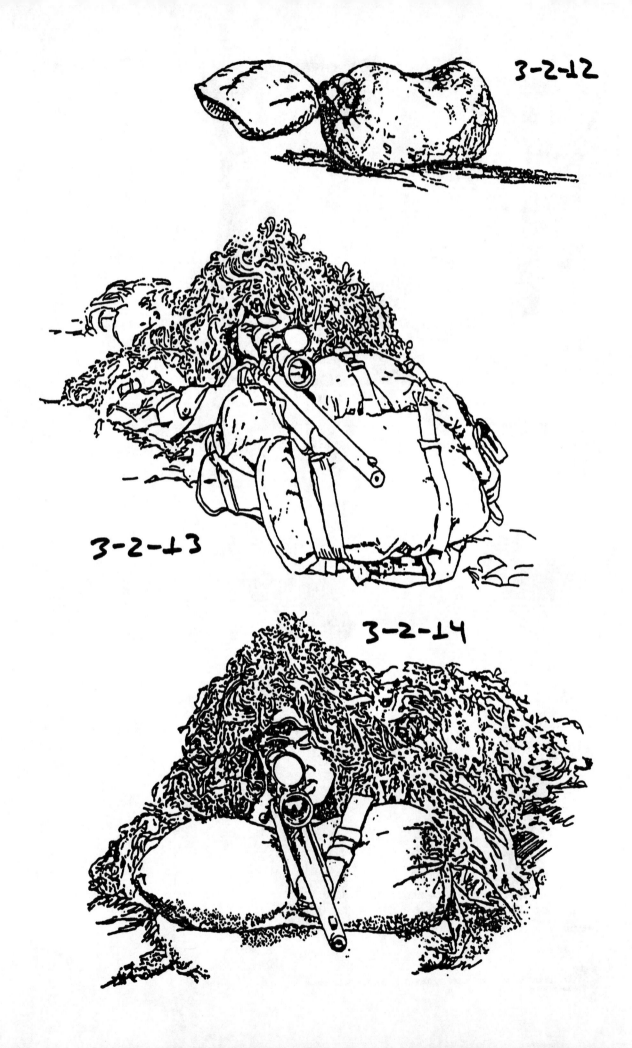

3-2-12

3-2-13

3-2-14

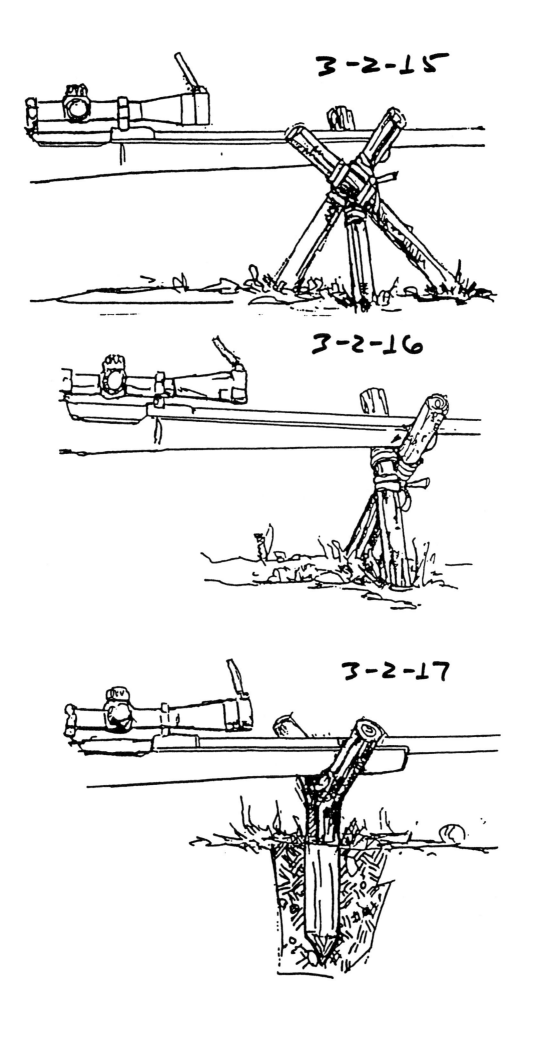

3-2-15

3-2-16

3-2-17

3-3-1

3-3-2

3-3-3

3-3-4

3-3-5

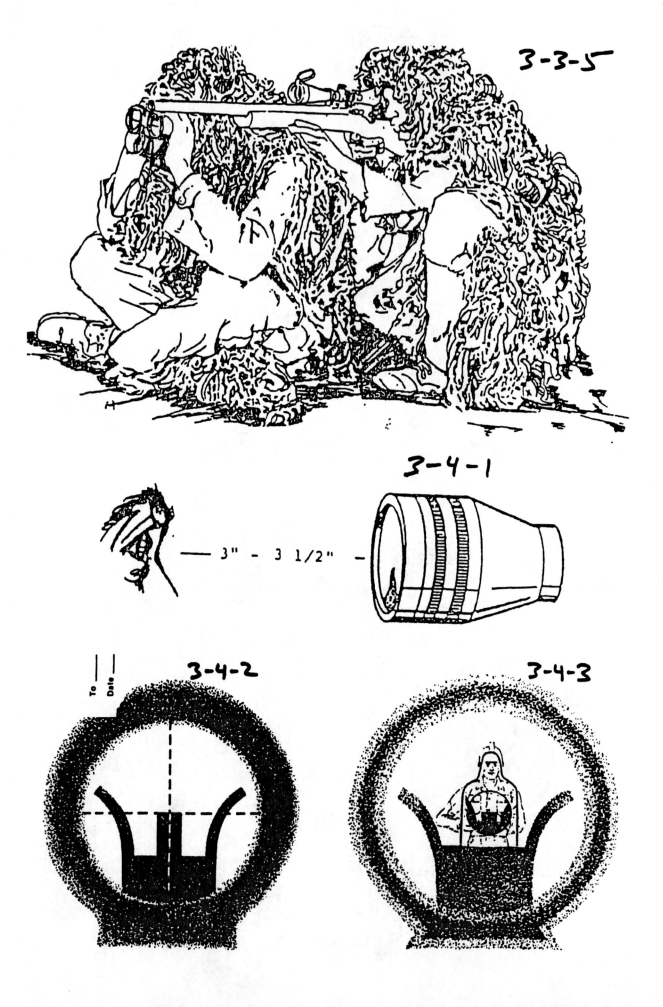

3-3-5

3-4-1

3" - 3 1/2"

3-4-2

3-4-3

3-4-4

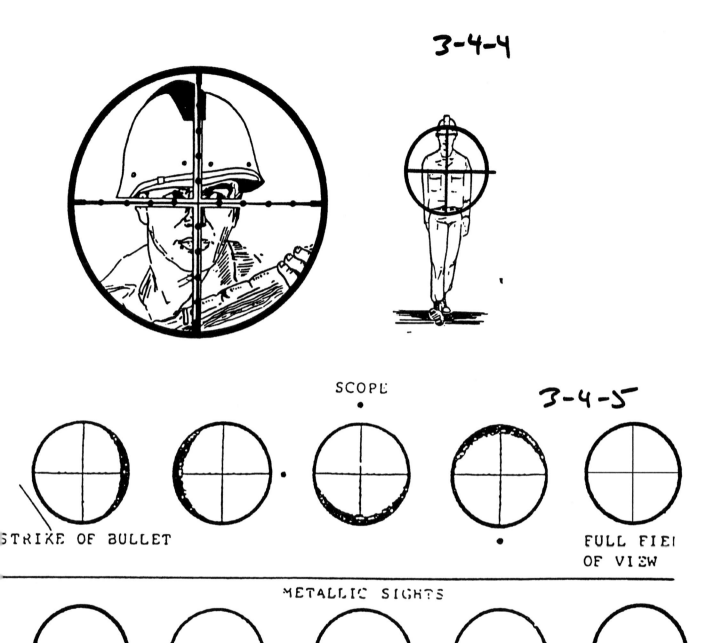

SCOPE

3-4-5

STRIKE OF BULLET

FULL FIEL
OF VIEW

METALLIC SIGHTS

FULL FIE
OF VIEW

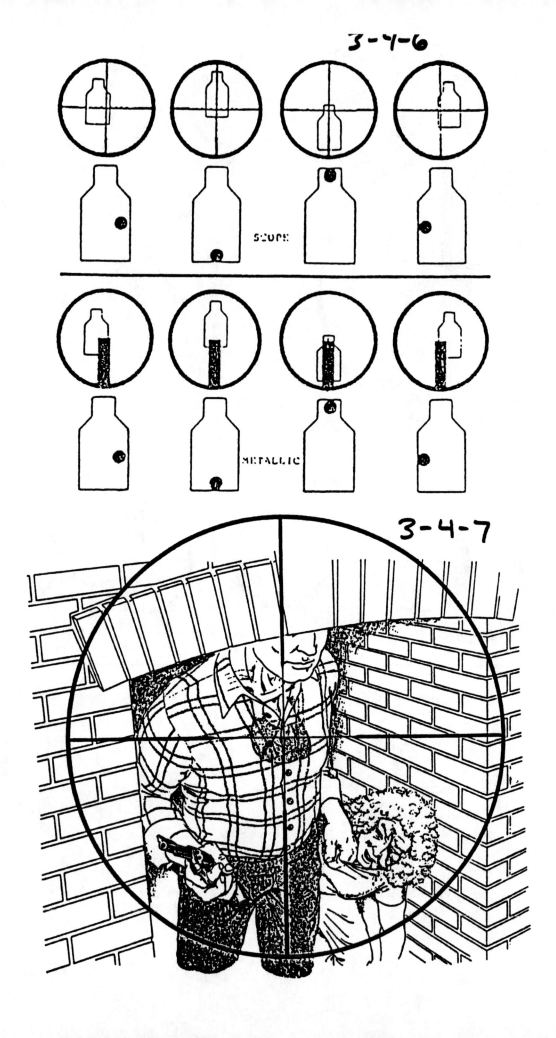

3-4-6

SCOPE

METALLIC

3-4-7

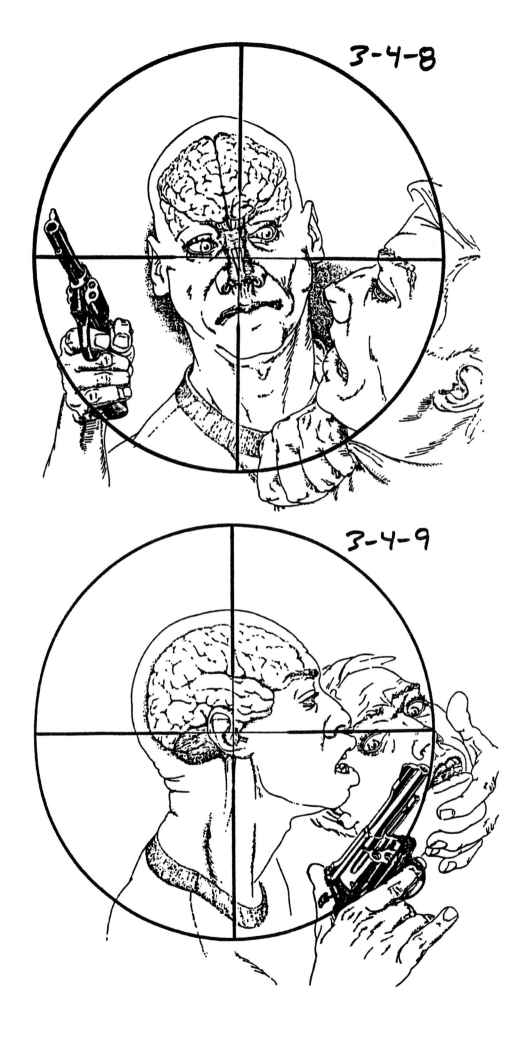

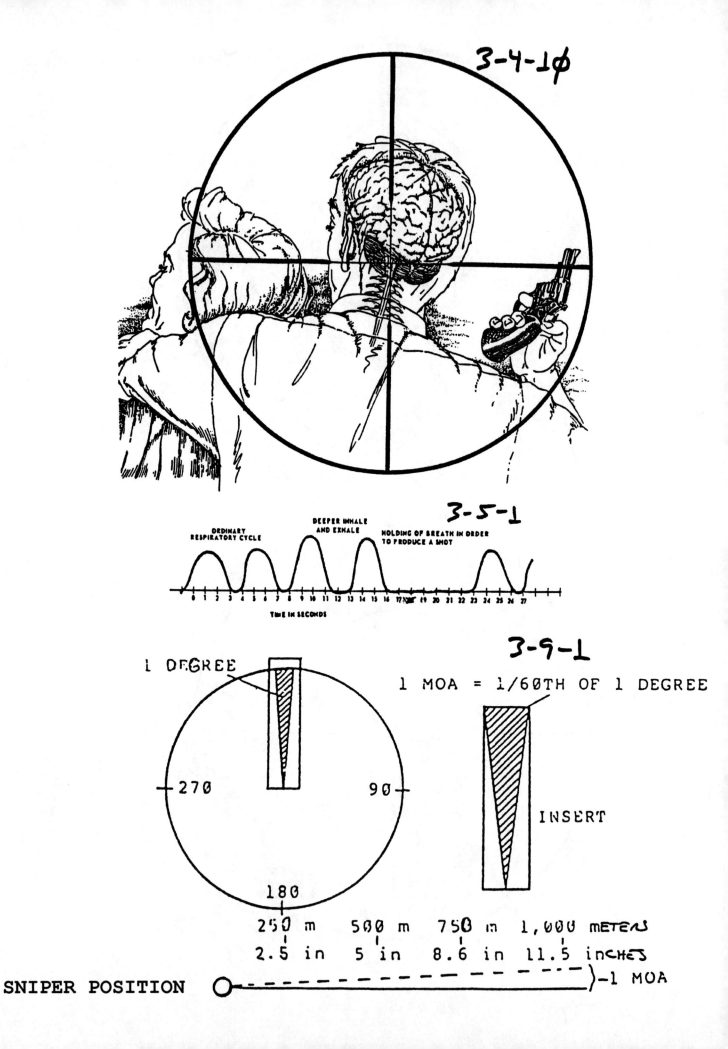

3-4-10

3-5-1

ORDINARY
RESPIRATORY CYCLE

DEEPER INHALE
AND EXHALE

HOLDING OF BREATH IN ORDER
TO PRODUCE A SHOT

TIME IN SECONDS

3-9-1

1 DEGREE

1 MOA = 1/60TH OF 1 DEGREE

270

90

INSERT

180

250 m    500 m    750 m   1,000 METERS

2.5 in   5 in    8.6 in   11.5 inches

SNIPER POSITION    O — — — — — — — — — — )–1 MOA

3-9-2

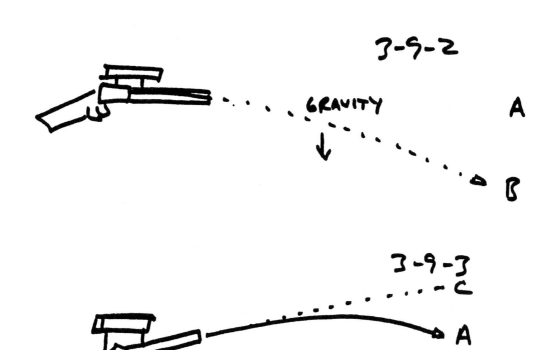

GRAVITY

A

B

3-9-3

C

A

3-12-1

WINDAGE INDICATOR PLATE

ELEVATION KNOB

WINDAGE KNOB

SPRING TENSION SCREW

SET SCREW

ELEVATION INDICATOR PLATE

EYEPIECE

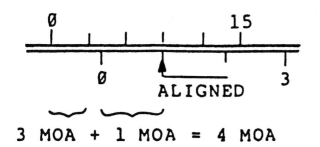

0                    15

0          ↑          3
    ALIGNED

3 MOA + 1 MOA = 4 MOA

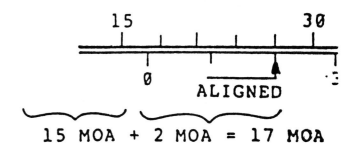

15                    30

0          ↑
    ALIGNED

15 MOA + 2 MOA = 17 MOA

| SNIPER'S DATA CARD | DISTANCE TO TARGET __600__ METERS |
|---|---|

For use of this form, see FM 23-10. The proponent agency is TRADOC
DATA REQUIRED BY PRIVACY ACT OF 1974
AUTHORITY: 10 USC 3012(g)/Executive Order 9397. PRINCIPAL PURPOSE(S): Facilitates individual's training on targets at varying ranges. ROUTINE USE(S): Evaluate individual proficiency. SSN is used for positive identification purposes only. MANDATORY OR VOLUNTARY DISCLOSURE AND EFFECT ON INDIVIDUAL NOT PROVIDING INFORMATION: Voluntary. Individuals not providing information cannot be rated/scored on a mass basis.

| LAST NAME | FIRST | MI | RANK | SSN | UNIT |
|---|---|---|---|---|---|
| Raitt | Scott | A. | E-5/SGT | 234-56-7891 | D 2/29 |

| RANGE | RIFLE AND SCOPE NO | | DATE | ELEVATION | | WINDAGE | |
|---|---|---|---|---|---|---|---|
| Burrought | 23456789 | 1234 | 12 Sep 91 | USED | CORRECT | USED | CORRECT |
| | | | | 6 | 6+1 | 0 | L 2½ |

| AMMO | LIGHT | MIRAGE | TEMP | HOUR | HOLD |
|---|---|---|---|---|---|
| 66.234 | Clear | heavy | 85° | 1000 | |

LIGHT / WIND

10 mph VELOCITY — E DIRECTION

| SHOT | 1 | 2 | 3 | 4 | 5 | 6 | 7 | 8 | 9 | 10 | REMARKS |
|---|---|---|---|---|---|---|---|---|---|---|---|
| ELEV | 6 | 6 | +1 | +1 | +1 | +1 | +1 | +1 | +1 | +1 | unexpected recoil on 10th shot |
| WIND | 0 | 5½ | 5½ | 5½ | 6½ | 5½ | 6 | 2½ | 2½ | 2½ | not feeling well today |
| CALL | | | | | | | | | | | Firing time 10 minutes |

NOTE: THE REQUIRED TARGETS WILL BE DRAWN IN BY HAND TO MEET THE NEEDS OF THE UNIT.

DA FORM 5785-R

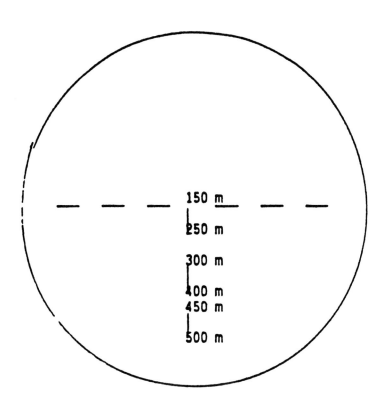

BLACK LINE RETICLE PATTERN


　　　　Through experience and test firing (zeroing), it has been determined
that the placement of the reticle index marks produce the above noted
range zeroing reference points.

　　　　Using these aiming points in the center of mass of a target will enable
the sniper to obtain a first-round hit.

Horizontal line from left
point of origin represents
20 feet at ranges shown.
Range is in hundreds of meters.

Vertical lines above or
below horizontal line
represent 6 feet at ranges
shown.  Range is in hundreds
of meters.

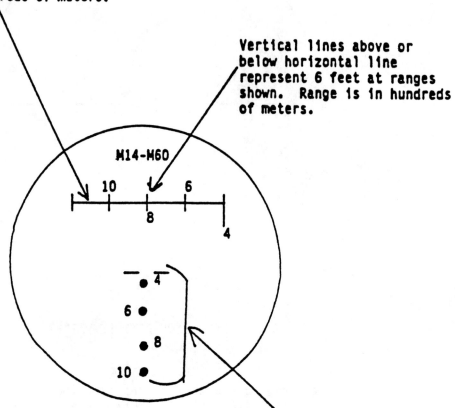

M14-M60

M14-M60 aiming points.
Range is in hundreds of
meters.

Use center of two horizontal
lines for 0-250 meters.

EXAMPLE:

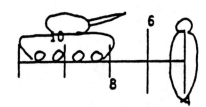

Distance to tank is 800 m

Distance to 6' man is 200 m

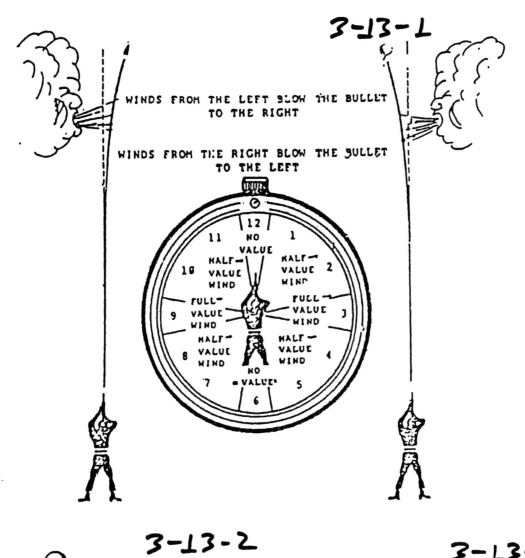

3-13-1

WINDS FROM THE LEFT BLOW THE BULLET
TO THE RIGHT

WINDS FROM THE RIGHT BLOW THE BULLET
TO THE LEFT

12
NO VALUE

11        1

HALF-        HALF-
VALUE        VALUE
WIND         WIND

10                    2

FULL-        FULL-
VALUE        VALUE
WIND         WIND

9                    3

HALF-        HALF-
VALUE        VALUE
WIND         WIND

8                    4

NO
7    VALUE    5

6

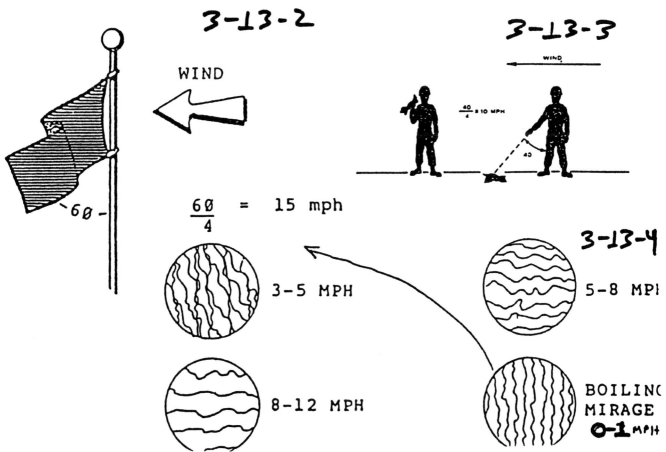

3-13-2

WIND

$\frac{60}{4} = 15$ mph

3-5 MPH

8-12 MPH

3-13-3

WIND

$\frac{40}{4} = 10$ MPH

3-13-4

5-8 MPH

BOILING
MIRAGE
0-1 MPH

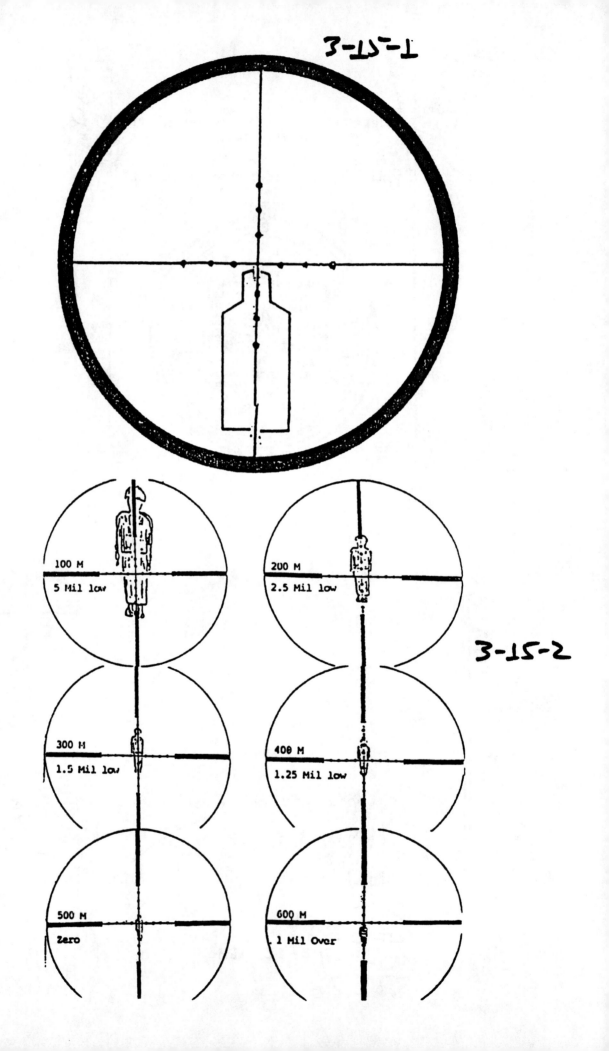

3-15-1

100 M
5 Mil low

200 M
2.5 Mil low

3-15-2

300 M
1.5 Mil low

400 M
1.25 Mil low

500 M
Zero

600 M
1 Mil Over

3-15-3

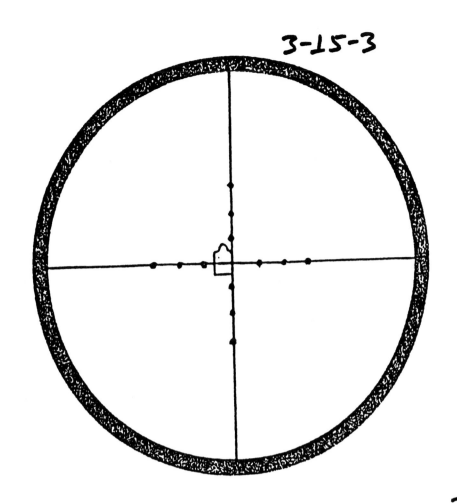

3-15-4

HOLDOFF FOR 7.62 (173 gr) IN INCHES (M21 SYSTEM)

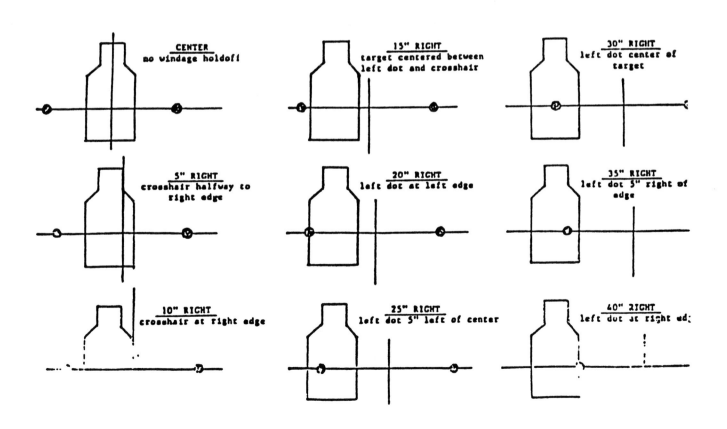

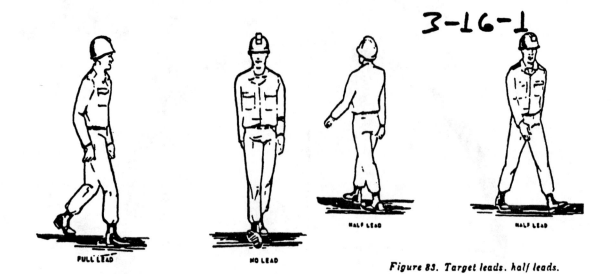

3-16-1

PULL LEAD  NO LEAD  HALF LEAD  HALF LEAD

*Figure 83. Target leads. half leads.*

4-1-1

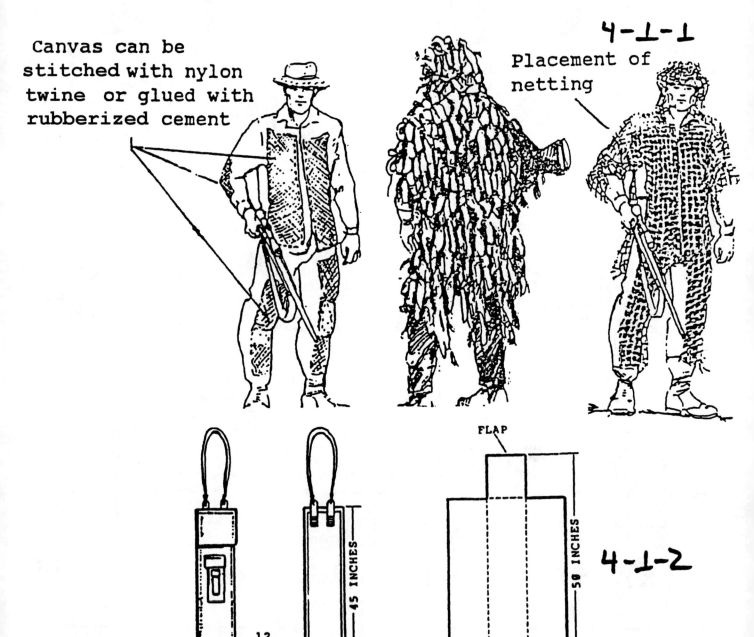

Canvas can be stitched with nylon twine or glued with rubberized cement

Placement of netting

FLAP

45 INCHES

12 INCHES

TOP VIEW  BOTTOM VIEW

50 INCHES

4-1-2

36 INCHES

# Chapter 4

## FIELD SKILLS

The sniper's primary mission is to reduce selected enemy targets with long-range precision fire. How well he accomplishes his mission depends on the knowledge, understanding, and application of various field techniques and skills that allow him to move, hide, observe, and detect targets. This chapter discusses the field techniques and skills that the sniper must learn before employment in support of combat operations. The sniper's application of these skills will affect his survival on the battlefield.

## 4-1. CAMOUFLAGE

Camouflage is one of the basic weapons of war. It can mean the difference between a successful or unsuccessful mission. To the sniper team, it can mean the difference between life and death. Camouflage measures are important since the team cannot afford to be detected at any time while moving alone, as part of another element, or while operating from a firing position. Marksmanship training teaches the sniper to hit a target, and a knowledge of camouflage teaches how to escape becoming a target. A sniper must be camouflage conscious from the time he departs on a mission until he returns. Paying attention to camouflage fundamentals is a mark of a well-trained sniper. See FM 5-20 for more details.

### Camouflage Fundamentals
The proper use of camouflage clothing and equipment, both artificial and natural, requires careful attention to the following fundamentals:

o    Take advantage of all available natural concealment, such as trees, bushes, grass, earth, manmade structures, and shadows.

o    Alter the form, shadow, texture, and color of objects.

o    Camouflage against ground and air observation.

o    Camouflage a sniper post as it is prepared.

 *    Study the terrain and vegetation in the area. Arrange grass, leaves, brush, and other natural camouflage to conform to the area.

 *    Use only as much material as is needed. Excessive use of material (natural or artificial) can reveal a sniper's position.

1

        *     Obtain natural material over a wide area. Do not strip an area, as this may attract the enemy's attention.

        *     Dispose of excess soil by covering it with leaves and grass or by dumping it under bushes, into streams, or into ravines. Piles of fresh dirt indicate that an area is occupied and reduces the effectiveness of camouflage.

        o     The sniper and his equipment must blend with the natural background. Remember, vegetation changes color many times in an area.

## Camouflage in Various Geographical Areas

One type of camouflage cannot be used in all types of terrain and geographic areas. Before operations in an area, a sniper should study the terrain, the vegetation, and the lay of the land to determine the best possible type of personal camouflage.

        o     In areas with heavy snow or in wooded areas with snow-covered brush, a full white camouflage suit with gray shading can be used. With snow on the ground and the brush not covered, white trousers and green-brown tops are worn. A hood or veil in snow areas is very effective, and equipment should be striped or totally covered in white. In snow regions, visibility during a bright night is nearly as good as during the day, giving snipers full-time capabilities, but movement must be undertaken along carefully concealed routes.

        o     In sandy and desert areas that have little vegetation, textured camouflage is normally not necessary. Still, proper coloring of a suit that breaks up the sniper's human outline is needed. Blending tan and brown colors is most effective. A bulky-type smock of light material with a hood works well. The hands, face, and all equipment should be blended into a solid pattern that corresponds with the terrain. The sniper must make full use of the terrain by using properly selected and concealed routes of movement.

        o     In urban areas, when deployed with regular troops in a built-up area, the sniper should be dressed like the troops in the area. When the sniper is in position, he should be camouflaged to match the area he is in. A bulky, shapeless, gray camouflage suit that has been colored to match rubble and debris of the urban area, making sure the outline of the head is broken up by some type of hood, can be used. Movement should be extremely slow and careful, if at all, during daylight hours because of the unlimited amount of possible enemy sniper positions.

        o     In jungle areas, foliage, artificial camouflage, and camouflage paint are used in a contrasting pattern that will blend with the texture of the terrain. In a very hot and humid area, only a light camouflaged suit can be worn. A heavy suit will cause a loss of too much body fluid. The vegetation is usually very thick in jungle areas, so the sniper can rely more on using the natural foliage for concealment.

## Camouflage During Movement
The sniper must be camouflage-conscious from the time he departs on a mission until the time he returns. The sniper must constantly observe the terrain and vegetation changes to pick the most concealed routes of advance and be certain he is camouflaged properly. He should utilize shadows caused by vegetation, terrain features, and man-made features to remain undetected. He must master the techniques of hiding, blending, and deceiving.

o  Hiding. Hiding is completely concealing the body from observation by lying in thick vegetation, lying under leaves, or even by digging a shallow trench and covering up in it. The technique of hiding may be used if the sniper stumbles upon an enemy patrol and immediate concealment is needed or if he wishes to "lay low" during daylight hours to await darkness.

o  Blending. Blending is the technique used to the greatest extent in camouflage, since it is not always possible to completely camouflage in such a way as to be indistinguishable from the surrounding area. A sniper must remember that his camouflage needs to be so nearly perfect that he cannot be recognized through optical gear or with the human eye. He must be able to be looked at directly and not be seen. This takes much practice and experience.

o  Deceiving. In deceiving, the enemy is tricked into a false conclusion regarding the sniper's location, intentions, or movement. By planting objects such as ammunition cans, food cartons, or something intriguing, the sniper decoys the enemy into the open where he can be brought under fire. Cutting enemy communications wire and waiting for the repair personnel is another technique. After a unit has left a bivouac area, a sniper can be left behind to watch for enemy scouts that may search the area. Mannequins can be used to lure the enemy sniper into firing, thereby revealing his position.

## Target Indicators
A target indicator is anything a sniper does or fails to do that will reveal his position to an enemy. A sniper must know these target indicators if he is to locate the enemy as well as prevent the enemy from locating him. These target indicators are grouped into four general areas: olfactory, tactile, auditory, and visual.

o  Olfactory. Olfactory indicators are those indicators that the sniper can smell. Cooking food, fires, cigarettes, aftershave lotion, soap, and insect repellents are examples. Most olfactory target indicators are caused by the sniper's bodily

3

functions. This target indicator can be eliminated by washing the body, burying body wastes, and eliminating the cause.

o    Tactile. Tactile indicators are those indicators that the sniper can touch, i.e., trip wire, phone wire, hide positions. The tactile indicator is used mainly at night. Tactile indicators are defeated through the proper construction of sniper hides.

o    Auditory. An auditory target indicator is a sound that can be made by movement, equipment rattling, or talking. These target indicators are most noticeable during hours of darkness. The enemy may dismiss small noises as natural, but when they hear someone speak, they know for certain that others are near. Equipment should be silenced before a mission so that no sounds will be made while the sniper is running or walking. Auditory indicators are defeated through noise discipline and proper equipment preparation.

o    Visual. The visual target indicator is the most important target indicator. The primary reason the sniper is detected is because he has been seen by the enemy. Subcategories of visual target indicators will aid the sniper in locating the enemy and will help prevent the sniper from being detected. Visual indicators are defeated through the proper use of the principles of concealment.

*    Movement. The human eye is attracted to movement. A stationary target may be impossible to locate; a slowly moving target may go undetected; but a quick or jerky movement will be seen quickly. This indicator is most noticeable during hours of daylight.

*    Improper camouflage. Improper camouflage is a contrast of colors that does not match the area of operation.

*    Shine. Shine comes from reflective objects exposed and not toned down. The lenses of optical gear will reflect light.

*    Outline. A sniper must disguise the outline of his body. The use of the ghillie suit will aid in breaking up the outline.

*    Geometric shapes. In this world, all shapes in the woods and forests are irregular. Weapons, optical gear, and buildings are geometric shapes that will stand out.

*    Silhouette. A sniper may silhouette himself against a lighter or darker background that will contrast, showing a distinct outline.

4

        *     Disturbance of wildlife. A sniper may give himself
away if any of the following occur: birds suddenly flying away, a
sudden stop of animal noises, or animals being spooked.

## Principles of Concealment

        o     Shape. Military equipment and personnel have familiar
outlines and specific shapes that are easily recognizable.  A
sniper must alter or disguise these revealing shapes and outlines.

        o     Shadows.   Shadows, if used correctly, can be very
effective in hiding a sniper's position.  Shadows can be found
under most conditions of day and night.

        o     Silhouettes.   Silhouettes can be easily seen in the
daytime as well as at night.  A sniper must break up the outline of
his body and his equipment so that it blends with the background in
order to reduce the possibility of his silhouette being recognized.

        o     Surface.   Reflections of light on shiny surfaces can
instantly attract attention and can be seen for great distances.
Objects that have a distinguishable surface, such as hats, gloves,
and shirt sleeves must be camouflaged in order to remain unseen.

        o     Spacing. Spacing will normally become a more important
factor when more than one sniper team is deployed together, but it
is still a factor with one sniper team.  A sniper team must
consider the spacing between team members when moving to an
objective and at the objective or firing position.  This will
normally depend on the terrain and the enemy situation.

        o     Color. Changing seasons cause vegetation to change.  A
sniper must be aware of the color of vegetation so that he does not
contrast with it.

        o     Movement. The most common reason why a sniper's position
is revealed to the enemy is due to movement.  Even if all other
indicators are absent, movement can give a sniper's position away.

        o     Siting.  Siting is dependent upon three factors:

        *     Mission.

        *     Dispersion    (more   than   one   sniper   team   per
objective).

        *     Terrain patterns (rural, urban, wooded, barren).

## Effect of Terrain Patterns and Weather Conditions
     Weather conditions for the duration of the mission must be
considered, since the weather changes.  Terrain patterns vary
during the mission.  The terrain pattern at the objective may be

quite different from the pattern of the routes to and from the objective.

## Types of Camouflage
The two types of camouflage that the sniper team can use to camouflage itself and its equipment are natural and artificial.

o    Natural. Natural camouflage is vegetation or materials that are native to the given area. The sniper team should always augment its appearance by using some natural camouflage. Natural foliage, properly applied, is preferred to artificial material, but the sniper must be aware of wilting.

o    Artificial. Artificial camouflage is any material or substance that is produced for the purpose of coloring or covering something in order to conceal it. Camouflage sticks or face paints are used to cover all exposed areas of skin, such as face, hands, and the back of the neck. The parts of the face that form shadows should be darkened. The sniper team uses three types of camouflage patterns:

*    Striping. Used when in heavily wooded areas, and leafy vegetation is scarce.

*    Blotching. Used when an area is thick with leafy vegetation.

*    Combination. Used when moving through changing terrain. It is normally the best all-round pattern.

## Camouflage Materials
The types of camouflage materials to be applied to exposed skin are as follows:

o    Artificial materials (or manufactured materials).

o    Army issued camouflaged paint sticks.

*    Loam and light green--used for light-skinned personnel, in all but snow regions.

*    Sand and light green--used for dark-skinned personnel, in all but snow regions.

*    Loam and white--used for all personnel in snow-covered terrain.

o    Commercial hunter's paint. There are many different colors.

o    Stage makeup.

6

o    Bear grease.

o    Natural materials (or self-made materials).

   *    Burnt cork.

   *    Charcoal.
   *    Lampblack (carbide).

   *    Mud.

CAUTION:  Dyes or paints should not be used, as they do not
         come off.

## Camouflage Clothing

o    US Army uniforms.

   *    Camouflage fatigues.

   *    Battle dress uniforms (BDUs).

   *    Desert BDUs.

   *    Overwhites.

   *    Desert night camouflage uniforms.

o    Foreign army uniforms.

o    Gloves/mittens.

o    Head masks.

   *    Balaclavas.

   *    Veils.

   *    Head covers.

   *    Kaffias.

   *    Ghillie or sniper hats.

## Ghillie Suit
     The term "ghillie suit" originated in Scotland during the
1800s.  Scottish game wardens made special camouflage suits in
order to catch poachers.  Today the ghillie suit is a specially
made camouflage uniform that is covered with irregular patterns of
garnish or netting (Figure 4-1-1).

7

Ghillie suits can be made from BDUs or one-piece aviator-type uniforms. Turning the uniform inside out places the pockets inside the suit. This protects items in the pockets from damage caused by crawling on the ground. The front of the ghillie suit should be covered with canvas or some type of heavy cloth to reinforce it. The knees and elbows should be covered with two layers of canvas, and the seam of the crotch should be reinforced with heavy nylon thread since these areas are prone to wear out more often. Shoo-goo is excellent for attaching the canvas to the uniform.

The garnish or netting should cover the shoulders and reach down to the elbows on the sleeves. The garnish applied to the back of the suit should be long enough to cover the sides of the sniper when he is in the prone position. A bush hat is also covered with garnish or netting. The garnish should be long enough to break up the outline of the sniper's neck, but should not be so long in front to obscur his vision or hinder movement. A cut-up hammock makes an excellent foundation for the garnish.

A veil can be made from a net or piece of cloth covered with garnish or netting. It covers the weapon and sniper's head when in a firing position. The veil can be sewn into the ghillie suit or carried separately. The veil can also be sewn into a boonie hat. Remember, a ghillie suit does not make one invisible and is only a camouflage base. Natural vegetation should be added to help blend with the surroundings.

## Camouflage for Equipment

The sniper must camouflage all the equipment that he will use. However, he ensures that the camouflage does not interfere with or hinder the operation of the equipment.

Rifles. The sniper weapon system and the M16/M203 should also be camouflaged to break up their outlines. The sniper must not bind the scope of the M21 to a point that it will not adjust properly or have loose garnish that will get caught in the bolt of the rifle. The sniper weapon system can be carried in a "drag bag" (Figure 4-1-2), which is a rifle case made of canvas and covered with garnish similar to the ghillie suit. However, the rifle will not be combat ready while it is in the drag bag.

Optics. Optics used by the sniper team must also be camouflaged to break up the outline and to reduce the possibility of light reflecting off the lenses. Lenses can be covered with mesh-type webbing or nylon hose material.

ALICE pack. If the sniper uses the ALICE pack while wearing the ghillie suit, he must camouflage the pack the same as the suit. He can use paints, dyes, netting, and garnish.

8

## Facial Camouflage Patterns

Facial patterns can vary from irregular stripes across the face to bold splotching. The best pattern, perhaps, is a combination of both strips and blotches. Avoid wild types of designs and colors that stand out from the background. Cover all exposed skin, to include:

The hands and forearms.

The neck, front and back.

The ears, as well as behind the ears.

The face.

    Forehead--darkened.

    Cheekbones--darkened.

    Nose--darkened.

    Chin--darkened.

    Under eyes--lightened.

    Under nose--lightened.

    Under chin--lightened.

## Use of Removable Camouflage Spray Paint on the SWS and Equipment

The sniper weapon should be painted with a removable paint ("Bow Flage") so that the colors can be changed to suit different vegetation and changing seasons. Bow-Flage spray paint will not affect the accuracy or performance of the weapon; however, care must be taken when applying this paint. Bow-Flage should not contact the lens of optical equipment, the bore of the weapon, the chamber, the face of the bolt, the trigger area, or the adjustment knobs of the telescope. Bow-Flage is easily removed with Bow-Flage remover or Shooters Choice cleaning solvent, but it will not damage the weapon to be stored with the paint on it.

## Field-Expedient Camouflage

The sniper team may have to use field-expedient camouflage if other methods are not available. Instead of camouflage sticks or face paint, the team may use charcoal, walnut stain, mud, or whatever works. The team will not use oil or grease due to the strong odor. Natural vegetation can be attached to the body by boot bands or rubber bands or by cutting holes in the uniform.

9

## 4-2. COVER AND CONCEALMENT

The proper understanding and application of the principles of cover and concealment used with the proper application of camouflage protects the sniper team from enemy observation.

## Cover

Cover is natural or artificial protection from the fire of enemy weapons. Natural cover (ravines, hollows, reverse slopes) and artificial cover (fighting positions, trenches, walls) protects the sniper team from flat trajectory fires and partly protects it from high-angle fires and the effects of nuclear explosions. Even the smallest depression or fold in the ground may provide some cover when the team needs it most. A 6-inch depression, properly used, may provide enough cover to save the sniper team under fire. It must always look for and take advantage of all cover the terrain offers. By combining this habit with proper movement techniques, the team can protect itself from enemy fire. To get protection from enemy fire when moving, it uses routes that put cover between itself and the places where the enemy is known or thought to be. The team uses natural and artificial cover to keep the enemy from seeing and firing at it.

## Concealment

Concealment is natural or artificial protection from enemy observation. The surroundings may provide natural concealment that needs no change before use (bushes, grass, and shadows). The sniper team creates artificial concealment from materials, such as burlap and camouflage nets, or it can move natural materials (bushes, leaves, and grass) from their original location. The sniper team must consider the effects of the change of seasons on the concealment provided by both natural and artificial materials.

The principles of concealment include the following:

o    Avoid unnecessary movement. Remain still--movement attracts attention. The sniper team's position may be concealed when it remains still, yet easily detected if it moves. This movement against a stationary background makes the team stand out clearly. When the team must change positions, it moves carefully over a concealed route to the new position, preferably during limited visibility. It moves inches at a time, slowly and cautiously, always scanning ahead for the next position.

o    Use all available concealment:

*    Background. Background is important; the sniper team must blend with it to prevent detection. The trees, bushes, grass, earth, and man-made structures that form the background vary in color and appearance. This makes it possible for the team to blend in with them. The team selects trees or bushes to blend with

the uniform and to absorb the figure outline. It must always assume that its area is under observation.

        *     Shadows. The sniper team in the open stands out clearly, but the sniper team in the shadows is difficult to see. Shadows exist under most conditions, day and night. A sniper team should never fire from the edge of a wood line; it should fire from a position inside the wood line (in the shade or shadows provided by the tree tops).

        o     Stay low to observe. A low silhouette makes it difficult for the enemy to see a sniper team. Therefore, the team observes from a crouch, a squat, or a prone position.

        o     Expose nothing that shines. Reflection of light on a shiny surface instantly attracts attention and can be seen from great distances. The sniper uncovers his rifle scope only when indexing and reducing a target. He uses optics cautiously in bright sunshine because of the reflections they cause.

        o     Avoid skylining. Figures on the skyline can be seen from a great distance, even at night, because a dark outline stands out against the lighter sky. The silhouette formed by the body makes a good target.

        o     Alter familiar outlines. Military equipment and the human body are familiar outlines to the enemy. The sniper team alters or disguises these revealing shapes by using the ghillie suit or outer smock that is covered with irregular patterns of garnish. The team must alter its outline from the head to the soles of the boots.

        o     Keep quiet. Noise, such as talking, can be picked up by enemy patrols or observation posts. The team silences gear before a mission so that it makes no sound when it walks or runs.

## 4-3. INDIVIDUAL AND TEAM MOVEMENT

In many cases the success of a sniper's mission will depend upon his being able to close the range to his target, engage or observe the target, and withdraw without being detected. To do this, he must be able to move silently through different types of terrain.

### Preparation for Movement
As with any mission, the sniper team must make preparations prior to movement. They must make a detailed study of large-scale maps and aerial photographs of the area, they must interview inhabitants and people who have been through the areas before, and they must review any other intelligence available about the area. Sand tables of the area of operations may be constructed to assist

11

in forming and rehearsing the plan. They must also select camouflage to suit the area. The sniper team must allow enough time for the selection of the proper camouflage, which should match the type of terrain the team will be moving through. Prior to movement, an inspection should be held for all personnel to ensure that all shiny equipment is toned down and that all gear is silenced. The sniper must ensure that only mission essential gear is taken along.

o    Route selection. In selecting routes of movement, a sniper should try to avoid known enemy positions and obstacles, open areas, and areas believed to be under enemy observation. The sniper should select routes that make maximum use of cover and concealment; trails should never be used. Advantage should be taken of the more difficult terrain--swamps, dense woods, etc.

o    Movement. The sniper team cannot afford to be seen at any time by anyone. Therefore, their movement will be slow and deliberate. The movement over any given distance will be considerably slower than infantry units. Stealth is a sniper's security.

## Rules of Movement
When moving, the sniper team should always remember the following rules:

o    Always assume that the area is under enemy observation.

o    Move slowly. A sniper counts his movement progress by feet and inches.

o    Do not cause the overhead movement of trees, bushes, or tall grasses by rubbing against them.

o    Plan every movement and move in segments of the route at a time.

o    Stop, look, and listen often.

o    Move during disturbances such as gunfire, explosions, aircraft noise, wind, or anything that will distract the enemy's attention or conceal the team's movement.

## Types of Movement
The sniper team will always move with caution; they will employ various methods of walking and crawling based upon the enemy threat and the speed of movement required.

o    Walking. Walking is the fastest and easiest way to move when extreme silence is desired. It is also the most expedient form of individual sniper movement. It is used when threat is low and speed is important. The sniper walks in a crouch to maintain a low profile with shadows and bushes so as not to be silhouetted (Figure 4-3-1). When walking, the sniper ensures that his footing is solid. He keeps his weight on one foot as he raises the other, being sure to clear all brush; then gently sets the moving foot down, toes first, and then the heel. Short steps are taken to maintain balance. The weapon is carried in line with the body by grasping the forward sling swivel. The muzzle is kept pointed down. At night, the weapon is held close to the body to free the other hand to feel for obstacles.

o    Hands and knees crawl. This crawl is used when cover is adequate or silence is necessary. It is self-explanatory in that the sniper uses his hands and knees to crawl (Figure 4-3-2). The rifle is held in one hand close to the chest in line with the body or placed on the ground along the side of the body. The weight of the upper body is supported by the opposite arm. While supporting the rifle in one hand, the sniper picks a point ahead to position the opposite hand and slowly and quietly moves the hand into position. When moving the hand into position, the sniper may support the weight of his upper body on the opposite elbow. The sniper then alternately moves his hands forward, being careful not to make any noise. Leaves, twigs, and pebbles can be moved out of the way with the hand if absolute silence is required.

o    High crawl. The high crawl is used when cover is more prevalent or when speed is required (Figure 4-3-3). The body is kept free of the ground and the weight rests on the forearms and the lower legs (shins). The rifle can either be carried as in the low crawl or cradled in the arms. Movement is made by alternately pulling with each arm and pushing with one leg. The sniper can alternate legs for pushing when cover is adequate. An alternate method is to pull with both arms and push with one leg. The sniper should ALWAYS keep in mind that the head and buttocks cannot be raised too high and the legs must not be allowed to make excessive noise when being dragged over brush and debris.

o    Medium crawl. The medium crawl is used in fairly low cover (Figure 4-3-4). It is faster than the low crawl and less tiring to the body. The medium crawl is similar to the low crawl, except that one leg is cocked forward to push with. One leg is used until tired; then the other leg is used. However, the sniper must not alternate legs, as this causes the lower portion of the body to rise into the air.

o    Low crawl. The sniper uses the low crawl when an enemy is near, when vegetation is sparse, or when moving in or out of position to fire or to observe (Figure 4-3-5). To low crawl, the sniper lies face down on the ground, legs together, feet flat on the ground, and arms to the front and flat on the ground. To carry the rifle, the sniper grasps the upper portion of the sling and lays the stock on the back of his hand or wrist, with the rifle lying on the inside of his body under one arm. The rifle can be

13

pushed forward as the sniper moves. However, care must be taken to ensure that the muzzle does not protrude into the air or stick into the ground. To move forward, the sniper extends his arms and pulls with his arms while pushing with his toes, being careful not to raise his heels or head. This type of movement is extremely slow and requires practice to keep from using quick or jerky movements.

o       Turning while crawling. It may be necessary to change direction or turn completely around while crawling. To execute a right turn, the sniper moves his upper body as far to the right as possible and then moves his left leg to the left as far as possible. The right leg is then closed to the left leg. This will create a pivot-type movement (Figure 4-3-6). Left turns are done in the opposite fashion.

o       Backward movement. The sniper moves backwards by reversing the crawling movement.

o       Assuming the prone position. The sniper assumes the prone position from a walk by stopping, tucking his rifle under his arm, and crouching slowly. Simultaneously, he feels the ground with the free hand for a clear spot. He then lowers his knees, one at a time, to the ground. He shifts his weight to one knee and lifts and extends the free leg to the rear. The toes are used to feel for a clear spot. Rolling onto that side, he then lowers the rest of his body into position.

o       Night movement. Movement at night is essentially the same as movement during the day, except that it must be slower and more deliberate because of the limited visibility. The sniper has to rely on the senses of touch and hearing to a greater extent. If at all possible, the sniper should move under the cover of darkness, fog, haze, rain, or high winds to conceal his movement. This is a safety factor; however, it makes the enemy harder to spot and specific positions or landmarks harder to locate.

## Stalking

Stalking is the sniper's art of moving unseen into a firing position within a range that will ensure a first-round kill and then withdrawing undetected. The stalk incorporates all aspects of field craft and can only be effectively learned by repeated practice over various types of ground.

o       Reconnaissance. The sniper should conduct a complete reconnaissance prior to his mission. Seldom will a sniper have an opportunity to view the ground. He must rely on maps and aerial photographs for his information. The sniper should address the following before stalking:

*       Location, position, or target to be stalked.

*       Cover and concealment.

14

* Best possible firing position to engage targets.

* Best line of advance to stalk.

* Obstacles, whether natural or artificial.

* Observation points along the route.

* Known or suspected enemy locations.

* Method of movement throughout the mission.
* Withdrawal route (to include method of movement).

o Conduct of the stalk.

* A sniper may lose his sense of direction while stalking, particularly if he has to crawl for any appreciable distance. The chances of this happening can be reduced if:

o A compass, map, and aerial photograph are used and the route, direction, and distance to various checkpoints are thoroughly and accurately planned.

o A distinct landmark or two, or even a series, have been memorized.

o The direction of the wind and sun are noted. However, the sniper must bear in mind that over a long period of time the wind direction can change and the sun will change position.

o The sniper has the ability to use terrain association.

* The sniper must be alert at all times. Any relaxation on a stalk can lead to carelessness, resulting in an unsuccessful mission and even death.

* Observation should be undertaken at periodic intervals. If the sniper is surprised or exposed during the stalk, immediate reaction is necessary. The sniper must decide whether to freeze or move quickly to the nearest cover and hide.

* The sniper must remember that disturbed animals or birds can draw attention to the area of approach. If animals are alarmed, the sniper should stop, wait, and listen. Their flight may indicate someone's approach or call attention to the sniper's position. However, advantage should be taken of any local disturbances or distractions that could enable the sniper to move more quickly than would otherwise be possible. It should be emphasized that such movement includes a degree of risk, and when the enemy is close, risks should be avoided.

15

*    While halted, the sniper identifies his next position.

   *    When moving through tall grass, the sniper should occasionally make a slight change of direction to keep the grass from waving in an unnatural motion.

   *    The sniper should be aware of any changes in local cover, since such changes will usually require an alteration to his personal camouflage.

   *    When crossing roads or trails, look for a low spot or cross on the leading edge of a curve. Avoid cleared areas, steep slopes, and loose rocks. The sniper should never skyline himself.

   o    Night stalking.

   Man is less adapted to stalking at night than during the day. He must use slower, more deliberate movement in order to occupy an observation post or a firing position. The principal differences between day stalking and night stalking are that at night:

   *    There is a degree of protection offered by the darkness against aimed enemy fire.

   *    While observation is still important, much more use is made of hearing, making silence vital.

   *    Cover is less important than background. The sniper should particularly avoid crests and skylines against which he may be silhouetted.

   *    Maintaining direction is much more difficult to achieve, which places greater emphasis on a thorough reconnaissance. A compass or knowledge of the stars may help.

## Silent Movement Techniques

   Stealthful movement is critical to sniper survival and mission success. This requires the sniper to learn the skills of: memorization of the ground and the surrounding terrain; silent and stealth movement; and movement over different terrain and various noise obstacles. The sniper must memorize the terrain, select a route, move, communicate using touch signals, and avoid or negotiate obstacles using stealth techniques. This is accomplished by:

   o    The sniper uses binoculars to observe the terrain to the front, simultaneously selecting a route of advance and memorizing the terrain.

16

o     The sniper partners plan signals for different obstacles. Considerations are:

     *     Finding the obstacles.

     *     Identifying the obstacles (barbed wire, explosives, mines).

     *     Negotiating the obstacles.   (Should the team go around, over, or under the obstacles?)

     *     Clearing the obstacles.   (Or getting caught in the obstacle.)

     *     Signaling partner.  A signal must be relayed to the sniper's partner.

o     Stealth and silent movement techniques are characterized by:

     *     Cautious and deliberate movement.

     *     Frequent halts to listen and observe.

     *     No unnecessary movement.

     *     Silent movement.  All equipment is taped and padded.

     *     Looking where the next move is going to be made.

     *     Clearing foliage or debris from the next position.

o     Passage of obstacles involves:

     *     Avoiding or by-passing noise obstacles.

     *     If noise obstacles must be moved through, checking the debris and clearing loose noise obstacles from the path.

     *     Memorizing locations of obstacles for night movement.

o     The basic elements of walking stealthily are:

     *     Maintaining balance.

     *     Shifting weight gradually from the rear foot to the front foot.

     *     Moving the rear foot to the front, taking care to clear brush, etc.  The moving foot may be placed either heel first, toe first, edge of foot first, or flat on the ground.

17

o     To move through rubble and debris:

        *        Test the debris with the hand.

        *        Remove debris that will break.

        *        Move forward as quickly as practical and as quietly
as possible.

        *        Putting the feet down flat-footed.  This will reduce
noise.

    o     Try to avoid moving through mud and muck.  If it cannot
be avoided, the boots should be wrapped with burlap rags or socks.

    o     Sand is noiseless to cross, so movement can be fairly
fast.

    o     To move over an obstacle, the sniper keeps a low
silhouette, ensuring that he does not brush or scrape against the
obstacle, lowers himself silently on the other side, and moves away
at a medium-slow pace.

    o     The sniper always maintains positive control of his
weapon.

**Detection Devices**
    The sniper must be constantly vigilant in his movements and
acts to defeat enemy detection.  These devices are:

    o     Passive and active light intensification devices.
Beyond direct enemy observation, the sniper must be aware of enemy
detection devices.  The enemy may employ these devices, and the
sniper may not know that he is under observation.  Where there is
the possibility that night vision devices are being used, the
sniper can combat them by moving very slowly and staying very low
to the ground.  In this way his dark silhouette will be broken up
by vegetation.  Preferably, the sniper will move in dark shadows or
tree lines that will obscure the enemy's vision.  Also, moving in
defilade through ground haze, fog, or rain will greatly benefit the
sniper by helping him to remain undetected.  Additionally, using
the new infrared reflecting material (used in equipment netting) as
a base for the ghillie suit will limit the enemy's infrared viewing
capabilities.

    o     Sensors.  Sensors are remote monitoring devices with
seismic sensors, magnetic sensors, motion sensors, infrared
sensors, or thermal sensors planted in the ground along likely
avenues of advance or perimeters.  These devices normally vary in
sensitivity.  They are triggered by vibration of the ground, metal,
movement, breaking a beam of light, or heat within their area of
influence.  The sniper can move past these devices undetected only

18

by using the slowest and most careful movement without mistakes. He can help combat the effects of seismic devices by moving when other actions that will activate the devices, such as artillery fire, low-flying aircraft, rain, snow, or even a heavy wind, are in progress or, in some instances, moving without rhythm. Most other sensors can be defeated if the sniper knows their limitations and capabilities.

o  Ground surveillance radars. Ground surveillance radars can detect troop or vehicle movement at an extended range, but only along its line of sight and only if the object is moving at a given speed or faster. It takes a well-trained individual to properly monitor the device. Snipers can combat the use of ground surveillance radars by moving in defilade, out of the direct line of sight of the equipment, or slower than the radar can detect. Movement should be extremely slow and low to the ground, using natural objects and vegetation to mask the movement.

o  Thermal imagers. Thermal imagers are infrared heat detectors that locate body heat. They may be used to detect the sniper. Even a motionless and camouflaged sniper could be located by these devices. One possible way to confuse such a detector would be to attach a space blanket (Mylar) to the inside of the camouflage suit. This would reflect the body heat inward and could possibly keep the sniper from being distinguished from the heat pattern of the surrounding terrain. This would work best when the temperature is warm and the greatest amount of radiant heat is rising from the ground.

## Selecting Lines of Advance
Part of the sniper's mission will be to analyze the terrain, select a good route to the target, use obstacles (manmade and natural) and terrain to their best advantage, and determine the best method of movement to arrive at his target. Once at the target site, he must be able to select firing positions and plan a stalk.

On the ground, the sniper looks for a route that will provide the best cover and concealment. Maximal use is made of low ground, dead space, and shadows. Open areas are avoided. Look for a route that will provide easy movement, yet will allow quiet movement at night. Select the route, then choose the movement technique(s) that will allow undetected movement over that specific terrain.

Position selection is critical to mission success. Do not select a position that looks obvious and ideal for a sniper. It will appear that way to the enemy. Select a position away from prominent terrain features of contrasting background. The position must give maximum cover and concealment. When possible, an area is selected that has an obstacle (natural or manmade) between the sniper and the target.

19

Stalk planning involves map and ground reconnaissance, selection of a route to the objective, selection of the type of movement, notation of known or suspected enemy locations, and selection of a route of withdrawal. Movement differs in many ways from that of the infantry squad. One of the most noticeable differences is the movement technique used by the sniper team. Movement by teams must not be detected or even suspected by the enemy. Because of this, a sniper team must master individual sniper movement techniques.

## Sniper Team Movement and Navigation

Snipers are employed in two-man teams consisting of one sniper and one observer. Normally, the sniper carries the sniper weapon system; the observer carries an M16/M203; and both have sidearms. Because of this lack of personnel and firepower, the sniper team cannot afford to be detected by the enemy nor can it successfully meet the enemy in sustained engagements.

When possible, the sniper team should have a security element (squad/platoon) attached. The security element allows the team to reach its area of operations quicker and safer than can be expected by the team operating alone. Plus, the security element provides the team a reaction force should the team be detected.

Snipers use the following guidelines when attaching a security element:

o    The security element leader is in charge of the team while it is attached.

o    Sniper teams always appear as an integral part of the element.

o    Sniper teams wear the same uniform as the element members.

o    Sniper teams maintain proper intervals and positions in all formations.

o    The sniper weapon system is carried in line and close to the body, hiding its outline and barrel length.

o    All equipment that is unique to sniper teams is concealed from view (optics, ghillie suits, and so forth).

o    Once in the area of operation, the sniper team separates from the security element and operates alone. Two examples of sniper teams separating from security elements are as follows:

*    The security element provides security while the team prepares for its operation.

20

o     The team dons the ghillie suits and camouflages itself and its equipment (if mission requires).

o     The team ensures that all equipment is secure and caches any nonessential equipment (if mission requires).

o     Once the team is prepared, it assumes a concealed position, and the security element departs the area.

o     Once the security element has departed, the team waits in position long enough to ensure neither itself nor the security element have been compromised. Then, the team moves to its tentative position.

*     The security element conducts a short security halt at the separation point. The sniper team members halt, ensuring they have good available concealment and know each other's location. The security element then proceeds, leaving the sniper team in place. The sniper team remains in position until the security element is clear of the area. The team then organizes itself as required by the mission and moves on to its tentative position. This type of separation also works well in MOUT situations.

When selecting routes, the sniper team must remember its strengths and weaknesses. The following guidelines should be used when selecting routes:

o     Avoid known enemy positions and obstacles.

o     Seek terrain that offers the best cover and concealment.

o     Take advantage of difficult terrain (swamps, dense woods, and so forth).

o     Avoid natural lines of drift.

o     Do not use trails, roads, or footpaths.

o     Avoid built-up or populated areas.

o     Avoid areas of heavy enemy guerrilla activity.

o     Avoid areas between opposing forces in contact with each other.

When the sniper team moves, it must always assume its area is under enemy observation. Because of this and the size of the team with the small amount of firepower it has, the team can use only one type of formation--the sniper movement formation. Characteristics of the formation are as follows:

o     The observer is the point man; the sniper follows.

21

o    The observer's sector of security is 8 o'clock to 4 o'clock; the sniper's sector of security is 2 o'clock to 10 o'clock (overlapping).

o    Visual contact must be maintained, even when lying on the ground.

o    An interval of no more than 20 meters is maintained.

o    The sniper reacts to the point man's actions.

o    The team leader designates the movement techniques and routes used.

o    The team leader designates rally points.

o    The team moves by using individual bounding techniques. They can move by successive bounds or alternating bounds.

o    Danger areas are crossed by changing movement techniques.

## Sniper Team Immediate Action Drills

A sniper team must never become decisively engaged with the enemy.  The team must rehearse immediate action drills to the extent that they become a natural and immediate reaction should they make unexpected contact with the enemy.  Examples of such actions are as follows:

Visual contact.  If the sniper team sees the enemy and the enemy does not see the team, the team freezes.  If the team has time, it will do the following:

o    Assume the best covered and concealed position.

o    Remain in position until the enemy has passed.

NOTE:  The team will not initiate contact.

Ambush.  In an ambush, the sniper team's objective is to break contact immediately.  One example of this involves performing the following:

o    The observer delivers rapid fire on the enemy.

o    The sniper throws smoke grenades between the observer and the enemy.

o    The sniper delivers well-aimed shots at the most threatening targets until smoke covers the area.

o     The observer then throws fragmentation grenades and withdraws toward the sniper, ensuring he does not mask the sniper's fire.

o     The team moves to a location where the enemy cannot observe or place direct fire on it.

o     If contact cannot be broken, the sniper calls for indirect fires/security element (if attached).

o     If team members get separated, they should either link up at the objective rally point or return to the next-to-last designated en route rally point.  This will depend upon the team SOP.

Indirect fire.  When reacting to indirect fires, the team must move out of the area as quickly as possible.  This sudden movement can result in the team's exact location and direction being pinpointed.  Therefore, the team must not only react to indirect fire but also take actions to conceal its movement once it is out of the impact area.

o     The team leader moves the team out of the impact area using the quickest route by giving the direction and distance (clock method).

o     Both members move out of the impact area the designated distance and direction.

o     The team leader then moves the team farther away from the impact area by using the most direct concealed route. They continue the mission using an alternate route.

o     If the team members get separated, they should either linkup at the the objective rally point or return to the next-to-last designated en route rally point.

Air attack.

o     Team members assume the best available covered and concealed positions.

o     Between passes of aircraft, team members move to a position that offers better cover and concealment.

o     The team does not engage the aircraft.

o     Team members remain in position until the attacking aircraft departs.

o     If team members get separated, they should linkup at the objective rally point or return to the next-to-last designated en route rally point.

23

## Navigational Aids

To aid the sniper team in navigation, the team should memorize the route by studying maps, aerial photos, or sketches. The team notes distinctive features (hills, streams, roads) and its location in relation to the route. It plans an alternate route in case the primary route cannot be used. It plans an offset to circumvent known obstacles to movement. The team uses terrain countdown, which involves memorizing terrain features from the start to the objective, to maintain the route. During the mission, the sniper team mentally counts each terrain feature, thus ensuring it maintains the proper route.

The sniper team maintains orientation at all times. As it moves, it observes the terrain carefully and mentally checks off the distinctive features noted in the planning and study of the route.

Many aids are available to ensure orientation:

o    The location and direction of flow of principal streams.

o    Hills, valleys, roads, and other peculiar terrain features.

o    Railroad tracks, power lines, and other man-made objects.


## 4-4.   TRACKING AND COUNTER-TRACKING

Tracking is the art of being able to follow a person or an animal by the signs that they leave during their movement. It is next to impossible to move cross country and not leave signs of one's passage. These signs, however, small, can be detected by a trained and experienced tracker. However, a person who is trained in tracking techniques can use deception drills that can minimize telltale signs and throw off or confuse trackers who are not well trained or who do not have the experience to spot the signs of a deception.

As a tracker follows a trail, he builds a picture of the enemy in his mind by asking himself questions: How many persons am I following? What is their state of training? How are they equipped? Are they healthy? What is their state of morale? Do they know they are being followed? To answer these questions, the tracker uses available indicators--that is, signs that tell an action occurred at a specific time and place (Figure 4-4-1). By comparing indicators, the tracker obtains answers to his questions.

## TRACKING

## Tracking Signs

24

Signs are visible marks left by an individual or an animal as it passes through an area. There are different categories of signs:

o     Ground signs. These are signs left below the knees. All ground signs are further divided into large and small ground signs.

*     Large ground signs. Are caused by the movement of 10 or more individuals through the area.

*     Small ground signs. Are caused by the movement of one to nine individuals through the area.

o     High signs. Also known as top signs. These are signs left above the knees. These signs are also divided into large and small top signs.

o     Temporary signs. Are those signs that will eventually fade with time (e.g., a footprint).

o     Permanent signs. Those signs that require weeks to fade or that will leave a mark forever (e.g., broken branches or chipped bark).

## Tracking Indicators

Any sign the tracker discovers can be defined by one of six tracking indicators: displacement, stains, weathering, litter, camouflage, and immediate-use intelligence.

## Displacement

Displacement takes place when anything is moved from its original position. A well-defined footprint in soft, moist ground is a good example of displacement. The footgear or bare feet of the person who left the print displaced the soil by compression, leaving an indentation in the ground. The tracker can study this sign and determine several important facts. For example, a print left by worn footgear or by bare feet may indicate lack of proper equipment. Displacement can also result from clearing a trail by breaking or cutting through heavy vegetation with a machete--such trails are obvious to the most inexperienced tracker. Individuals may unconsciously break more branches as they move behind someone who is cutting. Displacement indicators can also be made by persons carrying heavy loads who stop to rest; prints made by box edges can help to identify the load. When loads are set down at a rest halt or campsite, they usually crush grass and twigs. A reclining man can also flatten the vegetation.

Analyzing Footprints. Footprints can indicate direction, rate of movement, number, and sex, and whether the individual know he is being tracked.

o    If footprints are deep and the pace is long, rapid movement is apparent.  Extremely long strides and deep prints with toe prints deeper than heel prints indicate running (Figure 4-4-2).

o    Prints that are deep, short, and widely spaced, with signs of scuffing or shuffling indicate the person who left the print is carrying a heavy load (Figure 4-4-3).

o    If the party members realize they are being followed, they may try to hide their tracks.  Persons walking backward (Figure 4-4-4) have a short, irregular stride.  The prints have an unnaturally deep toe, and soil is displaced in the direction of movement.

o    To determine the sex of a member of the party being followed (Figure 4-4-5), the tracker should study the size and position of the footprints.  Women tend to be pigeon-toed, while men walk with their feet straight ahead or pointed slightly to the outside.  Prints left by women are usually smaller and the stride is usually shorter than that taken by men.

Determining Key Prints.  Normally, the last man in the file leaves the clearest footprints; these should be the key prints.  The tracker cuts a stick to match the length of the prints and notches it to show the length and widest part of the sole.  He can then study the angle of the key prints in relation to the direction of march.  He looks for an identifying mark or feature, such as worn or frayed footgear, to identify the key prints.  If the trail becomes vague, erased, or merges with another, the tracker can employ his stick-measuring device and identify the key prints with close study.  This method helps him to stay on the trail.  By using the box method, he can count up to 18 persons.  There are two ways the tracker can employ the box method:

o    The most accurate is to use the stride as a unit of measure (Figure 4-4-6) when determining key prints.  The tracker uses these prints and the edges of the road or trail to box in an area to analyze.

o    The tracker may also use the 36-inch box method (Figure 4-4-7) if key prints are not evident.  To use the 36-inch box method, the tracker uses the edges of the road or trail as the sides of the box.  He measures a cross section of the area 36 inches long, counting each indentation in the box and dividing by two.  This method gives a close estimate of the number of individuals who made the prints; however, this system is not as accurate as the stride measurement.

Recognizing Other Signs of Displacement.  Foliage, moss, vines, sticks, or rocks that are scuffed or snapped from their original position form valuable indicators.  Broken dirt seals around rocks, mud or dirt moved to rocks or other natural debris, and water moved onto the banks of a stream are also good indicators. Vines may be dragged, dew droplets displaced, or stones and sticks overturned to show a different color underneath. Grass or other vegetation may be bent or broken in the direction of movement (Figure 4-4-8).

o    The tracker inspects all areas for bits of clothing, threads, or dirt from footgear than can be torn or can fall and be left on thorns, snags, or the ground.

o    Flushed from their natural habitat, wild animals and birds are another example of displacement. Cries of birds excited by unnatural movement is an indicator; moving tops of tall grass or brush on a windless day indicates that someone is moving the vegetation.

o    Changes in the normal life of insects and spiders may indicate that someone has recently passed. Valuable clues are disturbed bees, ant holes covered by someone moving over them, or torn spider webs. Spiders often spin webs across open areas, trails, or roads to trap flying inspects. If the tracked person does not avoid these webs, he leaves an indicator to an observant tracker.

o    If the person being followed tries to use a stream to cover his trail, the tracker can still follow successfully. Algae and other water plants can be displaced by lost footing or by careless walking. Rocks can be displaced from their original position or overturned to indicate a lighter or darker color on the opposite side. The person entering or exiting a stream creates slide marks or footprints, or scuffs the bark on roots or sticks (Figure 4-4-9). Normally, a person or animal seeks the path of least resistance; therefore, when searching the stream for an indication of departures, trackers will find signs in open areas along the banks.

## Stains

A stain occurs when any substance from one organism or article is smeared or deposited on something else. The best example of staining is blood from a profusely bleeding wound. Bloodstains often appear as spatters or drops and are not always on the ground; they also appear smeared on leaves or twigs of trees and bushes. The tracker can also determine the seriousness of the wound and how far the wounded person can move unassisted. This process may lead the tracker to enemy bodies or indicate where they have been carried.

By studying bloodstains, the tracker can determine the wound's location:

o    If the blood seems to be dripping steadily, it probably came from a wound on the trunk.

27

o     If the blood appears to be slung toward the front, rear, or sides, the wound is probably in the extremity.

o     Arterial wounds appear to pour blood at regular intervals as if poured from a pitcher.  If the wound is veinous, the blood pours steadily.

o     A lung wound deposits pink, bubbly, and frothy bloodstains.

o     A bloodstain from a head wound appears heavy, wet, and slimy.

o     Abdominal wounds often mix blood with digestive juices so the deposit has an odor and is light in color.

Any body fluids, such as urine, or feces, deposited on the ground, trees, bushes, or rocks will leave a stain.

On a calm, clear day, leaves of bushes and small trees are generally turned so that the dark top side shows.  However, when a man passes through an area and disturbs the leaves, he will generally cause the lighter side of the leaf to show.  This is also true with some varieties of grass.  This causes an unnatural discoloration of the area, which is called "shine."  Grass or leaves that have been stepped on will have a bruise on the lighter side.

Staining can also occur when muddy footgear is dragged over grass, stones, and shrubs.  Thus, staining and displacement combine to indicate movement and direction.  Crushed leaves may stain rocky ground that is too hard to show footprints.  Roots, stones, and vines may be stained where leaves or berries are crushed by moving feet.

The tracker may have difficulty in determining the difference between staining and displacement since both terms can be applied to some indicators.  For example, muddied water may indicate recent movement; displaced mud also stains the water.  Muddy footgear can stain stones in streams, and algae can be displaced from stones in steams and can stain other stones or the bank.  Muddy water collects in new footprints in swampy ground; however, the mud settles and the water clears with time.  The tracker can use this information to indicate time; normally, the mud clears in about one hour, although time varies with the terrain.  Since muddied water travels with the current, it is usually best to move downstream.

## Weathering
Weathering either aids or hinders the tracker.  It also affects indicators in certain ways so that the tracker can determine their relative ages.  However, wind, snow, rain, or

28

sunlight can erase indicators entirely and hinder the tracker. The tracker should know how weathering affects soil, vegetation, and other indictors in his area. He cannot properly determine the age of indicators until he understands the effects that weathering has on trail signs.

By studying weathering effects on indicators, the tracker can determine the age of the sign. For example, when bloodstains are fresh, they are bright red. Air and sunlight first change blood to a deep ruby-red color, then to a dark brown crust when the moisture evaporates. Scuff marks on trees or bushes darken with time; sap oozes, then hardens when it makes contact with the air.

Weather greatly affects footprints (Figure 4-4-10). By carefully studying this weathering process, the tracker can estimate the age of the print. If particles of soil are just beginning to fall into the print, the tracker should become a stalker. If the edges of the print are dried and crusty, the prints are probably about one hour old. This process varies with terrain and is only a guide.

A light rain may round the edges of the print. By remembering when the last rain occurred, the tracker can place the print into a time frame. A heavy rain may erase all signs.

Trails exiting streams may appear weathered by rain due to water running from clothing or equipment into the tracks. This is especially true if the party exits the stream single file. Then, each person deposits water into the tracks. The existence of a wet, weathered trail slowly fading into a dry trail indicates the trail is fresh.

Wind dries out tracks and blows litter, sticks or leaves into prints. By recalling wind activity, the tracker may estimate the age of the tracks. For example, the tracker may reason "the wind is calm at the present but blew hard about an hour ago. These tracks have litter blown into them, so they must be over an hour old." However, he must be sure that the litter was blown into the prints and not crushed into them when the prints were made.

Wind affects sound and odors. If the wind is blowing down the trail (toward the tracker) sounds and odors may be carried to him; conversely, if the wind is blowing up the trail (away from the tracker), he must be extremely cautious since wind also carries sounds toward the enemy. The tracker can determine wind direction by dropping a handful of dust or dried grass from shoulder height. By pointing in the same direction the wind is blowing, the tracker can localize sounds by cupping his hands behind his ears and turning slowly. When sounds are loudest, the tracker is facing the origin.

In calm weather (no wind), air currents that may be too light to detect can carry sounds to the tracker. Air cools in the evening and moves downhill toward the valleys. If the tracker is moving uphill late in the day or night, air currents will probably be moving toward him if no other wind is blowing. As the morning sun warms the air in the valleys, it moves uphill. The tracker considers these factors when plotting patrol routes or other operations. If he keeps the wind in his face, sounds and odors will be carried to him from his objective or from the party being tracked.

The sun should also be considered by the tracker. It is difficult to fire directly into the sun, but if the tracker has the sun at his back and the wind in his face, he has a slight advantage.

## Litter
Litter consists of anything not indigenous to the area that is left on the ground. A poorly trained or poorly disciplined unit moving over terrain is apt to leave a trail of litter. Unmistakable signs of recent movement are gum or candy wrappers, ration cans, cigarette butts, remains of fires, urine, human feces, and bloody bandages. Rain flattens or washes litter away and turns paper into pulp. Exposure to weather can cause ration cans to rust at the opened edge; then, the rust moves toward the center. The tracker must consider weather conditions when estimating the age of litter. He can use the last rain or strong wind as the basis for a time frame.

The sniper should also know the wildlife in the area, because even sumps, regardless of how well camouflaged they are, are a potential source of litter. This is due to the fact that many animals can find the sump and dig it up for food. The best policy you can follow is to take out with you everything you brought in.

## Camouflage
Camouflage applies to tracking when the followed party employs techniques to baffle or slow the tracker--that is, walking backward to leave confusing prints, brushing out trails, and moving over rocky ground or through streams. This would indicate a trained adversary.

## Immediate-Use Intelligence
The tracker combines all indicators and interprets what he has seen to form a composite picture for on-the-spot intelligence. For example, indicators may show contact is imminent and require extreme stealth.

The tracker avoids reporting his interpretations as facts. He reports what he has seen, rather than stating these things exist. There are many ways a tracker can interpret the sex and size of the party, the load, and the type of equipment. Time frames can be determined by weathering effects on indicators.

Immediate-use intelligence is information about the enemy that can be used to gain surprise, to keep him off balance, or to keep him from escaping the area entirely. The commander may have many sources of intelligence: reports, documents, or prisoners of war. These sources can be combined to form indicators of the enemy's last location, future plans, and destination.

Tracking, however, gives the commander definite information on which to act immediately. For example, a unit may report there are no men of military age in a village. This information is of value only if it is combined with other information to make a composite enemy picture in the area. Therefore, a tracker who interprets trail signs and reports that he is 30 minutes behind a known enemy unit, moving north, and located at a specific location, gives the commander information on which he can act.

## Dog-Tracker Teams

There are three types of tracker dogs:

o    Visual dogs. Rely upon their acute vision.

o    Search dogs. Are allowed to run free and search using airborne scents.

o    Tracker dogs. Run on leashes and use ground scents.

Many myths surround the abilities and limitations of canine trackers. The first and perhaps greatest myth is that tracking involves only the dog's sense of smell. Canine tracking involves a team--a merging of man and dog. Dogs use both their eyes and ears; the tracker uses his eyes and knowledge of the quarry. Together, they create an effective team that maximizes their strengths and minimizes their weaknesses. The sniper team is not only trying to evade and outwit "just" a dog but also the dog's handler. The most common breed of dog used is the German Shepherd. These dogs are trained to respond independently to a variety of situations and threats. Good tracking dogs are a rare and difficult-to-replace asset.

A visual tracker assists the dog handlers in finding a track if the dog loses the trail. He can radio ahead to another tracker and give him an oral account of the track picture. A visual tracker is slower than dogs, because he must always use his powers of observation, which creates fatigue. His effectivensss is limited at night.

A misconception is that dogs can smell molecular-level deposits left by the quarry. While it is true that blood, oil, or linked trails of material can be followed, this is not the primary

31

scent that a dog tracks. Dogs smell microbes in the earth that are released from disturbed soil. The trail has no innate smell of a specific quarry, although trails do vary depending on the size and number of the quarry. For example, a scent is like the wake a ship leaves in the ocean, but no part of the ship is left in the wake. It is the white, foamy, disturbed water that is the trail. This is entirely different from a point smell of the quarry such as sweat, urine, cigarette smoke, and so forth. The same training that makes tracking dogs adept at tracking a scent trail applies to finding a point smell.

Smelling is a highly complex process and many variables affect it. The most important element in tracking is "living" ground such as earth and grass that has living microbes in it and are disturbed by the quarry's passage. Artificial surfaces (concrete and macadam) and mainly inorganic surfaces (stone) provide little or no living microbes to form a scent track.

A dog builds a scent picture of the person that he is tracking. Scent is short lived, and its life span is dependent upon the weather and the area that the person last passed through. The sun and the wind, as well as time, destroy the scent. There are both airborne and ground scents. Airborne scents can be blown away within minutes or a few hours. Ground scents can last as long as 48 hours under ideal conditions.

Wind and moisture are other major variables that affect tracking. Foggy and drizzly weather that keeps the ground moist is best. Too much rain can wash a trail away; depending on the strength of the trail, it takes persistent, hard rain to erase a scent rail. Usually, the scent is not washed away but only sealed beneath a layer of ground water. A short, violent rainful could deposit enough water to seal the scent track, but after the rain stops and the water layer evaporates, the microbe trail would again be detectable by dogs. Hard, dry ground releases the fewest microbes and is the most difficult terrain for dogs to track on. A dog may also have difficulty following a trail on a beach or dusty path, but his human tracker could easily follow the footprints visually. Snipers must always remember they are being tracked by a man and dog team.

Wind strength and direction are important factors in tracking. Basically, strong wind inhibits tracking a scent trail but makes it easier for a dog to find a point scent source--like a hide. A general rule is that a dog can smell a man-size source downwind out to 50 meters and a group-size source--a hide--out to 200 meters under ideal conditons. Upwind, a source 1 meter away could be missed.

Wind Direction -->

Wind Speed:                    Still          Windy

```
        D--X--------D------------D
```

Distance:        1 meter    30 to 50      Maximum 150 to 200 meters
                            meters

    D = Dog Team
    X = Sniper/Sniper Team

    A strong wind disperses microbes that arise from the ground,
hindering a dog's ability to follow a trail. However, a strong
wind increases the size of a point scent, helping a dog to find the
target in an area search.

    An inflexible rule for the life of a scent trail cannot be
provided. In West Germany, the trackers rate their chance of
following a trail that is more than three days old as negligible.
Terrain, weather, and the sensitivity of the tracking dog are some
of the many variables that affect the scent trail. A point smell
will last as long as the target emits odors.

    While dogs are mainly scent hunters, they also have good
short-range vision. Dogs are color blind and do not have good
distance vision (camouflage works extremely well against dogs);
they can, however, detect slight movements. Dogs also have a
phenomenal sense of hearing, extending far beyond human norms in
both the frequency range and in sensitivity. Dogs use smell to
approximate a target, and then rely on sound and movement to
pinpoint that target.

    Although dogs have tremendous detection abilities, they also
have limitations. Following a scent trail is the most difficult
task a tracking dog can perform. The level of effort is so intense
that most dogs cannot work longer than 20 to 30 minutes at a time,
followed by a 10-to-20 minute rest. Dogs can perform this cycle no
more than five or six times in an 24-hour period before reaching
complete exhaustion. The efficiency of the search also decreases
as the dog tires. In wartime, the situation will force the maximum
from men and equipment, but times should remain constant for dog
endurance. In war or peace, dogs always give 100 percent effort;
they enjoy tracking. If the snipers keep moving and stay out of
the detection range of the human handlers, then they could outlast
the dog-scent trackers.

    When looking for sniper teams, trackers mainly use woodline
sweeps and area searches. A woodline sweep consists of walking the
dog upwind of a suspected woodline or brush line--the key is
upwind. If the wind is blowing through the woods and out of the
woodline, trackers move 50 to 100 meters inside a wooded area to
sweep the wood's edge. Since woodline sweeps tend to be less
specific, trackers perform them faster. An area search is used
when a team's location is specific such as a small wooded area or
block of houses. The search area is cordoned off, if possible, and

                              33

the dog-tracker teams are brought on line, about 25 to 150 meters apart, depending on terrain and visibility. The handlers then advance, each moving their dogs through a specific corridor. The handler controls the dog entirely with voice command and gestures. He remains undercover, directing the dog in a search pattern or to a likely target area. The search line moves forward with each dog dashing back and forth in assigned sectors.

## Techniques to Defeat Dog-Tracker Teams

While dog and handler tracking teams are a potent threat, there are counters available to the sniper team. As always, the best defenses are basic infantry techniques: good camouflage and light, noise, and trash discipline. Dogs find a team either by detecting a trail or by a point source such as human waste odors at the hide site. It is critical to try to obscure or limit trails around the hide, especially along the woodline or area closest to the team's target area. Surveillance targets are usually major axes of advance. "Trolling the woodlines" along likely-looking roads or intersections is a favorite tactic of dog/tracker teams. When moving into a target area, the sniper team should take the following countermeasures:

o   Remain as far away from the target area as the situation allows.

o   Never establish a position at the edge of cover and concealment nearest the target area.

o   Minimize the track. Try to approach the position area on hard, dry ground or along a stream or river.

o   Urinate in a hole and cover it up. Never urinate in exactly the same spot.

o   Deeply bury fecal matter. If the duration of the mission permits, use MRE bags sealed with tape and take it with you.

o   Never smoke.

o   Carry all trash until it can be buried elsewhere.

o   Surround the hide with a 3- to 5-cm band of motor oil to mask odor; although less effective but easier to carry, garlic may be used. A dead animal can also be used to mask smell, although it may attract unwanted canine attention.

When dogs are being used against a sniper team, they use other odors left behind or around the team to find it. Sweat from exertion or fear is one of these. Wet clothing or material from damp environments holds in the scent. Soap or deodorant used prior to infiltration helps the dogs to find the team. Foreign odors, such as oils, preservatives, polish, and petroleum products, also aid the dogs. The sniper should ensure to change his diet to that of the local inhabitants prior to infiltration.

When the sniper team first arrives into its area of operations, it is best to move initially in a direction that is from 90 to 170 degrees away from the objective. Objects or items of clothing not belonging to any of the team members should be carried into the area of operations in a plastic bag. Once the team is on the ground, it should drop this item of clothing or piece of cloth out of the bag and leave it on a back trail when the team first starts moving. This can confuse a dog long enough to give the team more of a head start. Also, if dogs are brought in late, the team's scent will be very faint, while this scent will still be strong.

While traveling, the team should try to avoid heavily foliaged areas, as these areas hold the scent longer. Periodically, when the situation permits, move across an open area that the sun shines on during the day which has the potential of being windswept. The wind moves the scent and will eventually blow it away; the sun destroys scent very rapidly.

When the situation permits, make changes in direction at the open points of terrain to force the dog to cast for a scent.

If dogs are very close behind, moving through water does not confuse them, as scent will be hanging in the air above the water. Moving through water will only slow the team down. Also, throwing CS gas to the rear or using blood and spice mixtures or any other concoctions will prevent a dog from smelling the team's scent, but it will not be effective on a trained tracker dog. At the first sign of the substance the dog will avoid the area.

While a dog will not be confused by water if he is close, running water, such as a rapidly moving stream, will confuse a dog if he is several hours behind. However, areas with foliage, stagnant air, and little sunlight will hold scent longer. Therefore, swampy areas should be avoided.

Move through areas that have been frequently traveled by other people, as this will confuse the team's scent picture to the dog.

Team members should split up from time to time to confuse the dogs. The best place for this is in areas frequently traveled by indigenous personnel.

If a dog tracker team is on the team's trail, the team should not run, as this will cause the scent to become stronger. The team may attempt to wear out the dog handler and confuse the dog, but should always be on the lookout for a good ambush site that the team can fishhook into. If it becomes necessary to ambush the tracking party, fishhook into the ambush site and kill or wound the handler, NOT the dog. Tracker dogs are trained with their handler,

35

and a trained tracker dog will protect his wounded handler.  This has the potential of allowing the team to move off and away from the area while the rest of the tracking party tries to give assistance to the handler.  Also, that dog will not work well with anyone other than his handler.

If a dog search team moves into the area, the team can employ several actions but should first check wind direction and strength.  If the team is downwind of the estimated search area, the chances are minimal that the team's point smells will probably be detected.  If upwind of the search area, the team should attempt to move downwind.  Terrain and visibility dictate whether the team can move without being detected visually by the handlers.  Remember, sweeps are not always conducted just outside of a woodline.  Wind direction determines whether the sweep will be parallel to the outside or 50 to 100 meters inside the woodline.

The team has options if caught inside the search area of a line search.  The handlers rely on radio communications and often do not have visual contact with each other.  If the team has been generally localized through enemy radio detection-finding equipment, the search net will still be loose during the initial sweep.  A sniper team has a small chance of hiding and escaping detection in deep brush or in woodpiles.  Larger groups will almost certainly be found.  Yet, the team may have the opportunity to eliminate the handler and to escape the search net.

The handler hides behind cover with the dog.  He searches for movement and then sends the dog out in a straight line toward the front.  Usually, when the dog has moved about 50 to 75 meters, the handler calls the dog back.  The handler then moves slowly forward and always from covered position to covered position.  Commands are by voice and gesture with a backup whistle to signal the dog to return.  If a handler is eliminated or badly injured after he has released the dog, but before he has recalled it, the dog continues to randomly search out and away from the handler.  The dog usually returns to another handler or to his former handler's last position within several minutes.  This creates a gap from 25 to 150 meters wide in the search pattern.  Response times by the other searchers tend to be fast.  Given the high degree of radio "chatter", the injured handler will probably be quickly missed from the radio net.  Killing the dog before the handler will probably delay discovery only by moments.  Dogs are so reliable that if the dog does not return immediately, the handler knows something is wrong.

If the sniper does not have a firearm, human versus dog combat is a hazard.  One dog can be dealt with relatively easily if a knife or large club is available.  The sniper must keep low and strike upward using the wrist, never overhand.  Dogs are quick and will try to strike the groin or legs. Most attack dogs are trained to go for the groin or throat.  If alone and faced with two or more dogs, the sniper should flee the situation.

36

Dog-tracker teams are a potent threat to the sniper team. While small and lightly armed, they can greatly increase the area that a rear area security unit can search. Due to the dog-tracker team's effectiveness and its lack of firepower, a sniper team may be tempted to destroy such an "easy" target. Whether a team should fight or run depends on the situation and the team leader. Eliminating or injuring the dog-tracker team only confirms to threat security forces that there is a hostile team operating in the area. The techniques for attacking a dog-tracker team should be used only in extreme situations or as a last measure.

## COUNTERTRACKING

There are two types of human trackers:  combat trackers and professional trackers. Combat trackers look ahead for signs and do not necessarily look for each individual sign. Professional trackers go from sign to sign. If they cannot find any sign, they will stop and search till they find one. The only way to lose a trained professional tracker is to fishhook into an area and then ambush him.

If an enemy tracker finds tracks of two men, this tells him that a highly trained speciality team may be operating in his area. However, a knowledge of countertracking enables the sniper team to survive by remaining undetected.

As with the dogs, to confuse the combat tracker and throw him off the track, the sniper always start his movement away from his objective. Travel in a straight line for about an hour and then change directions. This will cause the tracker to cast in different directions to find the track.

### Evasion
Evasion of the tracker or pursuit team is a difficult task that requires the use of immediate-action drills mostly designed to counter the threat. A team skilled in tracking techniques can successfully employ deception drills to minimize signs that the enemy can use against them. However, it is very difficult for a person, especially a group, to move across any area wthout leaving signs noticeable to the trained eye.


### Camouflage
The followed party may employ most used and least used routes to cover its movement. It also loses travel time when trying to camouflage the trail.

o    Most Used Routes. Movement on lightly-travelled sandy or soft trails is easily tracked. However, a person may try to confuse the tracker by moving on hard-surfaced, often-traveled roads or by merging with civilians. These routes should be carefully examined; if a well-defined approach leads to the enemy, it will probably be mined, ambushed, or covered by snipers.

o    Least Used Routes.  Least used routes avoid all man-made trails or roads and confuse the tracker.  These routes are normally magnetic azimuths between two points.  However, the tracker can use the proper concepts to follow the party if he is experienced and persistent.

Reduction of Trail Signs.  A soldier who tries to hide his trail moves at reduced speed; therefore, the experienced tracker gains time.  Common methods to reduce trail signs are:

o    Wrap footgear with rags or wear soft-soled sneakers, which make footprints rounded and less distinctive.

o    Brush out the trail.  This can rarely be done without leaving signs.

o    Change into footgear with a different tread immediately following a deceptive maneuver.

o    Walk on hard or rocky ground.

## Deception Techniques

Evading a skilled and persistent enemy tracker requires skillfully executed maneuvers to deceive the tracker and to cause him to lose the trail.  An enemy tracker cannot be outrun by a sniper team that is carrying equipment, because he travels light and is escorted by enemy forces designed for pursuit.  The size of the pursuing force dictates the sniper team's chances of success in employing ambush-type maneuvers.  Sniper teams use some of the following techniques in immediate-action drills and deception drills.

o    Backward Walking.  One of the most basic techniques is that of walking backward (Figure 4-4-11) in tracks already made, and then stepping off the trail onto terrain or objectives that leave little sign.  Skillful use of this maneuver causes the tracker to look in the wrong direction once he has lost the trail.

o    Large Tree.  A good deception tactic is to change directions at large trees (Figure 4-4-12).  To do this, the sniper moves in any given direction and walks past a large tree (12 inches wide or larger) from 5 to 10 paces.  He carefully walks backward to the forward side of the tree and makes a 90-degree change in the direction of travel, passing the tree on its forward side.  This technique uses the tree as a screen to hide the new trail from the pursuing tracker.  A variation used near a clear area is as follows.  The sniper must pass by the side of the tree that he wishes to change direction to on his next leg.  He walks past the tree into a clear area for 75 to 100 meters and then walk backwards to the tree. At this time he moves 90 degrees and passes on the side away from the tracker. This could possibly cause the tracker to follow his sign into the open area where, when he loses the track, he might possibly cast in the wrong direction for the track.

NOTE:     By studying signs, an observant tracker can determine if an attempt is being made to confuse him. If the sniper team trys to lose the tracker by walking backward, footprints will be deepened at the toe and soil will be scuffed or dragged in the direction of movement. By following carefully, the tracker can normally find a turnaround point.

o     "Cut the Corner". This deception is used when approaching a known road or trail. About 100 meters from the road, the team changes its direction of movement, either 45 degrees left or right. Once the road is reached, the team leaves a visible trail in the same direction of the deception for a short distance down the road. The tracker should believe that the team "cut the corner" to save time. The team backtracks on the trail to the point where it entered the road, and then it carefully moves down the road without leaving a good trail. Once the desired distance is achieved, the team changes direction and continues movement (Figure 4-4-13). A combination using the big tree method here would improve the effectiveness of this deception.

o     "Slip the Stream". The sniper team uses this deception when approaching a known stream. It executes this method the same as the "cut the corner" maneuver. The team establishes the 45-degree deception maneuver upstream, then enters the stream. The team moves upstream to prevent floating debris and silt from compromising its direction of travel, and the team establishes false trails upstream if time permits. Then, it moves downstream to escape since creeks and streams gain tributaries that offer more escape alternatives (Figure 4-4-14). False exit points can also be used to further confuse. However, the sniper must be careful not to cause a false exit to give away his intended travel direction.

o     Artic Circle. The team uses this deception in snow-covered terrain to escape pursuers or to hide a patrol base. It establishes a trail in a circle (Figure 4-4-15) as large as possible. The trail that starts on a road and returns to the same start point is effective. At some point along the circular trail, the team removes snowshoes (if used) and carefully steps off the trail, leaving one set of tracks. The large tree maneuver can be used to screen the trail. From the hide position, the team returns over the same steps and carefully fills them with snow one at a time. This technique is especially effective if it is snowing.

o     Fishhook. The team uses this technique to double back (Figure 4-4-16) on its own trail in an overwatch position. It can observe the back trail for trackers or ambush pursuers. If the pursuing force is too large to be destroyed, the team strives to eliminate the tracker. It uses hit-and-run tactics, then moves to another ambush position. The terrain must be used to advantage.

Dog and visual trackers are not infallible, and they can be confused with simple techniques and clear thinking. The sniper should not panic and try to outrun a dog or visual tracker. This only makes it easier for the tracking party. The successful sniper keeps his head and always plans two steps ahead. Even if trackers are not in the area, it is best to always use counter-tracking techniques. This will prevent possible grief in the long run. Remember: **THERE IS NO WAY TO HIDE A TRAIL FROM A PROFESSIONAL TRACKER!**

## 4-5. OBSERVATION AND TARGET DETECTION

The sniper's mission requires that he deliver precision fire to selected targets. This mission could not be accomplished without first observing and detecting the target. In the process of observing and detecting, the sniper team is concerned with the significance of the target rather than the number of targets. The sniper team will record the location identification of all targets observed and then fire at them in a descending order of importance.

### Use of Target Indicators

As discussed in the section on camouflage and concealment, the sniper team must protect themselves from target indicators that could reveal their presence to the enemy. The team can also use these target indicators to locate the enemy, using the process of observation, which is planned and systematic. The first consideration is toward the discovery of any immediate danger to the sniper team. The sniper team begins with a "hasty search" of the entire area. This is followed by a slow, deliberate observation, which is called a "detailed search." As long as the sniper team remains in position, they will maintain constant observation of the area, using the hasty and detailed search methods as the situation requires.

### Hasty Search

The hasty search is the first phase of observing a target area. The observer conducts a hasty search immediately after the team occupies the firing position. This is a very rapid check for enemy activity and is conducted in a very short time, about 10 seconds. The search is carried out by making quick glances at specific points, terrain features, or other areas that could conceal the enemy. The sniper should not sweep his eyes across the terrain in one continuous movement; this will prevent him from detecting motion. The observer views the area closest to the team's position first since it could pose the most immediate threat. The observer then searches farther out until the entire target area has been searched. The hasty search is effective because the eyes are sensitive to the slightest movement occurring within a wide arc of the object upon which they are focused. This is called "side vision" or "seeing out of the corner of the eye". The eye must be focused on a specific point to have this sensitivity. When the observer sees or suspects a target, he uses the binoculars or the M49 telescope for a detailed view of the suspected target area.

## Detailed Search

After completing the hasty search, the designated observer then begins a systematic examination known as the detailed search using the overlapping strip method of search. Normally, the area nearest the sniper team offers the greatest potential danger. Therefore, the search should begin with the terrain nearest the sniper. The detailed search begins at either flank. The observer systematically searches the terrain to his front in a 180 degree arc, 50 meters in depth. After reaching the opposite flank, the observer searches the next area nearest his post. The search should be in overlapping strips of at least 10 meters to ensure complete coverage of the area as far out as the observer can see, usually of areas of interest that attracted the observer during the hasty search (Figure 4-5-1).

The observer must memorize the area as much as possible and make mental notes of prominent terrain features and other areas that may offer cover and concealment for the enemy. In this way, he becomes familiar with the terrain as he searches.

This cycle of a hasty search followed by a detailed search should be repeated three or four times. This allows the sniper team to become accustomed to the area; additionally, the team will look closer at various points with each consecutive pass over the area. After the initial searches, the observer should view the area, using a combination of both hasty and detailed searches. While the observer conducts the initial searches of the area, the sniper should record prominent features, reference points, and distances on a range card. The team members should alternate the task of observing the area about every 30 minutes. When searching or maintaining observation, the observer keeps movement of his head and body to a minimum. The observer should not expose his head any higher than is necessary to see the area being observed.

## Maintaining Observation

Method. After completing his detailed search, the observer will be required to maintain observation of the area. To do this he should use a method similar to the hasty search. He should glance quickly at various points throughout the entire area, focusing his eyes on specific features.

Sequence. In maintaining observation of the area, the observer should devise a set sequence for searching to ensure coverage of all terrain. Since it is entirely possible that his hasty search may fail to detect the enemy, the observer should periodically repeat a detailed search.

## Why Objects Are Seen

The relative ease or difficulty in seeing objects depends upon several factors:

o    Shape.  Some objects can be recognized instantly by their shape, particularly if it contrasts with the background. Experience teaches people to associate an object with its shape or outline.  At a distance, the outline of objects can be recognized well before the details of makeup can be determined.  The human body and the equipment that a soldier carries are easily identified unless the outline has been altered.  Areas of importance when considering shape during observation are:

*    The clear-cut outline of a soldier and/or his equipment, either partially or fully exposed.

*    Man-made objects, which have geometric shapes.

*    Geometric shapes, which do not occur in nature on a large scale.

o    Shadow.  In sunlight an object or a man will cast a shadow that can give away his presence.  Shadows may be more revealing that the object itself.  Care must be taken to detect alterations of the natural shape of a shadow.  Where light is excessively bright, shadows will look especially black.  Contrast will be extreme, and in this exaggerated contrast the observer's eye cannot adjust to both areas simultaneously.  This requires the observer to "isolate" the shadowed area from the bright sunlight so that his eye can adapt to the shadow.

o    Silhouette. Any object silhouetted against a contrasting background is conspicuous.  Any smooth, flat background, such as water, a field, or best of all, the sky, will cause an object to become well delineated.  However, special care must be taken when searching areas with an uneven background, as it is more difficult to detect the silhouette of an object.

o    Surface.  If an object has a surface that contrasts with its surroundings, it becomes conspicuous.  Objects with a smooth surface will reflect light and become more obvious than an object with a rough surface that casts shadows on itself.  An extremely smooth object becomes shiny, and the reflections from a belt buckle, watch, or optical device can be seen over a mile away from the source.  Any shine would attract the observer's attention.

o    Spacing.  Nature never places objects in a regular, equally spaced pattern.  Only man uses rows and equal spacing.

o    Siting.  Objects that do not belong in the immediate surroundings are obvious and become readily detectable.  This should arouse the observer's curiosity and cause him to investigate the area more thoroughly.

o    Color.  The greater the contrasting color, the more visible the object becomes.  This is especially true when the color is not natural for that area.  Color alone will usually not identify the object, but is often an aid in locating it.

o    Movement.  This final reason why things are seen will seldom reveal the identity of an object, but it is the most common reason an enemy's position is revealed.  Even when all other indicators are absent, movement will give a position away.  A stationary object may be impossible to see and a slow-moving object difficult to detect, but a quick or jerky movement will be seen.

## Elements of Observation
Four elements in the process of observation include: awareness, understanding, recording, and response.  Each of these elements may be construed as a separate process or as occurring at the same time.

Awareness.  Awareness is being consciously attuned to a specific fact.  A sniper team must always be aware of the surroundings and take nothing for granted.  The team also considers certain elements that influence and distort awareness.

o    An object's size and shape can be misinterpreted if viewed incompletely or inaccurately.

o    Distractions can occur during observation.

o    Active participation or degree of interest can diminish toward the event.

o    Physical abilities (five senses) can be limited.

o    Environmental changes can affect or occur at the time of observation.

o    Imagination or perception can cause possible exaggerations or inaccuracies when reporting or recalling facts.

Understanding.  Understanding is derived from education, training, practice, and experience.  It enhances the sniper team's knowledge about what should be observed, broadens its ability to view and consider all factors, and aids in its evaluation of the information.

Recording.  Recording is the ability to save and recall what was observed.  Usually, the sniper team has mechanical aids, such

43

as writing utensils, logbooks, sketch kits, tape records, and cameras, to support the recording of events; however, the most accessible method is memory. The ability to record, retain, and recall depends on the team's mental capacity (and alertness) and ability to recognize what is essential to record. Added factors that affect recording include:

o    The amount of training and practice in observation.

o    Skill through experience.

o    Similarity of previous incidents.

o    Time interval between observing and recording.

o    The ability to understand or convey messages through oral or other communication.

Response.    Response is the sniper team's action toward information. It may be as simple as recording events in a logbook, making a communications call, or firing a well-aimed shot.

NOTE:    See Chapter 4-9 for discussion on the keep-in-memory (KIM) game.

**Target Indication at Unknown Distances**
Whenever possible, snipers should be deployed in pairs. Because of this, it is vital that they are able to recognize and direct each other to targets quickly and efficiently. In order to be able to recognize targets quickly, the sniper uses standard methods of indication, with slight variations to meet his individual needs.

There are three methods of indicating targets. These are, in order of simplicity, the direct method, the reference point method, and the clock ray method. Also, it is easier to recognize a target if the area of ground in which it is likely to appear is known. Such an area of ground is called an "arc of fire". An arc of fire is indicated in the following sequence:

o    The axis (i.e., the middle of the arc).

o    The left and right limits of the arc.

o    Reference points (prominent objects). These should be as permanent as possible (woods, mounds, etc.), a reasonable distance apart, and easy to identify. A specific point of the object is nominated and given a name and range (i.e., "mound--bottom left corner--to be known as mound--range 400") the same as on your range card.

Direct Method. The direct method is used to indicate obvious targets. The range, where to look, and a description of the target are given. Terms used for where to look are:

      o     "Axis of arc" for targets on or very near the axis.

      o     "Left" or "right" for targets 90 degrees from the axis.

      o     "Slightly", "quarter", "half", or "three-quarters" and "left" or "right" for targets between the axis and the left or right limits.

Reference Point Method. To indicate less obvious targets, a reference point may be used together with the direct method, and perhaps the words "above" and "below" as well. For example:

      o     "300-mound (reference point--slightly right--small bush" (the target)).

      o     "200-mound (reference point--slightly right and below--gate" (target)).

Clock Ray Method. To indicate less obvious targets, a reference point target with a clock ray may be used. During indication it is imagined that there is a clock face standing up on the landscape with its center on the reference point. To indicate a target, the range, the reference point and whether the target is to the left or to the right of it, and the approximate hour on the clock face are given, i.e., "300-mound--right--4 o'clock--small bush".

When indicating targets, the following points must be considered:

      o    Range. This should be given as accurately as possible, though its main purpose is to give an indication of how far to look. The sniper alone should decide on his sight setting, and it may not necessarily be the same one as the indicated range.

      o    Corrections. This should be considered in conformance with the wind table. The observer's opinion of the wind allowance is given to assist the sniper in deciding which setting to use. Between the two opinions, fairly accurate range and windage settings should be decided, although with trained snipers little difference should exist.

      o    Detailed indication. This may require more detail than a normal indication; nevertheless, it should still be as brief and as clear as possible.

Mil measurements can be used along with the methods of indication to specify the distance between an object and the reference point used (i.e., "mound--reference point; go left 50 mils; lone tree; base of tree; target"). The mil scale in binoculars can assist in accurate indication, although occasionally the use of hand angles will have to suffice. It is important that each sniper is conversant with the angles subtended by the various parts of his hand when the arm is outstretched.

Sniper teams must always be aware of the difficulties that can be caused when the observer and the sniper are observing through instruments with different magnifications and fields of view (i.e., telescope, binoculars). If time and concealment allow it, the observer and the sniper should use the same viewing instrument, particularly if the mil scale in the binoculars is being used, to give accurate measurements from a reference point.

It is necessary that both the observer and the firer know exactly what the other is doing and what he is saying when locating the target. Any method that is understandable to both snipers and is fast to use is acceptable. They must use short and concise words to locate the target. Each must always be aware of what the other is doing so that the sniper does not shoot before the observer is ready. They must set a routine that both are comfortable with. An example of this dialogue would be:

Observer: "600--half right, barn, right 50 mils, 2 o'clock, large rock, bottom left corner, target."

Firer: "Target identified, ready."

Observer: "Hold on edge of right shoulder" (wind correction).

The firer should have a round downrange within 1 second after the wind call.

It is extremely important that the shooter fires as soon as possible after the wind call to preclude any wind change that could affect the impact of his bullet. If the wind does change, then it is necessary for the observer to stop the firing sequence and give new wind readings to the shooter. The shooter and the observer must not be afraid to talk to each other, but they should keep everything said as short and as concise as possible.

## Indexing Targets

There are several reasons why the sniper must have some system for remembering or indexing target locations. The sniper may want to shoot at the highest priority target first. This requires patience. The sniper must be selective and not shoot at a target just to have a kill. Indiscriminate firing may alert more valuable and closer targets. Engagement of a distant target may result in disclosure of the sniper post to a closer enemy.

46

Since several targets may be sighted at the same time, some system is needed to remember all of the locations. To remember the locations of targets, the observer uses aiming points and reference points and records this information on the sector sketch/range card and observer's log.

To index targets, the sniper team uses the prepared range card for a reference since it can greatly reduce the engagement time. When indexing a target to the sniper, the observer locates a prominent terrain feature near the target. He indicates this feature and any other information to the sniper to assist in finding the target. Information between team members varies with the situation. The observer may sound like an forward observer (FO) giving a call for fire to a fire direction center (FDC), depending on the condition of the battlefield and the total number of possible targets from which to choose.

Considerations:

o      Exposure time. Moving targets may expose themselves for only a short time. The sniper team must be alert to note the points of disappearance of as many targets as possible before engaging any one of them. By doing so, the sniper team may be able to take several targets under fire in rapid succession.

o      Number of targets. When the number is such that the sniper team is unable to remember and plot all target locations, the sniper team must concentrate only on the most important targets. By concentrating only on the most important targets, they will not fail to effectively locate and engage high priority targets and/or those targets that represent the greatest threat.

o      Spacing. The greater the space interval between targets, the more difficult it is to note their movements. In such cases, the sniper team should accurately locate and engage the nearest target.

o      Evaluating aiming points. Targets that disappear behind good aiming points are easily recorded and remembered. Targets with poor aiming points are easily lost. If two such targets are of equal value and threat to the team, the poor aiming point target should be engaged first, until the target with a good aiming point becomes a greater threat.

**Target Selection**
Snipers select targets according to their value. Certain enemy personnel and equipment can be listed as key targets, but their real worth must be decided by the sniper team in relation to the circumstances in which they are located.

Consideration in target selection. As stated in the discussion of recording targets, the choice of targets may be forced on the sniper team. They may lose a rapidly moving target if they wait to identify it in detail, and they must consider any enemy threatening their position as an "extremely high value" target. When forced to choose a target, the sniper team will consider many factors:

o    Certainty of target's identity. The sniper team must be reasonably certain that the target it is considering is the key target.

o    Target effect on the enemy. The sniper team must consider what effect the elimination of the target will have on the enemy's fighting ability. It must determine that the target is the one available target that will cause the greatest harm to the enemy.

o    Enemy reaction to sniper fire. The sniper team must consider what the enemy will do once the shot has been fired. The team must be prepared for such actions as immediate suppression by indirect fires and enemy sweeps of the area.

o    Effect on the overall mission. The sniper team must consider how the engagement will affect the overall mission. The mission may be one of intelligence gathering for a certain period. Firing will not only alert the enemy to a team's presence, but it may also terminate the mission if the team has to move from its position as a result of the engagement.

o    Probability of first-round hit. The sniper team must determine the chances of hitting the target with the first shot by considering the following:

*    Distance to the target.

*    Direction and velocity of the wind.

*    Visibility of the target area.

*    Amount of the target that is exposed.
*    Amount of time the target is exposed.

*    Speed and direction of target movement.

o    Distance. Although the sniper may be capable of hitting a human target at a range of 900 meters, he should not risk such a distant shot without a special reason.

o    Multiple targets. The sniper should carefully weigh the possible consequences of shooting at one of a number of targets, especially when the target cannot be identified in detail. The sniper may trade his life for an unimportant target by putting himself in a position where he must fire repeatedly in self-defense.

o    Equipment as targets.  A well-placed shot can disable crew-served weapons, radios, vehicles, or other equipment. Such equipment may serve as "bait" and allow the sniper to make repeated engagements of crew members or radio operators while keeping the equipment idle, to be disabled at the sniper's convenience.

o    Intelligence collection.  Intelligence is an important collateral function of the sniper team.  When in a location near to the enemy, the sniper team must be very judicious in its decision to fire.  The sniper may interrupt a pattern of activity which, if observed longer, would allow the pair to report facts that would far outweigh the value of a kill.  The well-trained sniper team will carefully evaluate such situations.

o    Key target selection.  A sniper selects targets according to their value.  A target's real worth is determined by the sniper and the nature of his mission.  Key personnel targets can be identified by: actions, mannerisms, positions within formations, rank or insignias, and/or equipment being worn or carried.  Key targets are as follows:

*    Snipers.  Snipers are the number one target of a sniper team.  The enemy sniper not only poses a threat to friendly forces, but he is also the natural enemy of the sniper. The fleeting nature of a sniper is reason enough to engage him because he may never be seen again.

*    Dog-tracking teams. Dog-tracking teams pose a great threat to sniper teams and other special teams that may be working in the area.  It is hard to fool a trained dog; therefore, the dog-tracking team must be stopped.  When engaging a dog-tracking team, the sniper should engage the dog's handler first. This confuses the dog, and other tracking team members may not be able to control the dog without its handler.

*    Scouts.  Scouts are keen observers and provide valuable information about friendly units.  This, along with their ability to control indirect fires make them dangerous on the battlefield.

*    Officers (military and political).  Officers are another key target of the sniper team.  Losing key officers in some forces is such a major disruption to the operation that forces may not be able to coordinate for hours.

*    Noncommissioned officers.  Losing NCOs not only affects the operation of a unit but also affects the morale of lower ranking personnel.

* Vehicle commanders and drivers. Many vehicles are rendered useless without a commander or driver.

* Communications personnel. In some forces, only highly trained personnel know how to operate various types of radios. Eliminating these personnel can be a serious blow to the enemy's communication network.

* Weapon crews. Eliminating weapon crews reduces the amount and accuracy of enemy fire on friendly troops.

* Optics on vehicles. Personnel who are in closed vehicles are limited to viewing through optics. The sniper can blind a vehicle by damaging these optic systems.

* Communication and radar equipment. The right shot in the right place can completely ruin a tactically valuable radar or communication system. Also, only highly trained personnel may attempt to repair these systems in place. Eliminating these personnel may impair the enemy's ability to perform field repair.

* Weapon systems. Many high-technology weapons, especially computer-guided systems, can be rendered useless by one well-placed round in the guidance controller of the system.

## Principles of Vision

In order to fully understand and accomplish the principles of training the eye, the sniper must know the capabilities and limitations of the eye. The parts of the eye correspond to the parts of the camera and react in much the same way as the camera (Figure 4-5-2). The eye has a lens much the same as a camera lens; however, the lens of the eye focuses automatically and much more rapidly than the lens of a camera. The eye also has a diaphragm, called the iris, that regulates the amount of light into the eye. This permits the individual to see in bright light or in dark shadows. Just as with the camera, the eye cannot accomplish both at the same time. The eye's film is the photoreceptor cells located on the back wall, or retina, of the eye. There are two types of cells:

o The cone cells are located in the central portion of the retina. They are for day vision, and enable one to distinguish color, shape, and sharp contrast. A great deal of light is required to activate the cone cells, so they are blind during periods of low light.

o The other cells are the rod cells. These cells are always active and surround the central portion of cone cells. They produce a substance called "visual purple". As the light level decreases, this substance increases the rod cells' ability to register light. However, visual purple is destroyed by light and requires time to build up. The rod cells are sensitive to movement, and this causes the detection of movement out of "the corner of the eye" to register better than when looking directly at the movement.

## Observation Techniques

Training of the eye requires training of the mind as well. The sniper's proficiency as an observer will come from a good mental attitude and a trained eye. As an observer, just like a hunter, the eye must be trained to notice little things, such as the bending of grass when there is no wind, the unnatural shape of a shadow, or the wisp of vapor in cold air. Even when the enemy cannot be seen, little things can give his location away, such as a window that is now open when it was closed before, a puff of smoke, signs of fresh soil, or disturbed undergrowth.

Learn the habits of the animals in the area, or watch the domestic animals. A chicken suddenly darting from behind a building; sheep, goats, or cows suddenly moving or just becoming more alert in a field; wild birds flying or becoming quiet; insects becoming quiet at night; or animals startled from their positions should alert the observer of possible enemy activity in his area.

The area of operation should be studied and memorized. Any change will alert the prepared mind to the possibility of the enemy. All changes should be closely inspected to determine the cause of the change.

An observer should keep certain rules in mind at all times while observing:

o Learn to look for objects that seem out of place. Almost every object in the wild is vertical; only man-made objects, such as a gun barrel, are horizontal.

o Learn to see things in the proper perspective at distances. Learn to see movement, color, shape, and contrast in miniature.

o Learn to look through vegetation, not at it. The observer should not be satisfied until he has seen as far as possible into the vegetation.

Due to the constant changing of clouds and the position of the sun, light is a constantly changing factor in observation. Always be ready to watch the changing contrast and shadows. An area that the sniper previously thought held no enemy may prove to be an enemy position when the light changes. When the sun is to the sniper's back, light will reflect from the enemy's optical devices. But beware, when the light changes and is to the front, the enemy will be able to see the light reflected from the sniper's optical devices.

51

When the sun is to the sniper's front, it is also more tiring for him to observe due to the light being in his eyes. He should be prepared to change personnel more frequently at this time if possible. If not, the use of some type of shading to cut down on the amount of light coming into the eyes will help.

## Limited Visibility Techniques

Twilight is another time of light changes. The eye begins to produce visual purple, and the cone cells begin shutting down. Also, the iris opens more to let more light in. This causes the eye to constantly change focus, and consequently, this is more tiring for the eye. However, during twilight the enemy will usually become more careless, allowing an alert observer to spot that last change in position or that last cigarette before dark. The sniper should remember that this is not a time for him to become relaxed as well.

Limited visibility runs the gamut from bright moonlight to utter darkness. But no matter how bright the night is, the eye cannot function with daylight precision. For maximum effectiveness, an observer must apply the principles of night vision when training the eye.

o    Night adaptation. Allow approximately 30 minutes for the eye to adjust.

o    Off-center vision. Never look directly at an object at night. This will cause the object to disappear. When it reappears, it could appear to change shape or move.

o    Scanning. When scanning, it is important that the eye stops movement for a few seconds during the scan to be able to see an object. When scanning around an object, the temptation to look directly at the object "just to make sure" should be resisted.

The following factors affect night vision:

o    Lack of Vitamin A.

o    Colds, headaches, fatigue, narcotics, alcohol, and heavy smoking.

o    Exposure to bright light. This will destroy night vision for about 10 to 30 minutes, depending on the brightness and duration of the light.

Darkness blots out detail, so the eye must be trained to recognize objects by outline alone.

While some people can see better than others at night, everyone can use techniques to improve their vision at night.

52

o     The eye can be trained to actually see all the detail possible at nighttime. When the sniper sees a tree, he actually <u>sees</u> the tree, not a faint outline that he thinks may be a tree.

o     Open the iris. While the iris of the eye is basically automatic, the eye can be trained to open the iris up even more to gather more light, thus allowing more detail to be seen.

o     Practice roofing. Roofing is silhouetting objects against a light background.

o     Maneuver to catch the light. At night, noticeable light will only be in patches where it filters through the trees. The      sniper must maneuver to place an object between his eyes and that patch of light.

o     Lower the body. By lowering the body or even lying down, the sniper will be able to pick up more light and therefore see things that might otherwise go unnoticed.

## Observation by Sound

Many times sound will warn the sniper long before the enemy is actually seen. Also, the sounds or lack of sounds from birds or animals may alert one to the possible presence of the enemy. It is therefore important to train the ears along with the eyes.

The ear nearest the origin of the sound will pick up the sound first and will hear it slightly louder than the other ear. This is what enables the sniper to detect the direction of the sound. However, if the sound reaches both ears at the same time and with the same intensity, the direction that the sound came from will not be discernable.

Sound also loses its intensity with distance traveled. The ears must be trained to become familiar with the different sounds at different distances so that the distance to the sound can be estimated. This would then give the sniper a general location of the sound.

The sniper must learn to actually hear all sounds. Most people rely on sight for most of their information. A trained sniper must learn to use his ears as well as his eyes. The observer must make a conscious effort to hear all of the sounds, so that when a sound changes or a new one occurs, he will be alerted to it.

By cupping his hand behind one ear, the sniper can increase his ability to hear and pinpoint the direction of a sound.

## Target Location by the "Crack-thump" Method

53

Through training of the ear, the sniper will be able to determine the approximate location of a shot being fired. This is done by the "crack-thump" method. When the sniper is being fired at, he will hear two distinct sounds. One sound is the crack of the bullet as it breaks the sound barrier as it passes by his position. The other sound is the thump created by the muzzle blast of the weapon being fired. The crack-thump relationship is the time that passes between the two sounds. This time interval can be used to estimate the distance to the weapon being fired.

When the sniper hears the crack, he does not look into the direction of the crack. This will give him a false location because the sonic waves of the bullet strike objects perpendicular to the bullet's path. The sniper would mistakenly look 90 degrees from the enemy's true position. The crack should instead alert the sniper to start counting seconds.

The second sound heard is the thump of the weapon being fired. This is the enemy location. The time passed in seconds is the distance to the enemy. Sound travels at 340 meters per second at 15 degrees centigrade. Therefore, half a second is approximately 300 meters, and a full second 600 meters. It becomes easier to distinguish between the two sounds as the distance increases. By listening for the thump and then looking in the direction of the thump, it is possible to see the flash of a second round or the smoke of the weapon being fired. The speed of light is far greater than the speed of sound or of bullets. Remember that the "crack-thump" is a double edged sword that may be used against the sniper.

The speed, size, and shape of the bullet will produce different sounds. Initially, they will sound alike, but with practice the sniper will be able to distinguish between different types of weapons. A 7.62x39mm bullet is just going subsonic at 600 meters. Since the crack-thump sounds differ from weapon to weapon, with practice the experienced sniper will be able to distinguish enemy fire from friendly fire. The sniper should always be keep in mind the three objectives of fire:

o    To kill.

o    To wound.

o    To suppress.

The crack-thump method has the following limitations:

o    Isolating the crack and thump is difficult when many shots are being fired.

o    Mountainous areas and tall buildings cause echoes and make this method ineffective.

To overcome these limitations, the innovative sniper team can do the following:

o     Dummy Targets.  During World War I, snipers used paper-mache or wooden heads to lure enemy snipers into firing.  If the head was hit, they placed a pencil into the hole and noted the direction the pencil pointed.  Today, the sniper team may use this technique with polystyrene plastic heads or mannequins dressed to resemble a soldier.  The head is placed on a stick and slowly raised into the enemy's view while another team observes the area for muzzle blast or flash.

o     Shot-Hole Analysis.  Locating two or more shot holes in trees, walls, dummy heads, and so forth may make it possible to determine the direction of the shots.  The team can use the dummy-head pencil method and triangulate on the enemy sniper's position.  However, this method only works if all shots come from the same position.

## Observation Device Use and Selection

The sniper team's success in selecting and engaging targets without betraying itself depends upon its powers of observation. In addition to the telescope, the sniper team has an observation telescope, binoculars, night vision sight, and night vision goggles to enhance its ability to observe and engage targets.  Team members must relieve each other when using this equipment since prolonged use can cause eye fatigue, greatly reducing the effectiveness of observation.  Periods of observation during daylight should be limited to 30 minutes followed by at least 15 minutes of rest. When using night vision devices, the observer should limit his initial period of viewing to 10 minutes followed by a 15-minute rest period.  After several periods of viewing, he can extend the viewing period to 15 and then 20 minutes.

The M19 binoculars are the fastest and easiest aid to use when great magnification is not needed.  The M19 binoculars also have a mil scale that can aid the sniper in judging sizes and distances. The M19 binoculars can also be used to observe at twilight by gathering more light than the naked eye.  Using this reticle pattern aids the sniper in determining range and adjusting indirect fires.  The sniper uses the binoculars for:

o     Observing target areas.

o     Observing enemy movement and positions.

o     Identifying aircraft.

o     Improving low-light level viewing.

o     Estimating range.

o     Calling for and adjusting indirect fires.

The M22 binoculars are the latest in the inventory, but have several fatal flaws. The M22's flaws are directly attributable to its anti-laser protective coating. This coating reflects light like a mirror, and is a excellent target indicator. Also, this coating reduces the amount of light that is transmitted throught the lens system and greatly reduces the observation capability of the sniper during dawn and dusk.

The M49 observation spotting telescope is 20x and can be used to discern much more detail at a greater distance than the binoculars or the sniper telescope. With good moonlight, targets up to 800 meters away can be detected. However, the high magnification of the observation scope decreases its field of view. Moreover, the terrain will not be in focus unless it is near the object being inspected. The observation scope should be used only for the inspection of a specific point and not for observation of an area. More modern, and higher quality spotting scopes are available in limited quantities. The sniper team should research the availability of these improved observation devices.

## 4-6. RANGE ESTIMATION

Range estimation is the process of determining the distance between two points. In most situations, one of these points will be the observer's position, while the other may be the target or a prominent feature. The ability to accurately determine range is the key skill needed by the sniper to accomplish his mission. Range can be determined by measuring or by estimating. There are three main factors that affect the appearance of objects when determining range by eye.

### Factors Affecting Range Estimation

o    Nature of the target. Objects of regular outline, such as a house, will appear closer than one of irregular outline, such as a clump of trees. A target that contrasts with its background will appear to be closer than it actually is. A partially exposed target will appear more distant than it actually is.

o    Nature of the terrain.

*    Observing over smooth terrain, such as sand, water, or snow, causes the observer to underestimate distance targets. Objects will appear nearer than they really are when the viewer is looking across a depression, most of which is hidden from view. They will also appear nearer when the viewer is looking downward from high ground. They will also appear nearer when the viewer is looking down on a straight, open road or along railroad tracks.

*    As the observer's eye follows the contour of the terrain, he tends to overestimate distance targets. Objects will

appear more distant than they really are when the viewer is looking across a depression, all of which is visible. They also appear more distant than they really are when the viewer is looking from low ground toward high ground and when the field of vision is narrowly confined, such as in twisted streets or on forest trails.

o    Light conditions. The more clearly a target can be seen, the closer it will appear. A target viewed in full sunlight appears to be closer than the same target viewed at dusk or dawn or through smoke, fog, or rain. The position of the sun in relation to the target also affects the apparent range. When the sun is behind the viewer, the target appears closer. When the sun appears behind the target, the target is more difficult to see and appears farther away.

## Units of Measure

o    Human target. When ranging on a human target, the sniper may use two different methods. The first method is to range on the target using the vertical cross hairs and mil dots. The second method is to use the horizontal cross hairs and mil dots.

*    Vertical method. This is the most common method of range finding when using the M3A. The sniper must become very good at estimating the height of the target in either meters or feet and inches. The sniper has the option of using a 1-meter (head to crotch) target frame or using the entire target (head to toe) as the target frame. To use the vertical method, the cross hairs are placed at either the feet, crotch, of top of the head of the target. The mil value is then read for that target. The sniper must determine the height of the target if he is not using the 1-meter target frame. Since the telescope is cammed out in meters, the height of the target must be converted into meters. The range is then calculated using the mil relation formula. The estimation of the height of the target may be the most important factor in this formula. An error of 3 inches on a 5-foot 9-inch target that is actually 5 feet 6 inches results in a 25 meter error at a reading of 4 mils.

Normal height of the human head is 10 inches.

$$\frac{10 \text{ inches} \times .0254 \times 1,000}{\text{Size of target in mils}} = \text{Range to target in meters}$$

This example may prove to be of specific use when facing an enemy entrenched in bunkers or in dense vegetation.

*    Horizontal method. The horizontal method is based upon a target width of 19 inches at the shoulders. This technique can be very accurate out to ranges of 350 meters, and is very effective in an urban environment. Beyond this range it is no longer effective. When using this method, the sniper must be

57

sure to have on hand the chart that shows the various ranges for the mil dot readings obtained. A good rule of thumb is that if the target is smaller than 1 1/2 mils (322 meters), it is more accurate to use the vertical method.

The mil dots in the M3A are 3/4 MOA in diameter. Therefore, it is important to note where on the dots the bottom or the top of the target falls within the mil dot. <u>The mil dots are spaced 1 mil from center to center</u>.

o    Building or Vehicle. When range finding on a building or a vehicle using a vertical scale, place the zero value at the lowest visible point; the top of the vehicle or building should be on the upper scale of numbers. Read the value at the highest point of the structure or vehicle.

When ranging on a vehicle or a structure using the horizontal scale, place the zero value at the far left of the structure and read the value located at the far right of the structure. When objects are at an oblique angle, the sniper may obtain ranges that are a little farther than they actually are. This is something to remember; this must be compensated for.

## Range Estimation Techniques

### Sniper Telescope

The M3A has a mil dot reticle and the mil relation formula is used for range determination. With the adjustable ranging feature of the ART I or ART II telescope, the sniper can accurately determine the range to any visible object or point out to 900 meters. The only requirement is that the sniper is familiar with the observed targets to determine or estimate a 30-inch portion of the target for the ART I or a 1-meter portion for the ART II. The sniper can then read the range/power index number opposite the white reference dot on the top of the telescope tube by the power ring; this will be the range in hundreds of meters. For example, the number 4 indicates a range of 400 meters. When the power ring stops between two reference numbers, the sniper merely interpolates. Using the telescope for range estimation is especially helpful when establishing known ranges for a range card or a reference mark. The sniper rifle's inherent stability helps to improve the accuracy of the measurements. Using the ranging feature of the sniping telescopes, the sniper may determine range by using the following:

o    Personnel. The distance from the individual's head to his waist is normally 30 inches; from the top of his head to his groin is 1 meter (39.4 inches).

o    Tanks. The distance from the ground line to the deck or from the deck to the turret top of a Soviet tank is approximately 30 inches.

o    Vehicles.    The distance from the ground line to the fender above the wheel is approximately 30 inches.  The distance to the roofline is approximately 3 1/2 to 4 feet.

o    Trees.    The width of the trees in the vicinity of the sniper will be a good indication of the width of the trees in the target area.

o    Window frames.    The vertical length of a standard frame is approximately 60 inches.  This distance is 1.5 meters by 2.0 meters in Europe.

NOTE:    Through the process of interpolation, the sniper can range on any object of known size.  For example, the head of any individual will measure approximately 12 inches. This can be ranged on by placing the head between the top vertical stadia line and the reticle horizontal line, which represents 15 inches for the ART I.  The M3A has a mil dot reticle.  On this telescope a mil dot equals 3/4ths of an MOA, while the space between mil dots equals 1 mil or 3.375 MOA.

Mil Relation Formula
    The mil relation formula can also be used to determine ranges. The M3A rifle telescope has 10 mils vertical and horizontal measurement between the heavy duplex reticle lines; the space between each dot represents 1 mil.  Military binoculars also have a mil scale in the left ocular eyepiece.  By using the known measured sizes of objects, the sniper can use the mil relation formula to determine the range.

NOTE:    The size of objects in meters yields ranges in meters; the size of objects in yards yields ranges in yards. Other relationships must also be understood:    1 mil equals 3.375 MOA or 3.375 inches at 100 yards, 1 meter at 1000m, or approximately 1 yard at 1,000 yards.

    The sniper uses the following formula to determine the range to the target:

Range to target = <u>Size of object in meters or yards X 1000</u>
                            Size of object in mils

Examples:  1)  Object = 2 meters, Mils = 4 mils (as measured in the M3A scope)

$$\frac{2 \times 1000}{4} = \frac{2000}{4} = 500 \text{ meters} = \text{range to target}$$

2)  Object = 2 yards, Mils = 5 mils (as measured in the M3A scope)

59

$$\frac{2 \times 1000}{5} = \frac{2000}{5} = 400 \text{ yards} = \text{range to target}$$

NOTE:   The distance to the target in yards must be converted to meters in order to correctly set the M3A's ballistic cam.

Once he understands the formula, the sniper must become proficient at estimating the actual height of the target in his scope.   At longer ranges the measurements must be accurate to within 1/2 mil.   Otherwise the data will be more than the 10 percent allowable error.   The ability of the sniper team to accurately estimate the height of the target is the single most important factor in using this formula.

## Calculating Ranges Using Military Binoculars
The range to a target can be calculated using the M3, M19, M22 binoculars, or any other optical device that has vertical and horizontal mil reticles.

o   M3 Binoculars

The graduations between the numbers on the horizontal reference line are in 10-mil graduations.

The height of the vertical lines along the horizontal reference line is 2 1/2 mils.

The graduation of the horizontal reference lines on the left of the reticle is 5 mils (vertical) between the reference lines.   These lines are also 5 mils long (horizontal).

The small horizontal lines located above the horizontal reference line in the center of the reticle are 5 mils apart (vertical) and are also 5 mils long (horizontal).

The vertical scale on the reticle is not to be used for range finding purposes.

o   M19 Binoculars

The graduation between the number lines on the horizontal and the vertical lines on the reticle is 10 mils (Figure 4-6-1).

The total height of the vertical lines on the horizontal reference lines is 5 mils.   These lines are further graduated 2 1/2 mils above the horizontal line and 2 1/2 mils below the line.

The total width of the horizontal lines on the vertical reference line is 5 mils.   These lines are further graduated into 2 1/2 mils on the left side of the line and 2 1/2 mils on the right side of the vertical reference line.

o   M22 Binoculars

60

The graduation between the numbered lines on the horizontal and vertical reference lines is 10 mils.

There are 5 mils between a numbered graduation and the 2 1/2 mil tall line that falls between the numbered graduations.

The value of the longer lines that intersect the horizontal and vertical lines on the reticle is 5 mils.

The value of the shorter lines that intersect the horizontal and vertical reference lines on the reticle is 2 1/2 mils. These are the lines that fall between the 5 mil lines.

Estimation

There will be times, however, when the sniper must estimate the range to the target. This requires no equipment and can be accomplished without exposing the observer's position. There are two methods of estimation that meet these requirements: the 100-meter unit-of-measure method and the appearance-of-objects method.

o    The 100-Meter Unit-of-Measure Method

To use this method, the sniper must be able to visualize a distance of 100 meters on the ground. For ranges up to 500 meters, he determines the number of 100-meter increments between the two points that he wishes to measure. Beyond 500 meters, the sniper must select a point halfway to the target, determine the number of 100-meter increments of the halfway point, and then double this number to find the range to the target (Figure 4-6-2).

During training exercises, the sniper must become familiar with the effect that sloping ground has on the appearance of a 100-meter increment. Ground that slopes upward gives the illusion of greater distance, and the observer's tendency is to overestimate a 100-meter increment. Conversely, ground that slopes downward gives the illusion of shorter distance. In this case, the sniper's tendency is to underestimate.

Proficiency in the 100-meter unit-of-measure method requires constant practice. Throughout the training in this technique, comparisons should continuously be made between the range as determined by the sniper and the actual range as determined by pacing or other more accurate means of measurement. The best training technique is to require the sniper to pace the range after he has visually determined it. In this way he discovers the actual range for himself, which makes a much greater impression than if he were simply told the correct range.

The greatest limitation of the 100-meter unit of measure is that its accuracy is directly related to how much of the terrain is visible at the greater ranges. This is particularly true at a range of 500 meters or more when the sniper can only see a portion of the ground between himself and the target. It becomes very

61

difficult to use the 100-meter unit-of-measure method of range determination with any degree of accuracy.

o    The Appearance-of-Objects Method
The appearance-of-objects method is the means of determining range by the size and other characteristic details of the object in question. This is a common method of determining distances and is used by most people in their everyday living. For example, a motorist attempting to pass another car must judge the distance of on-coming vehicles based on his knowledge of how vehicles appear at various distances. Of course, in this example, the motorist is not interested in precise distances, but only that he has sufficient road space to safely pass the car in front of him. This same technique can be used by the sniper to determine ranges on the battlefield. If he knows the characteristic size and detail of personnel and equipment at known ranges, then he can compare these characteristics to similar objects at unknown ranges. When the characteristics match, so does the range.

To use the appearance-of-objects method with any degree of accuracy, the sniper must be thoroughly familiar with the characteristic details of objects as they appear at various ranges. For example, the sniper should study the appearance of a man when he is standing at a range of 100 meters. He fixes the man's appearance firmly in his mind, carefully noting details of size and characteristics of uniform and equipment. Next, he studies the same man in a kneeling position and then in a prone position. By comparing the appearance of these positions at known ranges from 100 to 500 meters, the sniper can establish a series of mental images that will help him determine range on unfamiliar terrain. Training should also be conducted in the appearance of other familiar objects such as weapons or vehicles. Because the successful use of this method depends upon visibility, anything that limits the visibility (such as weather, smoke, or darkness). will also limit the effectiveness of this method.

o    Combination of Methods
Under proper conditions, either the 100-meter unit-of-measure method or the appearance-of-objects method is an effective way of determining range. However, proper conditions do not always exist on the battlefield. Consequently, the sniper will be required to use a combination of methods. The terrain might limit using the 100-meter unit-of-measure method, and the visibility could limit using the appearance-of-objects method. For example, an observer may not be able to see all of the terrain out to the target; however, he may see enough to get a general idea of the distance within 100 meters. A slight haze may obscure many of the target details, but the observer should still be able to judge its size. Thus, by carefully considering the approximate ranges as determined by both methods, an experienced observer should arrive at a figure close to the true range.

## Range Calculation by Triangulation

One of the primary fallacies of sniper operations is the assumption that the sniper will be determining distance based on exposure of the target. This has led, in recent times, to reliance on the mil relation method. Under field conditions it is highly unlikely that the sniper will have a target exposure that will permit the use of the mil dot system or binoculars to obtain a reading. Even with a pre-calculated table on hand, the sniper will still need approximately 20 seconds to work out the mil relation formula. The sight picture will be lost as the sniper consults his data. Without the table, as much as two minutes are required to work out the mil relation formula.

To engage targets quickly, the sniper must have predetermined points on the field of view where the ranges are known. There are two points, at a minimum, that the sniper should have determined and ranged on. The first key distance is the weapon's point blank zero. The second key distance should be a point on the field where the sniper can quickly take a reference. This second key distance may be based on several factors. An enemy's expected avenue of approach or the possible dead space from which an enemy may approach are but two of the factors that may influence the selection of the second key distance.

The method for determining the key distance using triangulation is as follows:

1) The sniper picks a prominent terrain feature in his field of observation.

2) Facing his reference feature, he lays a base line 90 degrees out from his position. The base line should be a minimum of 10 meters in length. The longer the base line, the more accurate the determination will be.

3) Given that the angle from the reference feature to the sniper's position to the end of the base line is 90 degrees, the angle from the end of the base line to the reference feature is measured. This angle may be measured either in mils or degrees. However, the use of degrees will be difficult unless the sniper has binoculars with a built-in compass to aid in interpolation to one-tenth of a degree. Mils are much easier to work with and are more accurate.

4) The problem then becomes one of finding the length of one side of a triangle when all the angles are known (Figure 4-6-3). The length of one side (the base line) is also known>

$$AC = \frac{(AB) \times \sin B}{\sin C}$$

AC = Key distance or range.

63

AB = Base line length.

Note 1:     The sum of the three angles in a triangle is equal to 180 degrees or 3200 mils. A triangle with a right angle (of a known value of 90 degrees or 1600 mils), the sum of the two other angles must therefore be 90 degrees or 1600 mils. In this formula, angle A is a right angle and measures 1600 mils (90 degrees). The sum of angles B and C will always equals 1600 mils (90 degrees).

Note 2:     When this method is used, rarely will angle C exceed 53.333 mils (3 degrees). Nor will angle B measure less than 1546.666 mils (87 degrees). The sniper is recommended to carry a base line of cord (preferably a material that has little stretch) that is 50 meters long and is marked in 5-meter increments. This is sufficient to meet most contingencies.

Note 3:     Experience has shown that the following length cords work well at the ranges indicated:

| | |
|---|---|
| 0-400 meters | 10-meter cord |
| 400-600 meters | 20-meter cord |
| 600-700 meters | 30-meter cord |
| 700-infinity | 40-meter cord |

## SIN TABLE

| DEGREES | SIN | DEGREES | SIN | DEGREES | SIN |
|---------|-----|---------|-----|---------|-----|
| 0.1 | .00175 | 1.1 | .01920 | 2.1 | .03664 |
| 0.2 | .00349 | 1.2 | .02094 | 2.2 | .03839 |
| 0.3 | .00524 | 1.3 | .02269 | 2.3 | .04013 |
| 0.4 | .00698 | 1.4 | .02443 | 2.4 | .04188 |
| 0.5 | .00873 | 1.5 | .02618 | 2.5 | .04362 |
| 0.6 | .01047 | 1.6 | .02792 | 2.6 | .04536 |
| 0.7 | .01222 | 1.7 | .02967 | 2.7 | .04711 |
| 0.8 | .01396 | 1.8 | .03141 | 2.8 | .04885 |
| 0.9 | .01571 | 1.9 | .03316 | 2.9 | .05059 |
| 1.0 | .01745 | 2.0 | .03490 | 3.0 | .05234 |
| 87.0 | .9986 | 88.0 | .9994 | 89.0 | .9998 |
| 87.1 | .9988 | 88.1 | .9995 | 89.1 | .9999 |
| 87.2 | .9988 | 88.2 | .9995 | 89.2 | .9999 |
| 87.3 | .9989 | 88.3 | .9996 | 89.3 | .9999 |
| 87.4 | .9990 | 88.4 | .9996 | 89.4 | .9999 |
| 87.5 | .9990 | 88.5 | .9997 | 89.5 | 1.0000 |

| 87.6 | .9991 | 88.6 | .9997 | 89.6 | 1.0000 |
| 87.7 | .9992 | 87.7 | .9997 | 89.7 | 1.0000 |
| 87.8 | .9993 | 88.8 | .9998 | 89.8 | 1.0000 |
| 87.9 | .9993 | 88.9 | .9998 | 89.9 | 1.0000 |

NOTE:     Rarely will any angle used in this method exceed 3 degrees at the reference feature, or be less than 87 degrees at the baseline unless the sniper carries a baseline of considerable length. It is recommended that the sniper carry a baseline of suspension line 50 meters long, marked in 5 meter increments. This is sufficient to meet most contingencies.

## Measuring
Measuring distance can be accomplished in two ways: measuring distance on a map or pacing the distance between two points.

o    Map (Paper-strip Method)
The paper-strip method is useful when determining longer distances (1,000 meters plus). When using this method, the sniper places the edge of a strip of paper on the map and ensures it is long enough to reach between the two points. Then he pencils in a tick mark on the paper at the team position and another at the distant location. He places the paper on the map's bar scale, located at the bottom center of the map, and aligns the left tick mark with the 0 on the scale. Then he reads to the right to the second mark and notes the corresponding distance represented between the two marks.

o    Actual Measurement
This method is to actually pace the distance on the ground. Pacing the distance between two points is one method a sniper can use, provided the enemy is not in the vicinity. This obviously has limited applications and can be very hazardous to the sniper team. This is one of the least desirable methods.

## Bracketing Method
The bracketing method is used when the sniper assumes that the target is no less than "X" meters away, but no more than "Y" meters away. The sniper then uses the average of the two distances as the estimated range. Snipers can increase their accuracy of range estimation by eye by using an average of both team members' estimation.

## Halving Method
The halving method is used for distances beyond 500 meters. The sniper selects a point midway to the target, determines the number of 100-meter increments to the halfway point, and then doubles the estimation. Again, it is best to average the results of both sniper team members.

## Range Card

The range card method is a very accurate means of estimating range. The mere fact that the sniper has had time to establish a range card means that he has been in the area long enough to become familiar with the target area. He has had the time to determine ranges to indicated reference points in the target area. The observer will give his targets to the sniper by giving deflections and distances from known reference points in the target field of view. The sniper can adjust his telescope for a good median distance in the target area and simply adjust fire from that point. There are two key distances that should be calculated and noted with references on the range card. The first is the point blank zero of the weapon. With a 300 meter zero the point blank zero of the M118 ammunition is 375 meters. Targets under this range do not need to be corrected for. The second key distance is merely a point of reference against which further distance determinations can be judged. This distance is determined by triangulation.

## Speed of Sound

The approximate distance from the observer to a sound source (bursting shell, weapon firing, etc.) can be estimated by timing the sound. The speed of sound in still air at 50 degrees F is about 340 meters per second; however, wind and variations in temperature alter this speed somewhat. For practical use the sniper may assume the speed of sound is 350 meters per second under all conditions. The sound can be timed either with a watch or by counting from the time the flash appears until the sound is heard by the observer. The sniper counts "one-1,000, two-1,000" etc., to determine the approximate time in seconds. The time in seconds is then multiplied by 350 to get the approximate distance in meters to the source of the fire.

## Measurement by Bullet Impact

Another undesirable but potentially useful method is to actually fire a round at the point in question. This is possible if you know your target is coming into the area at a later time and you plan to ambush the target. However, this method is not tactically sound and is also very hazardous to the sniper team.

## Laser Range Finders

Laser range finders can also be used to determine range to a very high degree of accuracy. When aiming the laser at a specific target, the sniper should support it much the same as his weapon to ensure accuracy. If the target is too small, aiming the laser at a larger object near the target will suffice--that is, a building, vehicle, tree, or terrain feature. The range finder must be used with the yellow filter to keep it eye safe for the sniper and observer. This limits the range; however, the limitations are well within the range of the sniper, i.e., 20,000 meters. Rain, fog, or smoke will severely limit the use of laser range finders.

Sniper Cheat Book

The sniper team should keep a "cheat book" complete with measurements. The team fills in the cheat book during its area analysis, mission planning, isolation, and once in the area of operations. A tape measure will prove invaluable.

o   Average height of human targets in area of operation.

o   Vehicles.
    *       Height of road wheels.
    *       Vehicle dimensions.
    *       Length of main gun tubes on tanks.
    *       Lengths/sizes of different weapon systems.

o   Urban environment.
    *       Average size of doorways.
    *       Average size of windows.
    *       Average width of streets and lanes (average width of a paved road in the United States is 10 feet).
    *       Height of soda machines.

As the sniper team develops its cheat book, all measurements are converted into constants and computed with different mil readings. An example of this can be found in Appendix C, which has already been computed for immediate use. This table should be incorporated into the sniper's log book.


## Mil Relation (Worm Formula) Sample Problems:

Problem No. 1:

As a member of a sniper team, you and your partner are in your sniper hide and are preparing a range card. To your front you see a Soviet truck that you determine to be 4 meters long. Your team is equipped with an M24 system. Through your binoculars the truck is 5 mils in length. Determine the range to this reference for your system.

SOLUTION: STEP 1.    No conversion needed.

STEP 2.    Determine the range.

$$\text{Width} = \frac{4 \text{ meters} \times 1{,}000}{5 \text{ mils}} = 800 \text{ meters}$$

Problem No. 2:

You are a member of a sniper team assigned to cover a certain area of ground. You are making a range card and are determining ranges to reference points in that area. You see a tank located to your front. Through your binoculars you find the width of the tank to be 8 mils. You determine the length of the tank to be 5 meters. You are equipped with an M21 system with an ART I telescope. Determine the correct range for your system.

SOLUTION: STEP 1.    No conversion needed.

STEP 2.    Determine the range.

Width = $\dfrac{5 \text{ meters} \times 1{,}000}{8 \text{ mils}} = 625$ meters

## 4-7.    SELECTION AND PREPARATION OF HIDES

To effectively accomplish its mission or to support combat operations, the sniper team must select a position from which to observe and fire. This position is called a sniper hide or post. Once constructed, it will provide the sniper team with a well-concealed post from which to observe and fire without fear of enemy detection. Selecting the location of a position is one of the most important tasks a sniper team must accomplish during the mission planning phase of an operation. After selecting the location, the team must also determine how it will move into the area and locate and occupy the final position.

### Hide Selection

Upon receiving a mission, the sniper team locates the target area and then determines the best location for a tentative position by using one or more of the following sources of information: topographic maps, aerial photographs, visual reconnaissance before the mission, and information gained from units operating in the area.

In selecting a sniper hide, maximum consideration is given to the fundamentals and principles of camouflage/cover and concealment. Once on the ground, the sniper team ensures the position provides an optimum balance between the following considerations:

o    Maximum fields of fire and observation of the target area.

o    Maximum concealment from enemy observation.

o    Covered routes into and out of the position.

o    Located no closer than 300 meters from the target area.

o    A natural or man-made obstacle between the position and the target area.

A sniper team must remember that a position that appears to be in an ideal location may also appear that way to the enemy. Therefore, it avoids choosing locations that are:

o   On a point or crest of prominent terrain features.

o   Close to isolated objects.

o   At bends or ends of roads, trails, or streams.

o   In populated areas, unless it is required.

The sniper team must use its imagination and ingenuity in choosing a good location for the given mission. The team must choose a location that not only allows the team to be effective but also must appear to the enemy to be the least likely place for a team position. The following are examples of such positions:

o   Under logs in a deadfall area.

o   Tunnels bored from one side of a knoll to the other.

o   Swamps.

o   Deep shadows.

o   Inside rubble piles.


## Hide Site Location
Determine the area location by the three factors of site location:

o   Mission.

o   Dispersion.

o   Terrain patterns.

Select tentative sites and routes to the objective area by utilizing:

o   Aerial photographs.

o   Maps.

o   Reconnaissance/after-action reports.

o   Interrogations of assets, indigenous personnel, and prisoners of war.

o    Weather reports.

o    Area studies.

When utilizing these tools, look for:

o    Terrain patterns (urban, rural, wooded, barren).

o    Soil type (to determine tools).

o    Population density.

o    Weather conditions (snow, rain).

o    Drainage.

o    Types of vegetation.

o    Drinking water.

Conduct a reconnaissance of the area to determine:

o    Fields of fire.

o    Cover and concealment.

o    Avenues of approach.

o    Isolated and conspicuous patterns.

o    Terrain features lying between your position and the objectives.

## Sniper Hide Checklist

There are many factors to consider in the selection, construction, and use of a sniper hide. The sniper team must remain alert to the danger of compromise and consider their mission as an overriding factor. The sniper team should use the following guidelines when selecting a site and constructing the sniper hide.

o    When the situation permits, select and construct a sniper hide from which to observe and shoot. Because the slightest movement is the only requirement for detection, construction is usually accomplished at night. Caution still must be exercised, as the enemy may employ night vision devices, and sound travels greater distances at night.

o    Do not place the sniper hide against a contrasting background or near a prominent terrain feature. These features are usually under observation or used as registration points.

o    In selecting a position for the sniper hide, consider those areas that are least likely to be occupied by the enemy.

o    Ensure that the position is located within effective range of the expected targets and that it affords a clear field of fire.

o    Construct or employ alternate hides where necessary to effectively cover an area.

o    Assume that the sniper hide is under enemy observation.

o    Avoid making sounds.

o    Avoid unnecessary movement.

o    Avoid observing over a skyline or the top of cover or concealment that has an even outline or contrasting background.

o    Avoid using the binoculars or telescope where light may reflect from the lenses.

o    Observe around a tree from a position near the ground. The snipers should stay in the shadows when observing from a sniper hide.

o    Give careful consideration to the route into or out of the hide. A worn path can easily be detected. The route should be concealed and covered, if possible.

o    Use resourcefulness and ingenuity to determine the type of hide to be constructed.

o    When possible, choose a position that has a terrain obstacle (e.g., a river, thick brush, etc.) between it and the target and/or known or suspected enemy location.

## Hide Site Occupation
During the mission planning phase, the sniper also selects an objective rally point (ORP). From this point, the sniper team reconnoiters the tentative position to determine the exact location of its final position. The location of the ORP should provide cover and concealment from enemy fire and observation, be located as close to the selected area as possible, and have good routes into and out of the selected area.

From the ORP, the team moves forward to a location that allows the team to view the tentative position area. One member remains in this location and covers the other member while he reconnoiters the area to locate a final position. Once a suitable location has been found, the covering team member moves to the position. While conducting the reconnaissance or moving to the position, the team:

71

o    Moves slowly and deliberately, using the sniper low crawl.

o    Avoids unnecessary movement of trees, bushes, and grass.

o    Avoids making any noises.

o    Stays in the shadows, if there are any.

o    Stops, looks, and listens every few feet.

When the sniper team arrives at the firing position, it:

o    Conducts a hasty and detailed search of the target area.

o    Starts construction of the firing position, if required.

o    Organizes equipment so that it is easily accessible.

o    Establishes a system of observing, eating, resting, and latrine calls.

## Hasty Sniper Hide

A hasty position is used when the sniper team will be in position for a short time, when it cannot construct a position due to the proximity of the enemy, or when it must immediately assume a position. Due to the limited nature of most sniper missions and the requirement to stalk, the sniper team will, in most cases, use a hasty position.

A hasty position (fast find) provides protection from enemy fire or observation. It may be natural or artificial. Natural cover (ravines, hollows, reverse slopes, etc.) and artificial cover (foxholes, trenches, walls, etc.) protect the sniper from flat trajectory fires and enemy observation. Snipers must form the habit of looking for and taking advantage of every bit of cover and concealment the terrain offers. They must combine this habit with proper use of movement techniques to provide adequate protection from enemy fire and observation.

Cover and conncealment in a hasty position provide protection from enemy fire and observation. The cover and concealment may be artificial or natural. Concealment may not provide protection from enemy fire. A sniper team should not make the mistake of believing they are protected from enemy fire merely because they are concealed from enemy eyes.

There should be no limitation on ingenuity of the sniper team in selecting a hasty sniper hide. Under certain circumstances it may be necessary to fire from trees, rooftops, steeples, logs, tunnels, deep shadows, buildings, swamps, woods, and an unlimited variety of open areas. How well the sniper team accomplishes the mission depends to a large degree on the sniper team's knowledge, understanding, and application of the various field techniques or skills that allow them to move, hide, observe, and detect the enemy.

Advantages:

o    Requires no construction. The sniper team uses what is available for cover and concealment.

o    Can be occupied in a short time. As soon as a suitable position is found, the team need only prepare loopholes by moving small amounts of vegetation or by simply backing a few feet away from the vegetation that is already there to conceal the weapon's muzzle blast.

Disadvantages:

o    Affords no freedom of movement. Any movement that is not slow and deliberate may result in the team being compromised.

o    Restricts observation of large areas. This type of position is normally used to observe a specific target area (intersection, passage, or crossing).

o    Offers no protection from direct or indirect fires. The team has only available cover for protection from direct fires.

o    Relies heavily on personal camouflage. The team's only protection against detection is personal camouflage and the ability to use the available terrain.

Occupation time. The team should not remain in this type of position longer than eight hours, which will only result in loss of effectiveness. This is due to muscle strain or cramps as a result of lack of freedom of movement combined with eye fatigue.

## Expedient Sniper Hide
When a sniper team is required to remain in position for a longer time than the hasty position can provide, an expedient position (Figure 4-7-1) should be constructed. The expedient position lowers the sniper's silhouette as low to the ground as possible, but it still allows him to fire and observe effectively. The expedient position is characterized by the following:

Advantages:

o    Requires little construction. This position is constructed by digging a hole in the ground just large enough for the team and its equipment. Soil dug from this position can be placed in sandbags and used for building firing platforms.

73

o    Conceals most of the body and equipment.  The optics, rifles, and heads of the sniper team are the only items that are above ground level in this position.

o    Provides some protection from direct fires due to its lower silhouette.

Disadvantages:

o    Affords little freedom of movement.  The team has more freedom of movement in this position than in the hasty position.  However, teams must remember that stretching or reaching for a canteen causes the exposed head to move unless controlled. Team members can lower the head below ground level, but this should be done slowly to ensure a target indicator is not produced.

o    Allows little protection from indirect fires.  This position does not protect the team from shrapnel and debris falling into the position.

o    Exposes the head, weapons, and optics.  The team must rely heavily on the camouflaging of these exposed items.

Construction time:  1 to 3 hours (depending on the situation).

Occupation time:  6 to 12 hours.


## Belly Hide
The belly hide (Figure 4-7-2) is similar to the expedient position, but it has overhead cover that not only protects the team from the effects of indirect fires but also allows more freedom of movement.  A belly hide is best used in mobile situations or when the sniper does not intend to be in the position for extended periods of time.  This position can be dug out under a tree, a rock, or any available object that will provide overhead protection and a concealed entrance and exit.  The belly hide is characterized by the following:

Advantages:

o    Allows some freedom of movement.  The darkened area inside this position allows the team to move freely.  The team must remember to cover the entrance/exit hole with a poncho or piece of canvas so outside light does not silhouette the team inside the position.

o    Conceals all but the rifle barrel.  All equipment is inside the position except the rifle barrels, but the barrels could be inside, depending on the room available to construct the position.

74

o    Provides protection from direct and indirect fires. The team should try to choose a position that has an object that will provide good overhead protection (rock, tracked vehicle, rubble pile, and so forth), or prepare it in the same manner as overhead cover for other infantry positions.

o    The hide is simple and can be quickly built. This hide can be used when the sniper is mobile, because many can be built.

Disadvantages:

o    The hide is uncomfortable.

o    The hide cannot be occupied for long periods of time.

o    The sniper is exposed while firing.

o    The hide provides limited protection from the weather or fire.

o    The sniper has to enter the position from the front.

o    Requires extra construction time.

o    Requires extra materials and tools. Construction of overhead cover will require saws or axes, waterproof material, and so forth.

o    Has limited space. The sniper team will have to lay in the belly hide without a lot of variation in body position due to limited space and design of the position.

Construction.

o    Dig a pit (shallow) for the prone position.

o    Omit the parapet.

o    Build an overhead cover using:

*    Dirt/sod.
*    A drop cloth.

*    Woven saplings.

*    Corrugated metal, shell boxes, scrap metal, doors, chicken wire, scrap lumber, etc.

Construction time: 4 to 6 hours.

Occupation time:  12 to 48 hours.

## Semipermanent Sniper Hide

The semipermanent hide (Figure 4-7-3) is used mostly in a defensive or outpost situation.  This position requires additional equipment and personnel to construct.  However, it will allow sniper teams to remain there for extended periods or be relieved in place by other sniper teams.  Like the belly hide, this position can be constructed by tunneling through a knoll or under natural objects already in place.  This prepared sniper hide should provide sufficient room for movement without fear of detection, some protection from weather and overhead or direct fire, and a covered route to and from the hide.

A semipermanent hide can be an enlargement of the standard one- or two-man fighting position with overhead cover (Figure 4-7-4).  This type of hide is constructed when in a defensive posture, since considerable time is required for its construction, and it would be suitable when integrated into the perimeter defense of a base camp, during static warfare, or during a stay-behind infiltration.  It can be constructed as a standing or lying type of hide.

The construction of loopholes requires care and practice to ensure that they afford an adequate view of the required fields of fire.  The loopholes should be constructed so that they are wide at the back where the sniper is and narrow in the front, but not so narrow that observation is restricted.  Loopholes may be made of old coffee cans, old boots, or any other rubbish, provided that it is natural to the surroundings or that it can be properly and cleverly concealed.

Loopholes may be holes in windows, shutters, roofs, walls, or fences, or they may be constructed by the sniper team.  Loopholes must blend in with the surrounding area.

Advantages:

o     Offers total freedom of movement inside the position.  The team members can move about freely.  They can stand, sit, or even lie down.

o     Protects against direct and indirect fires.  The sniper team should look for the same items as mentioned in the belly hide.

o     Is completely concealed.  Loopholes are the only part of the position that can be detected.  They allow for the smallest exposure possible; yet, they still allow the sniper and observer to view the target area.  The entrance/exit to the position must be covered to prevent light from entering and highlighting the loopholes.  Loopholes that are not in use should

76

be covered from the inside with a piece of canvas or suitable material.

      o    Is easily maintained for extended periods. This position allows the team to operate effectively for a longer period.

    Disadvantages:

      o    Requires extra personnel and tools to construct. This position requires extensive work and more tools. Very seldom can a position like this be constructed near the enemy, but it should be constructed during darkness and be completed before dawn.

      o    Increases risk of detection. Using a position for several days or having teams relieve each other in a position always increases the risk of the position being detected. Snipers should never continue to fire from the same position.

    Construction time:  4 to 6 hours (4 personnel).

    Occupation time:  48 hours plus (relieved by other teams).

## Types of Deliberate Sniper Hides

    Enlarged fire trench hides. An enlarged fire trench hide is an enlarged fighting position (Figure 4-7-5).

    Advantages:

      o    The sniper team is able to maintain a low silhouette.

      o    The hide is simple to construct.

      o    The hide can be occupied for a moderate period of time with some degree of comfort.

    Disadvantages:

      o    The hide is not easily entered into or exited from.

      o    The sniper team has no overhead cover when in firing position.

      o    The sniper team is exposed while firing or observing.

    Construction.

      o    Enlarge and repair the sides and the parapet.

o     Camouflage the hide with a drop cloth.

<u>Shell hole hides</u>.  A shell hole hide is a crater improved for kneeling, sitting, or prone firing positions (Figure 4-7-6).

Advantages:

o     Construction of the hide does not require much digging.

Disadvantages:

o     The hide requires material to secure the sides.

o     There is no drainage.
Construction.

o     Dig platforms for either the prone, the kneeling, or the sitting positions.

o     Reinforce the sides of the craters.

<u>Tree or stump hides</u> (Figure 4-7-7).

Advantages:

o     The hide can be rapidly occupied.

o     The sniper team is protected from fire and shrapnel.

o     The sniper team has freedom of movement.

o     The hide provides comfort.

Disadvantages:

o     The hide takes time to construct.

o     The sniper team requires pioneer equipment for construction of the hide (picks, shovels, axes, etc.).

Construction.  In selecting trees for hides, use trees that have a good, deep root such as oak, chestnut, or hickory. During heavy winds these trees tend to remain steady better than a pine tree, which has surface roots and sways a bit in a breeze.  A large tree that is back from the woodline should be used.  This may limit the view, but will provide better cover and concealment.

## Hide Site Construction Considerations

A sniper mission always requires the team to occupy some type of position. These positions can range from a hasty position, which a team may use for a few hours, to a more permanent position, which the team could remain in for a few days. When choosing and constructing positions, the sniper team must use its imagination and ingenuity to reduce the time and difficulty of position construction. The team should always plan to build its position during limited visibility.

Sniper Position Considerations. Whether a sniper team will be in a position for a few minutes or a few days, the basic considerations in choosing a type of position remain the same.

o    Location:

*    Type of terrain and soil. Digging and boring of tunnels can be very difficult in hard soil or in fine, loose sand. The team needs to take advantage of what the terrain offers (gullies, holes, hollow tree stumps, and so forth).

*    Enemy location and capabilities. Enemy patrols in the area may be close enough to the position to hear any noises that may accidentally be made during any construction. The team also need to consider the enemy's night vision and detection capabilities.

o    Time:

*    Amount of time to be occupied. If the sniper team's mission requires it to be in position for a long time, the team must consider construction of a position that provides more survivability. This allows the team to operate more effectively for a longer time.

*    Time needed for construction. The time needed to build a position must be a consideration, especially during the mission planning phase.

o    Personnel and equipment:

*    Equipment needed for construction. The team must plan the use of any extra equipment needed for construction (bow saws, picks, axes, and so forth).

*    Personnel    needed    for    construction. Coordination must take place if the position requires more personnel to build it or a security element to secure the area during construction.

## Steps Used In the Construction Of a Sniper Hide

When the sniper team is en route to the objective area, material that can be used for constructing the hide should be marked. The team should establish an objective rallying point, reconnoiter the objective area, select a site, and mark the fields of fire and observation. After collecting additional material, the team returns to the sniper hide site under the cover of darkness and begins construction of the hide.

o    Post security.

o    Remove the top soil (observe construction discipline).

o    Dig a pit. Dispose of soil properly and reinforce the sides. Ensure that the pit has:

*    Loopholes.

*    A bench rest.

*    A bed.

*    A drainage sump (if appropriate).

o    Construct an overhead cover.

o    Construct an entrance/exit by escape routes noted.

o    Camouflage the hide.

o    Inspect the hide for improper concealment (continuous).

## Hide Site Construction Techniques
o    Frontal protection. Regardless of material, every effort is made to bulletproof the front of the hide position. The team can use the following techniques:

*    Pack kevlar flak jackets around the loophole areas.

*    Emplace an angled armor plate with a loophole cut into it behind the hide loophole.

*    Sandbag the loopholes from the inside.

o    Pit. Hide construction begins with the pit since it protects the sniper team. All excavated dirt is removed (placed in sandbags, taken away on a poncho, and so forth) and hidden (plowed fields, under a log, or away from the hide site).

o    Overhead cover. In a semipermanent hide position, logs should be used as the base of the roof. The sniper team places a dust cover over the base (such as a poncho, layers of empty sandbags, or canvas), a layer of dirt, and a layer of gravel, if

80

available. The team spreads another layer of dirt, and then adds camouflage. Due to the various materials, the roof is difficult to conceal if not countersunk.

   o    Entrance. To prevent detection, the sniper team should construct an entrance door sturdy enough to bear a man's weight.

   o    Loopholes. The construction of loopholes (Figure 4-7-8) requires care and practice to ensure that they afford adequate fields of fire. These loopholes should have a large diameter (10 to 14 inches) in the interior of the position and taper down to a smaller diameter (4 to 8 inches) on the outside of the position. A position may have more than two sets of loopholes if needed to cover large areas. Loopholes must be camouflaged by foliage or other material that blends with or is natural to the surroundings.

   o    Approaches. It is vital that the natural appearance of the ground remains unaltered and camouflage blends with the surroundings. Remember, construction time is wasted if the enemy observes a team entering the hide; therefore, approaches must be concealed whenever possible. Teams should try to enter the hide during darkness, keeping movement around it to a minimum and adhering to trail discipline. In built-up areas, a secure and quiet approach is needed. Teams should avoid drawing attention to the mission and carefully plan movement. A possible ploy is to use a house search with sniper gear hidden among other gear. Sewers may be used for movement also.

WARNING: WHEN MOVING THROUGH SEWERS, TEAMS MUST BE ALERT FOR BOOBY TRAPS AND POISONOUS GASES.

## Tools, Materials, and Equipment Needed To Construct a Sniper Hide
The tools needed to build a sniper hide depend on the soil, the terrain, and the type of hide to be built. Some considerations are:

   o    Entrenching tools.

   o    Bayonets.

   o    GP nets.

   o    Ponchos.

   o    Waterproof bags.

   o    Rucksacks.

   o    Shovels.

   o    Picks.

o    Axes/hatchets.

o    Hammers.

o    Machetes.

o    Chisels.

o    Saws (hacksaws, etc.)

o    Screwdrivers, pliers, garden tools.

Materials for the construction of a hide are varied. Some of the materials that will be needed are:

o    Garbage bags.

o    Wood glue.

o    Nails.

o    Chicken wire, newspapers, flour, water.


## Hide Site Routines

Although the construction of positions may differ, the routines while in position are the same. The sniper and the observer should have a good firing platform. This gives the sniper a stable platform for the sniper weapon and the observer a platform for the optics. When rotating observation duties, th sniper weapon should remain in place, and the optics are handed from one member to the other. Data books, observation logs, range cards, and the radio should be placed within the team where both members have easy access to them. A system of resting, eating, and latrine calls must be arranged within the team. All latrine calls should be done during darkness, if possible. A hole should be dug to conceal any traces of latrine calls.


## 4-8.  SNIPER RANGE CARD, OBSERVATION LOG, AND MILITARY SKETCH

The sniper team uses range cards, observation logs, and military sketches to enable it to rapidly engage targets and maintain a record of its employment during an operation.

## Range Card

The range card represents the target area drawn as seen from above with annotations indicating distances throughout the target area. Information is recorded on DA Form 5787-R (Sniper's Range Card) (Figure 4-8-1). (A blank copy of this form is located in Appendix N for local reproduction). The range card provides the sniper team with a quick-range reference and a means to record target locations, since it has preprinted range rings on it. These cards can be divided into sectors by using dashed lines (Figure 4-8-2). This provides the team members with a quick reference when locating targets. A field-expedient range card can be prepared on any paper the team has available. The sniper team position and distances to prominent objects and terrain features are drawn on the card. There is not a set maximum range on either range card, because the team may also label any indirect fire targets on its range card. Information contained on both range cards includes:

o    Sniper's name and method of obtaining range.

o    Left and right limits of engageable area.

o    Major terrain features, roads, and structures.

o    Ranges, elevation, and windage needed at various distances.

o    Distances throughout the area.

o    Temperature and wind. (Cross out previous entry whenever temperature, wind direction, or wind velocity changes.)

o    Target reference points (azimuth, distance, and description).

Relative locations of dominant objects and terrain features should be included. Examples are:

o    Houses.

o    Bridges.

o    Groves

o    Hills.

o    Crossroads.

The sniper team will indicate the range to each object by estimation or measuring. All drawings on the range card are from the perspective of the sniper looking straight down on the observation area.

## Observation Log
The observation logbook is a written, chronological record of all activities and events that take place in a sniper team's area. It is used with military sketches and range cards; this combination not only gives commanders and intelligence personnel information about the appearance of the area, but it also provides an accurate

record of the activity in the area. Information is recorded on DA Form 5786-R (Sniper's Observation Log) (Figure 4-8-3). (A blank copy of this form is located in Appendix N for local reproduction). Information in the observation logbook includes:

o    Grid coordinates of the sniper team's position.

o    Observer's name.

o    Date and time of observation and visiblity.

o    Sheet number and number of total sheets.

o    Series number, time, and grid coordinates of each event.

o    The event that has taken place.

o    Action taken.

The sniper log will always be used in conjunction with a military sketch. This helps to serve as a pictorial reference to the written log. If the sniper team is relieved in place, a new sniper team can easily locate earlier sightings using these two documents as references. The observer's log is a ready means of recording enemy activity, and if properly maintained, it enables the sniper team to report all information required.

Sniper observation logs will be filled out using the key word SALUTE for enemy activity and OCOKA for terrain. When using these key words to fill out the logs, the sniper should not use generalities; he should be very specific (i.e., give the exact number of troops, the exact location, the dispersion location, etc.).

The range card is a record of the sniper's observations and preparations. Its proper preparation and use provides a quick reference to key terrain features and targets. It also allows the sniper team to quickly acquire new targets that come into their area of observation. The sniper's range card and the observation log are always used in conjunction with each other.

The key word "SALUTE":

S - Size.

A - Activity.

L - Location.

U - Unit/Uniform.

T - Time.

84

E - Equipment.

The key word "OCOKA":

        O - Observation and fields of fire.

        C - Cover and concealment.

        O - Obstacles.

        K - Key terrain.

        A - Avenues of approach.

## Military Sketch

DA Form 5788-R (Military Sketch) is used to record information about a general area, terrain features, or man-made structures that are not shown on a map. Military sketches provide intelligence sections a detailed, on-the-ground view of an area or object that is otherwise unobtainable. These sketches not only let the viewer see the area in different perspectives but also provide detail such as type of fences, number of telephone wires, present depth of streams, and so forth. There are two types of military sketches as stated in FM 21-26: road/area sketches and field sketches. Both types of sketches are recorded on DA Form 5788-R. (A blank copy of this form is located in Appendix N for local reproduction.)

**Road/Area Sketch.** A road/area sketch (Figure 4-8-4) is a panoramic representation of an area or object drawn to scale as seen from the sniper team's perspective. It shows details about a specific area or a man-made structure. Information considered in a road/area sketch includes:

o     Grid coordinates of sniper team's position.

o     Magnetic azimuth through the center of sketch.

o     Sketch name and number.

o     Scale of sketch.

o     Remarks section.

o     Name and rank.

o     Date and time.

o     Weather.

Field Sketches. A field sketch (Figure 4-8-5) is a topographic representation of an area drawn to scale as seen from above. It provides the sniper team with a method for describing large areas while showing reliable distance and azimuths between major features. This type of sketch is useful in describing road systems, flow of streams/rivers, or locations of natural and man-made obstacles. The field sketch can also be used as an overlay on the range card. Information contained in a field sketch includes:

o    Grid coordinates of the sniper team's position.

o    Left and right limits with azimuths.

o    Rear reference with azimuth and distance.

o    Target reference points.

o    Sketch name and number.

o    Name and rank.

o    Date and time.

o    Weather and visibility.

The field sketch serves to reinforce the observation log. A military sketch is either panoramic or topographic.

o    Panoramic sketch. The panoramic sketch is a picture of the terrain in elevation and perspective as seen from one point of observation.

o    Topographic sketch. The topographic sketch is similar to a map or pictorial representation from an overhead perspective. It is generally less desirable than the panoramic sketch because it is difficult to relate this type of sketch to the observer's log. It is drawn in a fashion similar to the range card.

## Guidelines for Drawing Sketches
As with all drawings, artistic skill is an asset, but satisfactory sketches can be drawn by anyone with practice. The following are guidelines when drawing sketches:

o    Work from the whole to the part. First determine the boundaries of the sketch. Then sketch the larger objects such as hills, mountains, or outlines of large buildings. After drawing the large objects in the sketch, start drawing the smaller details.

o    Use common shapes to show common objects. Do not sketch each individual tree, hedgerow, or woodline exactly. Use common shapes to show these types of objects. Do not concentrate on the fine details unless they are of tactical importance.

o    Draw in perspective; use vanishing points. Try to draw sketches in perspective. To do this, recognize the vanishing

86

points of the area to be sketched. Parallel lines on the ground that are horizontal vanish at a point on the horizon (Figure 4-8-6). Parallel lines on the ground that slope downward away from the observer vanish at a point below the horizon. Parallel lines on the ground that slope upward, away from the observer, vanish at a point above the horizon. Parallel lines that recede to the right vanish on the right and those that recede to the left vanish on the left (Figure 4-8-7).

## Panoramic Sketching

In order for the sniper team to effectively observe their entire area of responsibility thoroughly, they must be aware of the slightest change in the area. These otherwise insignificant changes could be an indicator of targets or enemy activity that needs to be reported. By properly constructing a panoramic sketch, the snipers have a basis for comparing small changes in the surrounding terrain. This permits the team to better report intelligence and complete their mission.

### General principles of sketching:

o    The panoramic sketch is initiated only after the observer's log and range card have been initiated and after the sniper team has settled into the area of operations.

o    The terrain is studied with the naked eye first to get an overall impression of the area. After the overall impression has been obtained, those areas that attracted the sniper's attention is studied in further detail with binoculars before the first mark is made on a sketch pad.

o    Too much detail is not desirable, unless it is of tactical importance. If additional detail is required on a specific area, the sniper can make subdrawings to supplement the main drawing.

### Principles of perspective and proportionality:

o    Sketches are drawn to perspective whenever possible. To accomplish this, he must remember that the farther away an object is, the smaller it will appear in the drawing.

o    Vertical lines will remain vertical throughout the drawing; however, a series of vertical lines (such as telephone poles or a picket fence) will diminish in height as they approach the horizon.

### Use of delineation to portray objects or features of the landscape (Figure 4-8-8):

o      The horizontal line is the line formed by the intersection of the ground or sky with the horizontal plane at the height of the sketcher's eye.

o      The skyline or the horizon and crests, roads, and rivers form the "control lines" of the sketch. These areas are drawn first to form the framework within which the details can be placed.

o      Represent features with a few, rather than many, lines. Create the effect of distance by making lines in the foreground heavy and making distance lines lighter as the distance increases.

o      A light "hatching" may be used to distinguish wooded areas, but the hatching should follow the natural lines of the object (Figure 4-8-9).

Use of the conventional methods to portray objects:

o      If possible, the actual shape of all prominent features that may be readily selected as reference points when describing targets are shown. These features may be accepted with an arrow and with a line to a description; e.g., a prominent tree with a withered branch.

o      Rivers and roads are drawn as two lines that diminish in width to the vanishing point as they recede.

o      Railroads in the foreground are shown as a double line with small cross lines (which represent ties). This will distinguish them from roads. To portray railroads in the distance, a single line with vertical ticks to represent the telegraph poles is drawn. When rivers, roads, and railroads are all present in the same sketch, they may have to be labelled to show what they are.

o      Trees are represented in outline only, unless a particular tree is to be used as a reference point. If a particular tree is to be used as a reference point, the tree must be drawn in more detail to show why it was picked.

o      Woods in the distance are shown by outline only. If the woods are in the foreground, the tops of individual trees can be drawn.

o      Churches are shown in outline only, but it should be noted whether they have a tower or a spire.

o      Towns and villages are drawn as definite rectangular shapes to denote houses. The location of towers, factory chimneys, and prominent buildings shown in the sketch. Again, detail, if necessary, can be added in subdrawings.

o    Cuts, fills, depressions, swamps, and marshes are shown by using the usual topographic symbols.

A legend is used to label the sketch:

o    Included in the legend is the title of the sketch, the DTG (date, time, group), and the sketcher's signature.
o    Included in the legend is an explanation of the topographic symbols used in the sketch.

## 4-9. KIM GAMES

Sniper operations encompass a much larger scope than hiding in the woods, spotting targets of opportunity and engaging them. The sniper must observe vast areas and accurately record any and all information of his area and what occurs in his assigned area. Because many situations occur suddenly and do not offer prolonged observation, snipers must train themselves to observe situations for short periods of time and extract the maximum amount of information from any given situation.

Keep-in-memory (KIM) games are a series of exercises with the intent of increasing the sniper's abilities to both perceive reality and retain information. KIM games can be conducted anywhere, in very little time, with a large return for the trainer's investment of effort and imagination. Although the various time limits of viewing, waiting, and recording the objects are often not reflected in tactical reality, KIM games are designed to exercise the mind through overload (much the same as weight training overloads the muscles).

Advancement in Kim's Games is measured by shortening the viewing and recording times and lengthening the waiting time. Greater results can be realized by GRADUALLY adding additional elements to increase confusion and uncertainty. In the sniper's trade, the perception of reality often means penetrating the enemy's deception measures. These measures may include, but are not limited to:

o    Misdirection.

o    Disguise.

o    Exchange.

There is a marked similarity between the above list and the principles of stage magic. Just as knowing how a magician performs a trick takes the "magic" from it, knowing how one is being deceived negates the deception.

The Basic Game

The instructor will require a table, a cover, and an assortment of objects. Ten objects are selected and placed randomly on the table. The objects should not be placed in orderly rows, since studies have shown that objects that are placed in rows make memorization easier. The objects are then covered. The students must be briefed on the rules prior to each iteration:

- No talking is allowed.

- Objects may not be touched.

- Students will not write until told to do so.

The students are gathered around the table. The cover is removed, and the time for viewing begins. When the time is up, the cover is replaced, and students return to their seats. After a designated interval, the students will begin to write their observations within a designated time limit. To aid in retaining and recording their observations, standardized categories are used throughout:

- Appears to be (ATB).

- Size.

- Color.

- Condition.

It must be stressed that the above categories are not intended for use in a tactical setting.

## The Savelli Shuffle
A variation of the KIM game that trains the eyes to "look. faster" and coordinates hand to eye is the Savelli Shuffle. Two individuals face each other approximately 5 meters apart. The first man has a bag containing a number of yellow rubber balls and a smaller number of red rubber balls. The second man has an empty bag. The first man reaches into his bag and picks out a ball, concealing it from the second man. The first man tosses the ball to the second man. Velocity will depend on level of experience.

The second man has a quick decision to make: catch yellow balls with the left hand, red balls with the right hand. The second man then places the caught balls into his bag.

This process is repeated until the first man's bag is emptied. Positions of the first man and the second man are exchanged. Advancement in this exercise is measured by the speed at which the balls are thrown and the distance between men.

## Interest and Attention

90

When learning to observe, a distinction must be made between interest and attention. Interest is a sense of being involved in some process, actual or potential. Attention is a simple response to a stimulus, such as a loud noise. Attention without interest cannot be maintained for very long. During long periods of uneventful observation, attention must be maintained through interest. Deception at the individual level can be thought of as manipulation of interest.

## 4-10. NIGHT OPERATIONS

Without night vision devices, the sniper team must depend upon eyesight. Regardless of night brightness, the human eye cannot function at night with daylight precision. For maximum effectiveness, the sniper team must apply the following principles of night vision:

    o    Night Adaptation. The sniper team should wear sunglasses or red-lensed goggles in lighted areas before departing on a mission. After departure, the team makes a darkness adaptation and listening halt for 30 minutes.

    o    Off-Center Vision. In dim light, an object under direct focus blurs, appears to change, and sometimes fades out entirely. However, when the eyes are focused at different points, about 5 to 10 degrees away from an object, peripheral vision provides a true picture. This allows the light-sensitive portion of the eye, that not used during the day, to be used.

### Factors Affecting Night Vision
The sniper team has control over the following night vision factors:

    o    Lack of vitamin A impairs night vision. However, an overdose of vitamin A will not increase night vision capability.

    o    Colds, fatigue, narcotics, headaches, smoking, and alcohol reduce night vision.


    o    Exposure to bright light degrades night vision and requires a readaption to darkness.

### Illumination Aids
The sniper team may occasionally have artificial illumination for observing and firing. Examples are artillery illumination fire, campfires, or lighted buildings.

    o    Artillery Illumination Fire. The M301A2 illuminating cartridge provides 50,000 candlepower.

o    Campfires.   Poorly disciplined enemy soldiers may use campfires, or fires may be created by battlefield damage.   These opportunities give the sniper enough illumination for aiming.

o    Lighted Buildings.   The sniper can use lighted buildings to eliminate occupants of the building or personnel in the immediate area of the light source.

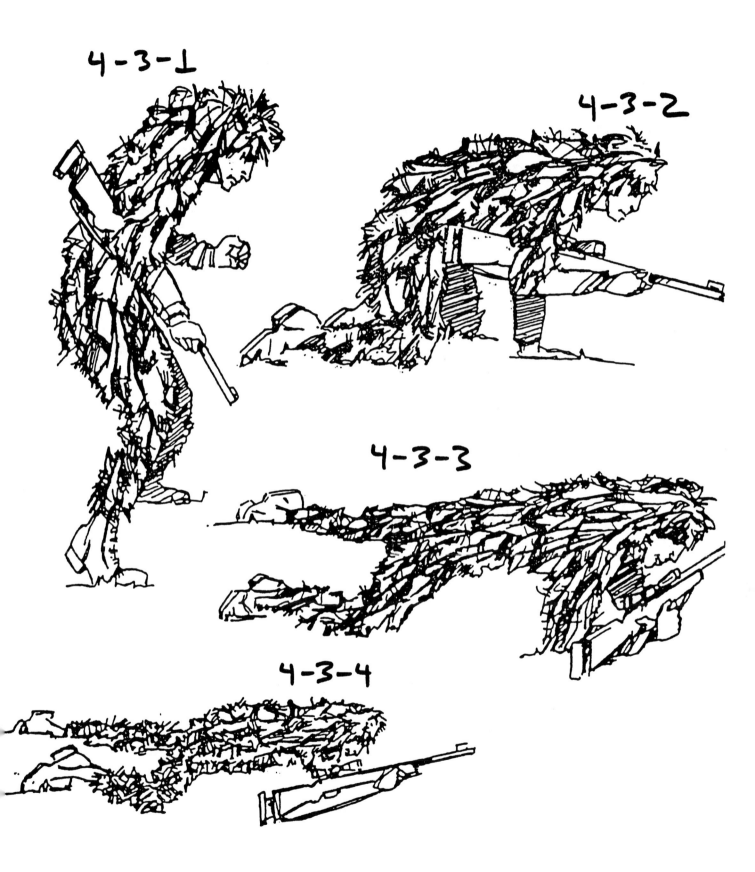

4-3-1

4-3-2

4-3-3

4-3-4

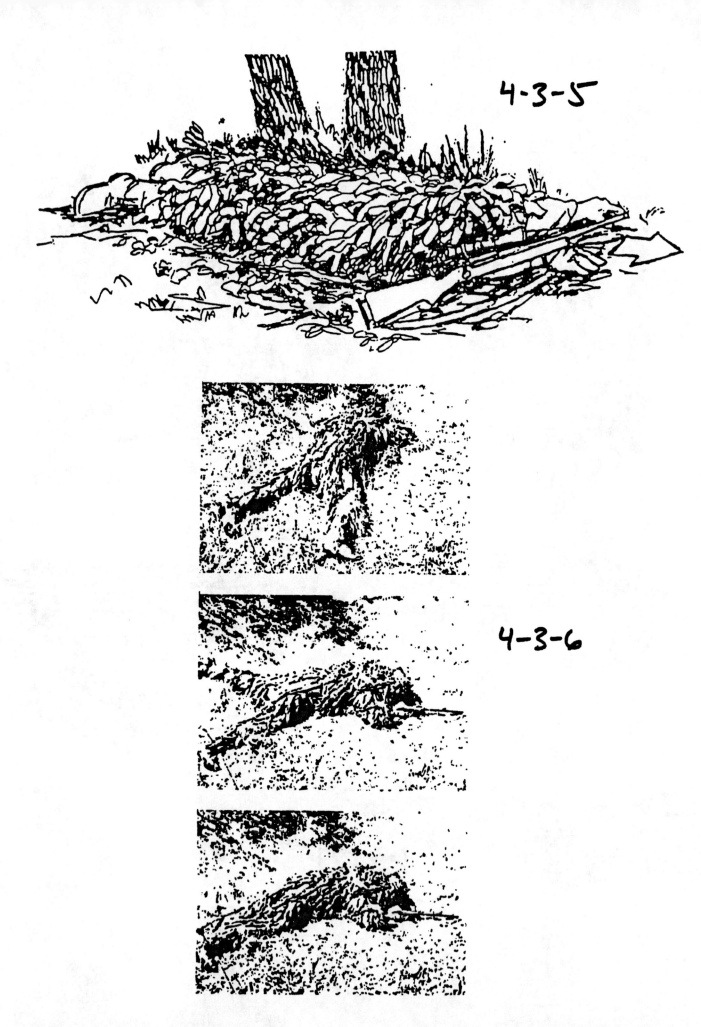

4-3-5

4-3-6

4-4-1

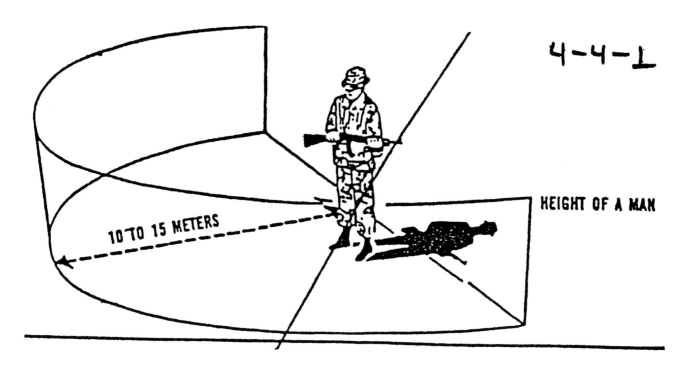

HEIGHT OF A MAN

10 TO 15 METERS

Area being surveyed for indicators.

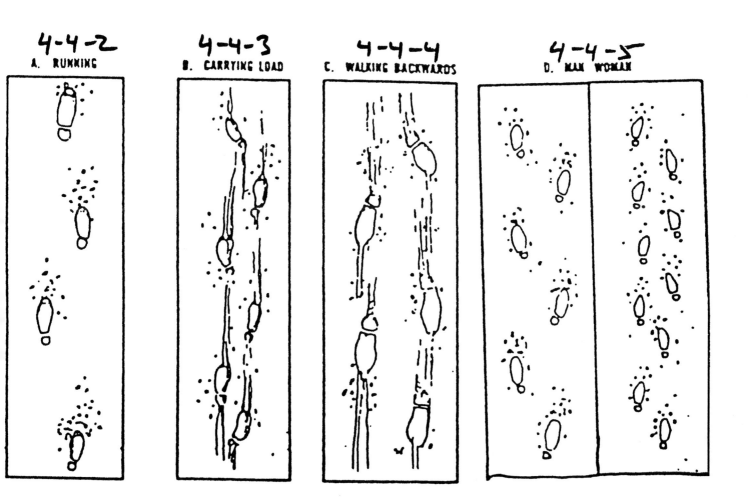

4-4-2
A. RUNNING

4-4-3
B. CARRYING LOAD

4-4-4
C. WALKING BACKWARDS

4-4-5
D. MAN  WOMAN

4-4-6

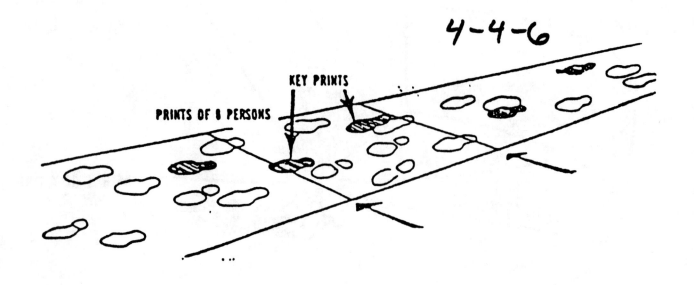

PRINTS OF 8 PERSONS

KEY PRINTS

4-4-7

36 INCHES

4-4-8        4-4-8        4-4-9

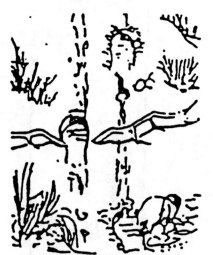

A. TURNED OVER ROCKS
AND STICKS

B. CRUSHED AND DISTURBED
VEGETATION

C. SLIP MARK AND WATERFILLED
FOOTPRINTS ON STREAM BANKS.

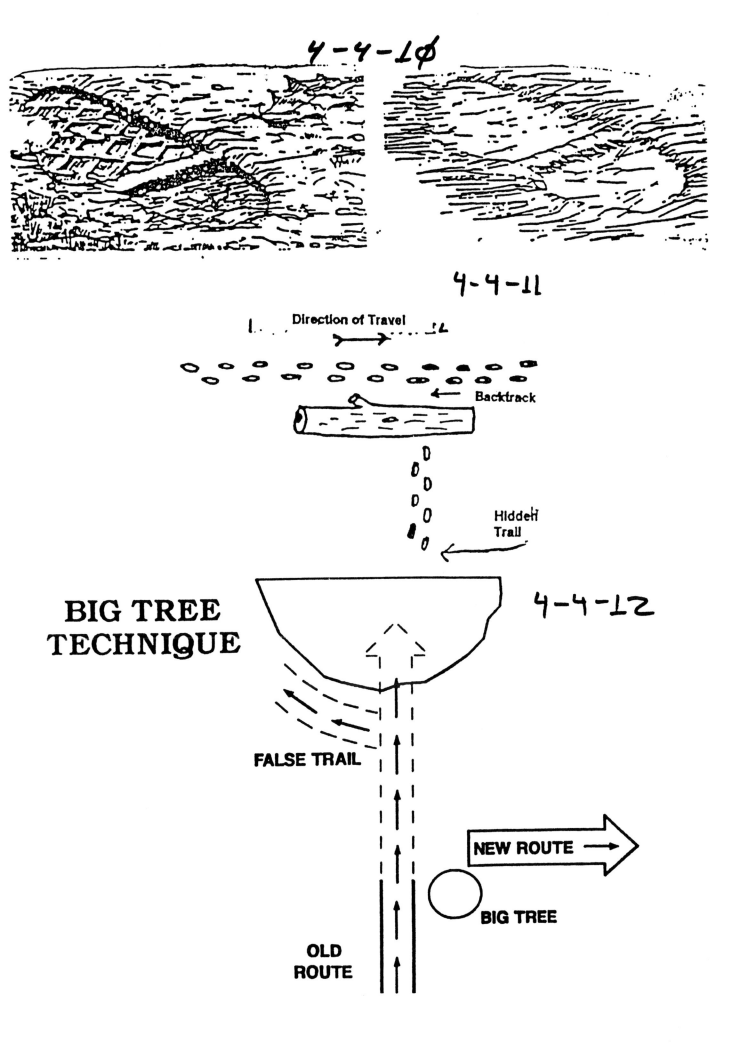

4-4-10

4-4-11

Direction of Travel

Backtrack

Hidden Trail

4-4-12

BIG TREE
TECHNIQUE

FALSE TRAIL

NEW ROUTE

BIG TREE

OLD
ROUTE

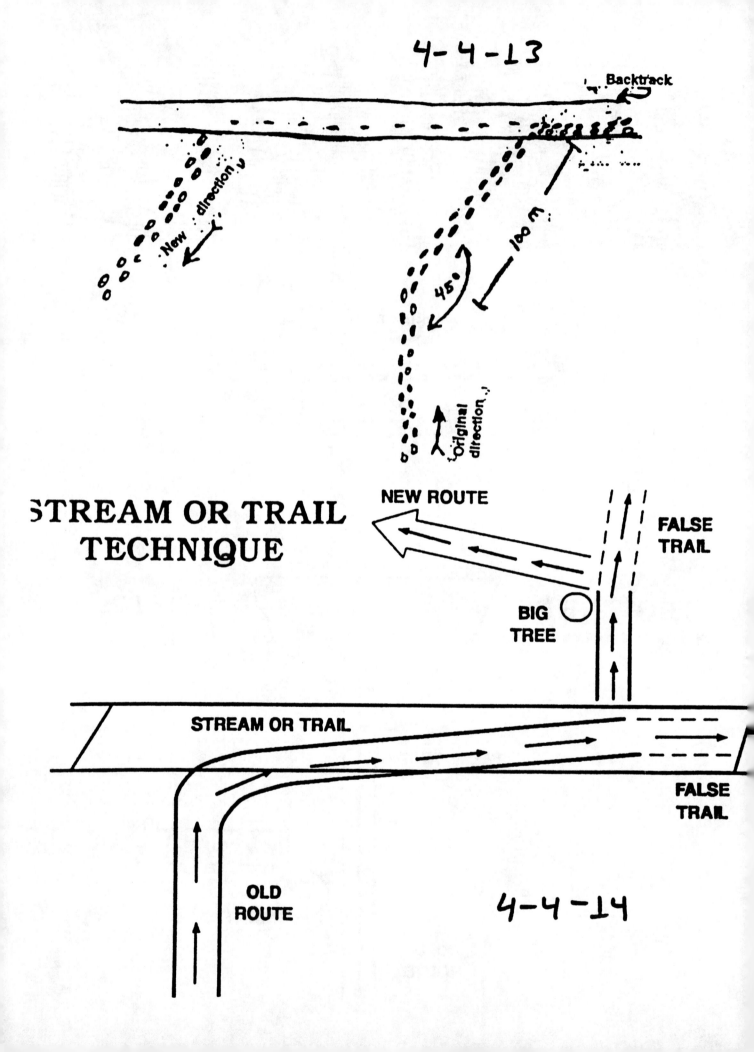

4-4-13

Backtrack

New direction

100 m

45°

Original direction

# STREAM OR TRAIL
# TECHNIQUE

NEW ROUTE

FALSE TRAIL

BIG TREE

STREAM OR TRAIL

FALSE TRAIL

OLD ROUTE

4-4-14

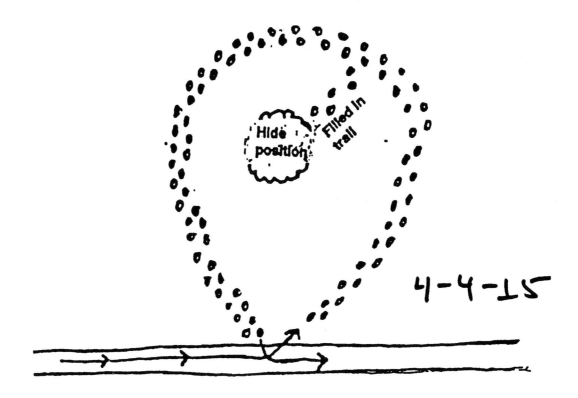

Hide
position

Filled in
trail

4-4-15

4-4-16

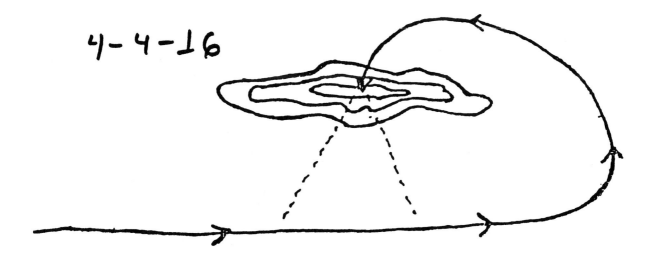

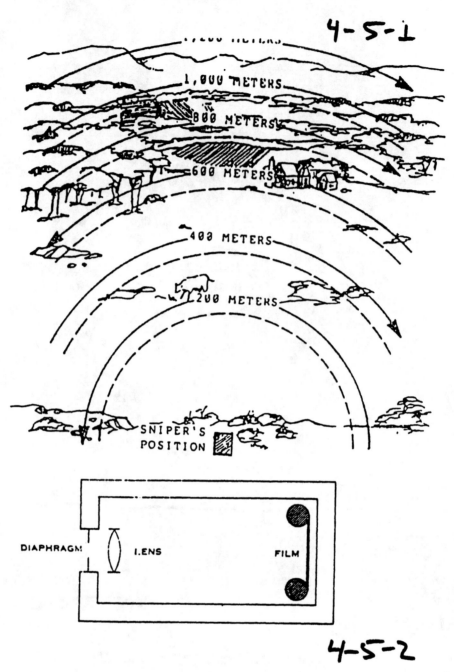

4-5-1

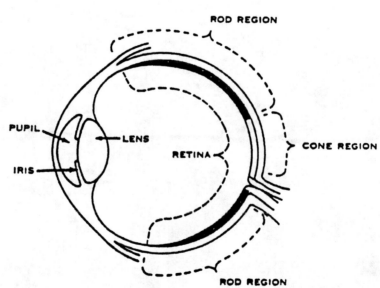

4-5-2

4-6-1

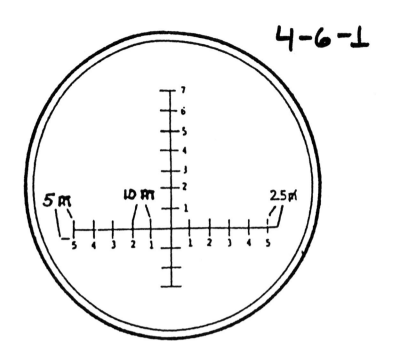

M19 binocular reticle.

4-6-2

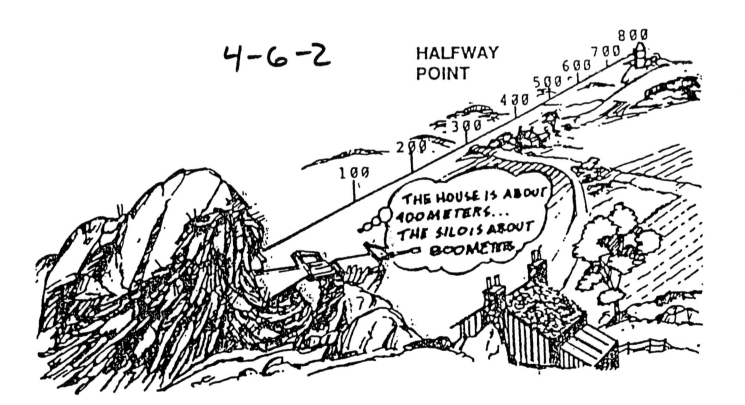

SAMPLE PROBLEM #1.  Base line length is 20 meters.

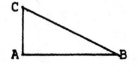

Angle B = 1,560 mils

C = 3,200 mils - (A + B)
C = 3,200 mils - (1,600 + 1,560)
C = 3,200 - 3,160
C = 40 mils

---

$$AC = \frac{(AB) \times \sin B}{\sin C} \qquad AC = \frac{(20) \times \sin 1,560}{\sin 40}$$

$$AC = \frac{(20) \times .9992292}{.0392598} \qquad AC = \frac{19.984584}{.0392598}$$

AC = 509.03 meters

---

SAMPLE PROBLEM # 2   Base line length is 30 meters.

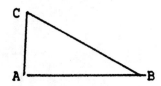

Angle B = 1,585 mils

C = 3,200 mils - (A + B)
C = 3,200 mils - (1,600 + 1,585)
C = 3,200 mils - 3,185 mils
C = 15 mils

---

$$AC = \frac{(AB) \times \sin B}{\sin C} \qquad AC = \frac{(30) \times \sin 1,585}{\sin 15}$$

$$AC = \frac{(30) \times .9998915}{.014725} \qquad AC = \frac{29.996745}{.014725}$$

AC = 2037.13 meters

---

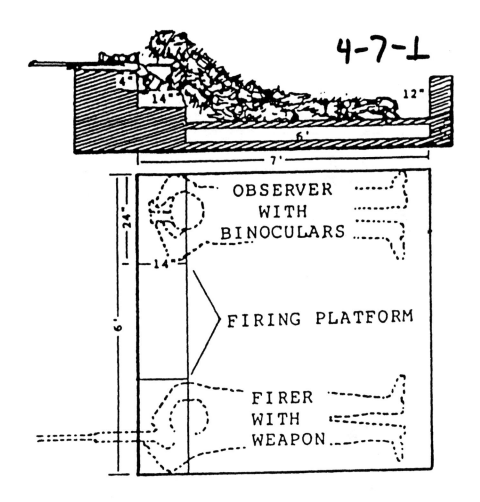

4-7-1

OBSERVER WITH BINOCULARS

FIRING PLATFORM

FIRER WITH WEAPON

Expedient position.

4-7-2

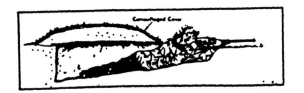

Figure 4-35. Belly Hide (Side View).

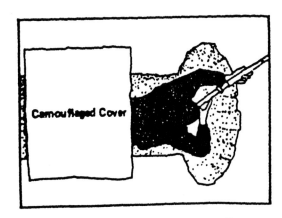

Camouflaged Cover

Figure 4-36. Belly Hide (Top View).

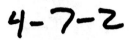

4-7-2

4-7-3

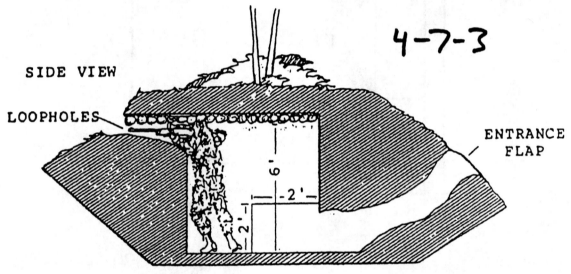

SIDE VIEW

LOOPHOLES

6'

2'

2'

ENTRANCE FLAP

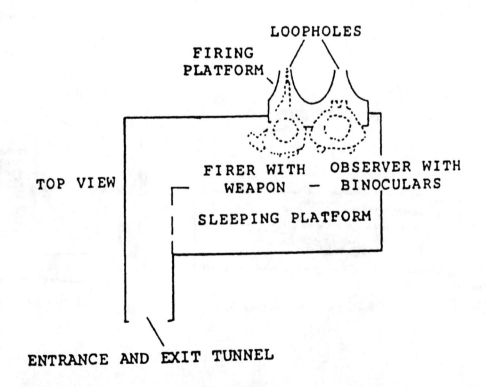

LOOPHOLES

FIRING PLATFORM

FIRER WITH WEAPON  —  OBSERVER WITH BINOCULARS

TOP VIEW

SLEEPING PLATFORM

ENTRANCE AND EXIT TUNNEL

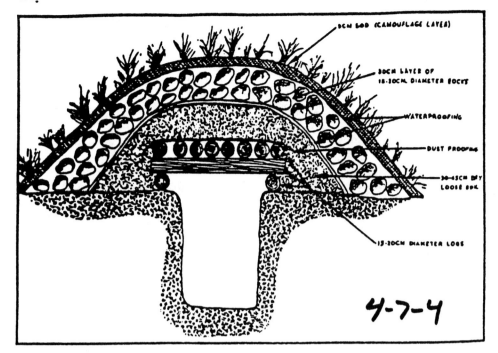

Figure 4-34. Overhead Cover.

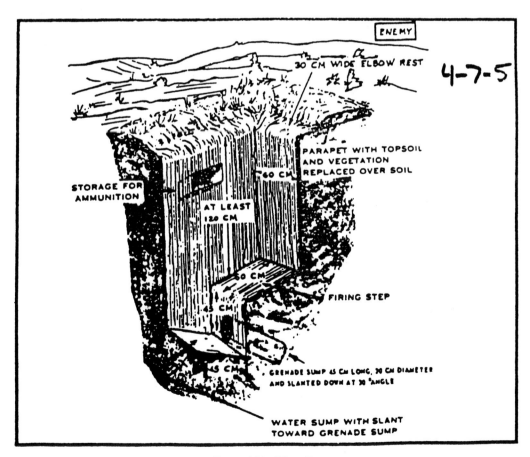

Figure 4-32. Elbow Rest.

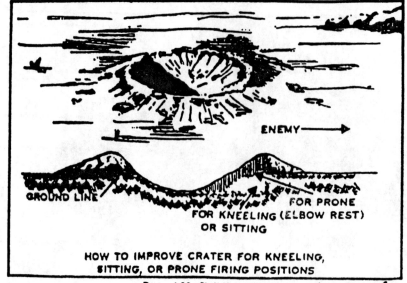

HOW TO IMPROVE CRATER FOR KNEELING,
SITTING, OR PRONE FIRING POSITIONS

Figure 4-39. Shell Hole Hide.

4-7-6

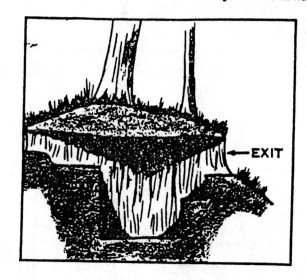

4-7-7

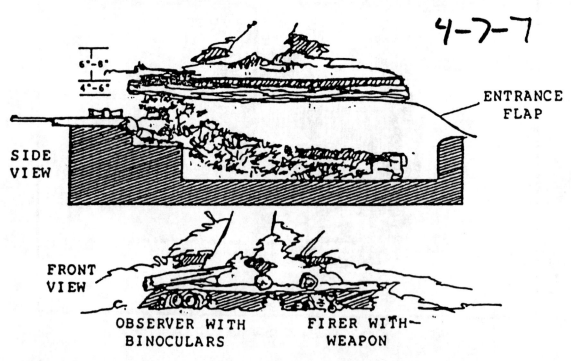

TYPICAL LOOPHOLE CONSTRUCTION

FRONT VIEW          VIEW FROM INSIDE POST          SIDE VIEW

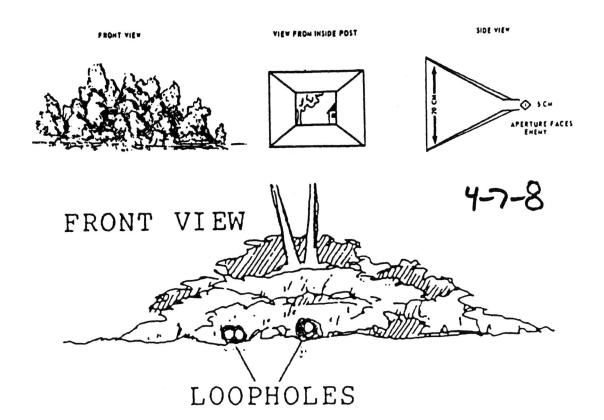

# FRONT VIEW

## LOOPHOLES

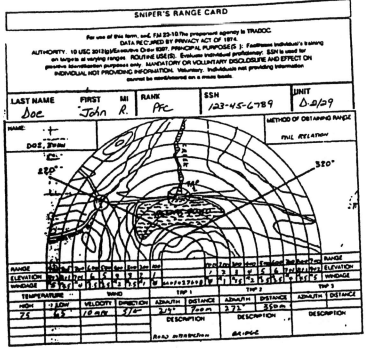

DA FORM 5787-R

**SNIPER'S RANGE CARD**
For use of this form, see FM 23-10. The proponent agency is TRADOC.

| NAME | | METHOD OF OBTAINING RANGE |
|---|---|---|
| DOE, JOHN | | MIL RELATION |

| RANGE | | | | | | | RANGE |
|---|---|---|---|---|---|---|---|
| ELEVATION | | | | | | | ELEVATION |
| WINDAGE | | | | | | | WINDAGE |

| TEMPERATURE | | WIND | | TGT 1 | | TGT 2 | | TGT 3 | |
|---|---|---|---|---|---|---|---|---|---|
| HIGH | LOW | VELOCITY | DIRECTION | AZIMUTH | DISTANCE | AZIMUTH | DISTANCE | AZIMUTH | DISTANCE |
| | | | | | | | | | |
| | | | | DESCRIPTION | | DESCRIPTION | | DESCRIPTION | |

DA FORM 5787-R

**SNIPER'S OBSERVATION LOG**   SHEET 1 OF 1 SHEETS

For use of this form, see FM 23-10. The proponent agency is TRADOC.
DATA REQUIRED BY PRIVACY ACT OF 1974.
AUTHORITY: 10 USC 3012(g)/Executive Order 9397. PRINCIPAL PURPOSE(S): Facilitates individual's training on targets at varying ranges. ROUTINE USE(S): Evaluate individual proficiency. SSN is used for positive identification purposes only. MANDATORY OR VOLUNTARY DISCLOSURE AND EFFECT ON INDIVIDUAL NOT PROVIDING INFORMATION: Voluntary. Individuals not providing information cannot be admitted/scored on a class basis.

| LAST NAME | FIRST | MI | RANK | SSN | UNIT |
|---|---|---|---|---|---|
| Doe | John | R | PFC | 123-45-6789 | D 3/29 |

| ORIGINATOR: | DATE/TIME: | LOCATION: |
|---|---|---|
| Doe, John | 1 Oct 91 | GL 03427648 |

| SERIAL | TIME | GRID COORDINATE | EVENT | ACTIONS OR REMARKS |
|---|---|---|---|---|
| 1 | 0300 | GL03427648 | Occupied Position | Observation |
| 2 | 0340 | Same | PFC Judson rested | None |
| 3 | 0430 | Same | PFC Judson assumed observation duties | I rested |
| 4 | 0530 | Same | Both of us awake | None |
| 5 | 0630 | Same | Prepared Range Card, and topographic sketch | Light enough to see |
| 6 | 0655 | GL03117631 | BMM crossed bridge going South | observed |
| 7 | 0700 | GL03427648 | Prepared sketch of bridge GL 03117631 | Complete |
| 8 | 0900 | GL03427648 | mission completed — return to CP | End of mission |

DA FORM 5786-R

## MILITARY SKETCH

| LAST NAME | FIRST | MI | RANK | SSN | UNIT |
|---|---|---|---|---|---|
| Ode | John | L | SPC/E-4 | 987-65-4321 | D 2/29 |

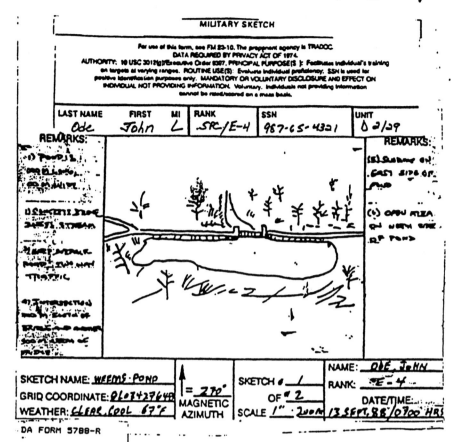

**REMARKS:** (1) Pond is controlled by military. US military side of military stream near portable pond - low road traffic. (4) Intersection roads east of bridge road near south area of pond.

**REMARKS:** (5) Swamp on east side of pond. (6) Open area on north side of pond.

SKETCH NAME: WEEMS POND
GRID COORDINATE: QL0342764B
WEATHER: CLEAR, COOL 67°F
↑ = 270° MAGNETIC AZIMUTH
SKETCH # 1 OF 2
SCALE 1" = 200m
NAME: Ode, John
RANK: E-4
DATE/TIME: 13 SEPT 88 / 0700 HRS

DA FORM 5788-R

## MILITARY SKETCH

| LAST NAME | FIRST | MI | RANK | SSN | UNIT |
|---|---|---|---|---|---|
| Anderson | Teddy | A | SGT | 456-78-9012 | D 2/29 |

**REMARKS:**

**REMARKS:**

SKETCH NAME: Weems Rd bridge
GRID COORDINATE: QL0322764B
WEATHER: Clear/warm 90°F
↑ = 270° MAGNETIC AZIMUTH
SKETCH # 1 OF 1
SCALE 1 = 50m
NAME: Anderson, Teddy A.
RANK: SGT
DATE/TIME: 11 SEP 91 / 1245 hrs

DA FORM 5788-R

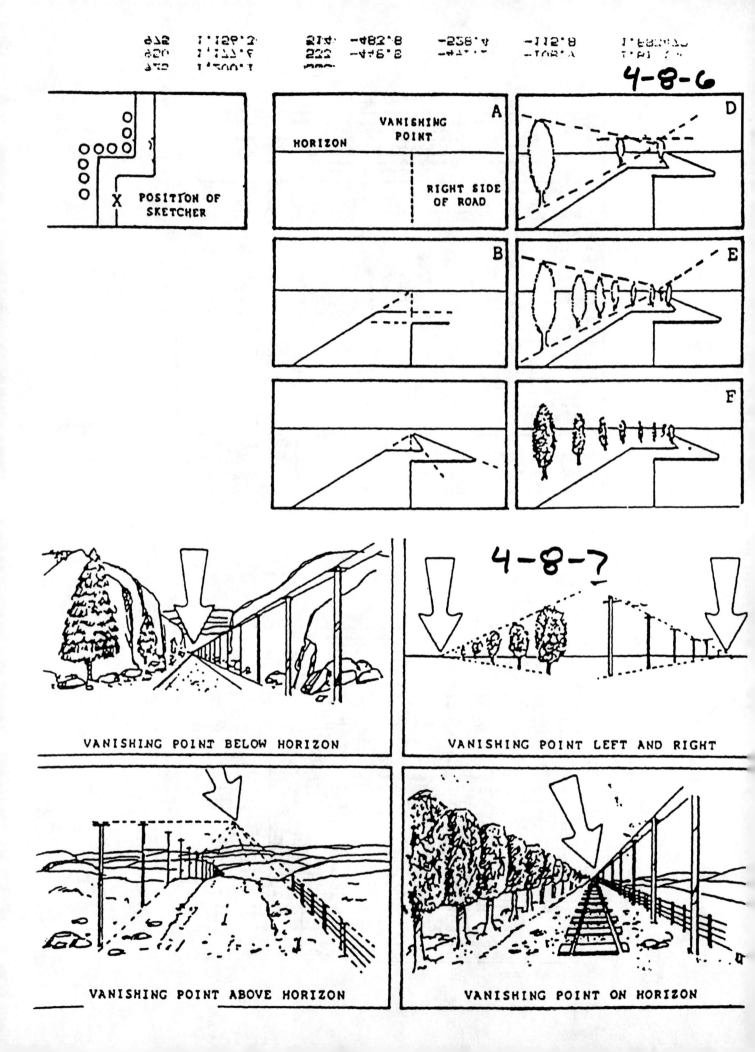

**4-8-6**

POSITION OF SKETCHER

A — HORIZON · VANISHING POINT · RIGHT SIDE OF ROAD

B

C

D

E

F

**4-8-7**

VANISHING POINT BELOW HORIZON

VANISHING POINT LEFT AND RIGHT

VANISHING POINT ABOVE HORIZON

VANISHING POINT ON HORIZON

4-8-8

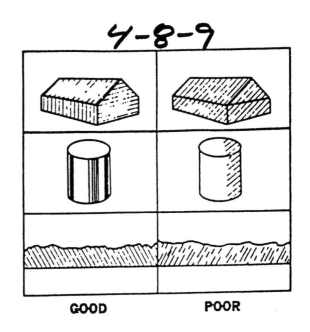

4-8-9

GOOD          POOR

6-3-1

6-3-2

# Chapter 5

## EMPLOYMENT

Special operations sniper employment is complex. When employed intelligently, skillfully, and with originality, the special operations sniper will provide a pay-off far greater than would be expected from the assets used. For this to happen, though, the planner must have more than a basic knowledge of the sniper weapon system. He must understand the capabilities and limitations of the special operations sniper. However, sniping is an individual talent and skill that varies with each individual sniper. This compounds the planner's challenge, but these variables can be minimized with careful planning. The special operations sniper, when properly trained and employed, can be one of the special operation forces' most versatile weapon systems.

## 5-1.  EMPLOYMENT CONSIDERATIONS

### Methods of Employment
The sniper planner must apply methods of interdiction in relation to the necessary target and the desired effects against it. The employment of SO snipers generally falls into several distinct categories:

   o   <u>Surveillance and reconnaissance</u>. Sniping, by nature of its execution (stealthful movement, infiltration, use of long-range optics, and limited-visibility operations), is closely related to reconnaissance and surveillance. The techniques a sniper uses to hunt a target are similar to those the scout uses to conduct surveillance--only the end results are different. In addition, human intelligence (HUMINT) collection is a secondary function to sniping. Operational planners should refrain from employing snipers in solely HUMINT roles but should take advantage of the HUMINT function when possible. Combining both functions would be analogous to using a long-range guard: the sniper provides needed information and can intercede if necessary.

   o   <u>Point interdiction</u>. A point interdiction is essentially hunting a specific target. The SO sniper can interdict both personnel and materiel point targets in support of SO missions in all levels of conflict. Such missions tend to be complex and may require: difficult infiltration; precise navigation to the target; evasion of enemy forces; the broaching of sophisticated security systems; and external mission support systems (safe houses, special intelligence, etc.). Normally, the more complex the target or the more protected it is, the greater the degree of sophistication required to defeat it. For instance, a protected personnel target may require detailed intelligence and a highly skilled sniper for

1

successful interdiction. Point interdiction also includes shooting situations like those encountered in counterterrorist situations.

o       Long-range harassment. Sniper harassment differs from point interdiction in its objective--the sniper's goal being to interdict targets for the purpose of impeding, destroying, or preventing enemy influence in a particular area. Snipers normally conduct harassment at extended ranges to take advantage of their ability to engage targets at distances beyond the enemy's small arms fire. This normally means the sniper will not engage targets closer than 400 meters--100 meters beyond the common effective-fire range of conventional small arms. Long-range harassment is not intended to be decisive; creating psychological fear in the enemy and restricting his freedom of action are the sniper's primary goals. The sniper has the greatest latitude of employment in harassment missions. He can often engage opportunity targets at his discretion but always within the constraints of the mission. This may include harassment of specific kinds of targets to disrupt key functions such as C2 procedures. In some situations, the sniper can afford to engage targets at extreme ranges and risk nonfatal or missed shots. This maximizes harassment by interdicting more targets.

o       <u>Security operations</u>. Snipers can provide long-range security in order to deny an enemy freedom of action in a particular area. The sniper security mission can take the form of a series of mutually supporting sniper outposts or cordons. An example of security operations where snipers proved invaluable was during the USMC operations in Beirut, Lebanon when Marine snipers were interwoven with traditional defenses and proved to be effective in long-range protection of local US facilities and interests. Security and cordon missions normally entail static, defense-like operations. However, with the austere firepower of sniper teams and their inability to maneuver in defensive warfare, they are vulnerable to becoming decisively engaged. Therefore, security operations are best integrated into conventional security and reaction forces to help snipers increase their defensive capability. Without such support, the sniper can easily be suppressed and maneuvered upon with fire and maneuver tactics.

**Employment Planning**

When employing snipers, operational planners must consider many factors. Tactical planning considerations of primary concern to the sniper include hide selection, deception plans, movement techniques, and so forth. However, the operational planner must consider sniper employment from an even higher level of operational perspective. They must realize that snipers are a unique weapon system and possess entirely different attributes from conventional forces, among which, (and the one most frequently misunderstood) is the sniper's firepower. Unlike conventional small arms fire that emphasizes volume, the sniper's firepower emphasizes precision. Sniper fire is most effective when combined with a mind that can exploit long-range precision. A two-man sniper team can deliver only limited volumes of fire, and no matter how accurate, the volume will seldom equal that of even the most austere military units. If employed incorrectly, the sniper easily becomes just another soldier on the battlefield--except that he is handicapped with a slow-firing weapon.

The sniper's unique employment considerations should be guided by the following considerations:

o   Stand-off.   Employment should be built around the sniper's ability to engage targets at extended ranges. The maximum effective range will vary with each sniper. However, planners can establish nominal engagement ranges based on the sniper's ability to group his shots into a specified area or shot group. This measurement can, in turn, be applied to specific targets. The sniper should be able to keep his fire within two minutes-of-angle (2 MOA) shot groups under simulated combat conditions. (The MOA is a universal measurement of shot-group size and is calculated by multiplying the MOA times the range in meters to equal the group size in inches. For example, 2 MOA times 500m equals 10 inches; therefore the sniper would be expected to group his shots within a 10-inch circle at a range of 500m).

The application of group size is important for determining maximum stand-off in relation to target size. For planning, SO snipers should be expected to provide instant incapacitation (non-reflexive impact) shots on personnel to 200m; personnel interdiction with 100 percent probability to 600m on stationary targets; and 70 percent probability to 900m. Engagement of more complicated targets, such as those moving or in adverse environmental conditions, depends on the individual sniper's skill, his willingness to take risks, and his weapon's capability. Sniper employment planning should take into account the probability of error against the risks incurred if the shot misses. Such analysis will help determine the minimum stand-off range for a reliable chance of a hit on the target.

o   Deception.   The sniper's most critical tools are his deceptive talents, including all aspects of his deception operations from infiltration to movement within the target area. To planners, deception is also important for operational needs. The SO sniper may use a weapon from another country in order to duplicate that weapon's characteristic signature (ballistic characteristics, cartridge case, bullet, and so forth) for cover. Operational deception may be centered around infiltrating the target area using a clandestine (concealed) sniper weapon. Operational deception may also require plausible deniability of the operation and possibly lead the enemy to believe the target damage was the result of normal failure, accident, or some other form of sabotage. With such interdiction requirements, the sniper can employ special weapons and munitions and aim for vulnerable points to purposely obtain such results. (Such targets include those that

3

tend to burn, detonate, or self-destruct when shot.) However, this kind of deception is not possible with many targets and is especially difficult to conceal in personnel interdiction. Deception also means a sniper can seldom fire more than once from any location as the sound of shots (even suppressed) is increasingly easier to locate with repetition. (This concept differs greatly from many media and war stories, where the sniper engages his enemy on a protracted basis from the same location-- firing shot after shot with apparent impunity.) In reality, snipers locked in decisive duals with enemy forces and firing defensively will normally lose as sniping seldom succeeds in such situations. Planners should refrain from employing snipers in missions that will not allow deception or concealment after firing.

o    <u>Operational security</u>. The sniper's use of tactical deception is often his only real security. Employment planners must consider security from operational aspects of the mission when using snipers. These include infiltration means, communications procedures, and methods of command and control. These procedures are important because the sniper must remain covert prior to interdiction to assure success. Normally, once the sniper fires, he is no longer covert and must rely on other plans to facilitate escape. Many environments may permit sniper employment, but few allow plausible denial for the sponsor or operation after interdiction. In other words, such covert operations may be easy to perform, but the risk of compromise, no matter how small, may overshadow the mission. Missions to collect information concerning another country's hostile intentions may themselves provoke serious repercussions if discovered. Moreover, using snipers will assuredly indicate an alternative motive to actually interdicting a target--which could compromise the mission even more.

o    <u>Time</u>. The sniper's mission normally requires more time than conventional operations. Because the sniper normally moves on foot with stealth, his only defense is that of remaining unseen. If the sniper has not been given enough time to execute the mission, he may hurry and unnecessarily compromise the mission or fail to reach the target.

o    <u>Team employment</u>. Special operations always employ snipers in a team of two qualified snipers, because two-man employment has proven much more successful than single-sniper employment. Teams provide limited security for self-protection, allow near-continuous operations, yet are small enough to allow concealment for execution. In practice, one sniper fires while the other observes. The sniper-observer identifies and selects targets, adjusts the sniper-shooter to environmental factors, provides security, and helps correct missed shots. However, the greatest advantage is the sniper-observer's detachment from the firing process, leaving the sniper-shooter to concentrate on the act of shooting. In other words, the act of shooting does not complicate the sniper-observer's decision process--a task requiring

4

total concentration. Mission needs may also require snipers to be employed as part of a larger force or in multiple sniper teams to engage the same target. Both techniques of employment can enhance the sniper's affect; however, the basic sniper team should always be retained.

     o    <u>Terrain</u>. The terrain characteristics for any given area are extremely important to the sniper's mission. Some areas, such as those that are densely wooded, tightly compartmented, or heavily vegetated, are not suitable for sniper employment because they reduce the sniper's ability to employ the full stand-off capability of his weapons system. The threat can quickly suppress snipers that engage targets inside their minimum stand-off envelope (usually 400m). Moreover, restrictive terrain offers the threat cover and concealment in which to mask his attack against the sniper.

     o    <u>Innovation</u>. A sniper's most important attribute is his ability to improvise. The operational planner must also be innovative in the planning process. The sniper is a weapon of opportunity, not one to be employed as a matter of course. Planners must actively seek missions and opportunities in which to apply the sniper's unique attributes of long-range precision rifle fire and concealment. Often the sniper's greatest handicap is the planner's inability to fully exploit his potential because of the planner's lack of familiarity with the sniper's true role and capability. Staff officers with little practical sniper experience or lacking innovative thought will never be able to fully exploit sniping capabilities.

## 5-2. ORGANIZATION

Organizational grouping of snipers above the sniper-team level is normally accomplished through expedient pooling of sniper pairs into larger organizations. Such centralized grouping of sniper assets can prove beneficial to their employment for specific missions. In all cases, centralized control should be managed by the sniper specialist within the unit. Regardless of any provisional or temporary sniper grouping, sniper teams should not be split; they are best employed in the pairs in which they have trained, with all members being fully qualified snipers.

The level at which sniping is organized and managed directly influences the ability of sniping to provide direct or indirect support to friendly operations. Centralized organization and management of sniping provides a great degree of flexibility regarding deployment. This permits snipers to be deployed to areas or locations where they are most needed. Snipers are deployed where they will have the greatest influence on the enemy and provide the maximum possible support to friendly operations.

The organization of sniper teams will magnify their effectiveness against the enemy. Sniping, like any other supporting arm, is an individual specialty requiring independence of action to achieve its greatest potential effect on the enemy. Requiring special organization, snipers may be organized into teams, squads, sections, and platoons.

## Sniper Team

The base element of any sniper unit is the sniper team, which consists of two equally trained snipers. When organized into a team, snipers are able to:

o      Provide mutual security.

o      Engage targets more rapidly.

o      Lengthen their duration of employment.

o      Diminish stress.

## Sniper Squad

A sniper squad is composed of three to four sniper teams and is located at company level. The organization of the sniper squad is as follows:

o      Squad leader
                                          Command element
o      Assistant squad leader

o      Senior sniper
                                          Two to three sniper teams
o      Junior sniper

The mission of the sniper squad is to support the operations of the company. The company is the lowest level at which sniping can be centralized and still maintain operational effectiveness. Sniper teams should not be attached to the tactical subunits of the company.

## Sniper Section

The mission of the sniper section is to directly or indirectly support the combat operations of a battalion's subordinate units. In direct support, sniper teams are attached to company headquarters elements as needed, and employment considerations are identical to those of company sniper teams. In indirect support, sniper teams are assigned sectors of responsibility as part of the battalion fire plan. The sniper section is attached to the battalion headquarters S2/S3, and the section commander would act as the battalion sniper coordinator. The sniper section is composed of 8 to 10 sniper teams and consists of:

o      Section commander

o    Assistant section commander        Command element

o    Armorer
                                          Support element
o    Radio operator


o    Senior sniper
                                          Operational team(s)
o    Junior sniper

## Sniper Platoon

The mission of a sniper platoon is to support regiment/brigade combat and intelligence operations independently or by attachment to regiment/brigade subunits. When attached, sniper squads should remain intact and should be attached no lower than battalion level. The sniper platoon is composed of a platoon leader, a platoon sergeant, a radiotelephone operator/driver, an armorer, and three sniper squads consisting of a squad leader and five two-man sniper teams. The sniper platoon falls under direct operational control of the regiment/brigade intelligence officer or indirect control through liaison with the sniper platoon leader. Sniper platoon operations may include deep penetration of the enemy rear areas, stay-behind operations, and rear area protection.


## 5-3. COMMAND AND CONTROL

Command and control of snipers is accomplished using indirect and direct control procedures. These procedures complement the sniper's self-discipline in executing his assigned mission. The sniper team will often operate in situations where direct control methods will not be possible. Therefore, the sniper must prosecute his mission, within the parameters of the commander's intent, on personal initiative and determination. This is a major reason (in the sniper-selection process) why personnel with motivation and self-determination are required as snipers. Without these personal traits, the sniper's decentralized execution allows total disregard for the mission and its completion. In other words, he can go out to perform a mission and merely "lay low" until time to return.

## Indirect Control of Snipers

Commanders can accomplish indirect control of snipers through a variety of methods, the simplest being rules-of-engagement (ROE) and fire control measures. Even with strict direct control (voice radio, wire, and so forth) of sniper teams, commanders should establish ROE and fire control to maximize flexibility, and to prevent unnecessary engagements. The ROE will normally designate combatant forces and situations that will allow the sniper to engage the enemy.

One significant problem with contemporary ROE is the restrictive measures used in low-intensity conflicts. Often, such ROE will specify enemy personnel as only those presenting a direct threat to friendly forces or requiring verbal warning prior to engagement. The paradox is that a sniper's modus operandi is to engage targets that are not a direct threat to him (outside small arms effective fire range) at the moment, but which later may be. To stay within the guidance of the ROE is extremely difficult for the sniper, as once the enemy gets within the sniper's minimum stand-off, the conflict can become one of close-quarters battle, and a twelve-pound, scope-sighted sniper rifle is no match for an AK-47 or M-16 at close quarters--despite the fact that it may be a semiautomatic rifle. Therefore, ROE for snipers must provide for the sniper's safety by adding security forces or by removing him from the operation.

Fire control measures are just as important for the sniper as they are for indirect-fire weapons and aircraft. As with any long-range weapons system, positive target identification is difficult at extended ranges--even with the advanced optics the sniper will carry. Establishment of no-fire zones, fire coordination lines, and free-fire zones will help in sniper command and control by establishing guidelines for when and where the sniper can fire.

## Direct Control of Snipers

Direct control of SO snipers can be accomplished through the use of technical and nontechnical systems, including radio and wire communications. In some circumstances, direct control means may include commercial telephones or other nontraditional tactical forms of communications. The exact methods of control, technical or nontechnical, will be determined by the mission and the operational environment.

Nontechnical control of snipers is accomplished through the use of prearranged methods including rendezvous, message pick-ups and drops, and other clandestine methods of secure communications. In denied areas, or those with electronic interception capabilities, these methods may be the only secure techniques for communicating with the sniper teams. These systems, although often quite secure, tend to be slow and require more elaborate procedures for execution.

Snipers can also employ many forms of technical communications systems such as radio and wire. Both radio and wire offer near-instant message traffic and facilitate command and control with two-way communications. Radio is a common method of communications for most sniper missions; it is responsive and provides real-time control and reporting capabilities. In addition, radio (voice, burst, satellites) allows the mobility snipers require for their mobile-employment methodology. The major advantage to radio is its ability to transmit mission changes, updates, and intelligence in a timely manner. However, when properly arrayed, enemy-direction finding assets can determine the location of even the most focused and directional transmissions. To avoid this, SO must use specialized communications techniques and procedures. But even then, the deployed teams will still have the problem of transmitting from their location to confirm messages or send data.

The major drawback to radio communications is the transmitter's electronic signature. In the case of the SO sniper's operational environment, enemy detection of any electronic signature can be just as damaging as reception of a message. Once the enemy is aware of the sniper's presence (through spurious transmissions), it becomes an academic problem to hunt him down. Even with successful evasion from efficient threats (for example, scent- and visual-tracking dogs), the sniper team will be preoccupied with escape and evasion instead of the target. Of course, this can also be an objective--to divert enemy internal security forces to a rear-area sniper threat.

Wire communications can provide protection from enemy deception, jamming, and interception. Static security operations, defensive positions, and extended surveillance posts are suitable for the use of wire communications. However, the disadvantages of wire must also be calculated--time to emplace, lack of mobility, and relative ease of compromise if found by the enemy. When possible, wire communications should be backed up by more flexible forms of control, such as radio.

Certain environments, such as found during foreign internal defense and counterterrorism missions, may allow for more flexible technical communications techniques. For example, the use of commercial telephones may be more appropriate than traditional military communications. In addition, many of these environments possess a low threat from actual message interception or direction-finding assets, allowing the sniper team more liberal use of the radio. However, planners would be wise to remember the time-tested proverb--never underestimate your enemy.

Coordination
There must be meticulous coordination with both supported and unsupported units that fall within the sniper team's area of operations. This coordination is the primary responsibility of the sniper coordinator. Coordination with supported and unsupported units includes:

o     Nature, duration, and extent of local and extended patrols.

o     Friendly direct and indirect fire plans.

o     Local security measures.

o     Location and extent of obstacles and barrier plan.

9

o    Rendezvous and/or linkup points.

o    Passage and re-entry of friendly lines.

o    Unit mission and area of responsibility.

o    Routes and limits of advance.

o    Location and description of friendly units.

o    Communication plan.

While it is important that the sniper team receives as much information as possible to ensure mission success, the sniper coordinator must not give the team so much information that, in the event of capture, the entire sector would be compromised. This demands that everyone involved: the sniper team, the sniper coordinator, supported and unsupported units in the area of operations, all communicate and remain "coordinated."

Once coordination is initiated, control measures to protect the sniper and the supported and unsupported friendly units must be planned. Also, in the event of a situation change, there must be a recall capability to prevent the sniper team from being subjected to undue danger. The sniper team must also be advised of friendly operations in their area that could subject them to friendly fire. The snipers must be allowed enough latitude within these controls to avoid decisive engagement with the enemy by remaining mobile, elusive, and unpredictable.

## Support Relationships

Sniping is a combat support activity. As with any other forms of support, sniping should be used to augment only those units that have a specific need for it. Sniping provides either indirect or direct support. Deployed as HUMINT assets, snipers indirectly support friendly units and operations. Direct support is of two types:

o    Operational control. Snipers are under the operational control (OPCON) of the supported unit only for the duration of a specific operation. After completion of the mission they return to the control of the parent unit. This is the optimal method of supporting operations, as it is flexible and efficient toward the unit to which the snipers are attached.

o    Attachment. For extended operations or distances snipers may be attached to a specific unit. The unit of attachment assumes control of sniping for the duration of attachment. The sniping specialist/coordinator should also be attached to advise the unit on assignment of proper employment methods. If it is not possible to attach the sniper coordinator, then the senior and most experienced sniper on the attachment orders must assume the job as sniper coordinator for the period of attachment. The receiving unit must also be made aware of the status of the sniper coordinator and the importance of his position. Normally, attachment for extended periods will include supply and logistical support to the sniper element from the unit of attachment.

Planning, coordination, and control are also dictated by the support given to the unit and by the support received from the unit. Support given to a unit can be classified into four broad types:

(1) Offensive operational support.

(2) Defensive operational support.

(3) Retrograde operational support.

(4) Special operations.


## 5-4. TARGET ANALYSIS

There are two general classes of sniper targets: personnel and materiel. These targets can be further categorized as either of tactical or strategic value. Tactical targets have local, short-term value to the current battle or situation. Tactical personnel targets for the sniper are normally of enough significance to warrant the risk of detection when firing. Such targets include: enemy snipers, key leaders, scouts, and crew-served weapon crews. Tactical materiel targets are of particular importance to the war effort or operation.

Strategic personnel targets are not as well-defined. as tactical personnel targets because of problems with the concept and definition of assassination. The definition of assassination versus the elimination of a military target is a complex problem unrelated to the scope of this manual. Strategic materiel targets consist of all types of objects of a military nature, including components or systems within a target (such as a turbine in an aircraft).

### Target Systems and Critical Nodes

SO snipers should be directed at the enemy's C2 facilities and the critical nodes supporting them. Snipers can frequently regard targets as being in an interrelated system; that is, any one component may be essential to the target's entire operation. These interrelated, and essential, components are known as critical nodes. Critical C2 nodes are components, functions, or systems that support a military force's command and control. These will differ for each target, but they will generally consist of the following:

o    <u>Procedures</u>. Snipers can easily interdict the procedures, routines, and habits the enemy uses to conduct operations. Of most significance, snipers can create fear in the enemy which will cause him to take extreme measures in security or to modify procedures to keep from being shot. The enemy may curtail certain functions, divert assets for security, or restrict movement in his own rear areas to prevent interdiction.

o    <u>Personnel</u>. Personnel targets are critical, depending on their importance or function. The target does not necessarily need to be a high-ranking officer but may be a lower-ranking person or a select group of people, such as a skill or occupational group, who are vital to the enemy's war-fighting apparatus.

o    <u>Equipment</u>. Equipment is critical when the loss of it will impact the enemy's conduct of operations. Seldom will singular equipment targets be so critical as to impact the enemy in any significant fashion. However, targets or components that are not singularly critical may, collectively, be vital to the enemy. Common targets include objects common to all other similar targets or systems vulnerable to interdiction, such as a particular component (a radar antenna) which is common to many other radars. Interdicting only one antenna would have limited effect; it would merely be replaced. However, interdicting every possible radar antenna would significantly impair the enemy's logistics.

o    <u>Facilities</u>. Facilities include activities and complexes that support the enemy's operations or C2 functions. In the larger context, snipers are not suited for such interdiction. However, where possible, the sniper can focus on critical elements, such as C2 nodes or logistic capabilities, of the larger facility (power generation systems or transportation equipment, for example).

o    <u>Communications</u>. The most fragile components of C2 systems are often the communications nodes, which include all the systems providing information to the enemy. Snipers can usually interdict these nodes because they are easily recognizable and, frequently, quite vulnerable. Attacking other targets, not critical in some fashion, serves no purpose in the employment of SO snipers and only wastes resources without a definable objective. Target analysis helps determine which critical nodes to interdict and predict how effective the sniper will be.

## Target Analysis

Target analysis includes selecting the appropriate method to use against a target. This includes aircraft, a strike force, snipers, etc. In doing so, the planner can match the sniper's capabilities to the potential target. Sniper capabilities include using special weapons and performing covert execution of operations.

Attacking targets by sniper fire requires detailed planning and coordination; SO sniper targets should not be attacked indiscriminately. Interdiction must be conducted within the parameters of the assigned mission from higher headquarters, the desired results of the interdiction, the target's vulnerabilities, and the priorities of interdiction (on multiple targets or components.)

The target analysis system used considers the target's criticality, accessibility, recuperability, vulnerability, effect, and recognizability (CARVER). The CARVER analysis process is a generic model for special operations interdiction missions. It is also suitable for sniper interdiction, particularly during materiel interdiction planning, which is similar to interdiction with special munitions or demolitions. Sniper fire can be applied within the framework of the CARVER model to better determine if sniping would be the appropriate interdiction method, and precisely how and where to apply it. The CARVER analysis is applied to sniper interdiction based on the following criteria:

o   Criticality. A target is critical in relation to the impact its destruction would have on the enemy. The mission order will largely determine critical targets. However, within a target system there may be components that may be critical for the operation of the entire target. For example, a turbine is a critical component of a jet aircraft. The concept of attacking a critical component (using accurate fire) allows the sniper to engage a much greater variety of targets than commonly accepted.

o   Accessibility. Accessibility to a target is based on how readily the target can be attacked. For the sniper, target accessibility includes getting through the target's security systems (security police or intrusion detectors) and knowing what the reaction will be to the sniper's stand-off interdiction. Accessibility for sniper interdiction is unique, because the sniper can frequently engage targets without violating security systems, which, in turn, reduces the enemy's ability to detect the sniper before the interdiction.

o   Recuperability. The recuperability of a target is measured in the time it takes the target to be repaired, replaced, bypassed or substituted. The concept of recuperability is essential to sniping. Frequently, planners think only in terms of total destruction as opposed to a lesser degree of destruction. Frequently, however, the same effect can be achieved by simply shutting down the target or destroying one vulnerable component. The advantage of interdiction short of total destruction is in the application of force; complete destruction normally requires a more elaborate force and more units. In addition, the ability to control target destruction with precision fire can prevent unnecessary damage or limit adverse effects to systems on which the local populace may depend for electrical power, food, water, and so forth.

      o    <u>Vulnerability</u>. A target (or component) is vulnerable to the sniper if he has the weapons and skill required to interdict the critical points that the target analysis has identified. The key to target vulnerability is identifying the weakest critical link in the target system and destroying it.

      o    <u>Effect</u>. The effect of interdiction includes a wide range of results incident to the interdiction. Target effect is the desired result of attacking the target, including all possible implications--political, economic, and social effects of the interdiction. Occasionally, the planner must decide what the desired effect is; it may be the removal of key personnel, the psychological impact of the interdiction, or the threat of interdiction.

      The fear of interdiction is evident in the German attempts to kill Churchill in World War II, which forced him to remain hidden for periods of time. Conversely, John M. Collin's book, <u>Green Berets, SEALs, and Spetsnaz</u>, detail the political implications of a direct-action mission to kill a figure such as Emperor Hirohito of Japan, the "emperor-god", during World War II. Such action, Collins, states, would have had an adverse impact by rallying the Japanese people. A similar reaction was seen when the US bombed Libya in 1986. During the raid, US bombs seriously injured one of Colonel Muammar Qaddafi's children and resulted in negative media and international backlash. (Despite Qaddafi's own unscrupulous acts, endangering his family was unacceptable to the international public.)

      Materiel target interdiction by sniper fire is much more limited than it is with personnel targets. The SO sniper's abilities might be enhanced by his choice of special weapons to interdict materiel targets, but he might still be limited by the relative vulnerability of the target. The greatest obstacle for successful interdiction of materiel target rests primarily with the identification of the vulnerable nodes. The goal of the sniper's fire on these nodes is to be as effective as more powerful weapons--using precision fire at key points instead of brute force in the general area.

      o    <u>Recognizability</u>. A target is recognizable if it can be effectively acquisitioned by the sniper. A target may be well within the sniper's stand-off range but cannot be effectively engaged because the target is masked or concealed. For example, the sniper's recognition of targets using night-vision equipment might be restricted because of the technological limitations of the device. Positive identification of targets, as well as small target components, is difficult given the characteristics of the phosphor screen in night-vision devices. Other factors complicating recognizability include the time of day, light conditions, terrain masking, and environmental factors.

## 5-5. MISSION PLANNING

Successful accomplishment of a sniper mission relates directly to the planning and preparation that takes place.

### Levels of Mission Planning

The two levels of mission planning are above-team level and team level. At above-team level the sniper employment officer (SEO) or sniper leader is responsible for planning and coordinating the actions of more than one sniper team. This is done with the intent of having several teams carry out coordinated or independent missions toward the same objective. At team level the two members of the sniper team will carry out the planning, preparation, and coordination for the mission. Therefore, warning orders are not necessary at this level, and the sniper operation order itself is a mission planning tool.

### Sniper Operation Order (OPORD)

1. SITUATION

    A.    Enemy Forces.
         1). Weather. Light data, precipitation, temperature, effect on the enemy and the sniper team.
         2). Enemy. Type unit(s), identification, training, presence of countersnipers, significant activities, and effect on the sniper team.
         3). Terrain. Terrain pattern, profile, soil type, vegetation, effect on the enemy and the sniper team.

    B.    Friendly Forces. Adjacent units, left, right, front, and rear. Since sniper teams are vulnerable to capture, they should not be given this information. Rather, they should be given information such as the location of free fire and no fire zones.

2. MISSION

    Who, what, where, when, and **WHY**. The **WHY** is extremely important for the sniper to successfully accomplish this mission and future missions. The sniper must understand the importance of taking the life of the target.

3. EXECUTION

A.    Commander's Intent.   This paragraph relates specifically what is to be accomplished, in a short, precise statement.   This should include the **Commander's measure of success.**

B.    Concept of the Operation.   This paragraph relates step by step how the mission will be carried out.   This is best done by breaking the mission down into phases.   Specific tasks will be carried out in each phase, usually starting from infiltration to exfiltration.

C.    Fire Support.   Normally in a deep operation, fire support will not be available.   However, in other situations, the assets may exist.

D.    Follow-on Missions.   This paragraph will outline any follow-on missions that may be needed.   Once the primary mission is accomplished, the sniper team may be called upon to carry out another mission in the area of operation (AO) before exfiltration. This may consist of another sniper mission or a link-up with another team, a unit, or indigenous persons as a means of exfiltration.

E.    Coordinating Instructions.   Consists of the following:

1).    Actions at the objective.   This paragraph contains specifically the duties of each member of the team and their rotation to include:

a.    Security.

b.    Selection and construction of the hide.

c.    Removal of spoils.

d.    Camouflage and fields of fire.

e.    Observer's log, range card, and military sketch.

f.    Placement of equipment in the hide.

g.    Maintenance of weapons and equipment.

h.    Observation rotation.

2).    Movement techniques.   This paragraph will cover the movement techniques, security at halts, and responsibilities during movement to and from the objective rallying point (ORP) and the hide and during the return trip.

3).    Route.   This paragraph covers the primary and alternate routes to and from the objective area.   It may also include the fire support plan if it is not covered in the fire support annex.

4). Departure and reentry of friendly positions. This is normally used in the support of conventional units, but it could be used when dealing with indigenous persons, such as during a link-up.

5). Rally points and actions at rally points. This can be used in some instances, but for a two-man element a rendezvous is much more advisable. For example, several rendezvous points en route should be preplanned with a specific time or period for link-up. This is done so that movement is constantly toward the objective, preventing the lead man from backtracking and wasting time.

6). Actions on enemy contact. Avoid contact; do not engage in a firefight. It is best to avoid contact, even in an ambush; evade as best as possible. Do not attempt to throw smoke or lay down a base of fire. This only calls attention to your position, and soon the enemy will be pursuing you with a much larger element. In the event of an air attack, hide. It is not possible for a two-man element to successfully engage an enemy aircraft. You will only call attention to your position if you try to engage the aircraft.

7). Actions at danger areas. Avoid danger areas by moving around them, unless this is not possible or time is critical. When moving across large open areas, stalk across; do not move in an upright posture. Linear danger areas are best crossed by having both team members move across the area at the same time to avoid splitting the team in case of enemy contact.

8). Actions at halts. Security is critical even when taking a break and nobody is expected in the area. Stay alert.

9). Rehearsals. If time is not available, at the minimum, always practice actions at the objective. During rehearsals, practice immediate action drills (IADs) and discuss actions at rally and rendezvous points. Know their locations and your routes on the map.

10). Inspections. Inspect each other's equipment. Use a checklist for equipment and ensure that everything works. Ensure that you have the proper equipment and camouflage for the terrain and the environment you will be encountering.

11). Debriefing. This paragraph covers who will attend the briefing, where the briefing will be conducted, and when the debriefing will take place. This is where the observer's log and military sketches find their use, as information-gathering tools.

12). Priority intelligence requirements (PIR)/information requirements (IR). These requirements are passed down to the sniper team as information that should be gathered when the team is employed.

13). Annexes. This section contains specific maps and sketches showing items such as routes, the fire support plan, the tentative ORPs, and the hide sites.

4. SERVICE SUPPORT

This paragraph covers, but is not limited to, administrative items such as:

A. Rations.

B. Arms and ammunition that each team member will carry.

C. Uniform and equipment that each team member will carry.

D. Method of handling the dead and wounded.

E. Prisoners and captured equipment. This paragraph is not likely to be used, unless the equipment can be carried, photographed, or sketched.

F. Caches, mission support sites (MSSs).

5. COMMAND AND SIGNAL

A. Frequencies and call signs. It is not necessary to list all the frequencies and call signs. You need only to refer to the current Communications-Electronics Operating Instructions (CEOI).

B. Pyrotechnics and signals, to include hand and arm signals. It is best to have a team standing operating procedure (SOP) to which you can refer. Otherwise, you must list all the pyrotechnics and hand and arm signals.

C. Challenge and password. The challenge and password will be necessary when linking up at rendezvous points and passing through friendly lines.

D. Code words and reports. This refers to any contact made with higher headquarters or possibly a link-up with indigenous persons.

E. Chain of command.

## Terrain Profile
A terrain profile is an exaggerated side view of a portion of the earth's surface between two points. The primary purpose is to

determine if line of sight is available. Line of sight is used to determine:

o    Defilade positions.

o    Dead space.

o    Potential direct fire weapon positions.

A profile can be constructed from any contoured map. Its construction requires the following steps:

o    Draw a line from where the profile begins to where it ends.

o    Find the highest and lowest value of the contour lines that cross or touch the profile line. Add one contour value above the highest and one below the lowest to take care of hills and valleys.

o    Select a piece of notebook paper with as many lines as contours on the profile line. The standard Army green pocket notebook or any paper with quarter-inch lines is ideal. If lined paper is not available, draw equally spaced lines on a blank sheet.

o    Number the top line with the highest value and the rest of the lines in sequence with the contour interval down to the lowest value.

o    Place the paper on the map with the lines parallel to the profile line.

o    From every point on the profile line where a contour line, a stream, an intermittent stream, or a body of water crosses or touches, drop a perpendicular line to the line having the same value. Where trees are present, add the height of the trees to the contour.

o    After all perpendicular lines have been drawn and tick marks placed on the corresponding elevation line, draw a smooth line connecting the marks to form a horizontal view or profile of the terrain.

o    The profile drawn may be exaggerated. The space of lines on the notebook paper will determine the amount of exaggeration.

o    Draw a straight line from the start point to the finish point on the profile. If the straight line intersects the curved profile, line of sight is not available.

## Sunrise/Sunset Overlay

19

A sunrise/sunset overlay (SSO) is a graphic representation of the angle to the rising and setting sun and the objective. An SSO enables a team to plan a line of advance or tentative hide sites to take best advantage of the light. An SSO requires a table showing the true azimuth of the rising sun and the relative bearing of the setting sun for all months of the year. An SSO is constructed in the following manner:

o    Using the projected date of the mission and the latitude of the target, determine the true azimuth of the sunrise from Table 5-5-1.

o    Using a protractor and a straightedge, draw a line from the objective along the true azimuth.

o    Subtract the true azimuth from 360 to find the sunset azimuth.

o    Using a protractor and a straightedge, draw another line from the objective along the sunset azimuth.

o    Convert each azimuth to a back azimuth and write it on the appropriate line.

o    Label the appropriate lines SUNRISE and SUNSET.

o    Write down the latitude and the date that was used to construct the overlay.


5-6.  SPECIAL FORCES MISSIONS/COLLATERAL ACTIVITIES

Special Forces Missions include:

    o    Unconventional Warfare (UW)

    o    Foreign Internal Defense (FID)

    o    Direct Action (DA)

    o    Special Reconnaissance (SR)

    o    Counterterrorism (CT)

    o    Security Assistance (SA)

    o    Humanitarian Assistance (HA)

    o    Antiterrorism/Security Activities

    o    Counternarcotics (CN)

o    Search and Rescue (SAR)

o    Special Activities

o    Deception Operations

o    Demonstrations and Shows of Force

## Effects of SO Sniper Operations on Civil Affairs and Psychological Operations

Civil Affairs (CA) and civic action programs sponsored by friendly organizations can be adversely affected if sniper interdiction is misused. The sniper is a very efficient killer, and given a target, the sniper will go to extreme efforts to interdict it. Therefore, planners must temper the use of force with common sense and the future goals of the operation. It may be easier to eliminate threats than to negotiate, but in the long run, negotiations may open the door for settlment where sniping may close it or may set the stage for undesirable reactions.

Planners must also consider the psychological operations (PSYOP) aspects of the mission, including both positive and negative impacts. The sniper can project not only accurate weapons fire but tremendous psychological destruction. Such impact was given as rationale for the Viet Nam Mai Lai massacre. There, in defense of their actions, some soldiers claimed that enemy sniper fire (and friendly casualties) over a protracted period of time drove them to commit the war crimes. On the other end of the spectrum, US use of snipers can also cause adverse reaction on enemy forces. As at Mai Lai, the enemy may focus on innocent noncombatants and commit inappropriate reprisals in response to intense sniper pressure. This is especially true in unconventional warfare and foreign internal defense environments where US special operations forces may use local populations as guerrillas and security forces.

The psychological impact of sniping has received little attention in the overall scheme of war. Historians often focus on the large weapons systems and overlook the stress and fear that sniping adds to the battlefield. Yet, this psychological impact can ruin the fibre and morale of an entire army, much like that which occurred in World War I where the sniper's bullet was often feared far more than many other ways of dying.

Only recently in US history has the military recognized the psychological impact of sustained combat, although the sniper has always contributed as much to fear as he has to fighting. Operational planners may consider this PSYOP capability when planning sniper missions, especially when using PSYOPs in unconventional warfare where it plays a vital role.

21

## 5-7.  UNCONVENTIONAL WARFARE

Unconventional Warfare (UW) is a broad spectrum of military and paramilitary operations, normally of long duration, predominantly conducted by indigenous or surrogate forces who are organized, trained, equipped, supported, and directed in varying degrees by an external source.  UW includes guerrilla warfare (GW) and other direct offensive low-visibility, cover, or clandestine operations, as well as the indirect activities of subversion, sabotage, intelligence collection, and evasion and escape (E&E).

### Sniper Employment in UW Operations

The primary mission of the SO sniper in UW is to organize and train the resistance force into an effective fighting force.  The primary mission of the resistance force is to support conventional forces during times of war.,  Therefore, the SO sniper must know conventional sniper tactics as well as unconventional techniques in order to effectively train a US-sponsored resistance force.  During peacetime, training of foreign military or paramilitary forces may be accomplished by mobile training teams (MTTs).  In times of war, the training would take place during the organization/training phase of the resistance force after linkup.

The importance of a sniper in UW cannot be measured alone by the number of casualties he inflicts upon the enemy.  Realization of the sniper's presence instills fear in enemy troops and influences their decisions and actions.  Selective and discriminate target interdiction not only instills fear in the enemy, but can lead to general confusion and relocation of significant enemy strengths to counter such activity.

In UW and FID roles, the SO sniper can perform both as a fighter and a trainer.  Not only can he teach sniper skills to the force he is training, he can act as a direct-action asset when needed.  The sniper's ancillary skills in camouflage, stalking, surveillance, and deception are also useful in UW and FID environments.  The impact of these talents is magnified when the sniper is employed as a trainer.  By training others he is, in effect, performing interdiction much more efficiently than he could alone.

Unconventional warfare or guerrilla warfare is characterized by three major phrases:  build-up, consolidation, and link-up. Snipers will play an important role in all three phases.

### Build-up.

During initial contact and build-up SO snipers will be mainly involved in training the indigenous force snipers and then acting as sniper coordinators.

During the build-up snipers are extremely effective when used in the harassing and sniper ambush role.  By utilizing the snipers' ability to deliver long-range precision rifle fire, the UW force can accomplish several objectives all at once: the snipers will be able to strike at the enemy forces while minimizing their own exposure; they will deny the comfort of a secure area to the enemy; they will build UW force morale with successes while minimizing the amount of UW force exposure; and since the fires are discriminatory, the effect on the civilian population should be mainly positive, as civilian casualties will be minimized.

It is, however, very important that the snipers go after targets with a military objective only. The line between sniper ambush and assassination at this point can be blurred. It must be remembered that an ambush is for military gain, while an assassination is for political gain. Assassination, under any guise, is illegal and against Presidential Executive Order 12333, Part II, para 2-11, dtd 4 Dec 1981.

During the end of the build-up and prior to the consolidation phase, the UW force snipers will be used the same as strike operations snipers, that is, in support of small raids and ambushes. As the size of the UW force grows, so will the size of the missions that are similar to strike missions.

Consolidation.
During consolidation, as the UW force becomes larger, the role of the sniper reverts to that of the conventional sniper. The same missions, tactics, and employment principles apply.

Link-up.
During link-up and after, the snipers' role will mainly become that of security force snipers and rear area protection force snipers. The UW force snipers will be particularly suited for this role. They have spent their time in that area and should know most, if not all, of the main areas that could support the enemy during infiltration and rear area attacks.

During the initial contact phase of a resistance movement, sniper employment will normally be limited to supporting small-unit operations and will include such actions as:

o     Harassment of enemy personnel. When performed at ranges greater than 500 meters, harassment serves to lower the enemy's morale and inhibit his freedom of movement.

o     Infiltration. Prior to an attack, snipers may infiltrate enemy units' positions and establish themselves in the enemy's rear area. During the attack the infiltrated snipers engaged specific targets of opportunity in order to divert the enemy's attention from the attacking units and to disrupt his freedom of movement in his rear areas.

23

o    Interdiction.    The snipers will delay or interdict reinforcing elements to a target and deny the enemy use of an area or routes by any means.

o    Sniper ambush.  This is the use of multiple sniper teams operating together to engage targets by timed or simultaneous fire. A fixed number of rounds will be fired by each sniper, and the ambush will be terminated when either the targets have been successfully engaged or the predetermined number of shots have been fired.  Planning considerations must include how the ambush is to be initiated, how the snipers will communicate with each other, and what methods the snipers will use to engage the targets.

o    Security and surveillance.    Snipers are employed to gather information or to confirm existing intelligence by long-term surveillance of a target site, or they may be used to provide early warning  of  impending  counterattacks.    Snipers  will  normally establish a hide position to conduct their surveillance.

o    Offensive/defensive operations.    During the advanced stages of the combat phase of a resistance movement, snipers may be used to detect and shoot long-range targets that could impede the progress of the offense.

o    Defensive operations.  Snipers are best used in defensive operations outside the forward line of troops (FLOT) to provide early warning of the approaching enemy, disorganize his attack, and cause him to deploy early.  Snipers may also be used to delay the enemy's advance by interdicting enemy movements using a series of interlocking delay positions, thus allowing the friendly forces to withdraw.

## Sniper Element Organization in UW and FID

When organizing sniper elements in a UW or FID role, the sniper elements must be organized above team level with elements under the control of the commander and the S2, as the scout or recon platoons are.  Depending upon the availability of trained personnel, the sniper elements should be organized as a squad at battalion level (10 men or five teams) and as a platoon at regimental or brigade level.  The regimental level must have a sniper coordinator, and this is also desirable at battalion level. The sniper coordinator should be assigned to the S2/G2 staff for intelligence purposes; however, he must work closely with the S3/G3 staff for planning purposes.  The sniper coordinator should be a sniper-qualified senior NCO, warrant officer, or officer who is well versed in mission planning.  He must also be forceful to ensure that the sniper teams are not improperly deployed.  All other members of the squads, the platoon, and the platoon headquarters element must be sniper qualified.

5-8.   FOREIGN INTERNAL DEFENSE

Foreign Internal Defense (FID) is the participation by civilian and military agencies of a government in any of the action programs taken by another government to free and protect its society from subversion, lawlessness, and insurgency. The primary SF mission in this inter-agency activity is to organize, train, advise, and assist host nation military and paramilitary forces.

## Sniper Employment In FID Operations

The primary role of SO snipers in FID is the same as in UW, primarily that of a teacher. During the passive FID role, SO snipers will be in-country for the purpose of training and advising only, and will not have an active role. During active FID, the SO snipers could find themselves in both a trainer's role and an active role. In either case, passive or active, the primary tactics will be that of conventional warfare: offense, defense, and withdrawal.

During active FID, the SO sniper will conduct the following missions: counter-guerrilla operations, sniper cordons/periphery OPs, sniper ambushes, urban sniper hides, and civil disorders.

Counterguerrilla operations. One of the primary means to accomplish this mission is to employ snipers in rear area protection (RAP). Snipers are used to enhance the protective measures surrounding sensitive facilities or installations by setting up observation posts along routes of access, acting as part of a reaction force to rear area penetration, or patrolling the area (as members of established security patrols). The role of the sniper in RAP operations includes protecting critical installations and sites, covering gaps between units to avoid infiltration, preventing removal of obstacles, and tracking enemy patrols known to have penetrated into the rear area.

The sniper's ancillary skills in camouflage, stalking, surveillance, and deception are also useful in the FID environment. The impact of these talents is magnified when the sniper is employed as a trainer. By training others he is, in effect, performing interdiction much more efficiently than he could alone.

When organizing sniper elements in a FID role, the sniper elements must be organized above team level with elements under the control of the commander and the S2, as the scout or recon platoons are. Depending upon the availability of trained personnel, the sniper elements should be organized as a squad at battalion level (10 men or five teams) and as a platoon at regimental or brigade level. The regimental level must have a sniper coordinator, and this is also desirable at battalion level. The sniper coordinator should be assigned to the S2/G2 staff for intelligence purposes; however, he must work closely with the S3/G3 staff for planning purposes. The sniper coordinator should be a sniper-qualified senior NCO, warrant officer, or officer who is well versed in mission planning. He must also be forceful to ensure that the sniper teams are not improperly deployed. All other members of the squads, the platoon, and the platoon headquarters element must be sniper qualified.

## 5-9. DIRECT ACTION

DA operations are short-duration strikes and other small-scale offensive actions by SOF to seize, destroy, or inflict damage on a specified target or to destroy, capture, or recover designated personnel or materiel. In the conduct of these operations, SOF may:

o    Employ direct assault, raid, or ambush tactics.

o    Emplace mines and other munitions.

o    Conduct standoff attacks by fire from air, ground, or maritime platforms.

o    Provide terminal guidance for precision-guided munitions.

o    Conduct independent sabotage.

SF DA operations are normally limited in scope and duration and have a planned exfiltration. They are designed to achieve specific, well defined, and often time-sensitive results of strategic or operational significance. They usually occur beyond the range (or other operational capabilities) of tactical weapons systems and conventional maneuver forces. DA operations typically involve the:

o    Attack of critical targets.

o    Interdiction of critical LOC or other target systems.

o    Capture, rescue, or recovery of designated personnel or materiel.

The major type of DA operations include:

o    Raids against strategic objectives or targets that have a high tactical value or are time-sensitive in nature.

o    Seizure of key facilities.

o    Interdiction of major lines of communications (LOCs).

o    Recovery operations.

o    Deception operations.

26

o    Show-of-force operations.

## Sniper Employment in DA Operations

When employed in direct action missions, snipers will perform one or more of the following four functions:

o    Harassment.  Deliberate harassment of the enemy through sniping is designed to impede, destroy, or prevent movement of enemy units.  The degree of harassment depends on the amount of time and planning put into the operation.  Harassment is best suited for protracted or unconventional operations.  During such operations sniper casualties will be high, and provisions for their replacement must be included in the harassment plan.

o    Sniper ambush.  The term "sniper ambush" refers to the use of multiple sniper teams operating together to engage targets by timed or simultaneous fire.  A fixed number of rounds are fired by each sniper, and the ambush is terminated either after the targets have been successfully engaged or after the predetermined number of shots has been fired.  Planning considerations important to the sniper ambush include how the ambush will be initiated, how the snipers will communicate with each other, and how targets in the kill zone will be engaged.

o    Sniper cordon.  A sniper cordon is a series of outposts surrounding an area in a general or a specific location. A sniper cordon is designed to prevent the enemy from entering or leaving a target location.  Snipers may be employed in cordon operations by being integrated into the overall fire plan as a supporting force or in cordon areas as independent elements.  During cordon operations snipers should be employed so as to maximize their precision long-range fire capabilities.  Due to the snipers' limited volume of fire and reliance on stealth, they possess little capability to become decisively engaged during such operations. Once the snipers have been located, they may be suppressed by fire and maneuver and/or indirect fire.  Therefore, the snipers' ability to hold or cordon an area will be directly commensurate to the enemy force encountered and the support from friendly units.

o    Interdiction.  Interdiction is preventing or hindering enemy use of an area or route by any means.  When deployed for the purpose of interdiction, snipers are emplaced to interdict dismounted avenues of approach.  The snipers' ability to interdict vehicular traffic would be limited to harassment unless armed with large caliber sniper weapons systems.  Snipers can be deployed with vehicular interdiction elements to harass the enemy when he is forced to dismount.

## Sniper Employment in Strike Operations

27

Strike operations are normally limited-scope operations with a planned exfiltration. Using snipers in strike operations depends largely on the operation's scope and objectives. Often strike operations consist of an overt, forced infiltration and overwhelming firepower to suppress the target area. In such cases, using snipers should be weighed against the requirements for suppressive fire. Automatic weapons may provide better long-range suppressive fire--only in volume. However, snipers can use semiautomatic sniper weapons to provide accurate long-range suppressing and interdicting fire, which is especially advantageous when weight, collateral structural damage, and threats to noncombatants are concerns. Given the nature of direct-action operations, it is difficult to imagine a strike operation in which snipers could not contribute in some way.

## Elements of the Strike Force

The size of the strike force will depend on the mission, location of the target, and enemy situation. A strike force is tailored in size and capability to perform a specific mission; the force can be a small team to interdict a personnel target, or a larger force to destroy a large facility or plant. Regardless of size, most strike operations consist of command, security, support, and assault elements. Snipers can provide support to any of these elements depending on the objectives and needs of the commander. The requirements for the SO sniper in strike operations may be applied as follows:

o    Command element. The command element forms the primary command post and is normally composed of the strike force commander and, as a minimum, his S2/S3 and fire support element controllers. The sniper coordinator should also be assigned to the command element. The snipers assigned to the command element are formed by the expedient pooling of strike force snipers under the control of the sniping specialist. Regardless of their origin, pooled snipers are kept in their original teams. Centralized under the command element, snipers will be able to conduct reconnaissance and direct-action missions supporting the entire strike force or multiple missions supporting one or more strike force elements throughout the operation. Examples of specific sniper missions under centralized control of the command element include: reconnoitering the objective rally points, routes, and/or exfiltration sites; reconnoitering and observing the objective (once action is initiated, covert OP snipers may perform a direct-action function in support of the strike force); establishing a reserve to intervene or reinforce elements with precision rifle fire; and screening danger areas and vulnerable flanks or sealing off the enemy rear.

o    Security element. The security element's mission in strike operations includes securing rally points; providing early warning of enemy approach; blocking avenues of approach into the objective area; preventing enemy escape; and acting as left, right, and rear security elements for the strike force. Snipers may be employed in conjunction with a larger security force or independently in support of the security mission. This employment will generally be determined by the scope of the strike operation and personnel constraints.

In smaller operations the security element may be made up in part or entirely by the snipers, which would reduce personnel requirements. In larger operations a larger, more flexible (anti-armor, demolitions, etc.) security force will normally be required. In this regard, snipers would serve to complement the security element's capabilities. For example, armored threats require augmentation by appropriate antiarmor weapons. Snipers can provide accurate long-range suppressive fire to separate infantry from their armored units and to force tanks to "button-up" which will hinder their ability to detect the launch of wire-guided missiles. The sniper team can employ large-bore sniper weapons to help delay and interdict light materiel targets.

Snipers performing security missions in strike operations are particularly well suited to perform successive or simultaneous missions in addition to providing early warning of, delaying, and harassing reaction forces. Reaction forces located some distance from the objective will approach using vehicles or air. The mobility assets of the reaction force can be dedicated to that mission and can subsequently present an actual threat to the strike force. Snipers may be employed a part of the security force to interdict or harass reaction force avenues of approach or landing zones (if known or obvious).

In addition to the main role of security, the snipers may also be used secondarily to report information prior to the assault, support the assault force by fire (caution must be used here), assist in sealing the objective during the assault, maintain contact after the assault, and act as a rear guard during the withdrawal of the assault force.

o    Support element. The support element of the strike force must be capable of placing accurate supporting fire on the objective. The support element must deliver a sufficient volume of fire to suppress the objective and provide cover to the assault element. The support element also provides fire support to cover the withdrawal of the assault element from the objective.

Snipers in the support element provide discriminate fire in support of the assault force. The sniper's optics facilitate positive target identification and acquisition, which allows snipers to fire in close proximity to friendly forces with reduced risk of fratricide. This is opposed to more traditional automatic or indirect supporting fire that must be terminated or shifted as friendly forces approach the target area ("lift and shift"). At night, friendly troops can wear distinctive markings such as reflective tapes or infrared devices, visible to the sniper's night-vision equipment, to aid identification.

When assigned to the support element, snipers should be organized into four-man sniper teams (two pairs working together). There are several reasons for this type of organization. First, the rate and control of the snipers' supporting fire can better be controlled by the sniper team leader. Second, sniper elements centrally located are better able to redeploy to critical locations to delay pursuing forces. Third, limited vantage points from which to deliver precision rifle fire may exist. Concentrating snipers at these vantage points may be the only effective way to maximize their capabilities of long-range precision rifle fire.

When snipers are assigned to the support element, the mission that they will perform should be specific. The effectiveness of sniper fire is not in the volume, but the precision with which it is delivered. Sniper missions include: disrupting command and control by engaging officers or NCOs directing the defense; suppressing guards and enemy security forces; providing precision covering force to the assault element; delaying pursuing forces after withdrawal; and maintaining contact with displaced enemy forces after the attack. This includes observing for enemy counterattacks or continued harassment of the enemy in order to disorganize any counterattack efforts. One advantage of snipers in the support is that snipers do not have to lift and shift as crew-served weapons do once the assault element is on the objective. The snipers can continue to support through precision rifle fire.

o  <u>Assault force</u>. Snipers are seldom assigned to the assault force, primarily because of the need for rapid movement combined with suppressive fire. This type of maneuver seldom allows for the snipers' deliberate (sedentary) firing process. In addition, the assault force is often employed in close-quarter battle--nullifying the snipers' stand-off capability. However, snipers can be assigned to the assault element when command and control will be better effected or in circumstances where the sniper can enhance the assault force's mission. They may be attached to the assault element to provide cover fire when the assault element must pass through an area that is dead space from other supporting elements. However, the snipers are then used in the support of the assault element's movement to the objective and are not an actual part of it.

## Enemy Considerations during Strike Operations
o  <u>Enemy Security Forces</u>. The type and number of enemy security forces likely to be manning the target or available for reaction must be considered in the plan. These forces may be static, foot mobile, vehicle mounted, or airmobile. Armored vehicles will generally be positioned on the perimeter, while light vehicles will normally be located in a vehicle park. Armored vehicles are likely to become centers of resistance, around which

defenders will concentrate during the action. This will present the snipers with a high density of targets, particularly officers and NCOs who will tend to use static armored vehicles as rally points. The lack of vehicular mobility on the part of the strike force renders them vulnerable to a mobile threat. In such circumstances, snipers should be delegated the task of interdicting routes of access to vehicle parks. Drivers of light vehicles are the primary targets; track or tank commanders are the prime armored vehicle targets.

o  <u>On-site defensive positions</u>. Strike targets deep within enemy lines will generally have less protection and a lower defensive posture than those located nearer to the main battle area. Target site defenses can be characterized as either hasty or permanent.

*  Hasty defensive positions will be characterized by less protection to defending personnel than prepared ones. Strike force snipers will be able to engage such positions at a greater distance with more effectiveness due to the limited protection to the targets. Snipers should consider any object or location at the target site that affords protection to the enemy (e.g., behind light vehicles or in buildings) as a hasty defensive position.

*  Permanent defensive positions will be characterized by bunkers, sandbagged fighting positions, prepared buildings, etc. Such targets present unique circumstances to the snipers. These well-protected targets, which often have narrow firing ports and are mutually supportive, make engagement difficult and require the snipers to approach much closer to the protective targets than normal. As the range to the targets decreases, the probability of detection and engagement from the enemy forces is increased.

o  <u>Enemy reaction force</u>. Strike force snipers functioning in a support capacity, or as part of the strike force security element, will be targeted primarily against the enemy reaction force.

## 5-10. SPECIAL RECONNAISSANCE

Special Reconnaissance (SR) is reconnaissance and surveillance conducted by SOF to obtain or verify, by visual observation or other collection methods, information concerning the capabilities, intentions, and activities of an actual or potential enemy. SOF may also use SR to secure data concerning the meteorological, hydrographic, or geographic characteristics of a particular area. SR includes target acquisition, area assessment, and post-strike reconnaissance.

Special reconnaissance operations are the most complex missions of SOF. In fact, special reconnaissance is so complex that much controversy remains over its very definition. The problem stems from the operational environments and geographic areas in which special reconnaissance is performed. To a SOF commander in Central Europe, an SR mission may entail infiltration, HAHO parchute operation deep in enemy rear areas to collect information on the movement of a second-echelon front army. To a SOF commander in Central America, the SR team may infiltrate by commercial carrier or on foot to conduct surveillance of a guerrilla force in a rural environment. Simply stated, the circumstances surrounding the mission govern the execution. Special reconnaissance is as much a technique as it is a mission, that technique being to collect information on a target or objective. The execution of special reconnaissance will be prosecuted commensurate to the environment.

Special reconnaissance consists of infiltration (land, air, and sea) into an area to collect target information. Reconnaissance teams (normally four to six men) employ advanced information-collection equipment and have the ability to process some information. In addition, SR missions may require nondescript uniforms and equipment (with appropriate legal oversight) and may employ some type of communications to transmit information if needed. Teams can communicate with secure radio transmission unless the electronic signature presents a compromising threat. If so, the team must establish alternate clandestine communications.

One problem unique to the SR mission is the frequent requirement for the SR team to perform some sort of additional mission other than reconnaissance. The proximity of the SR team to the target often causes planners to add requirements for the team to perform more than reconnaissance. These missions (known as follow-on missions) can take the form of terminal guidance operations to bombing aircraft on a target or of direct intervention by the reconnaissance team itself. The problem with follow-on missions is the overwhelming amount of equipment required. The reconnaissance teams already carry heavy loads for the reconnaissance mission, and the added burden of radio beacons and transponders (used to vector aircraft) consume room in a rucksack that force some other baggage to be sacrificed (food and water often being the victims).

The SO sniper offers some advantages to special reconnaissance missions; he is well trained in surveillance, and his ability to interdict materiel targets at extended range is often complementary to follow-on SR missions. If interdiction of C2 systems is the goal of the follow-on mission, then snipers can carry much more potential destruction in the form of large-bore sniper rifles than the same number of persons can in conventional demolitions.

## Sniper Employment in SR Operations

Surveillance is the systematic observation of areas, places, persons, or things by visual, aural, electronic, photographic, or other means. Snipers make extensive use of fixed and roving surveillance to acquire targets or assess target vulnerabilities. Snipers will normally establish a hide position to conduct their surveillance. Once they are in the hide, the snipers will prepare an observation log. Information should be described in detail. The observation log will serve as a record of events and assist in mission debriefing. All priority intelligence requirements (PIRs) and information requirements (IRs) will be reported as required.

Reconnaissance is a mission to obtain information about the activity and resources of an enemy or potential enemy or to secure data concerning the meteorological, hydrographic, or geographic characteristics of a particular area. Because of their mission-essential equipment, snipers are ideally suited to perform reconnaissance in conjunction with their primary direct-action mission.

Snipers may be employed to reconnoiter enemy positions that are of specific interest to supported units. Information gathered by snipers includes, but is not limited to:

o    Locations of crew-served weapons.

o    Gaps in enemy wire.

o    Locations and sizes of LP/OPs.

o    Gaps between enemy units and positions.

o    Locations of infiltration routes.

Snipers may be used to infiltrate through enemy positions in support of offensive operations or to harass enemy rear areas. Once sniper teams have infiltrated enemy positions, they may be employed to report information on:

o    Troop strength and movements.

o    Concentrations and reserve locations.

o    Observation posts and weapons locations.

o    Command, control, and communications facilities.


## 5-11.  COUNTERTERRORISM

Counterterrorism (CT) is offensive measures taken by civilian and military agencies of a government to prevent, deter, and respond to terrorism. The primary mission of SOF in this interagency activity is to apply specialized capabilities to preclude, preempt, and resolve terrorist incidents abroad. SOF involvement in CT is limited by HN responsibilities, Department of

33

Justice (DOJ) and Department of State (DOS) lead agency authority, legal and political restrictions, and appropriate DOD directives. When directed by the National Command Authority (NCA) or the appropriate unified commander, designated SOF units conduct or support CT missions that include:

o    Hostage rescue.

o    Recovery of sensitive material from terrorist organizations.

o    Attack of the terrorist infrastructure.

Because of the very low profile of most terrorist organizations, identifying targets for CT missions can be extremely difficult.  While a preemptive strike against terrorists may be preferred, CT missions must often be conducted after the terrorists have already initiated a terrorist incident.  For SF, CT is a special mission, not a generic mission applicable to all SF units. SF participation in CT is limited to those specially organized, trained, and equipped SF units designated in theater contingency plans.  These designated SF units respond as directed by the NCA or unified commander to resolve specific situations arising from a terrorist incident.  As part of the counterterrorist enhancement program (CTEP), these designated SF units may also train selected HN forces to perform CT missions.

## Sniper Employment in CT Operations
In CT operations, snipers provide three primary functions:

o    They can deliver discriminate fire to interdict hostile targets.

o    They can cover the entry teams into the objective area with rifle fire.

o    They can provide the CT force commander with his most accurate target intelligence.  In this case, snipers are normally positioned to have ideal observation of the enemy.  Most frequently, this will be the commander's only view of the target.

## Background Information
Counterterrorist operations play a significant role in the world today.  Incidents, such as the assassination of President Kennedy, demonstrated to the world how vulnerable even the most protected people are.  The notorious Texas Tower Sniper of the mid-60s, Charles Whitman, proved that existing law-enforcement capabilities against snipers were inadequate.  In the late 1960s and early 1970s, hostage barricade situations (aircraft and buildings) became commonplace, the growth of sniping (or countersniping as the police prefer to call it) was a logical

reaction on the part of law-enforcement agencies to counteract such threats.

Today there are not only formal police sniper programs (such as those for the Federal Bureau of Investigation, Secret Service, National Rifle Association, and many local agencies), but there are many commercial outgrowths as well. Major firearms companies now market police "sniper rifles" and private literature is replete with material for would-be snipers. Law-enforcement application of sniping coincided with the Vietnam conflict and served to feed the sniper industry.

After Vietnam, for the first time in US history, the US maintained active sniper programs--if only in law enforcement. The military was slower to learn; it abolished almost all of its sniper capability only to have to revive it in the late '70s in response to the demands of modern warfare--low intensity conflicts, terrorist situations, and selected applications in the nuclear age. (Interestingly, the popularity of law-enforcement sniping has diminished significantly since the terrorist bomb has become a more favored terror technique. Bombs are impersonal and efficient--if collateral damage to innocents is of no concern.)

Counterterrorist operations require extensive training and coordination. Most important, the sniper teams must know the plans and actions of the entry teams to avoid possible injury to friendly personnel, and they must fire when told to do so. Failure to engage and neutralize a target can have devastating consequences, as that which occurred in the 1973 Olympic games in Munich, Federal Republic of West Germany, when snipers did not neutralize their terrorist targets on command. The result was that the terrorists were free to exterminate the hostages. To compound the problem, the snipers were so confused that they shot and killed several of their own men. Of course, overzealous snipers can create results similar to what occurred in Los Angeles, California. Police snipers shot and killed a bank present who was indicating a gunman by pointing his finger. The overanxious police sniper thought the man was pointing a gun and shot him. Obviously, the line between shoot and don't shoot is thin and can be stretched thinner by haste of indecisiveness.

Part of the solution to these problems lies in the selection and training process. During the selection process, an individual's mind is the one variable that cannot be effectively measured. In fact, psychologists cannot agree on what traits to look for in a sniper. How does one pick a man to deliberately kill another man who presents no immediate threat to him personally? Unfortunately, the real test of a sniper comes only when it is time to pull the trigger. Only then will the sniper's reliability definitely be known.

Another problem that seems to manifest itself in CT scenarios is what is known as the Stockholm Syndrome. This is the sniper's inability to shoot a person who has become familiar to him. This syndrome manifests itself when the sniper has conducted constant surveillance of his target and becomes so familiar with the target's actions, habits, and mannerisms that the target becomes more human, almost well acquainted--too familiar to shoot. On the other hand, some reports have indicated the opposite to be true; some snipers hope to have the opportunity to shoot someone from some twisted, personal motivation. Perhaps this happened in Los Angeles. Nevertheless, these psychological extremes, eager or reluctant shooters, are inappropriate to the sniper's function; the sniper must be somewhere in-between.

## 5-12.  COMBAT SEARCH AND RESCUE

In Combat Search and Rescue (CSAR) operations, the role of Special Operations snipers is extremely limited, because the mission is intended to rescue and not to interdict. However, SO snipers can provide traditional long-range security and early warning to rescue forces. The sniper's ability to operate effectively in denied areas can greatly assist the rescue forces by providing accurate information regarding the rescue. Snipers can infiltrate before the rescue and conduct surveillance of the rescue area unnoticed. The USAF is considering using snipers with their pararescue units (in place of machine guns) to provide long-range security during rescue operations. This would give them the benefit of selectively interdicting threat targets while not endangering innocent bystanders.

## 5-13.  COUNTERSNIPER

A sniper team is the best asset available to a commander for a countersniper operation. Countersniper operations eliminate the enemy sniper threat. These operations are planned and coordinated by the sniper team. A countersniper operation occurs between two highly trained elements--the sniper team and the enemy sniper--each knowing the capabilities and limits of the other.

A sniper team's first task is to determine if there is a sniper threat. If so, it then identifies information that may be gained from the unit in the operations area, such as:

o    Enemy soldiers in special camouflage uniforms.

o    Enemy soldiers with weapons in cases or drag bags.

  *    Long barrel lengths.

  *    Mounted telescopes.

36

> * Bolt-action receivers.

o Single-shot fire at key personnel (commanders, platoon leaders, senior NCOs, or weapon crews).

o Lack or reduction of enemy patrols during single-shot fires.

o Light reflecting from optical lenses.

o Reconnaissance patrols reporting of small groups of enemy (one to three men) by visual sighting or tracking.

o Discovery of single, expended casings, such as a 7.62x54mm Rimmed ammunition.

The sniper team next determines the best method to eliminate the enemy sniper. To accomplish this, the team:

o) Gathers information:

> * Time(s) of day precision fire occurrences.

> * Location(s) where enemy sniper fire was encountered.

> * Location(s) of enemy sniper sightings.

> * Material evidence of enemy snipers such as empty brass casings or equipment.

o Determines patterns: The sniper team evaluates the information to detect the enemy's established patterns or routines. It conducts a map reconnaissance, studies aerial photos, or carries out a ground reconnaissance to determine travel patterns. The sniper must consider himself from the enemy position and ask, "How would I accomplish this mission?"

Once a pattern or routine is detected, the sniper team determines the best location and time to engage the enemy sniper. The team can also request:

o Coordinating routes and fires.

o Additional preplotted targets (fire support).

o Infantry support to canalize or ambush the sniper.

o Additional sniper teams for mutual supporting fire.

o Baiting of likely engagement areas to deceive the enemy sniper into commitment by firing.

37

o     All elements be in place 12 hours before the expected engagement time.
       During a countersniper operation, the team must ignore battle activity and concentrate on one objective--the enemy sniper.

When an enemy sniper is operating in a unit's area, the sniper team ensures that the unit employs passive countermeasures to defend against enemy sniper fire:

o     Do not establish routines--for example, consistent meal times, ammunition resupply, assembly area procedures, or day-to-day activities that have developed into a routine.

o     Conduct all meetings, briefings, or gatherings of personnel under cover or during limited visibility.

o     Cover or conceal equipment.

o     Remove rank from helmets and collars.  Do not salute officers. Leaders should not use authoritative mannerisms.

o     Increase OPs and use other methods to increase the unit's observation capabilities.

o     Brief patrols on what to look for, such as single, expended rounds or different camouflage materials.

o     Do not display awareness of the enemy's presence at any time.

o     Be aware that 50 percent of enemy snipers are women; many Third World countries follow suit.  Patrols and OPs must not be misled when sighting a woman with a mounted telescope on her rifle. She is a deadly opponent.


5-14.  CONVENTIONAL OFFENSIVE OPERATIONS

Many planners have resisted SOF interface with conventional forces and operations.  Much of this resistance is due to petty rivalries within the military.  However, special operations can significantly enhance conventional operations when correctly applied.  Special operations forces can add depth to the conventional battlefield by extending the deep battle in the enemy's rear area while protecting the friendly rear area.  The SO sniper can add deception to the battlefield and provide economy-of-force to allow the conventional commander to focus combat power elsewhere.

Conventional missions with SOF interface require thorough coordination and planning.  In addition, sniper operations must be thought of in unilateral terms.  The effect of snipers on a scale of ones and twos is small; when employed in coordinated actions on a broad front, their effect can be substantial. Of course, this is true with most any weapon system; a cannon is not very useful as an individual piece; however, when massed, artillery is devastating.

## Offensive operations that the sniper can support are:

o    Movement to contact.

o    Attack of built-up or fortified areas.

o    River crossings.

o    Support of reconnaissance and combat patrols.

o    Extended ambushes.

o    Cordon operations.

o    Deception operations.

## Sniper Employment in Offensive Operations

Special operations support to offensive operations can be useful not only throughout the battlefield but also before, during, and after the battle. SO snipers can provide support to conventional units in the following four critical phases of offensive operations:

o    *Preoffensive missions*. Missions prior to offensive operations will primarily be in the deep battle area to gather information on the enemy's disposition. Snipers can help collect this information and interdict selected targets, if necessary. If the objective is to divert enemy assets from the main effort, then snipers can imitate the actions that the Russian partisans conducted against the Germans in World War II. The result of such actions can impair logistics operations and demoralize enemy soldiers in their own rear areas. The preoffensive missions are generally HUMINT oriented. However, several direct-action functions can be performed as a natural consequence of the snipers' proximity to the enemy as a HUMINT asset.

*    Reconnoitering. Snipers are employed to:
o    Gather (real-time) information on enemy dispositions, terrain, and weather.

o    Penetrate enemy security zones in an effort to determine the extent and nature of enemy deception efforts.

o    Confirm or deny existing intelligence as requested by the commander or S2.

o    Locate securable routes/axes of advance.

39

o    Locate enemy reserve forces and the possible routes they could use to reinforce the objective.

o    Establish or modify preplanned fires of indirect weapons.

o    Locate enemy security measures, i.e., mines, obstacles, barriers, etc.

*    Harassment. As a preoffensive function, harassment serves to lower the enemy's morale and inhibit his freedom of movement within his own lines. It takes the feeling of a secure area away from the enemy and inhibits his ability to rest his troops. This form of harassment is generally performed at ranges greater than 500 meters.

*    Infiltration. Prior to an attack, snipers infiltrate the gaps between enemy units and positions and establish themselves in the enemy's rear area. During the attack the infiltrated snipers will engage specific targets and targets of opportunity both on the main line of resistance and in the rear area. This serves to divert the enemy's attention from the attacking units and to disrupt his freedom of movement in his own rear areas. Specific targets engaged by infiltrating snipers include:

o    Enemy snipers.

o    Command, control, and communications facilities and personnel.

o    Crew-served weapons crews.

o    Artillery and forward air controllers.

o    Dismounted reserve forces.
o    Military policemen.

o    Wire repair and resupply parties.

o    Missions during the offense. Sniping during the offensive is direct-action oriented. Snipers are attached to friendly units to provide immediate direct support by means of precision rifle fire. The main function of attached snipers will be the suppression of enemy crew-served weapons, enemy snipers, and command and control personnel. Snipers can also support the offensive by interdicting follow-on or reserve forces (such as second-echelon combat forces or logistics). Conventional snipers, assigned to their parent units, can also be used to interdict key targets in the main battle area. Also, attached snipers can be used to screen the flanks of advancing units, cover dead space from supporting crew-served weapons, and engage specific selected targets of the defending enemy units.

    o    <u>Postoffensive missions</u>. Snipers' postoffensive role begins during the consolidation of the objective. Snipers are deployed forward of the consolidating unit's OP/LP line to interdict the advance of dismounted counterattacking forces or button up advancing armor. This will give the antitank weapons a better chance of success and survival. When sufficient numbers of snipers are available, hasty sniper ambushes are established to interdict patrols and probing elements and enemy sniper teams that normally precede a counterattack. These ambushes can also be used to harass the displaced enemy to prevent him from establishing a base to counterattack.

    *    Interdiction. In the interdiction mission, snipers push out beyond the range of friendly support in an effort to prein-filtrate reestablished first echelon defenses, infiltrate second echelon defenses, or engage counterattacking forces from the rear.

    *    Security. Because of their ability to remain undetected in close proximity to the enemy, snipers are employed to maintain contact with displaced enemy forces. During consolidation snipers range ahead of the main OP/LP line, determine the enemy's whereabouts, and continue to harass until the attack is resumed. Forward deployment also permits snipers to provide early warning of impending counterattacks.

    *    Countersniping. Displaced enemy forces will often result in individuals or small groups getting cut off from their parent units. Often snipers will be left behind to disrupt the attacker's consolidation efforts. As these threats are small, snipers should be employed to track down and eliminate stay-behinds and isolated pockets of resistance. At the very least snipers will be capable of suppressing them until suitable forces can be spared to deal with them.

    o    <u>Reserve missions</u>. In a reserve role, snipers can give support where needed. They can reinforce success, or they can be used to react to enemy incursions or to provide stop-gap measures until the commander can rally more appropriate forces. Snipers can also be used to maintain security in their own rear areas, using stealth and unconventional skills to seek out enemy special forces.

    *    Reinforcement involves attaching themselves directly to the unit engaged and adding their fires to those of the unit.

    *    Intervention is a means of outflanking local resistance and suppressing it with precision rifle fire.

## Sniper Support to Dismounted Movement to Contact

Snipers may be used in a dismounted movement to contact by deploying prior to the movement. Once deployed, they will move along the route to reconnoiter the route and select sniper hide positions to secure the route for the moving element. Depending on the number of snipers available, it is possible to secure a corridor over 1,500 meters wide at the widest, depending on the terrain, and as deep as permitted by the number of sniper teams and terrain.

## Sniper Support to Reconnaissance Patrols

During reconnaissance and combat patrols, snipers may be used as part of the security or support elements.

## 5-15. CONVENTIONAL DEFENSIVE OPERATIONS

Special operations sniper support to conventional defensive operations is similar to offensive operations. The sniper can lend support anywhere on the battlefield including deep, rear, and main battle areas. However, conventional snipers normally operate in the main battle area in concert with their parent units--making SO sniper support seldom necessary in this area. The SO sniper's most important role is in the deep battle area. The rear battle area is also an area of employment, providing a rear area threat exists.

Sniper operations in the deep battle area can be used to keep enemy efforts off-balance and directed toward rear-area protection. The more enemy assets the sniper eliminates from the deep battle area, the fewer forces the enemy will have to execute attacks against our main effort. The sniper can also provide information on enemy strengths, location of reserves and intentions. Just as in offensive operations, SOF units using snipers should be deployed on a broad front to disrupt the enemy's order of battle. Key to this is the disruption of follow-on forces in the deep battle area. Snipers can assist in interdicting the enemy's soft underbelly--his unarmored logistics columns, fragile C2 nodes, and critical military weapons such as missiles and fire control equipment.

Threat doctrine calls for simultaneous attacks at critical nodes located in US rear areas. The sniper is ideally suited to locate and interdict the threat of enemy special operations units which conduct such operations.

## Defensive operations that could involve the sniper are:

o    Area defense.

o    Perimeter defense.

o    Security forces.

42

o      Reverse slope defense.

o      Defense of built-up or fortified positions.

o      River line defense.

o      Mobile defense.

o      Economy of force.

o      Withdrawal operations.

## Sniping Employment in Defensive Operations

o      Harassment.

Snipers are best employed in defensive operations beyond the forward line of troops (FLOT) to provide early warning of the approaching enemy, disorganize his attack, and cause him to deploy early and, in the event of armored vehicles, cause the vehicle commanders to button up early. Snipers should be integrated in the security force while performing this mission.

Snipers may be employed directly into the FLOT defensive positions or assume their positions after withdrawal of the security fire. Snipers in the defense of the FLOT should be employed similarly to the crew-served weapons. Optimum results from the snipers will be obtained by maximizing their standoff range to the targets, positioning on lucrative avenues of approach, and engaging targets of opportunity. Sniper positions should not be emplaced near obvious indirect fire targets. No matter how well concealed a hide is, if it is in the bursting radius of an indirect fire weapon, it can be compromised and destroyed.

The use of skilled marksmen will enhance the overall combat effectiveness of the defensive positions. Skilled marksmen are not necessarily snipers. They are simply skilled rifle shots who, for whatever reason, have neither the inclination nor the background skill to be successful snipers. However, they do possess the ability to engage targets at long ranges. When equipped with special weapons, such as .50 caliber or high-powered target rifles, they are particularly useful for conducting long-range harassment.

o      Delay.

When it is necessary for friendly forces to withdraw from contact with the enemy, snipers are employed to delay and impede the enemy's advance. Snipers are deployed throughout the withdrawing unit's sector. By using a series of interlocking delay positions, a handful of snipers can interdict dismounted avenues of approach and severely impede advancing enemy forces. By using successive delay positions, snipers permit withdrawing forces to reassemble and establish new defensive positions. Sniper elements must remain mobile to avoid decisive engagement with the attacking enemy. Snipers can be employed during the withdrawal to cover obstacles with precision rifle fire and thus increase the effectiveness of the obstacles. Snipers can also be employed in the stay-behind role and attack the enemy forces' rear area and supply columns.

   o   <u>Rear area protection</u>.

       In this mission snipers are used to enhance the protective measures surrounding sensitive facilities or installations. This is accomplished either through the establishment of observation posts along routes of access, as a reaction force to rear area penetrations, or by means of patrolling. Snipers will not normally patrol by themselves, but as members of established security patrols.

       The role of sniping in security operations is that of extending the depth and scope of the security effort. Specific roles include:

           o   Protecting critical installations, sites, or projects from infiltration.

           o   Dominating the gaps between units to prevent infiltration by enemy combat elements or patrols.

           o   Preventing the removal or breaching of obstacles.

           o   Tracking enemy patrols known to have penetrated into the rear area.

## Sniper Support to Defensive HUMINT Collection

The employment of snipers in defensive operations permits a variety of means to maintain a constant offensive pressure on the enemy. Sniping in the defense is dependent on the collection and use of information. When the snipers collect information for their personal use, this is known as targeting. Information collected for organizational use is but an element of the total HUMINT collection effort of the snipers' unit. Observation posts (OPs) are the snipers' primary means of collecting information in the defense. In the role of the observers, the snipers establish a series of OPs that dominate their sector. These OPs are of two types: overt and covert.

       o   Overt OPs. An overt sniping OP is not overt in the sense that its location or function is known to the enemy, but in that the snipers may engage high-priority targets from the OP itself. While firing from the OP may not necessarily reveal its exact location, it will certainly reveal the snipers' presence and the fact that such a location exists.

o    Covert OPs.    OPs that offer a particularly commanding view of enemy positions that should remain unknown to the enemy and should never be fired from, regardless of the temptation to do so.  The information that is collected from a well-sited covert OP is far more valuable than any targets that may appear.

## 5-16.  CIVIL DISTURBANCE ASSISTANCE

Military assistance to civil authorities in civil disturbances is provided by the US Army when such assistance is requested or directed in accordance with prevailing laws.  When such assistance is requested, the mission of military forces is to assist local authorities in the restoration and maintenance of law and order.

Military assistance is considered as a last resort.  When committed, involvement is to the degree justified by the circumstances to restore law and order with a minimum loss of life and property.  When using force, the guiding principle should be minimum force consistent with mission accomplishment.

The sniper team's precision fire and observation abilities give authorities a way to detect and eliminate criminal threats with low risk to innocent personnel.  The use of sniper teams in civil disorders must be planned and controlled.  The use may be an important factor in the control and elimination of weapons fire directed against riot control authorities.

### Characteristics of Urban Violence
o    Crowd behavior during a civil disturbance is essentially emotional and without reason.  This, and the momentum generated, has the tendency to reduce the behavior of the total group to that of its worst members.  Skillful agitators or subversive elements exploit these psychological factors during these disorders.  Regardless of the reason for violence, whether the result of spontaneous reactions or deliberate incitement, the results may consist of indiscriminate looting and burning, or open and violent attacks on officials, buildings, and innocent passers-by.  Rioters may set fire to buildings and vehicles to block the advance of troops, to create confusion and diversion, or to achieve goals of property destruction, looting, and sniping.

o    Organized rioters or agitators may use sniper fire to cause government forces to overreact.

### Considerations for Sniper Employment during Civil Disturbances
o    Briefings.  Sniper teams must be thoroughly briefed on the areas and routes within the riot area.  Representatives of

local authorities should be assigned to the sniper teams for protection and communications with local indigenous personnel.

     o     Adequate Personnel. Sufficient sniper teams should be allocated to provide maximum versatility to the riot control authorities.

     o     Observation Areas and Field of Fire. Observation areas and fields of fire are clearly defined by streets and highways. However, surveillance and detection are complicated by the numerous rooftops, windows, and doorways from which hostile fire may be directed. Sniper teams take maximum advantage of dominant buildings or rooftops to maintain continuous observation of a riot scene. Mutually supporting teams cover blind spots or dead space within the area.

     o     Cover and Concealment. Built-up areas offer excellent cover and concealment for both the rioters and the sniper teams.

     o     Avenues of approach. The best avenues of approach to a riot scene, or to points of observation and firing positions, are through building interiors. Movement through streets may be difficult and easily detected by rioters.

     o     Operations. Sniper teams should operate in each established area. The teams remain at a sufficient distance from control troops to keep from getting involved in direct riot actions.

     o     Firing Positions. The firing position should provide the maximum stability, because precision fire is employed to wound and not to kill. A stray shot that wounds or kills a woman, child, or unarmed rioter may only inflame an already riotous situation. When firing from a window, the sniper team should, if possible, fire from a supported position in the back of the room. This will muffle the muzzle blast, and the muzzle flash will not be noticed. If the sniper shows his rifle or part of his body, this may invite fire from weapons-equipped rioting personnel. When possible, a silencer should be used on the sniper rifle.

     o     Camouflage. Sniper teams should be dressed in drab or blending clothing to prevent identification or observation.

     o     Civil Authorities. Since civil authorities are in charge, snipers maintain a direct line of communication with the civilian who permits or directs snipers to engage. Civil authorities also determine the caliber of weapon as well as the type of ammunition. Usually, however, anything within 300 meters is engaged with 5.56mm ammunition unless special penetration capability is required.

o    Sniper Team Control. A key to effective sniper team utilization is control. When directed to engage in countersniping activities, the sniper team's actions must be swift and precise.

o    Rules of Engagement. When directed to countersnipe, the sniper team should direct its precision fire to wound rather than to kill, if possible.

## Sniper Employment in Civil Disturbances

Snipers employed to counteract sniper fire from a street disorder require quick and decisive action. When directed to support the control forces during a street disorder, the sniper team reacts as follows:

o    Deploys to rooftops or vantage points providing observation and fields of fire into the riot area.

o    Institutes communications with the commander.

o    Begins observation immediately and continues it.

o    Relays information continuously to the commander.

o    Conducts countersniping actions as directed.

During civil disorders, rioters may seize control of buildings for the purpose of utilizing the vantage points of rooftops or windows from which to direct hostile sniper fire on riot control forces. The sniper team may be called upon to provide covering fire to allow the search/clearing team to approach and clear the building. Or, the sniper may be directed to use precision fire to wound the hostile sniper if the hostile sniping is directed at control authorities in mob control actions.

Hostile snipers may fire against unarmed firefighting personnel. Upon the identification or location of a riotous sniper who is directing fire at firefighting personnel, the sniper immediately reacts to reduce the hostile sniper fire. This countersniper fire is directed with accuracy to kill.

Looting must be controlled quickly because it may also lead to more serious acts of murder and arson, often against innocent nonparticipants. The sniper team's employment to assist in looting control is mainly for observation, communication, and to act as a covering force should the looters fire upon the control forces. In instances where control forces are fired upon, the sniper team immediately engages the riotous sniper(s) to facilitate apprehension by the control forces.

The sniper team's role in support of riot control forces is equally important during the hours of darkness.

47

o    Optical equipment, to include night vision devices, allows the sniper team to provide prolonged night observation.

o    During darkness, sniper teams are best employed to accompany patrol forces, to man observation posts and roadblocks, or to cover control troops during mob control activities.

TABLE 5-5-

**Angle to North from the rising or setting sun (level terrain)**

| DATE | | 0° | 5° | 10° | 15° | 20° | 25° | 30° | 35° | 40° | 45° | 50° | 55° | 60° |
|---|---|---|---|---|---|---|---|---|---|---|---|---|---|---|
| JANUARY | 1 | 113 | 113 | 113 | 114 | 115 | 116 | 117 | 118 | 121 | 124 | 127 | 133 | 141 |
| | 6 | 112 | 113 | 113 | 113 | 114 | 115 | 116 | 118 | 120 | 123 | 127 | 132 | 140 |
| | 11 | 112 | 112 | 112 | 113 | 113 | 114 | 115 | 117 | 119 | 122 | 125 | 130 | 138 |
| | 16 | 111 | 111 | 111 | 112 | 112 | 113 | 114 | 116 | 118 | 120 | 124 | 129 | 136 |
| | 21 | 110 | 110 | 110 | 111 | 111 | 112 | 113 | 115 | 117 | 119 | 122 | 127 | 133 |
| | 26 | 109 | 109 | 109 | 109 | 109 | 110 | 111 | 112 | 113 | 115 | 117 | 124 | 130 |
| FEBRUARY | 1 | 107 | 107 | 108 | 108 | 108 | 109 | 110 | 111 | 113 | 115 | 117 | 121 | 126 |
| | 6 | 106 | 106 | 106 | 106 | 107 | 107 | 108 | 109 | 111 | 113 | 115 | 118 | 123 |
| | 11 | 104 | 104 | 105 | 105 | 105 | 106 | 107 | 108 | 109 | 110 | 112 | 116 | 120 |
| | 16 | 103 | 103 | 103 | 103 | 103 | 104 | 105 | 106 | 107 | 108 | 110 | 113 | 116 |
| | 21 | 101 | 101 | 101 | 101 | 101 | 102 | 102 | 103 | 104 | 105 | 107 | 109 | 112 |
| | 26 | 99 | 99 | 99 | 99 | 100 | 100 | 100 | 101 | 102 | 103 | 104 | 106 | 108 |
| MARCH | 1 | 98 | 98 | 98 | 98 | 99 | 99 | 99 | 100 | 100 | 101 | 102 | 104 | 106 |
| | 6 | 96 | 96 | 96 | 96 | 96 | 97 | 97 | 97 | 98 | 98 | 99 | 100 | 102 |
| | 11 | 94 | 94 | 94 | 94 | 94 | 94 | 95 | 95 | 95 | 96 | 96 | 97 | 98 |
| | 16 | 92 | 92 | 92 | 92 | 92 | 92 | 92 | 92 | 93 | 93 | 93 | 93 | 94 |
| | 21 | 90 | 90 | 90 | 90 | 90 | 90 | 90 | 90 | 90 | 90 | 90 | 90 | 90 |
| | 26 | 88 | 88 | 88 | 88 | 89 | 88 | 88 | 88 | 87 | 87 | 87 | 87 | 86 |
| APRIL | 1 | 86 | 86 | 86 | 86 | 85 | 85 | 85 | 85 | 84 | 84 | 83 | 82 | 81 |
| | 6 | 84 | 84 | 84 | 83 | 83 | 83 | 83 | 82 | 82 | 81 | 80 | 79 | 77 |
| | 11 | 82 | 82 | 82 | 82 | 81 | 81 | 81 | 80 | 80 | 79 | 77 | 76 | 74 |
| | 16 | 80 | 80 | 80 | 80 | 79 | 79 | 78 | 78 | 77 | 76 | 74 | 72 | 70 |
| | 21 | 78 | 78 | 78 | 78 | 78 | 77 | 76 | 76 | 74 | 72 | 71 | 69 | 66 |
| | 26 | 77 | 77 | 76 | 75 | 74 | 75 | 75 | 75 | 74 | 71 | 69 | 66 | 63 |
| MAY | 1 | 75 | 75 | 75 | 74 | 74 | 73 | 73 | 72 | 70 | 69 | 66 | 63 | 59 |
| | 6 | 74 | 74 | 73 | 73 | 73 | 72 | 71 | 70 | 68 | 67 | 64 | 61 | 56 |
| | 11 | 72 | 72 | 72 | 72 | 71 | 70 | 69 | 68 | 67 | 64 | 62 | 58 | 52 |
| | 16 | 71 | 71 | 71 | 70 | 70 | 69 | 68 | 67 | 65 | 63 | 60 | 55 | 49 |
| | 21 | 70 | 70 | 70 | 69 | 69 | 68 | 67 | 65 | 63 | 61 | 58 | 53 | 47 |
| | 26 | 69 | 69 | 69 | 68 | 68 | 67 | 66 | 64 | 62 | 60 | 56 | 51 | 44 |
| JUNE | 1 | 68 | 68 | 68 | 67 | 66 | 66 | 64 | 63 | 61 | 58 | 54 | 49 | 41 |
| | 6 | 67 | 67 | 67 | 67 | 66 | 65 | 64 | 62 | 60 | 57 | 53 | 48 | 40 |
| | 11 | 67 | 67 | 67 | 66 | 65 | 64 | 63 | 62 | 59 | 56 | 53 | 47 | 39 |
| | 16 | 67 | 67 | 67 | 66 | 65 | 64 | 63 | 62 | 59 | 56 | 53 | 47 | 39 |
| | 21 | 67 | 67 | 67 | 66 | 65 | 64 | 63 | 62 | 59 | 56 | 53 | 47 | 39 |
| | 26 | 67 | 67 | 67 | 66 | 65 | 64 | 63 | 62 | 59 | 56 | 53 | 47 | 39 |
| JULY | 1 | 67 | 67 | 67 | 66 | 65 | 64 | 63 | 62 | 59 | 56 | 53 | 48 | 39 |
| | 6 | 67 | 67 | 67 | 66 | 66 | 65 | 64 | 62 | 60 | 57 | 53 | 48 | 40 |
| | 11 | 68 | 68 | 68 | 67 | 66 | 65 | 64 | 63 | 61 | 58 | 54 | 49 | 41 |
| | 16 | 69 | 68 | 68 | 68 | 67 | 66 | 65 | 64 | 62 | 59 | 55 | 50 | 43 |
| | 21 | 69 | 69 | 69 | 69 | 68 | 67 | 66 | 65 | 63 | 60 | 57 | 52 | 45 |
| | 26 | 70 | 70 | 70 | 70 | 69 | 68 | 67 | 66 | 64 | 62 | 59 | 54 | 48 |
| AUGUST | 1 | 72 | 72 | 72 | 71 | 71 | 70 | 69 | 68 | 66 | 64 | 61 | 57 | 51 |
| | 6 | 73 | 73 | 73 | 73 | 72 | 71 | 71 | 69 | 68 | 66 | 63 | 60 | 55 |
| | 11 | 75 | 75 | 74 | 74 | 74 | 73 | 72 | 71 | 70 | 68 | 66 | 63 | 58 |
| | 16 | 76 | 76 | 76 | 76 | 75 | 75 | 74 | 73 | 72 | 70 | 68 | 65 | 61 |
| | 21 | 78 | 78 | 77 | 77 | 77 | 76 | 76 | 75 | 74 | 72 | 71 | 68 | 65 |
| | 26 | 79 | 79 | 79 | 79 | 79 | 78 | 78 | 77 | 76 | 75 | 73 | 71 | 68 |
| SEPTEMBER | 1 | 80 | 80 | 80 | 81 | 81 | 81 | 80 | 80 | 79 | 78 | 77 | 75 | 73 |
| | 6 | 83 | 83 | 83 | 83 | 83 | 83 | 82 | 82 | 81 | 81 | 80 | 78 | 77 |
| | 11 | 85 | 85 | 85 | 85 | 85 | 85 | 85 | 84 | 84 | 83 | 83 | 82 | 81 |
| | 16 | 87 | 87 | 87 | 87 | 87 | 87 | 87 | 86 | 86 | 86 | 85 | 85 | 84 |
| | 21 | 89 | 89 | 89 | 89 | 89 | 89 | 89 | 89 | 89 | 89 | 88 | 86 | 88 |
| | 26 | 91 | 91 | 91 | 91 | 91 | 91 | 91 | 91 | 91 | 91 | 92 | 92 | 92 |
| OCTOBER | 1 | 93 | 93 | 93 | 93 | 93 | 93 | 93 | 94 | 94 | 94 | 95 | 95 | 96 |
| | 6 | 95 | 95 | 95 | 95 | 95 | 96 | 96 | 96 | 99 | 99 | 100 | 102 | 104 |
| | 11 | 97 | 97 | 97 | 97 | 97 | 98 | 98 | 99 | 100 | 102 | 104 | 105 | 108 |
| | 16 | 99 | 99 | 99 | 99 | 99 | 100 | 100 | 101 | 101 | 102 | 104 | 105 | 108 |
| | 21 | 101 | 101 | 101 | 101 | 101 | 102 | 102 | 103 | 104 | 105 | 107 | 109 | 112 |
| | 26 | 102 | 102 | 103 | 103 | 103 | 104 | 104 | 105 | 106 | 108 | 109 | 112 | 115 |
| NOVEMBER | 1 | 104 | 104 | 105 | 105 | 105 | 106 | 107 | 108 | 109 | 110 | 113 | 115 | 123 |
| | 6 | 106 | 106 | 106 | 107 | 107 | 108 | 109 | 110 | 111 | 113 | 115 | 121 | 126 |
| | 11 | 107 | 107 | 108 | 108 | 108 | 109 | 110 | 111 | 113 | 115 | 117 | 124 | 130 |
| | 16 | 108 | 108 | 109 | 109 | 110 | 111 | 112 | 113 | 115 | 117 | 120 | 124 | 130 |
| | 21 | 110 | 110 | 110 | 111 | 111 | 112 | 113 | 114 | 116 | 119 | 122 | 126 | 133 |
| | 26 | 111 | 111 | 111 | 112 | 112 | 113 | 114 | 116 | 118 | 120 | 124 | 128 | 135 |
| DECEMBER | 1 | ·· | ·· | 112 | 113 | 113 | 114 | 115 | 117 | 119 | 122 | 125 | 132 | 140 |
| | 6 | ·· | ·· | 113 | 113 | 114 | 115 | 116 | 118 | 120 | 123 | 127 | 133 | 141 |
| | 11 | ·· | ·· | 113 | 114 | 115 | 116 | 117 | 118 | 121 | 124 | 127 | 133 | 141 |
| | 16 | ·· | ·· | 113 | 114 | 115 | 116 | 117 | 118 | 121 | 124 | 127 | 133 | 141 |
| | 21 | ·· | ·· | 113 | 114 | 115 | 116 | 117 | 118 | 121 | 124 | 127 | 133 | 141 |
| | 26 | ·· | ·· | 113 | 114 | 115 | 116 | 117 | 118 | 121 | 124 | 127 | 133 | 141 |

NOTE: When the sun is rising, the angle is reckoned from East to North.

# Chapter 6

## SNIPER OPERATIONS ON URBANIZED TERRAIN

### 6-1. URBAN OPERATIONS

Snipers are extremely effective in urban terrain. Their long-range precision fire can engage targets at a distance; their advanced optics can discriminate individual point targets to save innocent bystanders or protect property; and their observation skills can offer superior intelligence-collection capabilities. In an urban environment the sniper is both a casualty producer and an intimidating psychological weapon.

#### Tactical Implications of Urban Terrain

Urban terrain consists mainly of man-made structures. Buildings are the main components of urban terrain. Buildings provide cover and concealment, limit fields of fire and observation, and impair movement. Thick-walled buildings provide excellent protection from hostile fire.

Urban streets are generally avenues of approach. However, forces moving along streets are often canalized by buildings and terrain that offer minimal off-road maneuver space. Obstacles on streets prove difficult to bypass, due to these restrictive avenues of approach.

Underground systems found in some urban areas are easily overlooked but can be important to the outcome of operations. They include subways, sewers, cellars, and utility systems.

Civilians will be present in urban operations, often in great numbers. Concern for the safety of noncombatants may restrict fire and limit maneuver options available to the commander.

#### Categories of Urban Terrain

Urban terrain may be categorized as large cities, towns and small cities, villages, or strip areas.

   o    Large cities (population greater than 100,000). In Europe, other than the Soviet Union, there are approximately 410 cities with a population in excess of 100,000. Large cities frequently form the core of a larger, densely populated urban complex consisting of the city, its suburban areas, and small towns. Such complexes have the appearance of a single large and continuous city containing millions of people and occupying vast areas of land.

   o    Towns and small cities (population of 3,000 to 100,000). These areas are mostly located along major lines of communications and situated in river valleys. Similar to larger

1

cities, these areas are continuing to expand and will eventually form new concentrations or merge with existing ones.

o     Villages (population of less than 3,000).  In most cases, villages are agriculturally oriented and are usually distributed among the more open cultivated areas.

o     Strip areas.  These built-up areas generally form connecting links between villages and towns.  They are also found among lines of communications leading to larger complexes.

## Descriptions of Urban Terrain
Within the city, urban terrain differs based on size, location, and history.  These areas within the city are generally categorized as:

o     Industrial areas and residential sprawl.  Residential areas consist of some houses or small dwellings with yards, gardens, trees, and fences.  Street patterns are normally rectangular or curving.  Industrial areas consist of one- to three-story buildings of low, flat-roofed factories or warehouses, generally located on or along major rail and highway routes.  In both regions, there are many open areas.

o     Core periphery.  The core periphery consists of narrow streets (12 to 20 meters wide) with continuous fronts of brick and heavy-walled concrete buildings.  The height of the buildings is generally uniform: 2 to 3 stories in small towns; 5 to 10 stories in large cities.

o     City cores and outlying high-rise areas.  Typical city cores of today are made of high-rise buildings, which vary greatly in height and allow for more open space between buildings than that allowed in the old city cores.  Outlying high-rise areas are dominated by this open-construction style to a greater degree than city cores.  Generally, streets form a rectangular pattern.

o     Commercial ribbons.  These are rows of stores, shops, etc., built along either side of major streets through the built-up areas.  Generally, these streets at 25 meters wide or wider.  The buildings are uniformly two to three stories tall.

## Nature of Urban Combat
Urban combat usually occurs when a city is between two natural obstacles, and it cannot be bypassed; the seizure of the city contributes to the attainment of an overall objective; or political or humanitarian concerns require the seizure or retention of the city.

In the city, the ranges of observation and fields of fire are reduced by the structures as well as the smoke and dust of combat.

Targets will generally be exposed briefly at ranges of 200 meters or less.

Units fighting in urban areas often become isolated by an enemy; therefore, snipers must have the skill, initiative, and courage to operate effectively while isolated from their unit. As combat in modern nations can no longer be avoided in urban areas, snipers must be trained and psychologically prepared for the demands of urban combat.

The defender will generally have the advantage over the attacker in urban combat. The defender occupies strong positions, whereas the attacker must expose himself to advance. In addition, the greatly reduced line-of-sight ranges, built-in obstacles, and compartmented terrain require the commitment of more troops for a given frontage. Troop density may be three to five times greater for both attacker and defender in urban combat than in natural environments.

Due to the density of structures, radio communications are degraded. This, combined with limited observation, makes control of forces difficult. The well-established defender will probably employ wire communications to enhance control, thus adding to his advantage.

Soldiers may encounter a greater degree of stress during urban combat. Continual close combat, intense pressure, high casualties, the fleeting nature of targets, and fire from an unseen enemy may produce increased psychological strain and physical fatigue.

Commanders may be restricted in the weapons and tactics that they are allowed to employ to minimize collateral damage. This may be necessary to preserve a natural cultural heritage and gain the support of the population. In such cases, snipers are ideally suited to deliver discriminatory fire against selected targets.

Attacks will generally limit artillery fires to the direct fire mode. This is done to prevent reducing the city to rubble--an action that produces few casualties and tends to enhance the defender's fortifications, concealment, and restrict the attacker's avenues of approach.

Forces engaged in urban fighting use large quantities of munitions. Units committed to urban combat must also have special equipment, such as grappling hooks, ropes, snaplinks, construction materials, axes, sandbags, and ladders.

Urban combat historically has presented chances for looting. Looting can break down discipline, reduce alertness, increase vulnerability, and delay the progress of the unit. Looting also alienates the civilian population.

## Evaluating Urban Terrain

When the sniper evaluates urban terrain, he should consider the following factors:

o    <u>Observation and Fields of Fire</u>. Buildings on the edge of a city provide better fields of fire than buildings in the interior. In the city, tall buildings with numerous windows often provide the best fields of fire, especially if the buildings have spaces between them.

o    <u>Cover and Concealment</u>. Buildings with brick walls and few, narrow windows provide the best balance between cover and concealment and fields of fire. Roofs provide little protection; snipers are better protected in the lower stories than directly under the roof. (An exception to this rule is the parking garage.) Floor layouts with many small rooms provide more protection than floor layouts with larger rooms.

o    <u>Obstacles</u>. Doors and fire barriers are common in commercial buildings. They become obstacles if they are shut and secured. Furniture and appliances can also become obstacles in a building. Barbed wire can be used effectively inside a building because it further restricts movement.

o    <u>Key Control Points</u>. Key control points in a building are entrances, hallways, and stairs; troops that control these areas control the building.

o    <u>Avenues of Approach</u>. The best way to gain entry into a building is from the top. Therefore, the most important avenue of approach to look for is one that quickly leads to the top (fire escapes, drainpipes, or adjacent buildings).

o    <u>Intra-city Distribution of Building Types</u>. The layout of a city can generally be determined by the distribution of the buildings within the city.

    *    Mass construction buildings (modern apartments and hotels) are the most common structures in built-up areas (two-thirds of the total area) and are usually constructed of bricks.

    *    Steel- and concrete-framed multistory buildings are found in the core area--a city's most valuable land--where, as centers of economic and political power they have potentially high military significance.

    *    Open spaces (i.e., parks, athletic fields, and golf courses) account for about 15 percent of an average city's area. Most of this area is suitable for airmobile operations.

4

## Line-of-Sight Factors

Streets serving areas composed mostly of one type of building normally have a common pattern. Street widths are grouped into three major classes:

o    Narrow (7 to 15 meters). Found in such places as medieval sections of European cities.

o    Medium (15 to 25 meters). Found in newer, planned sections of most cities.

o    Wide (25 to 50 meters). Where buildings are located along broad boulevards or set far apart on large parcels of land.

When a street is narrow, observing or firing into windows of a building across the street can be difficult because an observer is forced to look along the building rather than into the windows. When the street is wide, the observer has a better chance to look and fire into and out of the window openings.

## Sources of Information on Urban Terrain

Operations in urban terrain require detailed intelligence. Snipers should have the following materials for planning operations:

o    Maps and aerial photos. Although tactical maps do not show manmade objects in enough detail for tactical operations in urban terrain, they do show the details of terrain adjacent to urban areas. Tactical maps should be supplemented with both vertical and oblique air photos.

o    Civil government and local military information. Considerable current information on practically all details of a city can be obtained from civil governments and local military forces:

*    Large-scale city maps.

*    Diagrams of underground sewer, utility, transport, and miscellaneous systems.

*    Information on key public buildings and rosters of key personnel.

*    Information on the size and density of the population.

*    Information on police and security capabilities.

*    Information on civil defense, air raid shelters, and firefighting capabilities.

5

\*    Information on utility systems, medical facilities, and mass communications facilities.

## Camouflage Techniques for Urban Terrain

To survive in urban combat, the sniper must supplement cover and concealment with camouflage. To properly camouflage himself, the sniper must study the surroundings in the area. He must make the firing positions look like the surrounding terrain. For instance, if there is no damage to buildings, the sniper will not make loopholes for firing. The sniper will use only the materials needed; excess material can reveal his position. He will get the materials from a wide area. For example, if defending the city park, the sniper will use all of the park for resources; he will not denude a small area near the position for camouflage material.

Buildings provide numerous concealed positions. Thick masonry, stone, or brick walls offer excellent protection from direct fire and provide concealed routes. If the tactical situation permits, the sniper will inspect positions from the enemy's viewpoint. He will conduct routine checks to see if the camouflage remains material-looking and actually conceals the position. Shirts should not be removed, as exposed skin reflects light and could attract the enemy's attention.

When using urban camouflage techniques, the sniper must consider the following:

o    Use of shadows. Buildings in urban areas throw sharp shadows. The sniper will use the shadow to aid in concealment during movement. He will avoid lighted areas around windows and loopholes. A lace curtain or a piece of cheesecloth provides additional concealment to snipers in interiors of rooms, if curtains are common in the area.

o    Color and texture. The need to break up the silhouette of helmets and individual equipment exists in urban areas as elsewhere. In urban areas, however, burlap or canvas strips are a more effective camouflage garnish than foliage. Predominant colors are normally browns, tans, and sometimes grays, rather than greens, but each camouflage location should be evaluated separately.

o    Dust. In weapons emplacements a wet blanket, canvas, etc., should be used to keep dust from rising when the weapons are fired.

o    Background. Snipers must pay attention to the background to ensure that they are not silhouetted or skylined, but rather blend into their surroundings.

o    Common camouflage errors. To defeat enemy urban camouflage, the sniper should look for errors such as tracks or other evidence of activity, shine or shadows, unnatural or peculiar

6

colors or textures, muzzle flash smoke or dust, unnatural sounds and smells, and, finally, movements.

o    Deception. Dummy positions can be used effectively to distract the enemy and make him reveal his position by firing.

o    Use the terrain and alter camouflage habits to suit the surroundings.

o    Do not forget deceptive camouflage of buildings.

o    Continue to improve positions. Reinforce fighting positions with sandbags or other shrapnel and blast absorbing material.

o    Do not upset the natural look of the area.

o    Do not make positions obvious by clearing away too much debris for fields of fire.

o    Choose firing ports in inconspicuous spots when available.

## Infiltration and Exfiltration in Urban Terrain

One method is infiltration into the outskirts of a town. The outskirts of a town may not be strongly defended. Its defenders may only have a series of antitank positions, security elements on the principal approach, or positions blocking the approaches to key features in the town. The strong points and reserves are deeper in the city.

As part of a larger force, the sniper moves by stealth on secondary streets, using cover and concealment of back alleys and buildings, and assists in seizing key terrain features and isolating enemy positions, thus aiding following units' entry into the urban area. Sniper teams may also infiltrate into the city after the initial force has seized a foothold and move into their respective sniper positions.

Mortar and artillery fire may be used to attract the enemy's attention and cover the sound of infiltrating troops. Infiltration should be done when visibility is poor; chances of success are greater if there are no civilians in the area.

Sniper teams may also infiltrate into a city as part of a larger force during an airborne or airmobile operation.

During exfiltration, extreme care must be taken to avoid detection. As in infiltration, stealth and use of all available cover and concealment must be used when leaving the sniper position. Exfiltration should be performed during darkness to avoid detection.

## Movement Techniques in Urban Terrain

Movement in urban areas is one of the first fundamental skills that a sniper must master. Movement techniques must be practiced until they become second nature. To minimize exposure to enemy fire, the urban sniper must move so that he:

o    Does not silhouette himself, but keeps low at all times.

o    Avoids open areas (streets, alleys, parks).

o    Selects the next covered position before moving.

o    Conceals movement by using buildings, rubble, foliage, smoke, or limited visibility.

o    Advances rapidly from one position to another, but not so rapidly that he creates dust clouds or noise that will help the enemy to locate him.

o    Does not mask his covering fire.

o    Remains alert, ready for the unexpected.

Specific movement techniques used frequently in urban operations must be learned by all snipers. They are:

o    Crossing a wall. After the sniper has reconnoitered the other side, he quickly rolls over the wall, keeping a low silhou- ette. The speed of this and the low silhouette will deny the enemy a good target.

o    Moving around a corner. Corners are dangerous. The area around the corner must be observed before the sniper moves beyond the corner. The most common mistake that a sniper makes at a corner is allowing his weapon to extend beyond the corner, exposing his position ("flagging"). Also, a sniper should not show his head at the height an enemy soldier would expect to see it. When using the correct technique for looking around a corner, the sniper lies flat on the ground and does not extend his weapon beyond the corner of the building. He exposes his head or a hand-held mirror (at ground level) only enough to permit observation around the corner.

o    Moving past windows. When using the correct technique for passing a window, the sniper stays below the window level, taking care not to silhouette himself in the window. He hugs the side of the building. An enemy gunner inside the building would have to expose himself to fire from another position if he wished to engage the sniper.

o    Moving past basement windows. When using the correct procedure of negotiating a basement window, the sniper stays close to the wall of the building and steps or jumps over the window without exposing his legs.

o    Using doorways. Doorways should not be used as entrances or exits.  If a sniper must use a doorway as an exit, he should move quickly through it to his next covered position, staying as low as possible to avoid silhouetting himself.

o    Moving parallel to a building.  At times, it may not be possible to use interiors of buildings for a route of advance.  To correctly move along the outside of a building, the sniper hugs the side of the building, stays in the shadows, presents a low silhouette, and moves rapidly to his next position.

o    Crossing open areas.  Open areas such as streets, alleys, and parks should be avoided whenever possible.  However, they can be crossed safely if certain fundamentals are applied by the sniper.  In using the correct method for crossing an open area, the sniper may employ a distraction or limited visibility to conceal his movement.  He crosses the open area at the shortest distance between two points.

*    Before moving from one position to another, a sniper should make a visual reconnaissance and select the position that will give him the best cover and concealment.  At the same time, he should select the route that he will take to that position.  He must take care to use existing cover and concealment.

*    The sniper team should not move together when crossing from one building to another or across an open area.

## Building Entry Techniques

When entering a building, a sniper may be required to enter by means other than through doorways, or reach top levels of buildings by means other than stairs.

Various means, such as ladders, drainpipes, vines, helicopters, or the roofs and windows of adjoining buildings, may be used to reach the top floor or roof of a building.  A sniper team may use the following aids and methods to accomplish this:

o    The two-man lift, supported and unsupported; the two-man lift with heels raised; the one-man lift; the two-man pull; and individual climbing techniques.  These techniques are more commonly used to gain entry into areas at lower levels.

o    Ladders or grappling hooks with knotted ropes.  By attaching a grappling hook to the end of a scaling rope, a sniper can scale a wall, swing from one building to another, or gain entry to an upstairs window.
o    Rappelling. Rappelling is a combat technique that snipers can use to descend from the roof of a tall building to other levels or a window.

9

## 6-2. SNIPER EMPLOYMENT IN URBAN OPERATIONS

**Employment Considerations**

A sniper should be given general areas (buildings or a group of buildings) in which to position himself, but he selects the best positions for engagements. Sniper positions should cover obstacles, roofs, gaps in the final protective fires, and dead space. The sniper also selects numerous secondary and supplementary positions to cover his areas of responsibility. The sniper should think 3-dimensionally.

Engagement priorities for snipers are determined by the relative importance of the targets to the effective operations of the enemy. The following are normally sniper targets:

o   Tank commanders.

o   Direct fire support weapons crewmen.

o   Crew-served weapons crewmen.

o   Key leaders.

o   Forward observers.

o   Radiotelephone operators.

o   Protected equipment.

The characteristics of built-up areas and the nature of urban warfare impact on both the effectiveness of the sniper weapons system and how the system may be employed. The sniper must consider the following basic factors during urban operations:

o   <u>Relative location of the firer and the target</u>. Both the target and the firer may be inside or outside of buildings, or either one may be inside a building while the other is outside.

o   <u>Structural configuration of buildings</u>. The basic classes of structures encountered in a built-up area can generally be classified as concrete, masonry, or wooden. However, any one building may include a combination of these materials. All buildings offer concealment, even though the degree of protection varies with the material used.

o   <u>Firing ranges and angles</u>. Engagement ranges may vary from distances of less than 100 meters up to the maximum effective range of a sniper system. Depression and elevation limits may create deadspace. Target engagement from oblique angles, either vertical or horizontal, demands increased marksmanship skills. Urban areas often limit snipers to firing down or across streets, but open spaces of urban areas permit engagements at long ranges.

o    <u>Visibility limitations</u>. Added to the weather conditions that limit visibility are the urban factors of target masking and increased deadspace caused by buildings and rubble. Observation through smoke, dust, and concealment offered by shaded areas, rubble, and manmade structures influence visibility.

## Sniper Employment During an Attack on or Defense of Urban Terrain

Snipers employed during the attack of a built-up area are usually divided into three phases:

o    Phase I is designed to **isolate** the battle area by seizing terrain features that dominate the approaches to it. Snipers deliver long-range precision fire at targets of opportunity.

o    Phase II consists of the advance to the built-up area and seizure of a **foothold** on its edge. It is during this period that snipers displace forward and assume their initial position from which to support continuation of the attack.

o    Phase III consists of the **advance** through the built-up area in accordance with the plan of attack. Sniper teams should operate in each zone of action, moving with and supporting the infantry units. They should operate at a sufficient distance from the riflemen to keep from getting involved in firefights, but close enough to kill more distance targets that threaten the advance. Some sniper teams can operate independently of the infantry on missions of search for targets of opportunity, particularly the search for enemy snipers.

Snipers employed in a defensive posture in an urban area should be positioned in buildings that offer the best long-range fields of fire and all-round observation. They are assigned various missions such as countersniper fire, firing at targets of opportunity, denying the enemy access to certain areas or avenues of approach, providing fire support over barricades and obstacles, surveillance of the flank and rear areas, supporting counterattacks, and prevention of enemy observation.

## Sniper Employment in Internal Security Operations
Snipers are employed in internal security operations during urban guerrilla warfare and hostage situations.

<u>Urban guerrilla warfare</u>. The role of the sniper in an urban guerrilla environment is to dominate the area of operations by delivery of selective, aimed fire against <u>specific</u> targets as authorized by local commanders. Usually this authorization only comes when such targets are about to employ firearms or other lethal weapons against the peacekeeping force or innocent civilians. The sniper's other role, almost equally as important as his primary role, is the gathering and reporting of intelligence.

Within the above roles, some specific tasks that may be assigned include:

        o     When authorized by local commanders, engaging dissidents/urban guerrillas who are involved in hijacking, kidnapping, holding hostages, etc.

        o     Engaging urban guerrilla snipers as opportunity targets or as part of a deliberate clearance operation.

        o     Covertly occupying concealed positions to observe selected areas.

        o     Recording and reporting all suspicious activities in the area of observations.

        o     Assisting in coordinating the activities of other elements by taking advantage of hidden observation posts.

        o     Providing protection for other elements of the peacekeeping force, including firemen, repair crews, etc.

     Limitations. In urban guerrilla operations, there are several limiting factors that snipers would not encounter in a conventional warfare:

        o     There is no forward edge of the battle area (FEBA) and therefore no "no man's land" in which to operate. Snipers can therefore expect to operate in entirely hostile surroundings in most circumstances.

        o     The enemy is covert, perfectly camouflaged among, and totally indistinguishable from, the everyday populace that surrounds him.

        o     In areas where confrontation between peacekeeping forces and the urban guerrillas takes place, the guerrilla dominates the ground entirely from the point of view of continued presence and observation. Every yard of ground is known to him; it is ground of his own choosing. Anything approximating a conventional stalk to and occupation of a hide is doomed to failure.

        o     Although the sniper is not subject to the same difficult conditions as he is in conventional war, he is subject to other pressures. These include not only legal and political restraints but also requirements to kill or wound without the motivational stimulus normally associated with the battlefield.
        o     Normally in conventional war the sniper needs no clearance to fire his shot. In urban guerrilla warfare the sniper must make every effort possible to determine in each case the need

to open fire, and that it constitutes reasonable/minimum force under the circumstances.

Hostage situations. Snipers and commanding officers must appreciate that even a well-placed shot <u>may not always</u> result in the instantaneous incapacitation of a terrorist. Even the best sniper when armed with the best weapon and bullet combination <u>cannot guarantee</u> the desired results. Even an instantly fatal shot <u>may not</u> prevent the death of a hostage when muscle spasms in the terrorist's body trigger his weapon. As a rule then, the sniper should be employed only when all other means of solving this situation have been exhausted.

o   <u>Accuracy requirements</u>. Consider the size of the target in a hostage situation. The only place on a man where if struck with a bullet instantaneous death will occur is the head. (Generally, the normal human being will live 8-10 seconds after being shot directly in the heart.) The entire head of a man is a relatively large target, measuring approximately 7 inches in width and 10 inches in height. But in order to narrow the odds and be more positive of an instant killing shot, the size of the target greatly reduces. The portion of the brain that controls all motor reflex actions is located directly behind the eyes and runs generally from ear lobe to ear lobe and is roughly 2 inches wide. In reality then, the size of the sniper's target is 2 inches, not 7 inches.

By applying the windage and elevation rule, it is easy to see then that the average sniper cannot and should not attempt to deliver an instantly-killing head shot beyond 200 meters. To ask him to do so requires him to do something that the rifle and ammunition combination available to him cannot do.

o   <u>Position selection</u>. Generally, the selection of a firing position for a hostage situation is not much different from selecting a firing position for any other form of combat. The same guidelines and rules apply. Remember, the terrain and situation will dictate the choice of firing positions.

Although the sniper should be used only as a last resort, he should be moved into his position as early as possible. This will enable him to precisely estimate his ranges, positively identify both the hostages and the terrorists, and select alternate firing positions for use if the situation should change.

o   <u>Command and control</u>. Once the decision has been made by the commander to employ the sniper, all command and control of his actions should pass to the sniper team leader. At no time should the sniper receive the command to fire from someone not in command. He should be given clearance to fire, and then he and the sniper team leader alone would decide exactly when.

If more than one sniper team is used to engage one or more targets, it is imperative that the same rules of engagement apply to all teams. But it will be necessary for snipers to communicate with each other. The most reliable method is to establish a "land line" or TA-312 phone loop much like a gun loop used in artillery battery firing positions. This enables all teams to communicate with all the others without confusion about frequencies, radio procedures, etc.

## Sniper Ambush in Urban Terrain

In cases where intelligence is forthcoming that a target will be in a specific place at a specific time, a sniper ambush is frequently a better alternative than a more cumbersome cordon operation.

Close reconnaissance is easier than in normal operations, as it can be carried out by the sniper as part of a normal patrol without raising any undue suspicion. The principal difficulty is getting the ambush party to its hide undetected. To place snipers in positions that are undetected will require some form of deception plan. This often takes the form of a routine search operation in at least platoon strength. During the course of the search, the snipers position themselves in their hide. They remain in position when the remainder of the force withdraws. This tactic is especially effective when carried out at night.

Once in position the snipers must be prepared to remain for lengthy periods in the closest proximity to the enemy and their sympathizers. Their security is tenuous at best. Most urban observation posts (OPs) have "dead spots", and this, combined with the fact that special ambush positions are frequently out of direct observation by other friendly forces, makes them highly susceptible to attack, especially from guerrillas armed with explosives. The uncertainty about being observed on entry is a constant worry to the snipers. It can and does have a most disquieting effect on the sniper and underlines the need for highly trained men of stable character.

If the ambush position cannot be directly supported from a permanent position, a "backup" force must be placed on immediate notice to extract the snipers after the ambush or in the event of compromise. Normally, it must be assumed that during the ambush the snipers cannot make their exit without assistance. They will be surrounded by large, extremely hostile crowds. Consequently, "backup" forces must not only be close at hand but also sufficient in size to handle the extraction of the snipers.

## 6-3. URBAN HIDES

14

A sniper team's success or failure in an urban area will greatly depend on each sniper's ability to place accurate fire on the enemy with the least possible exposure to enemy fire. Consequently, the sniper must constantly seek firing positions, and he must use them properly when he finds them. Positions in urban terrain are quite different than positions in the field. The sniper team normally has several places to choose from. These can range from inside attics to street-level positions in basements. This type of terrain is ideal for a sniper, and a sniper team can stop an enemy's advance through its area of responsibility. However, one important fact for the team to remember is that in this type of terrain the enemy will use every asset he has to detect and eliminate them. There are two types of firing positions: hasty and prepared.

## Hasty Hide

A hasty hide is normally occupied in the attack or the early stages of the defense. It is a position from which a sniper can place fire upon the enemy while using available cover to gain some degree of protection from enemy fire. Some of the more common hasty firing positions in a built-up area and techniques for occupying them are:

o  <u>Firing from corners of buildings</u>. The corner of a building provides cover for a hasty firing position if it is used properly. A sniper must be capable of firing his weapon from either shoulder to minimize body exposure to the enemy. A common mistake when firing around corners is firing from the standing position. The sniper exposes himself at the height the enemy would expect a target to appear and risks exposing the entire length of his body as a target for the enemy.

o  <u>Firing from behind walls</u>. When firing from behind a wall, the sniper must fire around cover when possible, not over it.

o  <u>Firing from windows</u>. In a built-up area windows provide readily accessible firing ports. However, the sniper must not allow his weapon to protrude beyond the window; it is an obvious sign of the firer's position, especially at night when the muzzle flash can easily be observed. A sniper should position himself as far into the room as possible to prevent the muzzle flash from being seen. He should fire from a supported position (table and sandbag) low enough to avoid silhouetting himself. He should use room shadow during darkness and leave blinds or shades drawn to a maximum to avoid being observed.

o  <u>Firing from an unprepared loophole</u>. The sniper may fire through a hole torn in the wall, thus avoiding the windows. He should stay as far from the loophole as possible so that the muzzle does not protrude beyond the wall, thus concealing the muzzle flash.

o   <u>Firing from the peak of a roof</u>.   The peak of a roof provides a vantage point for snipers that increases their field of vision and the ranges at which they can engage targets.   A chimney, a smokestack, or any other object protruding from the roof of a building can reduce the size of the target exposed and should be used.

o   <u>Firing when no cover is available</u>.   When no cover is available, target exposure can be reduced by firing from the prone position; firing from shadows, presenting no silhouette against buildings, skyline, etc.; and using tall grass, weeds, or shrubbery for concealment if available.

**Prepared Hide**
A prepared hide is one built or improved to allow the sniper to engage a particular area, avenue of approach, or enemy position while reducing his exposure to return fire.   Common sense and imagination are the sniper team's only limitation in the construction of urban hides.   There are several principles which must be followed in urban and field environments.   In urban environments the sniper must still avoid silhouetting, take into account refections and light refraction, and take particular care to minimize muzzle blast effects on dust, curtains, and other surroundings.   The team constructs and occupies one of the following positions or a variation thereof:

o   **Chimney hide**.   A chimney, or any other structure protruding through the roof of a building, provides a base from which a sniper position can be built (Figure 6-3-1).   Part of the roofing material is removed to allow the sniper to fire around the chimney while standing inside the building, on beams or a platform, with only his head and shoulders above the roof (behind the chimney).   Sandbags are used on the sides of the position to protect the sniper's flanks.

o   <u>Roof hide</u>.   When preparing a sniper position on a roof that has no protruding structure to provide protection, the position should be prepared underneath on the enemy side of the roof (Figure 6-3-2).   A small piece of roofing material should be removed to allow the sniper to engage targets in his sector.   The position is reinforced with sandbags and prepared so that the only sign that a position exists is the missing piece of roofing material.   Other pieces of roofing should be removed to deceive the enemy as to the true sniper position.   The sniper should not be visible from outside the building.   Care must be taken to hide the muzzle flash from outside the building.

o   <u>Room hide</u>.   In a room hide, the sniper team uses an existing room and fires through a window or loophole (Figure 6-3-3).   Weapon support may be achieved through the use of existing furniture--that is, desks or tables.   When selecting a position, teams must notice both front and back window positions.   To avoid

16

silhouetting, they may need to use a backdrop, such as a dark-colored blanket, canvas, carpet, and a screen. Screens (common screening material) are important since they allow the sniper teams maximum observation and deny observation by the enemy. They must not remove curtains; however, they can open windows or remove single panes of glass. Remember, teams can randomly remove panes in other windows so the position is not obvious. (For discussion on how glass affects ballistics, see Chapter 3).

o   <u>Crawl space hide</u>. The sniper team builds this position into the space between floors in multistory buildings (Figure 6-3-4). Loopholes are difficult to construct, but a damaged building helps considerably. Escape routes can be holes knocked into the floor or ceiling. Carpet or furniture placed over escape holes or replaced ceiling tiles will conceal them until needed.

o   <u>Rafter hide position</u>. The sniper team constructs this position in the attic of an A-frame-type buiding. These buildings normally have shingled roofs (Figure 6-3-5). Firing from inside the attic around a chimney or other structure helps prevent enemy observation and fire.

## Principles for Selecting and Occupying Sniper Firing Positions

o   Make maximum use of available cover and concealment.

o   Carefully select a new firing position before leaving an old one.

o   Avoid setting a pattern. The sniper should fire from both barricaded and unbarricaded windows.

o   The sniper position must never be subjected to traffic of other personnel, regardless of how well the sniper is hidden. Traffic will invite observation, and the sniper may be detected by optical devices. The sniper should be aware of backlighting that might silhouette him to the enemy.

o   Abandon a position from which two or three misses have been fired; detection is almost certain.

o   Operate from separate positions. In built-up areas, it is desirable that sniper team members operate from separate positions. Detection of two men in close proximity is very probable, considering the number of positions from which the enemy may be observing. The snipers should position themselves where they can provide mutual support.

o   Select alternate positions as well as supplementary positions to engage targets in any direction.

o   Always plan the escape route ahead of time.

17

o    Minimize the combustibility of selected positions (fireproofing).

o    A secure and quiet approach route.  This should, if possible, be free of garbage cans, crumbling walls, barking dogs, and other impediments.

o    A secure entry and exit point.  The more obvious and easily accessible entry/exit points are not necessarily the best, as their constant use during subsequent relief of sniper teams may more readily lead to compromise.

o    Good arcs of observation.  Restricted arcs are inevitable, but the greater the arc, the better.

o    Security.

o    Comfort.  This is the lowest priority, but still important.  Uncomfortable observing and firing positions can be maintained only for short periods.  If there is no adequate relief from observation, hides can rarely remain effective for more than a few hours.

## Characteristics of Urban Hides

o    The overriding requirement of a hide is that it must dominate its area of responsibility.

o    When selecting a suitable location, there is always a tendency to go for height.  In an urban operation this can be a mistake.  The greater the height attained, the more the sniper has to look out over an area and away from his immediate surroundings. For example, if a hide were established on the tenth floor of an apartment building, in order to see a road beneath, the sniper would have to lean out of the window, which does little for security.

o    The locations of incidents that the sniper might have to deal with are largely unpredictable, but the ranges are usually relatively short.  Consequently, a hide must cover its immediate surroundings as well as middle and far distances.  In residential areas this is rarely possible, as hides are forced off ground floor levels by passing pedestrians.  But, generally, it is not advisable to go above the second floor because to go higher greatly increases the deadspace in front of the hide.  This is not a cardinal rule, however.  Local conditions, such as being on a bus route, may force the sniper to go higher to avoid direct observation by passengers.

o    In view of this weakness in local defense of urban hides, the principle of mutual support between hides assumes even greater importance.  This need for mutual support is one reason why coordination and planning must take place at battalion level.

## When Constructing an Urban Position, the Sniper Team Must:

o     Always be aware of the outside appearance of the structure. Shooting through loopholes in barricaded windows is preferred; but, the team must make sure all other windows are also barricaded. Building loopholes in other windows also provides more than one position to fire from. When building loopholes, the team should make them different shapes (not perfect squares or circles). Dummy loopholes also confuse the enemy. Positions in attics are also effective. The team removes the shingles and cuts out loopholes in the roof; however, they must make sure there are other shingles missing from the roof so that the firing position loophole is not obvious.

o     Not locate the position against contrasting background or in prominent buildings that automatically draw attention. The team must stay in the shadows while moving, observing, and engaging targets.

o     Never fire close to a loophole. The team must always back away from the hole as far as possible to hide the muzzle flash and to muffle the sound of the weapon when it fires. Some positions can be located in a different room than the one the loophole is in by making a hole through a wall to connect the two and firing from inside the far room. Thus, the sniper is forming a "double baffle" with his loopholes by constructing two loopholes in succession. This will further reduce his muzzle flash and blast, and improve his concealment from enemy observation. The team must not fire continually from one position. (This is why more than one position should be constructed if time and the situation permit.) When constructing other positions, the team makes sure the target area can be observed. Sniper team positions should never be used by any personnel other than a sniper team.

## Possible Hide/OP locations

o     Old derelict buildings. Special attention should be paid to the possibility of encountering booby traps. One proven method of detecting guerrilla booby traps is to notice if the locals (especially children) move in and about the building freely.

o     Occupied houses. After careful observation of the inhabitants' daily routine, snipers can move into occupied homes and establish hides/OPs in basements and attics. This method was used very successfully by the British in Northern Ireland.

o     Shops.

o     Schools and churches. When using these buildings as hide/OP locations, the snipers risk possible damage to what might already be strained public relations.

o    Factories, sheds, and garages.

o    Basements and between floors in buildings. It is possible for the sniper team to locate itself in these positions, although there may be no window or readily usable firing port available. These locations require that the sniper remove bricks or stones without leaving any noticeable evidence outside the building. To do this, the sniper must carefully measure the width of the mortar around a selected brick/stone. He must them construct a frame exactly the size of the selected brick with the frame edges exactly the size of the surrounding mortar. He then carefully removes the brick from the wall and places it in his frame. Next, he crushes the mortar and glues it to the frame so that it blends perfectly with the untouched mortar still in place. He then places the brick/frame combination back into the wall. From the outside nothing appears abnormal, while inside the sniper team has create an extremely difficult-to-detect firing port. Care must be taken, however, when firing from his position that dust does not get blown about by the muzzle blast and that the brick/frame combination is immediately replaced. Another difficulty encountered with this position is that it offers a very restricted field of view.

o    Rural areas from which urban areas can be observed.

## Manning the Sniping Hides/OP

Before moving into the hide/OP, the snipers must have the following information:

o    The exact nature of the mission (observe, shoot, etc.).

o    The length of stay.

o    The local situation.

o    Procedure and timing for entry.

o    Emergency evacuation procedures.

o    Radio procedures.

o    Movement of any friendly troops.

o    Procedure and timing for exit.

o    Any special equipment needed.

The well-tried and understood principle of remaining back from windows and other apertures when in buildings has a marked effect on the manning of hides/OPs. The field of view from the back of a room through a window is limited. To enable a worthwhile area to be covered, two, or even three, men may have to observe at one time from different parts of the room.

## Sniper Techniques in Urban Hides

o      The second floor of a building is usually the best location for the position.  It presents minimal dead space but provides the team more protection since passersbys cannot easily spot it.

o      Normally, a window is the best viewing aperture/loophole.

*      If the window is dirty, do not clean it for better viewing.

*      If curtains are prevalent in the area, do not remove those in the position.  Lace or net-type curtains can be seen through from the inside, but they are difficult to see through from the outside.

*      If strong winds blow the curtains open, staple, tack, or weigh them down.

*      Firing a round through a curtain has little effect on accuracy; however, ensure the muzzle is far enough away to avoid muzzle blast.

*      When area routine indicates open curtains, follow suit.  Set up well away from the viewing aperture; however, ensure effective coverage of the assigned target area.

o      Firing through glass should be avoided since more than one shot may be required.  The team considers the following options:

*      Break or open several windows throughout the position before occupation.  This can be done during the reconnaissance phase of the operation; however, avoid drawing attention to the area.

*      Remove or replace panes of glass with plastic sheeting.

o      Other loopholes/viewing apertures are nearly unlimited.

*      Battle damage.

*      Drilled holes (hand drill).

*      Brick removal.

*      Loose boards/derelict houses.

21

o       Positions can also be set up in attics or between the ceiling and roof.  (See rafter hide positions).

        *       Gable ends close to the eaves (shadow adding to con-cealment).

        *       Battle damage to gables and/or roof.

        *       Loose or removed tiles, shingles, or slates.

        *       Skylights.

o       The sniper makes sure the bullet clears the loophole. The muzzle must be far enough from the loophole and the rifle boresighted to ensure the bullet's path is not in line with the bottom of the loophole.

o       Front drops, usually netting, may have to be changed (if the situation permits) from dark to light colors at BMNT/EENT due to sunlight or lack of sunlight into the position.

o       If the site is not multi-roomed, partitions can be made by hanging blankets or nets to separate the operating area from the rest/administrative area.

o       If sandbags are required, they can be filled and carried, inside of rucksacks or can be filled in the basement, depending on the situation/location of the position site.

o       Always plan an escape route that leads to the objective rally point.  When forced to vacate the position, the team meets the reaction force at the ORP.  Normally, the team will not be able to leave from the same point at which it gained access; therefore, a separate escape point may be required in emergency situations. The team must consider windows (other than the viewing apertures); anchored ropes to climb down building or a small, preset explosive charge situation on a wall or floor for access into adjoining rooms, buildings, or the outside.

o       The type of uniform or camouflage to be worn by the team will be dictated by the situation, how the team is employed, and area of operation.  The following applies:

        *       Most often, the normal BDU uniform and required equipment are worn.

        *       Urban-camouflaged uniforms can be made or purchased. Urban areas vary greatly in color (mostly gray <cinder block>; red <brick>; white <marble>; black <granite>; or stucco, clay, or wood).  Regardless of area color, uniforms should include angular-line patterns.

*      When necessary, most woodland-patterned BDUs can be worn outside as they are a gray or green-gray color underneath.

*      Soft-soled shoes or boots are the preferred footwear in the urban environment.

*      Civilian clothing can be worn (native/host country populace).

*      Tradesmen's or construction workers' uniforms and accessories can be used.

NOTE:      It is advisable to include a heavy-duty staple gun and wasp spray.

## 6-4. WEAPONS CHARACTERISTICS IN URBAN TERRAIN

The characteristics of built-up areas and the nature of urban warfare impact on both the effectiveness of sniper systems and how they may be employed. The following basic factors must be considered by the sniper during urban operations:

o      <u>Structural Configuration of Buildings</u>. The basic classes of structures encountered in a built-up area can generally be classified as concrete, masonry, or wooden. However, any one building may include a combination of these materials. All buildings offer concealment, even though the degree of protection varies with the material used. The 7.62x51mm NATO ball cartridge will penetrate at 200 meters:

*      Fifty inches of pinewood boards.

*      Ten inches of loose sand.

*      Three inches of concrete.

o      <u>Glass Penetration</u>. If the situation should require firing through glass, the sniper should know two things:

*      When the M118 ammunition penetrates glass, in most cases, the copper jacket is stripped off its lead core and the core fragments. These fragments will injure or kill should they hit either the hostage or the terrorist. The fragments show no standard pattern, but randomly fly in a cone-shaped pattern, much like shot from a shotgun. Even when the glass is angled to as much as 45 degrees, the lead core will not show any signs of deflection up to <u>6 feet</u> past the point of impact with the glass.

*      When the bullet impacts with the glass, the glass will shatter and explode back into the room. The angle of the bullet impact with the glass has absolutely no bearing on the

23

direction of the shattered glass. The shattered glass will always fly perpendicular to the pane of the glass.

## 6-5.   ENGAGEMENT TECHNIQUES

### Simultaneous Shooting

Shooting simultaneously with another sniper is a very important skill to develop, and requires much practice. Procedure as follows:

o       Team leader requests, "Sniper status."

o       Snipers respond by numbers, "One on," "Two on," "Three off." "Four on."

o       Team leader will respond with "Fire," or "Hold."

o       If it is the Green Light, "Fire," all snipers will shoot simultaneously (within 1/4 second).

o       Or the team leader may indicate, "One and four Fire."

o       All commands should be repeated twice, "Command Fire, Fire."

o       After shooting the sniper will acknowledge, "Shot out."

o       This is an exercise best practiced on balloons for a visual indication of simultaneous impact.

### Green Light Command

Also known as the "Fire Command", this command will generally be given by the senior man in the command post (CP). He may make the decision but then leave the command to the assault element team leader, so that it may be better coordinated with the rescue effort. The actual command must be given twice, "Command Fire, Fire!", to avoid any misunderstanding. The controller may just be saying, "Wait for me to say "Fire," but when the sniper hears, "...fire" he may shoot.

During a Continuous Green Light the sniper will radio "Shot out" after firing each time.

### Count-Down System

This is a verbal count-down by the CP or team leader.
For simultaneous fire:
        5
        4
        3
        2
        1-all snipers fire immediately

24

Sniper-initiated assault:
       5
       4
       3-sniper fire
       2-blast from stun grenades or breaching charge
       1-assault team moves in

Night Shot:
       5
       4
       3
       2-lights on target
       1-snipers fire
             Snipers #1 & #2 immediately relocate after muzzle
             flash.

Window Shot:
       5
       4
       3
       2-first sniper fires and breaks glass
       1-second sniper engages target
             If glass must be shattered to provide a clear shot
             for the primary sniper to engage his priority
             target, it is best if the support sniper also
             aims his "window breaking" bullet at the
             target. This way, two projectiles have been
             aimed at the target, increasing the likelihood
             of a hit.

## Stockholm Syndrome

This is a problem that can affect a sniper required to watch
a suspect for long periods through a high magnification telescope.
Limit the amount of information the sniper is given about the
suspect during the briefing period. Personal information that has
no impact on the tactical situation of the operation should be
minimized. The syndrome can manifest itself by the sniper
developing sympathies and feelings toward the suspect, caused by
long periods of very close observation. A sniper must almost psych
himself in the opposite direction to combat this.

## 6-6.  URBAN TRICKS OF THE TRADE

       o    Urban camouflage:  A bulky, light-weight hooded smock
works best in the urban areas. Select colors for the smock that
will blend with the colors and types of building materials in the
area.

       o    Avoid movement during daylight, but if necessary, keep
movements slow and deliberate.

o     During movements through or occupation of building rooms, be alert to the principles of camouflage and concealment.  Do not allow "Being Inside" lull you into a reduced awareness of the surroundings.

o     Stay in shadows, match clothing to blend with the room/area; hang black sheets to eliminate backlighting against openings or light sources.

o     Don't be the only open window in an air-conditioned building.  Use existing curtains and leave windows intact.  To make a "shooting hole", remove one pane or small corner of the glass.

o     Move into the area with help from the host nation.

o     Blend into the activities of the area, i.e., maintenance crew, etc., civilian clothing and civilian luggage (guitar cases will always look out of place).

o     You will have the ability to carry in more equipment.

o     You will be working in sniper teams and with multiple sniper teams to cover the entire area.

o     Choose a position (if possible) that is naturally in a shadow; if not possible, make your own shadows by building a "cave" with dark cloth.

o     Wear dark clothing to match the background.

o     Stay back from the window.

o     Don't flag your weapon in your loophole.

o     If time allows, make crawl holes from room to room.

o     Avoid background light, such as doors opening behind you.

o     Be careful of neutral personnel; handle with care.

o     Firing positions (roof tops):

     *     Stay below peak line as much as possible.

     *     Don't overhang barrel.

     *     If you are going to be in position a long time, put up some type of shade.

     *     Try to find a position that has a background of some type.

o   Equipment for urban operations

    *    Camera.

    *    Commo equipment (snipers and command).

    *    Food and water.

    *    Spotting scope with stand.

    *    Binoculars.

    *    Dark cloth.

    *    Roofing hammer with nails.

    *    Tape.

    *    Glass cutter.

    *    Complete cleaning kit.

    *    Multi-purpose knife.

    *    Silenced pistol.

    *    Notebook, pencils, and tape recorder.

    *    Sleeping/shooting pad.

**6-3-3**

**6-3-4**

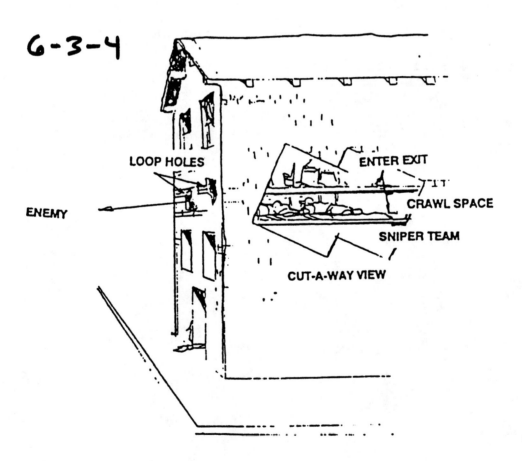

LOOP HOLES

ENTER EXIT

ENEMY

CRAWL SPACE

SNIPER TEAM

CUT-A-WAY VIEW

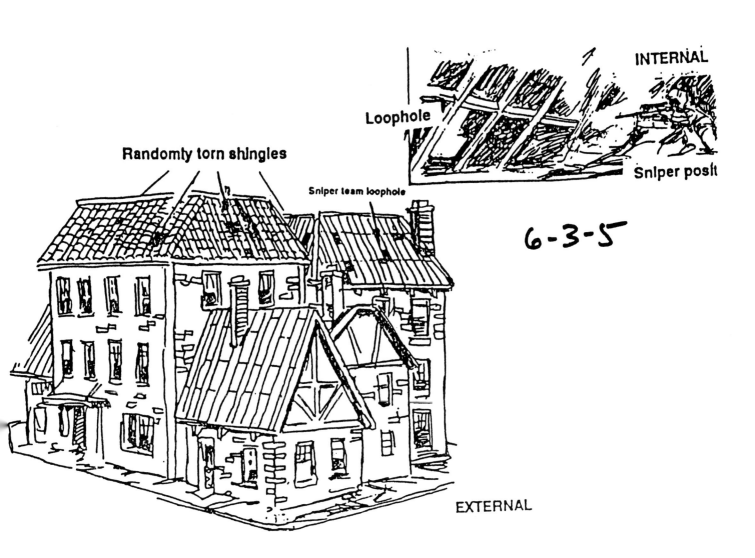

Randomly torn shingles

Sniper team loophole

Loophole

INTERNAL

Sniper posit

EXTERNAL

6-3-5

# Chapter 7

## SELECTING AND TAILORING AMMUNITION

### 7-1. GENERAL

WARNING: The Special Operations Target Interdiction Course, of the United States Army John F. Kennedy Special Warfare Center and School, Fort Bragg, N.C. cannot and does not accept any liability, either expressed or implied, for results of damage or injury arising from or alleged to have arisen from the use of data contained in this manual.

Because of the nature of special operations sniping, the SO sniper may not always have a steady supply of ammunition. If this is the case, the sniper himself will have to reload the best bullet/powder combination available from battlefield recovery. At other times, certain situations may arise in which issued ammunition will not do the job, for example, against hard/materiel targets. Therefore, the SO sniper must have an in-depth knowledge of what actually makes one round of ammunition more accurate than another. To acquire this knowledge, the sniper must learn how to reload ammunition. The guiding principle of marksmanship that also applies to reloading is: **ACCURACY IS THE PRODUCT OF UNIFORMITY!**

### 7-2. COMPONENTS OF THE RIFLE CARTRIDGE

The rifle cartridge has four basic components: cartridge case, bullet, powder, and primer. Three of these components (bullet, powder, and primer) are consumed during firing. The case remains after firing is completed. This case is the base component used in all reloading.

Cartridge Case. The cartridge case normally is made of brass, a malleable metal alloy. The case can be resized and reloaded repeatedly, up to 15 to 20 times, with proper care, cleaning, and trimming.

Primers. Primers are of two types: berdan and boxer (Figure 7-2-1). All USA-made cases are boxer primed. The boxer-primed case has one flash hole in the center of the case base. This case can be deprimed with a small pin punch. However, the sniper should be able to identify both types of primers. The berdan-primed case (European) has two or three small flash holes off center in the base of the case. This case can only be deprimed by using hydraulic pressure or by prying the primer out of the case.

Powder. Powder is made in three common forms: ball, extruded (tubular), and flake. Powder is made by two different processes:

single base and double base. For this reason powder can never be identified by its appearance alone.

   Bullet. The bullet is the most important part of the rifle cartridge. There are many designs available for reloading, but full metal-jacketed bullets are used primarily for military purposes. To obtain the best possible accuracy, the bullet design and weight must be matched to the rifle barrel diameter and rate of twist. Also, the flight characteristics of the bullet, which are controlled by the bullet's sectional density and ballistic coefficient, must be known.

## Characteristics of Cartridge Components

Cartridge Case Designs (Figure 7-2-2):

- o  Rimmed.
- o  Semirimmed.
- o  Rimless.
- o  Belted.
- o  Bottlenecked.
- o  Straight walled.

Cartridge Case Materials:

- o  Brass.
- o  Aluminium.
- o  Steel (lacquered).
- o  Steel (copper washed).

   Headspace: The measurement of the cartridge case that determines the safety and accuracy of ammunition (Figure 7-2-3). A cartridge's headspace is unique to its case design and caliber as follows:

- o  Rimmed.  Headspaces on the rim thickness.

- o  Rimless and bottlenecked.  Headspaces from the base of the case to the datum line (middle) of the shoulder.

- o  Rimless and straight walled.  Headspaces from the base of the case to the edge of the case mouth.

- o  Belted.  Headspaces from the base of the case to the edge of the front shoulder of the belt.

Bullet Styles and Ballistic Characteristics (Figure 7-2-4):

- o  Round nose.  Rapid deceleration, high arc.

- o  Spitzer nose.  More aerodynamic, flattens trajectory.

2

 o Flat base. Less aerodynamic than the boat tail.

 o Boat tail. More aerodynamic, more effective shape.

 o Combinations. Spitzer/boat tail, most aerodynamic shape.

Priming Systems:

 o Rimfire. Non-reloadable.

 o Centerfire. Boxer or berdan, reloadable.

Propellant Types and Forms:

 o Types:

  * Black powder.
  * Smokeless powder.

 o Forms:

  * Ball.
  * Tubular.
  * Flake.

## Metric System of Cartridge Designations

 o The first numerical designation is the projectile diameter in millimeters.

 o The second numerical designation is the case length in millimeters.

 o Rimmed cases may be further designated with an "R" suffix denoting that the casing design is rimmed.

 Example: 7.62x51mm = .308 Winchester (7.62mm/.308 inch diameter bullet with a 51mm/2.00 inch case length)

## 7-3. RELOADING

 In this manual two types or methods of reloading the rifle cartridge will be covered: the Lee Loader reloading kit and the bench-mounted compound press reloading system. The concepts, principles of operation, and general procedures are the same, but they differ in depth, and the quality of the final product.

## Lee Loader
 The first method of reloading is done with the Lee Loader reloading kit. This is a small, lightweight, hand-held reloading system that can easily fit into a rucksack. Yet, if used

3

carefully, this reloading kit will produce a satisfactory rifle cartridge. The steps are as follows:

(1)  Deprime the case.

(2)  Resize the case neck.

(3)  Prime the case.

(4)  Tap the case loose from the resizing die.

(5)  Put the correct amount of powder in the case.

(6)  Seat the bullet in the case to the proper depth.

(7)  Check to see if the round will chamber in the rifle.

## Lee Loader Reloading Instructions

The Lee Loader reloading kit instructions are reprinted here in case the instructions in the issued kit are missing or incomplete.

(1)  Knock out the old primer.

(2)  With a plastic mallet or piece of wood, drive the case into the tool flush with the end.

(3)  Insert a primer into the locating ring.  Place the tool, with shell inside, on the priming chamber.  Lightly tap on the priming rod several times until the primer is home.  NEVER TRY TO SEAT A PRIMER DEEPER AFTER THE POWDER HAS BEEN ADDED.

(4)  Place the tool on the decapping chamber and tap the rod to free the case.  LEAVE THE CASE IN THIS POSITION FOR THE NEXT THREE STEPS.

(5)  Add 1 level measure of powder.  BE SURE YOU HAVE THE CORRECT MEASURE AND POWDER.  SEE THE CHARGE TABLE.

(6)  TO AVOID CONTACT WITH THE PRIMER AND POSSIBLE EXPLOSION, CASE MUST BE FREE FROM DIE AND RESTING IN THE DECAPPING CHAMBER. Insert the bullet through the top.

(7)  TO AVOID CONTACT WITH THE PRIMER AND POSSIBLE EXPLOSION, CASE MUST BE FREE FROM DIE AND RESTING IN THE DECAPPING CHAMBER. Insert the bullet seater and tap until it contacts the stop collar. The stop collar is adjustable so you can seat the bullet as required.

## Bench-mounted Compound-press Reloading System

The second method of reloading is done with the bench-mounted compound-press (R.C.B.S., Lyman, or Pacific).  This is the best, most precise, and most efficient method to use. Unfortunately, the press system is expensive, requires more space, and is heavy because of the amount of equipment required. The specific instructions in the owner's manuals should be followed in detail. The general steps of reloading ammunition using the bench-mounted press are as follows:

(1) Wipe the case clean to prevent dirt from scratching the case and the inside surface of the sizer die. Inspect the case for cracks, splits, and other obvious flaws. If any flaws are present, discard the case.

(2) Lubricate the outside of the case lightly by rolling the case over the lubricating pad. This permits the case to be inserted into the sizer die without sticking.

(3) Lubricate the inside of the case neck with the case neck brush.

(4) Screw the sizer die into the press and adjust the press. Put the shell holder in the press.

(5) Raise the press handle and slide the case into the shell holder.
(6) Gently but firmly lower the press handle and run the case all the way into the die. This operation will resize the case and punch out the fired primer from the bottom of the case.

(7) While the case is still inside the die, insert a live primer, open end up, into the cup of the primer arm.

(8) Push the primer arm forward into the shell holder priming arm slot and hold it there.

(9) Gently and slowly raise the press handle. As the case is drawn out of the die, it will be lowered onto the live primer, which will be seated into the primer pocket. Inspect the primer to make sure it is properly seated. Wipe the case clean of lubricant.

(10) Using a deburring tool, remove any rough edges from inside and outside the brass mouth. The case is now ready for powder charging.

(11) Consult one of the many reloading manuals to learn what kind and weight of powder should be used for the specific cartridge and bullet style and weight. Then weigh the recommended powder charge on the scale.

(12) After you have accurately weighed the powder, pour it into the case through a powder funnel.

(13) Most reloaders use a powder measure for powder charging cases. This tool saves the time of weighing every powder charge when reloading a quantity of cases.

(14) You are now ready for the final step of reloading the cartridge: seating the bullet. Unscrew the sizer die from the press and push the press handle down as far as it will go.

(15) Screw the bullet seater die into the press unit until it touches the raised shell holder. Then unscrew the die about three-quarters of a turn and tighten the main lock ring.

(16) Unscrew the seater plug seven or eight turns.

(17) Raise the press handle and insert the case into the shell holder.

(18) Holding the bullet over the mouth of the case with one hand, lower the press handle with the other hand and run the bullet and case into the die.

(19) Screw the seater plug downward until it touches the bullet. Raise the press handle and check the bullet and case for overall length. Repeat this procedure, lowering the seat plug until the overall cartridge length is correct and the cartridge will function reliably through the magazine of the rifle. Tighten the lock rings. A few adjustments may be necessary to get the proper and final bullet seating depth.

(20) The reloaded rifle cartridge is now ready to be fired.

## Accuracy Reloading Techniques

Accuracy reloading techniques center around the principle of making all of the rounds of ammunition as identical as humanly possible to each other. **ACCURACY IS THE PRODUCT OF UNIFORMITY!** As these techniques are equipment and time intensive, an overview only is given to provide a background and stimulate further exploration and research.

Component Selection

o    All components of the same lot number (printed on the box).

o    Components of "Match" grade or quality.

o    Powder selection based on case-filling capacity and velocity.

Case Preparation

o    Neck-sized is best if used in a bolt action rifle.

6

o   Square off the case head.

o   Trim cases to the same length.

o   Deburr case mouth.

o   Uniform flash hole.

o   Uniform primer pocket.

o   Remove crimp from primer pocket of US military brass.
o   Weigh cases. Discard cases that do not fall within the average weight +/- 2.0 grains (7.62x51mm NATO).

## Cartridge Assembly

o   Seat primers with hand-held priming tools.

o   Seat bullet with a floating-chamber type seater.

## Cartridge Measurements

o   Cartridge case resized 0.001 inches shorter than headspace measurement to minimize case stretching and ensuring reliability. This is for semiautomatic rifles. For bolt action rifles, neck sizing with a collet-type die is best.

o   Neck run-out is 0.002 inches or less.

o   Bullet run-out is 0.002 inches or less.

o   Bullet seated out to within 0.005 inches of the rifling lead. This minimizes the bullet "jump." Ensure that the cartridge fits into the magazine and feeds reliably.

## Ammunition Testing

o   Chronograph testing can be conducted simultaneously with the grouping capability. The hand-loaded ammunition must provide the same trajectory as issue M118 for the ballistic cam to work properly. The standard deviations (SD) of the velocity averages should be 12 fps or less. If the SDs are greater than 12 fps, check the grouping capability.

## Ballistic Information

| Ammunition | Bullet | Muzzle Velocity | Remarks |
|---|---|---|---|
| M118 | 173 FMJBT | 2610 fps | issue |
| Federal 308M | 168 HPBT | 2650 fps | accurate |
| Handload | 168 HPBT | 2625 fps | (1) |
| Handload | 180 HPBT | 2600 fps | (2) |

Remarks:

(1). This handload duplicates the M118 out to 700 meters. It is only 3 inches (0.4 MOA) below the M118 at this distance. This is the maximum range for this bullet. Bullets undergo increased turbulence when they decelerate through the sound barrier ("going sub-sonic"). This destabilizing effect occurs between 900-1300 fps. This effect determines the "maximum effective range" of a bullet. Sierra rates their 168 HPBT MatchKing bullet effective out to 600 yards.

(2). This handload duplicates the M118 out to 1000 meters. It is 3.1 inches below the M118 at 1000 meters (0.31 MOA). It can be considered a ballistic duplicate but with a higher quality bullet.

## Barrel Twist and Bullet Compatibility

For optimal accuracy, the barrel twist must be compatible with the bullet selected. As a general rule, as the bullet weight increases, barrel twist must "speed up." For a given bullet diameter, as the weight increases, the bullet becomes longer. As the bullet increases in length (and weight) it must be spun faster for adequate stabilization. For example, consider the .308 Winchester with 150 and 190 grain bullets. The 150 grain bullet is well stabilized in a barrel with a 1 turn in 12 inch twist (1/12). The 190 grain bullet can be stabilized in a 1/12 twist, but it provides better long-range accuracy and stability with a 1/10 twist. To determine an approximation for the bullet's correct twist rate, the Greenhill formula is quite accurate:

$$\text{Barrel Twist} = \frac{(150)(\text{Bullet Diameter})(\text{Bullet Diameter})}{\text{Bullet Length}}$$

## Reloading Manuals and Reference Books

Many manuals and books have been published on the subject of reloading ammunition. The following are recommended for reading and studying:

o    <u>Sierra Bullets Rifle Reloading Manual</u>, 3rd Edition.

o    _Hornady Handbook of Cartridge Reloading._

o    _Hand Loader's Digest._

o    _ABC's of Reloading._

## 7-4.  BATTLEFIELD RECOVERY OF AMMUNITION

Any 7.62mm/.308-inch diameter bullet found throughout the world may be used to reload the 7.62x51mm NATO (.308 Winchester) cartridge case.  This reloaded cartridge, with the correct powder and primer combination, can then be fired in the 7.62x51mm NATO SWS.  Although satisfactory, this ammunition would not be of high quality and should be used only in the event that M118 Special Ball ammunition is not available.

Using the above principle, a SO sniper can use an expended case from his own rifle and a captured enemy round of the appropriate caliber, broken down for its bullet and powder, to create a 7.62x51mm cartridge.  With this capability, the sniper needs to carry only an 11-ounce Lee Loader and a supply of large rifle primers.  (A thousand primers will fit into a box 2 inches by 2 inches by 4 1/2 inches and will weigh only 9 ounces.)

The extreme variance between different countries' specifications for ammunition makes the listing of specific load data beyond the scope of this handbook.  Specific load data would, however, be suitable for inclusion in an area study.

**Battlefield Recovery Guidelines:**

o    A lighter bullet may be substituted for a heavier bullet, but never vice versa.

o    A slower burning powder may be substituted for a faster burning powder but never vice versa.

o    A 7.62x54mm R 180 gn FMJBT bullet with 42 grains of powder can be loaded into a 7.62x51mm NATO cartridge case.

o    A 7.62x39mm 120-123 gn FMJFB (flat base) bullet with 42 grains of powder can be loaded into a 7.62x51mm NATO cartridge case.

9

7-2-1

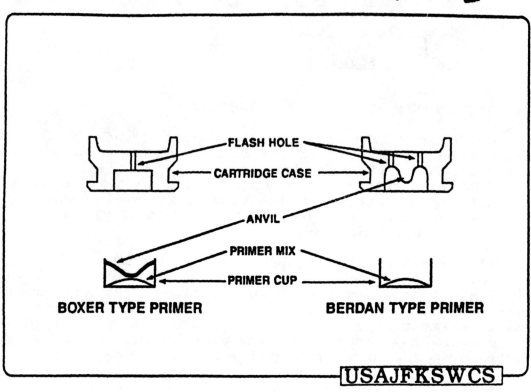

FLASH HOLE

CARTRIDGE CASE

ANVIL

PRIMER MIX

PRIMER CUP

BOXER TYPE PRIMER

BERDAN TYPE PRIMER

USAJFKSWCS

7-2-2

# CASE TYPES

RIMMED          SEMI-RIMMED          RIMLESS          REBATED          BELTED

USAJFKSWCS

# HEAD SPACE

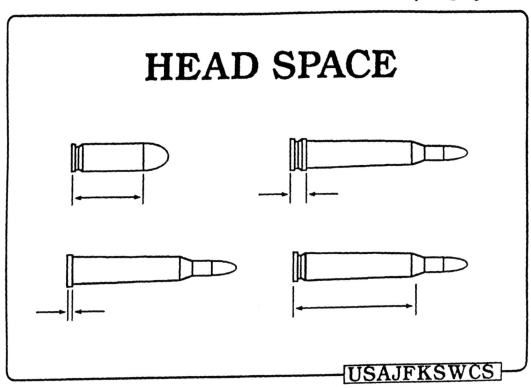

# BULLET SHAPE

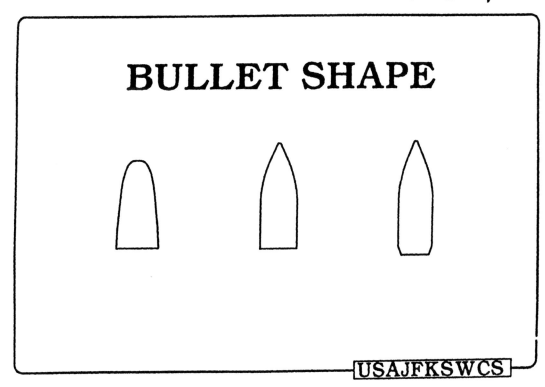

# Appendix A

## TRICKS OF THE TRADE

o  If several snipers are allocated to a high value target (HVT) and cannot agree on the range (with associated scope adjustments), the snipers can each place the range data on his telescope according to his own best estimate. The snipers would then fire simultaneously, and the percentage of obtaining a hit would be magnified.

o  When operating in a denied area, it sometimes is appropriate to use an indigenous weapon and ammunition. The evidence left (casings or recovered bullets) would disguise the true identity of the sniper, and the sponsor.

o  The sniper must be aware of the ground beneath the muzzle of his rifle. This is critical when the ground is sandy, dusty, or loose soil. The sniper should either wet the area (urinating will save valuable drinking water) or cover with a suitably sized cloth. Also, in damp conditions (early morning) the sniper should be aware of the possibility of the exhaust smoke indicating the position. An area with broken ground or foliage will help to conceal the smoke signature. But, the sniper should be aware of the muzzle blast moving tall grass and small plants. The sniper must choose his position carefully.

o  It is possible for thousands of bullets to pass by or come close to the sniper without doing any harm.

o  When in a static position, it is wise to build the sniper hide to provide a direction of fire at an angle to the front of the enemy. This provides cover and concealment, and the enemy that is hit by the sniper's fire will look to their front for his location.

o  If the sniper suspects that his system has lost its zero, and the situation allows sighting shots, the sniper should use "self-marking" targets that do not betray his direction of fire. The sniper may use pools of water, cement walls, brick, etc. He should not use cans, boxes, or other targets that can be used to sight back on azimuth to his location.

o  The sniper should locate his sniper hide in a location away from any obvious target reference points. If it looks like an obvious position, it is.

o  Before taking the shot, especially at longer ranges where the arc of the bullet will be quite high, the sniper should visualize the arc of the bullet. This ensures that there will be no obstacles in the path of the bullet. The sniper should consider this the "mask and over-head clearance" of the sniper rifle.

o Selection of the final firing point is critical to mission success. If the target is expected to be moving, the sniper should select a position that allows a shot at the target as it moves toward or away from him. Relative to the sniper's position, the target will be a stationary one, and therefore, require a no-lead hold.

o If it is necessary to engage a unit of enemy personnel, the sniper should engage the targets that are the greatest threat to him and his team's survival. If this is not a factor, he should engage the targets farthest away from him, and not in the front of the enemy formation. If he hits the front-most targets first, the remainder of the unit will deploy and conduct fire and movement to pin the sniper down and engage him. By eliminating the rear-most targets first, the sniper buys himself more time as their numbers will be decreased, possibly without their knowledge, and ensures the sniper with the best possible (least suspecting) targets.

o The sniper and his weapon can be of great help in the counter-ambush immediate action drill. The sniper should look for target indicators (muzzle flash, disturbed vegetation, ejecting brass, etc.) and use a "searching fire" technique where he fires rounds approximately nine inches from the ground, every six inches into the suspected enemy location. The M-21/LSR is best for this because of its capacity, and rapid fire capability.

o Recommended ammunition selection for the M-21/LSR for night operations: 1 tracer per two match rounds, with the last three rounds tracer to signify the necessity for a magazine change.

o When dealing with multiple targets, such as two hostage-takers covered by the sniper and another team sniper, he will need to coordinate with his colleague so that they fire simultaneously. Taking them out one at a time may allow the second suspect time to harm the hostages. One technique, if the snipers are within earshot or in radio contact with each other on a clear frequency, is for each of them to keep saying aloud in a steady, low voice,"Wait...wait...wait..." so long as they do not have a clear shot. When they do, they should stay silent and listen for the moment they are both silent. They should allow a one-second pause, then open fire together. In some cases, two snipers are assigned to engage a single suspect, particularly if he is behind heavy glass and there is fear that shots may be deflected. One option here is for one of the snipers to aim for his head, and the other for his chest, and fire simultaneously.

o CT situation: hostage-takers have been known to switch clothes with the hostages. This requires the sniper to distinguish facial features, and places a premium on higher-powered spotting scopes and rifle telescopes.
o The position behind a loophole should be darkened with a drape so that the sniper is not silhouetted or light allowed

through the loophole. The sniper should shut his loopholes when anyone enters or exits the hide.

o  The observer can tell if the target is hit. The target's response is similar to that of big-game. An animal which is fired at and missed always stands tense for the fraction of a second before it bounds away, but when an animal is struck by the bullet there is no pause. It bounds away at once on the impact, or falls. Thus, a stag shot through the heart commences his death rush at once, to fall dead within 50 yards, whereas a stag missed gives that tell-tale sudden start. If a human is hit well, he will fall forward or appear to crumple like a ragdoll. Continued activity or falling to the side indicates a superficial hit.

o  Speed is important. The sniper should practice for an aimed shot in 2 seconds or less.

o  The sniper should use armor-piercing (AP) rounds for anti-materiel missions to take out the weapon, not the crew. The crew is easier to replace.

Appendix B

BALLISTIC CHARTS

# SIERRA BALLISTICS III
**********************

```
DATA FOR: 7.62MM M118 M24        BC'S:   .515(H), .503(M), .491(L)
COMPANY: Sierra     TEMP:  59   PRESSURE: 29.53 IN.   HUMIDITY:  78%
ZERO: 100 meters        CROSSWIND: -10.00 mph      TAIL WIND:  +0.00 mph
ELEVATION ANGLE:   0 degs  ALTITUDE:       0 feet   SIGHT HGT. 1.7 IN
```

| RANGE METERS | VELOCITY (FPS) | ENERGY (FT-LB) | BULLET PATH(IN) | DROP (INCH) | DRIFT (INCH) | TIME OF FLIGHT(SEC) |
|---|---|---|---|---|---|---|
| 0 | 2,610.0 | 2,616 | -1.7 | +0.0 | +0.0 | 0.000000 |
| 25 | 2,561.9 | 2,521 | -0.7 | -0.2 | -0.1 | 0.031719 |
| 50 | 2,514.3 | 2,428 | -0.0 | -0.7 | -0.2 | 0.064037 |
| 75 | 2,467.2 | 2,338 | +0.2 | -1.7 | -0.5 | 0.096969 |
| 100 | 2,420.6 | 2,250 | +0.0 | -3.1 | -0.9 | 0.130533 |
| 125 | 2,374.4 | 2,165 | -0.6 | -4.9 | -1.3 | 0.164745 |
| 150 | 2,328.8 | 2,083 | -1.7 | -7.2 | -1.9 | 0.199625 |
| 175 | 2,283.7 | 2,003 | -3.3 | -9.9 | -2.7 | 0.235191 |
| 200 | 2,239.1 | 1,925 | -5.4 | -13.2 | -3.5 | 0.271464 |
| 225 | 2,194.9 | 1,850 | -8.0 | -17.0 | -4.5 | 0.308463 |
| 250 | 2,151.2 | 1,777 | -11.1 | -21.3 | -5.6 | 0.346210 |
| 275 | 2,108.0 | 1,707 | -14.8 | -26.2 | -6.9 | 0.384726 |
| 300 | 2,065.3 | 1,638 | -19.1 | -31.6 | -8.3 | 0.424036 |
| 325 | 2,023.2 | 1,572 | -24.0 | -37.7 | -9.8 | 0.464162 |
| 350 | 1,981.5 | 1,508 | -29.5 | -44.4 | -11.5 | 0.505128 |
| 375 | 1,940.4 | 1,446 | -35.6 | -51.8 | -13.3 | 0.546959 |
| 400 | 1,899.8 | 1,386 | -42.5 | -59.8 | -15.3 | 0.589681 |
| 425 | 1,859.7 | 1,328 | -50.1 | -68.6 | -17.4 | 0.633319 |
| 450 | 1,820.3 | 1,273 | -58.4 | -78.1 | -19.8 | 0.677901 |
| 475 | 1,781.2 | 1,219 | -67.5 | -88.4 | -22.2 | 0.723454 |
| 500 | 1,742.0 | 1,165 | -77.5 | -99.5 | -24.9 | 0.770022 |
| 525 | 1,703.4 | 1,114 | -88.2 | -111.5 | -27.8 | 0.817641 |
| 550 | 1,665.5 | 1,065 | -99.9 | -124.3 | -30.8 | 0.866341 |
| 575 | 1,628.4 | 1,018 | -112.5 | -138.1 | -34.0 | 0.916152 |
| 600 | 1,591.9 | 973 | -126.1 | -152.9 | -37.5 | 0.967102 |
| 625 | 1,556.3 | 930 | -140.7 | -168.7 | -41.1 | 1.019220 |
| 650 | 1,521.4 | 889 | -156.4 | -185.6 | -45.0 | 1.072533 |
| 675 | 1,487.3 | 850 | -173.2 | -203.6 | -49.0 | 1.127070 |
| 700 | 1,454.1 | 812 | -191.2 | -222.8 | -53.3 | 1.182854 |
| 725 | 1,421.8 | 776 | -210.4 | -243.2 | -57.8 | 1.239911 |
| 750 | 1,390.4 | 743 | -231.0 | -264.9 | -62.6 | 1.298263 |
| 775 | 1,360.0 | 710 | -252.8 | -287.9 | -67.5 | 1.357928 |
| 800 | 1,330.6 | 680 | -276.1 | -312.4 | -72.7 | 1.418923 |
| 825 | 1,302.2 | 651 | -300.8 | -338.3 | -78.2 | 1.481260 |
| 850 | 1,274.9 | 624 | -327.0 | -365.7 | -83.9 | 1.544946 |
| 875 | 1,248.8 | 599 | -354.9 | -394.8 | -89.8 | 1.609982 |
| 900 | 1,223.9 | 575 | -384.4 | -425.5 | -95.9 | 1.676366 |
| 925 | 1,200.1 | 553 | -415.7 | -458.0 | -102.3 | 1.744087 |
| 950 | 1,177.6 | 533 | -448.8 | -492.2 | -108.9 | 1.813130 |
| 975 | 1,156.3 | 514 | -483.8 | -528.4 | -115.8 | 1.883472 |

SIERRA BALLISTICS III
**********************

DATA FOR: 7.62MM M118 M24          BC'S:  .515(H), .503(M), .491(L)
COMPANY: Sierra    TEMP: 59    PRESSURE: 29.53 IN.    HUMIDITY: 78%
ZERO: 100 meters      CROSSWIND: -10.00 mph      TAIL WIND: +0.00 mph
ELEVATION ANGLE:  0 degs  ALTITUDE:    0 feet   SIGHT HGT. 1.7 IN
RANGE   VELOCITY   ENERGY   BULLET    DROP      DRIFT     TIME OF
METERS   (FPS)    (FT-LB)  PATH(IN)  (INCH)    (INCH)   FLIGHT(SEC)
-------------------------------------------------------------------
1,000   1,136.3     496   -520.7    -566.5    -122.9    1.955087

**********************************************************************

(CUT OUT AND SAVE FOR REFRENCE)

*************************************
*   RANGE      PATH      DRIFT    *
*-----------------------------------*
*      0       -1.7        0.0    *
*    100       +0.0       -0.9    *
*    200       -5.4       -3.5    *
*    300      -19.1       -8.3    *
*    400      -42.5      -15.3    *
*    500      -77.5      -24.9    *
*************************************

SIERRA BALLISTICS III
*********************


## ENVIRONMENTAL CONDITIONS
-------------------------

Actual Barometric Pressure at firing site:              29.53 IN.
Actual Speed of Sound at firing site:                   1,121 FPS
Effective ballistic coefficient at firing site:         0.514


## ANIMAL LEAD CALCULATIONS
-------------------------

Avg. lead for a running antelope at 100 meters is:          8 feet.
Avg. lead for a running deer at 100 meters is:              3 feet.
Avg. lead for a running elk at 100 meters is:              5 feet.

# Appendix C

## RANGE ESTIMATION TABLES

JUDGING DISTANCE

### RANGES IN METERS

| MIL | 19 INCHES | 1 METER | 1.67 METERS (5 ft, 6 in) | 1.75 METERS (5 ft, 9 in) | 1.8 METERS (6 ft) |
|---|---|---|---|---|---|
| 1 | 526.6 | 1000 | 1670 | 1750 | 1800 |
| 1 1/4 | 421 | 800 | 2446 | 1400 | 1440 |
| 1 1/2 | 351 | 667 | 1113 | 1167 | 1200 |
| 1 3/4 | 276 | 571 | 954 | 1000 | 1028.5 |
| 2 | 241 | 500 | 835 | 875 | 900 |
| 2 1/4 | 214 | 444 | 742 | 778 | 800 |
| 2 1/2 | 193 | 400 | 668 | 700 | 720 |
| 2 3/4 | 175 | 364 | 607 | 636 | 654.5 |
| 3 | 161 | 333 | 557 | 583 | 600 |
| 3 1/4 | 148 | 308 | 514 | 538 | 554 |
| 3 1/2 | 138 | 286 | 477 | 500 | 514 |
| 3 3/4 | 129 | 267 | 445 | 467 | 480 |
| 4 | 121 | 250 | 417.5 | 437.5 | 450 |
| 4 1/4 | 114 | 235 | 393 | 412 | 423.5 |
| 4 1/2 | 107 | 222 | 371 | 389 | 400 |
| 4 3/4 | 101 | 210 | 352 | 368 | 379 |
| 5 | 96.5 | 200 | 334 | 350 | 360 |
| 5 1/4 | | 190.5 | 318 | 333 | 343 |
| 5 1/2 | | 181.5 | 304 | 318 | 327 |
| 5 3/4 | | 173.9 | 290 | 304 | 313 |
| 6 | | 166.6 | 278 | 292 | 300 |
| 6 1/4 | | 160 | 267 | 280 | 288 |
| 6 1/2 | | 153.8 | 257 | 269 | 277 |
| 6 3/4 | | 148.1 | 247 | 259 | 267 |
| 7 | | 142.9 | 239 | 250 | 267 |
| 8 | | 125 | 209 | 219 | 225 |
| 9 | | | 186 | 194 | 200 |
| 10 | | | 167 | 175 | 180 |

1

NOTE:   At ranges exceeding 421 meters, the 19-inch (shoulder width) reference is not acceptable for use, as a 1/4 mil error in estimation, is beyond the ballistic capability of the M118 cartridge.   The same also applies to the 1 meter unit of measured beyond 571 meters.   These are for short range use only. REMEMBER, the point blank range for the M118 cartridge is 300 meters with a 250 meter zero.

# APPENDIX C

## TABLE OF MILS FOR OBJECTS

| FEET | 3 | 4 | 5 | 6 | 7 | 8 | 9 | 10 | 11 | 12 | 13 | 14 | 15 | 16 | 17 | 18 |
|---|---|---|---|---|---|---|---|---|---|---|---|---|---|---|---|---|
| YARDS | 1 | 1.3 | 1.7 | 2 | 2.3 | 2.7 | 3 | 3.3 | 3.7 | 4 | 4.3 | 4.7 | 5 | 5.3 | 5.7 | 6 |
| **MILS** | | | | | | | | | | | | | | | | |
| 2 | 500 | 650 | 850 | 1000 | 1150 | 1350 | 1500 | 1650 | 1850 | 2000 | 2150 | 2350 | 2500 | 2650 | 2850 | 3000 |
| 2.5 | 400 | 520 | 680 | 800 | 920 | 1080 | 1200 | 1320 | 1480 | 1600 | 1720 | 1880 | 2000 | 2120 | 2280 | 2400 |
| 3 | 333 | 425 | 566 | 665 | 766 | 900 | 999 | 1100 | 1230 | 1332 | 1433 | 1566 | 1665 | 1766 | 1900 | 1998 |
| 3.5 | 285 | 371 | 486 | 571 | 657 | 771 | 855 | 943 | 1057 | 1140 | 1229 | 1343 | 1425 | 1514 | 1629 | 1710 |
| 4 | 250 | 325 | 425 | 500 | 575 | 675 | 750 | 825 | 925 | 1000 | 1075 | 1175 | 1250 | 1325 | 1425 | 1500 |
| 4.5 | 222 | 289 | 370 | 444 | 511 | 600 | 666 | 733 | 822 | 888 | 950 | 1044 | 1110 | 1178 | 1267 | 1332 |
| 5 | 200 | 260 | 340 | 400 | 460 | 540 | 600 | 660 | 740 | 800 | 860 | 940 | 1000 | 1060 | 1140 | 1200 |
| 5.5 | 182 | 236 | 309 | 362 | 418 | 491 | 543 | 600 | 673 | 724 | 782 | 855 | 905 | 964 | 1036 | 1036 |
| 6 | 167 | 217 | 283 | 334 | 383 | 450 | 500 | 550 | 617 | 668 | 717 | 783 | 835 | 883 | 950 | 1000 |
| 6.5 | 154 | 200 | 262 | 308 | 354 | 415 | 432 | 503 | 569 | 616 | 662 | 723 | 770 | 815 | 877 | 924 |
| 7 | 143 | 186 | 243 | 286 | 329 | 386 | 429 | 471 | 529 | 572 | 614 | 671 | 715 | 757 | 814 | 858 |
| 7.5 | 133 | 173 | 227 | 266 | 307 | 360 | 399 | 440 | 493 | 532 | 573 | 627 | 665 | 707 | 760 | 795 |
| 8 | 125 | 163 | 213 | 250 | 288 | 338 | 375 | 413 | 463 | 500 | 538 | 588 | 625 | 663 | 713 | 730 |
| 8.5 | 118 | 152 | 200 | 234 | 271 | 318 | 351 | 388 | 435 | 468 | 506 | 553 | 585 | 624 | 671 | 702 |
| 9 | 111 | 144 | 189 | 222 | 256 | 300 | 333 | 367 | 411 | 444 | 478 | 522 | 555 | 589 | 633 | 646 |
| 9.5 | 105 | 137 | 178 | 210 | 242 | 284 | 315 | 347 | 389 | 420 | 453 | 495 | 525 | 559 | 600 | 630 |
| 10 | 100 | 130 | 170 | 200 | 230 | 270 | 300 | 330 | 370 | 400 | 430 | 470 | 500 | 530 | 570 | 600 |
| 10.5 | | | | | | | | 314 | 352 | 381 | 410 | 448 | 478 | 505 | 543 | 511 |
| 11 | | | | | | | | 300 | 336 | 367 | 390 | 427 | 455 | 482 | 518 | 545 |
| 11.5 | | | | | | | | | 322 | 348 | 374 | 409 | 435 | 461 | 496 | 522 |
| 12 | | | | | | | | | 308 | 333 | 353 | 392 | 417 | 442 | 475 | 500 |
| 12.5 | | | | | | | | | | 320 | 344 | 376 | 400 | 424 | 456 | 480 |
| 13 | | | | | | | | | | 308 | 331 | 362 | 385 | 408 | 438 | 462 |
| 13.5 | | | | | | | | | | | 319 | 348 | 370 | 393 | 422 | 444 |
| 14 | | | | | | | | | | | 307 | 336 | 357 | 379 | 407 | 429 |
| 14.5 | | | | | | | | | | | | 324 | 345 | 366 | 393 | 414 |
| 15 | | | | | | | | | | | | 313 | 333 | 353 | 380 | 400 |
| 15.5 | | | | | | | | | | | | 303 | 323 | 342 | 368 | 387 |
| 16 | | | | | | | | | | | | | 313 | 325 | 356 | 375 |
| 16.5 | | | | | | | | | | | | | 303 | 321 | 345 | 364 |
| 17 | | | | | | | | | | | | | | 312 | 335 | 353 |
| 17.5 | | | | | | | | | | | | | | 302 | 326 | 343 |
| 18 | | | | | | | | | | | | | | | 317 | 333 |
| 18.5 | | | | | | | | | | | | | | | 308 | 324 |
| 19 | | | | | | | | | | | | | | | 300 | 316 |
| 19.5 | | | | | | | | | | | | | | | | 308 |

1) ESTIMATE HEIGHT OF TARGET AND LOCATE ACROSS THE TOP

2) MEASURE HEIGHT OF TARGET IN MILS AND LOCATE DOWN THE SIDE

3) MOVE DOWN FROM THE TOP AND RIGHT FROM THE SIDE TO FIND THE RANGE IN YARDS

$$\frac{\text{HEIGHT OF TARGET (YARDS)} \times 1{,}000}{\text{HEIGHT OF TARGET (MILS)}} = \text{RANGE (YARDS)}$$

# Appendix D
# SNIPER RANGE LAYOUT

App. D

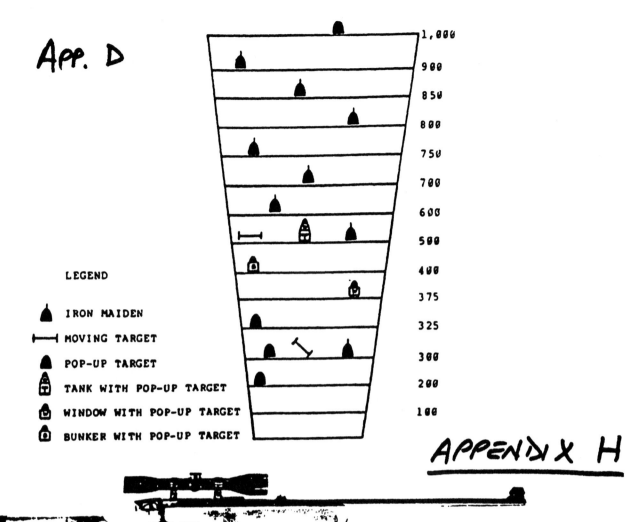

1,000
900
850
800
750
700
600
500
400
375
325
300
200
100

LEGEND

◆ IRON MAIDEN
 MOVING TARGET
◗ POP-UP TARGET
⬒ TANK WITH POP-UP TARGET
⬔ WINDOW WITH POP-UP TARGET
⬓ BUNKER WITH POP-UP TARGET

APPENDIX H

Steyr 7.62mm NATO Model SSG Rifle.

FN MODEL 30-11

The Canadian 7.62 × 51mm NATO Sniper Rifle C3 with telescopic sight.

**Model 54 Sniper Rifle**

French FR-F1 Sniper Rifle. Available in both 7.5 × 54mm and 7.62 × 51mm NATO.

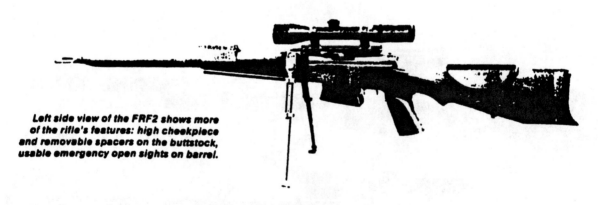

*Left side view of the FRF2 shows more of the rifle's features: high cheekpiece and removable spacers on the buttstock, usable emergency open sights on barrel.*

*Mauser 66-SP*

WA 2000

PSG-1

GALIL

BERETTA N/A

PRC - SEE SOVIET SVD

Romanian FPK sniper rifle.

SPAIN: C-75 N/A

SWITZERLAND SIG 510-4 N/A

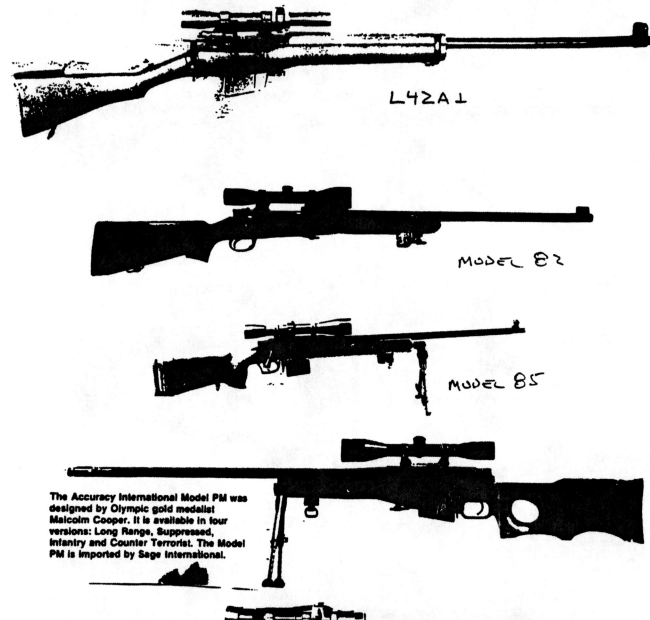

L42A1

MODEL 82

MODEL 85

The Accuracy International Model PM was
designed by Olympic gold medalist
Malcolm Cooper. It is available in four
versions: Long Range, Suppressed,
Infantry and Counter Terrorist. The Model
PM is imported by Sage International.

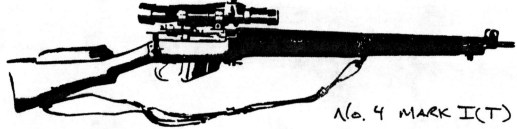

No. 4 MARK I(T)

Soviet Samozaridnyia Vintovka Dragunova (SVD) 7.62 × 54Rmm Sniper Rifle.

Soviet Sniper Rifles, SVT40 (top) and M1891 30 (bottom). Both are caliber 7.62 × 54Rmm.

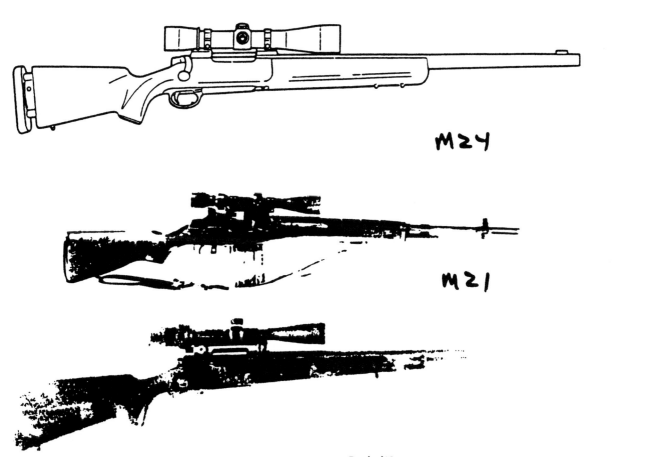

M24

M21

USMC M40A1 sniper rifle made by Remington.

BARRETT MODEL 82A1 N/A

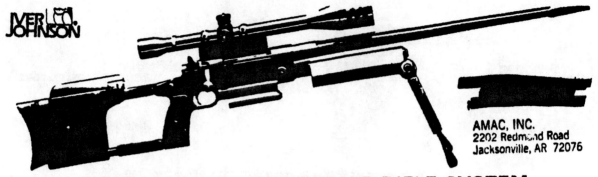

IVER JOHNSON

AMAC, INC.
2202 Redmond Road
Jacksonville, AR 72076

# CONVERTIBLE LONG RANGE RIFLE SYSTEM
## 7.62 ● 8.58 x 71

Caliber .30 M1903A4 Rifle.

Caliber .30 M1C Sniper Rifle.

Caliber .30 M1D Sniper Rifle.

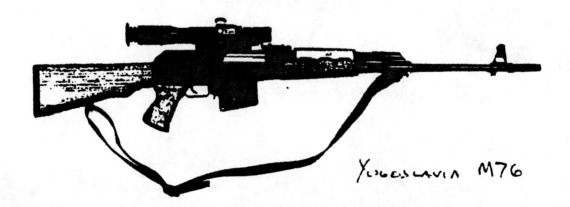

Yugoslavia M76

# Appendix E

## SUSTAINMENT PROGRAM

### E-1. SUPPORT FOR TRAINING/SUSTAINMENT TRAINING

The purpose of proficiency training is to enable the sniper to maintain the high degree of skill and proficiency required. Special emphasis should be placed on marksmanship and stalking because they are the most perishable of sniper skills.

Frequency of Training.
    The frequency of training is important to maintain sniper proficiency. The sniper should be tested or evaluated on all sniper skills at least annually; semi-annually is better. Marksmanship qualification should occur at least quarterly to the standards outlined in the SOTIC POI.

Time Devoted to Training.
    The time the unit will allow the sniper to devote to sustainment training will determine the sniper's overall proficiency. Experience has shown that to maintain the degree of familiarity with his weapon that is needed to engage targets at unknown distances, the sniper should devote at least eight hours a week in sniper marksmanship training. This amount of time spent in quality marksmanship training will sustain the sniper's proficiency in the art of precision long-range rifle fire.

Basic Ammunition Requirements.
    Basic ammunition requirements for sustainment type firing can be found in Table 5-34, Annual Ammunition Allocation and Training Strategy for the M21 Sniper Rifle, DA Pam 350-38 (Standards in Weapons Training) (page 106). This is the minimum ammunition requirement, not the maximum.

Training Exercises.
    The following exercises may be incorporated into team training to improve every team member's skills and enhance the team's overall capabilities.

    o Marksmanship exercises. Marksmanship training takes up a large amount of the sniper's overall proficiency training. The sniper must be proficient in all sniper-related skills, but without marksmanship, these other skills are useless. Some examples of marksmanship exercises are as follows:

        * Grouping exercises. These are simple exercises where the sniper fires five-round shot groups at various ranges, from 100 to 900 meters. Analysis of the shot groups helps the sniper to determine shooting errors and environmental effects in a more or less controlled environment. This also allows the sniper to

1

collect his cold bore shot and environmental data.

     * Moving target firing. Firing at moving targets helps
the sniper to maintain proficiency in this difficult skill.
Targets should be engaged from 300 to 800 meters. These exercises
are simple to run. Moving targets are provided by having personnel
"walk" silhouette targets on a stick or board held over their head
while protected in the pits of a traditional known distance range.
The targets must be cut to 12 inches in width to maintain realism.

     * Unknown distance firing. Unknown distance firing
helps the sniper to remain proficient in a variety of sniper
skills. The sniper pair must fill out a range card/sector sketch
and estimate the range to targets. The pair must then use the
information to engage targets of unknown distance.

     * Firing under artificial illumination and/or NVD. This
exercise includes both stationary and moving targets from 300 to
600 meters under artificial illumination or NVDs.

     * Stress shooting. All previous exercises can be
further enhanced with the additional application of a stress
factor. Applying a time limit, stalking to the target, or physical
effort prior to firing are but a few stresses that may be applied
to the sniper.

     * Firing air rifles. Match grade air rifles, (ex. the
RWS 75 or the Daisy Gamo), can be effectively used for marksmanship
training. Air rifles do not require any special ranges. Any area
with a minimum of 10 meters of distance can be used, indoors or
outdoors. This range, used in conjunction with .22 caliber bullet
traps and standing off-hand (unsupported), can be used to reinforce
marksmanship fundamentals. Ranges of up to 1,000 meters can be
simulated by using scaled targets and a good air rifle scope in an
outdoor area. Ranges of 10 meters to 50 meters and targets,
reduced in size to represent different ranges, can be used (see
Appendix E-3). Pellets may be purchased for about $4 per 500
pellets, rifles for between $150 and $300 each, and .22 caliber
bullet traps for approximately $25 each. Pellet traps should not
be used; they will not stand up to heavy use.
     o Stalking Exercises. Stalking exercises enable the sniper
to train and develop skills in movement, camouflage, map reading,
mission planning, and position selection. Live fire may be
incorporated to confirm the sniper's target engagement.

     o Range Estimation Exercises. There are many ways to conduct
this type of exercise. The sniper estimates ranges out to 1,000
meters and must be within 10 percent of the correct range. The
sniper should use only his binoculars and rifle telescope as aids.

     o Other Exercises. Other exercises may be developed or
incorporated into the sniper's training program to enhance his

2

observation, memory, and camouflage skills.

## E-2.  M24 SNIPER MILES TRAINING

MILES training is an invaluable tool in realistic combat training.  Other than actual combat, the sniper's best means of displaying effectiveness as a force multiplier is through the use of the M24/21 SWS with MILES.

Characteristics of the MILES Transmitter.
The M24 SWS MILES transmitter is a modified M16 transmitter. A special mounting bracket attaches the laser transmitter to the right side of the barrel (looking from the butt end) of the M24 and places it parallel with the line of bore.  The laser beam output has been amplified and tightened to provide precision fire capability out to 1,000 meters.  (For component information and instructions on mounting, zeroing, and operation, see TM 9-1265-211-10).

Training Value.
Using the M24/21 with MILES, the trainer can enhance sustainment training in target engagement such as:

o  Selection of firing positions.  Due to transmitter modifications, the sniper must attain a firing position that affords clear fields of fire.  Any obstruction (vegetation, terrain) can prevent a one-shot skill by deflecting or blocking the path of the laser beam.  By selecting this type of position, the sniper will greatly improve his observation and firing capabilities.

o  Target detection/selection.  Using MILES against multiple/cluster targets requires the sniper to select the target that will have the greatest effect on the enemy.  The trainer provides instant feedback on the sniper's performance.  Situations may be created such as bunkers, hostage situations, and MOUT firing.  The hit-or-miss indicating aspects of MILES are invaluable in this type of training.

o  Range estimation.  As indicated in Chapter 4, the sniper must be highly skilled in range estimation to properly use the M24 SWS.  The trainer's evaluation of this ability is as simple as the sniper pulling the trigger.  When the range to the target is properly computed and elevation dialed on the M3A, one shot, either hit or miss, indicates a strength or weakness in the sniper's range estimation ability (if the fundamentals of marksmanship were properly applied).

o  Marksmanship.  A target hit (kill) with MILES is the same as one with live ammunition.  Proper application of marksmanship fundamentals results in a first-round kill; the training value is

3

self-evident.

MILES Training Limitations.
     The concept of MILES is to provide realistic training;
however, MILES is limited in its capabilities as applied to the
sniper's mission of long-range precision fire.  These limitations
are as follows:

     o    Lack of external ballistics training.  A laser is a
concentrated beam of light emitted by the MILES transmitter.  It
travels from the sniper's weapon undisturbed by outside forces such
as temperature, humidity, and wind.  Lack of these effects may lull
the sniper into a false sense of confidence.  Without the sniper
correcting for these factors, their importance fades to disregard.
The trainers should constantly reinforce the importance of these
factors.  The sniper should make a mental note of changes that
should be applied to compensate for these effects.

     o    Engagement of moving targets.  The engagement of moving
targets (Chapter 3) requires the sniper to establish a target lead
to compensate for flight time of his bullet.  Travelling in excess
of 186,00 miles per second (speed of light), the MILES laser
nullifies the requirement for target lead.  Again, the sniper may
be lulled into a false sense of confidence.  The trainer should
enforce the principles of moving target engagement by having the
sniper note appropriate target lead for the given situation.

E-3.  REDUCED SCALE RANGE

     When using air rifles for marksmanship training, the sniper
can use one of several formulas to simulate distances for a reduced
or subcaliber range.  Listed below are several formulas and
explanations on how to use them.  Also listed is a chart based on
a 6-foot man at ranges to 1,000 yards/meters.

Reduced Scale Target Height Formula
     The formula to\ find the reduced height of a target at a given
range and a simulated range is as follows:

$$\frac{R\,1 \times H\,1}{R\,2} = H2$$

     R 1 = Reduced range+
     R 2 = Simulated range+
     H 1 = Height of actual target*
     H 2 = Reduced height of target*

NOTES:
     o    +Both the reduced range and the simulated range must
          agree in measurement, i.e., 1,000 meters and 35 meters
          or 1,000 yards and 35 yards.

4

o   *If the height of the real target is expressed in
    inches (i.e., 72 inches for a 6-foot man), the answer  is
in inches.  If the height is expressed in feet, the      answer
will be in feet.

<u>EXAMPLES:</u>

R 1 = 35 METERS     R 2 = 500 METERS     H 1 = 72 INCHES

$$\frac{35 \times 72}{500} = 5.04 \text{ INCHES}$$

R 1 = 25 YARDS     R 2 = 800 YARDS     H 1 = 6 FEET

$$\frac{25 \times 6}{800} = .1875 \text{ FEET}$$

To change the .1875 feet to inches, multiply by 12.

.1875 x 12 = 2.25 INCHES

<u>Reduced Scale Simulated Range Formula</u>
    The formula to find the simulated range of a given reduced
target height at a given reduced range is as follows:

$$\frac{R 1 \times H 1}{H 2} = R 2$$

<u>EXAMPLE:</u>

A 3-inch target at 35 meters will simulate what range?

R 1 = 35 METERS     H 1 = 72 INCHES     H 2 = 3 INCHES

$$\frac{35 \times 72}{3} = 840 \text{ METERS}$$

5

## Reduced Range Chart

Below is a table to simulate in inches a 6-foot man at various ranges on the given reduced ranges.

| Range | 15 yds/m | 20 yds/m | 25 yds/m | 30 yds/m | 35 yds/m |
|---|---|---|---|---|---|
| 1000 yds/m | 1.08" | 1.44" | 1.80" | 2.16" | 2.52" |
| 900 yds/m | 1.20" | 1.60" | 2.00" | 2.40" | 2.80" |
| 800 yds/m | 1.35" | 1.80" | 2.25" | 2.70" | 3.15" |
| 700 yds/m | 1.54" | 2.05" | 2.57" | 3.08" | 3.60" |
| 600 yds/m | 1.80" | 2.40" | 3.00" | 3.60" | 4.20" |
| 500 yds/m | 2.16" | 2.88" | 3.60" | 4.32" | 5.04" |
| 400 yds/m | 2.70" | 3.60" | 4.50" | 5.40" | 6.30" |
| 300 yds/m | 3.60" | 4.80" | 6.00" | 7.20" | 8.40" |
| 200 yds/m | 5.40" | 7.20" | 9.00" | 10.8" | 12.6" |
| 100 yds/m | 10.8" | 14.4" | 18.0" | 21.6" | 25.2" |

The center of the pellet strike should be the determining factor due to the size difference of the pellet diameter versus the range and simulated target size. It is also recommended that the ranges of 100 through 400 yards/meters be against a head or head and shoulders target and not the full body.

For example, at 35 meters the normal human head is simulated to be 2.8 inches high by 1.75 inches wide for a simulated range of 100 meters.

An additional advantage to the reduced range targets is that when the sniper utilizes the above table or formulas, a reduced scale unknown distance range for judging distance will be constructed at the same time. When he uses the mil scale in the Leupold M3A Ultra 10x scope, the targets will give the same mil readings as a real target at that distance. As an example, a 6-foot man at 500 yards is 4 mils high. A 3.60-inch target at 25 yards is 4 mils high, and simulates at 6-foot man at 500 yards.

6

# Appendix F

## SNIPER TRAINING EXERCISES

### F-1. Stalking Exercises

The purpose of stalking exercises is to give the sniper confidence in his ability to approach and occupy a firing position without being observed.

Description. Having studied a map (and aerial photograph, if available), individual students must stalk for a predesignated distance, which could be 1,000 yards or more, depending on the area selected. All stalking exercises and tests should be approximately 1,000 yards with a 4-hour time limit. The student must stalk to within 150 to 200 yards of two trained observers, who are scanning the area with binoculars and fire two blanks without being detected.

Reconnaissance by the Conducting Officer/NCO. The area used for a stalking exercise must be chosen with great care. An area in which a student must do the low crawl for the complete distance would be unsuitable. The following items should be considered:

 o As much of the area as possible should be visible to the observer. This forces the student to use the ground properly, even when far from the observer's location.

 o Where possible, available cover should decrease as the student nears the observer's position. This will enable him to take chances early in the stalk and force him to move more carefully as he closes in on his firing position.

 o The students must start the stalk in an area out of sight of the observer.

 o Boundaries must be established by means of natural features or the use of markers.

Conduct of the Exercise. In a location near the jumpoff point for the stalk, the student is briefed on the following:

 o Aim of the exercise.

 o Boundaries.

 o Time limit (usually 4 hours).

 o Standards to be achieved.

After the briefing, the students are dispatched at intervals

1

to avoid congestion.

In addition to the two observers, there are two "walkers", equipped with radios, who will position themselves within the stalk area. If an observer sees a student, he will contact a walker by radio and direct him to within 5 feet of the student's location. Therefore, when a student is detected, the observer can immediately tell the student what give him away.

When the student reaches his firing position, which is within 150 to 200 yards of the observer, he will fire a blank at an observer. This will tell the walker he is ready to continue the rest of the exercise. The walker will then move to within 10 yards of the student. The observer will search a 10-yard radius around the walker for the sniper student. If the student is undetected, the walker will tell him to chamber and fire his second blank. If the sniper is still unseen, the walker will then point in the student's direction, and the observer will search in detail for anything that indicates a human form, rifle, or equipment. If the sniper remains undetected, the walker will then move in and put his hand on the student's head. The observer will again search in detail. If the sniper student is not seen at this point, he must tell the walker which observer he fired at and what the observer is doing. The observer waves his hat, scratches his face, or makes some gesture that the student can identify when using his telescope. The sniper student must then tell the walker his exact range, wind velocity, and windage applied to the scope. If the sniper completes all of these steps correctly, he has passed the stalk exercise.

A critique is conducted at the conclusion of the exercise, touching on main problem areas.

Creating Interest. To create interest and to give the students practice in observation and stalking skills. one-half of the class could be positioned to observe the conduct of the stalk. Seeing an error made is an effective way of teaching better stalking skills. When a student is caught, he should be sent to the observation post (OP) to observe the exercise.

## F-2. Range Estimation Exercises

Range estimation exercises are to make the sniper proficient in accurately judging distance.

Description. The student is taken to an observation post, and different objects over distances of up to 1,000 meters are indicated to him. After time for consideration, he writes down the estimated distance to each object. He may use only his binoculars and rifle telescope as aids, and he must estimate to wtihin 10 percent of the correct range (a 6-foot man-sized target should be

2

utilized).

Reconnaissance by the Conducting officer/NCO. Each exercise must take place in a different area, offering a variety of terrain. The exercise areas should include dead space as well as places where the student will be observing uphill or downhill. Extra objects should be selected in case those originally chosen cannot be seen due to weather, or for other reasons.

Conduct of the Exercise. The students ae brought to the observation post, issued a record card, and given a review on methods of judging distances and causes of miscalculation. They are then briefed on the following:

- o   Aim of the exercise.

- o   Reference points.

- o   Time limit per object.

- o   Standard to be achieved.

Students are spread out and the first object is indicated. The student is allowed 3 minutes to estimate the distance and write it down. The sequence is repeated for a total of eight objects. The cards are collected, and the correct range to each object is given. The instructor points out in each case why the distance might be underestimated or overestimated. After correction, the cards are given back to the students. In this way, the student retains a record of his performance.

Standards. The student is deemed to have failed if he estimates three or more distances incorrectly.

## F-3. Observation Exercises

The purpose of observation exercises is to practice the sniper's ability to observe an enemy and accurately record the results of his observations.

Description. The student is given an arc of about 1,800 mils to observe for a period of not more than 40 minutes. He is ussed a panoramic sketch of his arc and is expected to plot on the sketch any objects he sees in his area. Objects are so positioned as to be invisible to the naked eye, indistinguishable when using binoculars, but recognizable when using the spotting telescope.

Reconnaissance by the Conducting Officer/NCO. In choosing the location for the exercise, the following points should be considered:

o    Number of objects in the arc.

o    Time limits.

o    Equipment which they are allowed to use (binoculars and spotting telescopes).

o    Standard to be attained.

Each student takes up the prone position on the observation line and is issued a panoramic sketch of the area. The staff is available to answer questions about the sketch if a student is confused. (If the class is large, the observation line could be broken into a right and left half. A student could spend the first 20 minutes in one half and then move to the other. This ensures that he sees all the ground in the arc.) At the end of 40 minutes, all sheets are collected and the students are shown the location of each object. This is best done by the students staying in their positions and watching while a member of the staff points out each object. In this way, the students will see why they failed to find an object, even though it was visible. (Students should view first with binoculars and then with spotting telescopes before the instructor picks the item up.)

A critique is then held, bringing out the main points.

Scoring. Students are given half a point for each object correctly plotted and another half point for naming the object correctly.

Standards. The student is deemed to have failed if he scores less than 8 points out of a total of 12 points (12 disguised military objects.)

4

## F-4. Hide Construction Exercise

The purpose of the hide construction exercise is to show the sniper how to build a hide and remain undetected while being observed. The purpose of a hide is to camouflage a sniper or sniper team which is not in movement.

Description. The sniper students are given 8 hours to build a temporary hide large enough to hold a sniper team with all their necessary equipment.

Reconnaissance by the Conducting Officer/NCO. The hide exercise area should be selected with great care. It can be in any type of terrain, but there should be more than enough prospective spots in which to build a hide. The area should be easily bounded by left and right, far and near limits so that when the instructor points out the limits to the students, they can be easily and quickly identified. There should be enough tools (i.e., axes, picks, shovels, and sandbags) available to accommodate the entire class. There must be sufficient rations and water available to the students to last the entire exercise, which is about 9 1/2 hours total--8 hours instruction, 1 1/2 hours testing.

Conduct of the Exercise. The students are issued a shovel, axe, pickaxe, and approximately 20 sandbags per team. The students are brought to the area and briefed on the purpose of the exercise, their time limit for construction, and their area limits. The students are then allowed to begin construction of their hides.

NOTE:     During the construction, an instructor should be present at all times to act as an advisor.

At the end of 8 hours, the students' hides are all checked to ensure that they are complete. An infantry officer is brought out to act as an observer. He is placed in an area 300 yards from the hide area, where he starts his observation with binoculars and a 20X M49 spotting scope. The observer, after failing to find a hide, is brought forward 150 yards and again commences observation.

An instructor in the field (walker with radio) then moves to within 10 yards of a hide and informs the observer. The observer then tells the walker to have the sniper in the hide to load and fire his only round (blank). If the sniper's muzzle blast is seen, or if the hide is seen due to improper construction, the team fails, but they remain in the hide. These procedures are repeated for all the sniper teams. The observer is then brought down to within 25 yards of each hide to determine whether they can be seen with the naked eye at that distance. The observer is not shown the hide. He must find it. If the sniper team is located at 25 yards, it fails and is allowed to come out and see its discrepancies. If the team is not seen, it passes.

Other Requirements.  The sniper teams should also be required to fill out a range card and a sniper's log book and make a field sketch.  One way of helping them achieve this is to have an instructor showing "flash cards" from 150 yards away, beginning when the observer arrives and ending when the observer moves to within 25 yards.  The sniper teams should record everything they see on the flash cards and anything going on at the observation post during the exercise.

Standards.  The sniper teams are required to pass all phases in order to pass the exercise.  All range cards, log books, and field sketches must be turned in for grading and a final determination of pass or fail.

## F-5.  Camouflage and Concealment Exercises

Camouflage and concealment exercises are held to help the sniper student to select final firing positions.

Description.  The student conceals himself within 200 yards of an observer, who, using binoculars, tries to find the student.  The student must be able to fire blank ammunition at the observer without being seen, and have the correct elevation and windage on his sight.  The student must remain unseen throughout the conduct of the exercise.

Reconnaissance by the Conducting Officer/NCO.  In choosing the location for the exercise, the instructor ensures that certain conditions are met.  These are:

o    There must be adequate space to ensure students are not crowded together in the area.  There should be at least twice the number of potential positions as there are students.  Once the area has been established, the limits should be marked in some manner (e.g., flags, trees, prominent features, etc.).  Students should then be allowed to choose any position within the limits for their final firing position.

o    The observer must be located where he can see the entire problem area.

As there will be several concealment exercises throughout the sniper course, different types of terrain should be chosen in order that the students may practice concealment in varied conditions. For instance, one exercise could take place in a fairly open area, one along a wood line, one in shrubs, and another in hilly or rough terrain.

Conduct of the Exercise.  The sniper is given a specified area with boundaries in which to conceal himself properly.  The observers turn their backs to the area and allow the students 5 minutes to conceal themselves.  At the end of 5 minutes, the observers turn and commence observation in their search for concealed snipers.  This observation should last approximately one-half hour (more time is allotted, if desired).  At the conclusion of observation, the observer will instruct, by radio, one of the two observers (walkers) in the field to move to within 10 meters of one of the snipers.  The sniper is given one blank.  If he cannot be seen after the walker moves within the 10 meters, the walker will tell him to load and fire his blank.  The observer is looking for muzzle blast, vegetation flying after the shot, and movement by the sniper before and after he fires.  If the student cannot be seen, the walker then extends his arm in the direction of the sniper, indicating his position.  If the sniper remains unseen after indication, the walker goes to the sniper's position and places his hand, palm facing the observer, directly on top of the

sniper's head.   If the sniper passess all of the above, he must
then state his elevation, windage, and what type of movement the
observer is making.

Creating Interest.   To create interest and to give students
practice in observation, one-half of the class may be positioned
with the observer in order that they can profit from the mistakes
of the other half of the class. When a student fails the exercise,
he should go to the observation post to observe.

## MISSION ESSENTIAL TASK LIST

1. Move Tactically (Sniper)                    7-5-1825

2. Select/Engage Targets (Sniper)              7-5-1869

3. Select/Occupy Firing Position (Sniper)      7-5-1871

4. Estimate Range (Sniper)                     7-5-1872

5. Debrief (Sniper)                            7-5-1809


**ELEMENT:  SNIPER TEAM**

**TASK:**  MOVE Tactically (7-5-1825) (FM 7-8, TC 23-14)

ITERATION  1  2  3  4  5  (circle)

TNG STATUS    T  P  U    (circle)

**CONDITION:**  The sniper team is given a mission to move with a security element.  Both friendly and OPFOR units have indirect fire and CAS available.

**TASK STANDARD:**

1. The sniper team moves undetected.

2. The sniper team moves tactically based on METT-T.

3. The sniper team complies with all graphic control measures.

4. The sniper team moves along the route specified in the order.

5. The sniper team arrives at the destination specified in the order.

6. The sniper team arrives at the specified time.

7. The sniper team sustains no casualties.

**SUBTASKS AND STANDARDS:**                           GO    NO-GO

**\*+1. The sniper team leader selects the movement routes, that:**

1

a. Avoids known OPFOR positions and obstacles.

b. Offers cover and concealment.

c. Takes advantage of difficult terrain, swamp, and dense woods.

d. Avoids natural lines of drift.

e. Avoids trails, roads, footpaths, or built-up or populated areas unless required by the mission.

2. **The sniper team personnel use the proper movement techniques: sniper low crawl, medium crawl, high crawl, hand-and-knee crawl, and walk.**

a. The observer is the point man; the sniper follows.

b. The observer's sector is from 9 o'clock to 3 o'clock; the sniper's position is from 3 o'clock to 9 o'clock.

c. The observer and the sniper must maintain visual contact even when lying on the ground.

d. The interval between the observer and the sniper is not more than 20 meters.

e. The sniper reacts to the point man's actions.

f. The sniper and the point man cross danger areas. (See T&EO 7-3/4-1028, Cross Danger Area <ARTEP 7-8-MTP>).

3. **The sniper team maintains operation security.**

a. Moves slowly and cautiously--not quickly or jerkily.

b. Uses camouflage.

c. Avoids making sounds.

4. **The sniper team maintains proper communication procedures.**

a. Maintains radio listening silence.

2

b.   Uses visual signals

**\*Leader task**
**+Critical task**

### TASK PERFORMANCE SUMMARY BLOCK

| ITERATION | 1 | 2 | 3 | 4 | 5 | TOTAL |
|---|---|---|---|---|---|---|
| TOTAL SUBTASKS AND STANDARDS EVALUATED | | | | | | |
| TOTAL SUBTASKS AND STANDARDS "GO" | | | | | | |

**OPFOR TASK and STANDARDS:**

**TASK:**  ENGAGE Sniper Team
**STANDARDS:**

1.   The OPFOR detects the moving sniper team.

2.   The OPFOR delays the team beyond its allotted time (leader evaluation).

3.   The OPFOR prevents the team from moving to its assigned destination or along its prescribed route (leader evaluation).

4.   The OPFOR inflicts one casualty on the sniper team.


**ELEMENT:**  SNIPER TEAM

**TASK:**  SELECT/ENGAGE Targets (7-5-1869) (TC 23-14)

                        ITERATION   1  2  3  4  5   (circle)

                        TNG STATUS     T  P  U    (circle)

**CONDITION:**  The sniper team is given a specific sniper mission (target criteria and priority), either by supporting a unit or by acting independently.  The sniper team observes the targets. Both friendly and OPFOR units have indirect fire and CAS available.


**TASK STANDARD:**

3

1.  The sniper team selects the priority target and destroys it within two rounds.

2.  The sniper team sustains no casualties.

**SUBTASKS AND STANDARDS:**                                      GO    NO-GO

1.  **The sniper team identifies the following priority targets that will limit the OPFOR's fighting ability:**

    a.  OPFOR sniper.

    b.  Officers, both military and political.

    c.  NCOs.

    d.  Scout or dog team.

    e.  Crew-served weapon personnel.

    f.  Vehicle commanders and drivers.

    g.  Communications personnel.

    h.  Forward observers.

    i.  Critical equipment such as optical sights or radios.

*2.  **The sniper team leader selects the priority targets to be engaged.**

    a.  The sniper team members select the target that is critical to the mission.

    b.  The sniper team does not become a target while searching for or firing on an OPFOR target.

    c.  The sniper team estimates their range from the target. (See T&EO 7-5-1872, Estimate Range). The range must be within 300 to 800 meters.

    d.  The sniper team leader choose to engage targets or continues the observation of the targets.

3.  **The sniper team engages the target.**

4

a.  The observer gives the wind adjustment.

b.  The sniper adjusts the scope on the
    target and informs the observer when
    completed.

**\*Leader task**

**SUBTASKS AND STANDARDS:**                                        GO    NO-GO

c.  The observer reconfirms the wind
    adjustment and notifies the sniper of
    any changes.

d.  The sniper fires.

e.  The observer watches the vapor trail
    and the strike of the round.  He then
    prepares to give an adjustment if the
    sniper missed.

f.  If the sniper misses, he checks the
    scope and fires again, or he may engage
    a second target.

### TASK PERFORMANCE SUMMARY BLOCK

| ITERATION | 1 | 2 | 3 | 4 | 5 | TOTAL |
|---|---|---|---|---|---|---|
| TOTAL SUBTASKS AND STANDARDS EVALUATED | | | | | | |
| TOTAL SUBTASKS AND STANDARDS "GO" | | | | | | |

**OPFOR TASK and STANDARDS:**

**TASK:**  REACT to Sniper Fire

**STANDARDS:**

1.  The OPFOR assumes covered and concealed positions within
three seconds of receiving sniper fire.

2.  The OPFOR detects the sniper team's location within five
seconds.

3.   The OPFOR returns fire within five seconds of receiving sniper fire.

4.   The OPFOR inflicts one casualty on the sniper team.

5.   The OPFOR sustains no more than one casualty.


**ELEMENT:  SNIPER TEAM**

**TASK:**   SELECT/OCCUPY Firing Position (7-5-1871) (TC 23-14)

ITERATION     1   2   3   4   5  (circle)

TNG STATUS        T    P    U      (circle)

**CONDITION:**  The sniper team is given a mission to engage a target and an area of operations.  Both friendly and OPFOR units have indirect fire and CAS available.


**TASK STANDARD:**

1.   The sniper team selects a final sniper position within 300 to 600 meters of the target area.

2.   The sniper team is not detected while occupying the position.

3.   The sniper team sustains no casualties.


**SUBTASKS AND STANDARDS:**                              GO    NO-GO

*1.  The sniper team leader selects a final firing position that has:

   a.   Maximum fields of fire and observation of the target area.

   b.   Maximum concealment from OPFOR observation.

   c,   Covered routes into and out of the position.

   d.   A position no closer than 300 meters to the target area.

   e.   A natural or man-made obstacle (if available) between the sniper team's position and the target.

6

2. The sniper team maintains operation security by avoiding:

   a. Prominent, readily identifiable objects and terrain features.

   b. Roads and trails.

   c. Objects that may make noise.

   d. Optical devices that may reflect light.

   e. Leaving a path that leads to their positions.

   f. Firing position(s).

3. The sniper team operates from a position by:

   a. Using shadows (if available).

   b. Using camouflage that does not contrast with the surrounding area.

4. The sniper team occupies the position.

   a. Moves into the position undetected.

   b. Scans ahead and watches for overhead movement.

   c. Keeps the body outline low to the ground.

**\*Leader tasks**

**SUBTASKS AND STANDARDS:**                                    GO   NO-GO

5. The sniper team sustains the firing position.

   a. Organizes the equipment.

   b. Establishes a system of observation and relief. (See T&EO 7-3/4-1058, Sustain <ARTEP 7-8-MTP>).

**TASK PERFORMANCE SUMMARY BLOCK**

| ITERATION | 1 | 2 | 3 | 4 | 5 | TOTAL |
|---|---|---|---|---|---|---|
| TOTAL SUBTASKS AND STANDARDS EVALUATED | | | | | | |
| TOTAL SUBTASKS AND STANDARDS "GO" | | | | | | |

**OPFOR TASKS and STANDARDS:**

**TASK:** DETECT Snipers

**STANDARDS:**

1.  The OPFOR detects movement of the snipers moving into the firing position.

2.  The OPFOR inflicts more than one casualty.

3.  The OPFOR engages the sniper team within five seconds.

4.  The OPFOR sustains no more than one casualty.


**ELEMENT:** SNIPER TEAM

**TASK:** ESTIMATE Range (7-5-1872) (TC 23-14)

ITERATION    1  2  3  4  5   (circle)

TNG STATUS    T  P  U    (circle)

**CONDITION:** The sniper team has to employ range estimation throughout the target area to engage targets. Both friendly and OPFOR units have indirect fire and CAS available.

**TASK STANDARD:**

1.  The sniper team agrees on range estimation.

2.  The averaged range estimation must be within 10 percent of the actual distance.

3.  The sniper team sustains no casualties.


**SUBTASKS AND STANDARDS:**                                    GO    NO-GO

8

1. Each member of the sniper team estimates the range to the target by selecting one or more of the following methods:

   a. The use of maps.
   b. A 100-meter increment.

   c. The appearance of objects.

   d. The mil-scale formula.

   e. The use of the sniper weapon system.

   f. The use of the range card.

   g. The bracketing method.

   h. A combination of methods.

2. The snipers estimate the range throughout the target area.

   a. Each sniper estimates the range to the target(s).

   b. The estimated range by individuals is averaged within 10 percent, plus or minus, of the true range.

\*+3. The team leader determines the estimated range to be used.

   a. Each sniper estimates the range to the target(s).

   b. The team leader compares the estimates.

   c. The team leader makes the final determination of the range to the target(s).

   d. The range to the target(s) is within 10 percent, plus or minus, of the true range.

\*Leader task
+Critical task

TASK PERFORMANCE SUMMARY BLOCK

| ITERATION | 1 | 2 | 3 | 4 | 5 | TOTAL |
|-----------|---|---|---|---|---|-------|

TOTAL SUBTASKS AND STANDARDS
EVALUATED

TOTAL SUBTASKS AND STANDARDS
"GO"

**OPFOR TASK and STANDARD:**

**TASK:**  MAINTAIN Operation Security

**STANDARD:**

The OPFOR does not present easily identifiable targets to the sniper.

**ELEMENT:**  SNIPER TEAM

**TASK:**       DEBRIEF (7-5-1809) (TC 23-14)

ITERATION    1  2  3  4  5  (circle)

TNG STATUS      T  P  U      (circle)

**CONDITION:**  The sniper team completes the mission and conducts a debriefing.  Both friendly and OPFOR units have indirect fire and CAS available.

**TASK STANDARD:**

1.    All team members and the sniper employment officer are present.

2.    All information is collected and recorded in the correct format.

**SUBTASKS AND STANDARDS:**                              GO    NO-GO

1.    The sniper employment officer designates an area for debriefing.

    a.    The size of the area is large enough for the personnel.

        o     S2.

        o     Sniper employment officer.

10

      o     Sniper team.

      o     Battalion commander or his
            representative.

  b.   The area is equipped with the necessary
      maps.

  c.   The debriefing is free from all
      distractions.

**\*2.  The sniper team links up with the sniper
employment officer.**

  a.   The sniper team links up with the sniper
      employment officer at the time specified
      in the patrol order.

  b.   The location is in a secure area behind
      the FLOT.

**3.  The team members and the sniper employment
officer conduct the debriefing.**

  a.   All members are present.

  b.   The sniper team has all recorded information.

      o     Range card.

      o     Field sketch.

      o     Log book.

  c.   The team leader conducts the debriefing in
      chronological order.

**\*Leader task**

**TASK PERFORMANCE SUMMARY BLOCK**

---

| ITERATION | 1 | 2 | 3 | 4 | 5 | TOTAL |
|---|---|---|---|---|---|---|
| TOTAL SUBTASKS AND STANDARDS EVALUATED | | | | | | |
| TOTAL SUBTASKS AND STANDARDS "GO" | | | | | | |

(NO OPFOR TASK OR STANDARDS)

# Appendix H

## FOREIGN/NON-STANDARD SNIPER WEAPON SYSTEMS DATA

**AUSTRIA**

Systems currently in use: Steyr Model SSG 69 and SSG-PII rifles
   w/Kahles ZF69, ZF84, or RZFM86 telescopes.

The Austrian Scharf Schutzen Gewehr (Sharp Shooter's Rifle) 69
(SSG-69) is the current sniper weapon of the Austrian Army and
several foreign military forces. It is available in either 7.62 x
51mm NATO or the .243 Winchester calibers. Recognizable features
are: a synthetic stock (green or black) that is adjustable for the
length of pull by a simple spacer system; hammer-forged, medium-
heavy barrel; two-stage trigger, adjustable for weight of pull (A
set trigger system is freqently seen); and a machined, longitudinal
rib on top of the receiver that accepts several types of optical
mounts. The mounting rings have a quick-release lever system that
allows removal and reattachment of the optics with no loss of zero.
The typical sighting system consists of the Kahles ZF69 6x42mm
telescope; iron sights are permanently affixed to the rifle for
emergency use. The SSG-PII (Politzei II) has a heavy barrel and
does not have iron sights. The telescope comes equipped with a
bullet drop compensator graduated to 800 meters, and a reticle that
consists of a post with broken cross hairs. The Steyr SSG-69 has
a well-deserved reputation for accuracy. The Kahles ZF-series of
telescopes are zeroed with the same procedure used for Soviet
telescopes. See Appendix I-4 for details.

**Steyr SSG-69 Characteristics:**
   System of Operation: bolt action
   Caliber: 7.62x51mm NATO
   Overall length: 44.5 inches
   Barrel length: 25.6 inches
   Rifling: 4 groove, 1/12 inch right hand twist
   Weight: 10.3 pounds
   Magazine capacity: 5- or 10-round detachable magazine
   Sights:
      Telescope: Kahles ZF-69 6x42mm; BDC: 100-800 m
      Front: hooded post
      Rear: notch
   Ammunition requirement: The ZF-69 is designed for the NATO
      ball ammunition: 147/150 gn FMJBT @ 2800 fps. Some
      models of this telescope were designed for export to the
      USA and the BDC is calibrated for Federal's 308M load
      (168 HPBT @ 2600 fps). The K-ZF84 telescope is
      available with the following ballistic cams:  .223/62
      gn; .308/143 gn; .308/146 gn; .308/168 gn; .308/173
      gn; .308/185 gn; and .308/190 gn.

**BELGIUM**

Systems currently in use: Fabrique Nationale Model 30-11.

The FN Model 30-11 is the current sniper rifle of the Belgian army. It is built on a Mauser bolt action with a heavy barrel, and a stock with an adjustable length of pull. The sighting system consists of the FN 4-power, 28-mm telescope and aperture sights with 1/6 MOA adjustment capability. Accessories include the bipod of the MAG machine gun, butt-spacer plates, sling, and carrying case.

**FN Model 30-11 Characteristics**:
    System of operation: bolt action
    Caliber: 7.62x51mm NATO
    Overall length: 45.2 inches
    Barrel length: 20.0 inches
    Rifling: 4 grooves, 1/12 inch right hand twist
    Weight: 15.5 pounds
    Magazine capacity: 10-round detachable magazine
    Sights:
        Telescope: 4x with post reticle, range-finding stadia, and BDC: 100-600 meters
        Front: hooded aperture
        Rear: Anschutz match aperture micrometer adjustable for W/E, and fitted to mount on the rifle's scope base with a quick detachable mount
    Ammunition requirement: 7.62x51mm NATO ball (147/150 gn FMJBT @ 2800 fps)

**CANADA**

Systems currently in use: Parker Hale Model C3.

The Parker Hale Model C3 is a modified target rifle (commercial Model 82 rifle, Model 1200 TX target rifle) built on the Mauser action. It was adopted in 1975. The receiver is fitted with two male dove-tail blocks, to accept either the Parker Hale 5E verner rearsight, or the Kahles 6x42mm telescope. The stock has a spacer system to adjust the length of pull.

**Parker Hale Model C3 Characteristics**:
    System of operation: bolt action
    Caliber: 7.62x51mm NATO
    Overall length: 48.0 inches
    Barrel length: 26.0 inches
    Weight: 12.8 pounds
    Magazine capacity: 4-round internal magazine
    Sights:
        Telescope: Kahles ZF-69 6x42mm; BDC: 100-800 m
        Front: detachable hooded post

Rear: detachable aperture
Ammunition requirement: 7.62x51mm NATO ball (147/150 gn FMJBT @ 2800 fps)


## CZECHOSLOVAKIA

Systems currently in use: Model 54.

The current sniper weapon system is the vz 54 sniper rifle ("vzor" is the Czech word for "model;" therefore, "vz 54" is the same as "Model 54"). It is a manually operated, bolt action, 10-round box, magazine-fed, 7.62x54mm Rimmed weapon. It is built with a free-floating barrel. This weapon is similar to the Soviet M1891/30 sniping rifle; it is shorter and lighter. The rifle is 45.2 inches long and weighs 9.0 pounds with the telescope. It has a muzzle velocity of 2,659 fps with a maximum effective range of 1,000 meters.


## FINLAND

Systems currently in use: Vaime Silenced Sniper Rifle Mark 2

The Finnish armed forces are using a 7.62x51mm NATO sniper rifle that is equipped with an integral barrel/silencer assembly. The SSR Mk2 has a fixed, self-cleaning, and non-corrosive silencer. It has a nonreflective plastic stock and an adjustable bipod. Through the use of adaptors, any telescopic or electro-optical sight may be mounted. The weapon is not equipped with metallic sights. With subsonic ammunition, the SSR Mk2 has a maximum effective range of 200m.

SSR Mk2 Characteristics:
    System of operation: bolt action
    Caliber: 7.62x51mm NATO
    Overall length: 46.5 inches
    Barrel length: 18.3 inches
    Rifling: not known
    Weight: 11 pounds
    Magazine capacity: 10-round internal magazine
    Sights:
        Telescope: various
        Front: none
        Rear: none
    Ammunition requirements: Subsonic (185 gn FMJBT @ 1050 fps)


## FRANCE

Systems currently in use: MAS-GIAT FR-F1 and FR-F2.

The FR-F1 sniping rifle, known as the Tireur d'Elite (sniper), was adopted in 1966. It is based on the MAS 1936 bolt action rifle. The length of pull may be adjusted with the removeable butt-spacer plates. This weapon's sighting system consists of the Model 53 bis 3.8x telescopic sight and integral metallic sights with luminous spots for night firing. Standard equipment features a permanently affixed bipod whose legs may be folded forward into recesses in the fore-end of the weapon. The barrel has an integral muzzle brake/flash suppressor. This weapon has a muzzle velocity of 2,794 fps and a maximum effective range of 800 meters.

## MAS-GIAT FR-F1 Characteristics:

System of operation: bolt action
Caliber: 7.62x51mm NATO or 7.5x54mm French
Overall length: 44.8 inches
Barrel length: 22.8 inches
Rifling: not known
Weight: 11.9 pounds
Magazine capacity: 10-round detachable box magazine
Sights:
Telescope: Model 53, 3.8x
Front: hooded post
Rear: notch
Ammunition requirement: not known

The FR-F2 sniping rifle is an updated version of the F1. Dimensions and operating characteristics remain unchanged; however, functional improvements have been made. A heavy-duty bipod has been mounted more toward the butt-end of the rifle, adding ease of adjustment for the firer. Also, the major change is the addition of a thick, plastic thermal sleeve around and along the length of the barrel. This addition eliminates or reduces barrel mirage and heat signature.

## MAS-GIAT FR-F2 Characteristics:

System of operation: bolt action
Caliber: 7.62x51mm NATO
Overall length: 47.2 inches
Barrel length: 22.9 inches
Rifling: 3 grooves, 1/11.6 right hand twist
Weight: 13.6 pounds
Magazine capacity: 10-round detachable magazine
Sights:
Telescope: 6x42mm or 1.5-6x42mm Schmidt and Bender;
BDC: 100-600 m
Front: post
Rear: notch
Ammunition requirement: 150 gn FMJBT @ 2690 fps

**GERMANY**

Systems currently in use: Mauser Model SP66, Walther WA 2000, and the Heckler & Koch PSG-1.

The Mauser Model SP66 is used by the Germans and also by about 12 other countries. This weapon is a heavy-barrelled, bolt-action rifle built upon a Mauser short action. It has a completely adjustable thumbhole-type stock. The muzzle of the weapon is equipped with a flash suppressor and muzzle brake.

**Mauser SP66 Characteristics**:
       System of operation: bolt action
       Caliber: 7.62x51mm NATO
       Overall length: not known
       Barrel length: 26.8 inches
       Rifling: not known
       Weight: not known
       Magazine capacity: 3-round internal magazine
       Sights:
               Telescope: Zeiss-Diavari ZA 1.5-6x
               Front: detachable hooded post
               Rear: detachable aperture
       Ammunition requirement: not known


The Walther WA 2000 is built specifically for sniping. The entire weapon is built around the 25.6-inch barrel; it is a semi-automatic gas-operated bull-pup design that is 35.6 inches long. This unique weapon is chambered for .300 Winchester Magnum, but it can be equipped to accommodate 7.62x51mm NATO or 7.5x55mm Swiss calibers. The weapon's trigger is a single- or two-staged type. It can be fitted with various optics, but is typically found with a Schmidt & Bender 2.5-10x56mm telescope. It has range settings from 100 to 600 meters and can be dismounted and mounted without loss of zero.

**Walther WA 2000 Characteristics**:
       System of operation: semiautomatic
       Caliber: .300 Win Mag, 7.62x51mm NATO, 7.5x55mm Swiss
       Overall length: 35.6 inches
       Barrel length: 25.6 inches
       Rifling: not known
       Weight: 18.3 pounds
       Magazine capacity: 3-round detachable magazine
       Sights:
               Telescope: Schmidt & Bender 2.5-10x56mm, BDC: 100-600 m
               Front: none
               Rear: none
       Ammunition requirement: not known


The Heckler & Koch Prazisions Schutzen Gewehr (Precision Marksman's Shooting Rifle) PSG-1 is an extremely accurate version of the G-3. It is a gas-operated, magazine-fed, semiautomatic

weapon with a fully adjustable, pistol-grip-style stock. Heckler
& Koch claims that this weapon will shoot as accurately as the
inherent accuracy of the ammunition. The 6x42mm Hensoldt has LED-
enhanced, illuminated crosshairs, elevation adjustments from 100 to
600 meters, and point blank settings from 10 to 75 meters. Sight
in requires loosening two small screws located in the center of the
windage and elevation knobs. Once the screws are loosened, the
adjustment can be made to center the shot group to correspond with
one of the range settings on the knobs. The adjustments for both
elevation and windage move the impact of the bullet one centimeter
(.4") at 100 meters.

## Heckler & Koch PSG-1 Characteristics:
        System of operation: semiautomatic
        Caliber: 7.62x51mm NATO
        Overall length: 47.5 inches
        Barrel length: 25.6 inches
        Rifling: polygonal, 1/12 right hand twist
        Weight: 17.8 pounds
        Magazine capacity: 5- and 20-round detachable magazine
        Sights:
                Telescope: 6x42mm Hensoldt with illuminated reticle, BDC:
                        100-600 m
                Front: none
                Rear: none
        Ammunition requirement: Lapua 7.62x51mm NATO Match: 185 FMJBT
                D46/D47 @ 2493 fps


## ISRAEL

Systems currently in use: Galil and M21 Sniping Rifle.

The Israelis copied the basic design, operational
characteristics and configuration of the Soviet AK-47 assault rifle
to develop an improved weapon to meet the demands of the Israeli
army. The Galil sniping rifle is a further evolution of this basic
design. Like most service rifles modified for sniper use, the
weapon is equipped with a heavier barrel fitted with a flash
suppressor; it can be equipped with a silencer and fired with
subsonic ammunition. The weapon features a pistol-grip-style
stock, a fully adjustable cheekpiece, a rubber recoil pad, a two-
stage trigger, and an adjustable bipod mounted to the rear of the
fore-end of the rifle. Its sighting system consists of a side-
mounted 6x40mm telescope and fixed metallic sights. When firing FN
Match ammunition, the weapon has a muzzle velocity of 2,672 fps;
when firing M118 special ball ammunition, it has a muzzle velocity
of 2,557 fps. The specifications on the M21 can be found in the US
section.

## Galil Sniper Rifle Characteristics:
        System of operation: semiautomatic

```
Caliber: 7.62x51mm NATO
Overall length: 43.9 inches
Barrel length: 20 inches
Rifling: 4 groove, 1/12 right hand twist
Weight: 18.3 pounds
Magazine capacity: 5- or 25-round detachable magazine
Sights:
        Telescope: 6x40mm Nimrod, BDC: 100-1000 m
        Front: hooded post with tritium night sight
        Rear: aperture with flip-up tritium night sight
Ammunition requirement: M118 (173 gn FMJBT @ 2610 fps)
```

## ITALY

Systems currently in use: Beretta Sniper Rifle.

The Beretta rifle is the Italian sniper rifle. This rifle is a manually operated, bolt-action, 5-round box, magazine-fed weapon that fires the 7.62x51mm NATO. Its 45.9 inch length consists of a 23-inch heavy, free-floated barrel, a wooden thumbhole-type stock with a rubber recoil pad, and an adjustable cheekpiece. Target-quality, metallic sights consist of a hooded front sight and a fully adjustable, V-notch rearsight. The optical sight consists of a Zeiss-Diavari ZA 1.5-6x variable telescope. The weapon weighs 15.8 pounds with a bipod, and 13.75 pounds without the bipod. The NATO-standard telescope mount allows almost any electro-optical or optical sight to be mounted to the weapon.

## PEOPLE'S REPUBLIC OF CHINA

Systems currently in use: Norinco Type 79.

The standard sniper rifle of the PRC is the Norinco Type 79, which was adopted in 1980. It is a virtual copy of the Soviet SVD. In many instances, they are nothing more than refinished and restamped Soviet SVDs that were once sold to the PRC. They have been imported into the U.S. under the designation of NDM-86. The specifications can be found under the Soviet SVD.

## ROMANIA

Systems currently in use: Model FPK.

The FPK was adopted in 1970. This sniper rifle fires the Mosin/Nagant M1891 cartridge which has a case length that is 15mm longer than the 7.62x39mm Warsaw Pact cartidge. Since the bolt of the AKM travels 30mm (1.18 inches) further to the rear than is necessary to accommodate the 7.62x39mm cartridge, the Romanian designers were able to modify the standard AKM-type receiver mechanism to fire the more powerful and longer-ranged 7.62x54mm rimmed cartridge. First, they altered the bolt face to take the larger rimmed base of the M1891 cartridge, added a new barrel, and lengthened the RPK-type gas piston system. The gas system of the Soviet SVD (Dragunov) sniping rifle is more like that of the obsolete Tokarev rifle. Second, the Romanians developed their own 10-shot magazine, and they fabricated a skeleton stock from laminated wood (plywood). This buttstock, with its molded cheek rest, is probably slightly better than the one used on the Dragunov. Third, the Romanians have riveted two steel reinforcing plates to the rear of the receiver to help absorb the increased recoil forces of the more powerful M1891 cartridge. Finally they have attached a muzzle brake of their own design. The standard AKM wire cutter bayonet will attach to this sniper rifle. The telescopic sight has English language markings.

**FPK Characteristics**:
    System of operation: semiautomatic
    Caliber: 7.62x54mm Rimmed
    Overall length: 45.4 inches
    Barrel length: 26.7 inches
    Rifling: not known
    Weight: 10.6 lbs
    Magazine capacity: 10-round detachable box magazine
    Sights:
        Telescopic: LSP (Romanian copy of the Soviet PSO-1);
            BDC: 100-1000 m with 1100, 1200, and 1300 m
                reference points
        Front: hooded post
        Rear: sliding u-shaped notch
    Ammunition requirements: see Soviet SVD comments


**SPAIN**

Systems currently in use: Model C-75.

The 7.62x51mm NATO C-75 special forces rifle is the current sniper rifle of Spain. This bolt-action weapon is built upon the Mauser 98 action. It is equipped with iron sights and has telescope mounts machined into the receiver to allow for the mounting of most electro-optic or optic sights. The weapon weighs 8.14 pounds.


**SWITZERLAND**

Systems currently in use: SIG Model 510-4.

The Swiss use the 7.62x51mm NATO SIG Model 510-4 rifle with a telescopic sight. The 510-4 is a delayed, blow-back-operated, 20-round, magazine-fed, semiautomatic or fully automatic weapon. With bipod, telescope, and empty 20-round magazine, the weapon weighs 12.3 pounds. It is 39.9 inches long with a 19.8-inch barrel, and has a muzzle velocity of 2,591 fps.


## UNITED KINGDOM

Systems currently in use: Lee Enfield Model L42A1, Parker-Hale Models 82 and 85, and the Accuracy International L96A1. The Lee Enfield No. 4 Mark 1 (T) is obsolete, but still found in use around the world

The L42A1 is the current standard sniper rifle. It is a conversion of the Lee Enfield No. 4 Mark 1 (T) .303, and was adopted in 1970. It has a heavy 7.62x51mm NATO barrel, and the fore-end is cut back. The original No. 32 telescope was renovated, regraduated, and redesignated the "Telescope Straight Sighting L1A1" which is marked on the tube along with the part number, O.S. 2429 G.A. The original No. 32 markings are usually still visible, cancelled out and painted over. New range graduations are read in meters instead of yards. Receivers from No. 4 Mark 1 (T) or Mark 1* (T) are used for this rifle. The magazine of the L42A1 is designed for 7.62mm NATO cartridges and has a capacity of 10 rounds. The butt stock has the same type "screw on" wooden cheek piece as used with the No. 4 Mark 1 (T). The left side of the receiver has a telescope bracket for the telescope No. 32 Mark 3. A leaf type rear sight and a protected blade type front sight are also used.

Lee Enfield L42A1 Characteristics:
     System of operation: bolt action
     Caliber: 7.62x51mm NATO
     Overall length: 46.5 inches
     Barrel length: 27.5 inches
     Rifling: 4 grooves, 1/12 right hand twist
     Weight: 12.5 pounds
     Magazine capacity: 10-round detachable magazine
     Sights:
          Telescope: L1A1, 3x, BDC: 0-1000 m
          Front: blade, with protecting ears
          Rear: aperture
     Ammunition requirement: NATO ball, 147/150 gn FMJBT @ 2800
          fps

The Parker Hale Model 82 sniper rifle is a bolt-action 7.62x51mm NATO rifle built upon a Mauser 98 action. It is a militarized version of the Model 1200 TX target rifle. It is equipped with metallic target sights and the Pecar V2S 4-10x variable telescope. An optional, adjustable bipod is also available.

Parker Hale Model 82 Characteristics:

System of operation: bolt action
Caliber: 7.62x51mm NATO
Overall length: 48.0 inches
Barrel length: 26.0 inches
Rifling: not known
Weight: 12.8 pounds
Magazine capacity: 4-round internal magazine
Sights:
    Telescope: Pecar V2S 4-10x
    Front: detachable hooded post
    Rear: detachable aperture
Ammunition requirement: 7.62x51mm NATO ball (147/150 gn FMJBT
  @ 2800 fps)

The Model 85 sniper rifle is a bolt action 7.62x51mm rifle designed for extended use under adverse conditions. It uses a McMillan fiberglass stock that is adjustable for length of pull. The telescope is mounted on a quick-detachable mount that can be removed in emergencies to reveal a flip-up rear aperture sight that is graduated from 100-900m.

**Parker-Hale M85 Characteristics**:
System of operation: bolt action
Caliber: 7.62x51mm NATO
Overall length: 47.5 inches
Barrel length: 24.8 inches
Rifling: 4 grooves, 1/12 right hand twist
Weight: 12.5 pounds
Magazine capacity: 10-round detachable magazine
Sights:
    Telescopic: Swarovski ZFM 6x42mm (BDC: 100-800 m) or ZFM
      10x42mm (BDC: 100-1000 m)
    Front: protected blade
    Rear: folding aperture
Ammunition requirement: NATO ball, 147/150 gn FMJBT @ 2800
  fps

The L96A1 sniper rifle is built by Accuracy International using a unique bedding system designed by Malcolm Cooper. It features an aluminium frame with a high-impact plastic, thumbhole-type stock; a free-floated barrel; and a lightweight-alloy, fully adjustable bipod. The rifle is equipped with metallic sights that can deliver accurate fire out to 700 meters and can use the L1A1 telescope. The reported accuracy of this weapon is 0.75 MOA at 1,000 meters. One interesting feature of the stock design is a spring-loaded monopod concealed in the butt. Fully adjustable for elevation, the monopod serves the same purpose as the sand sock that the US Army uses.

**Accuracy International Model PM/L96A1 Characteristics**:
System of operation: bolt action

```
Caliber: 7.62x51mm NATO, .243 Win, 7mm Rem Mag, 300 WM
Overall length: 47.0 inches
Barrel length: 26 inches
Rifling: 1/12 right hand twist
Weight: 15 pounds
Magazine capacity: 10-round detachable magazine
Sights:
        Telescope: 6x42mm or 12x42mm Schmidt and Bender
        Front: none
        Rear: none
Ammunition requirement: not known
```

The Lee Enfield Rifle No. 4 Mark 1 (T) and No. 4 Mark 1* (T) are sniper versions of the No. 4. They are fitted with scope mounts on the left side of the receiver and have a wooden cheek rest screwed to the butt. The No. 32 telescope is used on these weapons.

## Lee Enfield No. 4 Mark 1 (T) Characteristics:
```
        System of operation: bolt action
        Caliber: .303 British
        Overall length: 44.5 inches
        Barrel length: 25.2 inches
        Rifling: not known
        Weight: 11.5 pounds
        Magazine capacity: 10-round detachable magazine
        Sights:
                Telescope: No. 32, 3x, BDC: 100-1000 yards
                Front: blade with protecting ears
                Rear: vertical leaf w/ aperture battle sight or L type
        Ammunition requirement: .303 ball with a muzzle velocity (at
                date of adoption): 2440 fps
```

## UNION OF SOVIET SOCIALISTIC REPUBLICS

Systems currently in use: SVD (Dragunov).

The Self-loading Rifle, Dragunov (SVD) is a purpose-designed system that replaced the M1891/30 sniper rifle in 1963. The bolt operation of the SVD is similar to that of the AK/AKM. The principle difference is that the SVD has a short stroke piston system. It is not attached to the bolt carrier like that of the AK/AKM, and delivers its impulse to the carrier, which then moves to the rear. The remainder of the operating sequence is quite similar to the Kalashnikov-series assault rifle. The rifle has a somewhat unusual stock in that a large section has been cut out of it immediately to the rear of the pistol grip. This lightens the weight of the rifle considerably. It has a prong-type flash suppressor similar to those used on current US\small arms. It is equipped with metallic sights that are graduated to 2,000 meters and the PSO-1 4-power telescopic sight with a battery-powered,

11

illuminated reticle. The PSO-1 also incorporates a metascope that when activated, is capable of detecting an active, infrared source. The PSO-1 is designed for the ballistic trajectory of the "LPS" ball round. The windage knob provides 2 MOA per click and 4 MOA per numeral. The reticle pattern has 10 vertical lines to the left and right of the aiming chevron. These lines are spaced 4 MOA from each other, therefore providing 40 MOA to the left and right of the aiming chevron.

## SVD Characteristics:

System of operation: semiautomatic
Caliber: 7.62x54mm rimmed
Overall length: 47.9 inches
Barrel length: 24.5 inches
Rifling: 4 grooves, 1/10 right hand twist
Weight: 9.7 pounds
Magazine capacity: 10-round detachable magazine
Sights:
    Telescope: 4x PSO-1, BDC: 0-1300 m
    Front: hooded post
    Rear: tangent with notch
Ammunition requirement: LPS ball (149 gn FMJBT @ 2800 fps)

## Warsaw Pact Ammunition:
The standard M1908 Russian "L" ball cartridge features a 149 grain lead-core spitzer bullet with a gilding metal jacket and a conical hollow base. The "L" ball gives about 2800 fps from the M1891/30 rifles. It can be identified with a plain, unpainted, copper-colored bullet.

The "LPS" ball cartridge is a 149 grain boattail with a gilding metal-clad steel jacket and mild steel core. The LPS cartridge can be identified by a white or silver bullet tip, distinguishing it from the lead-core "L" ball. Velocity is around 2820 fps.

The M1930 heavy ball sniper load is known as the Type "D" and is sometimes identified by a yellow bullet tip. It features a 182 grain full metal jacket bullet with a hollow-base boat tail and develops 2680 fps from the M1891/30 or the SVD.

The general rule for identfying Soviet/Warsaw Pact ammunition is as follows: when the head of the cartridge case is oriented to that both numbers can be read, the factory number appears at 12 o'clock and the date of manufacture appears at 6 o'clock.

## Mosin-Nagant Bolt Action Sniper Rifle Model M1891/30:
The M1891 was adopted as the Russian army service rifle in 1891. It has a blade front sight with a leaf rear sight graduated in arshins (paces) from 100 to 3200, (2496 yards). In the 1930's the improved M1891/30 was fielded. The M1891/30 has a hooded front sight and a tangent rear sight graduated from 100 to 2000 meters. The M1891/30 sniper rifle was adopted shortly thereafter, with its only modification being the addition of a telescopic sight. Details on the telescope will be found in

Appendix I.

**M1891/30 Characteristics:**
    System of operation: bolt action
    Caliber: 7.62x54mm rimmed
    Overall length: 48.5 inches
    Barrel length: 28.7 inches
    Rifling: 4 groove, 1/10 right hand twist
    Weight: 11.3 pounds
    Magazine capacity: 5-round semi-fixed magazine
    Sights:
        Telescope: PU 3.5x or PE 4x telescope
        Front: hooded post
        Rear: tangent rear, graduated from 100-2000 m
    Ammunition requirement: L or LPS ball (149 gn FMJ @ 2800 fps)


**UNITED STATES OF AMERICA**

Systems currently in use: the M24 and M21 SWSs.

    The US Army sniper weapon systems are the M24 and M21. The USMC has adopted a product-improved version of the Remington 700 and is currently known as the M40A1. Special application sniper rifles such as the Barrett Model 82 and the RAI Model 500 are used on an organized, but limited basis. Numerous non-standard sniper rifles are used by different US Government and DOD agencies. Also, obsolete sniper rifles are still being used abroad. These include the M1903A4, M1C, and the M1D.

**M24 SWS:**
    The M24 entered service in 1988 to selected US Army units. It is the first purpose-built sniper rifle ever adopted by the Army. It is based on the Remington Model 700 long action; this will permit the later conversion to the .300 Winchester Magnum cartridge. The M3A Ultra telescope has the mil dot reticle system for range finding purposes. The ballistic cam is designed for the M118 ammunition and provides a one-revolution trajectory compensation for 100-1000 meters. The telescope can be removed in the field if necessary; detachable target sights are the back-up. H-S Precision makes the fiberglass/kevlar stock that is unique due to its aluminum bedding block. This stock eliminated the effects of weather and moisture on the system. A detachable Harris bipod can be attached to the additional sling swivel stud provided on the fore-end. The length of pull is adjustable to accommodate the assigned individual.

**M24 Characteristics:**
    System of operation: bolt action
    Caliber: 7.62x51mm NATO
    Overall length: 43-45.7 inches
    Barrel length: 24 inches

Rifling: 5 groove, 1/11.2 right hand twist
Weight: 14.1 pounds
Magazine capacity: 5-round internal magazine
Sights:
    Telescope: L&S M3A Ultra, mil dot, BDC: 100-1000m
    Front: detachable hooded post with replaceable inserts
    Rear: detachable aperture
Ammuntion requirement: M118 Match/Special Ball (173 gn FMJBT
    @ 2610 fps)

## M21 Sniper System:

In Sep 1968 the Army Materiel Command was directed to produce 1800 National Match M-14s for immediate shipment to Vietnam. From 1968 until 1975, when the XM-21 was adopted, several NM M-14 variants with different telescopes were shipped to Vietnam for use. The first XM-21s used the WW II-era M84 telescope. James Leatherwood, the designer of the ART-series provided most of the telescopes, although others were used. The M21 is carefully assembled to National Match standards with selected components. The stock was originally an epoxy-impregnated walnut or birch stock. The rifle has NM iron sights. The elevation and windage adjustments provide 1/2 MOA corrections. The scope mount is mounted to the side of the receiver with a large knurled knob. Later mounts provided two points of attachment with an additional knob threaded in to a modified clip guide. The M21 was type-classified with the ART I. The ART II was later used on a limited basis, and the M3A Ultra has been used to upgrade the M21 system.

NOTE: USSOCOM is currently developing an upgraded version of the M21 and it will be fielded as the new Light Sniper Rifle (LSR).

## M21 Characteristics:
System of operation: semiautomatic
Caliber: 7.62x51mm NATO
Overall length: 44.3 inches
Barrel length: 22 inches
Rifling: 4 groove, 1/12 right hand twist
Weight: 14.4 pounds
Magazine capacity: 20-round detachable magazine
Sights:
    Telescope: ART I or ART II, BDC: 300-900 m
    Front: protected post
    Rear: hooded aperture
Ammunition requirement: M118 Match or Special Ball (173 gn
    FMJBT @ 2610 fps)

## USMC M40A1:

The M40A1 is the current USMC sniping rifle that is the culmination of 20 years of use of the Remington Model 700 since the Vietnam War. It is built by match armorers to exacting standards using selected components. It uses Remington M700 and 40X receivers mated to a heavy McMillan/Wiseman stainless steel match

barrel. The stock is made by McMillan. The Unertl 10x USMC sniper
scope has the mil-dot reticle and a BDC designed to range from 100
to 1000 yards.

## M40A1 Characteristics:
        System of operation: bolt action
        Caliber: 7.62x51mm NATO
        Overall length: 44 inches
        Barrel length: 24 inches
        Rifling: 6 groove, 1/12 right hand twist
        Weight: 14.4 pounds
        Magazine capacity: 5-round internal magazine
        Sights:
                Telescope: Unertl 10x, BDC: 100-1000 yards
                Front: none
                Rear: none
        Ammunition requirement: M118 Match or Special Ball (173 gn
            FMJBT @ 2610 fps), or Federal Match with the 180 gn
            Sierra MatchKing bullet

## Barrett Model 82A1:
        The Barrett Model 82 sniping rifle is a recoil-operated, 11-
round detachable box, magazine-fed, semiautomatic chambered for the
.50 caliber Browning cartridge. Its 36.9-inch fluted barrel is
equipped with a six-port muzzle brake that reduces recoil by 30
percent. It has an adjustable bipod and can also be mounted on the
M82 tripod or any mount compatible with the M60 machine gun. This
weapon has a pistol-grip-style stock, is 65.9 inches long, and
weighs 32.9 pounds. The sighting system consists of a telescope,
but no metallic sights are provided. The telescope mount may
accommodate any telescope with 1-inch rings. Muzzle velocity of
the Model 82 is 2,849 fps.

## Iver Johnson Model 500:
        The Iver Johnson Model 500 is the current version of the
Research Armaments Industry (RAI) Model 500/Daisy Model 500. The
Model 500 long-range rifle is a bolt action, single-shot weapon,
that is chambered for the .50 caliber Browning cartridge. It has
a 33-inch heavy, fluted, free-floating barrel. With its bipod,
fully adjustable stock and cheekpiece, and telescope, it weighs a
total of 29.92 pounds. The weapon is equipped with a harmonic
balancer that dampens barrel vibrations, a telescope with a ranging
scope base, and a muzzle brake with flash suppressor. The USMC and
USN use this weapon, which has a muzzle velocity of 2,912 fps.

## NON-STANDARD U.S. SNIPER RIFLES

## Remington Models 40XB, 40XC, and 700 rifles:
        These variations of the Remington M700 bolt action rifle are
widely used. The M700 is the standard rifle. The M700 and its
variants have tubular/round actions which are preferred by many
competitors due to its ease of truing and bedding. It is most

frequently seen in the heavy barreled "Varmint Special" version. The 40XB is a single-shot competition rifle, and is extremely accurate. The 40XB has a solid magazine well that adds to the action's rigidity. The 40X or 40XC is similar to the XB except they have a magazine well, stripper clip guide, and are designed for use in high power rifle competition. The M24 SWS is built on a Remington M700 action marked M24 M700. It is built to the same exacting standards as the 40XB's are built with. The original M24 came with a Rock 5R barrel. The new M24s from Remington come with a Remington hammer-forged barrel. Most Remington .308 rifles (M700, 40XB, and 40XC) come with a short action, for reduced action size, increased action rigidity, and reduced bolt cycling distance. The M24 was adopted with a long action so that it could be converted to the .300 Winchester Magnum cartridge at a later date. This will be accomplished by replacing the barrel and bolt. In this magnum chambering the M24 will be designated the Medium Sniper Rifle (MSR), and be effective out to 1200 meters. The BDC on the Leupold & Stevens M3A will be replaced to match the different ballistic trajectory.

**Remington Models 40X/700 Characteristics:**
   System of operation: bolt action
   Caliber: 7.62x51mm NATO (.308 Win), .300 Win Mag, and others
   Overall length: approximately 42 inches (dependent on bbl
      length)
   Barrel length: 22-26 inches
   Rifling: 4-6 groove, 1/10-1/12 right hand twist
   Weight: 10-15 pounds
   Magazine capacity: 5-round standard calibers, 3 round magnum
      calibers, internal magazine; 40XB is single shot.
   Sights:
      Telescope: L&S Ultra/Mark IV M1A, M3A; Unertl 10x USMC;
         Bausch & Lomb 10x40mm Tactical; other
      Front: none
      Rear: none
   Ammunition requirement: varied

Winchester Model 70:
   The Model 70 in .308, or .300 Win Mag, when properly built, is also a very effective and accurate rifle, as proven by the multiple national and international competitors that use them. Winchester now makes a true short action, in caliber .308 as a varmint rifle which can be an alternative to the M700 Remington. The Winchester Model 70 has a square-bottomed action.

Other systems:

   A.   McMillan systems: The M-86SR (.308 Win), M-86LR
        (.300 Win Mag), and M-89 (.308 suppressed) are bolt-
        action rifles built on McMillan actions. The M-88ELR,
        M-87ELR, and M-87R are .50 cal bolt rifles. The
McMillan M-40 is a Remington short action barrelled          with a

McMillan .308 match barrel.  A variety of optics        a    r    e
available: L&S Ultra/Mark IV M1A, M3A, 3.5-10x Law
            Enforcement; the Bausch and Lomb 10x40mm tactical; and
            the Phrobis tactical rifle telescopes
    B.  Robar systems: Accurized Remington Model 700 rifle
    C.  Barrett Firearms: M82, M82A1 light semi .50 cal rifles,
        and the M90 bolt action .50 cal rifle
    D.  Iver Johnson Convertible Long Range Rifle System

**Iver Johnson Convertible Long Range Rifle Characteristics**:
        System of operation: bolt action
        Caliber: 7.62x51mm NATO, 8.58x71mm (.338/.416)
        Overall length: 46.5 inches
        Barrel length: 24 inches
        Rifling: 4 groove; 1/12 (7.62), 1/10 (8.58) right hand twist
        Weight: 15 pounds
        Magazine capacity: 4-round (7.62), 5-round (8.58),
            detachable magazine
        Sights:
            Telescope: varied
            Front: none
            Rear: none
        Ammunition requirement: 8.58x71mm; 250 gn HPBT 3,000 fps

**OBSOLETE U.S. SNIPER RIFLES**

**M1903A4 Springfield**:
        The M1903A4 was adopted in Dec 1942 as a sniper rifle during
WW II.  The only modification to the standard service rifle was the
addition of a pistol grip and optical sight.  There were numerous
telescopic sights used, but the most common were the M84 and the
Weaver Model 330C (marked M73B1 for the contract).  There are a few
1903's that were meticulously assembled with selected parts for
sniper use, but as a general rule, the majority were standard
service rifles.  The low magnification of the telescopes (2.2x for
the M84) made long-range target interdiction difficult.  The M84
scope will be discussed in Appendix I.  The Model 1942 is a Marine
Corps modification of the 1903A1, fitted with a 8x Unertl scope.
These rifles were manufactured by Remington, Springfield Armory,
and the L.C. Smith Corona Typewriter company.

**M1903A4 Characteristics**:
        System of operation: bolt action
        Caliber: Caliber .30 M1/M2 ball (7.62x63mm/30-06)
        Overall length: 43.5 inches
        Barrel length: 24 inches
        Rifling: 4 groove (and 2 groove), 1/10 right hand twist
        Weight: 9.4 pounds
        Magazine capacity: 5-round internal magazine
        Sights:
            Telescope: M84, M73B1 Weaver (Model 330C), or the M73
                Lyman Alaska; BDC: 0-900 yards

Front: none
Rear: none
Ammunition requirement: Caliber .30 M1/M2 ball (150 FMJ flat base @ 2800 fps

## Garand M1C and M1D:

In 1939 the Springfield Armory and Winchester began production of the M1. The M1 was the first self-loading rifle that withstood battlefield use. The M1C and M1D were developed for designated marksman use. The M1D was fitted with steel collar around the barrel in front of the receiver, which was tapped for a side-mounted scope mount, because the weapon loads through the top of the receiver. A M84 2.2x scope was used. A specially fabricated leather extension was affixed to the left side of the stock to provide a solid stock weld to accommodate the side-mounted telescope. This was so the shooter could rest his cheek and fire left eyed. Although the rifle can be fired right eyed it was designed to be fired left eyed. It is a fallacy to this day that the leather stock extension is a cheek piece; it is not. It was and is a rest for use with the side- mounted scope. The majority of the M1D's were also fitted with a prong-flash hider. The M1C is identical to the M1D except in one respect. The M1C has a side mount that was tapped into the left side of the receiver directly instead of using a collar around the barrel. Like the M1903A4, nothing was done to the majority of the rifles to accurize them. Eventually, hand-assembled M1D's and C's were made and used.

## M1C/D Characteristics:
System of operation: semiautomatic
Caliber: .30 Caliber M1/M2 ball (7.62x63mm/30-06)
Overall length: 43.6 inches
Barrel length: 24 inches
Rifling: 4 groove, 1/10 right hand twist
Weight: 11.8 pounds
Magazine capacity: 8-round en-bloc metallic clip
Sights:
    Telescope: M84, 2.2x, BDC: 0-900 yards
    Front: protected post
    Rear: aperture
Ammunition requirement: M1/M2 ball (150 gn FMJ flat base bullet @ 2800 fps)


## YUGOSLAVIA

Systems currently in use: Model M76.

The Yugoslav armed forces use the M76 semiautomatic sniping rifle. It is believed to be based upon the FAZ family of automatic weapons; it features permanently affixed metallic sights, a pistol-grip-style wood stock, and a 4x telescopic sight. The telescopic sight is graduated in 100-meter increments from 100 to 1,000 meters, and the optical sight mount allows the mounting of passive nightsights.  It has a muzzle velocity of 2,361 fps.

**M76 Characteristics**:
    System of operation: semiautomatic
    Caliber: 7.92x57mm (8mm Mauser), 7.62x54mm R, 7.62x51mm NATO
    Overall length: 44.7 inches
    Barrel length: 21.6 inches
    Rifling: not known
    Weight: 11.2 pounds
    Magazine capacity: 10-round detachable
    Sights:
        Telescope: 4x, BDC: 100-1,000m
        Front: hooded post
        Rear: tangent
    Ammunition requirement: 7.92x57mm (2361 fps); 7.62x51mm NATO
        (2657 fps)

# Appendix I

## SNIPER RIFLE TELESCOPES

### I-1. CHARACTERISTICS OF RIFLE TELESCOPES

#### Telescope Magnification

The average unaided human eye can distinguish 1-inch detail at 100 meters. Magnification, combined with quality lens manufacture and design, permits resolution of this 1-inch divided by the optical magnification. The general rule is 1x magnification per 100 meters. The magnification (power) of a telescope should correspond to the maximum effective range of the weapon system being used. This will enable the operator to identify precise corrections. For example, a 5x telescope is adequate out to 500 meters; a 10x is good out to 1000 meters. The best all around magnification determined for field-type sniping is the 10x because it permits the operator to identify precise corrections out to 1000 meters. The field of view of a 10x at close range, while small, is still enough to see large and small targets. Higher-powered telescopes have very limited field of views, making close range and snap target engagements difficult. Substandard high powered telescopes may be hard to focus and have parallax problems. Some marksmen still prefer lower-powered telescopes.

#### Parallax

Parallax results when the target is not focused on the same focal plane as the reticle. When parallax is present, the target will move in relation to the reticle when the sniper moves his head (changes his spot weld) while looking through the telescope. It is more apparent in high-powered telescopes. With parallax, the error will not effect the strike of the bullet more than 1/2 the diameter of the objective lens out to 2 times the zero distance. .For example, with a zero at 100m, the error would be less than approximately 1 inch at 200m. It is recommended that the sniper zero his system at the greatest distance possible. For a 1000m system, zero at 500m. The M1A and M3A Ultra/Mark IV by L&S have a focus/parallax knob on the left side of the telescope. With the M1A and M3A, it is imperative that the sniper adjust his focus/parallax when he zeros his system and never adjust it again until he re-zeros. If the focus/parallax is adjusted during shooting, the point of impact will change from the previously established zero.

#### Adjustable Objective Lens

Adjustable objective lenses for focusing at different magnifications and ranges are becoming quite common. Some target telescopes (such as the M1A and M3A) have a third turret knob on the side of the telescope that will focus the objective lens. Unfortunately, many telescopes have neither and must be dealt with on an individual basis.

Variable Power Telescopes
    Variable power telescopes have had a bad reputation for a shifting point of impact when the magnification is changed from the original magnification that the system was sighted in with. Modern, high quality, variable telescopes do not seem to have this problem anymore. This has been tested on Leupold's 6.5-20x target telescope. After zeroing it showed no variation in the point of aim versus the point of impact at any range or any power. Of course, it is prudent to test the system during live-fire exercises to establish the optic's reliability.

I-2.  TELESCOPE ADJUSTMENTS

Focusing
    Focusing the telescope to the individual assigned the weapon is important. Most telescopes' ocular lens can be adjusted for minor eye relief adjustments and to obtain a crisp, clear picture of the reticle. To do this, look at a distant object for several seconds without using the telescope. Then shift your vision quickly, looking through the telescope at a plain background. The reticle pattern should be sharp and clear before your eye refocuses. If you need to make an adjustment to match your eyes, hold the eyepiece lock ring and loosen the eyepiece by turning it counter-clockwise several turns. Then, with a quick glance recheck the image. To compensate for nearsightedness, turn the eyepiece clockwise; for farsightedness, turn the eyepiece counter-clockwise. After determining the precise focus for your eye, be sure to retighten the lock ring securely against the eyepiece to hold it in position.

    CAUTION: Never look at the sun through the telescope. Concentration of strong solar rays cay cause serious eye damage.

Eye Relief
    Proper eye relief is established very simply. First, loosen the scope rings' allen screws so that the telescope is free to move. Get into the shooting position that will be used most frequently and slide the scope forward or back until a full, crisp picture is obtained. There should be no shading in the view. This will be anywhere from 2-4 inches from the operator's eye depending on the telescope. Rotate the telescope until the reticle crosshairs are perfectly vertical and horizontal, then tighten the ring screws.

    The M-24 has a one-piece telescope base that has two sets of machined grooves that allow the telescope to be mounted either forward or back to adjust for personal comfort. If that range of adjustment is not sufficient, the telescope can be adjusted after the mounting ring lock screws are loosened.

## I.3 UNITED STATES TELESCOPES

### M84 Telescopic Sight

The M84 telescopic sight has a magnification of 2.2x. It has a field of view of 27 feet at 100 yards. The maximum field of view is obtained with an eye relief of 3 1/2 to 5 inches. The reticle consists of a vertical post and a horizontal crosshair (Figure I-3-1). The post is 3 MOA in width. The sight is sealed with rubber seals and may be submerged without damage (not recommended due to age). The windage knob has 60 MOA of adjustment, 30 MOA from center left or right. However, there is a total of 100 MOA adjustments available to zero the telescope for misalignment. To adjust the strike of the bullet vertically, turn the knob to the higher numbers to raise the point of impact, and to lower numbers to lower the point of impact. A complete turn of the elevation knob provides 40 MOA of adjustment. 1 click of the elevation or windage knob equals 1 MOA. The elevation scale starts at 0 yards and goes up to 900 yards with graduations every 50 yards. There is a numbered graduation every 100 yards.

Zeroing: To zero the scope, shoot at a target at 100 or 200 yards. Adjust the elevation and windage until the point of aim and point of impact are the same. Turn out the set screws on both the elevation and windage knobs to "zero" them. Rotate the windage dial until the windage (deflection) is on the zero marking for the no-wind zero. Set the range (elevation) knob to the distance used for the zeroing procedure. This telescope is mounted on both the M1C and D, and the M1903A4.

### Adjustable Ranging Telescope I (ART I)

The ART I automatically compensates for trajectory when a target of the proper size is adjusted between the stadia lines. It is a 3-9x variable that compensates for targets from 300 to 900 meters. It has a one-piece ballistic cam/power ring. The ballistic cam is set for the ballistic trajectory of the M118 Match or Special Ball ammunition (173 gn FMJBT @ 2610 fps). Each click or tick mark on the adjustment screws is worth 1/2 MOA in value. The ART I is zeroed at 300 meters. Set the power ring to 3 (3x/300m). Remove the adjustment turret caps. Fire the rifle and adjust the elevation and windage adjustment screws until the point of impact is the same as the point of aim. Screw the turret caps back on to maximize the water-proofing of the telescope.

The reticle has four stadia lines on it (Figure I-3-2). The two horizontal stadia lines are on the vertical crosshair, are 30 inches apart at the designated distance, and are used for ranging. The vertical crosshair and horizontal stadia lines are used to range targets from the beltline to the top of the head. Adjust the power/cam until the stadia lines are bracketing the target's beltline and top of head. The numeral on the power ring is the target distance. For example, if the power ring reads 5, the target is at 500m, and the scope is at 5x magnification. The

3

ballistic cam has automatically adjusted the telescope for the trajectory of the round by changing the telescope's point of aim. Aim center mass on the target to obtain a hit in a no-wind situation. The two vertical stadia lines are on the horizontal crosshair, are 60 inches apart at the designated distance, and are used for wind holdoffs and leads. If necessary, holdoff for environmental effects or target movement.

NOTE:        It is imperative to keep the scope base clean. The cam slides along the mount and pushes the telescope off from the bearing surface. Debris can interfere with the precise camming and ranging functions.

## Adjustable Ranging Telescope II (ART II)

The ART II is similar in operation and design to the ART I, with two major modifications. The ballistic cam and the power ring are now separable and can be moved independently of one another. This was done so that after ranging a target, the ballistic cam can be locked to permit the operator to increase the magnification for greater definition. The problem with this system is that it seldom works correctly. The two rings are locked together in poker-chip tooth fashion, and even when locked together, they can move independently. When unlocked, it is very difficult to move one without the other moving, creating a change in the camming action, and ultimately, causing misses. It is best to lock them together and keep them together. The mount is similar to the ART I mount, and the bearing surface must be kept clean. The ART II mount has two mounting screws, one of which is threaded into a modified clip guide. The reticle is the second major modification. The reticle pattern is a standard crosshair, with thick outer bars on the left, right, and bottom crosshairs (Figure I-3-3). The horizontal crosshair has two dots, one on each side of the crosshair intersection. Each dot is 30 inches from the center, and are a total of 60 inches apart. The heavy bars are one meter in height or thickness at the range indicated. To determine the range to a target, adjust the power ring and cam together until the target is of equal height to the bar. The correct placement of the bar is from the crotch to the top of head (one meter). Aim center mass for a no-wind hit. The cam can be read to determine the range.

## Leupold & Stevens M1A and M3A Ultra/Mark 4 10x or 16x

The M1A comes in either 10x or 16x. It has three large, oversize target knobs. The left knob (as seen from the sniper) is for focus/parallax adjustment. The top knob is for elevation adjustment. The right knob is for windage adjustment. The M3A is only available in 10x. It has the same knob arrangement as the M1A, but the knobs are smaller, and they have different click values. All L&S sniper telescopes use the mil dot reticle (Figure I-3-4). The M3A has a ballistic cam to compensate for the trajectory of the specified cartridge. The cam is calibrated for bullet drop compensation from 100m to 1000m. The following are available:

o   7.62mm NATO M118 (173 FMJBT @ 2610 fps)

o   .300 Win Mag (220 HPBT @ 2650 fps)

o   .30-06 Springfield (180 HPBT @ 2700 fps)

o   5.56mm M193/.223 Rem (55 FMJBT @ 3200 fps)

Adjustments of L & S telescopes:

| Model | Elevation | Windage | Complete Revolution |
|-------|-----------|---------|---------------------|
| M1A   | 1/4 MOA   | 1/4 MOA | 15 MOA              |
| M3    | 1 MOA     | 1 MOA   | 100-1000M           |
| M3A   | 1 MOA     | 1/2 MOA | 100-1000M           |

NOTE:   Due to the mechanics of the M1-M3 telescopes, when zeroing, set the focus/parallax adjustment knob and keep it in the zeroed location. It has been found that adjustment of the focus/parallax knob after the zero is established can change the point of impact.

## Bausch & Lomb Tactical Riflescope

The Bausch & Lomb Tactical Riflescope is a 10x40mm fixed magnification telescope with 1/4 MOA adjustments. It has two large, target-type knobs. The upper knob is for elevation, and the knob on the right is for windage. The eyepiece houses the range focus adjustment ring, that is calibrated from 50 yards to infinity. It has the same mil dot reticle pattern as the L&S series and USMC Unertl telescope (Figure I-3-4). Each revolution of the adjustment knobs provides 12 MOA.

## Unertl USMC Sniper Scope

This telescope was designed and built by the John Unertl Company. John Unertl was a USMC sniper during WWI and later became the manufacturer of some of the finest US-made optics. USMC sniper scope is a fixed 10x, steel-tubed, mil dot telescope with a ballistic drop compensator for the M118 ammunition. The lens are coated with a high efficiency, low-reflection (HELR) film that transmits up to 91 % of the ambient light. This telescope has 1/2 MOA adjustments for both elevation and windage. It has a fine tune elevation capability that permits +/- 3 MOA to adjust for differences in shooter's zeros, temperatures, ammunition lots, and ammunition. The windage adjustment has 60 MOA of main adjustment with +/- 4 MOA fine adjustment. This telescope also has a parallax adjusting capability. The reticle is identical to that of the L&S series and the Bausch and Lomb Tactical (Figure I-3-4).

## I-4.  SOVIET TELESCOPES

The Soviet telescopes are made on machinery purchased from Carl Zeiss of Germany during the 1930's. Their optical quality is therefore good to excellent. Their operation is straightforward, and rather simple. Only the PE series has the capability of individually focusing to the user. The top turret is for elevation adjustment, and has a ballistic cam that is calibrated for the 7.62x54mm Rimmed L ball ammunition (150 gn FMJ flat base @ 2800 fps). The turret on the left is for windage adjustments.

The zeroing procedures are identical for all Soviet telescopes. Zeroing should be done at 100 meters. Loosen the small screws on the turrets that hold the top plate to the cam that is engraved with the tick marks and numerals. Several turns are all that it necessary. Do not remove these screws completely; they are not captive, and are easily lost. Using a small screwdriver, gently pry the the top plate and cam apart so that the top plate can move independently of the cam. Firing three-shot groups, adjust the elevation and windage knobs until the point of aim and the point of impact are the same. When making adjustments, <u>move the reticle to the shot group</u>. This is the major difference from zeroing these telescopes when compared to zeroing modern, U.S.-style telescopes where the shot group is moved to the reticle (point of aim). When the rifle/telescope system is zeroed, "zero out" the cams. The elevation cam should be turned until the "1" which represents 100 meters is aligned with the reference tick mark. Ensure that the top plate does not rotate when the cam is moved. The windage cam is also centered on its "0" marking. Push down on the top plates until they mate with the cams. Carefully tighten the small metal screws. The telescope is now zeroed.

M1891/30 Sniper Telescopes:

| Model | Magnification | BDC | Tube Diameter |
|-------|---------------|---------|---------------|
| PE | 4x | 0-1400m | 1 inch |
| PU | 3.5x | 0-1300m | 30mm |
| PV | 3.5x | 0-1300m | 30mm |

## Translation of a Soviet Manual

The telescope is composed of a telescope tube and a mount.

o    <u>Telescope Tube</u>

On the top of the tube is an elevation range knob, consisting of a screw and a drum, marked with numbers from 1-14 on the PE scope and from 1-13 on the PU scope. Each graduation is equivalent to 100 meters in distance.

At the left rear side of the scope is a windage knob. The

components of the windage knob are the same as that of the elevation-range knob. The windage knob is used to compensate for the effects of wind on the trajectory of the bullet. The windage knob has 10 graduations: the middle one is marked with the number 0.

To move the strike of the bullet to the right, turn the windage knob to the direction of the mark "+", and conversely, turn the knob to the direction of the mark "-" to move the strike of the bullet to the left. Each click of windage corresponds to one mil.

The telescope tube contains a system of optical glasses including convex lenses, prisms and an eyepiece. The reticle is a cross-wire type. When aiming the rifle at the objective, place the vertical line of the reticle right on the objective. The horizontal line is used to adjust the aim. The two knobs provide horizontal and vertical movement of the reticle.

The telescope tube PE has adjusting devices. When taking aim, adjust the knobs on the tube to fit with the observer's eye.

The telescope tube PU has no adjusting (focusing) devices. Therefore, when aiming, the observer is required to look through the telescope and move his head until the sighted object is in focus.

When using a telescope to aim at the objective, place the eye at the center of the eyepiece, thus forming a sight alignment toward the objective. An accurate aim will not allow the observer to see any black spots in the telescope. (If aiming inaccurately, the observer will see a small, black, crescent-shaped spot in the telescope.)

o    Mount

Mounts used to fix the telescopes to the rifle: the mount for PE consists of a base and a body. Fix the base to the receiver of the rifle with six screws. The body of the mount, after being fastened to the base, is used to fix the telescope to the rifle.

The mount for PU also includes a base and a body. The base, after being screwed to the receiver of the rifle, is connected with the body of the mount by guide lugs and screws. The body of the mount may be moved up and down on the base thanks to the two screws on the upper side and the rear lower side of the base. The body is used to fix the telescope to the rifle.

We can loosen the three screws in order to rotate the sighting telescope, but we only loosen the screws when we fire for adjustment at the repair station of the regiment.

7

PSO-1:

The PSO-1 scope will be found mounted on the Soviet SVD and the Romanian FPK. The PSO-1 is 4x, and has an illuminated reticle powered by a small dry cell. The battery housing is located at the bottom rear of the telescopic sight mount. To change batteries, press in and rotate the battery housing counterclockwise. Remove the old battery and replace it with the same type. The reticle lamp can be replaced by unscrewing its housing and removing the bulb (The RPG-7 sight uses the same bulb). The reticle light is turned on or off by its switch. The lens cap should always be in place except when the telescope is in use. Two covers are issued with each rifle; one is for the telescopic sight alone and the other covers the sight and breech when the PSO-1 is mounted. A belt pouch is provided for carrying the telescope when dismounted from the rifle, four magazines, a cleaning kit, and an extra battery and lamp.

If the open sights are to be used, set the rear sight by pressing in the locks on the rear sight slide; then move the slide along the rear sight leaf. The front edge of the slide should be aligned with the numeral that corresponds in hundreds of meters. Use the same sight picture as for firing a pistol.

If the PSO-1 is used, rotate the elevation knob until the figure that corresponds to the range in hundreds of meters is aligned with the index. The range can be fairly accurately determined by use of the range finder located in the lower left of the telescopic reticle (Figure I-4-2). This range finder is graduated to the height of a man (5'7") from 200-1000m. Look through the telescope and place the horizontal line at the bottom of the target. Move the telescope until the upper (curved) line just touches the top of the target's head. The number indicates the range in hundreds of meters; if the target falls between numbers, the remaining distance must be estimated. When the range is determined and set into the elevation knob, use the point of the top chevron on the reticle as an aiming point. The three lower chevrons are used for firing at 1100, 1200, and 1300 meters with the elevation knob set at 10.

The horizontal scale extending out from the sides of the top chevron are used for hasty wind and lead corrections; each tick mark is worth 1 soviet mil (6000 soviet mills per 360 degrees). The horizontal scale is numbered every 5 and 10 mils. Deliberate changes are made by rotating the windage knob. The windage knob is graduated every 1/2 soviet mil. The windage knob scale has two (2) clicks per graduation, each click representing one half mil (.5 mil), each graduation one (1) mil. At 1000 meters each click moves the impact of the round .5 meters (20 in), each graduation moves the impact 1 meter (40 in). The numbers on the windage knob are colored. Right windage corrections are black, and are obtained when the knob is rotated clockwise. Left windage corrections are red, and are obtained when the knob is rotated counterclockwise.

For firing when the light is dim, illuminate the reticle by turning on the switch in the telescopic sight mount. If active infrared light sources are believed to be used by the enemy, set the range drum at 4 and switch the infrared detector into place. Scan the area to the front; if any active infrared light sources are in use, they will appear as orange-red blobs in the telescope. Align the point of the reticle on the light and fire. Turn off the reticle when not in use to conserve the battery and swing the infrared detector out of the way so that it will be activated by light during the day. Several hours of direct sunlight are required to activate the infrared detector.

If the correct dry cell batteries can not be obtained, a suitable expedient can be easily assembled (Figure I-4-3). The Soviet dry cell is 5.0 volts. . The following are required:

o    Two (2) 1.25 Volt/625 camera batteries (lithium)

o    One (1) 3.0 Volt/DL2025 camera battery (lithium)

o    One plastic bushing OD:0.85"; ID:0.60"; Length:0.73"

Place the batteries positive "+" side first into the battery compartment. The large, flat DL2025 is placed in first, then the bushing, then the two 625 batteries. Replace the battery compartment cap.

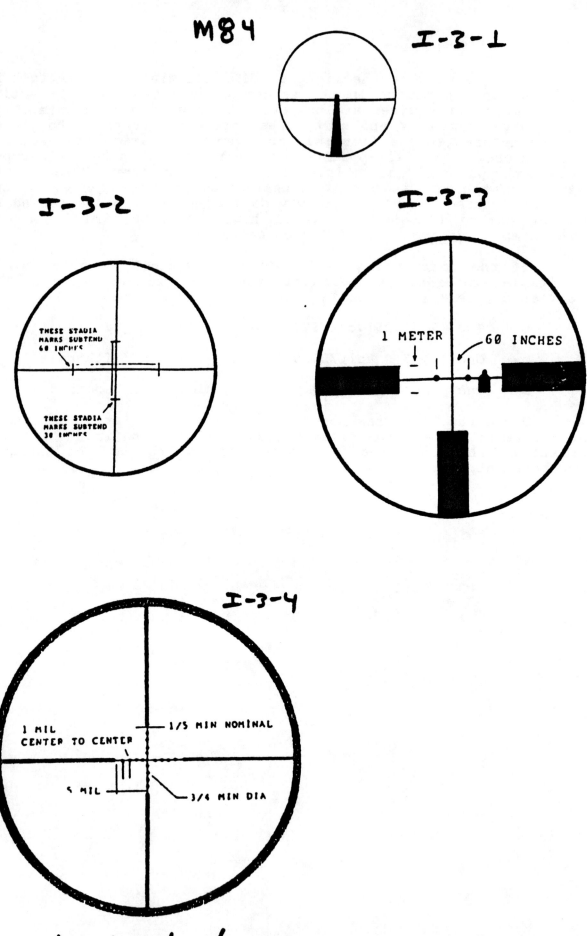

M84     I-3-1

I-3-2

I-3-3

THESE STADIA
MARKS SUBTEND
60 INCHES

THESE STADIA
MARKS SUBTEND
30 INCHES

1 METER    60 INCHES

I-3-4

1 MIL
CENTER TO CENTER

1/5 MIN NOMINAL

5 MIL

3/4 MIN DIA

L/S & B/L /UNERTL

AIMING POINT

I-4-1

SOVIET
PE/PU/PV

I-4-2

PSO-L

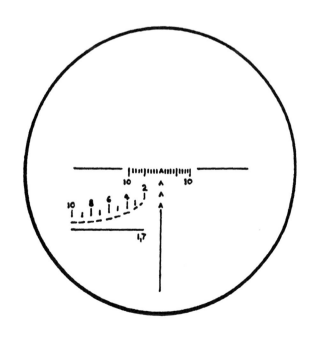

I-4-2

PSO-L

PSO-1 EXPEDIENT BATTERY
(NOT TO SCALE)

BUSHING

BATTERY PLACEMENT

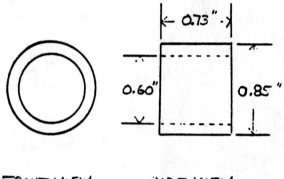

FRONT VIEW      SIDE VIEW

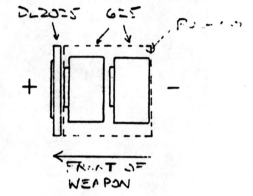

FRONT OF
WEAPON

# Appendix J

## SPECIAL OPERATIONS TARGET INTERDICTION COURSE
### 2E-F67/011-F19

## PROGRAM OF INSTRUCTION

FILE #     TITLE

### General Subjects

8301    Introduction to Special Operations Target Interdiction
        Course (SOTIC)

8302    Rigging of the Sniper Weapon System

8304    Mission Planning

8305    Sniping on Urbanized Terrain

8306    Training SOF Snipers

8307    Selecting and Tailoring Ammunition

8308    Considerations for Use of Special Operations (SO)
        Snipers

8310    Introduction to Tracking and Countertracking

### Marksmanship

8311    The M24 Sniper Weapon System (SWS) and Sniper Equipment

8312    Advanced Rifle Marksmanship

8313    Sniper Marksmanship

8314    Sight Adjustment and Zeroing

8315    Correcting for Meteorological Conditions

8318    Range Exercise #1 (Position Shooting)

8320    Judging Distances

8321    Judging Distances Demonstration

8322    Judging Distances Exercise

8323    Reading Wind and Spotting

1

| 8327 | Range Exercise #2 (Grouping and Zeroing - TS) |
| 8328 | Range Exercise #3 (Snapshooting) |
| 8329 | Range Exercise #4 (Moving Targets) |
| 8330 | Range Exercise #5 (Dawn and Dusk Shooting) |
| 8332 | Range Exercise #6 (Opposite Hand Shoot) |
| 8333 | Range Exercise #7 (Opportunity Targets) |
| 8334 | Introduction to Night Vision Devices (NVDs) |
| 8335 | Range Exercise #8 (Zero the NVD on the M24 SWS) |
| 8336 | Application of Fire |
| 8337 | Range Exercise #10 (Alternate U.S. SWS) |
| 8338 | Range Exercise #9 (Night Firing with the NVD) |
| 8341 | Field Shooting |

## Observation

| 8351 | Observation of Ground |
| 8352 | Observation Exercise |
| 8353 | Observer's Log and Range Card |
| 8354 | Panoramic Sketching |
| 8355 | Locating the Enemy |
| 8357 | Kim's Game |

## Concealment

| 8361 | Individual Camouflage and Concealment |
| 8362 | Concealment Exercise |
| 8364 | Ghillie Suits |
| 8365 | Individual Movement |
| 8369 | Selecting Lines of Advance |

8372    Stalking Exercise

8373    Silent Movement Course

8378    Sniper Hides and Loopholes

8379    Hides Demonstration

## Examination Annex

8381    Written Examination

8387    ARTEP 7-92 MTP MO 3, STX 15

8388    Advanced Rifle Marksmanship

8389    Sniper Marksmanship

Appendix K

SNIPER'S LOG BOOK

### 9 STEPS FOR A FIRST SHOT HIT

1. DETERMINE THE RANGE IN METERS--SET.
   TAKE SLOPE INTO ACCOUNT.
2. DETERMINE THE BASE WIND:
   A. IN MOA--SET.  OR:
   B. MILS FOR HOLDOFF.  1 MIL=3.375 MOA
   1/4m=.84 MOA, 1/2m=1.68 MOA, 3/4m=2.53 MOA
   NOTE: WHEN DETERMINING BASE WINDS, ENSURE YOU
        KNOW HOW THE MIRAGE LOOKS UNDER THE BASE
        CONDITION, SO YOU CAN SEE CHANGES.  FOR A
        CONSISTENT CHANGE, DIAL IN THE CHANGE.
        KEEP TRACK OF GUSTS AND LULLS.  GUSTS GO
        CLOCKWISE FROM THE BASE WIND DIRECTION,
        LULLS GO COUNTER-CLOCKWISE.  HOLD OR FAVOR
        INTO A GUST, HOLD OR FAVOR OUT OF A LULL.
        LULLS ARE MOST DANGEROUS--THEY REQUIRE THE
        LARGEST CORRECTION.
3. DETERMINE THE SPIN DRIFT CORRECTION:
   600-700 M - LEFT 1/2 MOA
   800-900 M - LEFT 3/4 MOA
   1000 M - LEFT  1  MOA    (M118)
4. DETERMINE THE TEMPERATURE CHANGE FROM "0" AND SET:
   100-500 M  +/- 20 DEGREES = -/+ 1 MOA
   600-900 M  +/- 15 DEGREES = -/+ 1 MOA
   1000 M  +/- 10 DEGREES = -/+ 1 MOA
5. DETERMINE THE PRESSURE CHANGE VERUS "0" PRESSURE
   AND SET.
6. DETERMINE THE ALTITUDE CHANGE FROM "0" AND SET.
7. DETERMINE LEAD (IF A MOVING TARGET).
8. ASSUME A GOOD POSITION:
   A. BONE SUPPORT
   B. MUSCULAR RELAXATION
   C. NATURAL POINT OF AIM ON THE AIMING POINT
9. FIRE THE SHOT:
   A. NATURAL RESPIRATORY PAUSE
   B. FOCUS ON THE FRONT SIGHT/RETICLE
   C. FOLLOW THROUGH
   NOTE: KEEP THE ROUNDS COVERED, SO THEY WILL
        STAY AT A CONSTANT TEMPERATURE.  A HOT
        GUN WILL STRING ROUNDS HIGH.  LOG ALL
        SHOTS AND SUBSEQUENT CHANGES.

## WIND DATA

1. DETERMINE <u>DIRECTION</u> OF:
   A. AVERAGE WIND
   B. GUSTS (ALMOST ALWAYS CLOCKWISE)
   C. LULLS
2. DETERMINE <u>VELOCITY</u> OF:
   A. AVERAGE WIND
   B. GUSTS
   C. LULLS
3. PUT THE <u>CORRECTION</u> FOR THE <u>AVERAGE</u>
   WIND ON THE SIGHT.
4. SLIGHTLY FAVOR, OR HOLD FOR GUSTS AND
   LULLS.
5. HOLD OR FAVOR <u>INTO</u> A GUST.
   HOLD OR FAVOR <u>OUT</u> OF A LULL.
6. IF A CONSISTENT HOLD OR FAVOR, PUT
   THE CORRECTION ON THE SIGHT.
7. REFERING TO YOUR TARGET DIMENSIONS IN
   MINUTES OF ANGLE.
   A. SLIGHTLY==1/2'
   B. FAVOR==1'
   C. HOLD==1 1/2-2'
8. LULLS ARE MORE DANGEROUS THAN GUSTS.
9. YOU CANNOT USE MIRAGE AS A VELOCITY
   INDICATOR UNTIL YOU KNOW WHAT IT
   LOOKS LIKE FOR THE AVERAGE WIND.
   THIS WILL CHANGE THROUGHOUT THE DAY.
10. SHOOT THE CONDITION.  DO NOT CHASE
    SPOTTERS.
11. IGNORE MINOR FLUCTUATIONS.  WAIT FOR
    THE CONDITION TO FULLY CHANGE.  MIRAGE
    WILL CHANGE BEFORE CONDITIONS ARRIVE.
12. GRASS WILL GIVE YOU MAGNITUDE OF THE
    WIND, BUT NOT DIRECTION OR VELOCITY,
13. OBSERVER COMPUTES CORRECTION IN
    <u>MINUTES</u>, AND GIVES IT TO SHOOTER IN
    <u>CLICKS</u> OR <u>MIL</u> HOLDOFF.

<u>CONSOLIDATED ZERO DATA</u>

| METERS: | 100 | 200 | 300 | 400 | 500 | 600 | 700 | 800 | 900 | 1000 |
|---|---|---|---|---|---|---|---|---|---|---|
| Temp.  E/W: | | | | | | | | | | |
| 50 | | | | | | | | | | |
| 55 | | | | | | | | | | |
| 60 | | | | | | | | | | |
| 65 | | | | | | | | | | |
| 70 | | | | | | | | | | |
| 75 | | | | | | | | | | |
| 80 | | | | | | | | | | |
| 85 | | | | | | | | | | |
| 90 | | | | | | | | | | |
| 95 | | | | | | | | | | |
| 100 | | | | | | | | | | |
| 105 | | | | | | | | | | |

NOTE:  This matrix is designed to compile data on the individual
SWS's zero at these ranges and temperatures.

3

The table below gives the inch equivalents of mils at the given ranges of 91 meters to 1,000 meters and 100 yards to 1,000 yards. This will aid the sniper in computing his sight change in mils for a given distance to the target with a given miss in estimated inches.

For example, a miss of 28 inches left at 400 yards would be a 2 mil hold to the right.

| RANGE | INCHES | RANGE | INCHES |
|---|---|---|---|
| 91 meters (100 yds) | 3.6 | 549 meters (600 yds) | 22.0 |
| 100 meters | 4.0 | 600 meters | 24.0 |
| 183 meters (200 yds) | 7.0 | 640 meters (740 yds) | 25.0 |
| 200 meters | 8.0 | 700 meters | 27.5 |
| 274 meters (300 yds) | 11.0 | 731 meters (800 yds) | 29.0 |
| 300 meters | 12.0 | 800 meters | 31.5 |
| 365 meters (400 yds) | 14.0 | 823 meters (900 yds) | 32.5 |
| 400 meters | 15.75 | 900 meters | 35.5 |
| 457 meters (500 yds) | 18.0 | 914 meters (1,000 yds) | 36.0 |
| 500 meters | 20.0 | 1,000 meters | 39.0 |

# METRIC ENGLISH EQUIVALENTS

| 1 MOA (CM) | YARDS | ENGLISH / METRIC METERS/YARDS | METERS | 1 MOA (IN) |
|---|---|---|---|---|
| 3 | 109 | 100 | 91 | 1 |
| 4.5 | 164 | 150 | 137 | 1.5 |
| 6 | 219 | 200 | 183 | 2 |
| 7.5 | 273 | 250 | 228 | 2.5 |
| 9 | 328 | 300 | 274 | 3 |
| 10.5 | 383 | 350 | 320 | 3.5 |
| 12 | 437 | 400 | 365 | 4 |
| 13.5 | 492 | 450 | 411 | 4.5 |
| 15 | 546 | 500 | 457 | 5 |
| 16.5 | 602 | 550 | 503 | 5.5 |
| 18 | 656 | 600 | 549 | 6 |
| 19.5 | 711 | 650 | 594 | 6.5 |
| 21 | 766 | 700 | 640 | 7 |
| 22.5 | 820 | 750 | 686 | 7.5 |
| 24 | 875 | 800 | 731 | 8 |
| 25.5 | 929 | 850 | 777 | 8.5 |
| 27 | 984 | 900 | 823 | 9 |
| 28.5 | 1039 | 950 | 869 | 9.5 |
| 30 | 1094 | 1000 | 914 | 10 |
| 31.5 | 1148 | 1050 | 960 | 10.5 |
| 33 | 1203 | 1100 | 1005 | 11 |

5

## LEADS IN MILS

| RANGE | WALKERS | FAST WALKERS | RUNNERS |
|---|---|---|---|
| 100 yds | LEADING EDGE | 7 /8 | 1 3/4 |
| 200 yds | 7/8 | 1 1/4 | 1 3/4 |
| 300 yds | 1 1/8 | 1 3/4 | 2 1/4 |
| 400 yds | 1 1/4 | 1 3/4 | 2 1/2 |
| 500 yds | 1 1/4 | 1 3/4 | 2 1/2 |
| 600 yds | 1 1/2 | 2 1/4 | 3 |
| 700 yds | 1 1/2 | 2 1/4 | 3 |
| 800 yds | 1 1/2 | 2 1/2 | 3 |
| 900 yds | 1 3/4 | 2 1/2 | 3 1/2 |
| 1,000 yds | 1 3/4 | 2 1/2 | 3 1/2 |

## LEADS IN MOA

| | | | |
|---|---|---|---|
| 100 yds | LEADING EDGE | 3 | 6 |
| 200 yds | 3 | 4.5 | 6 |
| 300 yds | 4 | 6 | 8 |
| 400 yds | 4.5 | 6 | 9 |
| 500 yds | 4.5 | 6 | 9 |
| 600 yds | 5 | 7.5 | 10 |
| 700 yds | 5 | 7.5 | 10 |
| 800 yds | 5.5 | 8 | 11 |
| 900 yds | 5.5 | 8 | 11 |
| 1,000 yds | 5.5 | 8 | 11 |

## LEADS IN FEET AND INCHES

| | | | |
|---|---|---|---|
| 100 yds | LEADING EDGE | 3" | 6" |
| 200 yds | 6" | 9" | 1' |
| 300 yds | 1' | 1.5' | 2' |
| 400 yds | 1.5' | 2.25' | 3' |
| 500 yds | 2' | 3' | 4' |
| 600 yds | 2.5' | 3.75' | 5' |
| 700 yds | 3' | 4.5' | 6' |
| 800 yds | 3.5' | 5.25' | 7' |
| 900 yds | 4' | 6' | 8' |
| 1,000 yds | 4.5' | 7.25' | 9' |

It is not recommended that you engage runners beyond 500 meters due to the excessive lead required. If a runner is engaged at distances beyond 500 meters, an immediate follow-up shot must be ready.

The classiftication of a walker, fast walker, and a runner is based on a walker moving at 2 miles per hour, a fast walker at 3 1/2 miles per hour, and a runner at 5 miles per hour.

It must be remembered that the above leads are guides only and starting point leads. Each individual will have hiw own leads based on how he perceives movement and his reaction time to it.

7

# SOTIC

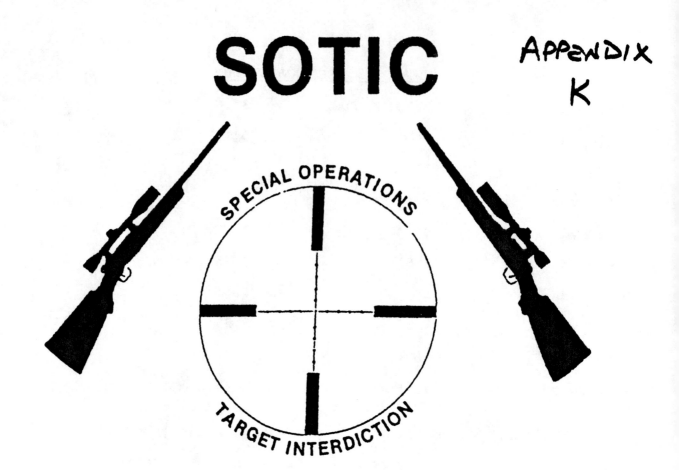

SPECIAL OPERATIONS

TARGET INTERDICTION

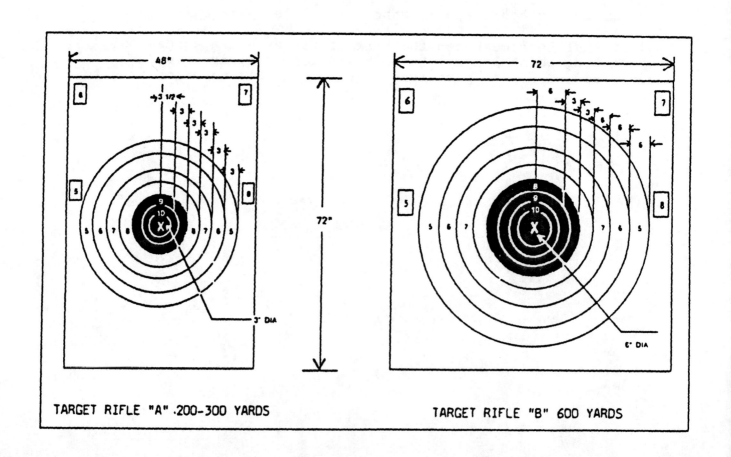

TARGET RIFLE "A" .200-300 YARDS          TARGET RIFLE "B" 600 YARDS

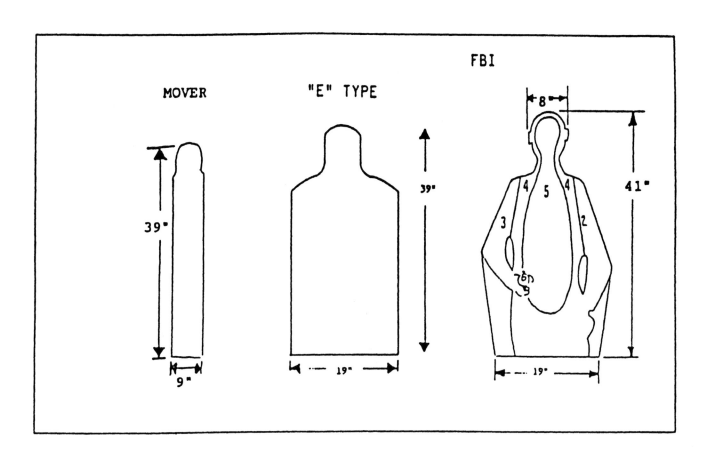

MOVER      "E" TYPE      FBI

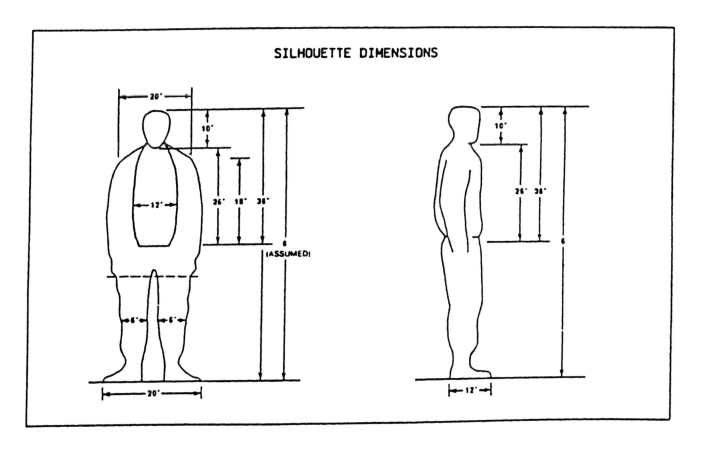

SILHOUETTE DIMENSIONS

| MIL | 1M | MOA | MIL/IN | 5 | 10 | 15 |
|---|---|---|---|---|---|---|
| 5 | 200 | 2" | 8 | .25 | .5 | .7 |
| 4.75 | 210 | | | | | |
| 4.5 | 222 | | | | | |
| 4.25 | 235 | | | .3 | .6 | .9 |
| 4 | 250 | | 9 | | | |
| 3.75 | 267 | 3" | 10 | | | |
| 3.5 | 286 | | 11 | .35 | .7 | 1 |
| 3.25 | 308 | 3.5 | 12 | .4 | .8 | 1.25 |
| 3 | 333 | | 13 | .45 | .9 | 1.35 |
| 2.75 | 364 | 4" | 14 | .5 | 1 | 1.5 |
| 2.5 | 400 | 4.5 | 16 | .55 | 1.1 | 1.65 |
| 2.25 | 444 | 5" | 18 | .65 | 1.3 | 1.95 |
| 2 | 500 | 5.5 | 20 | .75 | 1.5 | 2.25 |
| * 1.75 | 571 | 6.5 | 22 | .8 | 1.6 | 2.4 |
| * 1.66 | 600 | 7" | 24 | .95 | 1.9 | 2.85 |
| * 1.5 | 667 | 7.5 | 26 | 1 | 2 | 3 |
| * | 700 | 8" | 28 | 1.2 | 2.3 | 3.45 |
| * | 750 | 8.5 | 30 | 1.2 | 2.4 | 3.6 |
| **1.25 | 800 | 9" | 32 | 1.4 | 2.7 | 4 |
| ** | 900 | 10" | 36 | 1.6 | 3.2 | 4.8 |

100 - 5     under
200 - 2.5   under
300 - 1.5   under
400 - 1.25  under
500 - zero
600 - 1     over
700 - 1.25 over

W
-----
R | M

*spin .5L MOA
**spin 1L MOA

# HOW TO USE YOUR SLOW FIRE DATA SHEETS

PLOT AN ACCURATE SHOT LOCATION BY THE SHOT NUMBER AS INDICATED BY POSITION OF SPOTTING DISK ON THE TARGET. MARK SIGHTERS WITH AN ⑤

PLACE A DOT IN CALL CIRCLE WHERE YOU BELIEVE YOUR SHOT WILL APPEAR ON THE TARGET.

RECORD ELEVATION AND WINDAGE USED FOR EACH SHOT. MAKE CHANGES AS THEY OCCUR.

SHOT VALUE AS INDICATED BY POSITION OF SCORING DISK PLACED ON TARGET.

GRID OVERLAY INDICATES SIGHT MOVEMENTS IN MINUTES FROM CENTER OF TGT. FOR BOTH ELEVATION AND WINDAGE.

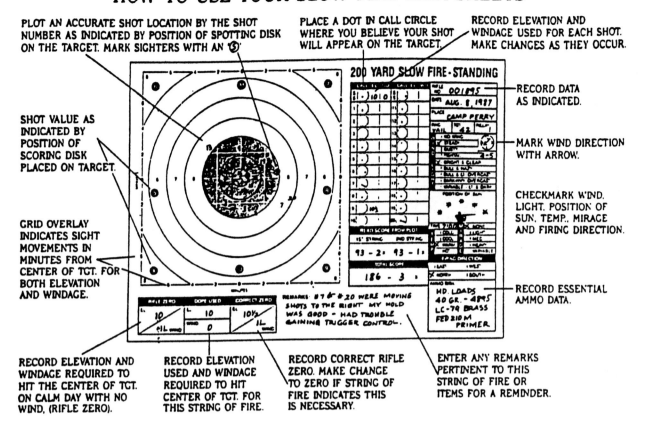

RECORD DATA AS INDICATED.

MARK WIND DIRECTION WITH ARROW.

CHECKMARK WIND, LIGHT, POSITION OF SUN, TEMP., MIRAGE AND FIRING DIRECTION.

RECORD ESSENTIAL AMMO DATA.

RECORD ELEVATION AND WINDAGE REQUIRED TO HIT THE CENTER OF TGT. ON CALM DAY WITH NO WIND, (RIFLE ZERO).

RECORD ELEVATION USED AND WINDAGE REQUIRED TO HIT CENTER OF TGT. FOR THIS STRING OF FIRE.

RECORD CORRECT RIFLE ZERO. MAKE CHANGE TO ZERO IF STRING OF FIRE INDICATES THIS IS NECESSARY.

ENTER ANY REMARKS PERTINENT TO THIS STRING OF FIRE OR ITEMS FOR A REMINDER.

# HOW TO USE YOUR RAPID FIRE DATA SHEETS

PLOT AN ACCURATE SHOT GROUP FOR EACH STRING OF FIRE BY MARKING AN X FOR EACH SHOT HOLE INDICATED ON THE TGT. WITH SPOTTING DISKS.

GRID OVERLAY INDICATES SIGHT MOVEMENTS IN MINUTES FROM CENTER OF TGT. FOR BOTH ELEVATION AND WINDAGE.

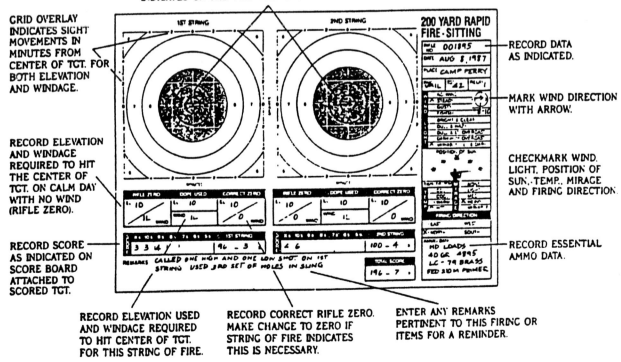

RECORD DATA AS INDICATED.

MARK WIND DIRECTION WITH ARROW.

CHECKMARK WIND, LIGHT, POSITION OF SUN, TEMP., MIRAGE AND FIRING DIRECTION.

RECORD ELEVATION AND WINDAGE REQUIRED TO HIT THE CENTER OF TGT. ON CALM DAY WITH NO WIND (RIFLE ZERO).

RECORD SCORE AS INDICATED ON SCORE BOARD ATTACHED TO SCORED TGT.

RECORD ESSENTIAL AMMO DATA.

RECORD ELEVATION USED AND WINDAGE REQUIRED TO HIT CENTER OF TGT. FOR THIS STRING OF FIRE.

RECORD CORRECT RIFLE ZERO. MAKE CHANGE TO ZERO IF STRING OF FIRE INDICATES THIS IS NECESSARY.

ENTER ANY REMARKS PERTINENT TO THIS FIRING OR ITEMS FOR A REMINDER.

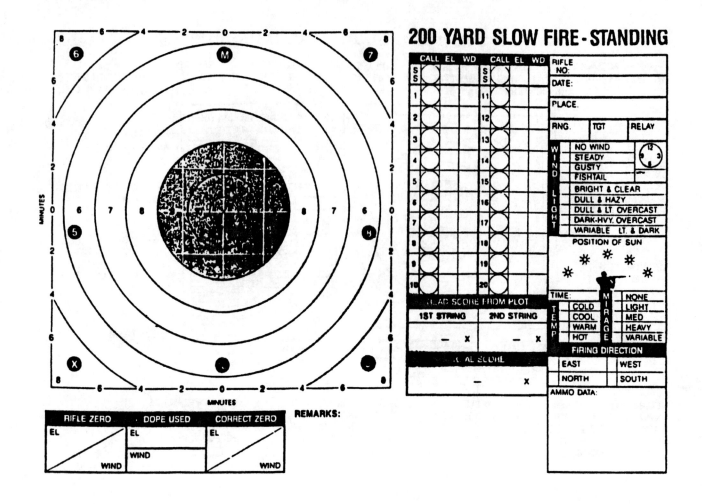

# 200 YARD SLOW FIRE - STANDING

| CALL | EL | WD | | CALL | EL | WD |
|---|---|---|---|---|---|---|
| S S | ○ | | S S | | ○ | |
| 1 | ○ | | 11 | | ○ | |
| 2 | ○ | | 12 | | ○ | |
| 3 | ○ | | 13 | | ○ | |
| 4 | ○ | | 14 | | ○ | |
| 5 | ○ | | 15 | | ○ | |
| 6 | ○ | | 16 | | ○ | |
| 7 | ○ | | 17 | | ○ | |
| 8 | ○ | | 18 | | ○ | |
| 9 | ○ | | 19 | | ○ | |
| 10 | ○ | | 20 | | ○ | |

READ SCORE FROM PLOT

| 1ST STRING | 2ND STRING |
|---|---|
| − x | − x |

TOTAL SCORE

| − x |
|---|

| RIFLE ZERO | DOPE USED | CORRECT ZERO |
|---|---|---|
| EL / WIND | EL / WIND | EL / WIND |

REMARKS:

RIFLE NO:

DATE:

PLACE:

| RNG. | TGT | RELAY |
|---|---|---|

| WIND | NO WIND |
|---|---|
| | STEADY |
| | GUSTY |
| | FISHTAIL |
| LIGHT | BRIGHT & CLEAR |
| | DULL & HAZY |
| | DULL & LT OVERCAST |
| | DARK-HVY. OVERCAST |
| | VARIABLE LT. & DARK |

POSITION OF SUN

| TIME: | | NONE |
|---|---|---|
| TEMP | COLD | LIGHT |
| | COOL | MED |
| | WARM | HEAVY |
| | HOT | VARIABLE |

FIRING DIRECTION

| EAST | WEST |
|---|---|
| NORTH | SOUTH |

AMMO DATA:

---

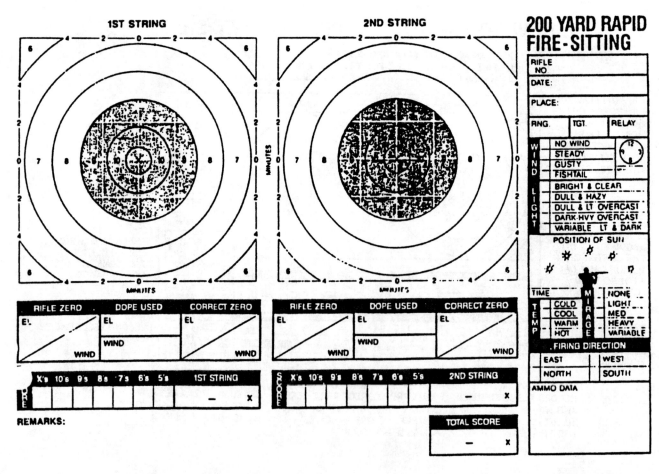

## 1ST STRING

## 2ND STRING

# 200 YARD RAPID FIRE - SITTING

RIFLE NO

DATE:

PLACE:

| RNG. | TGT | RELAY |
|---|---|---|

| WIND | NO WIND |
|---|---|
| | STEADY |
| | GUSTY |
| | FISHTAIL |
| LIGHT | BRIGHT & CLEAR |
| | DULL & HAZY |
| | DULL & LT OVERCAST |
| | DARK-HVY OVERCAST |
| | VARIABLE LT & DARK |

POSITION OF SUN

| TIME | | NONE |
|---|---|---|
| TEMP | COLD | LIGHT |
| | COOL | MED |
| | WARM | HEAVY |
| | HOT | VARIABLE |

FIRING DIRECTION

| EAST | WEST |
|---|---|
| NORTH | SOUTH |

AMMO DATA

| RIFLE ZERO | DOPE USED | CORRECT ZERO |
|---|---|---|
| EL / WIND | EL / WIND | EL / WIND |

| RIFLE ZERO | DOPE USED | CORRECT ZERO |
|---|---|---|
| EL / WIND | EL / WIND | EL / WIND |

| | X's | 10's | 9's | 8's | 7's | 6's | 5's | 1ST STRING |
|---|---|---|---|---|---|---|---|---|
| SCORE | | | | | | | | − x |

| S | X's | 10's | 9's | 8's | 7's | 6's | 5's | 2ND STRING |
|---|---|---|---|---|---|---|---|---|
| | | | | | | | | − x |

REMARKS:

TOTAL SCORE

| − x |
|---|

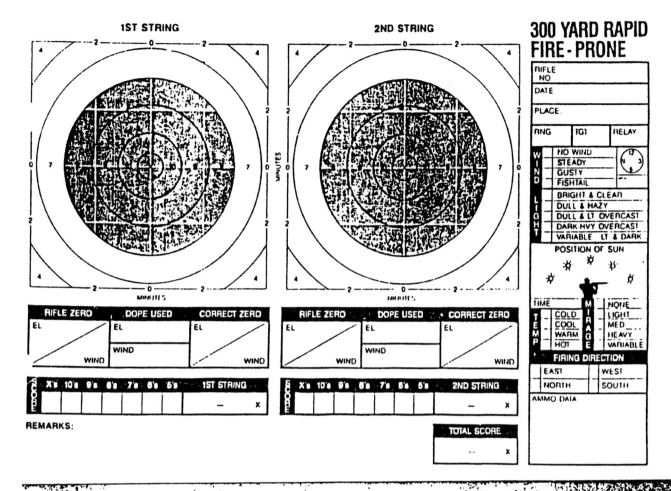

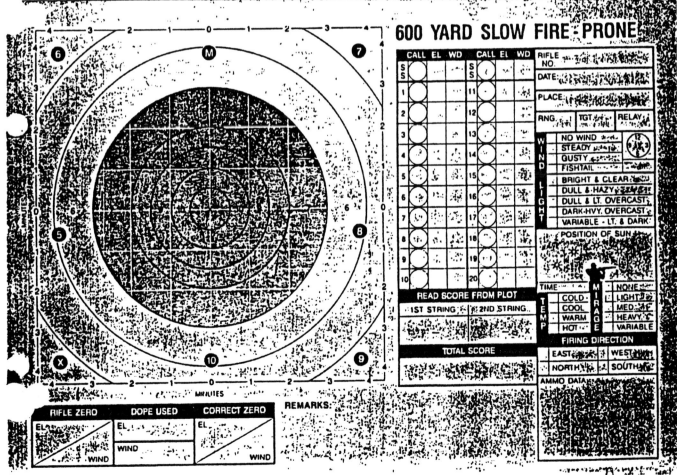

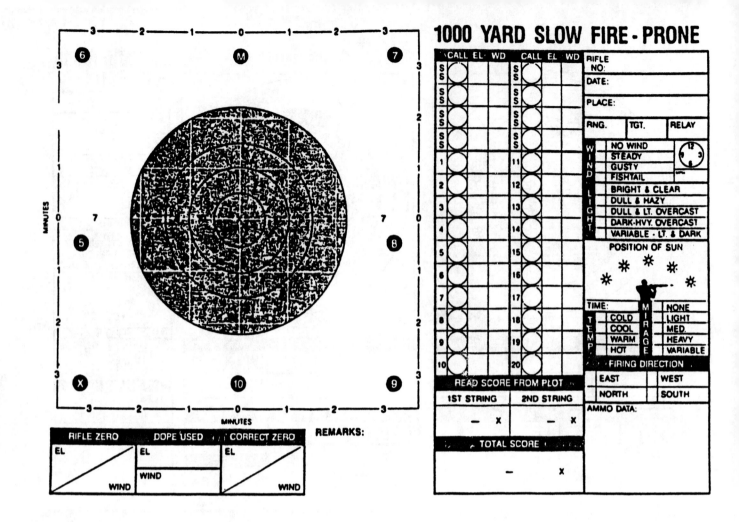

# 1000 YARD SLOW FIRE - PRONE

| CALL | EL | WD | CALL | EL | WD |
|---|---|---|---|---|---|
| S S ○ | | | S S ○ | | |
| S S ○ | | | S S ○ | | |
| S S ○ | | | S S ○ | | |
| S S ○ | | | S S ○ | | |
| S ○ | | | S ○ | | |
| 1 ○ | | | 11 ○ | | |
| 2 ○ | | | 12 ○ | | |
| 3 ○ | | | 13 ○ | | |
| 4 ○ | | | 14 ○ | | |
| 5 ○ | | | 15 ○ | | |
| 6 ○ | | | 16 ○ | | |
| 7 ○ | | | 17 ○ | | |
| 8 ○ | | | 18 ○ | | |
| 9 ○ | | | 19 ○ | | |
| 10 ○ | | | 20 ○ | | |

READ SCORE FROM PLOT

| 1ST STRING | 2ND STRING |
|---|---|
| —     X | —     X |

TOTAL SCORE

—     X

RIFLE NO:

DATE:

PLACE:

| RNG. | TGT. | RELAY |
|---|---|---|

| WIND | NO WIND | |
|---|---|---|
| | STEADY | |
| | GUSTY | |
| | FISHTAIL | |
| LIGHT | BRIGHT & CLEAR | |
| | DULL & HAZY | |
| | DULL & LT. OVERCAST | |
| | DARK-HVY. OVERCAST | |
| | VARIABLE - LT. & DARK | |

POSITION OF SUN

| TIME: | | NONE |
|---|---|---|
| TEMP. | COLD | LIGHT |
| | COOL | MED. |
| | WARM | HEAVY |
| | HOT | VARIABLE |

MIRAGE

FIRING DIRECTION

| EAST | WEST |
|---|---|
| NORTH | SOUTH |

AMMO DATA:

| RIFLE ZERO | DOPE USED | CORRECT ZERO |
|---|---|---|
| EL          WIND | EL     WIND | EL          WIND |

REMARKS:

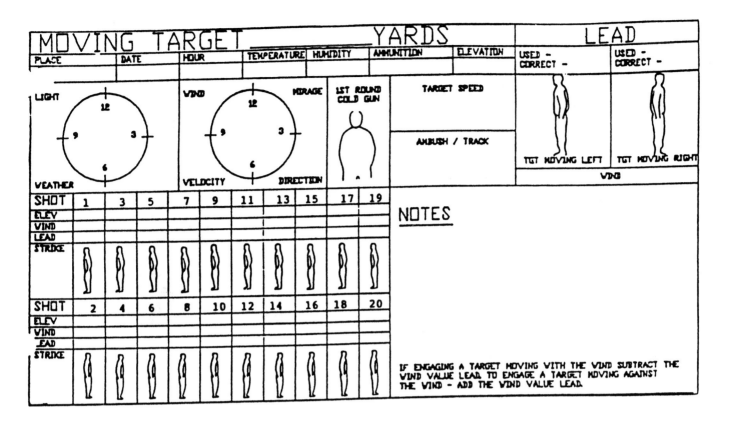

# MOVING TARGET _____ YARDS

| PLACE | DATE | HOUR | TEMPERATURE | HUMIDITY | AMMUNITION | ELEVATION |
|---|---|---|---|---|---|---|

## LEAD

USED – CORRECT –  |  USED – CORRECT –

TGT MOVING LEFT | TGT MOVING RIGHT

WIND

LIGHT

WIND / MIRAGE

1ST ROUND COLD GUN

TARGET SPEED

AMBUSH / TRACK

VELOCITY / DIRECTION

WEATHER

| SHOT | 1 | 3 | 5 | 7 | 9 | 11 | 13 | 15 | 17 | 19 |
|---|---|---|---|---|---|---|---|---|---|---|
| ELEV | | | | | | | | | | |
| VIND | | | | | | | | | | |
| LEAD | | | | | | | | | | |
| STRIKE | | | | | | | | | | |

| SHOT | 2 | 4 | 6 | 8 | 10 | 12 | 14 | 16 | 18 | 20 |
|---|---|---|---|---|---|---|---|---|---|---|
| ELEV | | | | | | | | | | |
| VIND | | | | | | | | | | |
| LEAD | | | | | | | | | | |
| STRIKE | | | | | | | | | | |

## NOTES

IF ENGAGING A TARGET MOVING WITH THE VIND SUBTRACT THE VIND VALUE LEAD. TO ENGAGE A TARGET MOVING AGAINST THE VIND – ADD THE VIND VALUE LEAD.

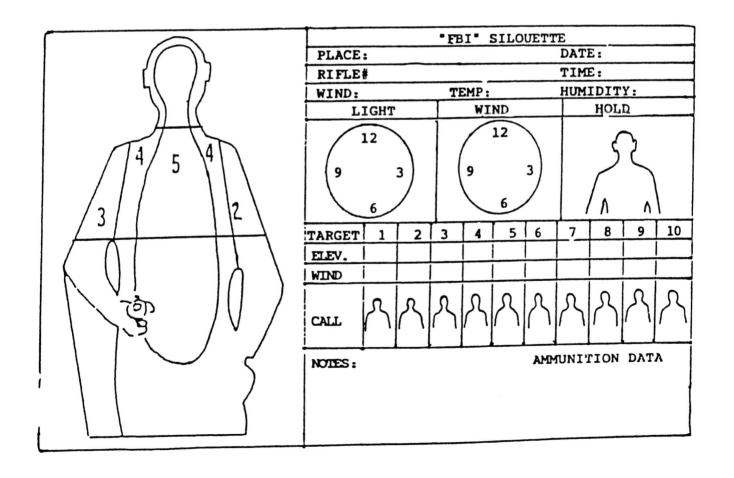

## "FBI" SILOUETTE

| PLACE: | | DATE: |
|---|---|---|
| RIFLE# | | TIME: |
| WIND: | TEMP: | HUMIDITY: |

| LIGHT | WIND | HOLD |
|---|---|---|

| TARGET | 1 | 2 | 3 | 4 | 5 | 6 | 7 | 8 | 9 | 10 |
|---|---|---|---|---|---|---|---|---|---|---|
| ELEV. | | | | | | | | | | |
| WIND | | | | | | | | | | |
| CALL | | | | | | | | | | |

NOTES:                 AMMUNITION DATA

## FULL SILHOUETTES

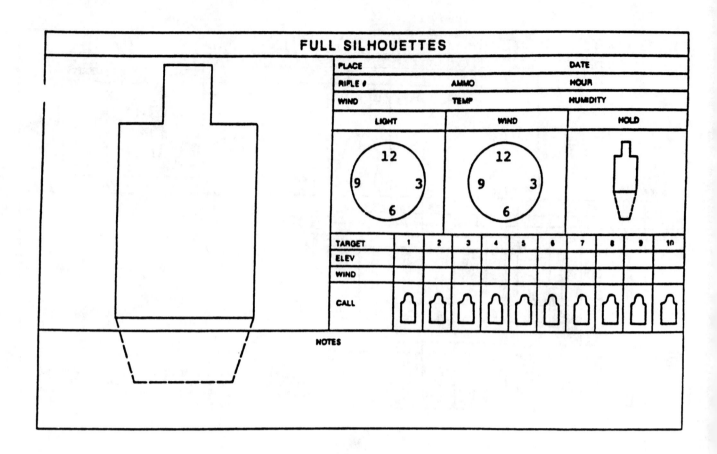

| PLACE | | | DATE | |
|---|---|---|---|---|
| RIFLE # | AMMO | | HOUR | |
| WIND | TEMP | | HUMIDITY | |

| LIGHT | WIND | HOLD |
|---|---|---|

| TARGET | 1 | 2 | 3 | 4 | 5 | 6 | 7 | 8 | 9 | 10 |
|---|---|---|---|---|---|---|---|---|---|---|
| ELEV | | | | | | | | | | |
| WIND | | | | | | | | | | |
| CALL | | | | | | | | | | |

NOTES

---

## 1st ROUND, COLD BORE SHOT

| EL: | WIND: | EL: | WIND: | EL: | WIND: | EL: | WIND: |
|---|---|---|---|---|---|---|---|

| RANGE: | RANGE: | RANGE: | RANGE: |
|---|---|---|---|
| DATE: | DATE: | DATE: | DATE: |
| TEMP: | TEMP: | TEMP: | TEMP: |
| AMMO: | AMMO: | AMMO: | AMMO: |
| CONDITIONS: | CONDITIONS: | CONDITIONS: | CONDITIONS: |

# MOVING TARGET
## _____ YARD LINE

| RANGE | RIFLE AND SCOPE NO. | | DATE/HOUR | MILS HT. | MILS HT. |
|---|---|---|---|---|---|
| | | | | | |

| AMMO | MIRAGE | TEMP | TGT SPEED | REMARKS | |
|---|---|---|---|---|---|
| | | | | | |

| LIGHT | | MPH WIND | |
|---|---|---|---|
| | | | |

| TGTS | 1 | 2 | 3 | 4 | 5 | 6 | 7 | 8 | 9 | 10 |
|---|---|---|---|---|---|---|---|---|---|---|
| ELEV | | | | | | | | | | |
| WIND | | | | | | | | | | |
| MILS | | | | | | | | | | |
| CALL | | | | | | | | | | |

| ELEV | WIND | ELEV | WIND |
|---|---|---|---|
| | | | |

# MOVING TARGET
## _____ YARD LINE

| RANGE | RIFLE AND SCOPE NO. | | DATE/HOUR | MILS HT. | MILS HT. |
|---|---|---|---|---|---|
| | | | | | |

| AMMO | MIRAGE | TEMP | TGT SPEED | REMARKS | |
|---|---|---|---|---|---|
| | | | | | |

| LIGHT | | MPH WIND | |
|---|---|---|---|
| | | | |

| TGTS | 1 | 2 | 3 | 4 | 5 | 6 | 7 | 8 | 9 | 10 |
|---|---|---|---|---|---|---|---|---|---|---|
| ELEV | | | | | | | | | | |
| WIND | | | | | | | | | | |
| MILS | | | | | | | | | | |
| CALL | | | | | | | | | | |

| ELEV | WIND | ELEV | WIND |
|---|---|---|---|
| | | | |

# SNIPERS RANGE CARD

| RANGE | 1000 | 900 | 800 | 700 | 600 | 500 | 400 | 300 | 200 | 100 | 200 | 300 | 400 | 500 | 600 | 700 | 800 | 900 | 1000 | RANGE |

GRID COORDINATE OF POSITIONS _____

METHOD OF OBTAINING RANGE _____

MADE OUT BY _____

DATE _____

## OBSERVATION LOG

SHEET____of____SHEETS

| ORIGINATOR | DATE | TOUR OF DUTY | POSITION | VISIBILITY |
|------------|------|--------------|----------|------------|

| SERIAL | TIME | GRID COORDINATE GR/BRG AND RANGE | EVENT | ACTION OR REMARKS |
|--------|------|----------------------------------|-------|-------------------|
| | | | | |

# SNIPER'S RECORD

| DATE | TYPE OF ROUNDS | NO. RDS. FIRED | TOTAL | DATE | TYPE OF ROUNDS | NO. RDS. FIRED | TOTAL |
|------|----------------|----------------|-------|------|----------------|----------------|-------|
|      |                |                |       |      |                |                |       |
|      |                |                |       |      |                |                |       |
|      |                |                |       |      |                |                |       |
|      |                |                |       |      |                |                |       |
|      |                |                |       |      |                |                |       |
|      |                |                |       |      |                |                |       |
|      |                |                |       |      |                |                |       |
|      |                |                |       |      |                |                |       |
|      |                |                |       |      |                |                |       |
|      |                |                |       |      |                |                |       |

| REMARKS | | TOTAL THIS PAGE | |
|---------|--|-----------------|--|
| | | TOTAL FROM PREVIOUS PAGES | |
| | | CUMULATIVE TOTAL | |

## SNIPER'S DATA CARD
For use of this form, see TC 23-14; the proponent agency is TRADOC

## DISTANCE TO TARGET_____ METERS

| RANGE | RIFLE AND SCOPE NO | | DATE | ELEVATION | | WINDAGE | |
|---|---|---|---|---|---|---|---|
| | | | | USED | CORRECT | USED | CORRECT |

| AMMO | LIGHT | MIRAGE | TEMP | HOUR | HOLD |
|---|---|---|---|---|---|

**LIGHT**

12
9   3
6

**WIND**

12
9   3
6

VELOCITY          DIRECTION

HOLD

| SHOT | 1 | 2 | 3 | 4 | 5 | 6 | 7 | 8 | 9 | 10 | REMARKS |
|---|---|---|---|---|---|---|---|---|---|---|---|
| ELEV | | | | | | | | | | | |
| WIND | | | | | | | | | | | |
| C A L L | | | | | | | | | | | |

NOTE: THE REQUIRED TARGETS WILL BE DRAWN IN BY HAND TO MEET THE NEEDS OF THE UNIT.

DA FORM 5785-R, JUN 89

---

## SNIPER'S OBSERVATION LOG
For use of this form, see TC 23-14; the proponent agency is TRADOC

SHEET_____OF_____SHEETS

| ORIGINATOR: | DATE/TIME: | LOCATION: |
|---|---|---|

| SERIAL | TIME | GRID COORDINATE | EVENT | ACTIONS OR REMARKS |
|---|---|---|---|---|
| | | | | |

DA FORM 5786-R, JUN 89

## Appendix L

## SNIPER TEAM DEBRIEFING FORMAT

### PREPARATION FOR DEBRIEFING

After the mission, the SEO or S3 representative directs the sniper team to an area where it prepares for a debriefing. The team remains in the area until called to the operations center.

A.  The sniper team will:

   (1)  Lay out and account for all team and individual equipment.

   (2)  Consolidate all captured material and equipment.

   (3)  Review and discuss the events listed in the mission logbook from insertion to return, including details of each enemy sighting.

   (4)  Prepare an overlay of the team's route, area of operations, insertion point, extraction point, and significant sighting locations.

B.  An S3 representative controls the debriefing. He directs the team leader:

   (1)  To discuss any enemy sightings since the last communications with the radio base station.

   (2)  To give a step-by-step account of each event listed in the mission logbook from insertion until reentry of the FLL, including the details of all enemy sightings.

   (3)  To complete a debriefing form (Table 5-2) and to draw an overlay as discussed.

The team leader either completes the form or has the observer complete different sections. He then returns the form and overlay to the S3 representative, while the observer performs post-mission maintenance tasks.

C.  When the debriefing is complete, the S3 representative releases the sniper team back to its parent unit.

1

# SNIPER TEAM DEBRIEFING FORMAT

## MISSION REPORT

TEAM NUMBER _____                     DATE-TIME-GROUP _____

TO _____

MAPS USED:  1:25,000:  _____
            1:50,000:  _____
            1:250,000: _____
            SPECIAL:   _____

A.  SIZE AND COMPOSITION OF TEAM:

    TEAM LEADER: _____
    OBSERVER: _____

B.  MISSION: _____
_____
_____

C.  ESSENTIAL ELEMENTS OF INFORMATION (USE ATTACHED SHEET):

D.  OTHER INTELLIGENCE REQUIREMENTS (USE ATTACHED SHEET):

E.  TIME OF DEPARTURE (DATE-TIME-GROUP):-

    METHOD OF INSERTION:_____

    POINT OF DEPARTURE (SIX-DIGIT GRID COORDINATES):
    _____

F.  ENEMY SPOTTING EN ROUTE (USE ATTACHED SHEET, IF NEEDED):

    1.  GROUND ACTIVITY: _____
    2.  AIR ACTIVITY: _____
    3.  MISCELLANEOUS ACTIVITY: _____

G.  ROUTES (OUT) (PROVIDE OVERLAY):

    1.  DISMOUNTED BY FOOT: _____
    2.  BY VEHICLE (STATE TYPE): _____
    3.  BY AIRCRAFT (STATE TYPE): _____

H.  TERRAIN (USE ATTACHED SHEET IN THE FOLLOWING FORMAT):

    KEY TERRAIN                TERRAIN COMPARTMENT
    SIGNIFICANT TERRAIN        TERRAIN CORRIDOR
    DECISIVE TERRAIN           MAP CORRECTIONS
    AVENUES OF APPROACH (STATE SIZE)

I.  ENEMY FORCES AND INSTALLATIONS (USE ATTACHED SHEET):

J.  MISCELLANEOUS INFORMATION (USE ATTACHED SHEET, IF NECESSARY):

    1.  LACK OF ANIMALS OR STRANGE ANIMAL BEHAVIOR: _____

    2.  MUTILATED PLANTS: _____
    3.  UNCOMMON INSECTS: _____
    4.  ABANDONED MILITARY EQUIPMENT (CHECK FOR AND INCLUDE NUMBER AND TYPE):
        A.  OUT OF FUEL: _____
        B.  UNSERVICEABLE (ESTIMATE WHY): _____
        C.  DESTROYED OR DAMAGED ON PURPOSE BY ENEMY FORCES: _____
        D.  OPERATIONAL EQUIPMENT LEFT INTACT: _____

    5.  ABANDONED TOWNS/VILLAGES: _____

K.  RESULTS OF ENCOUNTERS WITH ENEMY FORCE AND LOCAL POPULACE: _____

L.  CONDITION OF TEAM, INCLUDING DISPOSITION OF DEAD AND WOUNDED: _____

M.  ALL MAPS RETURNED OR ANY OTHER IDENTIFIABLE MATERIEL RETURNED WITH TEAM:  YES; NO; WHAT IS MISSING?; STATE ITEM AND WHERE APPROXIMATELY LOST: _____

N.  CONCLUSIONS AND RECOMMENDATIONS: _____

O.  CAPTURED ENEMY EQUIPMENT AND MATERIEL: _____

P.  TIME OF EXTRACTION (DATE-TIME-GROUP): _____

    METHOD OF EXTRACTION: _____

    EXTRACTION POINT (SIX-DIGIT GRID COORDINATES): _____

Q.  ROUTES (BACK) (PROVIDE OVERLAY):

    1.  DISMOUNTED BY GROUND (E&E): _____
    2.  FLIGHT ROUTE BACK: _____

R.  ENEMY SPOTTING EN ROUTE TO BASE (USE ATTACHED SHEET, IF NEEDED):

    1.  GROUND ACTIVITY: _____
    2.  AIR ACTIVITY: _____

3. MISCELLANEOUS ACTIVITY: _____

S. TIME OF RETURN (DTG): _____

POINT OF RETURN (SIX-DIGIT GRID COORDINATES): _____

TEAM LEADER: _____ _____
                           (PRINT NAME)          (GRADE)

_____ _____
             (UNIT)           (SIGNATURE)

ADDITIONAL REMARKS BY INTERROGATOR/DEBRIEFER: _____
_____
_____
_____

## Appendix M

### MISSION PACKING LIST

The sniper team determines the type and quantity of equipment it carries by a METT-T analysis. Some of the equipment mentioned may not be available. A sniper team, due to its unique mission requirements, carries only mission-essential equipment.

**ARMS AND AMMUNITION**

<u>Sniper</u>:

o   M24 sniper weapon system (SWS) with M3A telescope.

o   100 rounds M118/M852 ammunition.

o   Sniper's data book, mission logbook, range cards, wind tables, and slope dope.

o   M9/Service pistol.

o   45 rounds 9-mm ball ammunition.

o   3 each 9-mm magazines.

o   M9 bayonet.

o   4 M67 fragmentation grenades.

o   2 CS grenades; 2 percussion grenades (MOUT).

o   M18A1 mine, complete.

<u>Observer</u>:

o   M21 SWS/LSR/M-16A2/M203 (w/NVD as appropriate).

o   200-210 rounds ammunition.

o   5 to 7 magazines for rifle -- 5(M21) or 7(M16A2).

o   M9 9-mm pistol.

o   45 rounds 9-mm ball ammunition.

o   3 each 9-mm magazines.

o   M9 bayonet.

o   6 rounds 40mm high-explosive ammunition.

o    3 rounds 40mm antipersonnel ammunition.

o    4 M67 fragmentation grenades; 2 CS grenades; 2 percussion
     (MOUT).

## SPECIAL EQUIPMENT

<u>Sniper</u>:

o    M24 SWS cleaning kit.

o    M24 SWS deployment kit (tools and replacement parts).

o    M9 pistol cleaning kit.

o    Extra handset for radio.

o    Extra batteries for radio (BA 4386 or lithium, dependent
     on mission length).

o    SOI.

o    AN/PVS-5/7 series, night vision goggles.

o    Extra BA-1567/U or AA batteries for night vision goggles.

o    Pace cord.

o    E-tool with carrier.

o    50-foot 550 cord.

o    1 green and 1 red star cluster.

o    2 HC smoke grenades.

o    Measuring tape (25-foot carpenter-type).

<u>Observer</u>:

o    M16A1/A2 cleaning kit.

o    M203 cleaning kit.

o    AN/PRC-77/AN-PRC-119/AN/PRC-104 radio.

o    Radio accessory bag, complete with long whip and base,
     tape antenna and base, handset, and battery (BA-4386 or
     lithium).

o    M49 20x spotting scope with M15 tripod (or equivalent 15

2

to 20x fixed power scope, or 15-45x spotting scope)

o    M19/M22 binoculars (preferably 7 x 50 power with mil scale)

o    Range estimation "cheat book".

o    300-feet WD-1 field wire (for field-expedient antenna fabrication).

o    Olive-drab duct tape olive-drab ("100 mph") tape.

o    Extra batteries for radio (if needed).

o    Extra batteries (BA-1576/U) for AN/PVS-4.

o    Calculator with extra battery.

o    Butt pack.

o    10 each sandwich-size waterproof bags.

o    2 HC smoke grenades.

o    Lineman's tool.

## UNIFORMS AND EQUIPMENT

o    Footgear (jungle/desert/cold weather/combat boots).

o    2 sets BDUs (desert/woodland/camouflage).

o    Black leather gloves.

o    2 brown T-shirts.

o    2 brown underwear.

o    8 pair olive-drab wool socks.

o    Black belt.

o    Headgear (BDU/jungle/desert/cold weather).

o    ID tags and ID card.

o    Wristwatch (sweep second hand with luminous dial/waterproof).

o    Pocket survival knife.

o     Large ALICE pack, complete with frame and shoulder straps.

o     2 waterproof bags (for ALICE pack).

o     2 2-quart canteens with covers.

o     1 bottle water purification tablets.

o     LBE complete.

o     Red-lens flashlight (angle-head type with extra batteries).

o     MREs (number dependent on mission length).

o     9-mm pistol holster and magazine pouch (attached to LBE).

o     2 camouflage sticks (METT-T dependent).

o     2 black ink pens.

o     2 mechanical pencils with lead.

o     2 black grease pencils.

o     Lensatic compass.

o     Map(s) of operational area and protractor.

o     Poncho.

o     Poncho liner.

o     1 each ghillie suit complete.

o     1 each protective mask/MOPP suit.

o     Foot powder.

o     Toiletries.

## OPTIONAL EQUIPMENT

o     M203 vest.

o     Desert camouflage netting.

o     Natural-colored burlap.

o     Glitter tape.

o   VS-17 panel.

o   Strobe light with filters.

o   Special patrol insertion/extraction system harness.

o   12-foot sling rope.

o   2 each snap links.

o   120-foot nylon rope.

o   Lip/sun screen.

o   Signal mirror.

o   Pen gun with flares.

o   Chemical lights (to include infrared).

o   Body armor/flak jacket.

o   Sniper veil.

o   Sewing kit.

o   Insect repellant.

o   Sleeping bag.

o   Knee and elbow pads.

o   Survival kit.

o   Rifle drag bag.

o   Pistol silencer/suppressor.

o   2.5-pounds C4 with caps, cord, fuse, and igniter.

o   Rifle bipod/tripod.

o   Empty sandbags.

o   Hearing protection (ear muffs).

o   Thermometer.

o   Laser range finder.

o   Thermal imager.

o    KN-200-KN-250 image intensifier.

o    Pocket binoculars.

o    35-mm automatic loading camera with appropriate lenses and film.

o    1/2-inch camcorder with accessories.

o    Satellite communication equipment.

o    Short-range radio with earphone and whisper microphone.

o    Field-expedient antennas.

o    Information reporting formats.

o    Encryption device for radio.

o    SO sniper training/employment manual

## SPECIAL TOOLS AND EQUIPMENT (MOUT)

o    Pry bar.

o    Pliers.

o    Screwdriver.

o    Rubber-headed hammer.

o    Glass cutter.

o    Masonry drill and bits.

o    Metal shears.

o    Chisel.

o    Auger.

o    Lock pick, skeleton keys, cobra pick.

o    Bolt cutters.

o    Hacksaw or handsaw.

o    Sledgehammer.

o    Axe.

o   Ram.

o   Power saw.

o   Cutting torch.

o   Shotgun.

o   Spraypaint.

o   Stethoscope.

o   Maps/street plans.

o   Photographs, aerial and panoramic.

o   Whistle.

o   Luminous tape.

o   Flex cuffs.

o   Padlocks.

o   Instrusion detection system (booby traps).

o   Portable spotlight(s).

o   Money (US and indigenous).

o   Civilian attire.

## ADDITIONAL EQUIPMENT TRANSPORT

The planned use of air and vehicle drops and caching
techniques eliminates the need for the sniper team to carry extra
equipment. Another method is to use the stay-behind technique when
operating with a security patrol. (See Chapter 5).  Through
coordination with the security patrol leader, the team's equipment
may be broken down among the patrol members.  On arrival at the
ORP, the security patrol may leave behind all mission-essential
equipment.  After completing the mission, the team may cache the
equipment for later pickup, or it may be returned the same way it
was brought in.

## Appendix N

### REPRODUCIBLE FORMS

#### Concealed Movement Exercise

For use of this form, see FM 23-10. The proponent agency is
TRADOC.

DATA REQUIRED BY PRIVACY ACT OF 1974.
AUTHORITY: 10 USC 3012(g)/Executive Order 9397. PRINCIPAL
PURPOSE(S): Evaluates individual training. ROUTINE USE(S):
Evaluates individual proficiency. SSN is used for positive
identification purposes only. MANDATORY OR VOLUNTARY DISCLOSURE
AND EFFECT ON INDIVIDUAL NOT PROVIDING INFORMATION: Voluntary.
Individuals not providing information cannot be rated/scored on a
mass basis.

EXERCISE NUMBER: _____       DATE: _____
LAST NAME     FIRST    MI     RANK    SSN          UNIT

_____    ____  _____  _____
CONCEALED MOVEMENT EXERCISE AREA:    _____
WEATHER/VISIBILITY:    _____      SCORE: _____

_____          _____
TRAINER'S SIGNATURE                   SNIPER'S SIGNATURE

If the sniper                                         Points

    Was detected moving to the FFP...................    2

    Was detected moving in the FFP...................    3

    Fired first shot, not detected...................    4

    Was not detected when assistant trainer is within
    10 feet of firer.................................    5

    Properly identified number (within 30 seconds)....    6

    Failed to properly identify number..............    3

    Was not detected when assistant trainer is within
    5 feet of firer..................................    7

    Fired second shot, not detected..................    8

    Maintained stable firing position (support).......    9

    Properly adjusted weapon's scope for range and
    windage..........................................    10

NOTE:     1.    If muzzle blast/flash is detected, deduct
                1 point from the total score.

1

2. Failing to comply with training standards and objectives (such as unnecessary movement, premature fire, outside of prescribe boundaries) will result in termination of the exercise and a score of zero.

(Check one of the target indicators).

IMPROPER MOVEMENT TECHNIQUES     _____
IMPROPER CAMOUFLAGE     _____
SHINE     _____
OUTLINE     _____
CONTRAST TO BACKGROUND     _____
SOUND     _____
MUZZLE BLAST     _____
MUZZLE FLASH     _____

REMARKS: (EXPLAIN IN DETAIL THE REASONS FOR THE SNIPER'S DETECTION>)

_____
_____
_____

## Target Detection Exercise

For use of this form, see FM 23-10.  The proponent agency is TRADOC.

DATA REQUIRED BY PRIVACY ACT OF 1974.
AUTHORITY:  10 USC 3012(g)/Executive Order 9397.  PRINCIPAL PURPOSE(S):  Evaluates individual training.  ROUTINE USE(S): Evaluates individual proficiency.  SSN is used for positive identification purposes only.  MANDATORY OR VOLUNTARY DISCLOSURE AND EFFECT ON INDIVIDUAL NOT PROVIDING INFORMATION:  Voluntary. Individuals not providing information cannot be rated/scored on a mass basis.

EXERCISE AREA/NUMBER: _____    DATE: _____
LAST NAME    FIRST    MI              RANK    SSN        UNIT

WEATHER/VISIBILITY: _____         SCORE: _____

TRAINER'S SIGNATURE              SNIPER'S SIGNATURE

| NO. | SIZE | DESCRIPTION SHAPE | COLOR | COND | APPEARS TO BE | LOCATION | POSITION (Circle one-A-B |
|-----|------|-------|-------|------|---------|----------|------|
| 1. | | | | | | | |
| 2. | | | | | | | |
| 3. | | | | | | | |
| 4. | | | | | | | |
| 5. | | | | | | | |
| 6. | | | | | | | |
| 7. | | | | | | | |
| 8. | | | | | | | |
| 9. | | | | | | | |
| 10. | | | | | | | |
| 11. | | | | | | | |
| 12. | | | | | | | |

3

## Range Estimation Exercise

For use of this form, see FM 23-10.  The proponent agency is
TRADOC.

DATA REQUIRED BY PRIVACY ACT OF 1974.
AUTHORITY:  10 USC 3012(g)/Executive Order 9397.  PRINCIPAL
PURPOSE(S):  Evaluates individual training.  ROUTINE USE(S):
Evaluates individual proficiency.  SSN is used for positive
identification purposes only. MDNATORY OR VOLUNTARY DISCLOSURE
AND EFFECT ON INDIVIDUAL NOT PROVIDING INFORMATION:  Voluntary.
Individuals not providing information cannot be rated/scored on a
mass basis.

EXERCISE NUMBER: _____     DATE: _____
LAST NAME     FIRST      MI       RANK        SSN           UNIT

_____  _____   _____  _____
EXERCISE AREA: _____
WEATHER/VISIBILITY: _____   SCORE : _____

_____      _____
TRAINER'S SIGNATURE                      SNIPER'S SIGNATURE

| EYE ESTIMATION | BINOCULAR ESTIMATION | M3A TELESCOPE ESTIMATION |
|---|---|---|
| 1 _____ | 1 _____ | 1 _____ |
| 2 _____ | 2 _____ | 2 _____ |
| 3 _____ | 3 _____ | 3 _____ |
| 4 _____ | 4 _____ | 4 _____ |
| 5 _____ | 5 _____ | 5 _____ |
| 6 _____ | 6 _____ | 6 _____ |
| 7 _____ | 7 _____ | 7 _____ |
| 8 _____ | 8 _____ | 8 _____ |
| 9 _____ | 9 _____ | 9 _____ |
| 10 _____ | 10 _____ | 10 _____ |

1.   Within three minutes, estimate the range to the target at
each point, using the naked eye, binoculars, and M3A   telescope.
Estimations are performed in the order listed.
2.   Do not change eye or binocular estimates after recording, or
     these estimates will be counted as incorrect answers.
     However, the M3A telescope estimate may be changed before
     making the next set of estimates.
3.   The use of calculators is encouraged.
4.   This is an individual exercise.  Any sniper that talks or
     tries to look at another sniper's scorecard will be
terminated from the exercise.
5.   To ask a question, raise your hand, and the trainer will
     assist you.

## Qualification Table No. 1

For use of this form, see FM 23-10.  The proponent agency is TRADOC.

RECORD OR PRACTICE
(circle one)

EXERCISE NUMBER: _____        DATE: _____

LAST NAME    FIRST    MI    RANK    SSN              UNIT

_____  ____    _____  ____

EXERCISE AREA: _____

WEATHER/VISIBILITY: _____        SCORE: _____

TRAINER'S SIGNATURE                SNIPER'S SIGNATURE

| TARGET (meters) | 1st Round | 2nd Round | Miss |
|---|---|---|---|
| 200 | _____ | _____ | ____ |
| 300 | _____ | _____ | ____ |
| 325 | _____ | _____ | ____ |
| 375 | _____ | _____ | ____ |
| 500 | _____ | _____ | ____ |
| 600 | _____ | _____ | ____ |
| 500 | _____ | _____ | ____ |
| 375 | _____ | _____ | ____ |
| 600 | _____ | _____ | ____ |
| 700 | _____ | _____ | ____ |
| 500 | _____ | _____ | ____ |
| 400 | _____ | _____ | ____ |
| 325 | _____ | _____ | ____ |
| 400 | _____ | _____ | ____ |
| 600 | _____ | _____ | ____ |
| 500 | _____ | _____ | ____ |
| 700 | _____ | _____ | ____ |
| 325 | _____ | _____ | ____ |
| 300 | _____ | _____ | ____ |
| 200 | _____ | _____ | ____ |
| | x 10 = _____ | x 5 = _____ | ____ |

5

<u>Qualification Table No. 2</u>

For use of this form, see FM 23-10.  The proponent agency is
TRADOC.
DATA REQUIRED BY PRIVACY ACT OF 1974.
AUTHORITY:  10 USC 3012(g)/Executive Order 9397.  PRINCIPAL
PURPOSE(S):  Evaluates individual training.  ROUTINE USE(S):
Evaluates individual proficiency.  SSN is used for positive
identification purposes only.  MANDATORY OR VOLUNTARY DISCLOSURE
AND EFFECT ON INDIVIDUAL NOT PROVIDING INFORMATION:  Voluntary.
Individuals not providing information cannot be rated/scored on a
mass basis.

RECORD OR PRACTICE
(circle one)

EXERCISE NUMBER: _____    DATE: _____

| LAST NAME | FIRST | MI | RANK | SSN | UNIT |
|---|---|---|---|---|---|

EXERCISE AREA: _____
WEATHER/VISIBLITY: _____    SCORE: _____

TRAINER'S SIGNATURE                SNIPER'S SIGNATURE

| TARGET (meters) | 1st Round | 2nd Round | Miss |
|---|---|---|---|
| 300 | _____ | _____ | ____ |
| 325 | _____ | _____ | ____ |
| 375 | _____ | _____ | ____ |
| 600 | _____ | _____ | ____ |
| 500 | _____ | _____ | ____ |
| 600 | _____ | _____ | ____ |
| 700 | _____ | _____ | ____ |
| 750 | _____ | _____ | ____ |
| 800 | _____ | _____ | ____ |
| 850 | _____ | _____ | ____ |
| 900 | _____ | _____ | ____ |
| 850 | _____ | _____ | ____ |
| 800 | _____ | _____ | ____ |
| 750 | _____ | _____ | ____ |
| 700 | _____ | _____ | ____ |
| 900 | _____ | _____ | ____ |
| 500 | _____ | _____ | ____ |
| 400 | _____ | _____ | ____ |
| 325 | _____ | _____ | ____ |
| 300 | _____ | _____ | ____ |
| x 10 = | _____ | x 5 = _____ | ____ |

## SNIPER'S RANGE CARD
For use of this form, see TC 23-14, the proponent agency is TRADOC

NAME:

METHOD OF OBTAINING RANGE

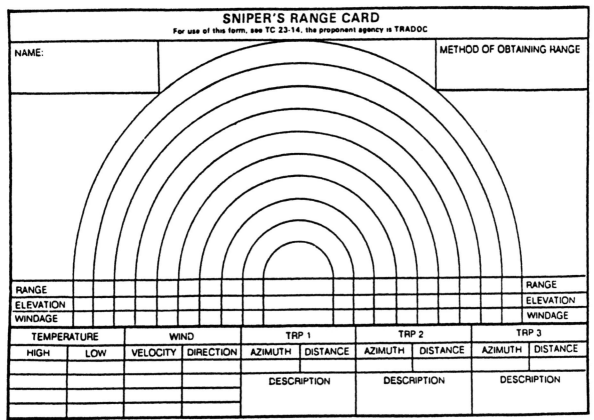

| RANGE | | | | | | | | | | | | | | | RANGE | |
|---|---|---|---|---|---|---|---|---|---|---|---|---|---|---|---|---|
| ELEVATION | | | | | | | | | | | | | | | ELEVATION | |
| WINDAGE | | | | | | | | | | | | | | | WINDAGE | |

| TEMPERATURE | | WIND | | TRP 1 | | TRP 2 | | TRP 3 | |
|---|---|---|---|---|---|---|---|---|---|
| HIGH | LOW | VELOCITY | DIRECTION | AZIMUTH | DISTANCE | AZIMUTH | DISTANCE | AZIMUTH | DISTANCE |
| | | | | DESCRIPTION | | DESCRIPTION | | DESCRIPTION | |

DA FORM 5787-R, JUN 89

## MILITARY SKETCH
For use of this form, see TC 23-14; the proponent agency is TRADOC

REMARKS:

REMARKS.

SKETCH NAME: _____

GRID COORDINATE: _____

WEATHER: _____

↑ = _____
MAGNETIC
AZIMUTH

SKETCH # _____

OF _____

SCALE _____

NAME:

RANK:

DATE/TIME.

DA FORM 5788-R, JUN 89

# Appendix O

## GLOSSARY

### O-1. ACRONYMS AND ABBREVIATIONS

| | |
|---|---|
| AAR | after action review/report |
| AMU | Army Marksmanship Unit |
| AP | anti-personnel or armor piercing |
| AR | Army Regulation |
| ARM | advanced rifle marksmanship |
| ART | adjustable ranging telescope |
| ARTEP | Army Training and Evaluation Program |
| ATB | appears to be |
| BMNT | beginning morning nautical twilight |
| BRM | basic rifle marksmanship |
| BTB | blind transmission broadcast |
| C | centigrade |
| C2 | command and control |
| C3 | command, control, and communications |
| C3I | command, control, communications, and intelligence |
| CA | civil affairs |
| CARVER | criticality, accessibility, recuperability, vulnerability, effect, recognizability (target analysis) |
| CAS | close air support |
| CLP | cleaner, lubricant, preservative |
| cm | centimeter |
| CMO | civil-military operations |
| CN | counter-narcotics |
| COMSEC | communications security |
| CSAR | combat search and rescue |
| CT | counterterrorism |
| DA | Department of the Army or direct action |
| DOD | Department of Defense |
| DODAC | DOD ammunition code |
| DTG | date-time group |
| E&E | escape and evasion |
| EEI | essential elements of information |
| EENT | ending evening nautical twilight |
| EW | electronic warfare |
| F | Fahrenheit |
| FC | field circular |
| FFL | final firing line |
| FFP | final firing position |
| FID | foreign internal defense |
| FLOT | forward line of troops |
| FM | field manual |
| fps | feet per second |
| FRAGO | fragmentary order |
| FSN | Federal Stock Number |

1

| | |
|---|---|
| FTX | field training exercise |
| GSR | ground surveillance radar |
| GTA | graphic training aid |
| HN | host nation |
| HUMINT | human intelligence |
| HVT | high value target |
| Hz | hertz |
| IAD | immediate action drills |
| IAW | in accordance with |
| IDAD | internal defense and development |
| INTSUM | intelligence summary |
| KD | known distance |
| kg | kilogram |
| KIM | keep-in-memory (exercise game) |
| km | kilometer |
| IPB | intelligence preparation of the battlefield |
| IR | intelligence requirements |
| JSOA | joint special operations area |
| LFX | live fire exercise |
| LIC | low intensity conflict |
| LOC | lines of communication |
| LP | listening post |
| m | meter |
| METL | mission essential task list |
| METT-T | mission, enemy, terrain, troops, and time available |
| MHz | megahertz |
| MIJI | meaconing, intrusion, jamming, and interference |
| MILES | multiple integrated laser engagement system |
| mm | millimeter |
| MMPI | Minnesota Multi-Phasic Personality Inventory |
| MOA | minute of angle (1.0472" at 100 yards) |
| MOPP | mission oriented protection posture |
| MOUT | military operations on urbanized terrain |
| mph | miles per hour |
| MTOE | modification table of organization and equipment |
| MTP | mission training plan |
| MTT | mobile training team |
| NATO | North Atlantic Treaty Organization |
| NBC | nuclear, biological, chemical |
| NCA | National Command Authority |
| NSN | national stock number |
| NVD | night vision device |
| OP | observation post |
| OPORD | operation order |
| OPSEC | operations security |
| PIR | priority intelligence requirement |
| POC | point of contact |
| POI | program of instruction |
| POL | petroleum, oils, and lubricants |
| PRI | preliminary rifle instruction |
| PSYOP | psychological operations |
| RETS | remote electronic target system |

| ROE | rules of engagement |
|---|---|
| RTO | radiotelephone operator |
| SALUTE | size, activity, location, unit, time, and equipment |
| SAR | search and rescue |
| SEO | sniper employment officer |
| SITREP | situation report |
| SO | special operations |
| SOF | special operations forces |
| SOI | signal operation instructions |
| SOP | standing operating procedure |
| SOTIC | Special Operations Target Interdiction Course |
| SR | special reconnaissance |
| SRT | special reaction team |
| ST | special text |
| STANAG | NATO Standardization Agreement |
| STANO | surveillance, target acquisition, and night observation |
| STP | soldier's training publication |
| SWS | sniper weapon system |
| TB | technical bulletin |
| TC | training circular |
| T&EO | training and evaluation outline |
| TFFP | tentative final firing position |
| TIP | target intelligence package |
| TM | technical manual |
| TOE | table of organization and equipment |
| TRP | target reference point |
| UBL | unit basic load |
| USAMU | US Army Marksmanship Unit |
| UW | unconventional warfare |

## O-2. DEFINITIONS

**Accuracy:** In sniping, the ability of the sniper and his weapon to deliver precision fire on a desired target. Accuracy can easily be measured as the ability to group all shots close to a desired impact point. The deviation from the desired impact point or the size of the group is a function of range. Accuracy is the product of uniformity.

**Action:** The mechanism of a sniper rifle or other firearm that normally performs loading, feeding, locking, firing, unlocking, extracting, and ejection. Also known as the receiver or frame.

**Adjustable objective:** Fine focussing ring on the objective lens of a telescope that helps to eliminate parallax.

**Adjusted aiming point:** An aiming point that allows for gravity, wind, target movement, zero changes, or MOPP firing.

3

**Ammunition lot:** A quantity of cartridges made by one manufacturer under uniform conditions from the same materials. Ammunition within a lot is expected to perform in a uniform manner.

**Ammunition lot number:** Code number that identifies a particular quantity of ammunition from one manufacturer. It is usually printed on the ammunition case, and the individual boxes in which the ammunition comes.

**Ball ammunition:** General-purpose standard service ammunition with a solid core (usually of lead) bullet.

**Ballistic coefficient:** A number used to measure how easily a bullet slips through the air (aerodynamic efficiency). Most bullets have BCs between .100 and .700. Higher BCs are required for long-range shooting.

**Ballistics:** A science that deals with the motion and flight characteristics of projectiles.

**Beat:** The sniper's operational area, where established control measures (boundaries, limits, etc.) define his territory.

**Berdan primer:** Form of primer that does not have an integral anvil. Still found in Europe, it is reloaded with difficulty.

**Boattail bullet:** A bullet with a tapered base to reduce aerodymanic drag. Drag partly comes from the effects of cavitation (turbulence), and the progressive reduction of the diameter toward the rear of the bullet allows the air to fill in the void.

**Boxer primer:** Standard primer with an integral anvil.

**Brass:** Empty cartridge case.

**Breech:** The chamber end of the barrel.

**Bullet drop:** The amount that a bullet falls due to the effect of gravity.

**Bullet drop compensator:** Any device that is integral to the rifle telescope that is designed to compensate for the bullet's trajectory.

**Caliber:** The measurement taken within the barrel from groove to groove or from the outside diameter of the bullet.

**Chamber:** Part of the bore, at the breech, formed to accept and support the cartridge.

**Chronograph:** An instrument used to measure the velocity of a projectile.

**Clandestine operation:** An activity to accomplish intelligence gathering, counterintelligence, or other similar activities sponsored or conducted by governmental departments or agencies, in such a way as to assure secrecy or concealment of the operation. It differs from covert operations in that the emphasis is placed on the concealment of the operation, rather than on the concealment of the sponsor's identity.

**Cold-bore shot:** The first shot from a clean, unfired weapon.

**Collimator:** Bore-sighting device.

**Concealment:** Protection from view. This is not necessarily the same as cover. Cover provides concealment, but concealment does not always provide cover.

**Cover:** Protection form hostile gunfire. Cover is a relative term. Cover that is thick enough to stop pistol bullets may not be adequate protection against rifle bullets. This is a crucial fact to keep in mind when selecting cover.

**Covert operation:** An operation that is planned and executed as to conceal the identity of, or permit plausible denial by, the sponsor(s). This differs from a clandestine operation in that emphasis is placed on the concealment of the sponsor's identity, rather than on the concealment of the operation.

**Crimp:** The bending inward of the mouth of the case in order to grip the bullet, or around the primer to seal it.

**Cross dominance:** A soldier with a dominant hand and a dominant eye that are not on the same side; for example, a right-handed firer with a dominant left eye.

**Crown:** The technique used to finish the barrel's muzzle. The rifling at the end of the barrel can be slightly relieved, or recessed. The purpose is to protect the forward edge of the rifling from damage which can ruin accuracy.

**Deflection:** The change in the path of the bullet due to wind or passing through a medium.

**Detailed search:** A systematic observation of a target area in detail, using overlapping observation in a 180 degree area, 50 meters in depth, starting in and working away from the observer.

**Drag:** The aerodynamic resistance to a bullet's flight.

**Drift:** The horizontal deviation of the projectile from its line of departure due to its rotational spin or the effects of the wind.

**Drop:** The distance that a projectile falls due to gravity measured from the line of departure.

**Dry firing:** Aiming and firing the weapon without live ammunition. This is an excellent technique to improve marksmanship skills, and does not cause any damage to a center-fire firearm. It is best done with an expended case in the chamber to cushion the firing pin's fall.

**Effective wind:** The average of all of the varying winds encountered.

**Exit pupil:** The small circle of light seen coming from the ocular lens of an optical device when held at arm's length. The exit pupil can be determined mathematically by dividing the objective lens diameter (in millimeters) by the magnification. The result will be the diameter of the exit pupil in millimeters. (example: for a 6 X 42mm telescope: 42mm divided by 6 = 7mm). The size of the exit pupil will help in determining the effectiveness of the optical device in low-light conditions. The human pupil dilates to approximately 7mm under low-light conditions, and a telescope with a 7mm exit pupil will provide the maximum light possible to the sniper's eye.

**Exterior ballistics:** What happens to the bullet between the time it exits the barrel and the time it arrives at the target.

**Eye relief:** The distance that the eye is positioned behind the ocular lens of the telescopic sight. A two to three inch distance is average. The sniper adjusts the eye relief to ensure a full field of view. This distance is also necessary to prevent the telescope from striking the sniper's face during recoil.

**Follow-through:** The continued mental and physical application of marksmanship fundamentals after each round has been fired.

**Fouling:** Build-up of copper and powder residue in the bore. These two types of fouling require different cleaning solvents for complete removal.

**Free-floating barrel:** A barrel that is completely free of contact with the stock. This is critical to accuracy because of barrel harmonics. As the bullet is travelling down the barrel, the barrel is vibrating like a tuning fork. Any contact with the barrel will dampen or modify these vibrations

6

with (usually) a negative impact on shot-group size or point of impact.

**Grain:** A unit of measure; 7,000 grains are equal to 1 pound. Used to describe bullet weight (ex., 173 grains) or powder charge.

**Grooves:** The low point of rifling within a barrel.

**Group:** Formed from numerous shots fired at a target using the same point of aim, for checking accuracy. For standardization, it is best to fire five-shot groups with the same aiming point. It is a statistical fact that group size will increase with the number of shots fired.

**Hand load:** Also called reload. Non-factory manufactured ammunition.

**Hand stop:** A device attached to the weapon's fore-end (modified with a metal rail) designed to prevent the supporting hand from sliding forward.

**Hasty search:** A very rapid check for enemy activity; primarily used as a security measure to determine immediate threats or danger to the sniper when occupying positions.

**Headspace:** In rifles, the distance from the shoulder of the cartridge case to the head of the case. For bottle-necked cases, the measuring point is centered on the shoulder, and is known as the datum line. For belted magnum cases, the headspace is measured from the front of the belt to the head of the case. This dimension is critical for the safety of the shooter, as well as the accuracy of the weapon system.

**Hide:** The term used to describe sniper positions, normally concealed from the enemy.

**Holdoff:** A shooting technique used to compensate for bullet trajectory by using a modified point of aim above or below the desired point of impact. Also used to describe the modified point of aim used to compensate for wind or target movement. Also known as "Kentucky windage."

**Hold-over:** The modified point of aim used above the target to compensate for bullet trajectory.

**Hold-under:** The modified point of aim used below the target to compensate for a projectile on its upward axis of its trajectory. This is also used when shooting at angles (slopes).

**Hollow-point:** Describes a bullet with a hollow cavity in the tip. The Sierra Matchking bullets have this design feature to

7

improve accuracy, not for improved terminal effects. This bullet type has been approved by the JAG for combat use.

**Indexing targets:** The method that a sniper team employs to identify targets within its effective field of fire.

**Interior Ballistics:** What happens to the bullet before it leaves the muzzle of the rifle. Calculations are used to measure pressure forces inside the cartridge and barrel during firing.

**Jacket:** The copper covering over the lead core of a bullet.

**Kentucky windage:** An estimate of the modified point of aim required to compensate for wind or for target movement. Synonymous with holdoff.

**Key hole:** When the bullet hits the target other than point first. Usually indicated by an elliptical bullet hole. Caused by inadequate rotational stabilization of the bullet (usually due to insufficient barrel twist; the twist is "too slow"), deflection of the bullet by objects in the bullet's path, or other factors.

**Lands:** The high points in the rifling of a barrel. This is the part of the barrel that actually engraves the bullet, imparts the spin to the bullet, and ultimately stabilizes the bullet.

**Lead:** The modified point of aim in front of a moving target needed to ensure a hit. This depends on the range to, and the speed of, the target.

**Loophole:** Firing port. A hole cut to conceal the sniper but allow him to engage targets in his sector.

**Mean radius:** The average radius of shot dispersion from the center of a shot group.

**Mid-range trajectory:** The highest point in the bullet's flight. This occurs, technically, slightly beyond the half-way mark of the distance at which the rifle is zeroed. This is the highest vertical distance of the bullet above the line of sight.

**Mil:** An angular unit of measurement equal to 1/6400 of a complete revolution (there are 6400 mils in 360 degrees). The mil is used to estimate distance and size based on the mil relation formula: 1 mil equals 1 meter at 1,000 meters. There are 3.375 MOA in 1 mil.

**Mil dot:** Used to descibe the reticle in telescopic sights (ex: the M3A) that has dots that are one mil apart.

8

**Minute of angle (MOA):** A unit of angular measurement equal to 1/60th of a degree. Although usually approximated as 1 inch per 100 yards of range, it is actually equal to 1.0472 inches per 100 yards of range.

**Mirage:** The heat waves or the reflection of light through layers of air of different densities and temperatures. With optical aids, mirage can be seen even on the coldest days. Mirage is used to estimate the effective wind to be applied to the sight of the SWS.

**Muzzle:** The end of the barrel where the bullet leaves the barrel.

**Muzzle velocity:** The speed of a projectile as it leaves the muzzle of the weapon.

**Natural point of aim:** The direction that the body/rifle combination is oriented while in a stable, relaxed firing position.

**Natural respiratory pause:** The temporary cessation of breathing after an exhalation and before an inhalation.

**Neck:** The portion of a cartridge case which holds the bullet.

**Objective lens:** The lens at the front of the telescope. It is usually larger in diameter than the ocular lens.

**Ocular lens:** The lens at the rear of the telescope, nearest the sniper's eye.

**Parallax:** The apparent movement of the target in relation to the reticle when the sniper moves his eye in relation to the ocular lens. When the target's image is not focused on the same focal plane as the telescope's reticle, parallax is the result. Current issue US Army rifle telescopes have a field parallax adjustment that makes parallax error an insignificant factor when proper eye relief and stock weld are used.

**Point of aim:** The exact location on a target with which the rifle sights are aligned.

**Point of impact:** The point that a bullet strikes; usually considered in relation to the point of aim.

**Powder:** The propellant material used in most ammunition.

**Primer:** A small explosive cap in the center of the head of the cartridge case that is struck by the firing pin to fire the round. It consists of a small cup filled with a detonating mixture that provides the flame (actually, a shock wave) that converts the propellant powder into a gas.

**Primer pocket:** The recess in the base of the cartridge case that accepts the primer. In military ammunition, it is usually crimped and sealed with a laquer sealant for water-proofing.

**Probability of hit (PH):** Refers to the chance (denoted as a percentage) that a given round will hit the target at a given range. PH values range from 0 to 1.0.

**Rail:** A metal track installed in the fore end of weapon to accept a hand stop or sling.

**Ranging:** The technique that a sniper uses to compensate for bullet trajectory by adjusting the ballistic cam of an adjustable/ranging telescope.

**Recoil lug:** The heavy metal protrusion beneath the front of the action designed to stabilize the action in the stock and transfer the recoil to the stock.

**Reload:** Hand-loaded ammunition.

**Reticle:** The sighting image, usually cross-hairs, in a telescopic sight.

**Retina:** The light-sensitive layer at the back of the eye. It consists of rod (black/white sensitive for night vision) and cone (color sensitive for day vision) cells.

**Rifle cant:** Any leaning of the rifle to the left or right from a vertical position during firing. This should be eliminated because of the potential for increasing misses at longer ranges.

**Rifling:** The spiral grooves in the bore of firearms that spin the bullet to provide it with rotational stability. This will ensure that the bullet flies true with a point-first attitude.

**Rimfire:** A cartridge whose priming compound is located in the rim of the cartridge case, and generally of .22 caliber. This type of ammunition is discharged by a strike of the firing pin to the rim. This ammunition is generally considered non-reloadable.

**Rimless:** The rim of the cartridge is the same diameter as the body of the case.

**Rimmed:** The rim of the cartridge is larger in diameter than the body of the cartridge case.

**Rings:**  The metal devices used to support the scope.  Usually 1" or 30mm in diameter.

**Round:**  Refers to a complete cartridge.

**Scout:**  An individual who is usually ahead of his parent organization to conduct surveillance on the enemy, conduct reconnaissance, and report information to his parent organization.

**Service rifle:**  The primary rifle of a military force.

**Silencer:**  See suppressor.

**Sniper specialist:**  An individual trained in sniper employment (preferably sniper qualified) who advises the commander or operations officer (S3) on proper sniper employment.

**Sniper team:**  Two snipers of equal training and ability; the foundation of sound sniper employment.

**Speed of sound:**  1120.22 fps at standard conditions.  Projectiles travelling faster than this pass through the sound barrier twice: once as it exceeds the sound barrier (within the barrel), and once when it re-enters sub-sonic speeds.  This effect causes a sonic crack that can be used to pin-point the firer.

**Stalking:**  The sniper's art of moving unseen into a firing position, engaging his target, and then withdrawing undetected.

**Stock weld:**  The contact of the cheek with the stock of the weapon.

**Suppressor:**  A device designed to muffle or eliminate the sounds of the discharging of a firearm.  It is usually fitted onto the muzzle, but can also be an integral assembly with the barrel.  This usually works best with sub-sonic ammunition to eliminate the bullet's sonic crack as well.

**Surveillance:**  The systematic observation of areas, places, persons, or things by visual, aural, electronic, photographic, or other means.  The sniper makes extensive use of fixed and roving surveillance to acquire targets or assess target vulnerabilities.

**Swivel:**  The attachment point for the sling to the stock.

**Target indicators:**  Any sign that can enable an observer to detect the location of the enemy, his installations, or his equipment.

**Terminal ballistics:** What happens to the bullet when it comes into contact with the target. The study of the effect of a bullet's impact on the target.

**Terminal velocity:** The speed of the bullet upon impact with the target. This will determine the effectiveness of the bullet because of its direct contribution to energy/energy transfer.

**Torque:** The turning force applied to screws or bolts.

**Trace:** The air turbulence created by the shock wave of a bullet as it passes through the air. This air turbulence can be observed (with an optical aid) in the form of a vapor trail as the bullet travels toward the target.

**Tracer:** Type of ammunition that is visible at night due to its phosphorous compound in the base of the bullet.

**Tracking:** Engaging moving targets where the lead is established and maintained; moving with the target as the trigger is squeezed. Also used to describe the technique of following the enemy by his markings left on the terrain.

**Trajectory:** The flight path the bullet takes from the rifle to the target. The path of a bullet in flight.

**Trapping:** A technique for engaging moving targets. The aiming point is established forward of the target. The rifle is held stationary and fired as the target approaches the aiming point.

**Twist:** The rate of pitch of the rifling in a firearm's bore. Usually measured by the length of barrel in inches required for the bullet to make one complete revolution, and expressed as a twist rate (ex., 1 turn in 11.2 inches; 1/11.2).

**Velocity:** The speed of the projectile.

**Windage:** The distance or amount of horizontal correction that a sniper must use to hit his target due to the effects of wind or drift. The adjustment on the telescope or iron sights to compensate for horizontal deflection of the bullet.

**X:** The power of optical magnification (ex., 10X, 3X-9X).

**Zero:** The range at which the point of aim and the point of impact are one and the same.

## Appendix P

## REFERENCES

**U.S. Army Publications:**

| | |
|---|---|
| AR 40-501 | Standards of Medical Fitness |
| AR 350-6 | Army-Wide Small Arms Competitive Marksmanship (1985) |
| AR 385-63 | Policies and Procedures for Firing Ammunition for Training, Target Practice and Combat |
| ARTEP 7-92-MTP | Mission Training Plan for the Infantry Scout Platoon/Squad and Sniper Team (1989) |
| ARTEP 31-807-31-MTP | Mission Training Plan for the Special Forces Company: Special Reconnaissance (1989) |
| ARTEP 31-807-32-MTP | Mission Training Plan for the Special Forces Company: Direct Action (1989) |
| DA Pam 350-38 | Standards in Weapons Training |
| FM 5-20 | Camouflage |
| FM 7-8 | Infantry Rifle Platoon and Squad (1992) |
| FM 7-70 | Light Infantry Platoon/Squad (1986) |
| FM 21-75 | Combat Skills of the Soldier (1984) |
| FM 23-8 | M14 and M14A1 Rifles and Rifle Marksmanship (1974) |
| FM 23-9 | M16A1 and M16A2 Rifle Marksmanship (1989) |
| FM 31-20 | Doctrine for Special Forces Operations (1990) |
| FM 90-10 (HTF) | Military Operations in Urbanized Terrain (MOUT) (How to Fight) (1979) |
| FM 90-10-1 | An Infantryman's Guide to Urban Combat (1982) |

1

| | |
|---|---|
| SH 23-9-5 | USAMU Marksmanship Instructors' and Coaches' Guide |
| ST 31-201 | Special Forces Operations (1978) |
| TC 19-16 | Countering Terrorism on US Army Installations (1983) |
| TC 23-13 | Crew-Served Weapon Night Vision Sight (1967) |
| TC 23-14 | Sniper Training and Employment (1989) |
| TC 31-29 | Special Forces Operational Techniques (1988) |
| TM 9-1005-222-35 | DS, GS, and Depot Maintenance Manual including Repair Parts and Special Tool Lists for Rifle, Caliber .30, M1, M1C (Sniper's) and M1D (Sniper's) (1966) |
| TM 9-1005-223-10 | Operator's Manual, Rifle, 7.62mm, M14, (1005-589-1271) (1972) |
| TM 9-1005-223-20 | Organizational Maintenance Manual Including Repair Parts and Special Tools Lists for Rifle, 7.62mm, M14, W/E (1005-589-1271) (1972) |
| TM 9-1005-223-35 | Direct Support, General Support, and Depot Maintenance Manual including Repair Parts and Special Tools List: Rifle, 7.62mm: M14, W/E (1005-589-1271) (1968) |
| TM 9-1005-306-10 | Operator's Manual, 7.62mm M24 Sniper Weapon System (SWS) (NSN 1005-01-240-2136) (1989) |
| TM 11-5855-203-10 | Operator's Manual for Night Vision Sight, Individual Served Weapon, AN/PVS-2, AN/PVS-2A, and AN/PVS-2B |
| TM 11-5855-213-10 | Operator's Manual for Night Vision Sight, Individual Served Weapon, AN/PVS-4 (NSN 5855-629-5334) |
| TM 11-5855-238-10 | Operator's Manual for Night Vision Goggles AN/PVS-5 and AN/PVS-5A (5855-150-1820) |

| USAMU | Accurized National Match M-14 Rifle "M-14 (MTU-NM)" Standards Procedures |
| USAMU | Service Rifle Marksmanship Guide |
| USSOCOM Reg 350-1 | Active Component Training |

**U.S. Marine Corps Publication:**

| FMFM 1-3B | Sniping |

**British Army Publications:**

Infantry Training Manual, Volume 2, Pamphlet 4, Sniping

Infantry Training Volume 1, Infantry Platoon Weapons Pamphlet No. 10 Sniping 1951

**Commercial Publications:**

The Accurate Rifle. Warren Page. Stoeger Publishing Company, 55 Ruta Court, South Hackensack, NJ 07606. 1973. ISBN 0 - 88317-023-X.

The Accurate Varmint Rifle. Boyd Mace. Precision Shooting, Inc., 37 Burnham Street, East Hartford, CT 06108. 1991.

Advanced Weapons Training for Hostage Rescue Teams. Mark V. Lonsdale. S.T.T.U. Training Division, P.O. Box 491261, Los Angeles, CA 90049. 1988. ISBN 0-939235-01-3.

A Rifleman Went To War. H.W. McBride. Lancer Militaria, PO Box 886, Mt. Ida, AR 71957. 1987. ISBN 0-935856-01-3.

The Australian Guerrilla: Sniping. Ion L. Idriess. Paladin Press, Boulder, CO 80306. 1978. ISBN 0-87364-104-3.

The British Sniper: British & Commonwealth Sniping & Equipments 1915-1983. Ian Skennerton. Ian D. Skennerton, PO Box 56, Margate Q. 4019 Australia. 1983. ISBN 0-949749-03-6.

The Cartridge Guide. Ian V. Hogg. Stackpole Books, Cameron and Kelker Streets, PO Box 1831, Harrisburg, PA 17105. 1982. ISBN 0-8117-1048-3.

Combat Loads for the Sniper Rifle. Ralph Avery. Desert Publications, Cornville, AZ 86325. 1981. ISBN 0-87947-544-7.

3

<u>The Complete Book of U.S. Sniping</u>.  Peter R. Senich.  Paladin Press, PO Box 1307, Boulder, CO  80306.  1988.  ISBN 0-87364-460-3.

<u>CQB: A Guide to Unarmed Combat and Close Quarter Shooting</u>.  Mark V. Lonsdale.  S.T.T.U. Training Division, PO Box 491261, Los Angeles, CA  90049.  1991.  ISBN 0-939235-03-X.

<u>Dear Mom: A Sniper's Vietnam</u>.  Joseph T. Ward.  Ivy Books (Ballantine Books), New York, NY.  1991.

<u>Death From Afar</u>.  Norman A. Chandler.  Iron Brigade Armory.  PO Box D. St. Mary's City, MD  20686.  1992.

<u>The Emma Gees</u>.  H.W. McBride.  Lancer Militaria, PO Box 886, Mt. Ida, AR  71957.  1988.  ISBN 0-935856-03-X.

<u>The German Sniper 1914-1945</u>.  Peter R. Senich.  Paladin Press, PO Box 1307, Boulder, CO  80306.  1982.  ISBN 0-87364-223-6.

<u>Handgun Stopping Power: The Definitive Study</u>.  Evan P. Marshall and Edwin J. Sanow.  Paladin Press, PO Box 1307, Boulder, CO 80306.  1992.  ISBN 0-87364-653-3.

<u>Handloading</u>.  Wm. C. Davis, Jr..  National Rifle Association of America, 1600 Rhode Island Ave., N.W., Washington, D.C. 20036.  1981.  ISBN 0-935998-34-9.

<u>Highpower Rifle Shooting, Volume III</u>,  Ellen Ross ed.  National Rifle Association of America, 1600 Rhode Island Ave., N.W., Washington D.C.  20036.  1985.

<u>Limited War Sniping</u>.  Peter R. Senich.  Paladin Press, PO Box 1307, Boulder, CO  80306.  1977.  ISBN 0-87364-126-4.

<u>Lyman Reloading Handbook, 46th Edition</u>.  C. Kenneth Ramage, ed. Lyman Publications, Rt. 147, Middlefield, CT  06455.  1982.

<u>Marine Sniper: 93 Confirmed Kills</u>.  Charles Henderson.  Stein and Day, Scarborough House, Briarcliff Manor, NY  10510.  1986.

<u>Modern Sniper Rifles</u>.  Duncan Long.  Paladin Press, PO Box 1307, Boulder, CO  80306.  1988.  ISBN 0-87364-470-0.

<u>NRA Highpower Rifle Rules</u>.  National Rifle Association of America, 1600 Rhode Island Ave., N.W., Washington, D.C.  20036.  1992.

<u>One Shot-One Kill</u>.  Charles W. Sasser and Craig Roberts.  Pocket Books/Simon & Schuster Inc., 1230 Avenue of the Americas, New York, NY 10020.  1990.

<u>Over the Top</u>. Arthur Guy Empey. A.L. Burt Company New York. 1917.

<u>The Police Sniper</u>. Burt Rapp. Loompanics Unlimited, PO Box 1197, Port Townsend, WA 98368. 1988. ISBN 0-915179-77-6.

<u>Position Rifle Shooting</u>. Bill Pullum and Frank T. Hanenkrat, Ph.D.. Winchester Press, 205 East 42nd Street, New York, NY 10017. 1973. ISBN 0-87691-097-5.

<u>Precision Shooting</u> (monthly periodical). Precision Shooting Inc., 37 Burnham St., East Hartford, CT 06108.

<u>The Rescuers: The World's Top Anti-Terrorist Units</u>. Leroy Thompson. Paladin Press, P.O. Box 1307, Boulder, CO 80306. 1986.

<u>Semi-Auto Rifles: Data & Comment</u>. Robert W. Hunnicutt, ed. National Rifle Association of America, 1600 Rhode Island Ave., N.W., Washington, D.C. 20036. 1988. ISBN 0-935998-54-3.

<u>Shots Fired in Anger</u>. Lt. Col. John George. National Rifle Association of America, 1600 Rhode Island Ave, N.W., Washington D.C. 20036. 1987. ISBN 0-935998-42-X.

<u>Sierra Rifle Reloading Manual, 3rd Edition</u>. Sierra Bullets, L.P. 1400 W. Henry, Sedalia, MO 65301. 1989.

<u>Silencers in the 1980s: Great Designs, Great Designers</u>. J. David Truby. Paladin Press, PO Box 1307, Boulder, CO 80306. 1983. ISBN 0-87364-269-4.

<u>Silencers, Snipers & Assassins</u>. J. David Truby. Paladin Press, PO Box 1307, Boulder, CO 80306. 1972. ISBN 0-87364-012-8.

<u>Small Arms of the World, 12th Edition</u>. Edward C. Ezell. Stackpole Books, Cameron and Kelker Streets, PO Box 1831, Harrisburg, PA 17105. 1983. ISBN 0-8117-1687-2.

<u>Sniper Counter Sniper: A Guide for Special Response Teams</u>. Mark V. Lonsdale. S.T.T.U. Training Division, P.O. Box 491261, Los Angeles, CA 90049. 1986. ISBN 0-939-235-00-5.

<u>Sniper Rifles of Two World Wars: Historical Arms Series No. 8</u>. William H. Tantum, IV. Museum Restoration Service, Bloomfield, Ontario, Canada K0K 1G0. 1967. ISBN 0-919316-08-5.

<u>Sniping in France</u>. Major H. Hesketh-Prichard D.S.O. M.C.. Hutchinson & Co. Paternoster Row E.C. London

<u>The Tactical Edge: Surviving High-Risk Patrol</u>.  Charles Remsberg.
    Calibre Press, Inc., 666 Dundee Road, Suite 1607, Northbrook,
    IL 60062.  1986.  ISBN 0-935878-05-X.

<u>The Ultimate in Rifle Accuracy</u>.  Glenn Newick.  Benchrest and
    Bucks, 6601 Kirby Drive #527, Houston, TX  77005.  1989.

<u>U.S. Rifle M14 from John Garand to the M21</u>.  R. Blake Stevens.
    Collector Grade Publications Incorporated.  PO Box 250 Station
    "E", Toronto, Canada M6H 4E2.  1991.  ISBN 0-88935-110-4.

<u>With British Snipers to the Reich</u>.  Captain C. Shore.  Paladin
    Press, PO Box 1307, Boulder CO  80306.  1988.  ISBN 0-87364-
    475-1.

**Film::**

<u>Sniper: The Invisible Enemy</u>.  International Historic Films.  1985.

# Appendix Q

## INDEX

tracking and holding
trapping/ambush
Environmental effects
effects of humidity
effects of light
effects of temperature
Exercises
dry fire
live fire
MOPP fire
target detection
Eye relief


# F

Factors affecting range estimation
Field sketching, panoramic sketch
conventional representation of features
delineation
other methods of field sketching
Fire support control
Firing positions
advanced positions
modified firing positions
MOUT firing positions
prone supported
prone unsupported
standing
Flag method
Focus
adjustment
Follow-through


# G

Gravity, effects of
aiming point, adjusted
on ammunition
trajectory
Grouping


# H

Hasty position
Hides
construction
deliberate
hasty
Holds and leads
angle of target movement

3

Principles of vision
Protective mask
Psychological evaluations


Q

Qualification


R

Range card
      field expedient range card
      use
Range estimation
      estimating by eye
            appearance of objects method
            bracketing method
            combination method
            range card method
            range estimation formula method
            100-yard increment method
      limitatons
Range estimation tables
      objects
      personnel
Ranges
      field fire
      grouping
      known distance
      procedures
      target detection
      zero
      25 meter
Reduced scale range
Requirements for possible sniper candidates
Reticle


S

SALUTE report
Savelli shuffle
Sniper, definition
Selection of personnel
Sight alignment
Sight picture
Sights
Silent moving techniques
SIMRAD
Skills, additionally trained in

6

# M80 Ball

7.62

147 gr
2750 fps

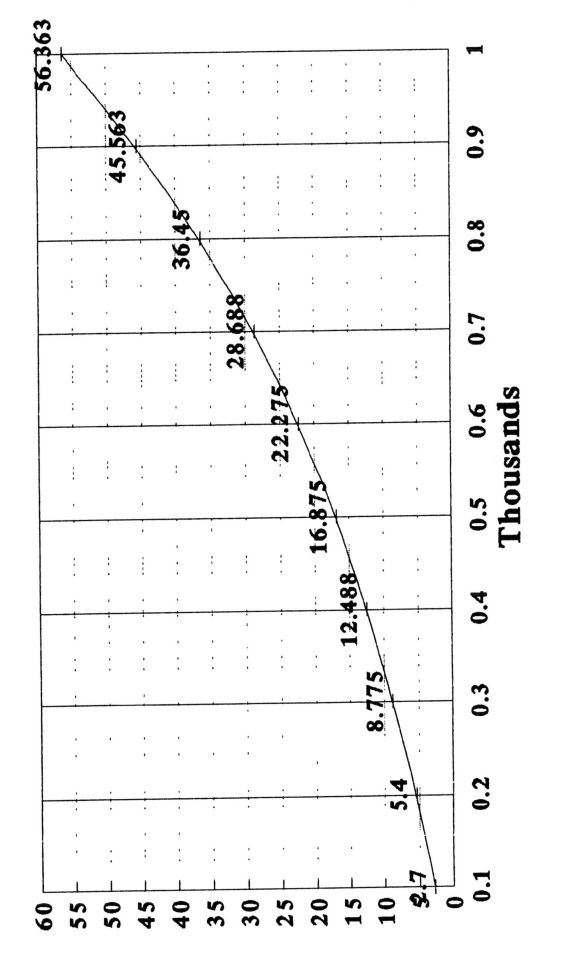

Thousands

─┼─ Elevation

# M852

168 gr
2600 fps

7.62

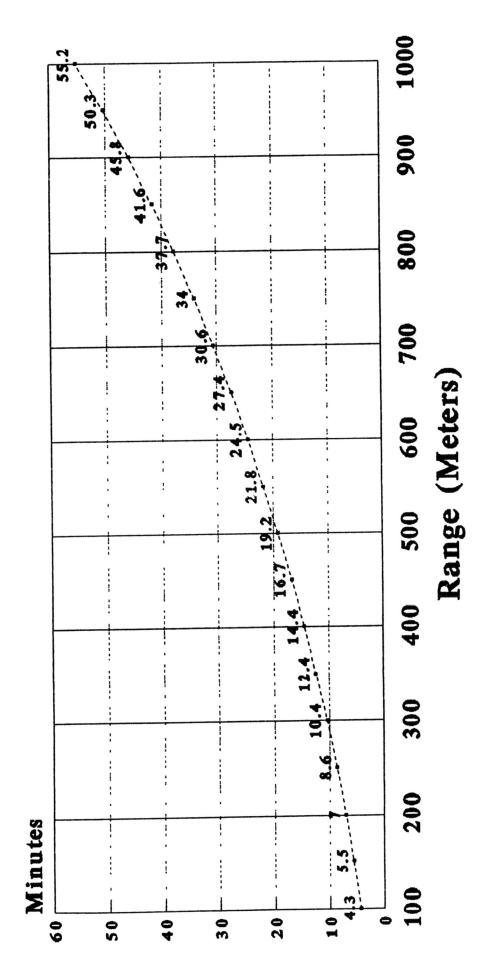

**Minutes**

**Range (Meters)**

----- M852

1.62

173

2550 fps

# M118 Special Ball

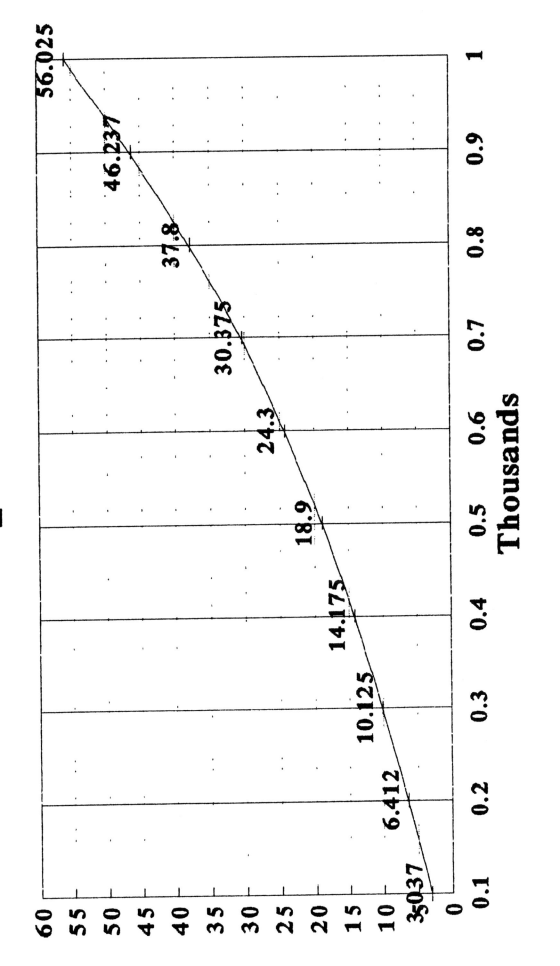

Thousands

—+— Elevation

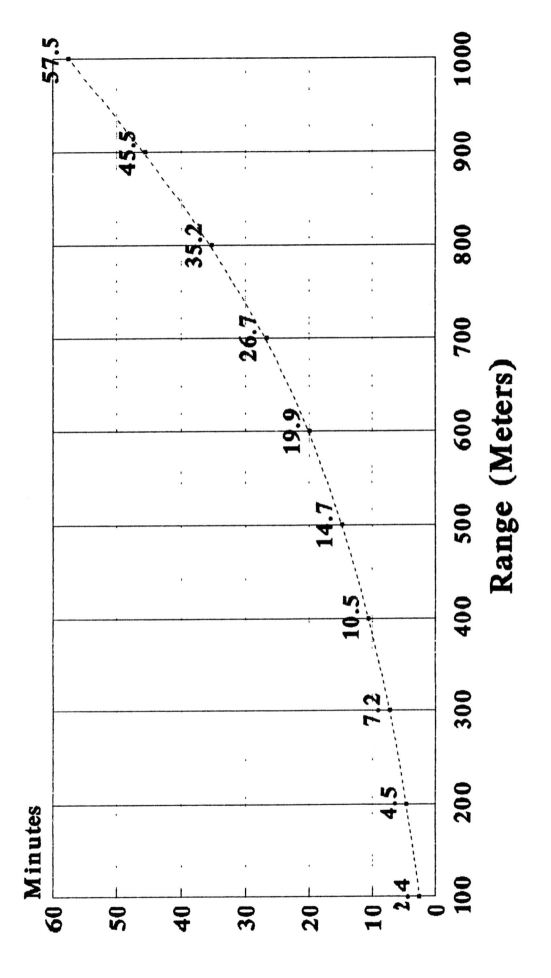

# M193 Ball

5.56

55 gr
3270 fps

**Range (Meters)**

----- Elevation

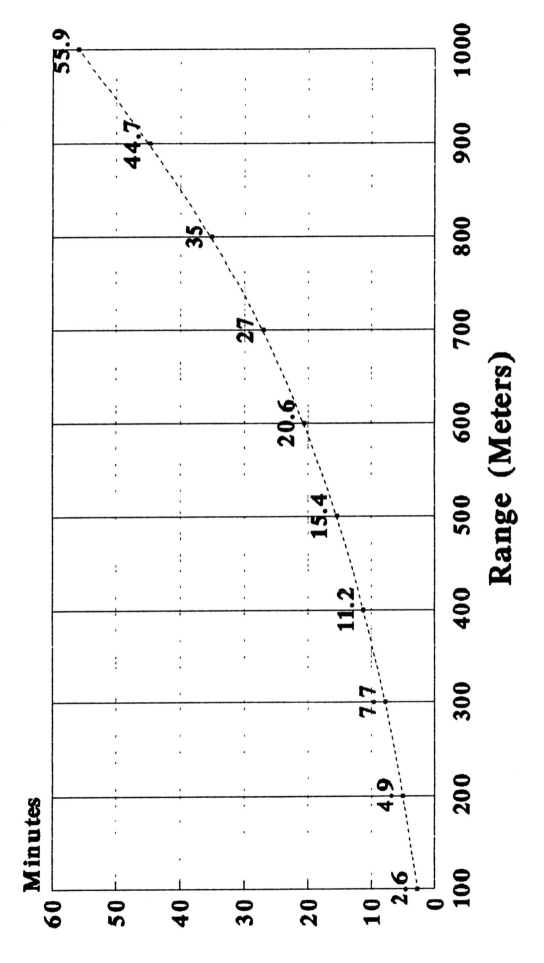

# M855 Ball

5.56 NATO

62 gr
3100 fps

**Minutes**

55.9
44.7
35
27
20.6
15.4
11.2
7.7
4.9
2.6

**Range (Meters)**

------- Elevation

# 500 Meter Danger Space
## 7.62mm M118

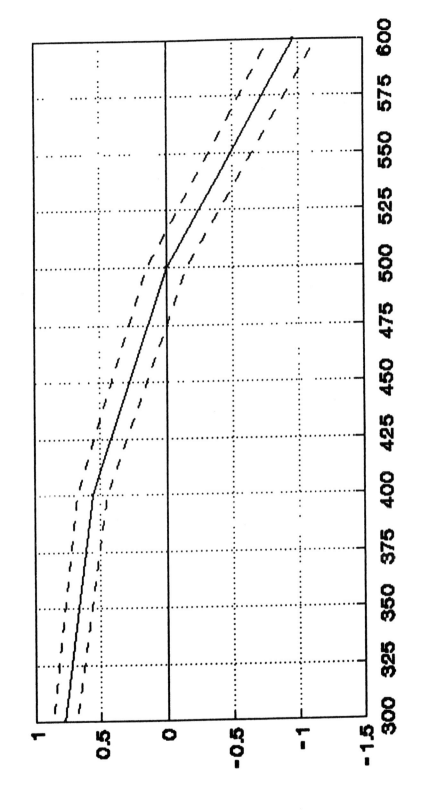

—— MPI

## 2 MOA Dispersion

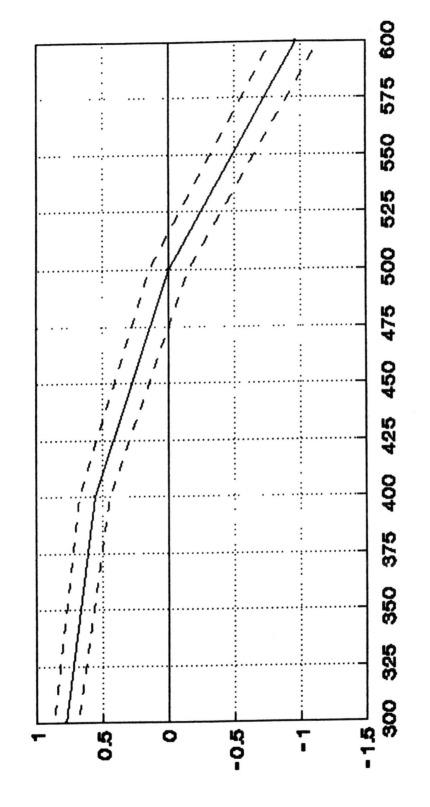

500 Meter Danger Space
7.62mm M118

——— MPI

2 MOA Dispersion

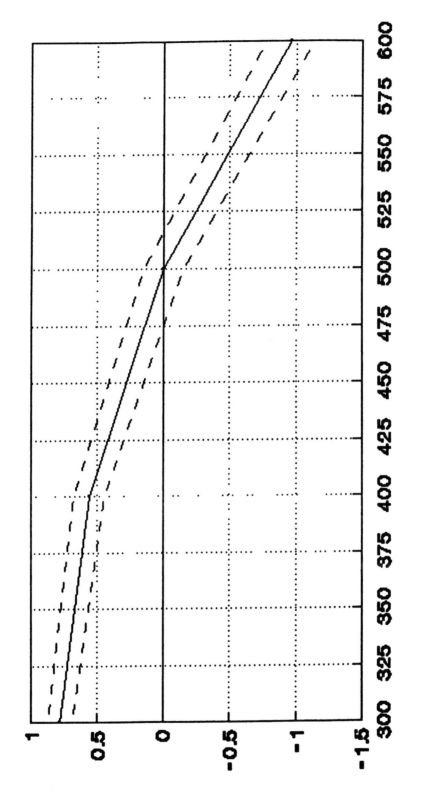

## 500 Meter Danger Space
## 7.62mm M118

——— MPI

## 2 MOA Dispersion

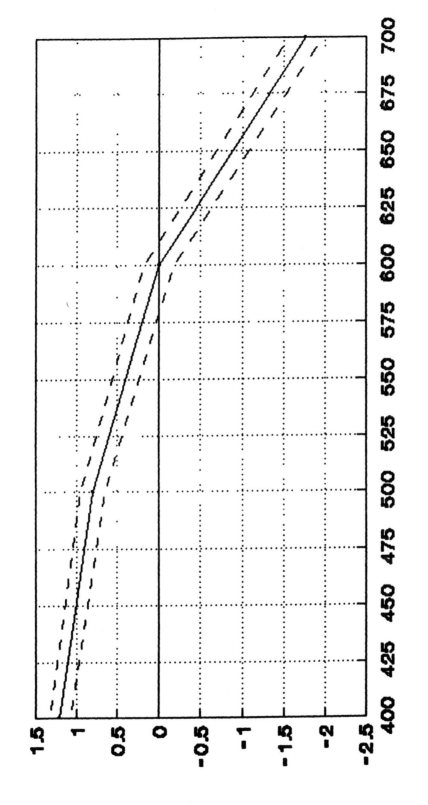

# 600 Meter Danger Space
## 7.62mm M118

—— MPI

2 MOA Dispersion

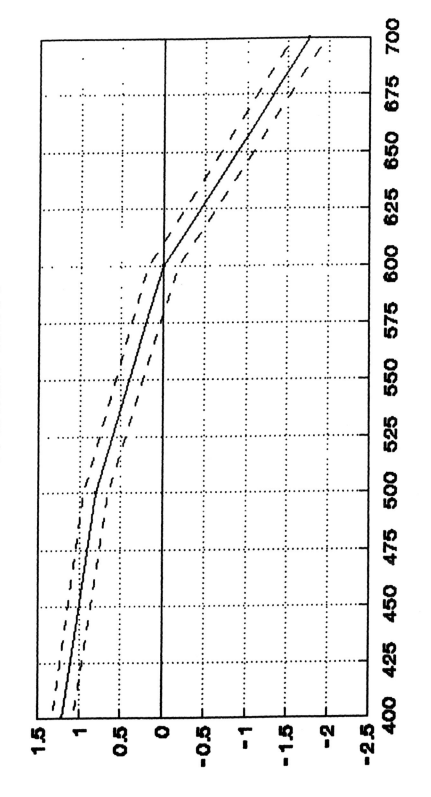

600 Meter Danger Space
7.62mm M118

——— MPI

2 MOA Dispersion

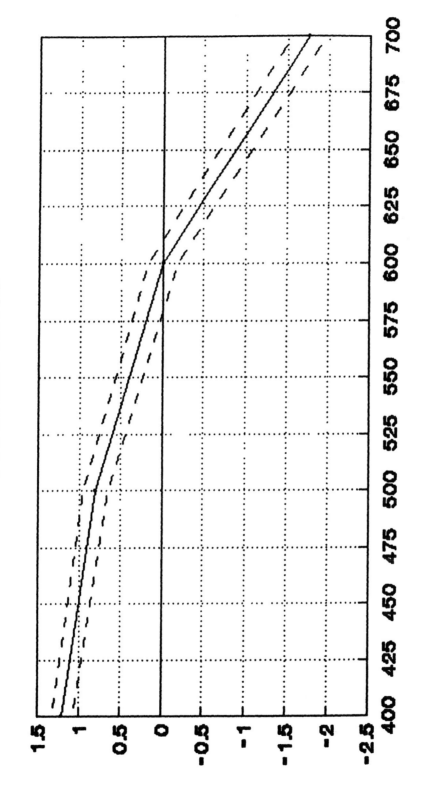

600 Meter Danger Space
7.62mm M118

—— MPI

2 MOA Dispersion

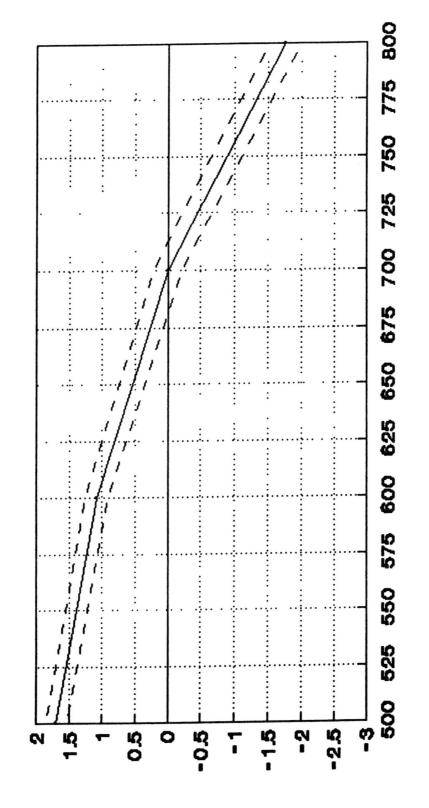

700 Meter Danger Space
7.62mm M118

——— MPI

2 MOA Dispersion

# 700 Meter Danger Space
## 7.62mm M118

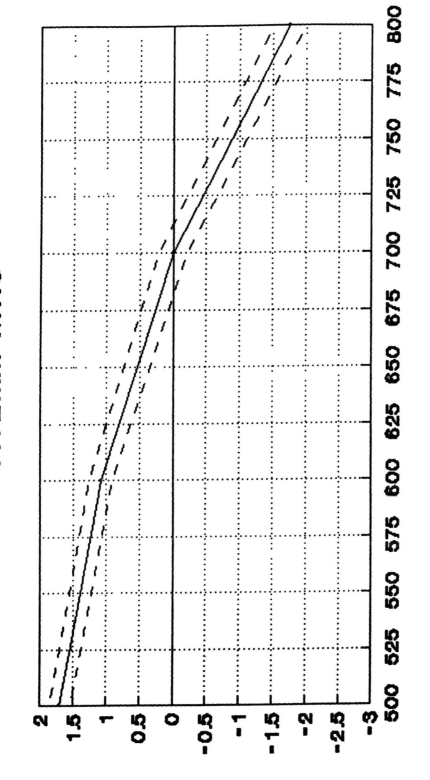

——— MPI

## 2 MOA Dispersion

# 700 Meter Danger Space
## 7.62mm M118

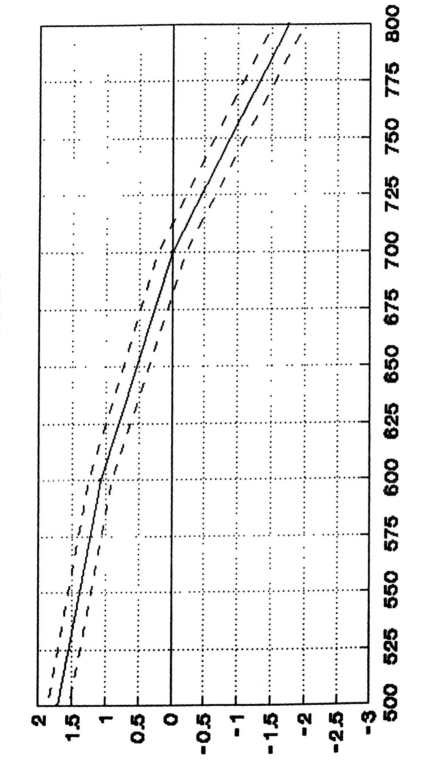

2 MOA Dispersion

—— MPI

# 800 Meter Danger Space
## 7.62mm M118

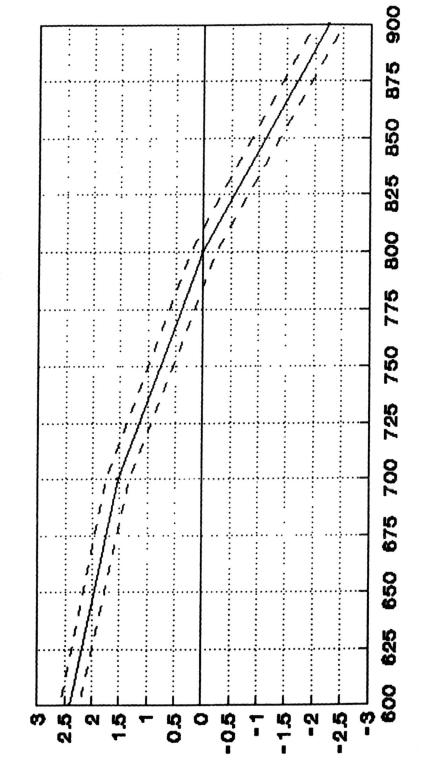

—— MPI

## 2 MOA Dispersion

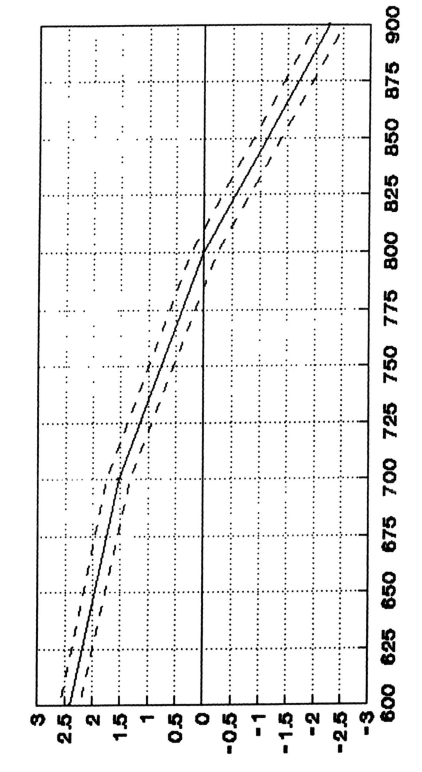

## 800 Meter Danger Space
## 7.62mm M118

—— MPI

## 2 MOA Dispersion

# 800 Meter Danger Space
## 7.62mm M118

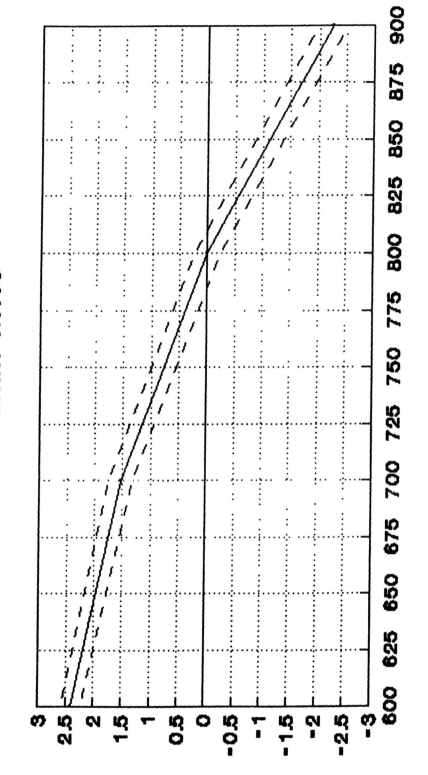

—— MPI

# 2 MOA Dispersion

# 900 Meter Danger Space
## 7.62mm M118

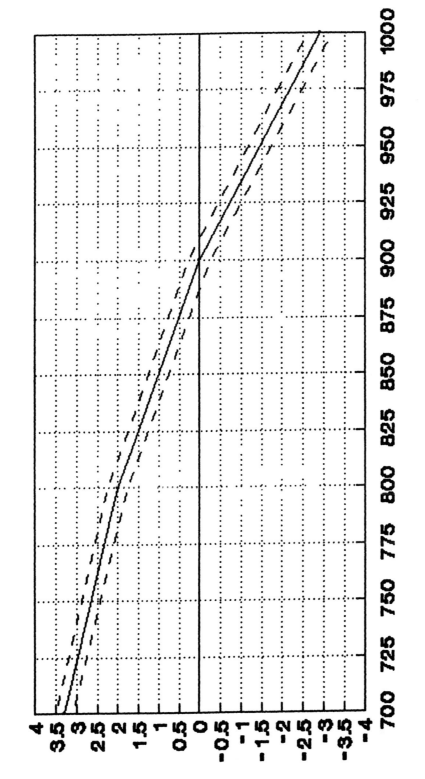

MPI

2 MOA Dispersion

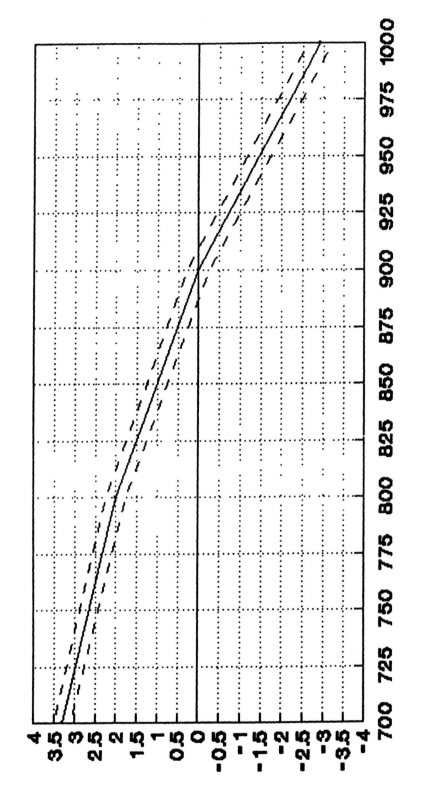

# 900 Meter Danger Space
## 7.62mm M118

—— MPI

2 MOA Dispersion